AN EXPLORER'S GUIDE

WITHDRAWN

Oregon

AN EXPLORER'S GUIDE

Oregon

YOLO COUNTY LIBRARY
226 BUCKEYE STREET
WOODLAND CA 95695

Denise Fainberg
with photographs by the author

THIRD EDITION

The Countryman Press ✷ Woodstock, Vermont

Copyright © 2003, 2006 by Mark Highberger
Copyright © 2010 by Denise Fainberg

Third Edition

All rights reserved. No part of this book may be reproduced in any form or by any electronic or mechanical means, including information storage and retrieval systems, without permission in writing from the publisher, except by a reviewer, who may quote brief passages.

Oregon: An Explorer's Guide

ISBN: 978-0-88150-863-5

Interior photographs by the author unless otherwise specified
Maps by Erin Greb Cartography, © The Countryman Press
Book design by Bodenweber Design
Composition by PerfecType, Nashville, TN

Published by The Countryman Press, P.O. Box 748, Woodstock, VT 05091

Distributed by W. W. Norton & Company, Inc., 500 Fifth Avenue, New York, NY 10110

Printed in the United States of America

10 9 8 7 6 5 4 3 2 1

To my children, Harell and Evan,
my first fellow travelers in Oregon exploration.

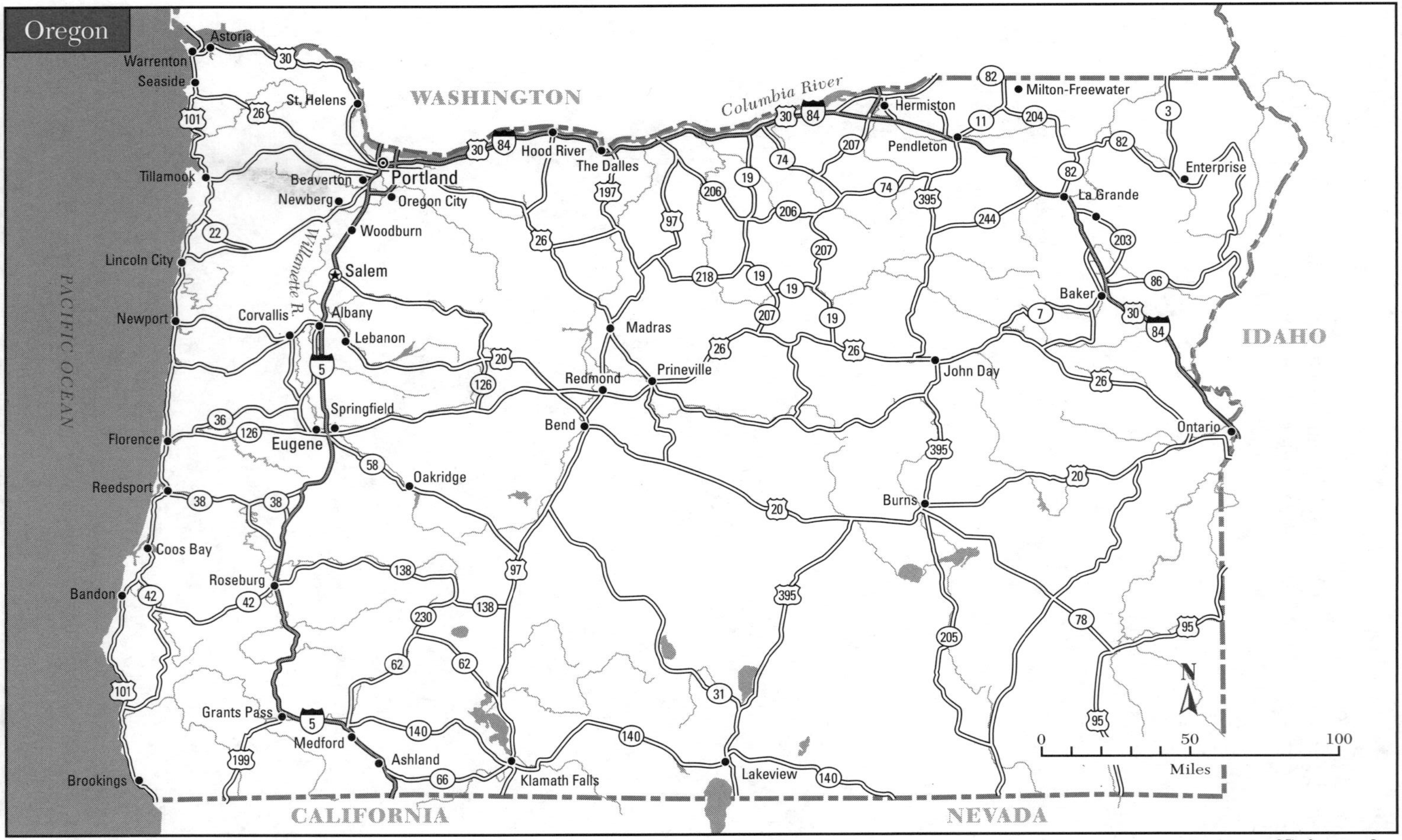

Oregon

©The Countryman Press

EXPLORE WITH US!

Welcome to the third edition of *Oregon: An Explorer's Guide.* This new edition will guide you not only to our state's better-known attractions, but also its back roads and hidden corners. With 98,386 wildly varied square miles of forest and farm, wine country, mountain ranges, sagebrush desert, and brooding coast, not to mention the city that practically invented microbrews, you have a lot of exploring to do. All listings here have been included on the basis of interest and merit; no payment is accepted for inclusion.

WHAT'S WHERE

This alphabetical section includes important information for quick reference and particular highlights.

LODGING

Innkeepers are **not charged for inclusion in this guide.** I have tried to include accommodations in a variety of price ranges, for travelers ranging from families to retirees to outdoorspeople, from the budget-conscious to the person of leisure. Listings concentrate on bed & breakfasts; independently owned, historic, or unique hotels; and some independent, friendly motels. Chains and franchises are included only where there are no, or few, other choices. Prices listed were current for 2009 and are subject to change. Unless otherwise indicated, they apply to double occupancy and do not include room tax, which may vary from 1 to 13 percent depending on the jurisdiction.

RESTAURANTS

In most sections, please note a distinction between *Dining Out* and *Eating Out.* By their nature, restaurants included in the *Eating Out* group are generally less expensive.

KEY TO SYMBOLS

- The crayon appears next to lodgings, restaurants, and attractions that accept or are geared to children. Many bed & breakfasts have age restrictions; when in doubt, ask.
- The wheelchair symbol appears next to lodgings and restaurants that are partially or fully wheelchair accessible.
- The paw appears next to accommodations that accept pets, always with prior approval and usually for a fee. Consult with the innkeeper.
- The blue ribbon appears by lodgings or restaurants that offer particularly good quality for the dollar.

We would appreciate any comments or corrections. Please address correspondence to Explorer's Guide Editor, Countryman Press, P.O. Box 748, Woodstock, VT 05091, or e-mail countrymanpress@wwnorton.com.

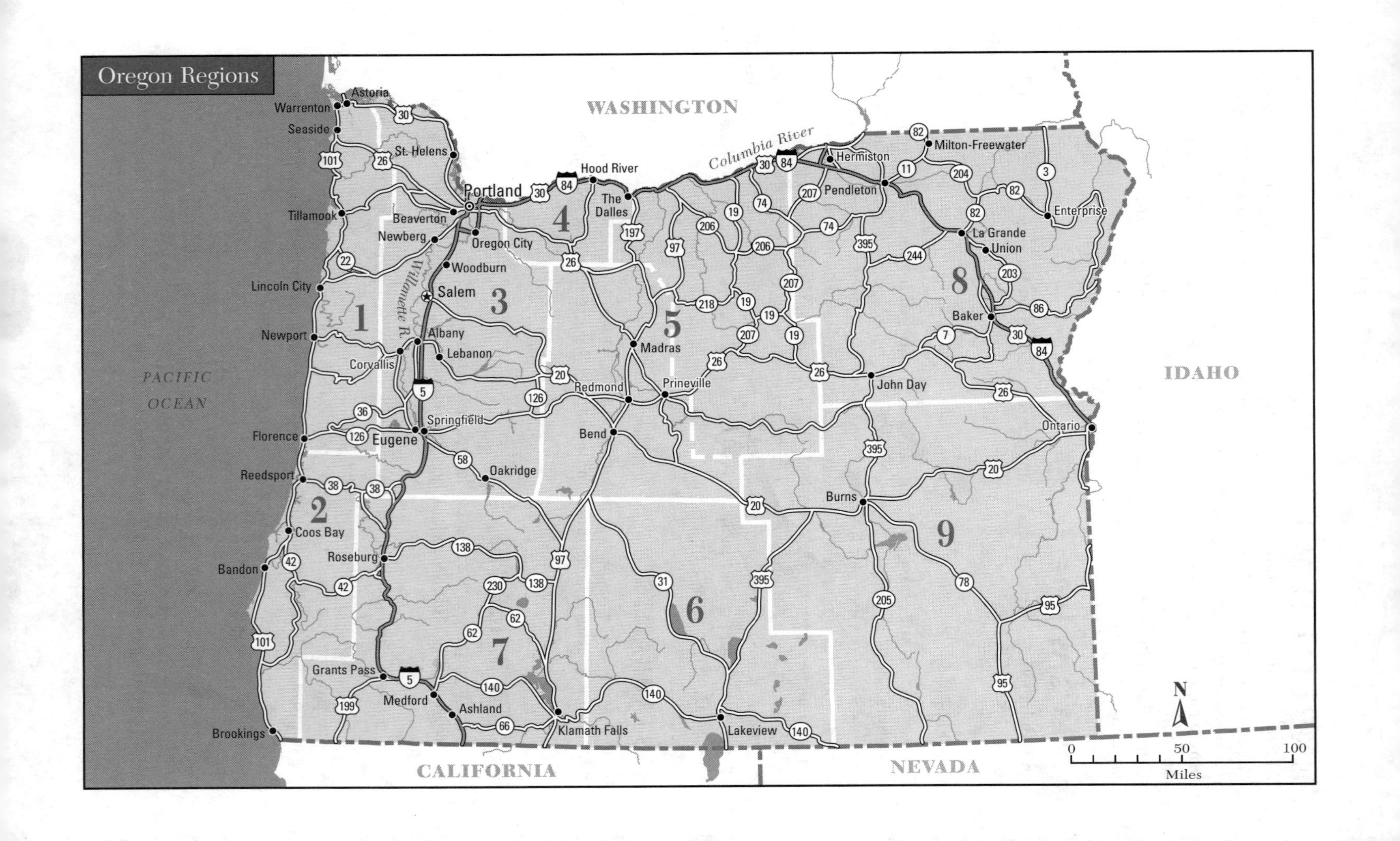
Oregon Regions
WASHINGTON
IDAHO
CALIFORNIA
NEVADA
PACIFIC OCEAN
Columbia River
Willamette R.
1
2
3
4
5
6
7
8
9
Astoria
Warrenton
Seaside
St. Helens
Tillamook
Portland
Beaverton
Newberg
Oregon City
Woodburn
Hood River
The Dalles
Lincoln City
Salem
Newport
Albany
Lebanon
Corvallis
Madras
Redmond
Prineville
Springfield
Eugene
Florence
Bend
Oakridge
Reedsport
Coos Bay
Roseburg
Bandon
Grants Pass
Medford
Ashland
Brookings
Klamath Falls
Lakeview
Hermiston
Pendleton
Milton-Freewater
Enterprise
La Grande
Union
Baker
John Day
Ontario
Burns
N
0
50
100
Miles

CONTENTS

8 Northeast Oregon / 373

9 Southeast Oregon / 423

ACKNOWLEDGMENTS

Thanks are due to the multitude of hoteliers, restaurateurs, and museum curators who allowed me to poke around their establishments and answered endless questions; to the employees of parks, state and national, and the Forest Service, who cheerfully replied to queries abstruse or commonplace; and to visitors centers and chambers of commerce around the state and their encyclopedias of information, especially to Travel Portland.

Thanks are also due to my family, who put up with a nearly unavailable relative for over a year, and likewise to friends in the same boat. Finally, and gratefully, thanks to my sons, Harell and Evan, who reminded me of some of their favorite places and pointed me to others.

INTRODUCTION

You don't lead by pointing and telling people some place to go. You lead by going there and making a case.

—Ken Kesey

Even the upper end of the river believes in the ocean.

—William Stafford

In a way that's what they did, the river of people—first Lewis and Clark, then Peter Skene Ogden and John Fremont—scoping out territory impossibly far and unimaginably different from their places of birth. Then came the Oregon Trail emigrants, most setting out on faith for country they had never seen. It's a part of the American mythos that has been enacted time and again. After all, who got to the moon? And in spite of all that flow, the state still only has 3.7 million inhabitants in an expanse of nearly 100,000 square miles.

Oregon is about half the size of Spain, with one-tenth the population. It's larger, in fact, than quite a number of small countries, which may explain why some citizens identify themselves first as Oregonians and then as Americans (though the rest of the world doesn't recognize that: often abroad, when telling people I'm from Oregon, they respond, "Oh, yes! Seattle!"). It certainly has the diversity of a country: from the air you see endless, seemingly uninterrupted forests, broken by white volcanic cones, and the broad Willamette Valley, then even greater expanses of desert relieved by the occasional canyon or weird rock formation. That's the macro view. Up close, you can commune with pristine rivers, glaciers, hot springs—not to mention fine wines and beers—vineyards, berry farms, and a wall-calendar-worthy coast. Socially, the more fertile western half is more densely inhabited and liberal leaning, while the dry eastern side is sparsely populated and a great deal more traditionalist. There's a strong streak of libertarianism throughout, though, which may explain why the state circles the wagons on issues as diverse as physician-assisted suicide and gun control.

Not as warm as California and lacking a deepwater port like Puget Sound, Oregon, for all its attraction, has never drawn the crowds of either. It's a sort of sober state. When gold was struck in California, or even Oregon, most folks stayed home and tended their fields. When, in 1970, fears of antiwar rioting surrounded an American Legion Convention, Governor Tom McCall arranged a rock concert to divert the putative rioters. Even the hippie-era Oregon Country Fair is now drug- and alcohol-free. Of course, there is the occasional contingent of self-styled anarchists or extremist environmental operation—we would get awfully sclerotic and complacent otherwise.

It was the aforementioned Tom McCall who famously said, "We want you to visit our State of Excitement often. Come visit us again and again. But for heaven's sake, don't move here to live!" Although Oregon's population has increased more than 50 percent since then, and the more garish development he sought to limit hasn't been entirely prevented, things still look different here. One caveat: distances on the ground are longer than they appear. Pull over and rest. Always carry water, and in winter carry tire chains and blankets. If a road is marked for high-clearance vehicles, pay attention. And another caveat: you may, in fact, be tempted to stay.

WHAT'S WHERE IN OREGON

AGRICULTURE This is what most Oregon Trail emigrants came for—farmland and more farmland, in the spectacularly fertile Willamette Valley. Beginning with truck farms feeding ambitious Portland, farming quickly spread south, taking advantage of "prairies" maintained by the Indians' controlled burns and clearing the intervening forest. When the valley filled up, there was a backwash over the mountains to the country straddling the Columbia River, where deep loess produces boatloads of wheat and legumes bound for U.S. and Pacific ports. Finally, ranching and sheepherding filled the dry eastern reaches. Cattle still roam widely east of the Cascades, while the numerous microclimates elsewhere make for a very diverse yield: dairy products from fat coastal cows; cherries, apricots, apples, and pears up the Hood River Valley; more pears in the Siskiyou foothills; berries in the northern Willamette Valley and grass seed to the south; and a great variety of nursery products. Willamette Valley groves produce 99 percent of the national hazelnut crop, making Oregon the world's third-largest hazelnut producer after Turkey and Italy. Then there are wine grapes (see *Wine*), and hops for the burgeoning microbreweries. Oregon ranks first in U.S. production of blackberries, Christmas trees, and hazelnuts, and second in hops.

AIR SERVICE **Portland International Airport (PDX)** (503-460-4040; www.portofportland.com/PDX), 7000 NE Airport Way, Portland, is Oregon's major air hub, served by most national and several international airlines. Smaller commercial airports are in Eugene (EUG), Redmond/Bend (RDM), Coos Bay/North Bend (OTH), Klamath Falls (LMT), Pendleton (PDT), and Medford (MFR). Most of these are served by the commuter branches of United, Alaska, or Delta Airlines.

AMTRAK (1-800-USA-RAIL; www.amtrak.com). Two or three AMTRAK lines serve Oregon, depending how you count: The Empire Builder out of Chicago has a terminus in Portland. The AMTRAK Cascades runs from Vancouver, British Columbia, to Eugene, while the Coast Starlight follows the same route from Seattle to Eugene, then veers across the Cascades to roll down to Los Angeles. Fundamentally, a single corridor of train service.

AREA CODES Most of Oregon has area code 541, except for Portland and the northwestern corner, including Salem, which have area code 503.

BEACHES All coastal beaches in Oregon are public. No, I mean really public—laws passed in 1911 and 1967 guarantee public access up to the vegetation line, not the high-tide line as in most public-beach states. Access is generally easy, from municipal parking lots or via one of the many coastal state parks. This means that all 363 miles of Oregon's wild and scenic coast are open to you, with such possibilities as surfing, hiking, kite-flying, and ocean contemplation—though hardly for swimming, with fierce surf and water temperatures between 45 and 55 degrees. A few areas are closed seasonally to protect nesting snowy plovers. You can even walk the entire Oregon Coast Trail (see *Hiking* in individual chapters) if you want. Watch the tide tables, though—Oregon's miles of sandy beach are punctuated by rocky tidal pools and promontories plunging forbiddingly to the sea. And you will see frequent warnings about "sneaker waves" and floating logs. Take these seriously.

BICYCLING Oregonians take biking seriously, for recreation and increasingly for transportation. The routes appearing here are mainly recreational and are just a sampling, from the flat and leisurely to the technical. The *Oregon Bicycling Guide,* a map of bike routes statewide, and bike maps of the Oregon Coast Route and the Columbia River Gorge, are available through the **Oregon Department of Transportation** (503-823-CYCL; www.odot.gov).

BIRD-WATCHING With habitats that range from High Desert to rain forest and alpine meadows to pounding surf, Oregon pulls in the birds and the watchers. Nearly five hundred species nest in, winter in, or migrate through the state, and there are plenty of places to catch them (figuratively speaking)—stellar wildlife refuges, state parks, and hot spots known only to the initiated (see *Wildlife Areas* sections). **Oregon Birding Trails** (www.oregonbirdingtrails.org) offers guides to Oregon's five long-distance birding trails, plus information on events and festivals. **Oregon Field Ornithologists** (www.oregonbirds.org) has a wealth of information for everyone, from the beginning birder to the obsessed.

BOATING There are a lot of waterways in Oregon. I've tried to steer readers to the unique, the picturesque, and the fun, whether on white-, flat, or salt water. Sailboats over 12 feet and motorized boats of any length must be registered. The **Oregon State Marine Board** (503-378-8587; www.boatoregon.com) takes care of such formalities and offers an online guide to marinas and other boating facilities.

BREWERIES Beer isn't exactly a new thing in the Northwest—German brewers began plying their craft here in the mid-1800s, and Henry Weinhard's brewery is still happily bubbling away in Hood River 150 years later. But since the 1980s microbreweries have been popping up like mushrooms around the Northwest, satisfying a new demand for distinctive beers reflecting their "terroir." Is it the hops (Oregon is the second-largest producer in the United States, between Washington and Idaho)? Or the mountain water? Or just eight months of rain and four months of damp weather? Whatever the case, Portland now has 30 breweries within the city limits, with many more scattered around the state. For a directory of breweries and brewpubs, contact the **Oregon Brewers' Guild** (www.oregonbeer.org).

BUREAU OF LAND MANAGEMENT Just about half of Oregon lands are public, and more than 15 million acres of those lands are administered by the Bureau of Land Management for multiple and sometimes competing uses. The Bureau wears many and diverse hats: it distributes grazing and mining permits, rounds up and sells the excess population of wild horses and burros roaming its lands, and provides lots of open space for camping, hiking, hunting, fishing, and OHV (off-highway vehicle) use. The upside is that most recreational use is free; the downside is that you may find a group conducting target practice uncomfortably close to your hiking trail or driving off-road vehicles where you want to camp. For information on activities and locations, go to www.blmgov/or, or contact one of the nine district offices listed under *Guidance* sections of this book.

BUS SERVICE **Greyhound** (1-800-231-2222; www.greyhound.com) still works the I-5 and I-84 corridors, but the vast intervening spaces are served by only a few regional lines: **Porter Stage Lines** (541-269-7183; www.kokkola-bus.com), running from North Bend and Florence on the coast to Burns in the southeastern desert; the **Valley Retriever** (541-265-2253; www.kokkola-bus.com), which serves the northern Willamette Valley; and **The POINT** (1-888-900-2609), operating between Klamath Falls and Brookings in the southwest. Lane County has a respectable public bus system (541-687-5555; www.ltd.org) connecting the coast to the high Cascades via Eugene. **Curry Public Transit** (1-800-921-2871; www.currypublictransit.org) runs a **Coastal Express** from Smith River, California, to North Bend. Some of these lines actually connect with each other or with Greyhound, but none has particularly frequent schedules.

CAMPGROUNDS Oregon's myriad campgrounds, ranging from primitive to family friendly, are a fine way to experience the state's natural diversity. I've concentrated on those found on public lands but include some private ones that offer a quiet or unique setting. Browse and reserve federal and state campgrounds online at www.oregon.com, or for a complete listing, check www.oregoncampgrounds.com.

CANOEING AND KAYAKING From serene mountain lakes to the adrenaline rush of whitewater to the 216-mile Willamette River Water Trail, there's plenty of choice in Oregon—the truly adventurous paddler can even try ocean kayaking. These sections offer suggestions for paddling some of the more accessible lakes and streams while avoiding those with a lot of motor traffic. For an exhaustive guide, consult *Soggy Sneakers: A Paddler's Guide to Oregon Rivers* by Pete Giordano and the **Willamette Kayak and Canoe Club** (www.wkcc.org), P.O. Box 1062, Corvallis 97339.

CITIES There are 241 incorporated cities in Oregon, if you consider Shaniko or Lonerock, population 20, cities. Portland, with about 570,000 inhabitants (though more than 2 million if you include the suburbs), is the commercial and cultural hub; the capital, Salem, vies with Eugene for second place, each having about 150,000. Then there are numerous small towns that, though unincorporated, may yet have post offices. Finally, there are the ghost towns (see *Ghost Towns*), remnants of extractive booms and busts or simply of a hardscrabble existence. Some still have a few living inhabitants.

CLAMMING AND CRABBING Combing the beaches for crabs, clams, and scallops is a popular activity and can usually be done year-round. However, some protected areas are closed to harvest, and occasionally a season will be closed due to a red tide or other outbreak, so it's essential to check with the **Oregon Department of Fish and Wildlife** (1-800-720-ODFW; www.dfw.state.or.us) before collecting. They can also furnish the required permit.

CLIMATE Oregon enjoys, if that is the right word, two starkly contrasting climates: the western third, from the Cascade crests across the Willamette Valley, over the Coast Range and down to the shoreline, is temperate and rainy as moist air continually pours in from the Pacific. (There's a reason why the state university teams are the Ducks and the Beavers.) Eastward, in the Cascades's rain shadow, the sagebrush country is high, dry, and cold, except during July and August, when it's hot, at least during the day. That said, there are climates within the climates. Summer days in the Willamette Valley can reach 90 degrees or more, while a hot day on the coast barely tops 70. Cape Perpetua gets near 120 inches of rain a year, but Eugene, an hour inland, gets 50. On the High Desert, rainfall averages 8 to 12 inches, but considerably more in the eastern mountain ranges. Summer temperatures often reach the hundreds, though in winter the mercury may dip well below zero, and frost can occur at any time of year—one reason that homesteading was generally unsuccessful east of the Cascades. The temperature gradients produce air flows for which the Columbia Gorge in particular functions as a large wind tunnel, festooned in places with wind farms.

COVERED BRIDGES Fifty-two covered bridges remain in the state, some rebuilt or moved. Most are in western Oregon, where the roof lengthened the life of the bridge in a wet climate. A directory is at www.coveredbridges.stateoforegon.com.

COUNTIES Oregon is composed of 36 counties, from Wallowa in the far northeast to Curry in the far southwest. Some are named for famous Americans (Jefferson, Lincoln), some for state and local luminaries (Lane, Gilliam, Benton), some for Native tribes (Clatsop, Clackamas), and some for geographic features (Deschutes, Lake).

DIVING The cold waters of some High Cascades lakes and a few places on the coast attract hardy divers for underwater wrecks and strange creatures; see the North Central Oregon and coastal chapters for venues.

EMERGENCIES Each chapter lists local hospitals under *Medical Emergency.* If in doubt, call 911. In some extremely isolated places, especially in eastern Oregon, you may be far from both hospitals and phone service. It's as well to be prudent and to carry first aid.

EVENTS Nearly every corner of the state has its festivals and events. Those selected here highlight local traditions, culture, and economy, whether of the general population, Native Americans, or immigrant groups.

FARMERS' MARKETS With Oregon's abundant produce, most localities have one or more farmer's markets, noted in each chapter. The **Oregon Farmers' Markets Association** (503-525-1035; www.oregonfarmersmarkets.org) keeps a list of those active around the state.

FISHING Salmon, steelhead, trout, or surf fishing—all have their adherents. Most fishing requires a license from the **Oregon Department of Fish and Wildlife** (503-947-6000; www.dfw.state.or.us), available online and at various sporting goods outlets. Be sure to check on seasons and limits, too, as these may vary from time to time.

GARDENS The western part of the state, mild and damp, allows for some riotous gardens. Those open to the public are indicated in the text.

GEOGRAPHY All Oregon is divided into six parts. Or is it eight? From the west is the **Coast,** with sandy beaches separated by rocky headlands, backed by the dense rain forest of the Coast Range, heavily logged in places. East of the range is the fertile **Willamette Valley,** a broad plain drained by the Willamette River extending from south of Eugene north to the Columbia. Then come the **Cascades,** a double row of volcanoes paralleling the valley—the Old, or West Cascades, and the snow-capped High Cascades. The southern Cascades merge with the **Siskiyous,** south of Roseburg and east of Klamath Falls, to form a hopeless geological jumble giving rise to a book aptly named *The Klamath Knot.* The range catches most of the precipitation flowing in from the Pacific, leaving precious little for the eastern half of the state, which is why it is mostly desert. **Central Oregon** tends to sagebrush plains on ancient lava flows, shading to wheat fields in the north, punctuated by river gorges and the occasional mountain poking up from the steppe. **Southeast Oregon** is dry and remote, containing some of the largest and least-populated counties, while the **Wallowa Mountains** and their attendant streams and grasslands grace the far northeast. Seven! For purposes of manageability, this book breaks it down a bit further.

GEOLOGY In few states does the earth show off its past so readily, from lava flows to canyons to the exploded cone of Mount Mazama, now Crater Lake. The history of Oregon is largely volcanic; but before that, about 130 million years ago, fragments of continental crust were carried in on tectonic plates as on a conveyor belt, bumping up on what was then the west coast—approximately eastern Idaho. Some of these became the Wallowas and the Blue Mountains. But the tectonic movement continues: North America rides westward, forcing the Juan de Fuca plate under its edge. The subducted plate edge melts and is forced up as magma. This created the Old Cascades and the High Cascades, as well as several more inland volcanoes; it also shut off moist air flows to interior Oregon, changing what was once a warm, damp forest to dry savanna and finally to desert. Besides this, massive lava flows erupted from fissures beginning about 17 million years ago, covering much of eastern Oregon with basalt hundreds and thousands of feet thick—this is what you see in the Columbia Gorge and in rimrock all over the dry side. Subsequent stretching and bending of the earth's crust created the basin and range province covering Nevada and southeastern Oregon, where it produced parallel fault-block mountains like the Steens, Hart Mountain, and Abert Rim. The earth here is still unsettled, as you can see from the many hot springs all over the state, from the tense southeast to the Cascades. Some mountain lava flows are only a thousand years old. Newberry Crater, south of Bend, is periodically the subject of geothermal energy exploration, and a section of the Three Sisters Wilderness is carefully watched since it started bulging several years ago. Sites of geological interest include **Lava Butte,** in Bend, in the **Newberry Crater National Volcanic Monument;** the **John Day Fossil Beds,** where the visitors center gives you a fine sense of the time scale and the biological and meteorological changes; and, last but certainly not least, **Crater Lake National Park.**

GHOST TOWNS Sometimes a hoped-for railroad passed by, so that the sheep and grain, however abundant, couldn't get to market. Or a mine deep in the mountains played out, rendering a roustabout town irrelevant. Or the rains promised by hucksters in Oregon's outback never came, and would-be homesteaders went home. For a variety of reasons ghost towns are scattered around the state, especially in the mining areas of northeastern Oregon and the dry southeast, but also near mineral deposits in the Old Cascades and north central Oregon, where dry-land farmers had a hard time of it. **Travel Oregon** (see *Travel Information*) lists 18 ghost towns in the state (abandoned homesteads are even more abundant); **www.ghosttowns.com** has an interactive map.

GOLF COURSES Golf courses are found all over the state, from the very professional greens of Bandon to a home-grown, nine-hole course in the far reaches of ranch country. Those listed here are public or semipublic. For a more complete listing, check www.oregongolf.com.

GUIDES AND OUTFITTERS Guides can be very helpful in situations where you don't know the terrain or conditions, or even if you just want advice. A complete state listing can be found at www.ogpa.org, the Web site of the **Oregon Guides and Packers Association.**

HIGHWAYS Oregon's main arteries are **I-5,** crossing the state north–south from Ashland to Portland; **I-84,** running from Portland east along the Columbia, veering southeast near Hermiston, and bisecting the northeastern corner of the state; **US 101,** hugging the entire length of the coast from California to Washington; **US 97,** crossing central Oregon north to south; **US 395,** which does the same for the eastern part of the state; and **US 20** and **26,** modest roads even if they are federal highways, crossing the whole width of Oregon. For information on safety, delays, and weather conditions, call the **Oregon Department of Transportation** at 511 or 1-800-977-6368 (503-5988-2941 from outside Oregon), or check www.tripcheck.com.

HIKING The hikes suggested in this volume represent only a fraction of the vast number of trails around the state. I have tried to select routes for various levels of skills and ability, including some wheelchair-accessible paths, and for appreciation of the nature and scenery unique to the area. Many hiking guides to Oregon exist; I find the series by William Sullivan (*100 Hikes in the Central Oregon Cascades,* etc.) particularly user friendly.

HISTORICAL MARKERS Those roadside plaques you often speed past actually contain interesting and pertinent information. You might learn about the construction of a military road from The Dalles to California, which gave rise to US 97, or about building World War I planes from Sitka spruce. The **Oregon Travel Information Council** (1-800-574-9397; www.oregontic.com) publishes a free guide to all state historical markers; call and ask for one or download it from their Web site. It covers heritage trees, too.

HISTORY From a cave south and east of Summer Lake come the earliest human remains yet found in the Americas: desiccated feces containing human DNA. Announced in 2008, the discovery predates Oregon's former oldest finds—sagebrush-fiber sandals nine thousand to thirteen thousand years old—by over a thousand years. Like the sandal makers, those early Oregonians were hunter-gatherers who roamed the large inland lakes and forests of the time, as did their descendants till the coming of Manifest Destiny.

Lonely European ships began tacking up the coast in the 1500s: the expedition of Juan de Fuca (a Greek, actually) went as far north as Vancouver Island; Francis Drake may have reached Oregon before turning west on his circumnavigation of the world; and Bruno de Heceta came up the coast in 1775, passing the Columbia River. But no one seems to have paid much attention to the country itself until Captain Cook came by on his 1778 Pacific explorations and noted the fine furs to be bought from the Indians. After that Europeans began trading regularly along the coast—to the point that Lewis and Clark, in 1805, noted that some Indians on the Lower Columbia spoke a smattering of English and were possessed of the occasional teapot or knife blade. In 1792 the American captain Robert Gray, followed shortly by the British captain Vancouver, entered the Columbia River, and search for the Northwest Passage reached fever pitch as Britain and the infant United States staked competing claims to the Northwest.

In far-off Washington, D.C., a president thought he had better get busy. Thomas Jefferson sent a small band of explorers off in 1804. Lewis and Clark's company spent the sodden winter of 1805–1806 on the northern Oregon coast—the first, albeit brief, nonnative settlement recorded—and reported that the Columbia River was not in fact the fabled Northwest Passage. But their accounts inspired furrier John Jacob Astor to establish the first permanent settlement in Oregon: Astoria.

For a time Americans and British shared the Oregon country uneasily. Trappers of various nationalities roamed freely north and south of the Columbia. Settlers trickled in: Methodist missionary Jason Lee set up his Willamette Valley mission in 1834, and the French Canadians built a Catholic chapel nearby in 1836. A motley skein of farming communities grew up in the northern Willamette Valley, some of them supplying the Hudson's Bay Company at Fort Vancouver just north of the Columbia. These maverick settlements were the nucleus of the Champoeg Declaration of 1843, by which the farmers narrowly voted for an American-style provisional government and, eventually, territorial status. This seemed to them preferable to the arbitrary administration of the Hudson's Bay Company.

Soon the Oregon Trail was discharging thousands of pioneers a year into the territory. British officials instructed John McLoughlin, factor of Fort Vancouver, to discourage Americans from settling in; instead he merely sent them south of the Columbia, often with provisions, earning himself the title of Father of Oregon. The British eventually withdrew north of the 49th parallel, leaving what is now Oregon and Washington in American hands.

Now the territory had to decide if it would long endure. Treaties "negotiated" in 1855 confining most Indians to reservations resulted in horrific "Indian wars" that lasted into the 1870s. And the path to statehood was vexed by the burning issue of the time: slave or free? Republicans, sympathetic with Lincoln, held slavery abhorrent; Democrats leaned toward the South and were far from comfortable with the thought of free blacks as neighbors. So they compromised: Oregon would not be a slave state; it would simply not allow permanent black residents at all. Thus Oregon reached statehood in 1859. Even after the Civil War the state showed extreme reticence in extending citizenship and voting rights to black people. In fact, it was only in 1927 that the clause forbidding black suffrage was expunged from the state constitution, though the Fifteenth Amendment had long since rendered it irrelevant. *Alis volat propriis* indeed (see *State Trivia*)—sometimes for better, sometimes for worse. Then again, Oregon's ornery streak also gave us pioneering legislation like the beach bills of 1913 and 1967 (see *Beaches*), the nation's first bottle bill in 1971, and, more ambiguously, the "death with dignity act" of 1997.

Sandwiched between busier California and Washington, Oregon is less populous and more laid-back than either, reveling in its one large small town (Portland), many small small towns, and vast natural environment. The ethos combines can-do self-sufficiency (think Bill Bowerman, founder of Nike) with a certain laid-back counterculturalism (think Matt Groening or Ken Kesey), sometimes but not always combined in the same individual (think Mel Blanc, voice of Bugs Bunny). You can read the state's rough-and-tumble development in the many "historic downtowns," the pioneer homes, the ghost towns, and last but not least, in Portland's **Oregon Historical Society Museum** (503-222-1741; www.ohs.org).

HOT SPRINGS Oregon is thin-skinned in places. Hot water bubbles up rock fissures, creating steamy springs in the back of, beyond, or just off the highway. Some are developed, some not, and some are on private land. Respect the owners and the environs, and be aware that some springs are clothing optional by common consent. A handy guide is *Touring Washington and Oregon Hot Springs* by Jeff Birkby (Falcon/Globe Pequot).

INDIAN RESERVATIONS The federal government recognizes 10 tribes in Oregon, though several of these are actually confederations of tribes—the **Warm Springs** reservation north of Madras, for instance, is home to the Warm Springs, Wasco, and Northern Paiute tribes: peoples of different cultures and languages, bound together by government order. This is the largest reservation, at 644,000 acres; the **Umatilla Reservation,** near Pendleton, is next at 172,000 acres; the **Siletz, Klamath, Burns Paiute, Cow Creek, Coquille,** and **Grande Ronde reservations** are much smaller. **Celilo Village,** while not a reservation, was ceded to tribes in 1947 in lieu of their usual and customary fishing sites at Celilo Falls, which were drowned by the dam at The Dalles. The history of removal to reservations is not a happy one. Nonetheless, most have powwows and other celebrations open to the public, and some have top-of-the-line museums or cultural centers (noted in the text under *Museums*). They all have casinos, too. **Travel Oregon** (see *Travel Information*) publishes a guide to the various reservations.

LEWIS AND CLARK When Thomas Jefferson dispatched the Corps of Discovery to the far reaches of the continent, it was to see what lay beyond the nebulous boundary of the 1803 Louisiana Purchase. With the crossing of the Continental Divide they entered the undefined Oregon country in early fall 1805. In mid-October they came to present-day Oregon near Umatilla, and their descent along the Columbia is marked with the campsites and landmarks they recorded on both sides of the river. On the coast, **Lewis and Clark National Historic Park** includes their winter camp at Fort Clatsop and associated sites. These are duly noted in the text under *Historic Sites.*

LIBRARIES Nearly every Oregon town has its library (or access to one in a neighboring town), and most of them have Internet access. Andrew Carnegie donated more than 30 in Oregon alone, between 1901 and 1915, some of which are still in service as libraries. A listing of all libraries is posted at www.publiclibraries.com.

MAPS Highway maps are distributed free at many interstate rest areas and can be ordered from the **Oregon Department of Transportation** (503-986-3154; www.oregon.gov/ODOT).

MILEAGE Mileages given here are as close as possible but remain approximate. Watch for signs and mileposts.

MUSEUMS The *Museums* listings in each chapter cover a variety of collections, from high art to small-town memorabilia. There are innovative museums of tribal art and history; there are specialized or hobbyist collections for lovers of trains or logging equipment; there are children's museums and museums devoted to forestry, museums of technology and natural history; in short, something for everyone. The **Oregon Museums Association** (www.oregonmuseums.org) publishes a list of museums by region.

MUSIC FESTIVALS Music festivals are listed under *Events* and run the gamut from blues to classical to folk to jazz. The Jacksonville **Britt Festival** (1-800-882-7488; www.brittfest.org), nearly 50 years old, is the mother of all Oregon music festivals, lasting most of the summer.

MUST-SEE SIGHTS Here are the top 10: Crater Lake; the Oregon coast, preferably an area like Port Orford/Gold Beach, Yachats, or Cannon Beach; Portland; the Columbia River Gorge; Hells Canyon; the Oregon Shakespeare Festival in Ashland; Steens Mountain and the Malheur National Wildlife Refuge; the John Day Fossil Beds; a Wild and Scenic River like the Rogue, Illinois, or Umpqua; one of the reservation museums, such as the Museum at Warm Springs or Tamasklilt; and, do go camping in the mountains. That makes 11.

NATIONAL FORESTS Oregon is home to 10 national forests: **Rogue-Siskiyou, Siuslaw, Umpqua, Deschutes, Willamette, Mount Hood, Fremont-Winema, Ochoco, Umatilla** (shared with Washington), **Malheur,** and **Wallowa-Whitman,** totaling over 17.5 million acres—a substantial expanse in which to camp, hike, ride a horse, and generally recreate. A **Northwest Forest Pass** ($5 daily, $30 annually) is now required to park at many national forest trailheads, the result of federal budget cuts in the 1990s and widely resented around the region. In the *To Do* sections I have tried not to neglect those few sites where a pass is not required.

NATIONAL PARKS Oregon has only one national park (but a stellar one),

Crater Lake. Also run by the Park Service are **Lewis and Clark National Historic Park, John Day Fossil Beds National Monument, Oregon Caves National Monument,** and part of **Fort Vancouver National Historic Site.** Fees at Crater Lake are $10 per vehicle, good for seven days; less or free at the other sites.

NEWSPAPERS There are dozens of local dailies and weeklies (it seems the first thing settlers did after building their cabins was to start a paper), but the principal newspapers are the ***Oregonian,*** out of Portland, established in 1850; the ***Register-Guard,*** Eugene's daily paper, established 1862; and the ***Statesman Journal,*** out of Salem, established 1851. East of the Cascades, the ***Bulletin*** (formerly the *Bend Bulletin*) got its start in 1903.

OREGON TRAIL From the 1840s to the end of the century, hundreds of thousands of hopeful farmers and fortune seekers took to the trail by foot, horse and wagon, and finally by train—all looking for fertile land and wide-open spaces. The trail entered Oregon along the Snake River a bit south of present-day Ontario and crossed northwestward over the Blue Mountains to reach the Columbia; from that point emigrants had to shoot the rapids or portage around them. There was thus a perennial search for shortcuts: the Barlow Trail avoided the worst rapids by climbing over the southern flank of Mount Hood, which was no walk in the park either; the Applegate Trail veered south into California, crossing the Siskiyous to enter the Willamette Valley from the south; and a few wagon trains struck east across the desert, hoping to save many miles of trail. These nearly ended up like the Donner party. Under *Historic Sites,* I have indicated places where ruts can be seen or where markers indicate the old trail.

PACIFIC CREST TRAIL The Pacific Crest Trail runs along America's roof—2,650 miles of hiking trail from Mexico to the Canadian border. A 430-mile segment crosses Oregon, entering the state in the mountains south of Ashland and departing over the Bridge of the Gods at Cascade Locks. Those who know say the Oregon segment is the least strenuous (certainly a relative statement), as it tends to stay along the crests without long rises and descents, except between Mount Hood and Cascade Locks.

PUBLIC LANDS More than half of Oregon's 97,131 square miles are in public hands, with more than 27,000 square miles held as national forests and 23,000 administered by the Bureau of Land Management. These are mostly multiple-use areas, used for grazing and lumber production as well as recreation, with the exception of designated wilderness. About 1,200 square miles are state forest, and a comparative handful of acres are held by the Park Service. These lands are owned by you and me, and we can be justly proud of their beauty and solicitous for their health.

RECOMMENDED READING Reub Long and E. R. Jackman include homespun reminiscences of running cows and horses on one of our last frontiers in *The Oregon Desert* (Caxton, 1964), a local classic. Try *Oregon's Promise: An Interpretive History* by David Peterson del Mar (Oregon State University, 2003) for an unconventional history of the state. David Rains Wallace's *The Klamath Knot* (Sierra Club, 1983) is a fascinating look at the unique natural history of the Siskiyous on the Oregon-California border. *Lis-*

tening for Coyote: A Walk across Oregon's Wilderness by William Sullivan (Morrow, 1988) is a terrific account of the author's east–west walk across the state; Bill is also Oregon's Mr. Hiking, having written a series of hiking guides to the state's different regions. Molly Gloss's novel *The Jump-Off Creek* (Houghton Mifflin, 1989) is an accurate and affecting portrait of a single woman pioneer in Oregon's northeastern mountains. David Alt's *Roadside Geology of Oregon* (Mountain, 1978) and *Hiking Oregon's Geology* by Ellen Bishop and John Allen (Mountaineers, 2004) are practical guides to the tectonic forces Oregon wears on its sleeve. Shannon Applegate, a descendant of the pioneering Applegate family, has written a powerful account of her ancestors' Oregon Trail experiences in *Skookum: A Pioneer Family's History and Lore* (Beech Tree, 1988). *River of the West: Stories from the Columbia* by Robert Clark (Picador, 1997) is a collection of essays on some of the Columbia River Basin's transforming personalities.

REST AREAS The Oregon Department of Transportation maintains 63 rest areas along interstate and U.S. highways, and many of the longer state highways. Most have restrooms, picnic tables, drinking water, and some handicapped-accessible facilities.

RESTAURANTS Food in Oregon naturally concentrates on its abundant (and often organic) produce, seafood, and locally grown meats. I have tried to include some interesting eats for all pocketbooks, as well as Oregon's increasingly diverse ethnic cuisines.

ROAD REPORTS If you're traveling outside the summer season, it's important to check road conditions. Mountain highways may close in winter, briefly or for the season; snow can fall nine months of the year, causing dangerous driving conditions; winter rains and spring snowmelt bring floods near the coast. You can check road conditions at www.tripcheck.com or by calling 511.

ROCKHOUNDING This is a rocky state (see *Geology*), and some spots are particularly propitious for rock collecting. You can dig for thundereggs, the state rock, at a private ranch in north central Oregon, or for sunstones (the state gem) at a BLM site in the desert of south central Oregon; see those sections for details.

RODEOS This is the Wild West, and each region has its rodeo. The larger ones are listed under *Events* in the relevant chapters, but you can find a more complete listing at www.oregonrodeo.org.

RV PARKS Few RV parks are listed in the guide, but if an RV is your mode of travel, guidance can be found at www.rvpark.com.

SCENIC BYWAYS There's certainly plenty of scenery to cover, and even Oregon's 39 National and State Scenic Byways, tour routes, and All-American Roads can't take in all of it. But driving one or two can be a peak experience, literally, as you look deep into Hells Canyon, admire the rugged Wallowa pinnacles, or contemplate the empty backcountry. While some, like the **Pacific Coast Scenic Byway,** have ready access to lodging, dining, and gas stations, many pass through quite remote areas, so be sure to fill your tank and take supplies. Several byways are inadvisable or even closed in winter. For details and directions check www.byways.org, and for closures check the listing of phone contacts for each byway at www.oregon.gov/ODOT/HWY/SCENICBYWAYS. I've included most of them in the relevant chapters, plus a few idiosyncratic favorites.

STATE FORESTS State forest acreage is rather paltry compared with that of the national forests, but **Tillamook, Clatsop,** and **Santiam state forests** offer similar recreational opportunities—camping, hiking, picnicking, and the like. Two smaller forests, Elliott and Sun Pass, offer only hunting, fishing, and snowmobiling. For details contact the **Oregon Department of Forestry** (503-945-7200).

STATE PARKS The state administers 189 state parks, recreation areas, and historic sites ranging from wayside rest areas to full-fledged parks with camping, interpretive programs, trails, and other amenities. The larger parks in this guide charge a day-use parking fee of $5 unless otherwise noted; many smaller ones are free. Thirty dollars buys you a year's pass, available at some parks or at www.oregonstateparks.org.

STATE TRIVIA Oregon's state bird is the western meadowlark, now sadly reduced in numbers west of the Cascades. Its state animal is the beaver (logically enough; the beaver is what brought the British and Americans here in the first place). The state fish is the chinook, or king, salmon, of course; the state insect is the Oregon swallowtail, a relative of the commoner tiger swallowtail; the state fruit is the pear; while the state flower is the Oregon grape, which is not a grape. The state tree is the Douglas fir, which is also natural since it has been the staple of the timber industry, and the state nut is the hazelnut, or filbert, of which Oregon is one of the world's largest producers. Oregon has an extraordinary number of state organisms—we even have a state fossil, the metasequoia, or dawn redwood. The state motto is *Alis volat propriis*, meaning "she flies with her own wings," readopted in 1987 though it originated in 1854 and was placed on the territorial seal. (From 1957 to 1978 the motto was "The Union," which appears on the state seal; an interesting shift.)

STATISTICS Oregon has a population of 3.7 million in an area of 97,131 square miles (although 1,129 square miles of that is water, which hardly counts toward population; though there are a few houseboat communities). About 550,000 people live in Portland, with about 2.2 million in the entire metropolitan area. Its geographic center lies near Post, 25 miles south-southeast of Prineville. Its highest point is the top of Mount Hood, 11,240 feet, and its lowest is sea level. The longest river entirely within the state is the John Day, at 281 miles. Bounded to the north by the Columbia River and the state of Washington and to the west by the Pacific, it is bordered to the east by Idaho and the Snake River, and to the south by California and Washington.

TAXES Of significance to travelers: Oregon has no sales tax. Its room tax is 1 percent, which is usually (but not always) augmented by local room taxes, which may raise the cost of your room as much as 13 percent. It has fairly hefty property taxes, which were capped some years ago, and a personal income tax, as well as a baroque corporate tax structure dating from the late 1800s, designed to draw employers to the state.

TIME ZONES Most of Oregon is on Pacific Time, except for an anomalous rectangle comprising most of Malheur County, which is on Mountain Time.

TRAVEL INFORMATION Local and regional visitors centers and chambers of commerce are listed in each chapter under *Guidance*. In addition, much information is available from the Oregon Tourism Commission, **Travel Oregon** (1-800-547-7842; www.traveloregon.com), 670 Hawthorne Avenue SE, Suite 240, Salem.

UNIVERSITIES Oregon's state system of higher education includes seven public universities: **Portland State University** (Portland), the **University of Oregon** (Eugene), **Oregon State University** (Corvallis), **Western Oregon University** (Monmouth), **Eastern Oregon University** (La Grande), **Southern Oregon University** (Ashland), and **Oregon Institute of Technology** (Klamath Falls). In addition there are 17 community colleges, often with satellite campuses to serve rural areas. However, Oregon's first university is the private **Willamette University** in Salem, founded by missionary Jason Lee—interesting to visit for its gardens and architecture. Other private universities of note are **Reed College** and **Lewis and Clark College** in Portland, and **Linfield College** in McMinnville.

WEATHER Generally, western Oregon is either cool and damp or warm and damp, while the east is dry and cold (sometimes very cold) or dry and hot (sometimes very hot). The highest temperature recorded in the state was 119 degrees in Pendleton on August 10, 1898, and the lowest was -54 in Seneca, on February 10, 1933. Frequently updated forecasts are online at www.tripcheck.com.

WHALE-WATCHING A favorite pastime is spotting Pacific gray whales as they migrate between their calving grounds in Mexico and their feeding grounds off Alaska. Auspicious lookout points, often staffed by volunteer naturalists, are noted in the text. Southward migration off Oregon occurs in December, and from early March through June they pass our coasts, heading north. A couple of hundred whales summer off the coast, so you have a chance of seeing one during much of the year.

WILD AND SCENIC RIVERS With its heavy rain and high mountains, Oregon possesses a long list of designated Wild and Scenic Rivers, from portions of the great Snake River to stretches of the John Day, Deschutes, Rogue, and Chetco rivers, to a rash of smaller but impressive streams like the Illinois, Sandy, Sixes, and Elk. Since the whole purpose of the designation is to keep a given watercourse clean and free flowing and to preserve its natural qualities (fish, scenery, wildlife), they are generally outstanding places to raft, kayak, picnic, or gaze upon.

WILDERNESS AREAS We are fortunate to have numerous designated wilderness areas comprising deep forest, alpine meadows, canyons, and wild streams, where humans leave only footprints (though horses leave considerably more). Wilderness areas are closed to mechanized equipment, meaning no mountain bikes, snowmobiles, chainsaws, etc. Be courteous to the next person by burying your waste, packing out your garbage, and leaving the wilderness as you found it; and be prudent. *Wilderness* means that help is not around the corner. Visitors are asked to fill out a free permit at trailheads.

WILDLIFE There is a lot of it. Birdlife is generous, and each chapter has notes on bird-watching sites. Among mammals, cheeky chipmunks and squirrels compete for a bite of your lunch. Mule deer and elk are common; scattered herds of pronghorn bound over the eastern scrublands, and bighorn sheep have been successfully reintroduced at Hart Mountain, Abert Rim, and Hells Canyon. Even mountain goats are occasionally seen in the northeastern wilderness. If you hang out on rivers, you may see otter, beaver, or mink. Cougars have increased, though they're more likely to see you than you are to see them (one lodged in downtown Bend for a few weeks in 2004, eluding the efforts of government dogs and hunters to eliminate it). Black bear inhabit the forests. They are fairly discreet except when it comes to food. Coyote yap the night away in the eastern desert. The grizzly is long gone, but one possible comeback creature is the wolf: a few have established themselves in the northeastern corner of the state, having crossed over from Idaho.

WILDLIFE AREAS Twenty-two national wildlife refuges and 22 state refuges protect all sorts of habitats and species around the state, from sea lions to butterflies. They are noted in the relevant chapters, but you can get further information from the **U.S. Fish and Wildlife Service** (503-231-6201; www.fws.gov) and the **Oregon Department of Fish and Wildlife** (1-800-720-ODFW; www.dfw.state.or.us).

WINE From a few cautious slips in the 1960s, the Oregon wine industry has sent tendrils all over the state. There are now 15 recognized growing areas producing wines from Albarino to Zinfandel (Oregon Pinot Noir has become quite celebrated); the Willamette Valley, where it all began, is the epicenter of Oregon's wine country, but fine vines and wineries can be found to the south in the Rogue, Umpqua, and Applegate valleys as well as the Columbia Gorge. There's even a wine district in the far east, on the banks of the Snake. Leisurely tasting tours offer fine scenery along with fine wines; plan your own with help from www.oregonwines.com or the **Willamette Valley Wineries Association** (www.willamettewines.com). Or leave the driving to someone else; a list of wine tour operators appears on the latter's Web site and at www.winetouroregon.com.

WINTER SPORTS Winter is anticipated with bated breath amid speculation on when the ski resorts will open. Of which there are several. They are listed under *Winter Sports* in the relevant chapters of this book. Timberline, on Mount Hood, is open for skiing year-round.

Northern Oregon Coast

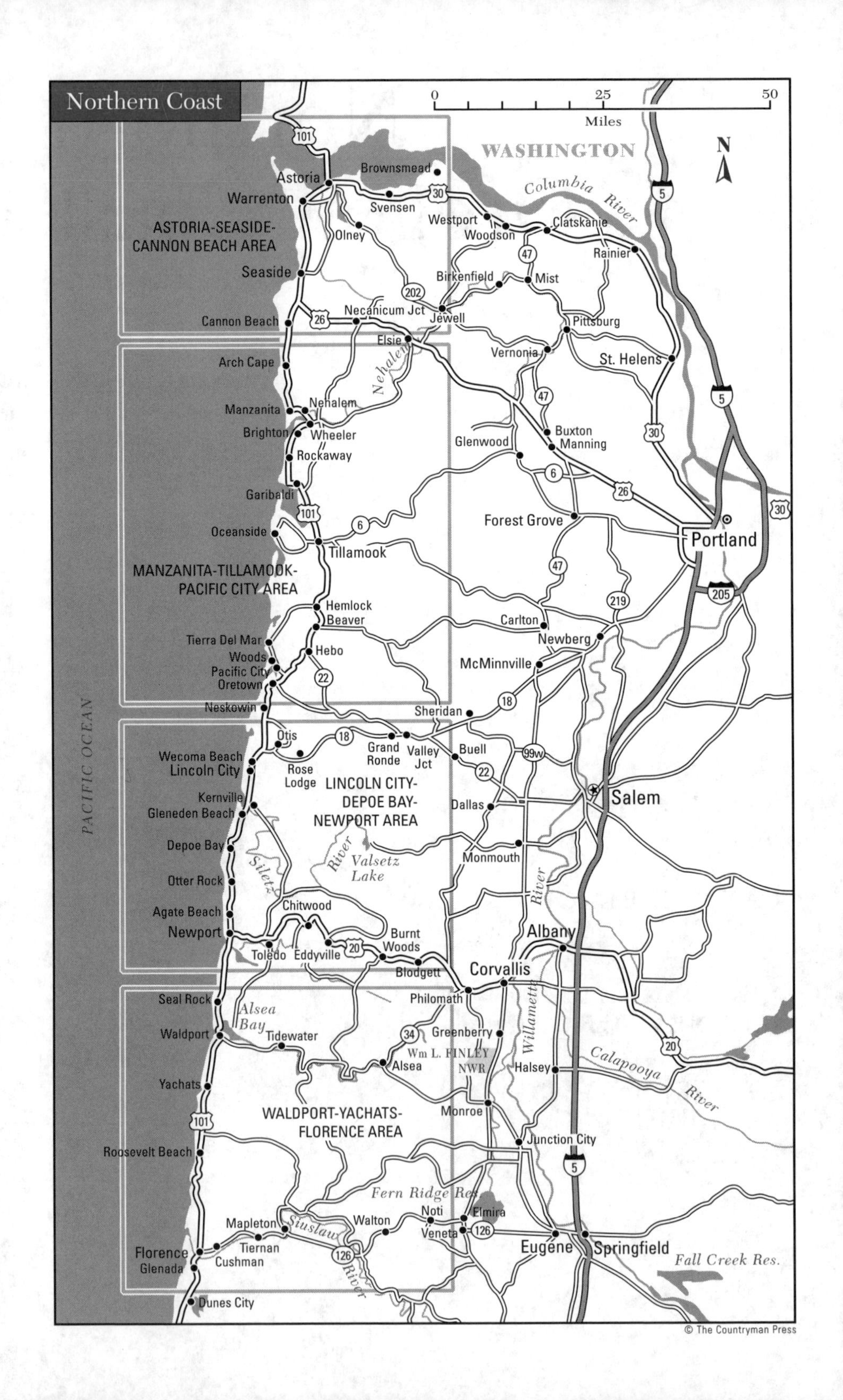
Northern Coast
0
25
50
Miles
N
WASHINGTON
Columbia River
PACIFIC OCEAN
ASTORIA-SEASIDE-CANNON BEACH AREA
MANZANITA-TILLAMOOK-PACIFIC CITY AREA
LINCOLN CITY-DEPOE BAY-NEWPORT AREA
WALDPORT-YACHATS-FLORENCE AREA
Astoria
Warrenton
Brownsmead
Svensen
Westport
Woodson
Clatskanie
Rainier
Olney
Seaside
Birkenfield
Mist
Cannon Beach
Necanicum Jct
Jewell
Pittsburg
Elsie
Vernonia
St. Helens
Arch Cape
Nehalem
Manzanita
Brighton
Wheeler
Rockaway
Garibaldi
Buxton
Manning
Glenwood
Forest Grove
Portland
Oceanside
Tillamook
Hemlock
Beaver
Carlton
Newberg
Tierra Del Mar
Woods
Pacific City
Oretown
Hebo
McMinnville
Neskowin
Sheridan
Otis
Grand Ronde
Valley Jct
Buell
Wecoma Beach
Lincoln City
Rose Lodge
Salem
Kernville
Gleneden Beach
Dallas
Depoe Bay
Siletz
River
Valsetz Lake
Monmouth
Otter Rock
Agate Beach
Chitwood
Newport
Burnt Woods
Albany
Toledo
Eddyville
Blodgett
Corvallis
Seal Rock
Philomath
Alsea Bay
Waldport
Tidewater
Greenberry
Wm L. FINLEY NWR
Alsea
Willamette River
Halsey
Calapooya River
Yachats
Monroe
Junction City
Roosevelt Beach
Fern Ridge Res.
Mapleton
Siuslaw River
Walton
Noti
Elmira
Veneta
Eugene
Springfield
Florence
Tiernan
Glenada
Cushman
Fall Creek Res.
Dunes City
101
30
5
47
202
26
6
219
205
22
18
99w
20
34
126
© The Countryman Press

NORTHERN OREGON COAST

Oddly, one reason the entire Oregon coastline is public is its history as a thoroughfare. Rare was the road, and rarer the train that penetrated the tangled Coast Range. The little coastal communities had been settled by sea, by following the beach, or, in some cases, by very patient overland pioneers. Once there, they pretty much had to fend for themselves, and to get from one to another—for supplies, for business, or to visit—people had to go by boat or along the beaches. So the beaches were public rights-of-way, with traffic in the form of horses and wagons or a few mules. Which was not as simple as it may sound. On the beaches you had to attend to high water and "sneaker waves," and getting around, or over, the rocky headlands was a nightmare, not to speak of river crossings. When US 101 came in with its bridges in the 1930s, it was a revolution.

Public access didn't survive unchallenged, of course, once the coast became accessible to tourists and thus to developers and landowners wanting their own piece of beach. However, it's now been enshrined in the "Beach Law" of 1967: anywhere below the vegetation line (legally defined) is the property of all Oregonians, with a few areas seasonally restricted to protect nesting birds. And what a beach. The Pacific, unimpeded by islands or reefs, drives in from Japan in long combers. Tall chunks of rock separated from the mainland by earthquakes or erosion stand offshore, rookeries for murres and rest stops for sea lions. Rivers surge from the temperate rain forest. Despite the towns and highway, there's nothing much wilder than this wild ocean, where the forested mountains come down to the sea. You can get your hot coffee in the morning, then go watch the rollers and know that you and your coffee are highly transitory.

On this northern half of the coast particularly are traces of Oregon's entry into the American orbit: Fort Clatsop, where the Corps of Discovery spent the winter of 1805–1806, and Fort Astoria, where John Jacob Astor set up his fur-trading operations (they were transitory, too; what you see now are replicas). Spanish explorers had started sailing by in the 16th century and named some landforms, otherwise showing little interest. But British, Russian, and American captains jostled for influence for years. By the late 1700s they were trading with the tribes at the mouth of the Columbia, who called them indiscriminately "Boston" and who succumbed in large numbers to smallpox, a by-product of trade.

US 101 is one of the great American roads, affording splendid views and connecting all the coastal villages and towns. But give yourself time. Get off the highway and meander through historic Astoria. Browse the small towns for their hidden treasures. And walk the beaches. Every so often storms or tides uncover something new, like a sunken forest or a lump of beeswax from a centuries-old Spanish shipwreck.

ASTORIA–SEASIDE–WARRENTON AREA

Astoria has the distinction of being the incorporated city with the highest rainfall in the contiguous United States. This doesn't mean you shouldn't go—there are some cozy places to come in from the cold—but try for summer or fall, when skies can be sunny and temperatures mild. This little corner of the state is distinctive in other ways, too. It's where the Columbia spectacularly meets the sea, which gave rise to a large fishing industry and to some historical firsts: first American permanent settlement in the Northwest (Fort Astor), and first beach resort in Oregon (Seaside). There's a lot of nature to enjoy, and if it does rain, pop into a fine museum, restaurant, or warm café.

GUIDANCE **Astoria and Warrenton Area Chamber of Commerce** (1-800-875-6807; www.oldoregon.com), 111 W. Marine Drive, Astoria 97103.

Clatsop County Parks (503-325-9306), 1100 Olney Avenue, Astoria 97103.

Oregon Coast Visitors Association (1-888-OCVA-101; www.visittheoregoncoast.com), 137 NE First Street, P.O. Box 74, Newport 97365.

Oregon State Parks (1-800-551-6949; www.oregon.gov), 725 Summer Street NE, Suite C, Salem 97301.

Seaside Visitors Bureau (1-888-306-2326; www.seasideor.com), 989 Broadway, Seaside 97138.

GETTING THERE *By car:* From Portland, take **US 26** west till you reach **US 101** along the coast; Cannon Beach will be 5 miles to your south, and Seaside 4 miles north. Fifteen more miles will take you to Astoria, just off **US 101** on **US 30.** Or take US 30 northwest out of Portland for a scenic meandering drive to Astoria (96 miles) along the lower Columbia.

GETTING AROUND *By bus:* The **Sunset Empire** (503-861-7433) runs buses between Astoria, Warrenton, Hammond, and Seaside. However, for most intents and purposes, you'll want a car.

MEDICAL EMERGENCY **Columbia Memorial Hospital** (503-325-4321), 2111 Exhange Street, Astoria.

Providence Seaside Hospital (503-717-7000), 725 S. Wahanna Road, Seaside.

✱ To See

FARMERS' MARKETS **Astoria Sunday Market** (503-325-1010), on 12th Street between Marine and Exchange, Astoria. Sun. 10–2, May–Oct.

Cannon Beach Farmers' Market (503-436-8044), at the intersection of Gower and Hemlock streets, Cannon Beach. Tues. 2–6, June–Sept. Includes wild-caught seafood.

FOR FAMILIES ✐ **Astoria Riverfront Trolley** (503-325-6311), Astoria riverfront. Daily noon–7, Memorial Day–Labor Day (except in the case of rain), and intermittently in fall and spring. One trip, $1; all-day pass, $2. See the Astoria waterfront without wearing your feet out or getting wet, with running commentary provided by the conductor. The 2.5-mile trip takes about an hour, but you can ride as long as you want. Board at any of nine stops along the route, or just flag it down.

✐ **Captain Gray's Port of Play** (503-325-8669; www.portofplay.org), 785 Alameda Avenue, Astoria. Tues.–Fri. 10–1 and 3–5, Sat. 1–4. Admission $3 per child. Children can play dentist, build, paint, create earthquakes (well, they can do that anywhere), and even learn a bit about Lewis and Clark.

✐ **Seaside Aquarium** (503-738-6211; www.seasideaquarium.com), 200 N. Promenade, Seaside. Daily from 9 AM. General admission $7.50, seniors $6.25, children 6–13 $3.25; families $25. One of the most venerable aquariums on the West Coast, this modestly shingled operation opened its doors in 1937. While lacking the "wow" effect of newer, higher-tech institutions, it's still a place to discover strange creatures of the sea, touch some of them, and get acquainted with an extended family of harbor seals.

HISTORIC HOMES **Flavel House** (503-325-2203), corner of Duane and Eighth streets, Astoria. Daily 10–5, May–Sept. and daily 11–4, Oct.–Apr. General admission $5, seniors $4, children $2. Captain Flavel could afford to build this wildly flamboyant mansion back in 1885. He was a Columbia Bar pilot, one of the hardy breed of seamen who dared to guide ships over the treacherous bar on which so many vessels have foundered. A good bar pilot could command high prices, as without his service there could be no shipping in or out of the Columbia's mouth. Flavel became a millionaire. The house is enormous: more than 11,000 square feet, with a large formal parlor, dining room, music room, and library downstairs, all ornate with fine woodwork and plaster molding. Upstairs are five capacious bedrooms, and bathroom with a tin tub, while the help slept in the attic. It was the height of luxury—indoor plumbing and gas lighting

WOOD AND ZINC BATHTUB AT THE FLAVEL HOUSE

throughout, and a basement furnace that heated the house with unimaginable quantities of logs (12- and 14-foot ceilings!) Captain and Mrs. Flavel lived in it with their two daughters, though the captain died after seven years; the family stayed on and eventually deeded it to the county. A visitors center and shop occupy the former carriage house behind the mansion. The entire neighborhood is composed of homes built in the late 1800s and early 1900s; a stroll takes you past some gems.

Hiram Brown House, 1337 Franklin Avenue, Astoria. This oldest surviving house in Astoria was built in 1852 by Capt. Hiram Brown. He had situated it a few miles east, but by 1862 it was clear that the city was developing to the west under a tall hill, so he had it barged along the river and pulled by oxen to its present site. Wings were added so that now it has five bedrooms. The current (private) owners painstakingly restored it, even to the gas lighting system. Please respect the owners' privacy.

HISTORIC SITES **Astoria Column** (503-325-2963; www.astoriacolumn.org), 2199 Coxcomb Drive, Astoria. Daily dawn–dusk; parking $1 per car. Never say that Oregon ignores the classics. Modeled after Trajan's Column in Rome, the 1926 Astoria Column was a pet project of Ralph Budd, president of the Great Northern Railroad. Scenes of Astorian history spiral up the column, depicting events from precontact times to the coming of the railroad in 1893 (well, fair enough), carved and colored by Attilo Pusterla, an Italian expert in the sgraffito style. Lewis and Clark appear soon after Captain Gray, crossing mountains, boiling salt, and having other adventures, followed by the arrival of John Jacob Astor after many mishaps, with some recognition of Indian fishing and canoeing techniques. It's a remarkable conceit. And even if you can't really see all the images from the ground, you can climb the 164 stairs inside and come out to a glorious view of the estuary, the Pacific, and a range of volcanoes. That is, if it isn't raining.

Fort Astoria, Fifteenth and Exchange Streets, Astoria. It didn't take long. Five years after Lewis and Clark returned with reports of abundant beaver, otter, bear, and other fur-bearing creatures, John Jacob Astor and his party arrived at the mouth of the Columbia and built a fort as the center of operations for their Pacific Fur Company. It was the first American-owned settlement in the Pacific Northwest, but in 1813 it was sold to the British North West Company—part of the fallout from the War of 1812. The British traders eventually moved upriver to Fort Vancouver, and Fort Astoria fell into disuse. It has since crumbled, but a replica of the blockhouse sits inconspicuously in a small park on part of the original site.

Fort Stevens State Park Military Site (503-861-1671), 100 Peter Iredale Road, Hammond. On the long spit of land separating the Columbia from the sea, the U.S. Army built one of three forts designed to protect the mouth of the river from entry by hostile parties (the others are Fort Canby and Fort Columbia, on the Washington side). Begun during the Civil War, its gun batteries and foritifications were modernized and expanded for defense during the Spanish-American War, the First World War, and World War II, after which they were decommissioned. Pick up a self-guiding brochure to the many points of interest at the park entrance, or sign up for a guided tour. Tours by army truck operate daily for $4 adults and $2 kids; tours of the 90-year-old underground battery likewise. You can visit the guardhouse Sat.–Mon. for free, and the museum is open daily 10–6. Living-history programs take place on summer weekends.

Seaside Promenade, along the beach in Seaside. Seaside has been a resort since 1870. From 1888 a "daddy train" brought Portland businessmen out to join their summering families on the weekends, and increased train service brought more growth and more summering or weekending families, promoting a carnival atmosphere that persists in today's video arcades and rides. The concrete promenade replaced an earlier wooden boardwalk in 1920.

***Peter Iredale* shipwreck,** a mile southwest of Hammond near **Fort Stevens State Park.** The mouth of the Columbia is called the graveyard of the Pacific for good reason. Since 1792, there have been two thousand recorded wrecks here, including more than two hundred big ships. On Oct. 25, 1906, the *Peter Iredale,* a four-masted tall steel ship bound for Portland, ran aground on Clatsop Spit in thick fog and strong westerly winds. Luckily all aboard were saved, even the two stowaways, and decaying remains of the hull are still visible in the sands, sometimes nearly buried, sometimes quite exposed.

Uniontown, along Astoria's western edge. In the heyday of Astoria's fishpacking industry, the Uniontown district was the domain of workers at the Union Cannery. Mostly Finnish immigrants, they lived in waterfront boardinghouses or modest homes on the hillside and brought food and folk traditions with them. Now huddled under a freeway, it has avoided gentrification and is the place to go for fresh fish and old-time cafés and bars.

MUSEUMS Camp 18 Logging Museum (1-800-874-1810; www.camp18restaurant.com), 42362 US 26, Elsie; 22 miles east of Seaside. Outdoor exhibits open daily; check at reception desk for key to indoor exhibits (open irregularly). Free. The history of the Northwest is in part a history of logging, and you can find it in this collection of vintage logging equipment. "Steam donkeys," tools, logging arches, even a wood-sided caboose are brought together in and around the spreading log museum, which is in itself is an example of woodcraft. An on-site restaurant serves logger-sized breakfasts, lunches, and dinners.

Columbia River Maritime Museum (503-325-2323; www.crmm.org), 1792 Marine Drive, Astoria. Daily 9:30–5. General admission $10, seniors $8, children 6–17 $5, under six free. Even the address is significant. It was in 1792 that American captain Robert Gray managed to cross the treacherous bar and became the first recorded nonnative to enter the Columbia River, claiming the surrounding territory for the United States and naming the river for his ship, the *Columbia Rediviva.* (Captain Vancouver followed soon after, advancing British claims that took decades to sort out.) Here you can see models of their boats and others occupy one of the galleries here, while other galleries are a guide to life on the river from pre-Columbian times to the present. Step onto some of the vessels that have

AT THE COLUMBIA RIVER MARITIME MUSEUM YOU CAN ALWAYS OBSERVE A RESCUE AT SEA.

made their living on the river—a 1914 gillnetter (in use till 1972), a World War II warship, a tugboat. Or, if you're in a more contemplative mood, take in the watercolors of George Davidson, who was signed on with Gray's crew to provide a visual record of the discoveries. Out on the wharf, visit the *Lighthouse Columbia.* This pilot boat used to guide ships safely across the bar—a job that is still done, albeit by newer boats. And in an ominous but striking two-story exhibit, a Coast Guard boat pitches into polymer waves at a frightening angle, intent upon a rescue (a short film on the river and its heroes is even more impressive). Visible through the sweeping glass front, the river itself is a constant presence.

Heritage Museum (503-325-2203), corner of Sixth and Exchange streets, Astoria. Daily 10–5 in summer, 10–4 in winter. General admission $3, seniors $2, youth $1. Everything you wanted to know about Clatsop County history: its native American heritage, geology, wildlife, and immigrants, through artifacts and ten thousand historic photographs.

Seaside Museum and Historical Society (503-738-7065), 570 Necanicum Drive, Seaside. Mon.–Sat. 10–4, May–Sept.; 10–3, Oct.–Apr. General admission $3, seniors $2, students $1; kids under six free. Not content with just depicting Seaside's glory days as Oregon's first coastal resort, the little museum also displays a collection of two thousand local Indian artifacts and a Clatsop longhouse, and details the activities of Lewis and Clark in the area. Next door, the 1907 Butterfield cottage has been restored as a beach house of the period, which would no doubt amuse the original owners.

NATURAL WONDERS **Columbia Estuary.** There are few more viscerally moving sights in nature than that of the Great River of the West emptying itself into the expansive Pacific. Having descended the heights of the Canadian Rockies, looped over the arid scablands of Washington, crossed the Cascade Range through the Columbia Gorge, and siphoned runoff from tributaries as large as the Snake and as small as Young's River, despite all the dams, it runs the last 150 miles of its journey wild and free to merge with the untrammeled sea. Yet some early mariners coming up the coast missed the rivermouth entirely because of fog or disbelief; the breadth of the estuary deceived several with the illusion of a large bay, and the breakers and contrary currents forbade entry until Captain Gray crossed the bar, with luck and patience, and navigated far enough to prove it was a river. Even Lewis and Clark, who certainly knew they were traveling down a river, thought they'd reached the sea a good 20 miles before they did—the waves and turbulence suggest as much. Flow at the river's mouth varies seasonally but averages 265,000 cubic feet per second, draining an area of 259,000 square miles. A fine view can be had from the cliffs Cape Disappointment, on the Washington side (take the bridge from Astoria), or from sea level at the breakwater on Clatsop Spit.

Klootchy Creek Spruce, about 5 miles from Seaside off US 26 at **Klootchy Creek State Park.** This majestic Sitka spruce used to be the largest in the United States, topping out at 200 feet. But a hurricane-force storm barreled in on Dec. 2, 2007, and the tree broke off 80 feet above the ground. The fallen champion is still visible on the forest floor, where chunks of it have been left to provide "nurse logs" for baby trees. Its 17-foot diameter and sheer mass still impress. It was estimated to be 500 to 750 years old.

SELF-GUIDING TOURS Two free **audio tours** of Astoria and Warrenton are downloadable from www.oldoregon.com, the area chamber of commerce: **Astoria and Warrenton's Historical Attractions,** with commentary and anecdotes on the canneries, Lewis and Clark, and other historic sites; and **The Reel Astoria,** a guide to locations featured in various movies.

Lewis and Clark sites: After a sodden, miserable two weeks encamped north of the river's mouth, the party took local advice and crossed the tumultuous estuary in canoes to find a more sheltered winter camp. (The captains put it to a vote, including the normally disenfranchised York, Clark's slave, and Sacagawea; not surprisingly, all were in favor.) They found a spot in the woods on a creek and built Fort Clatsop, a log square where the Corps lived, cooked, slept, ate, and grumbled from Dec. 1805 till the following Mar. At **Fort Clatsop National Memorial** (503-861-2471), 92343 Fort Clatsop Road, Astoria, a replica of the fort amid humid firs gives you some idea of their living conditions; living-history activities take place in summer. The adjacent visitors center houses fascinating displays of documents and rosters from the journey, their goals and tools, and what became of the members later in life. Open daily except Christmas, 9–6 in summer, 9–5 otherwise. Admission $5, children 4–16 $2. From the fort you can walk (or take a shuttle in summer) to **Netul Landing,** where the explorers came ashore after paddling up the Netul River (now Lewis and Clark River) to their new quarters.

Salt was a staple to preserve food and health. Several men were sent to the beach and commissioned to produce salt, which they did by boiling seawater. The **Seaside Saltworks** are commemorated with a cairn on Lewis and Clark Way, Seaside, near the promenade. In summer salt-boiling reenactments take place on the nearby beach.

Captain Clark called **Tillamook Head** "the steepest worst and highest mountain I ever ascended," which is hard to believe if you've read his account of crossing the Bitterroots. Maybe he was fed up. Still, it is a great lump of forested rock rising from the sea, and it stood between him and a whale beached just south of it. The

THE REPLICA OF LEWIS AND CLARK'S DIGS AT FORT CLATSOP NATIONAL HISTORIC PARK

great creature would enhance their food supply, and how often had the company seen a whale? A group including Sacagawea, who had no intention of missing this unique sight, took two weeks to reach the whale, crossing the Head in bad weather. They reached the whale near the mouth of **Ecola Creek** to find most of the whale stripped, and they traded with some Indians for some of the meat and blubber. Today **Ecola State Park** occupies much of the head and includes the 2.5-mile **Clatsop Trail Loop,** taking you along Clark's path from Indian Creek to Hiker's Camp.

A hunting party led by Patrick Gass, who also kept a journal, found 65-foot **Youngs River Falls** about 6 miles from the fort, now reachable by car about 8 miles south of Astoria via OR 202 and Young's River Road. View the falls from the parking lot or take a short trail to their base.

SCENIC DRIVES The **Pacific Coast Scenic Byway,** US 101, runs along the entire coast of Oregon, 363 miles. Often winding, especially around the headlands, it offers views of long Pacific combers, dunes, tidal pools, cliffs, and the chance to stop and explore any beach you like.

✷ To Do

BICYCLING The 1.5-mile wetland interpretive trail at **Cullaby Lake County Park** is a leisurely family-friendly ride, shared with walkers; likewise the 1.8-mile **promenade** in Seaside. For a longer jaunt, cycle out **Clatsop Spit** along NW Ridge Road or NW Warrenton Drive and continue through **Fort Stevens State Park** to the land's end, about 15 miles, or enjoy the 9 miles of bike trails winding through the park.

BIRD-WATCHING The **South Jetty** of the Columbia River, at **Fort Stevens State Park,** is a great (though windy) place for viewing species like shearwaters, puffins, auklets, loons, and wintering harlequin ducks riding the swells. In fall, thousands of migrating songbirds may fill the trees around the **Astoria Column** on Coxcomb Hill, Astoria. **Young's Bay,** between Astoria and Warrenton, draws thousands of migrating waterfowl in fall; luckily there's a causeway so you can virtually drive among them. Another good spot for such birds is along OR 202 just south of Astoria. **Mill Ponds Park** in Seaside, at the south end of Neawanna Natural Park, attracts a variety of species with both freshwater and brackish ponds.

CAMPING **Fort Stevens State Park,** on Clatsop Spit about 20 miles northwest of Astoria by US 101 and NW Ridge Road, is a large park with a large campground: 174 full hookup sites, 302 electrical hookup sites, 19 tent sites, and 15 yurts (hiker/biker sites by request), with all amenities like water, toilets, showers, etc. Reserve at 1-800-452-5687. A reduced number of sites is available Oct.–Apr. on a first-come, first-served basis.

Saddle Mountain State Park, back in the Coast Range 14 miles east of Seaside off US 26, offers 10 primitive campsites at the Saddle Mountain trailhead, open Mar.–Oct. Restrooms are available.

Ecola State Park (503-436-2844) has three primitive hike-in cabins 1.5 miles from Indian Beach parking area, each sleeping four on platforms; vault toilet; no water, heat, or electricity. Free, but day passes for each day of stay must be visible

OLD PILINGS AT NETUL LANDING ARE THE REMAINS OF FORMER LOGGING OPERATIONS.

on your car. No charge for through-hikers on the coastal trail system.

CANOEING AND KAYAKING The **Lewis and Clark River** meanders a scant 20 miles from its source to the Columbia estuary, offering a nice flat paddle; **Netul Landing,** a mile south of **Fort Clatsop,** is a convenient put-in point. The Park Service also offers short, guided kayak and canoe trips from the landing in summer; call 503-861-4425 for information or to reserve.

GOLF **Gearhart Golf Links** (503-738-3538), 1157 N. Marion Avenue, Gearhart. Eighteen holes.

The Highlands at Gearhart (503-738-5248), 33260 Highlands Lane, Gearhart. Nine holes.

Seaside Golf Club (503-738-5261), 451 Avenue U, Seaside. Nine holes.

HIKING From urban strolls to rugged mountain trails, here's a selection:

Astoria River Walk is a level, paved trail running for 4 miles along the Astoria waterfront, past the old canneries, piers, and slumbering sea lions. A shorter, but uphill, trail in Astoria starts at 28th and Irving, going up through fern and forest to the Astoria Column; the attraction of this trail is the **Cathedral Tree,** a three-hundred-year-old Sitka spruce. (This trail is partially closed at time of writing due to storm damage but is under repair.)

INSIDE FORT CLATSOP

The **Tillamook Head Trail** duplicates part of the journey Lewis and Clark took in search of a beached whale. They had a hard time of it. From the **Indian Beach** trailhead in **Ecola State Park** to the **Tillamook Head Trailhead** just south of Seaside, the trail rises through dense forest, then descends gradually from the promontory to Seaside, a distance of about 6 miles, with some spectacular ocean views. A hiker's camp with tent sites and three primitive cabins is about 3 miles from the Indian Beach trailhead. Also in **Ecola State Park, Clatsop Loop** is a 2.5-mile route that takes an old road up to Hiker's Camp, then turns back on a path along the brow of Tillamook Head for some ocean panoramas; elevation gain is 800 feet.

A pleasant walk at **Fort Stevens State Park** is the 2-mile path around **Coffenbury Lake.** Other park trails traverse seaside forest and wetlands.

From **Fort Clatsop,** the historic **Fort to Sea Trail** tries to retrace a route Lewis and Clark may have taken to the sea—6.5 miles through some hilly forest, wetlands, and dunes, and finally Sunset Beach. You will need a shuttle if you don't want to hike back; call **Fort Clatsop Visitor Center** to see if a shuttle is running. Or, you can shorten the trip by taking one of the side trails that loop back to the fort.

The **Saddle Mountain Trail** starts from a marked trailhead some 14 miles east of Seaside on US 26 and rises sharply—close to 3,000 feet in 2.5 miles—to the 3,283-foot peak. Most of the trail is in forest that opens out to a meadow at the top, with views of the surrounding Coast Range.

Shively Park, a wooded, landscaped urban park off Williamsport Road in Astoria, is popular for weddings and leisurely strolls.

Then, of course, there are **beach walks.** Remember, all ocean beaches are public to the vegetation line; look for access points along US 101 or at the state parks.

✷ Wilder Places

PARKS Del Ray Beach State Recreation Site (1-800-551-6949), off US 101, 2 miles north of Gearhart, is a day-use park where a short path leads over dunes to the beach. Walk, watch birds, fly a kite, or watch the waves. No fee.

Ecola State Park (503-436-2844), 2 miles north of Cannon Beach, occupies a large part of Tillamook Head. Just north of town the access road winds up, and up, through old forest, coming out on the top of the windy promontory for unbeatable views of the wide ocean and surf pounding the beaches below. Hike, camp, or picnic (see *Camping* and *Hiking*); explore tidal pools; or watch whales from the headland. It's a spectacular park in a state where that is no mean boast.

THE VIEW FROM TILLAMOOK HEAD IN ECOLA STATE PARK

Fort Stevens State Park (1-800-551-6949), on Clatsop Spit about 20 miles from Astoria. A military base for more than 80 years, Fort Stevens is now a 3,700-acre park encompassing a large historic site, freshwater ponds, hiking and biking trails, campgrounds (see the relevant categories above), and the long South Jetty between the Columbia River and the Pacific. Also a rewarding park for bird-watching and fishing.

Saddle Mountain State Park (1-800-551-6949), about 14 miles east of Seaside off US 26, is no ocean park but sits deep in the damp Coast Range. A steep and sometimes slippery trail leads to the mountaintop, with some primitive campsites at the trailhead. This is a place to enjoy dense rain forest (and often rain) and seasonal wildflowers.

WILDLIFE REFUGES The **Necanicum Estuary,** where the Necanicum and Neawanna rivers join to flow into the sea, is graced by **Neawanna Natural History Park** and the new **Necanicum Estuary Natural History Park** (North Coast Land Conservancy, 503-738-9126), designed to protect the estuary's complex ecology. Bald eagles nest alongside, endangered snowy plovers have nested there, and an entire estuarine web of life follows the tides. Access is from Seaside High School on N. Holladay or Alder Mill Road. Nature trails and observation platforms enhance the viewing experience.

✷ Lodging

BED & BREAKFASTS

Astoria

Astoria Inn Bed and Breakfast (1-800-718-8153; www.astoriaoregonbb.com), 3391 Irving Avenue. Set up against Coxcomb Hill, the 1890s house betrays builder Ole Haren's Norwegian roots with a simple gabled plan and subtle geometric details—a contrast with its more ornate neighbors. The four guest rooms, all with private baths, have a more Victorian decor. With its back to the woods, it's quiet, and you may see the occasional deer wander by. A wraparound porch looks out over the town. $80–95, with full breakfast.

Britta's Inn Bed and Breakfast (503-325-4940; www.brittasinn.com), 1237 Kensington Avenue. The clean lines of a Craftsman house couldn't present a greater contrast with, say, the nearby Flavel mansion, though the two are separated by only a generation. Fir interiors, oak furniture, and a homey elegance make you feel at home—well, it is a home. The two guest rooms have private bathrooms and all comforts. $120–135, with full organic breakfast.

Clementine's Bed and Breakfast (1-800-521-6801; www.clementines-bb.com), 847 Exchange Street. One of the city's imposing late-19th-century homes, this one is Italianate in style and dates from 1888. Today it holds five guest rooms, each comfortably appointed with feather beds, down comforters, fine linens, and its own bathroom; some have balconies or fireplaces. Children and pets welcome! (Well behaved, of course.) Owners Judith and Cliff Taylor have had the place since 1993 and can tell you all about the area; Judith also gives cooking classes at the Clementine, which tells you something about the breakfasts. $90–145, including full breakfast and afternoon hors d'oeuvres with wine. Next door, under the same ownership, is the **Moose Temple Lodge,** which happens to be the oldest building in Astoria (dating from the 1850s). It was, in fact, a Moose Lodge for 40 years and now welcomes guests with two suites and a loft. $110–135; the suites require a two-night minimum.

Franklin Station Bed and Breakfast (503-325-4314; www.astoriaoregonbb.com), 1140 Franklin Street. It was a shipbuilder's home when built in 1900, and it still stands square and solid just a couple of blocks from Astoria's historic center. Of the six rooms, all have private baths, some have balconies, and one even has a telescope for watching ships on the river. A friendly welcome and a hearty, hot breakfast make this an agreeable base for visiting Astoria's environs. $80–135, but ask about off-season specials.

Rose River Inn (1-888-876-0028; www.roseriverinn.com), 1510 Franklin Avenue. It sure has plenty of roses. Three luxurious guest rooms and two suites (one even has a sauna) enjoy period furnishings in this 1912 Craftsman house. $85–160, with full breakfast; children over 12 welcome.

Hammond

Officers' Inn (1-888-861-2524; www.officersinn.com), 540 Russell Place. Stay in the 1905 officers' housing at Fort Stevens. The original pressed tin ceilings still cover the living and dining rooms, and the nine rooms include two suites for families or friends. Pets okay in certain rooms. $85–150, with full breakfast.

Seaside

Tenth Street Inn (1-800-745-2378; www.10aveinn.com), 125 10th Avenue. With a piano, fireplace, and stuffed chairs in the parlor, it couldn't get much cozier. The 1908 home of a judge, it now offers three guest rooms with private bathrooms and ocean views, and it's a short walk to the beach. $109–160. The **Doll's House** cottage next door can accommodate families with two bedrooms and two baths. $160.

HOSTELS

Astoria

Hideaway Inn and Hostel (503-325-6989; www.hideawayinnandhostel.com), 443 14th Street. Above the Astoria Co-op, in a 1920s hotel, the Hideaway offers clean, comfortable rooms with private baths, rooms with shared baths, and four-bunked dorm rooms. All have access to the common kitchen and Wi-Fi. Here is Astoria's budget option. Dorm bunks $20, including linens.

Seaside

Seaside International Hostel (503-738-7911), 930 N. Holladay Drive. With a staff devoted to hosteling, the Seaside offers the camaraderie of the best hostels with a common kitchen, decks, gardens, and even singing around the fire. If you prefer more privacy than a bunk-bedded room affords, there are private rooms at your disposal. Rent one of the hostel kayaks for a paddle on the river or take a seaside stroll; you're few blocks from the beach. Private rooms $47–59; dorm bunks $23–26.

HOTELS AND MOTELS

Astoria

Cannery Pier Hotel (1-888-325-4996; www.cannerypierhotel.com), 10 Basin Street. Someone had to do it—build a hotel out on the water on the former site of the Union Fisherman's Cannery. Private balconies and fireplaces are standard room amenities, and hotel features include a Finnish sauna, Finnish-style continental breakfast, chauffeur service, and free bicycles. Okay, it's a far cry from the fishermen (many of them Finnish) who built the union and the cannery and settled Astoria's fringes, now Uniontown. But you can learn all about them in the hotel library and photo gallery, and they do run a number of programs to support the community. Lox and wine are served every afternoon. And your dog gets his own bottled water. $169–550.

✐ ♿ 🐾 **Elliott Hotel** (1-877-378-1924; www.hotelelliott.com), 357 12th Street. A complete makeover of a 1924 hotel resulted in this boutique hostelry, with a rooftop terrace, wine bar, and 32 rooms. Standard rooms include cedar closets, handmade cabinetwork, and lots of designer fixtures; the luxury suites go up from there. Pets allowed in two units. Rooms $109–229; suites from $179.

Seaside

🐾 **Beachside Inn** (1-800-845-1284; www.beachsideinnseaside.com), 300 Fifth Avenue. A small motel with some pleasant design touches, the Beachside has two-bedroom suites and a cottage as well as standard queen rooms. Pets welcome for a fee. Doubles $70–125.

INNS

Seaside

Gilbert Inn (1-800-410-9770; www.gilbertinn.com), 341 Beach Drive. After a colorful life involving the Franco-Prussian War, innkeeping in San Francisco, and operating a liquor store in rough-and-tumble Astoria, Frenchman Alexandre Gilbert "retired" to Seaside with his wife and went into real estate. Among other investments, the couple expanded their beach house to a sweeping hotel, ready for Seaside's booming summer and weekend traffic. Gilbert served guests wine of his own imported grapes and snails he bred of French stock. The house is much as it was, but for five new rooms added in the 1980s: tongue-and-groove fir walls and ceilings warm the common areas and some guest rooms, and a fireplace warms the parlor. The private bathrooms are an innovation, though. The decor claims to be, and in this case really is, French country: simple but good furniture with minimal, but tasteful, embellishment. Gilbert died in 1935 at the age of 92. Among his lasting impressions on the town was the donation of land for the promenade. $69–179.

✱ Where to Eat

DINING OUT

Astoria

✐ **Bridgewater Bistro** (1-877-357-6777; www.bridgewaterbistro.com), 20 Basin Street. Daily for lunch and dinner, and Sun. brunch. The former Union Cannery undergoes yet another transformation. The actual cannery is now a hotel (see *Hotels and Motels*), while the cannery offices and boat repair shops are now the Bridgewater Bistro—a recent metamorphosis realized by Tony and Ann Kischner, who ran the Shoalwater Restaurant in Seaview, Washington, for 28 years. Their reputation for fine Northwestern cuisine is being carried on here, with Columbia River salmon, halibut, and the gamut of Northwestern seafood, and a variety of meats including (in a nod to Astoria's heritage) Swedish meatballs. Usually there are several vegetarian options as well, and a kids' menu—though it comes with a warning that unruly children may be shanghaied. A nice option is the "small plates," if your appetite or purse is limited. The view is pretty good, too.

EATING OUT

Astoria

✐ **Andrew and Steve's Café** (503-325-5762), 1196 Marine Drive. Daily for breakfast, lunch, and dinner. Straightforward home cooking has been served up here since 1916—

including Greek home cooking, a legacy of the Greek immigrants who started it. American, Greek, and marine cuisine have been satisfying customers here since then and show no sign of stopping. It's busy just about every night.

Blue Scorcher Bakery Café (503-338-7473; www.bluescorcher.com), 1493 Duane Street. Daily 8–5. Here's a place to find artisanal breads, pastries, fair-trade coffee, and the Sun. *New York Times.* It's a warm place to come in out of the rain, especially if you have kids: they can entertain themselves in the play kitchen and kids' library while you read the paper over coffee and a croissant.

Cannery Café (503-325-8642; www.cannerycafe.com), 1 Sixth Street. Daily for lunch and dinner. Where yet another cannery used to be (Astoria was full of them), this is a little more than a café, offering dinner selections like filet mignon and halibut in cream sauce, and other goodies from land and sea. There's a full bar, too. Lunchtime brings soups, salads, and a children's menu; and the Sunny Side, under the same roof, serves breakfast from 7:30 daily.

The Columbian Café (503-325-2233; www.columbianvoodoo.com), 1114 Marine Drive. Mon.–Fri. 8–2 and Sat.–Sun. 10–2 for breakfast and lunch, and Wed.–Sat. 5–8 for dinner. Chef Uriah Hulsey has been developing vegetarian and vegan menus for 30 years at what is fundamentally a lunch counter, but it is always crowded. Dinner also finds local seafood on the menu. Quirky and eclectic (it's affiliated with the adjacent Columbia Theater and Columbia Voodoo nightclub), the place has gained a reputation for quality food at reasonable prices.

Uniontown Fish Market (503-325-9592; www.uniontownfishmarket.com), 229 W. Marine Drive. Mon.–Thurs. 11–3 and Fri.–Sat. 11–7. Buy your fresh or smoked seafood here or stop at the friendly, informal grill for lunch or dinner. Stuffed sandwiches, salads, crabs, oysters, fish—everything finny or shelled from the north Pacific. And a kids' menu, too.

Gearhart

Pacific Way Bakery and Café (503-738-0245), 601 Pacific Way. Café open Thurs.–Sun. from 11 for lunch and dinner, and the bakery opens at 7. Gearhart is a tiny place, but the Pacific Way is always packed—dinner reservations are a must, and you may run into lines at lunch and even outside the bakery at breakfast. Cinnamon rolls, danish, croissants—you name it—are snapped up fresh from the oven. Dinner concentrates on seafood, while lunch brings soup and creative sandwiches. This may be the best eatery you'll find between Cannon Beach and Astoria.

* Entertainment

Astor Street Opry Company (503-325-6104; www.shanghaiedinastoria.com), 129 W. Bond Street, Uniontown, Astoria. Now housed in the old Finnish meat market, the company presents theater for all ages, including annual performances of a local favorite, *Shanghaied in Astoria.*

Liberty Theatre (503-325-8108; www.liberty-theater.org), 1203 Commercial Street, Astoria. This 1920s vaudeville–movie house has been lovingly restored and again hosts musical, theatrical, and other performances.

* Shopping

Uniontown Fish Market (503-325-9592; www.uniontownfishmarket.com), 229 W. Marine Drive, Astoria (see *Eating Out*). Fresh, frozen, and canned

THE ORNATE LIBERTY THEATRE IN DOWNTOWN ASTORIA DATES FROM THE 1920S.

products of the north Pacific; come and see what's available, or place an order by phone.

✷ Events

February: **Fisher Poets Gathering** (503-325-6311), last weekend, locations around Astoria. Those who go down to the sea in ships sometimes come back to tell the tale in verse. Since 1997, fisherfolk on this coast have been gathering to share their poetry, hold workshops, listen to music, and eat and drink. Weekend admission $10.

June: **Scandinavian Midsummer Festival** (1-800-875-6807; www.astoriascanfest.com), weekend around June 21, Clatsop County Fairgrounds, Astoria. Celebrate Astoria's Scandinavian roots with folk music, dance, and especially food. Don't miss the running of the trolls. Three-day pass $6, children $2.

August: **Salt Makers Return,** Seaside Beach off Avenue U, Seaside. A living-history reenactment of salt production by the Corps of Discovery in the winter of 1805–1806. The volunteers remain in character; don't talk to them about Morton's.

September: **Pacific Commercial Fisherman's Festival** (503-325-1010), third weekend, Pier One at the Port of Astoria. Did you know Astoria is the third-largest fishing port in North America? Here's a festival designed to celebrate those who bring home the catch, with a filleting contest, search and rescue demonstrations, fisheries presentations, and, of course, music and food.

CANNON BEACH–TILLAMOOK–PACIFIC CITY AREA

Art, milk, and summer people constitute a summary of the three main towns on this bit of coast. Cannon Beach, with its unique offshore rocks, was an early haven for Portland vacationers and has capitalized on the influx to create an arts-oriented seaside community. Tillamook has grassy floodplains ideal for dairy cattle; as early as the 1850s farmers had formed a co-op for shipping their butter to Portland and today run the Tillamook Creamery. As for Pacific City, between the Nestucca River and the sea, its fishing heritage is still alive in its commercial dory fleet, but otherwise the shoreline seems to have been given over to beach homes and visitor accommodations (low profile, luckily) hidden along the scenic Three Capes Drive.

GUIDANCE **Cannon Beach Chamber of Commerce** (503-436-2623; www.cannonbeach.org), Second and Spruce, P.O. Box 64, Cannon Beach 97110.

Clatsop State Forest (503-325-5451; www.oregon.gov), 92219 US 202, Astoria 97103.

Nehalem Bay Area Chamber of Commerce (1-877-368-5100; www.nehalembaychamber.com), 327 Nehalem Boulevard, Wheeler 97147.

Oregon Coast Visitors' Association (1-888-628-2101; www.visittheoregoncoast.com), 137 NE Fourth Street, Newport 97365.

Oregon State Parks (1-800-551-6949; www.oregon.gov), 725 Summer Street NE, Suite C, Salem 97301.

Pacific City–Nestucca Valley Chamber of Commerce (503-392-4340; www.pcnvchamber.org), 34370 US 101 S., P.O. Box 75, Cloverdale 97112.

Rockaway Beach Chamber of Commerce (503-355-8108; www.rockawaybeach.net), P.O. Box 198, Rockaway Beach 97136.

Siuslaw National Forest (541-750-7000; www.fs.fed.us/r6/siuslaw), 4407 SW Research Way, Corvallis 97339; and 31525 US 22, Hebo 97122 (503-392-5100).

Tillamook Area Chamber of Commerce (503-842-7525; www.tillamookchamber.org), 3705 US 101 N., Tillamook 97141.

Tillamook State Forest (503-842-2545; www.oregon.gov), 5005 Third Street, Tillamook 97141.

GETTING THERE *By car:* Cannon Beach and Tillamook are on **US 101,** the latter also accessible from Portland via **OR 6.** For Pacific City, drive south from Tillamook on US 101 for 24 miles and turn west on Brooten Road.

GETTING AROUND *By bus:* The **Cannon Beach Shuttle** (1-800-776-6406) runs a dozen times a day from the north end of Cannon Beach to the south end, going as far as Seaside daily except Sun. Free.

Tillamook County Transportation District (503-815-8283; www.tillamookbus.com) runs buses Mon.–Sat. in and around Tillamook, as far as Cannon Beach and even Portland. Except within Tillamook, most buses run only a few times a day.

MEDICAL EMERGENCY **Tillamook County General Hospital** (503-842-4444), 1000 Third Street, Tillamook.

✷ To See

CHAMPION TREES A **Sitka spruce** at **Cape Meares** is the new state champion since the one at Klootchy Creek blew down, thought it's much shorter than the other: only 144 feet instead of 206. It's thought that the top of the new champion was torn off in a storm a century or so ago.

FARMERS' MARKETS **Cannon Beach Farmers' Market** (503-436-8044), in the parking area at the corner of S. Hemlock and E. Gower streets, Cannon Beach. Tues. 2–6, mid-June–Sept.

Manzanita Farmers' Market (503-368-3339), 467 Laneda Street, Manzanita. Fri. 5–8 PM, mid-June–mid-Sept.

Tillamook Farmers' Market (503-842-2146), Second Street and Laurel Avenue, Tillamook. Sat. 9–2, June–Sept.

FOR FAMILIES ✐ **Oregon Coast Scenic Railroad** (503-842-7972; www.ocsr.net), 403 American Way, Garibaldi. Take a ride around Tillamook Bay behind a 1910 Heisler steam locomotive. The round-trip between Garibaldi and Rockaway Beach takes an hour and a half; you can start at either end. Trains operate on summer weekends, and reservations are desirable. Adults $15–16, children 3–10 $7–10.

✐ **Whale-watching** is possible all along the coast. In Dec. the gray whales head south to their calving grounds in Baja California, and in Mar. they come back north. Pacific City is particularly blessed with a resident pod that often hangs about the bay, so you may see them even from the beach at any time of year. Generally, the best place to spot a whale is from one of the headlands, such as Cape Lookout or Cape Kiwanda. Just face out to sea and look for a sudden spout of vapor, and if you're lucky you'll catch a glimpse of a back, fin, or tail. During spring break—in Oregon, the last week of Mar.—guides are posted at several common viewing sites to help you.

HISTORIC SITES **Cape Meares Lighthouse,** 10 miles west of Tillamook, is the shortest lighthouse on the Oregon coast, only 38 feet high (but 200 feet above the sea). It also has the distinction of having had one of Oregon's few women lighthouse keepers: Augusta Hunt, who briefly replaced her husband after his death. Dating from 1890, the light is now open to visitors Apr.–Oct. (free) at **Cape Meares State Park.** Its actual function has been taken over by an adjacent automated beacon.

Tillamook Rock Lighthouse, about a mile out to sea off Tillamook Head. Imagine being a lighthouse keeper perched on an acre of basalt jutting from the sea. Imagine *building* a lighthouse on selfsame rock. Anything going from or coming onto the rock was lifted over in a sort of sling hung from a crane attached to a boat—something not always feasible in these stormy seas. But in 1881 a light out here was considered necessary for the safety of shipping, and so it was made. Terrible Tilly, they called it. Storms here are so violent that sometimes waves broke the windows and flooded the tower room 130 feet above the sea. Once, in 1934, they even broke the lens. The light was finally decommissioned in 1957, and the rock is part of the **Oregon Islands National Wildlife Refuge**—and a columbarium, a final resting place for human ashes.

MUSEUMS **Cannon Beach History Center and Museum** (503-436-9301; www.cbhistory.org), 1387 S. Spruce Street, Cannon Beach. Wed.–Mon 1–5. Free. People have come to Cannon Beach to relax for near a century now, but it wasn't always a carefree place. The center will remind you of good times and bad—blackouts during World War II, the tsunami of 1964—as well as earlier days when folks arrived by stagecoach. A replica Native American longhouse brings out the precontact way of life. And where's the cannon in Cannon Beach? Right here. It was discovered three times before landing in the museum: In Oct. 1846, a month after the Navy schooner USS *Shark* went down off the Columbia Bar (all hands were rescued), a ship fragment with three cannon was reported on Tillamook Head by tribal members; one cannon was dragged up the beach but subsequently lost. Mail carriers spotted it again just south of town in 1863 and 1894, and this last time it was brought into town. Excitingly, in 2008, two similar cannon were uncovered by a low tide in nearly the same location, and the three together are thought likely to be those reported in 1846.

✐ ♿ **Garibaldi Museum** (503-332-8411; www.garibaldimuseum.com), 112 Garibaldi Avenue, Garibaldi. Thurs.–Mon. noon–4, May–Oct. General admission $3, seniors and children 5–18 $2.50. The mission of this museum is to preserve and interpret the memory of Captain Gray's explorations of the Northwest coast. Models of both his ships, the *Columbia Rediviva* and *Lady Washington,* and displays on ship's provisions and sailors' daily lives, concretize what you learn in history books. Another wing sets out the history of the town of Garibaldi. Hands-on activities for kids bring the 18th century to life with hardtack, period clothes, and puzzles.

Latimer Quilt and Textile Center (503-842-8622; www.latimerquiltandtextile.com), 2105 Wilson River Loop Road, Tillamook. Mon.–Sat. 10–5 and Sun. noon–4, Apr.–Oct., and Mon.–Sat. 10–4 Nov.–Mar. Admission $3. Fiber enthusiasts, come here. Its collection of quilts runs from the mid-1800s to the present, as well as antique and contemporary crocheted items and woven textiles. A library lets you explore virtually all aspects of the fiber crafts. The place serves as a center for weavers, who work on the looms filling one room.

Tillamook Air Museum (503-842-1140; www.tillamookair.com), 6030 Tillamook Road, Tillamook. Daily 9–5. General admission $7.50, children 6–17 $4. More than 60 wartime aircraft inhabit a blimp hangar built in 1942 for coastal patrol dirigibles. You or your child can sit in the cockpit of some models.

Tillamook County Pioneer Museum (503-842-4553; www.tcpm.org), 2106 Second Street, Tillamook. Tues.–Sat. 10-4. General admission $3, seniors $2. Captain Gray made it to Tillamook Bay, and Kilchis Point, just north of town, held one of the most substantial Indian villages in the area. Mementos of these people, and of those who came after, fill this museum.

Tillamook Forest Center (503-815-6800; www.tillamookforestcenter.org), 22 miles northeast of Tillamook on OR 6. Wed.–Sun. 10–4, Mar.–Oct. Free. Run by the Oregon Department of Forestry, the decade-old forest center sits deep in the Tillamook State Forest. It sets out to provide an in-depth view of this piece of the Coast Range—its geology and ecology, how the indigenous Calapuyas and early settlers lived in and off it, and evolving forestry practices. Deep in local memory is the Tillamook Burn, a series of disastrous fires that destroyed much of the forest between 1933 and 1951. The fires, and the massive reforestation project that followed, are explored in film and exhibits. Outdoors are forest trails, picnic tables, a bridge over the Wilson River Gorge, and a watchtower you can climb for the view.

NATURAL WONDERS Two **Haystack Rocks** decorate this stretch of coast. One, just off Cannon Beach, stands 237 feet tall. You can walk out to it at low tide and explore the little pools at its base, but be very watchful; "sneaker" waves can and do rush in at any time, carrying off anything lighter than a boulder. The other, even higher at more than 300 feet, stands a mile offshore at Pacific City. Both house nesting seabirds in spring and fall and are very photogenic. They supposedly result from inland lava flows and look like—er—sugar loaves?

SCENIC DRIVES **Mount Hebo** was an Air Force radar station during the Cold War (though the radar domes did poorly in the mountain's high winds, and the station was eventually decommissioned). A steep, narrow road winds 12 miles up to the summit for a view of mountains and ocean. Take US 101 north for 5 miles from Tillamook, exit at Hebo, take OR 22 for 0.5 mile and turn left up the mountain.

Nestucca River Back Country Byway. From the town of Beaver, 4 miles north of Hebo on US 101, ascend the course of the Nestucca River through thick rain forest. This area gets about 120 inches of rainfall a year. Lichens festoon the 200-foot-tall Douglas firs, and sunlight falls dimly to the forest floor. The river is never far from the road, and there are numerous picnic areas and campsites along the way. The byway ends 48 miles from Beaver near the town of Carlton, in the Willamette Valley.

Three Capes Drive is a slower, gentler alternative to US 101 between Tillamook and Pacific City. While the highway runs inland, the scenic route follows the shoreline, visiting **Cape Meares, Cape Lookout,** and **Cape Kiwanda** before rejoining 101. There are plenty of places to stop and take in the breakers crashing on impressive cliffs and haystacks, or stroll a beach. You could actually spend a nice little getaway in this backwater, staying in one of the small towns or at **Cape Lookout State Park.** Entrances to the 40-mile route are well marked with brown signs.

✷ To Do

BICYCLING In the **Tillamook State Forest,** the 11.4-mile **Gales Creek Trail** and the 15-mile **Wilson River Trail** are open to mountain bikes for single-track forest riding; unfortunately, both are partially closed at time of writing due to storm damage. Call 503-357-2191 for information. For road biking, the **Three Capes Scenic Drive** between Tillamook and Pacific City takes in capes, headlands, lighthouses, and all Oregon's coastal spectacle on 40 miles of back road (see *Scenic Drives*). A 2-mile bike trail encircles **Nehalem Bay State Park,** south of Manzanita.

BIRD-WATCHING Check the two **Haystack Rocks** (Cannon Beach and Pacific City) for nesting murres, tufted puffins, guillemots, and lots of cormorants. **Nehalem Meadows,** south of Nehalem along Tideland Road, is a place to spot wintering peregrine falcons and even an occasional gyrfalcon, as well as wintering sparrows. All of **Tillamook Bay** is a bird haven, with winter alcids bobbing in the channel at **Barview Jetty** and wintering ducks and grebes at **Garibaldi Boat Basin. Bayocean Spit,** between the bay and the sea, is the state hot spot for sandpipers and other shorebirds in fall. **Cape Meares State Park** may—*may*—produce spotted owls and ancient murrelets. Puffins nest in the cliffs. See also *Wildlife Refuges*.

CAMPING In **Clatsop State Forest, Henry Rierson Spruce Run Campground** lies beside a creek with 32 drive-in sites, four walk-in tent sites, water, and toilets amid lichen-covered trees; turn south off US 26 near milepost 20 and drive 5 miles on Lower Nehalem River Road; open year-round. In **Tillamook State Forest, Nehalem Falls Campground** offers 14 drive-in sites, four walk-in tent sites, toilets, water, and access to fishing and swimming. Take OR 53 east 1.3 miles from its junction with US 101, turn south on Miami Foley Road for 1 mile, turn left on Foss Road, and go 7 miles. **Elk Creek Campground,** just off Wilson River Highway 28 miles east of Tillamook, has 15 walk-in sites with toilets, water, and hiking trails. **Reehers Camp** is an old CCC camp on Cochran Road 2.5 miles west of Timber, with 10 horse camp sites and six sites on another loop for campers without horses; toilets, but no water. These are generally open spring to early fall.

Two area state parks have campgrounds: **Nehalem Bay,** on a point about 3 miles south of Manzanita, has 265 electrical hookup sites, 18 yurts, a horse camp with 17 sites, and even a few primitive sites around an airstrip, plus all amenities, like restrooms, showers, and drinking water. **Cape Lookout,** 12 miles south of Tillamook off US 101, is another beachside park with 38 full hookup and one electric hookup site, 173 tent sites, 13 yurts, a hiker/biker camp, 3 cabins, and all conveniences. To reserve at these campgrounds, call 1-800-452-5687; some sites available year-round.

Several **Tillamook County Parks** have campgrounds: **Barview Jetty Campground** (503-322-3522), on the north side of the channel into Tillamook Bay, has 69 RV sites and 224 tent sites with restrooms, water, and hot showers; open year-round. **Kilchis River Park** (503-842-6694), on the Kilchis River, offers 63 RV/tent sites, hiker/biker sites, water, restrooms, and showers; open May–Sept. **Trask River Park** (503-842-4559), 8 miles northeast of Tillamook by US 101, Alderbrook Road, and Kilchis River Road, 18 miles east of Tillamook by OR 6 and Trask

River Road, has 63 RV/tent sites with restrooms, water, river access, and trails; open year-round. **Whalen Island Park** (503-965-6085), 4.5 miles north of Pacific City on the **Three Capes Scenic Loop,** has 34 campsites with water and restrooms; open May–mid-Oct. **Webb Park** (503-965-5001), at Cape Kiwanda just north of Pacific City, has seven RV sites and 31 tent sites, toilets, shower, and water; open year-round. **Woods Park** (503-965-5001), by Woods Bridge at the northern end of Pacific City, is 1 acre on the Big Nestucca River with five RV sites, seven tent sites, water, and restrooms. Summer only. To reserve at any of these, call the park number or reserve online at www.co.tillamook.or.us.

CANOEING AND KAYAKING There's lots of it, depending on your tastes. **Tillamook Bay, Nehalem Bay,** and the **Nestucca River and estuary** draw paddlers to their semiprotected waters. Sea kayakers take to the surf. **Lost Lake,** in **Clatsop State Forest,** is a quiet inland lake accessible from **Spruce Run Campground** (see *Camping*); there you won't have to compete with motorized boats. Book a kayak tour at **Kayak Tillamook County** (503-866-4808), or rent at one of many outlets, such as **Wheeler Marina** (503-368-5780), 278 Marine Drive, Wheeler—just south of Nehalem.

GOLF **Alderbrook Golf Course** (503-842-6413), 7300 Alderbrook Road, Tillamook. Eighteen holes.

Manzanita Golf Course (503-368-5744), off US 101 south of Manzanita. Nine holes.

HIKING **Ecola State Park,** just north of Cannon Beach, has hiking trails of all lengths and levels (see "Astoria–Seaside–Warrenton Area"). Ten miles south of Cannon Beach, in **Oswald West State Park,** the **Cape Falcon Trail** starts at a trailhead on the west side of the highway and runs 2 miles to Cape Falcon. A short (half-hour) trail from the same park leads to **Short Sands Beach.** Just north of the park at Arch Cape, the **Arch Cape Trail** also leads to Cape Falcon, crossing Arch Cape Creek and winding 5 miles through rain forest to connect with the **Cape Falcon Trail.** Climbing **Neah-Ka-Nie Mountain** yields tremendous views from the 1,631-foot peak; only about a mile each way. The trailhead is across from the Neah-Ka-Nie Golf Course, 2.6 miles south of the Short Sands parking area, off US 101.

At **Cape Lookout State Park,** about 6 miles south of Netarts, the **Cape Lookout Trail** runs along the headland for 2 miles, with the sea boiling under the cliffs. Two short (0.25-mile) trails lead to **Munson Falls,** south of Tillamook off US 101; one to the base and one up wooden walkways to a viewing platform. The waterfall is the highest in the Coast Range. **Bayocean Spit,** between Tillamook Bay and the sea, was the site of a hopeful seaside resort a hundred years ago. The resort was unfortunately washed away, and now the spit is popular for hiking, biking, and horseback riding. Deep in the Coast Range, on OR 6 about 20 miles east of Tillamook, a 2.5-mile trail up **King's Mountain** rises 2,800 feet through the reforested Tillamook Burn—strenuous, but rewarding, with fine wildflowers near the summit in spring.

Mount Hebo, some 20 miles east of Pacific City in Siuslaw National Forest, boasts several trails of varying sorts. From Hebo take FR 14 for 5 miles to **Hebo**

Lake Loop Trail, a handicapped-accessible, 0.5-mile trail in the Hebo Lake Campground; open spring through fall. A more adventurous trail from the same campground is the **Pioneer Indian Trail,** which runs 8 miles to South Lake, crossing Mount Hebo in the process. This route, rediscovered by Leonard Switmore of the Forest Service in 1975, used to be the "road" from the Tillamook area to the Willamette Valley from 1854 to 1862. More gently, the **Plantation Trail** traverses a replanted hillside forest for just under a mile, starting at the 4-mile point on FR 14. The fairly steep **Niagara Falls Trail** is harder to get to, but only a mile long, and leads to two 80-foot waterfalls in luxuriant forest. From Beaver, 4 miles north of Hebo, take Nestucca River Road 12 miles to FR 8533 and turn south, driving 4.3 miles to FR 8533-131; turn right and continue 0.7 mile to the trailhead.

Cascade Head is one of those great, windswept headlands jutting into the Pacific. Owned partly by the Nature Conservancy and partly by the Forest Service, its native coastal prairie backed by forest is home to several endangered species, including the Oregon silverspot butterfly. Two trails reach the top of the headland: One, from Knight Park just off Three Rocks Road, rises 6 miles to the point. A less steep, 1-mile trail starts from a parking lot off Cascade Head Road. About 10 miles south of Pacific City, Cascade Head is a good place to see migrating whales.

Finally, the **Oregon Coast Trail** is a 382-mile jaunt along the entire coastline, following the beach and headland trails whenever possible but often enough obliged to detour on roads or even the narrow shoulders of US 101. This is a glorious but arduous hike (it's not easy, walking on sand), taking in all the wildness of Oregon's shoreline; also all its weather. Maps can be downloaded from the Web site of the Oregon Department of Parks and Recreation (www.oregon.gov/OPRD/PARKS).

SURFING Devotees ride the waves at Cannon Beach and Cape Kiwanda, in wet suits, of course—the water temperature is suitable only for seals. Lessons and rentals can be had at **Kiwanda Surf Company** (503-965-3627), 6305 Pacific Avenue, Pacific City, or **Cleanline Surf Shop** (503-436-9726), 171 Sunset Boulevard, Cannon Beach.

UNIQUE ADVENTURES ✐ **Beach Horseback Rides** of varying lengths can be arranged with **Sea Ranch Stables** (503-436-2815), 415 Fir Street, Cannon Beach; a half-day ride runs about $65.

✐ **Tillamook Cheese Factory** (503-815-1300; www.tillamookcheese.com), 4175 US 101 North, Tillamook. Daily 8–8 in summer, 8–6 in winter. Between mountains and sea, the lush pastures of Tillamook County support some very contented cows. These cows give plenty of milk, much of which finds its way to the Tillamook Creamery, a hundred-year-old, farmer-owned cooperative. Tillamook cheeses, ice cream, butter, and yogurt are ubiquitous in Oregon, and a visit here is a sort of journey to the source. At the visitors center you can learn about and observe the cheese-making process and the history of dairying in the region—it goes back to the mid-1800s—and consume some of the product, including Tillamook Fudge, which you don't find everywhere. The Farmhouse Café is open for breakfast and lunch, serving (among other things) grilled cheese sandwiches, cheeseburgers, and cheese omelets.

✷ Wilder Places

PARKS A daisy chain of state parks dances down the coast, many simply small gateways to the beach, where you can walk forever: **Tolovana Beach,** a mile south of Cannon Beach, is in walking distance of **Haystack Rock.** No fee. Then comes **Arcadia Beach,** 3 miles south of Cannon Beach. No fee. Just north of the parking area at **Hug Point,** 5 miles south of Cannon Beach, you can see ruts left by the beach stagecoaches that used to provide transportation along the coast (the stage trail "hugged" the point). No fee. **Oswald West State Park** (1-800-551-6949), 10 miles south of Cannon Beach, honors Oregon's 14th governor (1911–1915), who passed the precursor to Oregon's 1967 public beaches law. Several trails meander the 0.25 mile to the beach.

Nehalem Bay State Park (503-368-5154 or 1-800-551-6949), 3 miles south of Manzanita Junction, is a bigger, full-service park with camping, picnic areas, playgrounds, and trails. Just behind the dunes, it has easy access to the beach while staying sheltered from the winds. Deer, elk, and other wildlife are often seen.

Manhattan Beach, 2 miles north of Rockaway, provides beach access and has picnic sites sheltered by shore pines. No fee.

Cape Meares State Scenic Viewpoint, 10 miles west of Tillamook, juts into the sea topped by the historic **Cape Meares Lighthouse.** Interpretive panels explain the history, and you can visit the lighthouse. No fee.

Oceanside Beach, 11 miles west of Tillamook in the small town of Oceanside, is a favored place for beachcombing and tidal pool exploration. In winter agates are often exposed. No fee.

Cape Lookout State Park (1-800-551-6949), 12 miles southwest of Tillamook, is out on a sand spit backed by old-growth forest, with 8 miles of trails and a campground. For some reason occasional fishing floats from Japan still wash up here. You may also spot paragliders floating overhead.

Cape Kiwanda, 1 mile north of Pacific City, is on the **Three Capes Scenic Drive.** Here you can view the other **Haystack Rock,** fly a kite, and see more paragliders. No fee.

Bob Straub State Park (1-800-551-6949), in Pacific City itself, is a jump-off point for long walks out Nestucca Spit. No fee. **Neskowin Beach,** Neskowin, is adjacent to Cascade Head and has access to the **Cascade Head Trail.** No fee.

Munson Creek Falls, 8 miles southeast of Tillamook via US 101 and Munson Creek Road, lies in old-growth cedar and Sitka spruce forest, with trails leading to a 319-foot waterfall. No fee.

Tillamook County (503-322-3522) also runs a nice network of beach and woodland parks; see *Camping.*

WILDLIFE REFUGES For more information on the refuges in this section, call 541-867-4550.♿ **Cape Meares National Wildlife Refuge,** 10 miles west of Tillamook on **Three Capes Scenic Drive.** This refuge protects a rare old-growth forest of western hemlock and Sitka spruce, which in turn shelter spotted owls and marbled murrelets—two endangered species unaware of the contention surrounding them. Peregrine falcons and lots more birds nest in the cliffs. Two wheelchair-accessible viewing platforms welcome the observer, who can also see two other refuges from this point: **Oregon Islands** and **Three Arch Rocks.**

♿ **Nestucca Bay National Wildlife Refuge,** 6 miles south of Pacific City off US 101. Where the Nestucca River flows down to the sea, it creates some varied and unusual habitat—the southernmost sphagnum bog on the Pacific coast, as well as salt marsh, meadows, upland forest, and surrounding pastures. The refuge was set aside to protect wintering grounds for threatened subspecies of Canada geese (yes, some of them actually are threatened) but harbors many other waterfowl and songbird species. The 0.5-mile, paved Pacific View Trail is wheelchair accessible and leads to an observation deck with panoramic views of the bay and ocean.

Oregon Islands National Wildlife Refuge consists of over a thousand islands, rocks, and reefs off the Oregon coast from Tillamook Head to the California border. These islands are nesting and resting grounds for millions of birds; seals also breed and give birth on many of them. They are off-limits to humans, but many are close enough to shore to observe with binoculars and see sea lions hauled out to rest and clouds of seabirds fishing to feed their families. There is an official viewing deck at **Cape Meares.**

Three Arch Rocks National Wildlife Refuge. Literally three big rocks (and six smaller rocks) 0.5 mile off Oceanside, this refuge was set aside in 1907 by President Roosevelt due to the research of two young conservationists, William Finley and Herman Bohlman. At that time people would row out from shore to kill sea lions for their oil and skins, and randomly shoot nesting birds—thousands at a time—for no use at all. After a century of protection, the rocks house the state's biggest breeding colony of tufted puffins and the biggest breeding colony of common murres south of Alaska, and also serve Steller's sea lions, petrels, and many other species. For obvious reasons, the rocks are closed to humans, but you can view them from Oceanside and Cape Meares.

✷ Lodging

BED & BREAKFASTS

Arch Cape

✐ ♿ 🐾 **Arch Cape Inn and Retreat** (1-800-436-2848; www.archcapeinn.com), 31970 East Ocean Lane. Here you can indulge your fantasy of living in a castle—a castle adapted to the 21st century and the timbered Oregon coast. Sort of a Northwest lodge, but with turrets, gables, and almost a suggestion of battlements. Indoors, alcoves and tapestries contribute to a medieval effect. But the amenities are definitely modern, from the Jacuzzis in some suites to free Wi-Fi. Plush mattresses, fireplaces, carpets, and high thread-count linens are de rigueur. Tucked in the woods above the sea, it's quite the spot for a romantic retreat. Doubles $219–329, with full breakfast; dinner available for an extra charge. Several rooms accommodate pets, and some are wheelchair accessible.

✐ **Shaw's Oceanfront Bed and Breakfast** (1-888-269-4483; www.shawsoceanfrontbb.com), 79924 Cannon Road. Four miles south of Cannon Beach, the Oceanfront is that—on the ocean, just through the garden gate. There's only one guest suite; it has one queen-sized bedroom, a living room with a queen sofa bed, and a window seat that sleeps one. There are two bathrooms to accommodate all those people, and a full kitchen if you want to make dinner; hosts Barbara and Jim Shaw come in to make you breakfast in the morning. $200 double occupancy, with a discount for stays of more than one night.

Cloverdale
Hudson House Bed and Breakfast Inn (1-888-835-3533; www.hudson house.com), 37700 US 101 South. Just north of Cascade Head, the 1906 farmhouse overlooks the Nestucca River valley—good for hiking the Head or enjoying the view from the porch. At day's end you can retreat to one of four cheerful, airy rooms (one twin-bedded). $95–125, with full breakfast.

Pacific City
The Craftsman Bed and Breakfast (503-965-4574; www.craftsmanbb .com), 35255 Fourth Street. Craftsman furniture in a Craftsman house makes for clean, quiet lines. There are no TVs or radios, so you're free to hike, read, or even converse. $110–150, with full breakfast.

Eagle's View Bed and Breakfast (1-888-846-3292), 37975 Brooten Road. This is a modern B&B, luxurious without being frilly, on 4 acres crossed by walking paths. An outdoor hot tub has views over the river. $135–170, with breakfast.

CABINS AND COTTAGES

Cannon Beach
🐾 **McBee Cottages** (1-800-328-4107; www.mcbeecottages.com), 888 S. Hemlock Street. These blue-shingled, attached units are a 1940s motor court, renovated to look nice and new while retaining a 1940s beach simplicity. White-painted Adirondack chairs adorn the lawn, and simple but crisp units ranging from basic studio size to small suites have either kitchens or a fridge and microwave. Check-in is at the Cannon Beach Hotel at 1116 S. Hemlock. $85–185 double occupancy, and pet friendly.

HOTELS AND MOTELS

Cannon Beach
♿ **Cannon Beach Hotel** (1-800-238-4107; www.cannonbeachhotel.com), 1116 S. Hemlock Street. This one has been around since 1914 and looks like a weathered but proud New England home. Ten rooms come in various shapes and sizes, some with fireplaces, all with private baths; one room is handicapped accessible. $80–240, includes a continental breakfast at the adjacent **Cannon Beach Café.**

Inn at Haystack Rock (1-800-507-2714; www.innathaystackrock.com), 487 S. Hemlock Street. Comprising just five rooms and three cottages around a Spanish-style courtyard, the inn brightens up the often cloudy coast with Mexican textiles and bedsteads. Most units have kitchens or kitchenettes. A block away is the beach. $70–169.

Gearhart
🖍 **Gearhart Ocean Inn** (1-800-352-8034; www.gearhartoceaninn.com), 67 N. Cottage Avenue. Gearhart is a small town—a village, really—and the Ocean Inn is proportional, with 14 units. The 1940s motel has been carefully restored to a more upscale, but still affordable, version of itself, with suite and studio units. Each has a kitchen or kitchenette and dining table, and some have fireplaces. $75–170. Children under 16 free, and cribs are supplied at no charge.

Manzanita
🖍 🐾 **Sand Dune Inn** (1-888-368-5163; www.sandune-inn-manzanita .com), 428 Dorcas Lane. Kid friendly, pet friendly, and people friendly, but

that's not all—there's a fleet of bikes at guests' disposal, as well as beach supplies, games, a library, and dollops of hospitality. Plus, last but not least, unpretentious, clean, and comfortable rooms, some with kitchenettes and separate living rooms. Doubles $65–110.

Oceanside

🐾 **Clifftop Inn** (503-842-6030; www.clifftopinn.com), 1816 Maxwell Mountain Road. A contemporary inn with 13 individually and sometimes whimsically decorated rooms, the Clifftop has (of course) clifftop views. Most rooms have a kitchen or kitchenette—even the bunkroom, which sleeps five and has two bathrooms. Rooms $95–157; bunk beds $45 each. Massage, yoga retreats, and use of the sauna are offered, but additional.

Pacific City

🐾 **The Inn at Pacific City** (1-888-722-2489; www.innatpacificcity.com), 35215 Brooten Road. Yes, it's a motor lodge, a shingled, family-run establishment right in town—close to restaurants and shopping as well as to the beach. $49–99, with discounts for seniors and on nights that are just slow.

Wheeler

Old Wheeler Hotel (1-877-653-4683; www.oldwheelerhotel.com), 495 US 101. Children over 10 are welcome. In the olden days, about 1920, Wheeler was a buzzing town. Literally. It was a town of lumber and shingle mills, with its own hotel, and trains took all those products away to Portland. In 1920 the Wheeler Hotel was built on the site of the previous inn. But then came the Depression and the Tillamook Burn. The hotel closed, and the building operated for a while as a clinic, then slid gently downhill until a passing couple bought and refurbished it in the 1990s. Current owners Katie Brown and Greg Nichols combine a traditional atmosphere with contemporary touches in the seven rooms (all have private baths, though a couple of the designated bathrooms are down the hall) and offer a complimentary continental breakfast. $65–145. Some rooms can be combined to create suites.

INNS

Nehalem

Nehalem River Inn (503-368-7708; www.nehalemriverinn.com), 34910 OR 53. Flop into one of the mission-style or four-poster beds above the Nehalem River—especially if you've enjoyed dinner at the restaurant (see *Dining Out*). Four very comfortable rooms and a cottage compose this country inn, away from it all. Rooms $100–185.

✷ Where to Eat

DINING OUT

Cannon Beach

Newman's at 988 (503-436-1151; www.newmansat988.com), 988 S. Hemlock Street. Tues.–Sun. 5:30–9 PM (and Mon. July–mid-Oct.). Not that Newman. Sandy and chef John Newman purchased an Italian restaurant in 2005 and blend John's French training with the establishment's Italian heritage to focus on the cuisine of southern France and northern Italy. Choose from the à la carte or the prix-fixe menu, which changes daily. Reservations recommended.

Manzanita

Bread and Ocean (503-368-5823; www.breadandocean.com), 154 Laneda Avenue. Dinner Fri.–Sat. 5–9, Sun. 5–8; bakery hours Wed.–Sat. 7:30–2, Sun. 8–2. Most of the time it's a bakery, selling bread, cakes, and panini, but on weekend evenings it morphs into a restaurant serving short but fresh and eclectic seasonal menus—duck and fig sausage with wild rice cakes, for example, or the homier meat loaf with sweet potato gratin.

Nehalem

Nehalem River Inn (503-368-7708; www.nehalemriverinn.com), 34910 OR 53. Open for dinner; call for seasonal hours. Chef Ryan Hamic believes in "food without borders." That's why his menu features dishes you don't often see together on one menu—Muscovy duck next to Japanese black bass, roast quail jostling gravlax salmon. The menu changes seasonally; Hamic believes in fresh, organic produce. Reservations recommended; children under 12 discouraged. If you want to sleep it off, there are guest rooms, too (see *Inns*).

Pacific City

Delicate Palate Bistro (1-866-567-3466), 35280 Brooten Road. Wed.–Sun. 5–closing. Fine seafoods and "natural" meats (i.e., no added antibiotics, hormones, or weird animal feeds) beside the sea. The wine list is extensive, and for smaller appetites, there's also a bar menu, complete with bar.

EATING OUT

Cannon Beach

Cannon Beach Bakery (503-436-0399; www.cannonbeachbakery.com), 240 N. Hemlock Street. Wed.–Mon. 6:30–5. The third generation of Danish bakers is now baking at Cannon Beach—trays and trays of luscious breads, tartlets, scones, and, er, Danish.

Cranky Sue's (503-436-0301), 308 Fir Street. Fri.–Tues. 11:30–7. "No shoes, no shirt, no problem"—well, that doesn't sound very cranky. In fact, it's downright refreshing. This is the beach, after all. And at Cranky Sue's you eat heartily among the usual beach decor—shells, nets, etc.—crabby cakes, No Bull chili, clams, oysters, and shrimp in all forms. Soups and salads, too. For some original choices try the horseradish-encrusted tuna or salmon in lobster sauce.

Ecola Seafoods Restaurant and Market (503-436-9130; www.ecolaseafoods.com), 208 N. Spruce Street. Daily 9–9 in summer, daily 10–7 in winter. Buy the latest catch or come in for lunch or dinner—chowder, seafood, grilled fish, whatever is in season. Fish are caught with hook and line only.

Lumberyard Rotisserie and Grill (503-436-0285; www.thelumberyardgrill.com), 264 Third Street. Daily noon–closing; happy hour 4–6 PM. Lumberyard roasts organic chicken, wild salmon, and natural Angus beef; you'll also find crab, ribs, potpie, and pizza on the menu. Kids and babies can enjoy their own selections.

Oceanside

Roseanna's Café (503-842-7351; www.roseannascafe.com), 1490 Pacific Avenue. Sun.–Thurs. 10–8, Fri.–Sat. 10–9. This is an intimate sort of place serving plenty of fish and seafood in varying forms, chowder, pastas, and a few dishes for landlubbers. If you ask, they'll try to accommodate your dietary restrictions. And you'll have a fine ocean view from the 1901 shingled house.

Pacific City

Grateful Bread (503-965-7337), 34805 Brooten Road. Thurs.–Mon. 8–4, bakery 8–5. The gray-shingled cottage offers fresh breads and pastries, plus breakfast, lunch, and pizza, made with their own freshly baked ingredients and with plenty of vegetarian options. Everything is available for take-out, too.

Pelican Pub and Brewery (503-965-7007; www.pelicanbrewery.com), 33180 Cape Kiwanda Drive. Daily for breakfast, lunch, and dinner. Yes, they do brew their own beer and ales on the spot, and the menu is a bit more ambitious than the average pub menu: fish-and-chips, yes, and bangers and mash, but also beer-poached salmon, curry-fried chicken—hmm—and more, including a child's menu.

✷ Entertainment

Coaster Theatre Playhouse (503-436-1242; www.coastertheatre.com), 108 N. Hemlock Street, Cannon Beach. Seven plays and musicals a season fill this playhouse, originally a 1920s skating rink.

✷ Shopping

Cannon Beach is full of **galleries,** from glass to bronze to paintings; check www.cbgallerygroup.com.

Blue Heron French Cheese Company (503-842-8281; www.blueheronoregon.com), 2001 Blue Heron Drive, Tillamook. Open daily. Oregon French cheeses, that is. Blue Heron produces several kinds of Brie and a Camembert. Their shop also carries their mustards, salad dressings, spices, racks of Oregon wines, and an eclectic selection of candies. And there's a petting zoo to amuse the children.

Cannon Beach Book Company (1-800-436-0906), 130 N. Hemlock Street, Cannon Beach. Open daily. What's a beach town without a bookstore? This one has been at it for 25 years, focusing on fine books for kids and adults (and lots of mysteries: perfect beach reading). There's a good regional selection, too.

✷ Events

April: **Pacific City Birding and Blues Festival** (503-392-4340), first weekend, Kiwanda Community Center, Pacific City. Field trips, workshops, and concerts.

June: **Blessing of the Dory Fleet,** early in the month, Cape Kiwanda Beach, Pacific City. Clergy of several denominations bless the dories as well as craft of more recent vintage.

Sandcastle Day (503-436-2623), mid-month, the beach, Cannon Beach. This is the day to give adults rein to childish fantasies. Competitions are judged in several age categories, from children to "masters," and it's worth going just to see the amazingly elaborate creations.

Tillamook County Dairy Parade and Festival (503-842-7525), last weekend, Tillamook County Fairgrounds, Tillamook. A celebration of the county's dairy heritage with a parade (Oregon's second largest, after the Rose Festival Parade), a rodeo, a Milk Run, wild cow milking, and other bovine-related activities.

November: **Stormy Weather Arts Festival** (503-436-2623), first full weekend, various venues around Cannon Beach. Just when the lowering clouds have settled in to stay, Cannon Beach enlivens spirits with events in all the arts.

LINCOLN CITY–DEPOE BAY–NEWPORT AREA

As you consider nature along US 101, you'll also wander through towns facing the gray sea: Lincoln City, a collection of former hamlets melded in a matrix of strip development; Newport, the port that the fishing industry hasn't forgotten, enriched by the Oregon Aquarium and Hatfield Marine Science Center; Depoe Bay, which has managed to capitalize on its tiny but scenic harbor; and several smaller, nearly hidden settlements. It's a short strip of coast but worth extra time to get out and explore.

GUIDANCE **Central Oregon Coast Association** (1-800-767-2064; www.coastvisitor.com), 137 NE First Street, P.O. Box 2094, Newport 97365.

Depoe Bay Chamber of Commerce (1-800-767-2064; www.depoebaychamber.org), 137 NE First Street, Depoe Bay 97365.

Lincoln City Visitors and Convention Bureau (1-800-452-2151; www.oregoncoast.org), 801 SW US 101, Suite 1, Lincoln City 97367.

Lincoln County Parks (541-574-1215), 880 NE Seventh Street, Newport 97365.

Newport Chamber of Commerce (1-800-262-7844; www.newportchamber.org), 555 SW US 101, Newport 97365.

Oregon State Parks (1-800-551-6949; www.oregon.gov), 725 Summer Street NE, Suite C, Salem 97301.

Toledo Chamber of Commerce (541-336-3183; www.visittoledooregon.com), 311 NE First Street, Toeldo 97391.

Waldport Chamber of Commerce Visitor Center (541-563-2133; www.waldport-chamber.com), 620 NW Spring Street, Waldport 97394.

GETTING THERE *By car:* Again, the towns are strung along **US 101,** Lincoln City being 15 miles north of Depoe Bay and 25 miles north of Newport. Newport is also reached by **US 20** from the east, while **OR 18** from Portland or **OR 22** and **18** from Salem will bring you to US 101 a few miles north of Lincoln City.

GETTING AROUND A car is needed.

MEDICAL EMERGENCY **Samaritan North Lincoln Hospital** (541-994-3661), 3043 North 28th Street, Lincoln City.

Samaritan Pacific Communities Hospital (541-265-2244), 930 SW Abbey, Newport.

✷ To See

COVERED BRIDGES Three of Lincoln County's four covered bridges are in this area:

The **Chitwood Bridge,** about 10 miles east of Toledo, was built in 1933 to cross the Lower Yaquina River. In 1984 it was rebuilt in the same style and painted the same dark red. It still carries traffic into Chitwood, though the town itself has been abandoned. From Newport take US 20 east and turn south at mile 17 onto the bridge.

Drift Creek Bridge is Oregon's oldest, dating from 1914, though rebuilt in 1933 after a flood. Deemed unsafe in 1997, it was almost demolished till Laura and Kerry Sweitz offered to move it to their property a few miles away. It was a community effort taking several years, but the bridge now spans Bear Creek on their acreage. Take OR 18 east from Lincoln City and turn south on Bear Creek Road; the bridge is a mile down on the left. Park on the road and walk to the bridge.

Fisher School/Five Rivers Bridge. Though the portal says 1927, records indicate this bridge went up in 1919. It has two names because it crosses a fork of Five Rivers and finds itself next to the old Fisher Elementary School. Take OR 34 east from Waldport and turn south at milepost 20 onto Five Rivers Road, and continue 9.4 miles to Crab Creek Road and the bridge.

FARMERS' MARKETS **Lincoln City Farmers' Market** (541-867-6293), 2168 NE Oar Place, Lincoln City. 9–2 Sat., May–Oct.

Newport Saturday Farmers' Market (541-961-8236), US 101 and Angle Street, Newport. 9–1 Sat.

FOR FAMILIES ✐ **Hatfield Marine Science Visitor Center** (541-867-0100; www.hmsc.oregonstate.edu), 2030 SE Marine Science Drive, Newport. Daily 10–5 in summer, Thurs.–Sun. 10–4 in winter. Admission by donation. While researchers study underwater volcanoes and the complexities of sea life, visitors comb the fruits of their findings with Magic Planet, a giant interactive globe; computers simulating consequences of environmental decisions; educational programs; and good old-fashioned squishy critters.

✐ **Oregon Coast Aquarium** (541-867-3474; www.aquarium.org), 2820 SE Ferry Slip Road, Newport. Daily 9–6 in summer, daily 10–5 Labor Day–Memorial Day. Entry is steep at $14.25 (seniors $12.25, kids 3–12 $8.75), but it's a pretty terrific aquarium; you never knew how beautiful jellyfish were, or how blown glass art can highlight truly weird ocean creatures. Contemplate sharks swimming overhead, then stroll the expansive open-air exhibits for close looks at the creatures inhabiting Oregon's coast, including elusive puffins and sea otters. Keiko, the whale who starred in the movie *Free Willy,* stayed here before being deported to Iceland. Bet she missed it.

✐ Whale-watching can be done all along the coast; in this region, good viewing sites are at Boiler Bay Scenic Viewpoint, the Depoe Bay seawall, the Whale Watching Center (541-765-3304) at Depoe Bay, Rocky Creek, Cape Foulweather, the Devil's Punchbowl at Otter Rock State Park, Yaquina Head Lighthouse, and Yaquina Bay Recreation Site. Whale-watch volunteers are present at most of these sites during peak migration times, which happen to occur in the week between Christmas and New Year's and the last week of Mar. (Oregon's spring break). To approach the creatures in their element, whale-watching charters depart Depoe Bay and Newport (see *Unique Adventures*).

GARDENS **Connie Hansen Garden** (541-994-6338; www.conniehansen garden.com), 1931 NW 33rd Street, Lincoln City. Daily dawn–dusk. Free. Constance Hansen started a garden on this property in the 1970s with irises in mind, but somehow it "just growed." A few ornamental trees here, a perennial bed there, then a mania for rhododendrons—by the time she died in 1993, all the lawn was gone but for a few grassy paths for access to the beds. Neighbors banded together to preserve the garden, so today you can admire Connie's azaleas, Himalayan ferns, flowers, and, yes, swales of irises, Japanese and Siberian. Guided tours are available by reservation.

HISTORIC HOMES **Bensell House,** 747 SW 13th Street, Newport. Possibly the oldest house in Newport, it appears in some very early photos of the waterfront and is thought to have been built by pioneer Royal Bensell. It is currently privately owned.

Hilan Castle, 620 SW 11th Street, Newport. The Roper family had a reputation for eccentricity, though whether it was prior to or after their castle's construction remains unclear. They had it built in 1913 to resemble a castle in Wales. It has been made over into apartments but still looks like a Hollywood castle from the outside.

HISTORIC SITES Newport has several art deco buildings—it even has designated an **Art Deco District**—in the city's business center, where some much-needed revitalization is under way. Most of these are still businesses, though perhaps not the original ones. Notable are the old **City Hall,** soon to become a Pig 'n Pancake, on Alder Street. Opposite is the **Lincoln County School District,** originally the Bank of Newport, next to the **Ark,** formerly the Midway Theater. The biggest art deco specimen of them all is Conde McCullough's arched and pyloned 1936 **Yaquina Bay Bridge,** soaring gracefully over the bay's mouth, carrying the traffic on US 101; a viewing plaza is accessible at the north base of the bridge. A printable walking tour can be downloaded from www.citycenternewport.com.

The **Nye Beach** district, in Newport, is a sort of village within the town, consisting of cottages, small businesses, and vacation homes, most of which date back to around 1910.

Newport Bayfront. Today the bayfront is an amalgam of commercial fishing and tourism, with fishery docks abutting newfangled cafés and old-fashioned bars, interspersed with galleries and restaurants. The tourism actually predates the fishery: one Sam Case, from Newport, Rhode Island, came west and built a hotel, the Ocean House, here on Yaquina Bay in 1866 (he also got to name the little town

MURALS DEPICT THE FISHING LIFE ALONG NEWPORT'S BAYFRONT.

that grew up around it, composed mainly of small resorts). "Summer people" arrived by train and ferry from the Willamette Valley. It was only in 1908, with the advent of electricity, that the town with its protected harbor became a major fishing port—still reportedly the largest in Oregon in dollar terms. Sea lions hang about on the docks, and murals tell stories of fishermen and the sea.

Yaquina Bay Lighthouse, at Yaquina Bay State Park, just north of the Yaquina Bay Bridge. Daily 11–5 in summer, daily noon–4 in winter. Free. Built in 1871 and decommissioned in 1874, when a better-placed lighthouse entered service, this is a neat cottage with a lantern room on top, 161 feet above the sea. The cottage, of course, was the keeper's residence, and you can walk in and make yourself at home (well, not too much; it does close at night). It is furnished with all the things a lighthouse keeper needed, and in summer docents can explain them all. In the basement is a rather extensive gift shop with books and other items related to area lighthouses. And the light functions again: in 1996 a group of volunteers restored it as an aid to navigation, operated by photocell.

SEA LIONS LIKE THE DOCKS AT NEWPORT.

Yaquina Head Lighthouse, off US 101 at the end of NW Lighthouse Drive, Newport. Grounds open daily sunrise–sunset; lighthouse open daily 9–4 in summer, daily noon–4 in winter; interpretive center open daily 9–5 in summer, daily 10–4 in winter. Closed Thanksgiving and Christmas. Admission $7 per vehicle, good for three days. This is the light that replaced Yaquina Bay Lighthouse, its height and placement on Yaquina Head making it visible over a greater area of ocean. At

YAQUINA BAY LIGHTHOUSE STANDS WATCH AT NEWPORT.

93 feet, it's the tallest in Oregon and has been working since 1873 (now fully automated), and it is within the **Yaquina Head Outstanding Natural Area** (see *Wildlife Areas*). You can tour the tower and climb the 110 steps to just below the lantern room, then wander the nearby trails to tidal pools.

Jason Lee Campsite, Lincoln City. Numerous young ladies, as well as men, heeded Jason Lee's call to help missionize the Oregon country. Among these was Anna Maria Pittman, who voyaged around the Horn and was introduced to Mr. Lee in May 1837 at Fort Vancouver. Two months later they were married and spent a honeymoon of several weeks camping with another missionary couple on the Oregon Coast, reporting that they much enjoyed the sunshine and fresh air (good thing it was Aug.). The site is thought to be near Devil's Lake in Lincoln City.

MUSEUMS ✐ **North Lincoln County Historical Museum** (541-996-6614; www.northlincolncountyhistoricalmuseum.org), 4907 SW US 101, Lincoln City. Wed.–Sun. noon–5 in summer, Wed.–Sat. noon–5 in winter. Ages 12 and up $2, under 12 $1, families $5. Japanese glass fishing floats, Native American baskets, homesteaders' artifacts, and displays on the dairy, fishing, and canning industries trace Lincoln County's early history and development. When roads came in, so did promoters; exhibits reproduce some of the inevitable roadside attractions and promotion schemes. A children's corner supplies puppets, books, and games.

Oregon Coast History Center (541-265-7509; www.oregoncoast.history.museum), 545 SW Ninth Street, Newport. Tues.–Sun. 10–5 in summer, Tues.–Sun. 10–4 in winter. Free. This is really a triad of museums. The original museum was in the log cabin, where you still find photos, displays on Native American history, the coming of coastal bridges, and rotating exhibits. Then, in 1976, the 1895 Burrows House was moved across the street to become the Oregon Coast History Center, housing exhibits on the life and history of the central coast; here are a restored period drawing room and early law office. Still under development is the new Pacific Maritime and Heritage Center, set in the 1925 home of World War I general McAlexander, just above the wharf. Plans call for an interactive center on boats and the sea. Unfortunately, an opening date is not yet set.

Toledo History Center (541-265-7509), 206 N. Main Street (City Hall), Toledo. Mon.–Thurs. 8–5. Free. Toledo was once the busiest spruce-milling site on the coast. During the First World War, the U.S. government established a huge mill to process billions of board feet of Sitka spruce surrounding the town for military planes. Learn all about it and related industries like boat building and railroads here.

Yaquina Pacific Railroad Historical Society (541-336-5256), P.O. Box 119, Toledo 97391. Tues.–Sat. 10–2. Mills sliced timber into lumber, and the train shipped it out. Four vintage train cars are on outdoor display down by the waterfront, including a 1922 steam locomotive and a 1907 wood-sided caboose, possibly the oldest in the Northwest. There's also an extensive library and archive on local railroad history.

NATURAL WONDERS **D River,** Lincoln City, is the world's shortest river, according to local wisdom. At 440 feet, it drains Devil's Lake into the ocean. It's not too short for a bridge, though, as US 101 has to cross it on its way up the coast.

Depoe Bay, 16 miles south of Lincoln City at Depoe Bay. This area seems to specialize in small wonders: Depoe Bay bills itself as the world's smallest navigable harbor. It is certainly small, at about 6 acres, and is navigated by fishing and cruising boats; watercraft shooting the narrow entrance from the breaking Pacific into the harbor provide excitement to onlookers, not to mention the boats' crews. It was originally named Depot Bay, for a person rather than a train station, but an early postmaster deemed that too prosaic and changed it to Depoe.

Valley of the Giants, 5 miles southwest of Dallas, is a 47-acre preserve of ancient forest deep in the Coast Range, administered by the Bureau of Land Management. Mostly western hemlock and Douglas fir, the trees are centuries old—four to six centuries—and reach heights of over 200 feet. There aren't many stands like this one around anymore, so it was designated a protected site in 1976, meaning no logging, no defacing, and leaving nothing but footprints. A steep 1.5-mile path winds through the behemoths. Access is by a labyrinth of graveled logging roads; the BLM gives directions at its Salem office (503-808-6002) and advises visiting on weekends to avoid close encounters with logging trucks.

SUNSET AT LINCOLN CITY

SCENIC DRIVES You can drive from Newport to Toledo in just 15 minutes, but why not take **Yaquina Bay Road,** hugging the bay's shoreline? It will take maybe half an hour, with bay views all the way.

✱ To Do

BICYCLING The **Lincoln City Bike Advocacy Group** (www.bikelincolncity.org) sponsors group rides monthly in "bike season."

Bike Newport (541-265-9917; www.bikenewport.net), 150 NW Sixth Street, Newport. Newport's source for bikes galore, repairs, and bike trail information, plus such amenities as showers, laundry, and a wireless lounge for long-distance cyclists. The associated **Yaquina Wheels Bicycle Club** (www.yaquinawheels.org), 1328 NW Nye Street, Newport, sponsors cycling events and group rides.

BIRD-WATCHING Virtually any headland, estuary, or bay along this coast will yield fine views of gulls, alcids, ospreys, and whatnot, depending on the season. **Taft Waterfront Park,** on SW 52nd Street off US 101 in Lincoln City, is good for gulls and terns following the fish in summer and loons and grebes in winter. At the **Inn at Spanish Head** (1-800-452-8127; www.spanishhead.com) at Lincoln City you get a bird's-eye view of the birds (and whales) from the 10-floor lounge or the lobby, and you can keep warm besides. **Salishan Nature Trails,** behind the shops at Salishan Marketplace at milepost 122.3 of US 101, run through varied habitat for a variety of songbirds, shorebirds, ducks, and seabirds. Down the road in **Depoe Bay,** the **seawall** and **Whale Watching Center** (541-765-3304) both offer good views of surfbirds, guillemots, turnstones, and whales. Just north of Depoe Bay is **Boiler Bay Scenic Viewpoint,** with various species of murreletes, auklets, shearwaters, and more. In Newport, **Yaquina Bay Natural Area** has incredible views and tidal pools; look for eagles, peregrine falcons, guillemots, and loons, plus intertidal species.

CAMPING Three state parks have campgrounds: **Devil's Lake,** in Lincoln City, with 28 full hookup and 5 partial hookup sites, 54 tent sites, 10 yurts, a hiker/biker camp, and water, restrooms, and showers. Being in the city, it's not far from shopping or rainy-day activities. **Beverly Beach,** off US 101, 7 miles north of Newport, has 53 full hookup, 75 partial hookup, and 128 tent sites (most of the tent sites will not accommodate any kind of RV or trailer); 21 yurts; and a hiker/biker camp, with all amenities. **South Beach,** 2 miles south of Newport, has 228 electrical hookup sites, 27 yurts, and a hiker/biker camp, with restrooms, water, and showers. To reserve at any of these, call 1-800-452-5687.

Three **Lincoln County Parks** (541-574-1215) offer camping: **Elk City Park,** about 8 miles east of Toledo, is an uncrowded riverside park with 12 campsites, water, and wheelchair-accessible restrooms; closed Dec.–Mar. **Jack Morgan Park** straddles OR 229 6 miles north of Siletz, with 13 sites, water, and restrooms; closed Dec.–Mar. **Moonshine,** along the Upper Siletz River, is 12 miles east of Siletz by Logsden Road and Moonshine Park Road, with 38 sites, handicapped-accessible campsites and restrooms, two RV sites (no hookups), and water. Open year-round.

CANOEING AND KAYAKING Have you ever felt like emulating the escaped prisoners of Ivan Doig's *Winter Brothers*? If so, an ocean kayak excursion may be just for you. **Ossie's Surf Shop** (see *Surfing*) offers a two-hour paddle for the brave and very fit from Depoe Bay to Otter Rock. For the rest of us, a paddle around **Depoe Bay** or **Devil's Lake** is quite adventurous enough. In summer there are guided kayak tours of **Devil's Lake** from **Devil's Lake State Park,** and of **Beaver Creek** from **South Beach State Park.**

GOLF **Agate Beach Golf Course** (541-265-7331; www.agatebeachgolf.net), 4100 N. US 101, Newport. Nine holes overlooking the ocean and Yaquina Head.

Crestview Hills Golf Course (541-563-3020), 1680 SW Crestline Drive, Waldport. Nine holes.

Lakeside Golf Club (541-994-8442), 3245 NE 50th Street, Lincoln City. Eighteen holes.

Ollala Valley Golf Course (541-336-2121), 1022 Ollala Road, Toledo. Nine holes.

HIKING First there are the beaches, especially those at Newport between Yaquina Bay and Yaquina Head, a glorious sweep of about 3 miles; and the beach at Lincoln City, which can make you forget the strip development over the rise. As always, watch the tides; you don't want to get stuck against a cliff or marooned in a cove when the sea comes in.

The hundred acres of **Yaquina Head Natural Area** are blessed with several miles of trails, some of which—Quarry Cove, the viewpoints over Cobble Beach, and the path from the lighthouse to the western edge—are wheelchair accessible. A longer trail (1.5 miles) mounts Salal Hill, where you can view the lighthouse against the vast ocean.

For a forest hike, go to the **Drift Creek Falls Trail** in **Siuslaw National Forest.** Take US 101 south from Lincoln City, turn left on Drift Creek Falls Road, and follow the signs for 12 miles. It's only a 3-mile round-trip walk, but it takes you through ferny rain forest and over a suspension bridge a hundred feet above the creek to a 75-foot-high waterfall. Open all year.

KITE FLYING **Lincoln City** bills itself as the kite-flying capital of the world, and it does have pretty reliable winds—enough for two kite festivals a year (see *Events*). There are plenty of kite shops, enabling you to indulge in case you forgot your own. The **D River Wayside** is one favorite kiting spot, but really any sandy beach in the neighborhood will be perfect.

SURFING **Ossie's Surf Shop** (541-574-4634; www.ossiessurfshop.com), 4860 N. US 101, Newport. Check out Ossie's for equipment and lessons on facing the north coast's surf, or kayak tours of Yaquina Bay if that's more your speed.

UNIQUE ADVENTURES **Whale-watching** is popular up and down the coast during the gray whales' migration (southward in Dec., northward Mar.–May). Particularly good views can be had from headlands like **Yaquina Head,** 3 miles north of Newport; whale-watching guides will often man these posts in season. Or, take the sport to their turf with the **Oregon Aquarium**'s own cruise line, **Marine Discovery Tours** (1-800-903-BOAT; www.marinediscovery.com), 345 SW Bay Boulevard, Newport; a two-hour wildlife cruise runs about $35 (seniors $33, children 4–13 $17). **Tradewinds Charters** (1-800-445-8730; www.tradewindscharters.com) and **Dockside Charters** (1-800-733-8915; www.docksidedepoebay.com) offer whale-watching trips out of Depoe Bay for $30–45 per two hours. It's also a great way to peek at seals, sea lions, and seabirds.

✷ Wilder Places

PARKS The procession of beach-access state parks continues down the coast with **Road's End,** a mile north of Lincoln City, a walking beach sheltered from some of the coastal winds; and **D River Wayside,** where the tiny river flows into the sea in Lincoln City (this is the place to fly a kite, as there is always wind). No fee for any of these; state parks: 1-800-551-6949, Lincoln County parks: 541-574-1215.

Devil's Lake State Park, right in Lincoln City, is a full-service park straddling the 3-mile lake and offers camping, picnicking, play areas, nature programs, boating, and wildlife. In summer the park offers two-hour guided kayak tours.

Gleneden Beach, 7 miles south of Lincoln City, is a day-use area where seals and surfers like to hang out; a nice walking beach, too. No fee. **Fogarty Creek,** where said creek flows into the sea, has a sheltered picnic area and walking trails through a windswept coastal forest. No fee. The **Whale Watching Center** (541-765-3304), on the seawall at Depoe Bay, is an interpretive center on the lives of whales with plenty of viewing from the windows and platform; volunteer interpreters are on duty during whale migration season. No fee. **Rocky Creek, Otter Crest,** and **Devil's Punchbowl** follow each other in rapid succession down US 101; the first two are viewpoints with spectacular panoramas of headlands, surf, and wild birds, while Devil's Punchbowl is a huge hollow in the rocky shore where surf pounds and swirls, especially in stormy weather. A trail goes down to tidal pools. Captain Cook is supposed to have named it when passing by in Mar. 1778. No fees for these three. **Beverly Beach** (541-265-9278) is a full-service park with campsites east of the road along forested Spencer Creek, and the beach to the west (reached by a tunnel under the highway). Picnicking, surfing, and kite flying are all popular here, and there's even a visitors center and playground. With **Agate Beach** we enter the beaches of Newport proper; at this one you may find agates, and you'll definitely have views of Yaquina Head to the north; it's a lovely beach for walking or contemplating. No fee. At **Yaquina Bay State Park** in Newport, you get to visit the town's first lighthouse and wander wooded trails; no fee. **South Beach** (541-867-6590), 2 miles south of Newport, has one of the area's fine beaches and comes complete with campground, showers, wheelchair-accessible restrooms and trails, and a visitors center. It's a popular spot for whale-watching, with volunteer naturalists in season. **Lost Creek,** 7 miles south of Newport, is primarily for beach access and has a picnic area; no fee. **Ona Beach,** 8 miles south of Newport, is a coastal wetland where you may actually swim; kayak tours are offered through South Beach State Park, which supplies the kayaks, gear, and guides. Reservations recommended (541-867-6590). No fee for park use (fee for kayak tour, $15). **Seal Rock,** 10 miles south of Newport, is a wayside with a picnic area sheltered by shore pines, tidal pools, and views of rock formations just offshore. These are habitat for seals, sea lions, and many seabirds. No fee. And **Driftwood Beach,** 3 miles north of Waldport, offers a wide, flat beach and picnicking amid shore pines. No fee.

Inland, **H. B. Van Duzer** is a wayside in ancient forest beside the 15 miles east of Lincoln City on OR 18. A mile to the east is a swimming hole.

Lincoln County also runs a network of parks (see *Camping*). Day-use parks of interest include **Cannon Quarry Park,** 22 acres on the Yaquina River with a mile-long nature trail, picnic area, and boat ramp. From Toledo take Butler Bridge Road, then take Elk City Road for 3 miles. **Mike Miller Park** is a 40-acre tract encompassing several ecosystems. Brochures guide you along a nature trail complete with benches, bridges, and observation decks. From Newport go south just over a mile to NE 50th Street, turn left, and go 0.25 mile to park.

WILDERNESS AREAS **Drift Creek Wilderness** (541-750-7000), Siuslaw National Forest. One of only three wilderness areas in the Siuslaw National Forest, Drift Creek is the biggest tract of old growth in the Coast Range. About 8 miles of trails cross the area, running from higher ridges to the dim gorge where ancient western hemlock and Sitka spruce tower over an undergrowth of lichens, mosses, ferns, and small hardwoods. From **Ona Beach,** 7 miles north of Waldport, turn east on N. Beaver Creek Road and turn left at a fork. After 3 miles turn right onto N. Elkhorn Road, after 6 miles turn left onto FR 50, and after 1.4 miles turn right onto FR 5087 and continue to the **Horse Creek** trailhead. Another trail, the **Harris Ranch Trail,** starts from FR 346, reached by FR 3446 from OR 34 about 7 miles east of Waldport.

WILDLIFE AREAS ♿ **Yaquina Head Outstanding Natural Area** (541-574-3100), 750 NW Lighthouse Drive, Newport. Daily sunrise–sunset; interpretive center daily 9–5 in summer, daily 10–5 in fall, daily 10–4:30 in winter. A $7 per vehicle fee includes day use and entry to the interpretive center and lighthouse (see *Historic Sites*). This rocky headland run by the Bureau of Land Management provides outstanding panoramas, several miles of trails, and, incidentally, fantastic wildlife viewing. From seals and sea lions bobbing in the waves below to eagles and ospreys, and many seabirds, soaring above, to passing whales, you have a grandstand seat. Well, a perch. After taking in all this, go to the micro level at the tide pools, some of which are wheelchair accessible, and see purple sea stars, anemones, snails, and other small tidal creatures.

✷ Lodging

BED & BREAKFASTS

Lincoln City

An Exceptional Place to B&B Inn (1-866-994-4920; www.anexceptionalbandb.com), 1213 SW 52nd Street. Nothing fancy or overblown here; Ed Kuntz opens his home, bordering Siletz Bay, with two guest rooms, each with private bath and Wi-Fi, and serves them breakfast. Two living rooms, a woodstove, a sunroom, and an herb garden provide ample space to sit and relax. $99–109, with breakfast (but ask about specials). Children over 10 welcome.

Brey House (1-877-994-7123; www.breyhouse.com), 3725 NW Keel. Five rooms a block from the beach in a three-story house with views, hot tub, and breakfast make for a cozy beach stay. Some rooms have fireplaces; some have access to a shared kitchen; all have private baths. And it's in walking distance of Chinook Winds Casino, if you are so inclined. $109–159.

Coast Inn Bed and Breakfast (1-888-994-7932; www.oregoncoastinn.com), 4507 SW Coast Avenue. Enjoy the outdoors from the deck or the sunroom, depending on the weather, or stay by the fire in the living room. The large Craftsman-style house has four guest rooms with nicely tiled private bathrooms. $109–198, with full breakfast; wine and snacks in the evening. Children over five welcome.

BEACH AND SILETZ BAY, JUST SOUTH OF LINCOLN CITY

Hidden Cove Bed and Breakfast (541-921-9754; www.hiddencovebedandbreakfast.com), 3445 NE 40th Court. This is really more of a duplex: two apartments beside Devil's Lake, one up and one down, where breakfast happens to be provided. The upstairs unit is a suite complete with full kitchen and bathroom, and the lower one is a bed-sitter with dining area. Each has a private entrance. $80–150.

Newport

Green Gables Bed and Breakfast (541-574-0986; www.greengablesbb.com), 156 SW Coast Street. Down comforters, easy chairs, and whirlpool tubs make the Gables's two rooms a snug retirement from what ails you, a block from the beach. A breakfast of pastries, quiche, and espresso is served at the coffee shop downstairs. Also downstairs is a bookstore that can best be termed eclectic; you're welcome to browse. $120–140, with breakfast.

Newport Belle Bed and Breakfast (1-800-348-1922; www.newportbelle.com), 2126 SE OSU Drive. Here's a twist: a stern-wheeler designed and built as a bed & breakfast. Five staterooms, a solarium, and a salon with woodstove keep guests cozy while they get a seal's-eye view of the marina. $125–165, with full buffet breakfast and beer or wine in the evening.

Ocean House Bed and Breakfast (1-866-495-3888; www.oceanhouse.com), 4920 NW Woody Way. Just north of town and south of Yaquina Head, the big contemporary house sits on a bluff with eight ocean-view rooms whose decor ranges from four-poster beds to a spare "Far East" room. Gardens and large living rooms give you plenty of elbow room. $99–250, with breakfast, though specials may be available. Across the way, the **Tyee Lodge,** under the same ownership, is even more up-to-date in architecture and design (which doesn't rule out stuffed armchairs and pillow-top mattresses). Five large, comfy rooms look out to sea, and one overlooks the garden ($99–200). Both facilities enjoy private trails to the beach and hearty breakfasts; the kitchen will cater to your special diet if you ask ahead of time.

Seal Rock

Caledonia House Bed and Breakfast (541-563-7337; www.caledoniabb.com), 6575 NW Pacific Coast Highway. Six thousand miles from the

Hebrides, Seal Rock (which is 12 miles south of Newport) must look a bit like home to Scotsman Dee Brodie. He and Belinda have created a cozy, elegant bed & breakfast with none of the frippery associated with a certain Southron monarch. Five rooms and suites named after Scottish coastal sites have comfortable contemporary furnishings and private bathrooms (attached or detached); guests have access to 2 acres of woods and gardens, a guest kitchen, sitting room, and hot tub. $110–165, with a buffet breakfast that may include such items as Kintyre quiche, Kinross crêpes, and Jacobite eggs. Children over 12 welcome.

Resting on the Rock Bed and Breakfast (1-800-313-5171; www.restingontherock.com), 8721 NW Grandview Street. This is a hypoallergenic house, meaning those with pesky allergies to dust, inhalants, and other airborne irritants should be comfortable. One guest room sleeps three, while the suite may sleep four (two large and two small), and both have window seats for watching the waves. $120, double occupancy.

HOTELS AND MOTELS

Depoe Bay

♿ **Inn at Arch Rock** (1-800-767-1835; www.innatarchrock.com), 70 NW Sunset Street. This hostelry runs the accommodation spectrum, from a little room for two to a penthouse suite. Light, airy rooms, each with its own color scheme, sleep two to seven on the edge of a bluff over the Pacific (whales sometimes appear right below). Children are welcome and even expected, and pets are allowed in several units with prior permission. One unit is handicapped accessible. $69–309, with continental breakfast.

Lincoln City

Historic Anchor Inn (1-800-582-8611; www.historicanchorinn.com), 4417 SW US 101. You could call this the little motel that time forgot, and it almost did. The oldest hostelry in Lincoln City, it opened in 1947 as the Taft Heights Motor Court, at the start of America's love affair with the road, and operated till nearly crumbling 70 years later. Its 14,000 square feet have been lovingly restored by the new owners to recover the ambience of the 1940s, and then some—period furniture, polished wood everywhere, stuffed sofas, and a definitely quirky decor featuring assorted marine memorabilia. Also clanking radiators and creaking timbers. This is not a luxury place, but it definitely has character, offering a guest kitchen, parlor, reading room, and pool room. In deference to the 21st century, each unit has free Wi-Fi, TV, and DVD player, though no phone. Lodge units and cabins both feature two-room suites, and the cabins have kitchenettes; pets allowed in cabins. Doubles from $39 in winter, $59 in summer.

Newport

Agate Beach Motel (1-800-755-5674; www.agatebeachmotel.com), 175 NW Gilbert Way. A stone's throw from Yaquina Head, the 1940s Agate Beach is a place to retreat from modern glitz and enjoy a beach walk with your dog. Or, borrow a bike and tool around the bay. The 10 suites, all with kitchen, deck, living room, and bedroom(s), front on the beach and sleep four to six people. $99–159.

Moolack Shores Motel (541-265-2326; www.moolackshores.com), 8835 N. US 101. A motel catering to those wanting a quiet retreat at reasonable rates? Here it is, set over 6 miles of beach with views from Yaquina Head to Cape Foulweather. Each of the 12 wood-paneled rooms and suites has its own theme, and most have fireplaces and vaulted ceilings (the Antique Room even has a toilet with an overhead wood tank). $75–149.

Sylvia Beach Hotel (1-888-795-8422; www.sylviabeachhotel.com), 267 NW Cliff Street. It's not about the beach. Sylvia Beach owned the landmark Shakespeare & Co. Bookstore in Paris in the 1920s and 1930s, and was adopted as a sort of patron saint by readers Sally Ford and Goody Cable when they opened their literary-themed hotel in 1987. Each of the 20 rooms is named and decorated for an honored writer, from Agatha Christie to Virginia Woolf by way of Tennessee Williams, J. R. R. Tolkien, and—well, you'll just have to read the book. Since most of the honored are nineteenth- and early-twentieth-century authors, the historic 1910 hotel fits nicely. Naturally there is a library, and for more mundane concerns, breakfast (included) and a prix-fixe $23.50 dinner are available at the hotel restaurant, **Table of Content** (dinner reservations required). To preserve the atmosphere, there are no TVs, radios, or phones in the rooms. Oh, and the hotel is right above the beach. $70–193.

Toledo

Yaquina Bay Hotel (541-336-2830; www.yaquinabayhotel.com), 160 N. Main Street. Built in the 1920s, when Toledo was a logging boomtown, the two-story renovated vintage hotel offers rooms with one or two beds and some kitchenette suites. Toledo is now a quiet, not to say depressed, community where a number of artists have chosen to settle; you can spend the day at the beach 7 miles west, then partake of Toledo's slower pleasures. $69–92.

RESORTS

Gleneden Beach

✐ **Salishan Spa and Golf Resort** (541-764-2371; www.salishan.com), 7760 US 101. As a resort, it has everything—golf, tennis, pool, spa, three restaurants—set on a hillside tastefully screened from the highway. It has spread since its inception in the 1960s, so that today a van takes you from the reception area to your room, and the older rooms are complemented by larger, more luxurious units with fireplaces, travertine floors, and the like. Families are welcome; children's activities are provided, yet somehow the place feels more oriented to the corporate guest. $159–239.

Otter Rock

Inn at Otter Crest (1-888-505-5375; www.innatottercrest.com), 301 Otter Crest Drive. Trails lead from this 35-acre property down to Devil's Punchbowl. One of Oregon's clifftop resorts, it offers activities, a pool, fitness room, playground, spa, and so on, and a scale of rooms from standard rooms to suites, all with private balconies. And it's big: 27 buildings with 144 units, basically condos owned by private parties that you rent. But then there's a tram to get you around. $71–251.

✷ Where to Eat

DINING OUT

Lincoln City

Fathoms (1-800-452-8127; www.spanishhead.com), 4009 SW US 101, at the Inn at Spanish Head. Daily for breakfast, lunch, and dinner. The inn looks like a ship's prow emerging from the cliff, and Fathoms is its 10th-floor restaurant and lounge. It's worth a visit just for the bird's-eye view of passing ships, whales, and eagles. The menu, not surprisingly, concentrates on seafood and steaks, and a daily 4–5:30 happy hour enables you to eat quite happily and economically, if a bit early. With reservations you can also stay over in one of the posh, privately owned condos, which run $205–319.

Newport

Panache (541-265-2929; www.panachenewport.com), 614 W. Olive Street. Daily from 4:30 PM. Relax and enjoy your food. At Panache you eat at hundred-year-old oak tables in a 1919 house smack in the middle of Nye Beach; it's not an environment for rushed meals. Wild seafoods and organic meats and produce appear in ever-changing seasonal menus, with a surprising number of entrées under $20, including vegetarian selections that are actually interesting. There is, of course, a wine list to match, and as for dessert . . . well, choose among homemade ice cream and a variety of pastries and sweets created by pastry chef Karen Edwards. Linger over a special meal without breaking the bank.

Saffron Salmon (541-265-8921; www.saffronsalmon.com), 859 SW Bay Boulevard. Daily (except Wed.) for lunch and dinner. Sandwiched (so to speak) between galleries and the bay, Saffron Salmon serves up crab, salmon, and other finny foods, sometimes in saffron, as fresh as it can get; in fact, some of your dinner may have been offloaded at the next pier. Watch the sea lions watch the fishing boats as the sun goes down. Reservations recommended.

EATING OUT

Gleneden Beach

Side Door Café (541-764-3825), 6675 Gleneden Beach Road. Daily for lunch and dinner. Halfway between Depoe Bay and Lincoln City, the café serves fusion dishes that change seasonally or even nightly in a theatrical setting (it shares space with Eden Hall, an intimate performing arts center). Vegetarians will find the menu adaptable to their needs.

Lincoln City

Andaman Thai Cuisine (541-996-THAI; www.andamancuisine.com), 660 SE US 101. In a town where it's not easy to find good, reasonably priced food, the chefs at Andaman Thai provide the real thing—Thai dishes made with fresh ingredients and an expert touch (for a hint of the Northwest, order the king salmon curry). Dishes are made to order, so a meal does take some time.

Blackfish Café (541-996-1007; www.blackfishcafe.com), 2733 NW US 101. Wed.–Sun. for lunch and dinner. Local seafood, of course, but also steaks, fowl, and pasta—some served as perennial beach favorites, others in dishes of chef Rob Pounding's own invention.

Newport

Café Mundo (541-574-8134), 711 NW Second Court. Tues.–Thurs. 4–10, Fri.–Sat. 4–midnight. Once upon a time, it was a food cart out in the open. Now it's a beach shack, also in the open, serving world fusion food: the place to go for tempeh or red lentil stew, but also fresh scallops, mesquite-grilled steak, and such coastal staples. The decor is eclectic, too, with dozens of individually painted tables and chairs. Music happens sometimes, as does belly dancing and puppet theater. It's become a sort of vocation for owners Greg and Laurie Card, who started cooking out of a trailer. And whatever you order, it's slow food, so be prepared to wait and enjoy the occasional entertainment.

Café Stephanie (541-265-8082), 411 NW Coast Street. Daily 7:30–3. This snug Nye Beach spot is a local favorite for a hearty breakfast or lunch. On offer are crêpes, omelets, quiches, fish tacos, and more, all homemade and served with a smile. You may even be served by Stephanie herself.

Chowder Bowl at Nye Beach (541-265-7477), 728 NW Beach Drive. Sun.–Thurs. 11–8, Fri.–Sat. 11–9. Go for the chowder and stay for dessert—bread pudding with brandy sauce, marionberry cobbler, and more. Of course, you don't have to have chowder. You might prefer fish-and-chips or oysters and chips. Some in your party may even want landlubber food. That's okay. It's a locals' favorite, which tells you something, and child friendly to boot.

✐ **Mo's Original Restaurant** (541-265-2979; www.moschowder.com), 622 SW Bay Boulevard. Daily 11 AM–9 PM. Mo (Mohava Marie Niemi) started her first chowder joint in 1946 on Newport's salty waterfront, and it quickly became a fixture with her reasonably priced seafood and warm though eccentric character (she installed a garage door on the café's street side in consideration of a customer who absentmindedly crashed through the storefront). The business is now run by Mo's granddaughter, Cindy McEntee, with branches in Florence, Cannon Beach, Lincoln City, and Otter Rock, not to mention a thriving mail-order business. The menus can vary but always include the signature chowder, a variety of oyster and clam dishes, and fish-and-chips, and are always family friendly.

Panini Bakery (541-265-5033), 232 NW Coast Street. Thurs.–Mon. 7–7. Pizza, breads, pastries, and sandwiches, all made on-site (and make a pretty nice sight, too). Eat in or to go.

✐ **Sandbar Sports Bar and Grill** (541-265-6032), 722 NW Beach Drive. Daily for lunch and dinner. Bring yourself, bring the family—the "sports bar" piece is downstairs, so you can eat upstairs television-free. Hold and cold sandwiches, seafood, steaks, and nightly specials, with an ocean view.

✐ **Whale's Tale** (541-265-8660), 452 SW Bay Boulevard. Open for breakfast, lunch, and dinner. This family-friendly restaurant on the waterfront can get crowded but serves Northwest seafood from chowder to halibut in a nautical decor.

Otis

Otis Café (541-994-2813), 1259 Salmon River Highway. Daily for breakfast, lunch, and dinner. Five miles north of Lincoln City, the café lures people slightly inland with hefty meals—soups, salads, sandwiches, and burgers, like home but more so. For instance, you can get not just regular burgers, but buffalo, salmon, tuna, veggie, or kids' burgers. Or comfort foods like pork chops and applesauce and liver and onions. Even more than these, though, people come for the pies: apple, peach, pumpkin, and on and on. A very popular place.

✷ Entertainment

Bijou Theatre (541-994-8255; www.cinemalovers.com), 1624 NE US 101, Lincoln City. Okay, it's raining and you don't feel like the offerings at the multiplex. The Bijou has been entertaining moviegoers since 1937 and shows art and independent films as well as first-run movies—but only one at a time. Matinees $5.50, evening shows $7.50 ($5.50 for kids and seniors).

Newport Performing Arts Center (541-265-2787; www.coastarts.org), 777 W. Olive Street, Newport. Two theaters entertain the public with music, comedy, talks, song, and dance.

✷ Shopping

Toledo, 8 miles east of Newport, has become something of an antiques center, with several outlets: **C&M Antiques and Collectibles** (541-336-0140), 281 N. Main Street; **This 'n That Antiques** (541-336-2222), 318 S. Main Street; and **Ada's Antiques and Collectibles** (541-336-2524), 123 N. Main Street.

Mossy Creek Pottery (541-996-2415;

www.mossycreekpottery.com), 483 Immonen Road, Gleneden Beach. Tucked in the woods a mile or so from US 101, the gallery is a small cottage welcoming the visitor with pots of all shapes and sizes, from the planters and platters decorating the garden to ware artistic and utilitarian indoors. Friendly owners Dan and Susan Wheeler are artists themselves (ceramics and glass) and will help you find what you want among works by potters around the Northwest.

Oregon Oyster Farms (541-265-5078; www.oregonoysterfarms.com), 6878 Yaquina Bay Road, Newport. Daily 9–5. Founded in 1907, Oregon Oyster Farms brought in Pacific oysters from Japan to replace the native oyster population, depleted a few years after the rich beds of Yaquina Bay had been handily subtracted from the Grande Ronde Indian Reservation. If you love oysters, this is the place to get them fresh, smoked, shucked, or in the shell, on the Yaquina River 7 miles east of Newport.

✷ Events

February: **Seafood and Wine Festival** (1-800-COAST44), last full weekend. Held, tellingly, near the Rogue Ales warehouse at the South Beach Marina parking lot. If you're over 21, you can spend a weekend pairing Northwest seafood and wines. Free shuttle buses are available from downtown. Admission $10 Fri., $15 Sat., and $5 Sun.

March: **Whale Watching Week** (541-765-3407), Mar. 20–27, Whale Watching Center, Depoe Bay. Volunteer docents are on hand to help you spot migrating whales.

Mystery Weekend, second full weekend, Nye Beach neighborhood, Newport. Clues around the district lead to a solution of murder most foul. There are prizes for the most successful detectives.

June: **Lincoln City Summer Kite Festival** (1-800-452-2151), last weekend, D River Wayside, Lincoln City. Fancy kite demonstrations and just plain fun. A similar festival takes place Columbus Day weekend.

August: **Port of Toledo Wooden Boat Show** (541-336-5207), mid-month, Toledo dock. Admire old and new wooden boats and build one yourself (or a toy one, if you're a child); plus games, races, and music.

November: **Lincoln City Seafood and Chowder Cookoff** (541-557-1125), second Sat., 801 SW US 101, Lincoln City. See how your choices match up against the judges', and have some good eating in the process.

December: **Newport's Lighted Boat Parade** (541-265-6200), early in the month, Newport. Boats bedecked with Christmas lights make their stately way around Yaquina Bay.

Whale Watching Week (541-765-3407), Dec. 26–Jan. 1, Whale Watching Center, Depoe Bay. Volunteer docents are on hand to help you spot migrating whales.

LOTS OF POTS BY REGIONAL POTTERS FILL THIS BUNGALOW SOUTH OF LINCOLN CITY.

WALDPORT–YACHATS–FLORENCE AREA

One of our former legislators once described the Oregon coast as a "virtual" coast; you can't swim at the beaches. This is unfortunately true. With average water temperatures of 55 degrees, heavy surf, and strong currents, rare is the place where you can actually get in the water. This is one reason why beaches are still fairly pristine: walk on a beach for a mile or so, and your solitude may be complete. Our beaches are made for walking, and kite flying, and beachcombing, and marveling. Here is nature in the raw, where lava flows from far-inland-created basalt headlands, and where the pounding ocean erodes them to form spouting horns and maelstroms like the Devil's Churn.

Cape Perpetua is a fine spot for admiring wild nature, then heading a few miles to a cozy Yachats café to warm up on a bowl of chowder. Sleep in a historic hotel (there are at least two) or a B&B, have a hearty breakfast, and enjoy the jewels of the coast—the view from Yachats Bay, the Siuslaw estuary, the towering Oregon Dunes, and the broad beaches in between.

GUIDANCE **Central Oregon Coast Association** (1-800-767-2064; www.centralcoast.com), 137 NE Fourth Street, Newport 97365.

Charleston Information Center (1-800-824-8486), Boat Basin Drive and Cape Arago Highway, Charleston 97420.

Dunes City Visitor Center (541-997-3338; www.dunescity.com), 82877 Spruce Street, Dunes City 97439.

Florence Area Chamber of Commerce (541-997-3128; www.florencechamber.com), 290 US 101, Florence 97439.

Lane County, Oregon, Convention and Visitors Association (1-800-547-5445; www.visitlanecounty.org), 115 W. Eighth Street, Eugene 97440.

Oregon State Parks (1-800-551-6949; www.oregon.gov), 725 Summer Street NE, Suite C, Salem 97301.

Siuslaw National Forest (541-750-7000; www.fs.fed.us/r6/siuslaw), 4077 SW Research Way, Corvallis 97339; also 1130 Forestry Lane, Waldport 97394 (541-563-3211) and 4480 US 101 Building G, Florence 97439 (541-902-8526).

LOWERING SKIES WHERE THE YACHATS MEETS THE SEA

Waldport Chamber of Commerce (541-563-2133; www.waldport-chamber.com), P.O. Box 669, Waldport 97394.

Yachats Chamber of Commerce (1-800-929-0477; www.yachats.org), 241 US 101, P.O. Box 728, Yachats 97498.

GETTING THERE *By car:* All along **US 101!** From the east, take **OR 34** from Corvallis to Waldport or **OR 126** from Eugene to Florence.

GETTING AROUND You'll want a car.

MEDICAL EMERGENCY **Peace Harbor Hospital** (541-997-8412), 400 Ninth Street, Florence.

✷ To See

COVERED BRIDGES **North Fork Yachats Covered Bridge,** about 9 miles east of Yachats via Yachats River Road and N. Yachats River Road. Built in 1938 and rehabilitated in 1989, the little bridge still carries road traffic from Yachats to homes up the valley. **Hayden Covered Bridge,** 2 miles west of Alsea, is the last of several that served the Alsea area.

FARMERS' MARKETS **Florence Old Town Market** (541-935-6600), on the boardwalk at Nopal and Bay streets, Florence. Arts and crafts and music, as well as fresh produce and seafood. Sat. 10–6 and Sun. 11–5, late May–Oct.

Yachats Farmers' Market (541-528-7192), at Yachats Commons. Sun. 9–2, mid-May–mid-Oct.

FOR FAMILIES ✐ **Sand Master Park** (541-997-6006; www.sandmasterpark.com), 87542 US 101, Florence. Daily 9–6:30 in summer, weekdays (except Wed.) 10–5 and Sun. noon–5 off season; closed Jan. 15–Mar. 1. Parking $5, or free with any rental. Too warm for snowboarding? Sand Master bills itself as the world's first sandboarding park. Forty acres of high, wind-sculpted dunes are open to the thrills of dry-land surfing. You can rent boards, and if simple sliding isn't enough, portable equipment will create jumps, rails, and boxes. Instruction is available, too. This is a nice alternative to noisy dune buggies.

HERITAGE TREES **Sitka spruce,** 185 feet, Cape Perpetua. This specimen would be even higher if its top 35 feet hadn't broken off in the great storm of 1962. It also survived the 9.0 earthquake and tsunami of 1700 and, somehow, the massive Sitka logging during the First World War. An easy, 2-mile-round-trip trail connects it to the Cape Perpetua Visitor Center.

HISTORIC SITES **Florence Old Town.** Florence's kernel is the few blocks along the Siuslaw River waterfront, with some of its more venerable buildings now become restaurants, galleries, or bed & breakfasts. The Bridgewater Restaurant at 1297 Bay Street was **William Kyle Mercantile** nearly a hundred years ago, when Kyle owned area lumber mills and canneries. The **Johnson House** at 216 Maple Street is Florence's oldest extant home, dating from 1892 (still private). The **Siuslaw Pioneer Museum** (see *Museums*) is in a 1905 schoolhouse. And from Old Town Park there is a view of the 1936 art deco **Siuslaw Bridge,** which put the local ferry out of business.

Heceta Head Lighthouse (541-547-3416), 11 miles north of Florence off US 101. Perched on its ledge 205 feet above the sea, photogenic Heceta shows up on calendars all over the country. It was no small feat to build it. Materials came from Portland and San Francisco and had either to be hauled from Florence or rowed in from ships anchored off the dangerous headland. The light began to shine in 1894 and is the brightest along the Oregon coast, which is a good thing: Bruno de Heceta, who surveyed the coast in 1775 for the Spanish navy, mentioned expansive shallows below the head. Tours are offered daily Mar.–Oct., and the 1893 keeper's house offers bed & breakfast accommodations (for reservations call 541-547-3696). Park facilities are also available (see *Parks*).

MUSEUMS **Little Log Church and Museum** (541-547-3976), 328 W. Third Street, Yachats. Daily noon–3 (closed Thurs.). Donations accepted. Built in 1930 of logs hauled down the Yachats River, it was transformed to a museum when the congregation outgrew the church. Now it showcases clothing and household items of Yachats settlers, photographs, fossil shells from beaches to the north, and other beloved mementos. In this setting they hardly seem of the past but blend into the present.

Siuslaw Pioneer Museum (541-997-7884), 278 Maple Street, Florence. Tues.–Sun. noon–4; closed Easter and Thanksgiving–Jan. Adults $3, children under 16 free. This 1905 schoolhouse gives you a glimpse of life not so long ago: a blacksmith's bellows, steam engine, a dugout canoe, and more implements of earlier Florence, with volunteers on hand to explain.

Waldport Heritage Museum (541-563-7092), 320 NE Grant Street, Waldport. Wed.–Fri. noon–4, Sat.–Sun. 10–4. Free. Waldport is a small town with a small museum that explains how the site was named (by German immigrants), its location (on an Indian burial ground), and its logging and canning history.

NATURAL WONDERS **Darlingtonia State Natural Site** (1-800-551-6949), 5 miles north of Florence. Just off US 101, this 18-acre site was created to protect the rare and carnivorous cobra lily, or *Darlingtonia californica.* A type of pitcher plant, it survives by trapping and dissolving unwary insects and likes damp sphagnum soils. After observing the plants from the boardwalk, you can picnic amid wild rhododendrons, Sitka spruce, and cedars.

Oregon Dunes, from Florence south nearly to Coos Bay. Remember the Saharan landscapes in *The English Patient*? Or in some of the *Star Wars* films? You can find similarly impressive scenery minus the heat here. A 40-mile-long system of dunes, some reaching heights of 400 feet, starts at the beach and reaches a mile or two inland—a very curious geology of sculpted, constantly shifting sand interspersed with marsh, lakes, and coastal forest, creating a fascinatingly plastic ecosystem. They are thought to have started forming about six thousand years ago as sand, having eroded off the Coast Range to the sea, was blown back by ocean currents and strong winds. They continue to march inland, changing shape and covering forests—occasional tree islands on dunes show where a wood used to be—and changing the landscape. Some of the many lakes and ponds here were formed when sand cut off an inlet of the sea or blocked a stream coming down from the hills. Winter winds create weird, freestanding sculptures from 2 to several feet high and may just as well destroy them in the next storm. Most of the dunes fall within the **Oregon Dunes National Recreation Area** (see *Guidance*), which regrettably allows OHV use in several large areas. For quieter exploration there are many trails (see *Hiking*). Be attentive to the path as the dunes can be disorienting, and watch for quicksand in the declivities between dunes.

SCENIC DRIVES A loop behind Yachats winds into the hills past dark forest and the occasional pasture, and safely back to US 101 just south of town. Take **Yachats River Road** for about a mile and a half, then turn right on Cape Ranch Road, which rises a couple of miles to meet FR 5553; turn right to stay on Cape Ranch, which twists and turns another couple of miles back down to the highway. You may meet some elk.

WALKING TOURS A walking tour of **Old Town Florence** is available from the chamber of commerce at 290 US 101, Florence (see *Guidance*).

✷ To Do

BICYCLING The **Cape Perpetua** trail system offers mountain bikers challenging rides through the rain forest: **Cummings Creek** is a 4.5-mile (each way) trail back into the woods from FR 1050, off US 101 just south of the cape itself; return by **Cummings Creek Loop** for variety. In the **Oregon Dunes,** the **Siltcoos Lake Loops** are 3 miles of two connected loops reaching Siltcoos Lake from US 101; trailhead 7 miles south of Florence at milepost 198.

BIRD-WATCHING So many birds, so little time . . . The mouth of the Siuslaw and complex dune habitats make for quite a variety. East of the **South Jetty** of the Siuslaw is a floodplain that draws quantities of shorebirds in late summer and early fall, plus waterfowl later in the season. The end of the jetty often provides views of kittiwakes, terns, loons, and other coastal birds. Another rivermouth is that of the

Siltcoos, about 7 miles south of Florence. Mudflats produce a variety of sandpipers, and snowy plovers may be seen on the nearby sandy beach. Look for songbirds around the lakes and coastal woods behind the **Oregon Dunes.** Farther north, the rocks and tidal pools below **Cape Perpetua** are a good spot for surfbirds and turnstones.

CAMPING What with the state parks, the fine network of Lane County parks, and the Siuslaw National Forest, there is no lack of camping opportunities. At **Beachside State Recreation Site,** 5 miles north of Yachats, there are 32 partial hookup sites (including two handicapped-accessible sites), 42 tent sites, 2 yurts, and a hiker/biker camp, with restrooms, showers, water, and beach access; open mid-Mar.–Oct.; to reserve call 1-800-452-5687. Fourteen miles north of Florence is **Carl G. Washburne State Park,** with 56 full and 2 partial hookup sites, 2 yurts, and 7 walk-in tent sites, in a wooded setting with a creek running through it, restrooms, water, and trails; open year-round, no reservations. And **Jessie M. Honeyman State Park,** 3 miles south of Florence, lies among the lakes and trees behind the **Oregon Dunes** with 47 full and 121 partial hookup sites, 187 tent sites, 10 yurts, and a hiker/biker camp, with water, shower, restrooms, trails, boating, and swimming; open year-round; for reservations call 1-800-452-5687. **Harbor Vista,** 87658 Harbor Vista Road, Florence, is a bucolic Lane County park tucked into fir and rhododendron groves above the North Jetty of the Siuslaw River, with 38 full hookup sites (including one handicapped-accessible site), water, showers, restrooms, views, and playground; open year-round; reserve at least three days ahead by calling 541-682-2000.

Siuslaw National Forest (541-750-7000) offers many sites in the district; where reservations are allowed, they may be made at www.recreation.gov or 1-877-444-6777. Near Waldport: **Blackberry Campground,** 18 miles east of Waldport on OR 34, lies along the Alsea River with 32 tent/trailer sites, water and toilets; reservations available; open mid-May through Labor Day. **Canal Creek Campground,** 11 miles east of Waldport by OR 34 and Canal Creek Road, has 11 sites with toilets and drinking water; open May–Sept.; no reservations. **Tillicum Beach Campground,** just off US 101, 5 miles south of Waldport, with 59 tent/trailer sites, water, and toilets, is right on the beach; with luck the surf will drown out highway noise. Open year-round (busy in summer); reservations available.

In the **Cape Perpetua Scenic Area,** 22 miles north of Florence, the **Cape Perpetua Campground** offers 38 tent/trailer sites in old-growth forest in an area outstanding even by Oregon coast standards, with water, toilets, trails, and the nearby visitors center. Open May–Sept.; reservations allowed. **Rock Creek Campground,** 14 miles north of Florence, has 15 tent/trailer sites, water, and toilets, beside US 101; open May–Sept.; some sites reservable.

Near Florence: **Alder Creek Campground,** 6 miles north of Florence off US 101, has 39 tent/trailer sites, water, and toilets, in a coastal forest beside Alder Lake with access to the dunes and the sea; open May–Sept.; reservations available. **Sutton Campground,** 4 miles north of Florence, has 80 tent/trailer sites, some with hookups, with water, toilets (some ADA accessible), and trails among the dunes. Open all year; reservations available. Inland, on OR 126, 18 miles east of Florence, is **Archie Knowles Campground,** with nine tent/trailer sites, water, toilets, and a creek; open May–Sept.; no reservations.

In the **Oregon Dunes** area: **Tyee Campground,** on Pacific Avenue 6 miles south of Florence on US 101, has 14 tent/trailer sites with toilets, showers, water, trail access, and a boat ramp on the Siltcoos River. Open May–Sept.; reservations possible. **Lagoon Campground,** 8 miles south of Florence via US 101 and Siltcoos Beach Access Road, offers 39 tent/trailer sites with water, toilets, an ADA-accessible trail, and bird-watching; open all year; reservations possible. Nearby **Waxmyrtle Campground** has 55 tent/trailer sites, water, toilets, and trails; open all year; reservations allowed. **Carter Lake Campground,** 11 miles south of Florence on US 101, has 23 sites with water, toilets, and trail access; open May–Sept.; reservations available.

CANOEING AND KAYAKING **Cleawox Lake,** in **Jessie Honeyman State Park,** is an 87-acre body of water nearly surrounded by tall dunes on which you can peaceably paddle a canoe or kayak (rentals available). Across the highway is larger **Woahink Lake,** but there you must compete with motorboats. The 3-mile **Siltcoos River Canoe Trail** is calm, flat water (though with some downed trees) flowing from Siltcoos Lake to the sea. One portage around a small dam is facilitated by a walkway. With varied scenery over its short length—woodlands, dunes, flowering shrubs, beach—it's a pretty, leisurely paddle. It's best to take out before reaching the beach, which is closed at this point from mid-Mar. to mid-Sept. to protect nesting snowy plovers. The **Kayak Shack** (541-563-4445), P.O. Box 370, Waldport 97394, is an enterprise of Waldport High School students who will take you on kayak tours of Alsea Bay and Lint Slough, teach you basic technique, or rent you equipment if you want to explore on your own.

GOLF **Avalon Park Pitch and Putt** (541-902-9478), 85208 US 101, Florence. A family course with nine holes.

Crestview Hills Golf Course (541-563-3020), 1680 SW Crestline Drive, Waldport. Nine to 18 holes.

Ocean Dunes Golf Links (541-997-3232; www.oceandunesgolf.com), 3345 Munsel Lake Road, Florence. Eighteen holes.

Sandpines Golf Links (541-997-1940; www.sandpines.com), 1201 35th Street, Florence. Eighteen holes.

HIKING Yachats area: The **804 Trail** follows a former county road right-of-way from Yachats Bay along the bluffs to **Smelt Sands State Park** just north of Yachats; 3 miles round-trip.

Cape Perpetua: A web of 26 miles of trails covers **Cape Perpetua Scenic Area,** running around the headland from base to summit and down to the churns, tidal pools, and spouting horns at sea level. All can become treacherously slippery in rain, so be cautious. **Cummins Creek Trail** and **Cummins Creek Loop** start from FR 1050 4 miles south of Florence for an exploration deep into the temperate rain forest; about 9 miles round-trip. **Cook's Ridge Trail** starts from the **Discovery Loop Trail** just east of the interpretive center and joins the **Gwynn Creek Trail** to loop back to the center by way of the **Oregon Coast Trail;** about 9 miles; challenging. The **Discovery Loop** climbs up from the interpretive center for some fine views; about 3.5 miles round-trip. **Saint Perpetua Trail** is also 3.5 miles round-trip, a stiff descent from the **Whispering Spruce** trailhead and a stiff climb back up. The **Whispering Spruce Trail** is a 0.25-mile, wheelchair-accessible trail from the trailhead on FR 55 11 miles south of Waldport; it runs along the brow of the headland with great ocean views and several rest areas. The **Giant Spruce Trail** leads from the interpretive center 1 mile to a huge Sitka spruce. **Gwynn Creek Trail** runs from its trailhead a mile south of the interpretive center off US 101 3 miles into the forest to connect with the **Cook's Ridge Trail.** To reach the rocky shore, take the **Cape Cove Trail** from US 101 11 miles south of Waldport, or the **Captain Cook Trail** from the same trailhead (0.3 and 0.6 mile respectively, each way). Also from this point you can pick up the **Restless Waters Trail,** an easy 1-mile loop with viewpoints.

Florence area: An easy 0.5-mile trail (each way) leads to **Heceta Head Lighthouse** from the parking area for tremendous views; about 13 miles north of Florence off US 101. Only 5.5 miles north of Florence, a sandy 1-mile trail loops around **Lily Lake;** turn west off US 101 onto Baker Beach Road. This trail is shared by equestrians. In fact, a whole network of horse trails is not far away: take Herman Peak Road east instead of Baker Beach Road west, and you'll come to the Dry Lake Trailhead of a 17-mile web of equestrian paths. Five miles north of Florence, turn west at the **Alder Dune Campground** entrance to find the 1-mile Alder Dune trail looping around tiny Alder Lake and through sand dunes to meet the **Sutton Lake** trail system that follows both sides of Sutton Creek, from the **Darlingtonia Bog Trail** near US 101 (wheelchair accessible) to **Holmen Vista,** also wheelchair accessible and reached by Sutton Beach Road as well as the trail. Slightly inland, the **Mapleton Pioneer Trail** covers the old North Fork Trail, part of an early road from Eugene to Florence; about 3 miles round-trip. From Florence drive 17 miles north on FR 5070 to the trailhead. At a similar distance, the **PAWN Trail** follows the banks of the North Fork Siuslaw River for a mile through an old-growth forest; PAWN stands for the surnames of four families who got a post office for their community in the early 1900s. From Florence take OR 126 east 1 mile to FR 5070 and follow it for 12 miles to FR 5084, at which point stay right and continue 5 miles to the trailhead.

Oregon Dunes area: Several miles of footpaths wind through **Honeyman State Park,** some skirting the shores of the several lakes, some connecting the various campgrounds. Within **Oregon Dunes National Recreation Area,** the **Taylor Dunes Trail** starts just off US 101 7.5 miles south of Florence to pass Taylor Lake and join the **Carter Dunes Trail** on its march to the sea; 1 mile from the trailhead to the Carter Trail. The latter is also accessible from the same turnoff, a couple of miles farther along, and makes its way through the dunes to the beach in 1.5 miles. Seven miles south of Florence, turn west on Siltcoos Access Road to find **Chief Siltcoos Trail,** a 1-mile loop starting at the Stagecoach Trailhead. Shortly before the Stagecoach you pass the **Lagoon Trailhead,** where you can take an easy walk along Siltcoos Lagoon's boardwalks, paths, and viewing platforms. Either the Lagoon or Stagecoach trailheads can be your jumping-off point for the **Waxmyrtle, Estuary,** and **Beach trails,** 1.5 miles along the Siltcoos estuary to the beach. Back at US 101, but on the eastern side, is access to **Siltcoos Lake Loops,** 3 miles to Siltcoos Lake (shared with mountain bikes).

UNIQUE ADVENTURES Sea Lion Caves (541-547-3111; www.sealioncaves.com), 91560 N. US 101, Florence (11 miles north of Florence). Daily 9–5, except

Christmas and Thanksgiving. General admission $12, seniors $11, children 3–12 $8, children under two free. This is the stuff of legend—caverns rising from the sea to a vault 12 stories high, a habitation of sea lions and wild sea birds. Of course, this being the United States, the legend comes complete with a gift shop selling fudge and the like. The cave was entered by mariner William Cox, who took his boat in several times (no small accomplishment) and was once reportedly marooned inside for several days while a storm raged. He bought the property from the state and grazed sheep on the meadows above. When rumors of a coastal road began, the holding was sold to entrepreneurs who knew an attraction when they saw it. Sea Lion Caves was opened in 1932. Access at that time was at low tide by a trail cut into the cliff and a 135-step wooden tower. Today you take an elevator down to the caves to observe some of the two hundred Steller's sea lions known to inhabit it—it is their only known haul-out and birthing place on the mainland. In spring and summer, adults and pups mostly hang out on the outside ledges; in winter they move into the cave. Birds spiral in and out of the high vault, uttering their wild cries. Despite the modernization, you still have to walk about 400 yards at a grade of 10 to 20 percent to reach the elevator, and go up and down 37 steps to reach outdoor trails.

✷ Wilder Places

PARKS One mile east of Waldport on OR 34, **W. B. Nelson State Recreation Site** is a small lake beside the Alsea River, popular for fishing and also for lots of waterfowl; no fee. A mile south of Waldport, **Governor Patterson Memorial Site** gives access to miles of beach; no fee. Two miles farther south is **Beachside State Recreation Site,** a small but pretty park for picnicking, camping, or just watching the waves.

Smelt Sands State Park and **Yachats State Park** bracket the town of Yachats, the former being a sandy beach to the north where the smelt run in winter, and the latter a promontory where Yachats Bay meets the sea; a fine place to watch for

ROAD TO THE SEA, YACHATS

whales and eat a picnic, firmly zipped into a fleece jacket. They are connected by the 0.75-mile **804 Trail** (see *Hiking*). No fee.

Three miles south of Yachats, **Neptune Scenic Viewpoint** hugs the south side of **Cape Perpetua** with fine views of wildlife and the surf. The mouth of Cummins Creek, which flows to the sea here, is a profitable place to look for agates. No fee. **Stonefield Beach,** 6 miles south of Yachats, is an access point to miles of sandy beach. No facilities; no fee. **Muriel Ponsler Memorial Park** is another such spot, but with picnic tables, 16 miles north of Florence; no fee. Close by, **Tokatee Klootchman** is a few feet above sea level with views and beach access; no fee.

Carl G. Washburne Memorial State Park (541-547-3416), 14 miles north of Florence on the east side of US 101, is set in second-growth forest thick with wild rhododendrons. Washburne offers full-service creekside camping and trails to miles of beach.

Heceta Head Lighthouse (541-547-3416), 11 miles north of Florence. If time is short, this park offers the quintessence of the Oregon coast: a photogenic lighthouse, forest-backed cliffs, tide pools, migrating whales, flocks of nesting seabirds, and on a clear day you can see—well, if not forever, maybe halfway to China. Take a lighthouse tour (see *Historic Sites*) or follow trails to viewpoints and a "hobbit forest" of wind-stunted Sitka spruce. Picnic tables allow you to lunch out of the wind. If you are particularly ambitious or lucky, you might stay in the old keeper's house, now operated as a bed & breakfast (541-547-3696).

♿ **Darlingtonia State Natural Site,** 5 miles north of Florence, is the home of a rare pitcher plant (see *Natural Wonders*), with wheelchair-accessible trails.

Jessie M. Honeyman Memorial State Park (1-800-551-6949), 4.5 miles south of Florence. This second largest of Oregon's state parks has its own historic district: day-use areas and the lodge built by the CCC in the 1930s. Honeyman sits on two freshwater lakes where the dunes meet the forest and is a favorite with families for its camping, fishing, berry picking, nature trails, and water sports; it's one place on the coast where you can actually swim, albeit not in the sea—2 miles of 500-foot dunes separate you from the Pacific. OHVs can access the dunes from the park in winter.

Harbor Vista, about 2 miles north of Florence on Rhododendron Drive, then left on Harbor Vista Drive. This is a lovely quiet Lane County park (541-682-2000) with camping, restrooms, showers (coin operated), and a view over the mouth of the Siuslaw.

Old Town Park, Laurel and Bay streets, Florence. Situated at the mouth of the Siuslaw River, this small but restful city park provides benches, pine trees, and river views in the midst of the gentrified waterfront.

WILDERNESS AREAS **Cummins Creek** and **Rock Creek wilderness areas,** slightly over 9,000 and 7,000 acres respectively, are tracts of ancient forest just south of Cape Perpetua—Cummins Creek is reported to have the only old-growth Sitka spruce forest left in the state. Besides tall evergreens, you'll find an understory of bigleaf maple and rhododendrons that come into riotous pink bloom in spring, and ferns and salmonberry galore. Salmon still run in the streams. **Cummins Ridge Trail** runs through Cummins Creek Wilderness; Rock Creek has no maintained trails.

WILDLIFE AREAS **Cape Perpetua Scenic Area** (541-547-3289), 2400 US 101, Yachats. Captain's log: "Each extreme of the land seemed to shoot out to a point; the one to the north we saw on the 7th it was called Cape Perpetua, on account of its first being seen on that day" (Captain Cook's log, Mar. 1778). That day being the feast of St. Perpetua; though some have suggested the cape was so named for being perpetually in view, as the boat could make little headway in the stormy weather. Which has some merit: he could have named it for St. Felicity, who shares the same day, but clearly did not feel felicitous. But we can. The cape is a superlative in a land of superlatives: a headland rising 800 feet above the waves, covered with giant Sitka spruce (one, a heritage tree, is six hundred years old), Indian middens, historic resonance, and churning waters below. Trails run down to the tide pools and spouting horns, through the rain forest, and up to the CCC-built shelter on top (though you can drive up, too) whence, on a clear day, you can see nearly 40 miles out to sea. Obviously this is a fine point to watch whales, though even better is the view from the interpretive center, which has the advantage of an enclosed observation room. The center contains exhibits on the cape's natural history and runs nature programs, including Whale Watch Week during the whales' migration seasons; open daily 10–5:30 in summer, 10–4 in winter. Cape Perpetua is a Forest Service site and requires a Northwest Forest Pass.

WILDLIFE REFUGES **Oregon Islands National Wildlife Refuge** (541-867-4550). More than 1,400 coastal islands, some no bigger than rocks, make up this refuge, designated a National Wilderness. They are out of bounds to human visitors, but **Heceta Head,** where some of said rocks seem nearly close enough to touch, is an official viewpoint.

✷ Lodging

BED & BREAKFASTS

Florence

Blue Heron Inn Bed and Breakfast (1-800-997-7780; www.blue-heroninn.com), 6563 OR 126. The Blue Heron sits on the Siuslaw River just east of Florence. The rambling house has five guest rooms with views of the garden or the river, a living room, and a lounge; a cozy place to come back to, or to spend the day watching eagles and sea lions. Doubles $100–160, with full breakfast.

Edwin K Bed and Breakfast (1-800-833-9465; www.edwink.com), 1155 Bay Street. This stately 1914 home narrowly escaped destruction when a Dairy Queen was planned on its site (to be fair, the house had fallen into disrepair). Prescient buyers moved it down the hill and had skilled woodworkers restore it to its former glory, so that guests now enjoy traditional grandeur plus private baths and high-speed wireless. Owners Marv and Laurie Vandestreek have named six rooms for the seasons (including fall, autumn, and Indian summer) and welcome you with tea and sherry in the afternoon and a five-course breakfast. Children must be over 14 to stay in the house; the adjacent apartment is open to families. $125–200.

✐ **Heceta Light Station** (541-547-3696), 92072 US 101. If you're lucky, you might sleep in the original lighthouse keeper's room, but the other five are just as nice, with view of the sea or the bay, and furnished with period pieces. Imagine, as you eat your seven-course breakfast, what it was like to live on this lonely headland before US 101 existed, and when any road was rudimentary. There's a long porch for considering the panorama and a fenced acre of yard for flying kites and other games. $133–315; children over 10 welcome.

Waldport

Cliff House Bed and Breakfast (541-563-2506; www.cliffhouseoregon.com), 1450 SW Adahi Road. Sink into an armchair or bed to watch the sea from one of three wood-paneled rooms in this large, antiques-furnished house. Or for an even more special occasion choose the suite, four-poster bed and all. All have ocean views, and there's a glass-enclosed deck for even better viewing. $125–225, with full breakfast.

Yachats

Ambrosia Gardens (541-547-3013; www.ambrosia-gardens.com), 95435 US 101. At Ambrosia you have nature and second nature: spruce forest on the one hand and a garden-lover's garden on the other. Lilies, jasmine, dahlias, and a multitude of fragrant flowers flourish in the mild sea air—nearly 3 acres on which to stroll. The accommodations are a room and a carriage house, both decorated with homemade quilts. Children are welcome in the carriage house. $110–125, with full breakfast.

Sea Quest Inn (541-547-3782), 95354 US 101. This is a spreading, contemporary cedar home overlooking the surf about 7 miles south of Yachats. Plenty of luxuries await the visitor—puffy beds, private Jacuzzi, etc.—though the best may be the wraparound deck for watching whales and whatever else comes along. Doubles from $170, with full breakfast; children over 12 welcome.

COTTAGES

Waldport

Edgewater Cottages (541-563-2240), 3978 SW US 101. One- to three-bedroom cottages have kitchens or kitchenettes, fireplaces, and beach access, and welcome well-behaved children and pets. A minimum stay applies, varying with the season. $110–200.

Westlake

Siltcoos Station Retreat (541-997-8444), 83036 Siltcoos Stations Road. On Siltcoos Lake south of Florence, Siltcoos Station sprang up along the new Eugene–Coos Bay rail line in the early 1900s. It had a grocery store, dance hall, post office, school, and eventually a number of cabins, before fading as so many railroad settlements did. The cabins and grounds now belong to Lane Community College, which rents them out for group classes and retreats but also accepts families. Each of the four cabins sleeps four to six and has its own kitchen and bathroom, and is simply but pleasantly furnished. At $50–60 a night it's hard to go wrong, and you're right on the lake for canoeing or kayaking.

Yachats

Rock Park Cottages (541-547-3214), 421 Second Street. The row of five shingled cottages backs onto a hobbit forest of wind-flattened Sitka spruce; beyond is the sea. They look much the same as they did when owner Virginia Gillmore bought them in the 1960s—wood paneling, wall heaters to dispel the damp, full kitchens and bathrooms, TV and games for the inevitable rainy day—and now are hosting third-generation vacationers. A cozier place for a quiet, unpretentious getaway with or without kids is hard to imagine. Some units accept dogs. Cottages $70–85, children under 16 free; an A-frame accommodates larger groups at $100–130.

🐾 **Shamrock Lodgettes** (1-800-845-5028; www.shamrocklodgettes.com), 105 US 101 S. Three 1950s log cabins at the south edge of Yachats Bay constitute the nucleus of the "lodgettes." Several newer cabins and six multiplex units have been added since, most with kitchenettes and wood-burning stoves or fireplaces. Well-behaved pets are welcome in the older cabins. $69–179.

HOTELS AND MOTELS

Florence

🐾 **Lighthouse Inn** (1-866-997-3221; www.lighthouseinn-florence.com), 155 US 101. This convenient little hotel has been taking care of Florence's guests since 1938, when it was built as the Hotel Ragan. It's undergone several renovations since then, but much of the furniture is original, including the rustic pine sofa and easy-chair set flanking the lobby's woodstove—a cozy spot to hunker down through Pacific storms or to come back to after a day exploring, and as tidy and shipshape as a coastal hotel ought to be. Twenty-six units of varying sizes and views welcome singles, couples, and families—even pets under 45 pounds. And old photos around the lobby show the hotel when US 101 was a dirt road. Doubles $50–84.

River House Inn (1-877-997-3933; www.riverhouseflorence.com), 1202 Bay Street. A newer hotel in Old Town, the River House has large modern rooms, some with balconies, right over the Siuslaw. No pets; children under 12 stay free. $75–160.

Yachats

🐾 **Fireside Motel** (1-800-336-3573; www.firesidemotel.com), 1881 US 101. Slightly older than its cliffside neighbors, the Overleaf and the Adobe, the Fireside has acquired a comfortable patina, enhanced by ocean-view rooms, some with fireplaces and balconies, and its welcome of pets. Doubles $60–140.

Ocean Haven (541-547-3583; www.oceanhaven.com), 94470 US 101, 8 miles south of Yachats. Not exactly a lodge, but not a hotel either, Ocean Haven offers four rustic studios and a cabin on a bluff over the sea. All have kitchen and bathrooms, and sleep two to six. Far from even small crowds, nature is your entertainment—there are no phones or TV, though there is Wi-Fi. You're a short, inclined walk to tide pools or woods. These folks are committed to protecting wildlife (no pets) and to diversity, welcoming all nature lovers (except those arriving in Hummers or RVs, or smokers). Double occupancy $95–145.

🐾 **Ya'tel Motel** (1-800-406-1338; www.yatelmotel.com), US 101 and Sixth Street. Karen and Dennis Lambert and their spaniel, Gidget, are your hosts at this friendly mom-and-pop motel in the heart of Yachats. Nine one- or two-room units welcome kids, pets, and singles or couples with lovely stitched quilts and all simple comforts; several have kitchens. A good deal at $50–100.

RESORTS

Yachats

♿ 🐾 **Adobe Resort** (1-800-522-3623; www.adoberesort.com), 1555 US 101. One of the first resorts to make its appearance on Yachats's scenic shores, the Adobe offers rooms in various shapes and sizes, from double-bedded rooms to suites with kitchen, Jacuzzi, and fireplace; also a restaurant and indoor swimming pool. While it lacks the personal character of some of the B&Bs or older accommodations, it is wheelchair friendly, allows pets in some rooms, and doesn't charge for children under 10. Doubles from $67.50.

Overleaf Lodge (1-800-338-0507; www.overleaflodge.com), 2055 US 101. Picture windows look out onto pounding surf, and your luxury room may have amenities ranging from robes and large-screen TV to balconies, gas fireplaces, and, strangely, a bathtub set right in said picture window. There's an on-site spa and exercise room, too. No pets. Doubles $120–265, including breakfast. Cottages at Overleaf Village next door go for $245–345 a night or $1,550–2,070 a week.

* Where to Eat

DINING OUT

Florence

Bridgewater Restaurant (541-997-1133), 1297 Bay Street. Daily for lunch and dinner. Once it was a mercantile store, owned by Florence promoter and businessman William Kyle. Now it specializes in classical American seaside dishes—steaks, fresh seafood, and clam chowder, in Florence's Old Town.

Feast (541-997-3284), 294 Laurel Street. Daily for lunch and dinner. It doesn't look like much, being a nondescript house of uncertain age a block off US 101, but chefs Evan and Jennifer Doughty were the cooking powerhouse behind the former Crave's. They have now taken it over, renamed it, and continue to focus their culinary chops on fine local foods. Here that means, of course, fish and seafood, but also mushrooms, Oregon meats, and plenty of fruits and vegetables. It may not be on the waterfront, but if what's on your plate is more important than what's outside the window, that's fine.

Waterfront Depot (541-902-9100), 1252 Bay Street. Dinner only; reservations recommended. It is a former railway depot, moved 14 miles from nearby Mapleton, but has become one the most appreciated restaurants in town for its cost-to-quality ratio. The menu's on a blackboard by the door and naturally rich in, but not confined to, seafood. The river view doesn't hurt either.

EATING OUT

Florence

Grape Leaf Wines and Bistro (541-997-1646; www.grape-leaf-wines.com), 1269 Bay Street. Open for lunch and dinner. Notice the wines come first. You can eat, and quite nicely, too, at small tables with the pleasant view of shelves and shelves of wine bottles, all available for the asking (well, for a small fee). The menu changes daily but always includes pizza and several hearty, homemade dishes.

Sidestreet Bistro (541-997-1195), 165 Maple Street. Daily for dinner; closed Jan. A small restaurant specializing in new, tenderly prepared American cuisine, especially Northwest seafood. It satisfies gastronomically and aesthetically without breaking the bank.

Yachats

Drift Inn (541-547-4477; www.the-drift-inn.com), 124 US 101 N. The Drift is considerably more respectable than it was in the '30s, when it reportedly served ice cream downstairs and drinks and gambling above. A legal tavern after Prohibition, it closed in 1994 and has now been reincarnated as a cozy family place serving breakfast, lunch, dinner, and live music. The creative cooking includes favorites like eggs Benedict, burgers, and chowder; several vegetarian choices; and experiments like the seafood lasagna. It's all good. The gleaming wood bar along one side recalls old times.

Green Salmon Coffee Shoppe (541-547-3077; www.thegreensalmon.com), 220 US 101. As tiny as it is, Yachats does not lack for coffeehouses. The Green Salmon specializes in organic, fair trade coffees and teas, and practices environmentalism to the point of mopping the floors with collected rainwater (well, there's no lack of that either). Pastries and sandwiches make it a stop for a casual breakfast or lunch.

Luna Sea Fish House (541-547-4794), 53 US 101. Daily 8 AM–9 PM in summer, daily 8–8 in winter. It's a hole-in-the-wall—which locals were raving about just a couple of months after it opened in 2008—serving fish-and-chips, fish sandwiches, steamers, and a rich and very fresh slumgullion: owner Robert Anthony goes out most days to catch the ingredients. Honest food prepared with a light touch by a man who knows his seafood. Also a place to buy fresh fish by the pound.

✷ Entertainment

Florence Events Center (541-997-1994; www.eventcenter.org), 715 Quince Street, Florence. The center hosts music, dance, and theater by visiting troupes and orchestras, as well as the local Last Resort Players, who spearheaded the center's creation in 1996.

✷ Shopping

Sure Beats Farmin' (541-997-7536), 185 Nopal Street, Florence. Tucked across from the marina parking lot, this candy store may just have the best fudge on the central coast. They also offer a selection of evangelical books and trinkets.

✷ Events

May: **Rhododendron Festival** (541-997-3128; www.florencechamber.com), third weekend, Florence. Almost uninterruptedly since 1908, the blooming of the wild rhododendrons has been celebrated with a parade, Rhododendron Queen, barbecue, and more.

September: **Chowder, Blues and Brews** (541-997-3128; www.florencechamber.com), third weekend, Florence Events Center. This combines two Northwest specialties—microbrews from all over the area and chowder by Oregon coast cooks—with live blues.

October: **Yachats Mushroom Festival** (541-547-3530), third weekend, Yachats. The moist forests looming above town abound in fungi. Scientific presentations, exhibits, mushroom walks, music, and food. Dinner $30; everything else is free.

Southern Oregon Coast

2

REEDSPORT–COOS BAY AREA

BANDON–PORT ORFORD AREA

GOLD BEACH–BROOKINGS AREA

Patrick Roberts

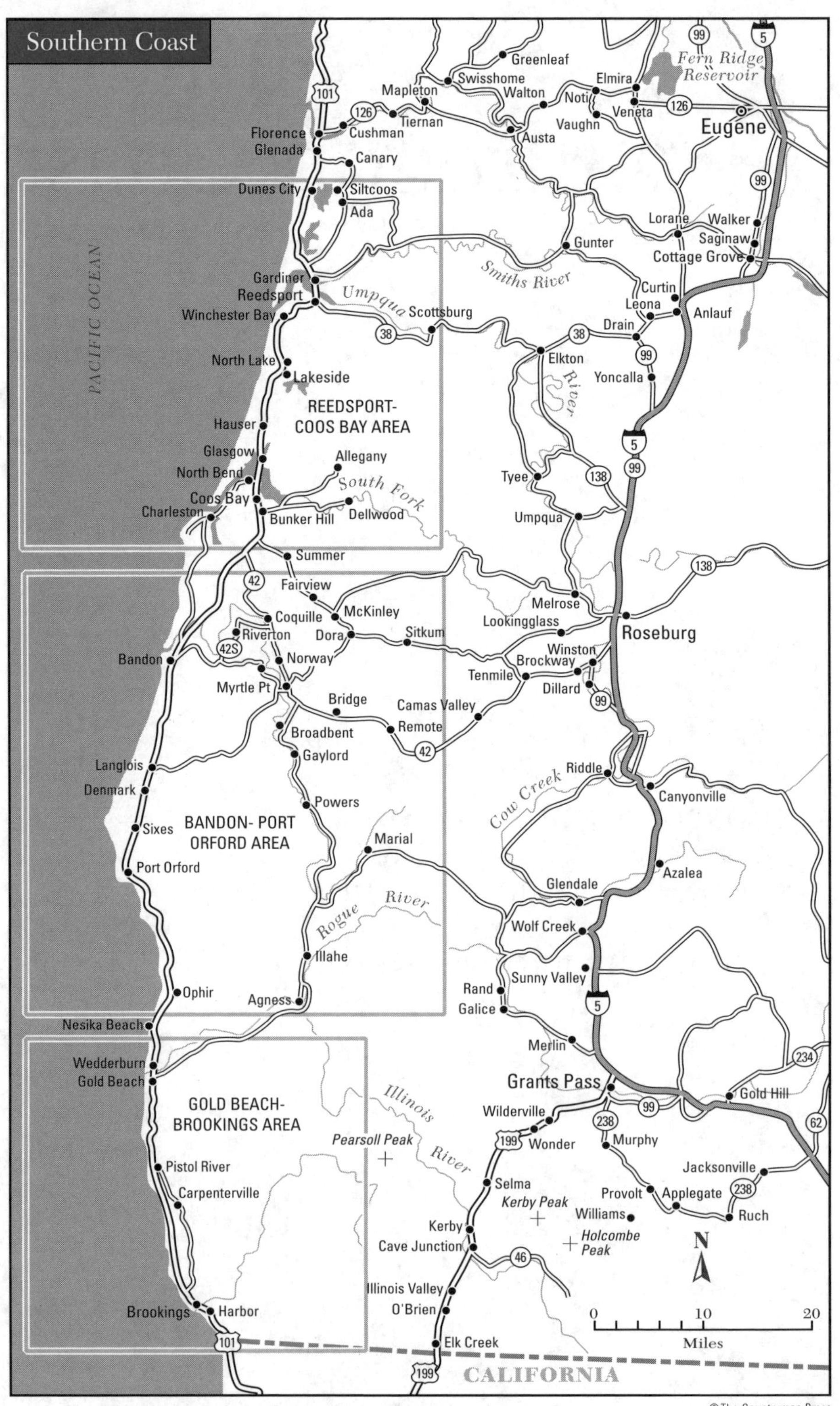
Southern Coast
PACIFIC OCEAN
REEDSPORT-COOS BAY AREA
BANDON- PORT ORFORD AREA
GOLD BEACH-BROOKINGS AREA
Florence
Glenada
Cushman
Canary
Mapleton
Tiernan
Swisshome
Greenleaf
Walton
Austa
Noti
Vaughn
Elmira
Veneta
Eugene
Fern Ridge Reservoir
Dunes City
Siltcoos
Ada
Lorane
Walker
Saginaw
Cottage Grove
Gunter
Smiths River
Curtin
Leona
Anlauf
Drain
Gardiner
Reedsport
Winchester Bay
Umpqua
Scottsburg
Elkton
River
Yoncalla
North Lake
Lakeside
Hauser
Glasgow
North Bend
Allegany
South Fork
Coos Bay
Charleston
Bunker Hill
Dellwood
Tyee
Umpqua
Summer
Fairview
McKinley
Coquille
Riverton
Dora
Sitkum
Norway
Bandon
Myrtle Pt
Melrose
Lookingglass
Roseburg
Winston
Brockway
Tenmile
Dillard
Bridge
Camas Valley
Broadbent
Remote
Gaylord
Langlois
Denmark
Sixes
Port Orford
Powers
Marial
Cow Creek
Riddle
Canyonville
Azalea
Glendale
Wolf Creek
Rogue River
Illahe
Sunny Valley
Rand
Galice
Ophir
Agness
Nesika Beach
Wedderburn
Gold Beach
Merlin
Grants Pass
Gold Hill
Illinois River
Wilderville
Wonder
Murphy
Pearsoll Peak
Pistol River
Carpenterville
Selma
Kerby Peak
Jacksonville
Provolt
Applegate
Williams
Ruch
Kerby
Cave Junction
Holcombe Peak
N
Illinois Valley
O'Brien
Brookings
Harbor
0
10
20
Miles
Elk Creek
CALIFORNIA
101
126
38
99
5
42
42S
138
234
238
62
199
46
©The Countryman Press

SOUTHERN OREGON COAST

Crash . . . whoosh, crash . . . whoosh. That's the sound of a well-behaved ocean beach in much of the world. Not so the Pacific; at least not on our coasts. Here it sounds more like a continuous express train, as the combers just keep rolling in without pause. With the whole expanse of the Pacific to gather strength and not much of a continental shelf to slow them down, they come in rows and break with a continuous roar. And that's in good weather. It can be disconcerting to campers trying to get some sleep.

On the other hand, the sound embodies the wildness of this wildest part of a wild coast. With the exception of the Coos Bay/North Bend agglomeration, towns are few and far between and get smaller the farther south you go. Coos Bay itself is known as Oregon's Bay Area: with the biggest harbor between San Francisco and Puget Sound, it became a massive shipping point for wood products, which means it has suffered badly with lumber's decline. Things cheer up as you head south, past the newly turned golf courses of Bandon and out to Cape Blanco with its lighthouse, the westernmost point in the continental United States. From Cape Blanco to the California line is Oregon's "banana belt"—something of an exaggeration, since it's hardly tropical, but some concatenation of topography and currents brings warmer temperatures and clearer weather than is common to the north. Which is not to say it doesn't rain; in winter it does, in buckets. But summer or winter, daytime temperatures hover between 60 and 75 degrees. Fog tends to stay offshore, and even in winter mild, sunny days are common. I'm told people take dips at Port Orford beaches in January. Though I wouldn't recommend it.

Settlement remained sparse in this area despite the discovery of gold in the rivers, and despite abundant lumber and fish (and despite the violent removal of Indians to reservations); it was just too remote, cut off from supplies and markets by the dense jumbled Siskiyous behind and the rough coast in front. Some of Oregon's most pristine rivers punctuate this coast: the Umpqua, falling from the Cascades to Reedsport; the Rogue, wild and scenic, at Gold Beach; the Chetco at Brookings; and a myriad of smaller but still impressive streams like the Coquille, Sixes, and Elk, which still carry respectable salmon runs. By all means use US 101, scenic in its own right, but amble along back roads to the beaches and headlands or upstream into the wilderness and the only redwood stands north of California. This is the coast's quiet corner of fishing villages, empty backcountry, small galleries, home-grown theater, hidden coves, and long, deserted beaches.

REEDSPORT–COOS BAY AREA

The Coast Road navigates between the continuing expanse of the **Oregon Dunes** and the freshwater lakes and sloughs behind them. Reedsport is the only town of any size; here the **Umpqua Discovery Center** puts it all in perspective, bringing forth the intertwined history and ecology of the river and marine environments. It's a watery world all the way to Charleston, at the southern end of Coos Bay, where the South Slough is a research area for estuarine systems.

GUIDANCE **Charleston Information Center** (1-800-824-8486), Boat Basin Drive and Cape Arago Highway, Charleston 97420.

Coos Bay–North Bend Visitors and Convention Bureau (1-800-824-8486; www.oregonsadventurecoast.com), 50 Central Avenue, Coos Bay 97420.

North Bend Information Center (1-800-472-9716), 1380 Sherman Avenue, North Bend 97459.

Oregon Dunes National Recreation Area (541-271-6000), 855 Highway Avenue, Reedsport 97467.

Reedsport/Winchester Bay Chamber of Commerce (1-800-247-2155; www.reedsportcc.org), US 101 and OR 38, Reedsport 97467.

GETTING THERE *By air:* **North Bend–Coos Bay Municipal Airport** (541-756-8531), 2348 Colorado Street, North Bend (also known as **Southwest Oregon Regional Airport**), allows air access to Oregon's "Bay Area"; it's served by Horizon Air, the commuter arm of Alaska Airlines, from Portland, and by SkyWest (United) from San Francisco.

By bus: **Curry Public Transit and Coastal Express** (1-800-921-2871; www.currypublictransit.org) runs three buses a day between North Bend and Brookings on Mon., Wed., and Fri. **Porter Stage Lines** (541-269-7183; www.kokkola-bus.porterstage2.html), 275 N. Broadway, Coos Bay, operates between Coos Bay and Florence several times daily.

By car: All towns lie along **US 101,** the coast's north–south artery; Reedsport is also accessible from the east via **OR 38,** a scenic but necessarily leisurely drive through the Coast Range.

MEDICAL EMERGENCY **Bay Area Hospital** (541-269-8111), 1775 Thompson Road, Coos Bay.

Lower Umpqua Hospital (541-271-3750), 600 Ranch Road, Reedsport.

✱ To See

FARMERS' MARKETS **Coos Bay Farmers' Market** (541-226-9706), Central Avenue and N. Fourth Street, Coos Bay. Wed. 9–3, May–Oct.

Umpqua County Farmers' Market (541-662-1527), Mid-Coast Mall, Reedsport. Fri. 2–5 and Sat. 10–3 year-round.

FOR FAMILIES ✐ **Umpqua Discovery Center** (541-271-4816; www.umpquadiscoverycenter.com), 409 Riverfront Way, Reedsport. Daily 9–5 June–Sept. and daily 10–4 Oct.–May. General admission $8.50, seniors $7.50, children 6–15 $4.50, under six free. Sitting on the Umpqua waterfront, this facility explores the estuarine environment and forest hinterland, and how both natives' and settlers' ways of life depended on them. Murals, soundtracks, a mock-up "tidewater town," and artifacts bring the time line to life.

GARDENS **Mingus Park** (541-269-8918), 10th and Commercial streets, Coos Bay. This multipurpose park has rhododendron and Japanese gardens as well as paths, play areas, and an outdoor pool.

Shore Acres State Park (541-888-3732), 4 miles south of Charleston. Shore Acres was the summer home of shipbuilder Louis Simpson, who collected plants and bulbs from around the world to create 5 acres of formal gardens. Abandoned during the Depression, the estate was bought by the state, which resurrected Simpson's Japanese lily pond along with acres of tulips and daffodils, and hundreds of rosebushes, azaleas, and rhododendrons. The whole place is extravagantly illuminated at Christmas.

HERITAGE TREES At **Shore Acres State Park** (see *Gardens*) a Monterey pine 95 feet tall is tied with one in California for the title of Champion Tree (the California tree is shorter, but broader).

HISTORIC SITES **Cape Arago Lighthouse.** The current light is the third incarnation of the Cape Arago light station—the first was born in 1866, and the latest dates from 1934 (it was deactivated in 2007). Set on a tiny island off the cape, it's not open to the public but is visible from **Sunset Bay State Park** (see *Parks*).

Egyptian Theatre (541-269-8650; www.egyptian-theater.com), 229 S. Broadway, Coos Bay. Things Egyptian were all the rage back in 1925, when the Egyptian Theatre opened as a vaudeville and movie house. Most of the original exotic decor remains in place, repainted and polished up to be sure—painted columns, "temple" entrances, even statuary—though the pride and joy is the Mighty Wurlitzer (not Egyptian) pipe organ, still functioning. And movies are still being shown Fri., Sat., and Sun., though not first-run films. Tickets $4, children and seniors $3.50.

Gardiner Historic District (541-271-4005), 2 miles north of Reedsport. Gardiner was founded in 1850 by shipwreck, when the merchatnt vessel *Bostonian* foundered at the mouth of the Umpqua River. Captain Gardiner was lucky: most of his goods washed ashore, and he decided he may as well start a center for river trade right there. Thirty-three buildings—homes, churches, commercial buildings—dating from 1874 to 1936 adorn the town center.

Umpqua River Lighthouse, off US 101, 6 miles south of Reedsport. Oregon's first lighthouse was built on the north spit of the Umpqua, which was expected to become a major shipping artery. But it didn't, and the 1855 structure, built on sand, crumbled only six years later. The current light dates from1894 and was sensibly placed on a ridge a hundred feet above the river. It's still operational and is right next to **Umpqua Lighthouse State Park.** Tours are given daily 10–6, May–Oct.

MUSEUMS **Coos Art Museum** (541-267-3901; www.coosart.com), 235 Anderson Avenue, Coos Bay. Tues.–Fri. 10–4, Sat. 1–4. Free. A permanent collection and temporary exhibits by Pacific Northwest artists fill this gallery in a former art deco post office.

Coos Historical and Maritime Museum (541-756-6320; www.cooshistory.com), 1220 Sherman Avenue, North Bend. Tues.–Sat. 10–4, and Sun. noon–4 in summer. General admission $4; children under 12 free. This facility is stuffed to the gills with items illuminating the history of the southern Oregon coast, from the artifacts of past daily life to photographs.

Marshfield Sun Printing Museum (541-267-3762), corner of Fronts Street and Bayshore, Coos Bay. Tues.–Sat. 1–4, Memorial Day–Labor Day. The *Sun,* a local newspaper, was printed from 1891 to 1944; here are the original presses.

Oregon Coast Historical Railway (541-297-6130; www.orcorail.org), 766 S. First Street, Coos Bay. Wed.–Sat. 9–3 in winter. As a port city in lumbering country, Coos Bay had its network of local railroads to bring wood in from the forests and ship it out to market. Here are several vintage locomotives and cars, including a caboose from the Eugene–Coos Bay line, which has been slated for reopening.

NATURAL WONDERS **Myrtlewood Groves.** Oregon myrtlewood is a tree in the laurel family that grows only in scattered groves along the southern Oregon and extreme northern California coasts. Today it's used for wood sculpture and gift items; it often has a burl that gives it a swirling grain, and it polishes to a nice sheen. For a time during the Depression myrtlewood coins were used as money in North Bend after the town's single bank had failed—they were issued in units from 5 cents to 10 dollars (one myrtlewood souvenir shop in Port Orford is called Wooden Nickel). One place to see them is at **Golden and Silver Falls State Park,** 24 miles northeast of Coos Bay via Coos River Highway.

SCENIC DRIVES The **Pacific Coast Scenic Byway,** US 101, continues its way along the Oregon coast, where nearly deserted beaches alternate with rugged headlands and broad estuaries. The farther south you go, the wilder it seems to get. It's also a popular stretch of coast for storm watching, but not in your car; find a cozy room or café to admire safely.

The **Cape Arago Beach Loop** covers 24 miles and three state parks, starting on Newmark Avenue in Coos Bay. At the end of Newmark, turn on the Cape Arago Highway for a tour of Sunset Bay, Cape Arago, and Shore Acres state parks, with beach and lighthouse lookouts and a view of Shell Island, where you may see seals, sea lions, elephant seals, and passing whales.

The **South Coast Lighthouse Tour** takes in five lighthouses in a stretch of 130 miles, from **Heceta Head** north of Florence to the **Umpqua River** and **Cape Arago lighthouses** (see *Historic Sites*) and the **Coquille River** and **Cape Blanco lighthouses** (see "Bandon–Port Orford Area"). All are within a few miles of US 101 and are indicated by highway signs.

✷ To Do

BICYCLING **Winchester Trail System** offers 30 miles of biking trails beginning at milepost 251 on US 101, some easy, some challenging. The **Eel Lake Trail** is a 5-mile loop around Eel Lake, dirt, gravel, and level, in **William Tugman State Park** (see *Parks*).

BIRD-WATCHING Some favorite spots are the **North Spit** of Coos Bay, where snowy owls are occasionally seen; **Pony Slough,** a branch of the bay, which brings in thousands of shorbirds, waterfowl, and the accompanying raptors; and **Shore Acres State Park,** especially for summer hummingbirds.

CAMPING State camping parks (for reservations, where available, call 1-800-452-5687): **Umpqua Lighthouse State Park,** 6 miles south of Reedsport off US 101, with 20 full hookup sites, 24 tent sites, 8 yurts, 2 cabins, and showers, restrooms, and water; **William Tugman State Park,** 8 miles south of Reedsport off US 101, is on Eel Lake, with 94 partial hookup sites (some handicapped accessible), 16 yurts, a hiker/biker camp, showers, water, and handicapped-accessible restrooms; and **Sunset Bay,** 12 miles southwest of Coos Bay, with 29 full hookup sites, 34 electrical sites, 66 tent sites, showers, restrooms, water, and a cliff-backed beach.

In the **Oregon Dunes National Recreation Area, Tahkenitch Campground** is open May–Sept. with 34 sites, water, and toilets; 7.5 miles north of Reedsport. Across US 101, **Tahkentich Landing** has 24 sites, a boat ramp, and toilets, but no water. **Eel Creek Campground,** 10 miles south of Reedsport off US 101, has 52 sites, water, toilets, and a trail through the dunes. **Bluebill Campground,** at the southern end of the dunes, has 18 tent/trailer sites, water, and toilets near Bluebill Lake, 1.5 miles north of North Bend. To reserve at any of these campgrounds, call 1-877-444-6777 or go to www.recreation.gov.

CANOEING AND KAYAKING **South Slough** (see *Wildlife Areas*) is a paddling paradise of channels and wetlands on Coos Bay. **Eel Lake,** in **Eel Lake State Park,** is quiet water; it does allow motorboats but with a 5 mph speed limit. **Lighthouse Beach** is a protected bay near Cape Arago popular with kayakers, but uncrowded. The two **Empire Lakes,** in **John Topits Park** on Lakeshore Drive in Coos Bay, are closed to motorized boats and open to paddlers.

GOLF **Forest Hills Country Club** (541-271-2626), 1 Country Club Road, Reedsport. Nine holes.

Kentuck Golf Course (541-756-4464), 94469 Golf Course Lane, North Bend. Eighteen holes.

Sunset Bay Golf Course (541-888-9301), 11001 Cape Arago Highway, Coos Bay. Nine holes.

HIKING Numerous trails wind through the **Oregon Dunes** both north and south of the Umpqua River: the **Oregon Dunes** and **Tahkenitch Loop trails** are interlocking paths leading from a trailhead at milepost 201 on US 101 to the ocean, about a mile; the first 0.5 mile is wheelchair accessible. Some parts are closed seasonally to protect snowy plover nesting habitat. The **Tahkenitch Creek Trail** starts at milepost 202, 9 miles north of Reedsport, and offers several loops along Tahkenitch Creek, ultimately meeting the beach after 3.5 miles. A 1-mile trail confusingly called **Threemile South** runs through a conifer forest to the south end of Threemile Lake; from US 101 4 miles north of Reedsort take Sparrow Park Road west for 2.5 miles. However, the **Threemile Lake Trail** actually is 3 miles long, from milepost 204 on US 101 past Threemile Lake (and two other lakes) to the beach. A wheelchair-accessible, vision-impaired-accessible 0.5-mile trail offers beach views; from US 101 at Reedsport take Salmon Harbor Drive for 2 miles. From a trailhead 10.5 miles south of Reedsport off US 101, the **John Dellenback Trail** traipses 3 miles over tall dunes to the sea. The **Bluebill Trail** is an easy 1.2 miles around Bluebill Lake, with lots of wildlife to see. From US 101, turn west on Jordan Cove Road 3 miles north of North Bend, then turn right onto Transpacific Highway and left on Horsfall Road and continue 2 miles. Across US 101 from **Tugman State Park,** the Hall/Shuttpelz Trail loops around two small lakes in 1.5 miles. Most of these paths are moderately difficult due to the sandy surfaces; most also require a fee, being on national forest lands.

SURFING The southern coast gets some mighty waves; on this stretch, **Bastendorff Beach** and **Lighthouse Beach** are the most popular spots.

✷ Wilder Places

PARKS Half a mile north of Reedsport, **Bolon Island Tideways** is an island in the middle of the Umpqua River (accessible by bridge) with a walking trail to a bird rookery; no fee.

Umpqua Lighthouse State Park (541-271-4118), 6 miles south of Reedsport, offers, of course, access to the lighthouse, but also a small swimmable, paddler-friendly lake, camping, and walking trails. Across the highway, **William Tugman State Park** (541-888-4902) embraces Eel Lake, also good for paddling, stocked with fish and surrounded by shore pines.

Go inland to find **Golden and Silver Falls State Park,** 24 miles northeast of Coos Bay on Coos River Highway. Here two creeks fall a hundred feet among alder, Oregon myrtle, and huge firs, accessible by trails through their canyons. No fee.

Sunset Bay State Park (541-888-4902), 12 miles southwest of Coos Bay, is a spectacular sandy beach backed by cliffs. There's camping, kayaking, and kite flying, and a network of trails connecting it to **Shore Acres** (541-888-2472) and **Cape Arago state parks,** for ocean and wildlife views.

Cape Arago State Park (1-800-551-6949) is one of the state's signature headlands. Sir Francis Drake is supposed to have come by, even anchoring for a while in a cove, in 1579. Captain Cook passed in 1778 and named it Cape Gregory, but it was eventually renamed Arago for a French geographer. With cliffs dropping 200 feet to the sea, trails to tidal pools, windswept vegetation, and views of seals and sea lions, it really shouldn't be missed. No fee.

Bastendorff Beach County Park (541-888-5353), 2 miles southwest of Charleston at the entrance to Coos Bay, is a beach favored by surfers, sunset viewers, and whale-watchers. It also offers camping and a playground.

♿ **John Topits Park** (541-269-8918), on Hull Street in Coos Bay, contains **Empire Lakes** and 120 acres of natural recreations: hiking, kayaking, biking, even swimming; some paths wheelchair accessible.

WILDLIFE AREAS **Dean Creek Elk Viewing Area** (541-756-0100), 8 miles east of Reedsport on OR 38. The bottomlands along the Umpqua River where it flows out of the hills support a herd of 60 to 100 Roosevelt elk, which are often visible from the road. In fall you'll see more activity as bulls compete for cows; in spring and summer calves graze beside their mothers. The Bureau of Land Management maintains viewing platforms just off the highway.

Simpson Reef Overlook, just south of **Shore Acres State Park.** The reef itself is an offshore rock shelf a stone's throw from nearby Shell Island, part of the **Oregon Islands National Wildlife Refuge.** From the overlook you can see both and, usually, thousands of marine mammals and wild birds. Interpretive panels, aided by docents in summer, help you pick out different species.

✐ **South Slough National Estuarine Research Reserve** (541-888-5558), 61907 Seven Devils Road, Charleston. Daily dawn–dusk; interpretive center open Tues.–Sat. 10–4:30. Administered by NOAA and the State of Oregon, the reserve was set aside in 1974 for the study of estuarine systems. They chose the right place; Coos Bay is the expansive estuary of the Coos River, and the slough reserve comprises 4,800 acres of tidelands, freshwater marshes, channels, river, and forest lands. At the interpretive center you can pick up trail maps and wildlife guides and check out the nature exhibits; then hit the trails with a paddle or a pair of hiking shoes. Activities and field trips for all ages are offered regularly.

✷ Lodging

BED & BREAKFASTS

Coos Bay

✐ 🐾 **Coos Bay Manor** (1-800-269-1224; www.coosbaymanor.com), 955 S. Fifth Street. Hjalte and Rolfe Nerdrum came to Coos Bay to work for the Coos Bay Pulp and Lumber Company. Apparently they did well, as Hjalte had this spacious house built in in 1912; but three years later the brothers packed it in and went back to Finland, and the company repossessed the house. It's a proud house indeed, with a two-story, round, pillared front porch; wide balcony; and five large, well-furnished guest rooms. Children are welcome, there's no extra charge for pets (though dogs over 30 pounds must be preapproved), and breakfast is included. $155 double occupancy.

The Old Tower House (541-888-6058; www.oldtowerhouse.com), 476 Newmark Avenue. Hole up in one of four cozy rooms right on the bay. The house is on the National Register of Historic Places and is furnished accordingly, with four-poster or brass beds and Victorian sofas by the fireplace. Doubles from $115, with continental breakfast.

This Olde House (541-267-5224; www.thisoldehousebb.com), 202 Alder Avenue. With a columned porch and balcony all along the front, the 1893 house perhaps reminded Joseph Bennett of Irish stately homes; at any rate, he and his father, George, emigrated here from the old sod. George founded Bandon, a bit down the coast, and Joseph had this grand house built, crystal chandeliers and all. Owner Sally White preserves the turn-of-the-20th-century flavor with antiques that are appropriate, not overwhelming. All rooms have private baths. $105–185, with full breakfast.

HOTELS AND MOTELS

Winchester Bay

♿ **Salmon Harbor Landing** (541-271-3742; www.salmonharborlanding.com), 265 S. Eighth Street. It's just a simple motel with six units, but it's independently owned and includes pillow-top beds and fireplaces in most rooms. One unit is handicapped accessible. Double occupancy from $49.

✱ Where to Eat

DINING OUT

Charleston

Portside Restaurant (541-888-5544; www.portsidebythebay.com), 63383 Kingfisher Road. Daily for lunch and dinner. This one has been around for nearly 50 years under various names, but always devoted to fresh seafood. At one point they went so far as to buy a fishing boat to eliminate the lag time of going to market, but it sank off Charleston. Now they rely on the local fishing fleet for everything from scallops to salmon, not forgetting oysters, shrimp, clams, and all the other coastal creatures, each prepared several different ways. A "small plates" menu accommodates those "under 12 and over 65."

North Bend

Porta (541-756-4900), 1802 Virginia Avenue. Tues.–Sat. 5–10. What could be more satisfying than a leisurely Italian dinner beside the sea, prepared by chefs Alex and Kaisa Bourgidu, formerly of Genoa, Italy. Their "slow food" principles are freshness, season, and simplicity. *Buon appetito.*

EATING OUT

Charleston

Oyster Cove Grille and Bar (541-888-0703; www.oystercovegrillebar.com), 63346 Boat Basin Road. Tues.–Sat. from 5 PM. Fresh Oregon seafood served with a slight Cajun touch, and steaks, steaks, steaks. Chase with dessert and/or port.

Coos Bay

Blue Heron Bistro (541-267-3933; www.blueheronbistro.com), 100 Commercial Avenue. Mon.–Sat. 11–9. Early-bird suppers for $5.95? Not bad, especially if the supper is sauerbraten with potatoes, red cabbage, and rye bread. Or any of the other German specialties. Yes, there is a restaurant in Coos Bay serving proper German food, knockwurst, Wiener schnitzel and all, as well as seafood dishes in case you came to the coast for that (you can't live on fish-and-chips alone). The full-price dinners are quite reasonable, too, with many entrées under $20.

Oregon Coast Culinary Institute (1-877-895-1540), 1988 Newmark Avenue. This cooking school opens its doors to the public for creative, $20 prix-fixe luncheons Fri. noon–1 during the academic year. Reservations required.

North Bend

Café Mediterranean (541-756-2299; www.cafemediterranean.net), 860 Union Street. Mon.–Sat. 11–9, Sun. 11–7. Family recipes from Greece to the Middle East—gyros, spanakopita, falafel, hummus—in short, all the goodies we've come to expect of that healthy Mediterranean diet. Orders to go, too.

✷ Entertainment

Egyptian Theatre (541-269-8650; www.egyptian-theater.com), 229 S. Broadway, Coos Bay. This 1920s cinema (see *Historic Sites*) presents second-run movies on weekends, as well as occasional concerts and lectures.

The Mill Casino (1-800-953-4800; www.themillcasino.com), 3201 Tremont Avenue, Coos Bay. Right in the middle of town, where nightlife is otherwise rather limited, the casino has a rotating calendar of performers.

✷ Events

July: **Oregon Coast Music Festival** (541-267-0938; www.oregoncoastmusic.com), last weekend, several indoor and outdoor venues around Coos Bay. This is the coast's premier music event, featuring three days of classical composers from Albeñiz to at least Vivaldi, plus jazz and pops.

August: **Charleston Seafood Festival** (541-269-0215), midmonth, Charleston Marina. Charleston celebrates its economic base with food, music, crafts, and a fish fling.

Oregon Shorebird Festival (541-867-4550), last weekend, Oregon Institute of Marine Biology, Charleston. Field trips, pelagic trips, even canoe trips, all timed to coincide with shorebird migration.

December: **Shore Acres Holiday Lights** (541-888-3778), Shore Acres State Park, Coos Bay. From Thanksgiving to New Year's Eve, the 7-acre gardens are illuminated.

BANDON–PORT ORFORD AREA

A few years ago, the world's golfing connoisseurs decided that Bandon closely resembled coastal Scotland, where the sport was born. This is not inaccurate: the cold sea cliffs, misty bluffs, and seaside grasslands do recall the old country, the main difference being that the old country is missing the dense evergreen forests backing the courses. The result has been the construction of several golf courses designed by the best experts in the field and, tangentially, the appearance of panini and at least one wine bar in humble Bandon. You don't have to be a golfer, though, to appreciate the landscape, or to enjoy the simple pleasures of kayaking a pristine river or hiking a headland. To the south, Port Orford remains the small town with the spectacular view that it has always been, a mélange of fisherfolk, craftspeople, and farmers, with a few eateries and hostelries thrown in for good measure. It also enjoys the distinctions of being the first town to be founded on the Oregon coast (1851), and the westernmost town in the state.

GUIDANCE **Bandon Chamber of Commerce** (541-347-9616; www.bandon.com), 300 Second Street, Bandon 97411.

Coquille Chamber of Commerce and Visitor Information Center (541-396-3414; www.coquillechamber.net), 119 N. Birch Street, Coquille 97423.

Myrtle Point Chamber of Commerce (541-572-5200; www.myrtlepointchamber.org), 424 Fifth Street, Myrtle Point 97458.

Port Orford and North Curry Chamber of Commerce (541-332-8055; www.discoverportorford.com), P.O. Box 637, Port Orford 97465.

Rogue River–Siskiyou National Forest (541-618-2200), 3040 Biddle Road, Medford 97504. **Powers Ranger District** (541-439-6200), 42861 OR 242, Powers 97466.

GETTING THERE *By bus:* **Curry Public Transit and Coastal Express** (1-800-921-2871; www.currypublictransit.org) stops in Bandon and Port Orford three days a week on its North Bend–Brookings run.

By car: All coastal towns here lie along the **US 101** north–south corridor. Bandon may also be reached from the east via **OR 42S.**

MEDICAL EMERGENCY **Coquille Valley Hospital** (541-396-3101), 940 E. Fifth Street, Coquille.

Southern Coos Hospital (541-347-2426), 900 11th Street SE, Bandon.

✷ To See

FARMERS' MARKETS **Coquille Farmers' Market** (541-396-3894), 115 N. Birch Street, Coquille. Thurs. 9–5, Apr.–Dec.

FOR FAMILIES ♂ ♿ **Game Park Safari** (541-347-3106), 46914 US 101 S., Bandon (7 miles south of town). Daily Mar.–Nov., weekends only Jan.–Feb.; hours vary seasonally. General admission $15, seniors $14, kids 7–12 $8.75, kids 2–6 $5.50; under two free. This is a petting zoo, though instead of lambs, goats, or calves, the kids get to cuddle impossibly cute leopard cubs and other fuzzy creatures—babies only: the adult animals are for looking at. And the viewing is nothing to sneeze at. Snow leopards, rare deer, bison, and monkeys are all on the park's "to see" list. The paths are wheelchair friendly.

♂ **Prehistoric Gardens** (541-332-4463), 36848 US 101, Port Orford. Daily 9–dusk. You can't miss it: a tyrannosaurus towers at the roadside entrance. Stroll the path back into the rain forest (yes, it is a real rain forest, though hardly what the dinosaurs would have known) to meet large and lifelike dinosaurs replicas peering at you from the misty vegetation.Call or contact the Port Orford Chamber of Commerce for hours and admission.

HERITAGE TREES The **Port Orford Cedar,** deep in the Siskiyou National Forest, is a national champion: 242 feet tall with a circumference of over more than feet. This is the species that put Port Orford on the map; untold numbers of board feet of its fine wood were shipped out of the tiny port and around the world. Which means old-growth stands are hard to come by. This one is 9.8 miles southeast of Powers: from Bandon take OR 42 to the junction with County Road 542, about 29 miles; take this to Powers, about 35 miles; and continue southeast on Elk Creek Road. For further information call the Powers Ranger District at 541-439-6200. It's a long way to go to see a tree, but the ride is quite beautiful. And you can picnic when you get there.

HISTORIC HOMES Modest **Myrtle Point** has quite a collection of homes dating from the 1860s to the early 1900s, in styles from the simple bungalow to Queen Anne. A **walking tour** is available from the chamber kiosk at OR 42 and Ash Street, or from www.coquillevalley.org.

Patrick Hughes House (541-332-0248), at the end of Cape Blanco Road, just north of Port Orford. Tues.–Sun. 10–3:30, Apr.–Oct. Adults $2, children under 12 $1, families $5 (includes admission to **Cape Blanco Lighthouse;** see *Historic Sites*). Jane and Patrick Hughes ranched along the Sixes River (surely as green and wet as their native Ireland) for 30 years and evidently prospered. In 1898 they moved into their fine new house on Cape Blanco—11 rooms and 3,000 square feet complete with gaslight and running water (though electricity wouldn't come in till 1942), and even its own chapel for their son John, who had become a priest. With an exterior of solid Port Orford cedar and lots of polished wood inside, it was as grand a house as you could find on that still-wild coast, and it is beautifully kept up by the Friends of Cape Blanco.

HISTORIC SITES **Battle Rock,** US 101, Port Orford. Port Orford dates its settlement from the events of 1851 on this heartbreakingly beautiful stretch of beach. On June 9, Capt. William Tichenor left nine men on the beach with some supplies with the idea of setting up a town to supply miners along the Rogue and Upper Klamath rivers. Local Indians attempted to drive the men away, whereupon the nine holed up on Battle Rock, a sea stack on the beach, and began firing. Two of the crew were wounded and 23 Indians were killed before a truce was called. The sailors then promised to leave within two weeks, probably assuming Tichenor would be back by then either to back them up or take them home. But he didn't, and after two weeks were up the tribe came back with reinforcements. Their chief, however, was killed in this skirmish; they set up a camp to regroup, and the sailors stole away during the night. Tichenor did return in July with a force of 70 men and established Port Orford, naming it after his friend, the Earl of Orford. These were the first salvos of the "Rogue River Wars" of 1855–1856. The Land Donation Act of 1850 had opened these lands to settlement before any treaties had been concluded with the Indians; and the tribes Vancouver had described half a century earlier as mild and peaceable were enraged at seeing their wild food sources plowed under and fenced in. The result, as so often, was a forced march to a reservation 125 miles up the coast.

Cape Blanco Lighthouse, at the end of Cape Blanco Road; turn off 4.5 miles north of Port Orford. Tues.–Sun. 10–3:30, Apr.–Oct. Adults $2, children under 12 $1, families $5 (includes admission to **Patrick Hughes House;** see *Historic Homes*). Sticking a mile and a half out to sea, and with reefs extending farther than that, the Cape was in definite need of a light as shipping increased along the coast. So much so that Louis Knapp, who owned a hotel in nearby Port Orford, kept a light burning in the large hotel window until the lighthouse was completed in 1870. The construction was no easy task: no road went out on the Cape, so most materials had to be brought in by sea through heavy surf. And the headland was shorn of its spruce forest, partly to avoid obstructing the light and partly to eliminate a fire hazard, so that even today it's mostly prairie. The first two keepers, James Langlois and James Hughes, served together for about 33 years, acquiring large families in the process; the two keeper's houses and ancillary buildings are gone, but you can still climb to the lantern room and admire the great Fresnel lens. Cape Blanco is the westernmost point in Oregon, so named by Spanish navigators for its whitish cliffs.

Coquille River Lighthouse, at the end of Park Road in **Bullard's Beach State Park** in Bandon, stands at the mouth of the Coquille River. Shipping traffic to and from Bandon's lumber-rich hinterland was heavy in the late 1800s, and the light was a double aid to navigation, with a foghorn complementing the lamp. It even put in a stint as emergency shelter after the Bandon fire of 1936. After years of faithful service its function was replaced by a jetty beacon in 1939; but one can visit the restored tower and octagonal foghorn room Wed.–Sun. 10–4, mid-Apr.–May; Mon.–Tues. 10–4 and Wed.–Sat. 9–6, June–Sept.; and daily 10–4 through Oct. No fee to visit lighthouse, beyond the $5 park day-use fee.

MUSEUMS **Bandon Historical Society Museum** (541-347-2164), US 101 and Fillmore Avenue, Bandon. Mon.–Sat. 10–4. Adults $2, children free. This little building was Bandon's first building to go up after the 1936 fire that burned down much of the town, and it served as the city hall until 1970. You can learn about the fire as well as the local cranberry industry, Coast Guard operations, and the fine points of Bandon's genesis and growth.

Coos County Logging Museum (541-572-5218), 705 Maple Street, Myrtle Point. Mon.–Sat. 10–4 and Sun. 1–4, June–Sept. Free. The peculiar onion-shaped building was originally intended as a church—more specifically, a scaled-down version of the Mormon Tabernacle in Salt Lake City, whose acoustics match its famous choir. Unfortunately, the change in size and shape played havoc with sound waves, which bounce chaotically off the walls like pinballs. Though it did serve local Mormons, and later a Foursquare Church (a square peg in a round hole, that), it's much better as a museum. Lumber was the mainstay here for many years, and antique logging equipment, photos, and a series of myrtlewood carvings tell the story.

Coquille Valley Museum (541-824-0076; www.coquillevalley.org), 153 N. Central Avenue, Coquille. Tues.–Sat. noon–4, Memorial Day–Labor Day and Sat. noon–4, Dec.–Mar. Admission $2. The Coquille River flows through remote territory in the Siskiyous to reach Myrtle Point and Coquille before finding the sea at Bandon. Settlement was rough and recent, and at this museum you can see implements and photos of this not-so-far-off era—antique carpentry tools, a forge, an old printing press (a newspaper was one of the first things a community would create), and other pioneering equipment.

Port Orford Lifeboat Station Museum (541-332-0521), 92331 Coast Guard Hill Road, Port Orford. Thurs.–Mon. 10–3:30, Apr.–Oct. Free. Port Orford, with its jutting headland, was an obvious place for a rescue station, though it took almost 40 years to get one built. Put into service in 1934, it served unlucky mariners till 1970. The cedar-shingled crew quarters still standing on 101 acres now houses exhibits on the history of sea rescue, especially here, and the open boats on display really did battle Pacific storm surges to save lives—instilling new respect, if you needed it, for the heroism of the surfmen. As the saying went, "You have to go out, but you don't have to come back." A network of trails wanders around the headland, now **Port Orford Heads State Park.**

NATURAL WONDERS **Myrtlewood groves.** The twisty Oregon myrtle grows in pockets along the Oregon–California coast (in California it's known as California bay laurel). You'll find plenty of opportunities to buy myrtlewood gifts and souvenirs, but here are a few places to see the live trees: **Hoffman Myrtle Grove,** 3 miles south of Myrtle Point on OR 42, boasts a majestic stand of ancient myrtles; a self-guiding brochure tells you all about it. At **Coquille Myrtle Grove,** on Powers Highway (CR 542) about 12 miles south of Myrtle Point, a picnic area and myrtle grove sit along the Coquille River. Myrtles are present at **Humbug Mountain State Park,** 6 miles south of Port Orford along US 101, where a 1.5-mile day-use trail ends in a pretty grove. **Myrtlewood Campground,** 8 miles south of Powers on Forest Road, has picnic tables and free campsites among the myrtles. Farther south, the myrtlewood state champion is an 88-foot tree 0.25 mile by trail from **Lobster Creek Campground;** from US 101 in Gold Beach, take County Road 595 and FR 33; about 10 miles. And **Alfred A. Loeb State Park,** 10 miles northeast of Brookings by North Chetco Road, is possessed of a grove two hundred years old or more.

SCENIC DRIVES **OR 42** follows the Middle Fork of the Coquille River from Roseburg to Coquille, 67 very unfrequented miles. The sparkling river winding between heavily forested crags, and a few small settlements like the appropriately named Remote, are all you're likely to see on this improbably beautiful route. I don't know why it hasn't been designated a National Scenic Byway. **OR 38,** from Drain to Reedsport, follows the much more powerful Umpqua River from farmlands at its eastern end and forest toward the west; a leisurely 57 miles. You may note a sea lion foraging far inland for a decent dinner. A few miles before Reedsport is the **Dean Creek Elk Viewing Area.**

Elk River Road winds along the **Elk River,** just north of Port Orford, with spectacular views of the river rushing through old-growth forest, picnic areas, fishing holes, and rafting put-ins; 8 miles from US 101 to the fish hatchery. The **Sixes River** is even more pristine. It's one of the state's prime salmon streams, and with no hatchery, its fish are wild. From US 101, take Sixes River Road about 5 miles north of Port Orford, or Elk River Road about 4 miles north. *Caution:* These become forest roads and are subject to washouts. Stick to the paved portions and drive slowly. And, of course, **US 101** continues to be spectacular with views of isolated beaches, headlands, and the great Pacific.

✷ To Do

BICYCLING The **Oregon Coast Bike Route** runs the length of the coast from Astoria to Brookings; from Bandon south is a particularly lovely section where towns are few and the scenery startles at every turn. The downside is that it mostly runs along US 101, which often has narrow or missing shoulders. However, there's a nice stretch of about 3 miles along the Old Coast Road between Otter Point and Gold Beach. A brochure with maps is available from the Oregon Department of Transportation (downloadable from the Web site www.oregon.gov/ODOT). The **Powers to Glendale Bike Route** is a challenging 74 paved miles (barring washouts) from Powers in the Coast Range to Glendale near I-5; there are a few campsites on the way.

BIRD-WATCHING **Bandon Marsh National Wildlife Refuge** (see *Wildlife Areas*) hosts tens of thousands of migrating shorebirds in Apr., May, and early Sept., including rare birds and vagrants. The mouth of the **Coquille River,** in Bandon, attract ducks and loons; surfbirds and turnstones explore the rocks at low tide. Observe from the south jetty. **Coquille Point,** at the end of 11th Street in Bandon, is the only mainland portion of **Oregon Islands National Wildlife Refuge** (see *Wildlife Areas*); a great place for spotting loons, grebes, tufted puffins, and thousands of seabirds nesting on the offshore rocks. At **Cape Blanco** (see *Historic Sites*) you may, if you're lucky, spot a pair of peregrine falcons that nest on the headland cliffs; even if you don't, you might see an endangered marbled murrelet or a variety of loons, ducks, alcids, and more. Songbirds, shorebirds, and raptors flock to the adjacent **Sixes River Estuary,** by the historic Hughes House. The forests of **Humbug Mountain,** 6 miles south of Port Orford, house warblers, dippers, thrushes, and pileated woodpeckers.

CAMPING State park campgrounds in this zone are: **Bullard's Beach State Park,** 2 miles north of Bandon off US 101, with 104 full and 81 electrical hookup sites, 13 yurts, an 8-site horse camp, and a hiker/biker camp, with ADA restrooms, water, and showers; **Cape Blanco State Park,** 9 miles northwest of Port Orford via US 101 and Cape Blanco Road, with 53 electrical hookup sites, 4 cabins, a hiker/biker camp, an 8-site horse camp, water, showers, and restrooms (reservations for cabins only); and **Humbug Mountain State Park,** 6 miles south of Port Orford, with 32 electrical hookup sites, 62 tent sites, a hiker/biker camp, water, and restrooms. To reserve call 1-800-452-5687.

Four miles up Sixes River Road is **Edson Creek Campground,** a meadow with 27 campsites, a boat ramp, and restrooms. Six miles farther on is the **Sixes River** recreation sites (see *Gold Panning*); both are rather rustic, but very scenic, along the rivers that tumble through thick forest to the sea. Fee $8. **Park Creek Campground,** about 15 remote miles east of Coquille, has 15 primitive campsites amid ancient myrtlewood and firs. For directions or information on any of these, call the Bureau of Land Management at 541-756-0100.

Back in the hills, the Powers Ranger District of Siskiyou National Forest operates several rustic campgrounds: **Eden Valley,** 33 miles southeast of Powers via FR 3300 and FR 3348, has 11 sites, restrooms, but no water; no fee. **Daphne Grove,** 15 miles south of Powers on FR 33, has 14 sites, restrooms, but no water. **Island Campground,** 17 miles south of Powers on FR 3300, offers five sites and a restroom, but no water. **Laird Lake,** 28 miles east of Port Orford on FR 5325, has four sites, one restroom, and no water; no fee (reduced service). **Rock Creek,** 19 miles southeast of Powers on FR 3348-080, has seven sites, a restroom, and no water. **Sru Lake,** 2 miles farther on the same road, offers six sites beside a mountain lake and a restroom; no water, no fee. **Sunshine Bar,** 19 miles east of Port Orford on FR 5325, has seven sites on the Elk River with a restroom but no water and no fee; service has been reduced. Also with reduced service is **Wooden Rock Creek,** with a single campsite and restroom; no water, no fee.

CANOEING AND KAYAKING Oregon paddlers enjoy the **New River,** which actually is a new river: it formed in 1890 when a terrific flood shifted the mouth of Floras Creek. Now it runs parallel to the sea, separated by a line of dunes from the breakers. Put in at **Floras Lake,** following signs 0.5 mile south of Langlois, and paddle 7 miles to Storm Ranch; or vice versa. This is a flat-water trip but best avoided on very windy days. Floras Lake itself is nice for a quiet morning paddle before the winds pick up.

A quiet stretch of the **Sixes River** is good for a winter or early spring paddle; launch at the **Edson Campground** (see *Camping*) and take out below the **Hughes House** (see *Historic Homes*). **Elk River,** too, is a favored paddle in season, which happens to be the rainy season; local folks appear to be used to that. Put-in is just below the fish hatchery, and take-out is along Elk River Road a mile from US 101. These two are too low for paddling in summer.

Garrison Lake is a small body of water accessed from boat ramps on 12th Street or 18th Street in Port Orford, with abundant wildlife; avoid the city water intake.

See also *Wilder Places.*

GOLD PANNING Gold was discovered on the **Sixes River** in 1856, giving rise to small but fast-growing settlements and bad blood between settlers and Indians. Mostly they didn't pan out, but flakes still appear, and the panners still try their luck at a Bureau of Land Management site 11 miles up Sixes River Road, which leaves US 101 5 miles north of Port Orford. If you don't see any "color," that's okay; you'll get a taste of the wild, scenic river in a completely undeveloped setting. A rustic campground fills early in summer.

GOLF Bandon has recently become a golfing mecca, with several courses designed to duplicate or exceed those in the game's birthplace. The following are public or semiprivate.

Bandon Crossings (541-347-3232), 87530 Dew Valley Lane, Bandon. Eighteen holes.

Bandon Dunes Golf Resort (1-888-345-6008), Bandon. Four courses with a total of 54 holes.

Old Bandon Golf Links (541-329-1927), 3235 Beach Loop Way, Bandon. Nine holes.

HIKING **Beach walks,** as usual; a lovely straight beach stretches from Bandon to Cape Blanco, and smaller beaches scallop the coast from Port Orford to Humbug Mountain. The farther south you go, the less developed the coast, till you might be walking primordial wilderness but for the proximity of US 101. As always, be aware of the tides and watch out for rogue waves.

Eight miles of hiking trails ramble over **Cape Blanco State Park** through woodland, wetland, and prairie. This may well be the most spectacular spot on the southern Oregon coast, with magnificent beach views north and south and the whole Pacific before you. It does tend to be quite windy, though. There are also 7 miles of equestrian trails.

Humbug Mountain, 6 miles south of Port Orford, is almost as impressive and has the virtue of a hike through dense coastal forest to the top, where a viewpoint has been cleared. At 1,756 feet, this is supposedly the highest mountain on the west coast to rise directly from the Pacific. Two loops offer the choice of a 5-mile or 5.5-

THE RAIN FOREST FLOOR AND CREEK, HUMBUG MOUNTAIN

Patrick Roberts

Patrick Roberts

THE VIEW UP THE COAST FROM HUMBUG MOUNTAIN

mile round-trip. Two lowland trails run along Brush Creek at the mountain's inland base: the 1.5-mile **Day Use Trail** past waterfalls to a myrtle grove and a 0.5-mile trail from the campground to Old 101. The **Old Highway 101 Trail,** as the name suggests, was part of US 101 before it was rerouted and is now a mostly paved walkway from the campground to the current highway, about 2.5 miles, with fine ocean views.

Short loop trails introduce the walker to the **New River Area of Critical Environmental Concern,** a new and varied estuarine habitat whose wetlands, meadows, woods, and water are still in transition. The river itself was formed only in 1890; before that Floras Lake drained through Floras Creek directly to the sea, but floods changed the channel so that it now flows north 15 miles, separated from the ocean by narrow dunes, before opening to the Pacific. Open year-round and free, but don't bring pets.

Roam the Coast Range in the **Siskiyou National Forest** (541-618-2200): the somewhat strenuous 1-mile **Big Tree Trail** takes you to some gigantic conifers, including the World Champion Port Orford Cedar (see *Heritage Trees*). From Powers take County Road 219, FR 33, and FRs 3353 and 3358-090. You can take a short (0.2-mile round-trip) detour on the **Elk Creek Falls Trail** to view Elk Creek Falls. A 5-mile round-trip trail climbs **Iron Mountain** through rhododendron, azalea, cedar, and white fir; from Port Orford take County Road 208 to FR 5325 and continue 25 miles to the trailhead. The **Grassy Knob Trail** enters the **Grassy Knob Wilderness;** just north of Port Orford take County Road 196 to FR 5105, ending at the trailhead. This is an uphill walk to an old lookout, where guards watched for Japanese incendiary bombs during World War II. The trail continues along the ridge for a 2-mile round-trip hike.

These trails are fairly remote, closed in winter, and some access roads may be closed year-round due to tree diseases; check with the Powers Ranger District (541-439-6200).

WATER SPORTS **Windsurfing** is a popular sport at Floras Lake, which gets reliable winds every afternoon and whose water is relatively warm (68 degrees in summer). Lessons and equipment are available at **Floras Lake Windsurfing** (541-348-9912), 92870 Boice Cope Road, Langlois, or **Big Air Windsurf and Surf Shop** (541-348-2213), 48435 US 101, Langois, both about 18 miles south of Bandon. For "regular" **surfing,** go to **Battle Rock Beach** in Port Orford, or **Hubbard Creek Beach** slightly to the south.

* Wilder Places

PARKS **Bullards Beach State Park** (541-347-3501), 2 miles north of Bandon, has a campground protected from westerly winds, but paths access the beach, where you can walk for miles. Within the park is the **Coquille River Lighthouse** (see *Historic Sites*), which is staffed May–Oct., where you have a view of the harbor, city, and sea. Just a mile south of Bandon is **Face Rock State Park** (1-800-551-6949), a beach access point where you have a view of Face Rock, a sea stack just beyond the breakers. According to legend, Chief Siskiyou, of a mountain tribe, came to visit coastal tribes with his daughter Ewauna. She couldn't resist walking into the ocean, whereupon the evil ocean spirit Seatka grabbed her to carry her off. She knew somehow that his power resided in his eyes, so she gazed resolutely at the sky—and she still does, in the form of the rock. No fee. Along Beach Loop Road in Bandon, three points provide access to **Bandon State Natural Area,** a long ribbon of seastack-strewn coast; no fee.

Nine miles north of Port Orford, **Cape Blanco State Park** (541-332-6774) boasts the westernmost point in Oregon, complete with lighthouse, a historic home, abundant wildlife, trails, camping, and calendar-quality scenery (see *Historic Sites, Camping,* and *Hiking*). Just north of Port Orford, **Paradise Point** sits above miles of beach running from Port Orford Head to Cape Blanco; no fee. This is reputed to be a good agate beach, as are the beaches just south of the town. Trails meander through the low forest on **Port Orford Heads,** though the centerpiece here is the 1934 Coast Guard station (see *Museums*). Right in the middle of Port Orford is **Battle Rock City Park** (see *Historic Sites*), with its signature sea stack, lovely beach, and ocean views. Six miles to the south is **Humbug Mountain** (541-332-6774), rising 1,756 feet straight out of the sea (see *Hiking*), complete with its coastal forest of spruce, myrtle, and azalea, as well as a campground and trails. And 5 miles south of that is **Arizona Beach State Park** (1-800-551-6949), a short beach bracketed by headlands; this keeps it warmer than most local beaches. Elk browse the wetland at the park's eastern end. Inland, **Hoffman Memorial Myrtle Grove** and **Coquille Myrtle Grove State Park** (1-800-551-6949), 3 miles and 14 miles south of Myrtle Grove respectively, boast old myrtle trees and picnic areas; the latter also offers a swimming hole.

Fifteen miles north of Coquille is **Laverne County Park** (541-396-2344), with swimming in the North Fork Coquille, picnicking, playgrounds, and camping on 350 acres; being a bit inland, it does get warm enough to swim.

Patrick Roberts

LOOKING UP THE COAST FROM GOLD BEACH TO HUMBUG MOUNTAIN

WILDERNESS AREAS **Grassy Knob** (541-618-2200), 17,200 acres in the Siskiyou National Forest, is thick rain forest in highly jumbled terrain. Difficult of access, its southern border is the Wild and Scenic Elk River—a major salmon-spawning stream—and it contains many pristine brooks that burble through stands of old Port Orford cedar. There are a few miles of trail and almost no visitors (and likely no cell phone reception either, so be prudent). Follow directions for Grassy Knob Trail (see *Hiking*).

WILDLIFE AREAS **Bandon Marsh National Wildlife Refuge** (541-347-1470), just north of Bandon, is a big tidal marsh in the Coquille estuary. The two units—Bandon Marsh and Ni-les'tun—protect mudflats and salt- and freshwater marsh, whose abundant shellfish, worms, and crustaceans support quantities of birds. Especially visible are brown pelicans, herons, raptors, and shorebirds. A viewing platform west of Riverside Drive allows you to observe the marsh. Ni-les'tun was added recently and has an observation area and a 4,500-year-old campsite. Just north of Bandon, turn west onto Riverside Drive for the Bandon Marsh unit or east onto Fahy Creek Road and North Bank Lane for Ni-les'tun. There are no hiking trails; hunting is allowed in season.

Coquille Point, at the end of 11th Street in Bandon, is part of the **Oregon Islands National Wildlife Refuge** (541-867-4550). From a parking area a path leads out along the point, where seals, sea lions, birds, and other creatures are visible, and you can observe even more creatures on the rocks just offshore.

New River Area of Critical Environmental Concern (541-756-0100) (see *Canoeing and Kayaking* and *Hiking*) is 1,100 acres along 9 miles of river, with sandflats, wetlands, and meadows in various stages of ecological succession. There's plenty of wildlife, depending on the season, from nesting snowy plovers (portions may be closed during nesting season) to peregrine falcons to deer to migrating salmon. Open dawn–dusk year-round.

✱ Lodging

BED & BREAKFASTS

Bandon

✐ 🐾 **Alder House Bed and Breakfast** (1-888-999-8829; www.alderhousebandb.com), 57586 Parkersburg Road. In the green hillocks a mile or so east of Bandon, Alder House welcomes you and your dog—not just with living space, but a fenced yard with a dog-friendly pond. Ask first, though, as there are size concerns. Two rooms, each with private bath, welcome guests, who are also welcome to relax on the deck (or dock) right on the Coquille River. An RV space and boat slip are also available. $100–125, with full breakfast. School-age children welcome.

Bailey's Cedar House Bed and Breakfast (541-347-3356), 58739 Seven Devils Road. A simple cedar house surrounded by woods and gardens offers a suite with kitchen and living room or a bed-sitter, plus a country breakfast. $85–100.

Bandon Ocean Guesthouse (1-888-253-1777; www.bandonguesthouse.com), 87141 Beach Lane. A very contemporary structure, this place contemplates the wide Pacific from the top of a bluff. Six guest rooms are named after Irish counties, each with its own deck and private bathroom, and in most cases a Jacuzzi as well; a luxurious coastal stay. $140–180, with full breakfast.

Lighthouse Bed and Breakfast (541-347-9316; www.lighthouselodging.com), 650 Jetty Road SW. This luxurious new house sits just across the Coquille River from the lighthouse, with five rooms, some of which have fireplaces and private decks (all have ocean or river views). $140–245, with full breakfast.

Port Orford

♿ **The Compass Rose** (541-332-7076; www.compassroseportorford.com), 42497 Gull Road. Above a breathtaking expanse of beach, the Compass Rose has its own birding trails encompassing (so to speak) forest, beach, and marsh habitats. But you're not coming just for the birds, right? Four large rooms, comfortably appointed with easy chairs and rugs, overlook the sea or Garrison Lake, all with private baths; one is wheelchair accessible. Doug's hearty breakfast will fortify you for the day; let him know of any dietary restrictions. $110–140, with full breakfast.

Home by the Sea (1-877-332-2855), 444 Jackson Street. Two rooms on a promontory overlooking the port and sea are ideal for storm watching and a base for strolling around town. Shuttle service is offered to Coast Trail hikers. $95–115, with full breakfast.

HOTELS AND MOTELS

Bandon

✐ **Inn at Old Town** (1-877-884-5900; www.innatoldtown.com), 370 US 101. A small shingled motel with a view of the waterfront, this one offers rooms in various configurations at reasonable rates (one even has a queen and bunk beds, for families). $50–110.

✐ 🐾 **La Kris Inn** (1-888-496-3610; www.lakrisinn.com), 940 Oregon Avenue. A motel, yes, but with quilts and other individual touches. $55–95.

Sea Star Guest House (1-888-732-7871; www.seastarbandon.com), 370 First Street. Some of us bemoan the loss of Bandon's hostel, the only one on the southern coast; it's been converted to four large rooms and a penthouse suite. Most rooms can sleep several guests, though, and some have kitchenettes, so it's still a good deal. Rooms $65–115; penthouse $125–150, with full kitchen, two bedrooms, living room, dining room, and deck. Pet and child friendly.

Port Orford

🐾 **Castaway by the Sea** (541-332-4502; www.castawaybythesea.com), 545 W. Fifth Street. Thirteen rooms and suites overlook the sea from this 1970s (but updated and clean) motel. Some units have full kitchens. An adjacent 1930s cottage, "The Lodge," sits on its own 7.5 acres and can accommodate up to 10. Rooms $65–145, cottage from $185.

RESORTS

Port Orford

♿ **WildSpring Guest Habitat** (1-866-333-9453; www.wildspring.com), 92978 Cemetery Loop Road. It's not a cabin; it's a home. Five cabins are outfitted with pillow-top beds, fine furnishings, and plump sofas, all as ecofriendly as the owners could possibly make them, set in lush gardens and forest. The idea here is to promote serenity and natural harmony (the slate hot tub should take care of that) with reverence for the environment. It doesn't come cheap, but both setting and cabins are lovely. $198–279, with "extended continental" breakfast. One cabin is wheelchair friendly. Massage, manicures, and pedicures are available at an extra charge.

✷ Where to Eat

DINING OUT

Bandon

Alloro Wine Bar (541-347-1850; www.allorowinebar.com), 375 Second Street SE. Opening in 2006, Alloro made a name for itself with an eclectic wine list and a menu where local seafood jostles with traditional Italian food, complemented but not dominated by handmade pasta. Both chef and sommelier studied in Florence and know their way around an Italian kitchen, from caprese to zucchini blossoms. Reservations recommended; call for hours, which vary seasonally.

Port Orford

Paula's Bistro (541-332-9378), 326 US 101. Tues.–Sat. 5–9. A cozy little place serving Northwestern and French cuisine is a bit of a surprise in a tiny coastal town. The menu changes often but may include dishes such as shiitake ravioli, quail, fresh tuna, apricot-glazed pork, and other interesting things. Reservations recommended.

EATING OUT

Bandon

Bandon Coffee Café (541-347-1144; www.bandoncoffee.com), 365 Second Street SE. Daily from 6 AM. The *whoosh* of an espresso machine fills the air, the barista hands you your brew, and you sit down and read the paper, or check e-mail . . . or order a breakfast or lunch sandwich.

🖍 **2 Loons Café** (541-347-3750; www.2loons.com), 120 Second Street SE. Daily 7–3 (winter weekdays 8–2:30). Homemade soups, sandwiches, and panini, not to mention a selection of cakes and pastries. And a kids' menu, too.

Langlois

Langlois Market (541-348-2476), 48444 US 101. Also known as Lee's Market, since Lee has been selling groceries here for years and is also renowned for his sandwiches, hot and cold, and old-fashioned hot dogs served up with homemade mustard.

Port Orford

🖍 **Crazy Norwegian's** (541-332-8601), 259 Sixth Street. Wed.–Mon. 11:30–8. To my mind (and not only to mine), this is where to find the best fish-and-chips on the southern Oregon coast. And the chowder isn't bad, either. Informal and family friendly.

Port and Starboard (541-332-4515; www.portandstarboard.com), 460 Madrona Avenue. Daily 7 AM–9 PM. This restaurant has been serving families breakfast, lunch, and dinner for more than four decades. No surprises here, but solid family fare—homemade soups and salads; tender, varied seafood; and plenty of landlubber dishes, too.

✷ Entertainment

Theatre 101 (541-332-PLAY; www.theatre101portorford.com), 1320 Oregon Street, Port Orford. A brand new (2007) theatrical company has brought down the house in Port Orford almost since its inception. Considering the town has a population of about one thousand, that's not bad! Not only does it have community support, but people come from miles around. Four productions a year take place in the tiny theater; try to catch one if you're there.

✷ Shopping

Second Street Gallery (541-347-4133), 210 Second Street SE, Bandon. Daily 10–5. Jewelers, potters, glass artists, painters, and sculptors from around the Northwest show their work here.

Wooden Nickel (541-332-5201; www.oregonmyrtlewood.com), 1205 Oregon Street, Port Orford. Weekdays 9–5. Here you can not only buy myrtlewood gifts, but visit the workshop and see how the dense wood with the swirling grain is worked.

✷ Events

July: **Coos County Fair** (541-260-1457), last week, fairgrounds at Myrtle Point. A rodeo, carnival, games, and lots of livestock. Admission fee.

September: **Bandon Cranberry Festival** (541-347-4830), second weekend, various locations around Bandon. The southern coast is cranberry country, and the harvest is celebrated all weekend with a quilt show, games, booths, antique cars, and a blessing of the harvest.

GOLD BEACH–BROOKINGS AREA

This sweeping southernmost coastline enjoys the most temperate weather in Oregon. The coastal vegetation begins to look slightly Mediterranean, and redwoods appear back in the hills. You might walk barefoot on the beach in December as well as in July; or you might not, if a sou'wester blows in. But it hardly matters. It's a magnificent place for either sunning or storm watching, quite possibly the finest stretch of coast in the state.

GUIDANCE **Brookings-Harbor Chamber of Commerce** (1-800-535-9469; www.brookingsor.com), 16330 Lower Harbor Road, Brookings 97415.

Gold Beach Visitors Center (1-800-525-2334; www.goldbeach.org), 94080 Shirley Lane, Gold Beach 97444.

Rogue River–Siskiyou National Forest (541-618-2200), 3040 Biddle Road, Medford 97504; **Gold Beach Ranger District** (541-247-3600), 29279 Ellensburg Avenue, Gold Beach 97444; **Crissey Field Welcome Center** (541-412-6000), 14433 US 101 S., Brookings 97415.

GETTING THERE *By bus:* **Curry Public Transit and Coastal Express** (1-800-921-2871; www.currypublictransit.org) stops in Gold Beach on its thrice-weekly North Bend–Brookings run. Takes bikes, too.

By car: Again, **US 101** is the sole artery. On a map you may see an unnumbered road running from Grants Pass to Gold Beach; avoid it. It is long, rugged, winding, and risky under the best of conditions.

GETTING AROUND *By bus:* **Curry Public Transit** (see *Getting There*) runs buses along the segment of coast from Smith River, California, to North Bend, Oregon. That said, most visitors will want a car.

MEDICAL EMERGENCY **Brookings Medical Center** (541-469-5377), 585 Fifth Street, Brookings.

Curry General Hospital (1-800-445-8085), 94220 Fourth Street, Gold Beach.

✱ To See

FOR FAMILIES ✐ **Jetboat rides.** Two companies take you deep into the Rogue River watershed, beating like salmon up the swift-flowing stream 30 to 50 miles into the wilderness. **Jerry's Rogue Jets** (1-800-451-3645; www.roguejets.com), 29880 Harbor Way, Gold Beach, offers lunch or dinner trips three times a day, May–mid-Oct., stopping at riverside lodges for meals; adults $45–87, children $20–40. Reservations recommended. **Mail Boat Hydro-Jets** (1-800-458-3511; www.mailboat.com), 94294 N. Bank Rogue River Road, Gold Beach, hark back to the days when mail was delivered by boat to remote upriver communities, a service begun in 1895. They cover the same routes. Adults $45–87, children $20–40. These are open boats, except Mail Boat's *Rogue Queen,* a glass-enclosed craft that keeps the tourists dry.

✐ **Whale-watching.** Like the rest of the coast, this belt has some perfect points for "catching" a whale. **Cape Sebastian,** 7 miles south of Gold Beach; **Cape Ferrelo,** 4 miles north of Brookings in **Sam Boardman State Park;** and **Harris Beach State Park,** just north of Brookings off US 101, are all staffed with volunteers during whale migration seasons. If you're there out of season, don't worry; several hundred whales stay along the Oregon coast July–mid-Nov. and come quite close to shore.

GARDENS **Azalea Park,** 617 Old County Road, Brookings. Azaleas bloomed throughout western Oregon before anyone thought of cultivating them. The mild, moist climate of the "banana belt" is especially propitious, and here banks of native azaleas, rhododendrons, and flowering bulbs fill this 33-acre park with brilliant color in spring and are bedecked with holiday lights in winter. A playground and softball field caters to those who may be less fascinated by azaleas.

Brookings Botanical Garden, US 101 and Constitution Avenue, Brookings. A tidy triangular garden is a little oasis complete with paths and plant labels, under the loving care of the Harbor Garden Club.

The short stretch of coast from Brookings to Smith River, California, is the nursery for most of the **Easter lilies** in the world. Many fields are visible (and smellable) from US 101—they bloom in July. Although many buds are removed to strengthen the bulbs, which are shipped worldwide, they still make a fine show and aroma.

HISTORIC SITES **Geisel Monument,** 7 miles north of Gold Beach, marks the burial site of the Geisel family, pioneers from Ohio. During the height of the Rogue Indian wars in 1856, nearly the entire family was killed in an Indian raid, as were several other settlers along the river. Mrs. Geisel and two daughters were taken captive and eventually rescued; strangely, she also was murdered in 1899 by a second-generation settler who stole her $75 pension check.

Mount Emily Bomb Site, 16 miles east of Brookings. This is the only site in the continental United States to have been bombed by plane during World War II (other sites were bombed by balloon; see "South Central Oregon"). On Sept. 9, 1942, a Japanese submarine 25 miles offshore released a miniature bomber, which dropped two incendiary bombs into the dense coastal forest. The idea was to start vast conflagrations; however, they failed to take the region's humidity into account. A 1.25-mile trail through redwoods takes you to the site; from the Chetco River Bridge take Chetco South Bank Road 8 miles, then take Wheeler Creek Road, following the signs to the trailhead. Meanwhile, back at the public library, the four-hundred-year-old samurai sword worn by the pilot hangs in a display case, donated by the pilot himself in 1962.

MUSEUMS Chetco Valley Museum (541-469-2753), 15461 Museum Road, Brookings. Fri.–Sun. 1–5, Memorial Day–Labor Day. Admission by donation. The 1857 frame house belonged to Harrison Blake, who was eventually elected to the legislature; it was not only his home, but a post office and stagecoach stop. Now it displays the gamut of local history, from the presettlement peoples to settlers' household goods. Some curiosities are an 1844 patchwork quilt and an iron cast of a woman's face. Nobody quite knows how that last got here, or where it came from, but it's thought to resemble the first Queen Elizabeth and so might have been dropped by Francis Drake, who is known to have come up the coast in the 1500s.

Curry Historical Society Museum (541-247-9396; www.curryhistory.com), 29419 Ellensburg Road, Brookings. Tues.–Sat. 10–4; closed Jan. Admission $2; children under 16 free. Native American basketry, photos, and archives document the vast changes sweeping this corner of the West in the last 150 years.

NATURAL WONDERS The **coastal redwood** reaches the northern edge of its range in the Brookings area. See some of these venerable trees along the **Redwood Nature Trail,** an easy 1-mile loop in the **Rogue River–Siskiyou National Forest.** From Brookings take the North Bank Chetco River Road 8 miles to **Loeb State Park,** then continue another 0.5 mile; the trailhead is on your left. A little farther is the **Oregon Redwoods Trail,** 11 miles southeast of Brookings via Winchuck Road and FR 1101, 1.2 miles out and back; it shares a trailhead with the **Oregon Redwoods Barrier Free Trail,** a wheelchair-friendly path among the big trees, about 1.5 miles round-trip.

SCENIC DRIVES US 101, aka the **Pacific Coast Scenic Byway,** continues its sinuous way around promontories and over mighty rivers—perhaps the most impressive stretch yet. Always a bit cut off (even today the most direct way from Brookings to inland Oregon is through California), the area is sparsely settled and less exploited than most of the coast, and its crescent beaches, cliffs, and recklessly tumbled sea stacks will keep your camera busy.

✷ To Do

BIRD-WATCHING From the marina at the **Rogue River mouth** in Gold Beach, spot plenty of gulls and terns as well as the occasional bald eagle and peregrine falcon. Hike through Sitka spruce at **Cape Sebastian State Park** for crossbills, wrentits, and hermit thrushes; scope out the ocean below for murres, loons, and other ocean birds. **Harris Beach State Park** is lovely in itself but also offers good views of Goat Island, part of the **Oregon Islands National Wildlife Refuge.** Puffins, auklets, and storm petrels nest on the island, and many seabirds frequent the surrounding waters. Mainland trails shelter warblers and hummingbirds.

CAMPING Two state parks offer camping in this area. **Alfred A. Loeb State Park,** about 10 miles northeast of Brookings along North Bank Chetco River Road, has 48 electrical hookup sites and three rustic cabins among fragrant myrtlewood. A 0.75-mile trail leads to the northernmost redwood grove in North America; no reservations. **Harris Beach State Park,** just north of Brookings off US 101, with sandy beaches between rocky promontories, offers 36 full and 50 partial hookup sites, 63 tent sites, and 6 yurts (and Wi-Fi), among coastal forest and meadow and abundant wildlife; reserve at 1-800-452-5687. Both are open year-round.

Several campgrounds dot pristine riverbanks in the **Gold Beach** and **Chetco Ranger districts** of **Siskiyou National Forest: First Camp,** along the Winchuck River 13 miles south of Brookings, offers dispersed camping and toilets but no water; from Brookings take Winchuck River Road to FR 1107; open May 15–Sept. 30. The adjacent **Winchuck Campground** is close to beaches and river, with 15 sites, a wheelchair-friendly campground, and toilets but no water; open May 15–Sept. 30 (but check for closures). No fee for these. **Foster Bar Campground,** in the woods 28 miles northeast of Gold Beach via County Road 595, FR 33, and County Road 375, has four tent/trailer and four tent-only sites with handicapped-accessible toilets, water, and a boat ramp on the Rogue River; open May–Nov. **Lobster Creek,** 10 miles east of Gold Beach by CR 595 and FR 33, has three tent sites and three tent/trailer sites, toilets, a boat ramp on the Rogue, and nearby myrtle and old-growth forest; open year-round. Four miles farther on FR 33 is **Quotasana Campground,** with 43 tent/trailer sites, three handicapped-accessible sites, water, toilet, and a wheelchair-accessible trail through myrtlewood; open year-round. **Ludlum Campground,** 14 miles south of Brookings by US 101, County Road 896, FR 1107, and FR 1108, is wheelchair friendly and has seven campsites, water, and toilets; open mid-May–Sept. **Miller Bar** is on the Wild and Scenic Chetco River, with dispersed camping and toilets but no water and no fee; from Brookings take North Bank Chetco River Road and FR 1376. A mile farther in is **Nook Bar,** also a dispersed site, with toilets, no water, and no fee; open May 15–Sept. 30. **Oak Flat Campground,** well in the forest about 30 miles from Gold Beach, has 15 sites and toilets but no water, and access to the Illinois River hiking and equestrian trail; open May–Nov. From Gold Beach take CR 595 and FRs 33 and 450. No fee. **South Fork Camps** is a dispersed-camping site along the Chetco with swimming, floating, sunbathing, and toilets but no water and no fee; open May–Sept. Take North Bank River Road to FR 1376 and continue 8 miles.

CANOEING, KAYAKING, AND RAFTING The Wild and Scenic **Rogue River,** with its pristine forest setting and swift current, is a world-class rafting and kayaking destination, as is its lesser-known tributary, the **Illinois** (also Wild and Scenic). The Rogue is unique in having several privately owned lodges along its lower reaches, so you can raft wildly and sleep comfortably. Unless you're very experienced, it's as well to go with an outfitter such as **Rogue Wilderness Adventures** (1-800-336-1647; www.wildrogue.com), 325 Galice Road, Merlin, or **Rogue River Raft Trips** (1-800-826-1963; www.rogueriverraft.com), 8500 Galice Road, Merlin. Part of the **Chetco,** which flows to the sea at Brookings, is also designated Wild and Scenic, with plentiful rapids and scenery; it's the river less traveled and beloved of local rafters and kayakers for that. A free permit is usually required to float Wild and Scenic Rivers; check with the Forest Service or Bureau of Land Management for availability and for water levels.

GOLF **Cedar Bend Golf Course** (541-247-6991), 34391 Cedar Valley Road, Gold Beach. Nine holes.

Edgebrook Golf Course (605-692-6995), 22nd Avenue S., Brookings. Eighteen holes and nine practice holes.

Salmon Run Golf Course (1-877-423-1234), 99040 South Bank Chetco River Road, Brookings. Eighteen holes.

HIKING This is one of the best areas to try a stretch of the **Oregon Coast Trail,** as several sections here follow paths over grassy bluffs and coastal woods, though it does return to the road at times. **Harris Beach State Park** is a good place to start and work north; the views are spectacular. Maps can be downloaded at www.oregon.gov/OPRD/PARKS.

The 1.5-mile **Frances Shrader Old Growth Trail** is an easy meander through dense virgin forest, where some of the state's biggest hardwoods and conifers can be found. A free brochure explains the forest's ecology and history. From Gold Beach take Jerry's Flat Road east 10 miles to Lobster Creek, then turn right on FR 090 and continue 2 miles. Also nearby is the **Myrtle Tree Trail,** where you can see the world champion Oregon myrtle; take Jerry's Flat Road to Lobster Creek, then turn left on FR 3310 and right onto FR 3533; park 0.25 mile down on the right. For an overnight backcountry trek, consider the **Lower Rogue River Trail,** 13 miles (each way) of rain forest and wildlife. The grade is level to moderate, passing waterfalls and ancient trees. From Gold Beach take Jerry's Flat Road, cross Lobster Creek Bridge, and turn right onto FR 3533; continue to FR 340 and follow signs. For more remote hikes contact the Gold Beach Ranger District or Crissey Field Welcome Center (see *Guidance*). (See also *Natural Wonders* and *Wilder Places.*)

WATER SPORTS **Surfers** head to **Sporthaven Beach** and **Harris Beach State Park,** near Brookings, for summer waves (though the hard-core go in winter). **Pistol River,** near Gold Beach, is a prime site for **windsurfing.**

UNIQUE ADVENTURES **Jetty cats.** For some reason the north jetty of the Rogue River in Gold Beach was a preferred site for dumping unwanted cats—the owners hoping, no doubt, that the sea would quickly wash away the evidence. But it didn't, and feral cats made it their territory. Cat lover Ursula Elliott joined with other locals to build kitty-sized shelters on the jetty and provide healthy food and veterinary care, including a spay and neuter program. The effort is supported by local volunteers and businesses. The cat, er, hotels are visible at the jetty off Wedderburn Loop.

Storm watching. Winter storms attack the Oregon coast with particular fury, and the driven waves pounding themselves to mist on the rocks are an impressive sight. Here particularly the sun may be shining while a storm rages offshore, so you may admire the effects in your shirtsleeves. As always, if on the beach, keep well back from the waterline, which may suddenly end up behind you.

✷ Wilder Places

PARKS **Otter Point,** 4 miles north of Gold Beach, draws the visitor into a web of walking trails above deserted beaches and rock formations. No fee.

Cape Sebastian, 7 miles south of Gold Beach, is a windswept park 200 feet above the sea. For the best views you don't even have to leave the parking area: from the south lot, on a clear day, you see rows and rows of combers stretching north to Humbug Mountain, 43 miles, and south to Crescent City, 50 miles. A 1.5-mile trail leads through Sitka spruce forest to the headland, where you may spot passing

Patrick Roberts

ROCK FORMATIONS ON THE BEACH SOUTH OF PORT ORFORD

whales and the multifarious marine birds and mammals that inhabit the rocks just offshore. No fee.

Pistol River State Park, where the Pistol River joins the sea 11 miles south of Gold Beach, is a favored spot of windsurfers and birdwatchers. River and dunes both shift, creating potholes that draw waterfowl and shorebirds, and the scenery's pretty good, too. Legend has it that a soldier lost his gun in the river during the wars with the Indians; hence the name.

Samuel Boardman State Scenic Corridor stretches along 12 miles of cliffs above the sea, from 4 to 16 miles north of Brookings; there are four access points from US 101. Boardman was Oregon's first parks superintendent. The vistas are astounding: sea-carved rocks, hidden coves, and always the waves. Luckily the Oregon Coast Trail runs through it, so you can walk a few or many miles through three-hundred-year-old Sitka spruce, along grassy bluffs, past old shell middens, and feasting your eyes. No fee.

Harris Beach State Park (541-469-2021), just north of Brookings, was the claim of Scotsman George Harris. He ran sheep and cattle. Today it's an enchanting park with camping, trails, beaches, forest, and plenty of wildlife viewing.

Just south of Brookings is **McVay State Recreation Site,** with a large lawn and long beach for walking, clamming, and whale-watching. No fee. **Winchuck State Recreation site,** 5 miles south of Brookings at the mouth of the Winchuck River, is similarly a beach-access park; no fee. Just south of it is **Crissey Field State Recreation Site,** on the Winchuck estuary, the domain of sea lions and seals, surrounded by dunes and old trees. No fee.

Inland, 10 miles northeast of Brookings, **Alfred A. Loeb State Park** (541-469-2021) preserves a grove of old-growth myrtle trees, whose fragrance permeates the park. Along the Chetco River, the park offers camping, hiking, boating, and nature programs.

WILDERNESS AREAS Several bits of **Oregon Islands National Wildlife Refuge** lie just offshore and are visible from **Cape Sebastian, Samuel Board-**

man, and **Harris Beach state parks** (Goat Rock, the largest of the chain, is just of Harris Beach). The primeval sounds of sea lion colonies and thousands of seabirds fill the air, and if you keep a bird checklist, you should be able to check a few off.

✷ Lodging

BED & BREAKFASTS

Brookings

Chetco River Inn (541-251-0087; www.chetcoriverinn.com), 21202 High Prairie Road. Eighteen miles outside Brookings, up the Chetco River, you're in a completely different biome—not the coast, but the coastal rain forest. The river surrounds the property on three sides, and summer birds frequent the garden and tall trees. This is a getaway for those who want to get away; power lines don't even come this far, and energy comes from solar panels and a generator. The contemporary cedar house has five guest rooms, comfortably furnished with brass beds and private bathrooms, $135–155; a separate cottage runs $200. If the weather is inclement, which is possible, curl up by the living-room fireplace; though even so, a little activity will help burn off a generous breakfast. Children welcome.

Lowden's Beachfront Bed and Breakfast (1-800-453-4768; www.beachfrontbb.com), 14626 Wollam Road. Perched on a headland between the Winchuck River and the ocean, Lowden's will let you watch passing whales from your deck. The suites include a living room, bedroom, spacious bathroom, and fine views. $109–139, with continental breakfast.

CABINS AND COTTAGES

Brookings

Holmes Sea Cove (1-888-290-0312), 17350 Holmes Drive. Just north of Harris Beach State Park, the Sea Cove offers a cottage with adjacent suite plus a two-bedroom apartment. Both are suitable for families or couples traveling together. A trail leads down to the beach. $120–250.

Gold Beach

Ireland's Rustic Lodges (1-877-477-3526; www.irelandsrusticlodges.com), 29346 Ellensburg Avenue. Rustic in the up-to-date, squeaky-clean sense: knotty pine cabins or lodge units with cozy furnishings, some with fireplaces and decks, look out to sea through the 19 acres of gardens. $75–169.

Rogue Pacific Motel (541-247-7444; www.roguepacificmotel.com), 29450 Ellensburg Avenue. Okay, it's not at first sight a promising location, being next to an RV park, but it does look out over the sea, and the price is right. Snug cottages dating from the 1930s or so go for $65–85 a night if they face the ocean, and $45–55 if they don't, each with its own kitchen and dining area. It's a short walk to the beach. Pets allowed in some units. Motel units from $35.

FOREST SERVICE RENTALS Old guard stations or watchtowers make for a remote but sheltered wilderness experience. Reservations are required; to reserve and get directions call 1-877-444-6444 or go to www.recreation.gov.

Bald Knob Lookout, about 16 miles from Powers, is a 16-by-16 room on a 20-foot tower, equipped with lights, a propane stove, refrigerator, heating, and a single bed (toilet facilities consist of an outhouse). Bring water, as there is none. High winds are possible on the 3,630-foot hilltop. Open Memorial Day–Oct. $35; no pets.

Lake of the Woods Lookout is about 21 miles east of Gold Beach. The one-room cabin stands on an 8-foot tower with a wraparound catwalk and has a double bed, propane stove, lights, and basic furniture (no cooking equipment). An outhouse is just, well, outside, and you'll need to bring your own water. $40. Open spring through fall.

An hour and a half from Brookings is **Packer's Cabin,** originally the station of an employee who supplied foresters by horse or mule train. Rustic but snug, it has one double bunk and 10 single bunks; bring your own bedding. There's a woodstove but no electricity or drinking water. The cabin and toilet are handicapped accessible. $40. Open spring through fall.

HOTELS AND MOTELS

Brookings

🐾 **Wild Rivers Motor Lodge** (1-877-469-5361; www.wildriversmotorlodge.com), 437 Chetco Avenue. Here's your affordable option for Brookings: a perfectly normal, centrally located 30-unit motel with standard amenities (refrigerator, hair dryer, etc.). $73–84, including tax. Pets allowed in some rooms.

Gold Beach

Azalea Lodge (1-866-381-6635; www.azalealodge.biz), 29481 Ellensburg Road. A basic but clean motel a couple of blocks from the beach, the Azalea also offers free Wi-Fi. $49–125.

Gold Beach Inn (1-888-663-0608; www.goldbeachinn.com), 29346 Ellensburg Avenue. Walk one of the paths down to the beach, or watch storms from your room; most have balconies overlooking the ocean. Units are motel-style but spacious, with queen or king beds, refrigerators, and microwaves. $69–149. A two-bedroom beach house sleeping up to seven goes for $109–169.

LODGES

Gold Beach

Rogue River Lodge (541-247-9070; www.rogueriverlodge.com), 94966 North Bank Rogue River Road. Open May–Oct. Up the river, six suites and

DESERTED SANDS SOUTH OF GOLD BEACH

Patrick Roberts

two snug guest rooms grace this secluded lodge. Suites have one or three bedrooms, living room, kitchen or kitchenette, private deck, and garden, while the rooms are much the same but for the kitchen and living room. Vaulted ceilings, lots of Port Orford cedar (either reclaimed from the ocean or from the Biscuit Fire), as well as other recycled wood and stone lend an updated Western lodge air. Double occupancy $199–548 per two-night stay.

✷ Where to Eat

DINING OUT

Gold Beach

Anna's by the Sea Wine Bar and Bistro (541-247-2100; www.annasbythesea.com), 29672 Stewart Street. Wed.–Sat. 5–8 in winter, Tues.–Sat. 5–8:30 in summer. Eight tables and seven seats at the cherry-maple bar make this an intimate place—as owner ChunYan Dower says, "Gold Beach's most fashionable/only wine bar." A little from here and a little from there: that's the wine list, and the cook, ChunYan's husband, Peter, is fixated on quality. Things you may not find elsewhere in Gold Beach include chopped chicken liver with truffle oil and veal meat loaf; then there's the local fish—not huge plates, but filling enough, and reasonably priced.

EATING OUT

Gold Beach

Barnacle Bistro (541-247-7799; www.barnaclebistro.com), 29805 Ellensburg Avenue. Mon.–Thurs. 11–8, Fri.–Sat. 11–9. Fish-and-chips, soup, salad, and burgers, with some imaginative twists like wasabi cod burrito or fish sandwich with tartar sauce and . . . pesto! Menu changes with what's in season.

Port Hole Café (541-247-7411; www.portholecafe.com), Harbor Way, Port of Gold Beach. Daily 11–9. Sandwiches and burgers for lunch, salads and seafood fresh from the docks for dinner, not to mention "Ma's" homemade soups.

✷ Shopping

Brandy Peak Distillery (541-469-0194; www.brandypeak.com), 18526 Tetley Road, Brookings. Tues.–Sat. 1–5, Mar.–first week of Jan., or by appointment. This tiny mom-and-pop distillery (no, they're not moonshiners; it's perfectly legal) has been producing brandies, marc, grappa, and liqueurs the old-fashioned way, on wood-fired pot still, since 1994. Stop by the tasting room for a sip of some award-winning spirits.

✷ Events

May: **Azalea Festival** (1-800-535-9469), Memorial Day weekend, various locations around Brookings. Flowers, arts, crafts, races, and much more. Check out the slug races.

Wild Rivers Coast Wine, Art and Music Festival (541-247-0923), second weekend, Event Center, Gold Beach. Just what it sounds like. Admission $10 for two days.

July: **Southern Oregon Kite Festival** (541-412-2941), second weekend, the beach at Brookings. Kites, food booths, crafts, and knickknacks.

Willamette Valley and Lower Columbia River

LOWER COLUMBIA RIVER

PORTLAND METROPOLITAN AREA

NORTHERN WILLAMETTE VALLEY

SOUTHERN WILLAMETTE VALLEY

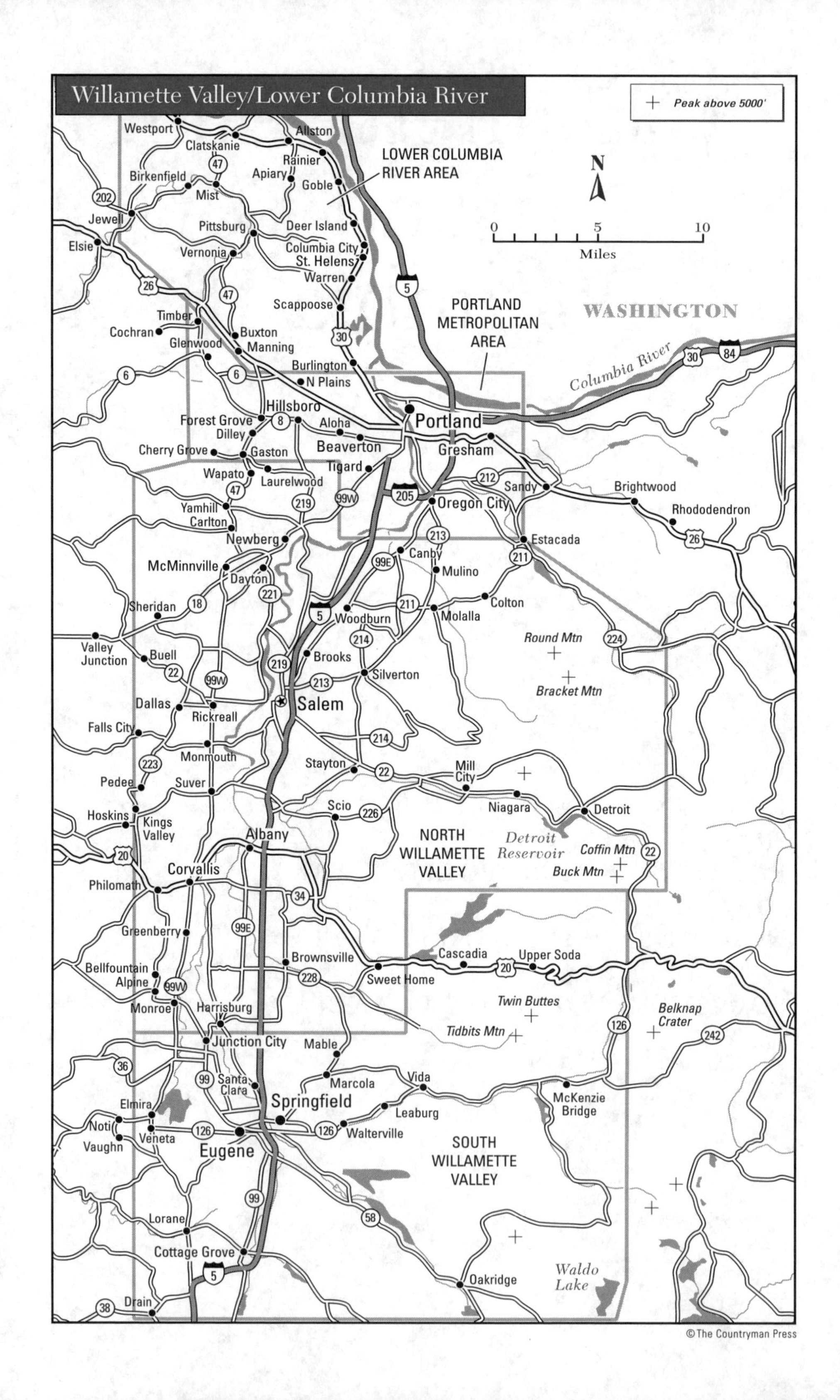

©The Countryman Press

WILLAMETTE VALLEY AND LOWER COLUMBIA RIVER

Somehow Lewis and Clark missed the entire Willamette River on their descent of the Columbia, a feat akin to missing the Columbia itself while sailing up the coast. Well, plenty of explorers did that, too. And admittedly the Willamette's mouth is camouflaged by shifting sandy islands. Still, it's a long and impressive river, draining a still larger valley. And it became the germ of the future state.

In spring of 1843 the first major wagon train set out on what would be called the Oregon Trail. Not that those emigrants were the first strangers to settle in Oregon. A smattering of retired trappers, missionaries, and fortune seekers had already sunk stakes along the lower river; coincidentally or not, that very spring the men of that loose community narrowly voted for self-government, American-style, and Oregon Country soon became the U.S.-held Oregon Territory. For decades they came: well-to-do farmers wanting to do better, poorer farmers hoping to do well, disgruntled Confederate veterans—hey, even Huckleberry Finn lit out for the Territory! They came by oxcart and foot and finally by train; they came despite death by cholera and drowning and accidental discharge of firearms; they set out despite the risks of having or losing a baby on the trail and the knowledge that they might end up buried on the lone prairie. Yet most of them weren't desperate economic refugees. What did they go to a wilderness to seek?

Rumors of a delightfully good and spacious land of biblical proportions had reached the Eastern states from the mouths of trappers and occasional explorers. Incredibly deep, rich, well-watered soil in almost endless supply—what better to entice America's yeomen farmers as the Midwest filled up? And it was mostly true, though the soil was perhaps a little more watered than they would have wished. Meadows and marsh were interspersed with oak and conifer groves, with a nice river system for bringing goods to market. There was the rain, and there was the little matter of the native inhabitants, but their numbers had already been greatly reduced by smallpox. A little pacification; a little clearing of woods and draining of swamps: Manifest Destiny couldn't have been clearer.

Though they couldn't have known it, the settlers had a catastrophe, also of biblical proportions, to thank for that fertile plain. A flood, in fact. The Missoula Floods of 15,000 to 12,000 years ago that tore the soil from Washington's Channeled Scablands and scoured out the Columbia River Gorge rushed up the valley between Cascades and coast and got trapped there long enough to drop much of that sediment. *Et voilà.* Perfect fruit-, grain-, and wine-growing country.

Take the secondary roads from Portland, the city that river trade built, to Oregon City, then meander among the hilly vineyards and berry farms of the lower Valley, the flat grass and grain fields from Salem to Eugene, the wetlands and wildlife refuges, and the never-distant forests. Oregon's largest cities, oldest universities, its agricultural epicenter, and a lingering wildness come together here. I have a surreal memory of barreling down I-5 late one afternoon somewhere south of Cottage Grove and, out of the corner of my eye, catching three elk standing on the shoulder, looking expectantly at the stream of eighteen-wheelers for a break in the traffic.

LOWER COLUMBIA RIVER

[It was] a Cloudy morning Som rain the after part of last night & this morning. I could not Sleep for the noise kept by the Swans, Geese, white & black brant, Ducks &c. on a opposit base, & Sand hill Crane, they were emensely numerous and their noise horid.

—*Capt. William Clark, journal entry, November 5, 1805*

Poor Lewis and Clark. Their party had arrived on the braided lower Columbia at the same time as thousands of waterfowl from the far north, all gabbling interminably. Silt dropped in the river's last surge to the Pacific forms marshy, shifting islands beloved of geese and ducks; several of these are now wildlife refuges for the quantities of birds that still winter here. And a few plaques mark spots where the Corps of Discovery camped on their extremely damp approach to the ocean (November is perhaps not the optimal time for a visit). Untrammeled by the dams that hold it back for most of its 1,200-mile length, here the river flows freely to the sea.

Tidal a hundred miles upstream, the Columbia harbored a teeming fauna into recent history: legendary salmon runs, seals and otter, even the California condor—of which the Corps depressingly shot a specimen—all of which supported thriving indigenous populations along both shores. The condor is gone and the salmon much diminished, but the sheer force of water and wood says it could all come back, given half a chance.

This is a landscape of dikes and low-lying farms, small towns that throve for a time on lumber and shipping, shimmering fields and tangled woods, with the dense Coast Range at its back and the runoff of a 259,000-square-mile watershed running past its feet. Untouristified, perhaps underappreciated (it *does* rain), this corner of Oregon is nearly uncharted territory for outdoors enthusiasts—with pleasant bed & breakfasts for sitting out the storms.

GUIDANCE **Clatskanie Chamber of Commerce** (503-728-2052; www.clatskanie.com), 155 W. US 30, Clatskanie 97016.

Columbia County Department of Forests, Parks and Recreation (503-366-3984), 1054 Oregon Street, St. Helens 97051.

South Columbia County Chamber of Commerce (503-397-0685; www.scc chamber.com), 2194 Columbia Boulevard, St. Helens 97051.

Travel Columbia County (503-804-0087; www.travelcolumbiacounty.com).

Vernonia Area Chamber of Commerce (503-429-6081; www.vernonia chamber.org), 1001 Bridge Street, Vernonia 97064.

GETTING THERE *By car/ferry:* **US 30** hugs the Columbia River from Portland to Astoria. At Westport, one of Oregon's few remaining **ferries** shuttles cars and people across the Columbia to Washington, departing at a quarter past the hour 6:15 AM–9:15 PM.

GETTING AROUND *By bus:* The **Columbia County Rider** (503-366-0199) provides bus service between Portland and Westport, with connections to Astoria and Seaside on the coast, but only three days a week.

MEDICAL EMERGENCY See *Medical Emergency* in "Portland Metropolitan Area."

✷ To See

FARMERS' MARKETS **Rainier Marina Market** (503-556-1220), 115 E. A Street, Rainier. Sat. 9:30–4, May–mid-Dec.

Scappoose Community Farmers' Market (503-543-3469), Second Street and East Columbia Avenue, Scappoose. Sat. 9–2, mid-May–mid-Oct.

GARDENS **Joy Creek Nursery** (503-543-7474; www.joycreek.com), 20300 NW Watson Road, Scappoose. Daily 9–5, Feb. 27–Oct. 31. Buy your plants here or just stroll the 4 acres of display gardens overlooking the confluence of the Willamette River with the Columbia.

HISTORIC HOMES **Caples House** (503-397-5390; www.capleshouse.com), 1915 First Street, Columbia City. Fri.–Sun. 1–5, Mar. 1–Oct. 31 and major holidays. General admission $4, children $3. Among the early waves of Oregon Trail emigrants, the Caples family settled in 1846 on this bluff overlooking the Columbia rather than in the fertile Willamette Valley. Joseph Caples built a log cabin on the site, where, 24 years later, his son Charles, grown and become a doctor, built the white two-story home that is now the Caples House Museum. Surrounded with the original apple and pear orchards, the place is a window into the life of a pioneer doctor—the office is there, as well as the kitchen, parlor, and three bedrooms, all furnished with period articles and household goods, while the carriage house has a fine collection of antique children's toys.

HISTORIC SITES **Columbia County Courthouse,** 230 Strand Street, St. Helens. In old photographs this imposing basalt monument looks like a New York landmark marooned on a desert island. The town has grown up around it since then, though not much, and it's now softened by trees and a plaza broken by a

THE HISTORIC COLUMBIA COUNTY COURTHOUSE AT ST. HELENS ON THE LOWER COLUMBIA RIVER

meandering line of tiles representing the Columbia River. Built in 1906, its sheer mass, columned portico, and bell tower surely betoken greater ambitions than were realized. But it has attained a degree of fame through its appearance in several melancholy movies, most recently *Twilight,* which used several locations in St. Helens as stand-ins for Forks and Port Angeles, Washington.

Prescott Beach, 5 miles south of Rainier; turn off US 30 onto Graham Road and continue 1.75 miles. The Corps of Discovery is thought to have camped here, as best historians can determine from their journals, on Nov. 5, 1805, where Clark wrote the entry at the beginning of this chapter. It actually referred to the previous night's camp near Sauvie Island, some 30 miles upstream, but no matter. Evidently he had unwittingly discovered the Pacific Flyway. A plaque near the end of the parking lot notes the event.

MUSEUMS ♿ **Vernonia Pioneer Museum** (503-429-3713), 511 E. Bridge Street, Vernonia. Fri.–Sun. 1–4, June–Sept. and Sat.–Sun. 1–4, Oct.–May. Free. The building houses exhibits on logging, the life of settlers in the long-remote Nehalem Valley, and local Indian artifacts. A good place for a rainy day in an outdoor town.

Watts House Pioneer Museum (503-260-4966), 52432 SE First Street, Scappoose. Sat. 10–2. Free, but donations are appreciated. James Grant Watts, first official mayor of Scappoose, built this ample home for his family in 1902. It also became the de facto library for 20 years; the town library burnt down in 1930 and wasn't replaced till the 1950s. In honor of its civic-minded owners, it has been largely restored and houses memories of Scappoose, including part of the first wooden water line and household items dating from the late 1800s to the mid-20th century. Hmm, you may recognize some.

WALKING TOURS Discover downtown St. Helens's colorful past with the **Olde Town St. Helens Historic Self-Guided Walking Tour,** available from the Historical Society of Columbia County (503-366-3650).

✷ To Do

BICYCLING **The Bike Shop** (503-397-4900), 315 S. Columbia River Highway, St. Helens. Bike rentals and information.

Banks-Vernonia Trail, from Banks, on OR 47, to Vernonia. This is Oregon's first rail-to-trail path. Used to haul lumber and passengers from remote Vernonia to Portland, the railway was abandoned in the 1970s, and the right-of-way is now owned by Oregon State Parks. Twenty-one miles of mostly paved trail open to walkers, cyclists, and horses (horses must walk a parallel path) run through woods and along burbling brooks for a bucolic outing—uphill from Banks to Vernonia, and vice-versa for a downhill ride.

BIRD-WATCHING **Scappoose Marine Park** (503-387-2888), 57420 Old Portland Road, Warren. Just offshore, Sand Island shelters Scappoose Bay from the mighty Columbia. A nature trail at the marina, between Scappoose and St. Helens, winds among creeks and trees by the water's edge. You might spot herons, eagles, warblers, and osprey, not to mention otters.

Twilight Creek Eagle Sanctuary (see *Wilder Places*) allows viewing of raptors, shorebirds, waterfowl, and more from its roadside perch off US 30.

CAMPING **Big Eddy** (503-366-3984), 64555 Nehalem Avenue N., Vernonia. Full hookups $17–20, partial hookups $15–18, without hookup $12–15; discounts for hiker/bikers.

Camp Wilkerson (503-366-3984), 65866 Apiary Road, Rainier. Cabins $35 up to six people, Adirondacks (three-sided shelters) $16–20, lodge $100.

L. L. "Stub" Stewart State Park (1-800-452-5687), 11 miles south of Vernonia on OR 47. Twelve one-room ($39) and three two-room cabins (one pet friendly), plus 35 walk-in sites ($6–13) and 94 full hookup sites ($18), some with corrals. Reservations accepted.

GOLF **St. Helens Golf Course** (503-397-0358), 57246 Hazen Road, Warren. Nine holes.

Vernonia Golf Course (503-429-6811), 15961 Timber Road E., Vernonia. Eighteen holes.

Wildwood Golf Course (503-621-3402), 21881 NW St. Helens Road, Portland; 15 miles northwest of Portland on US 30. Eighteen holes.

HIKING **Banks-Vernonia Trail** (see *Bicycling*). Obviously 21 miles is a stretch for hikers (though not impossible), but you can do all or part. Those wishing to do a through-hike may camp in **Stub Stewart State Park,** about halfway along.

Vernonia Lake, Vernonia. Formerly the pond for a huge lumber mill, the small lake today is as placid as, er, a millpond, with a mile-long paved trail around it. For a longer hike, connect to the Banks-Vernonia Trail via Webb Way. The mill itself was burned for a scene in the movie *Ring of Fire.*

KAYAKING **Lower Columbia River Water Trail** (503-226-1565; www.columbiawatertrail.org), a 146-mile nonmotorized-boat trail running from Bonneville Dam to the sea, presents several camping and launch sites in this area; check Web site for details.

Scappoose Bay Kayaking (1-877-2PADDLE; www.scappoosebaykayaking.com), 57420 Old Portland Road, Warren. Open year-round except Jan. Rentals, purchases, lessons, tours . . . this is your site on the lower Columbia for flatwater kayaking. Sheltered from the Columbia estuary by Sand Island (and therefore also home to lots of wildlife), the bay is an ideal place to learn or just enjoy a peaceful paddle among the otter and eagles. Owners Steve and Bonnie are dedicated to sharing the joys of paddling; they will find you the boat that fits and teach you skills if you need them. And for further adventure, you can book a guided tour, from three hours in the wetlands to a four-day trip down the Great River itself, with food, tents, and equipment provided. Rentals start at $15/hour; cruises from $45.

Vernonia Lake (see *Hiking*), near undiscovered Vernonia in the Coast Range, is just the right size for a quiet, unthreatening paddle. Motorboats are allowed, but only with nongas motors.

UNIQUE ADVENTURES **Dinosaurs Unlimited Scenic Tours and Aerobatic Flights** (503-939-0252 or 503-543-3121), 34442 Berg Road, Warren. Take a flight tailored to your adrenaline needs, calm and scenic or a little more exciting, in one of Dinosaurs's vintage aircraft; tours start at $100.

✷ Wilder Places

PARKS **Columbia County** (503-366-3984) runs a daisy chain of lovely and uncrowded parks, including:

Big Eddy Park (503-429-6982), 64555 Nehalem Highway N., Vernonia. Seven miles north of Vernonia, this restful county park along the Nehalem River offers camping, play areas, and canoeing.

Camp Wilkerson (503-366-3984), 65866 Apiary Road, Rainier. These 280 forested acres back in the woods hold lovely log shelters, including a day lodge, cabins, and three-sided camping shelters. Popular with youth groups, it's also a place for individuals or families to relax for a few hours or a day.

Prescott Beach (see *Historic Sites*). Besides its Lewis and Clark association, Prescott Beach is popular with windsurfers and fishing families.

Other parks:

L. L. "Stub" Stewart State Park (1-800-452-5687), 11 miles south of Vernonia on OR 47. This new park offers more than 1,600 acres of forest and field with streams, campsites, and miles of hiking and biking trails.

Pixie Park, corner of the Strand and I Street, Columbia City. It's not exactly wild, being a couple of hundred feet of riverfront maybe a hundred feet deep, but it has everything a minipark needs: a picnic table, a bench, little paths, and plantings, set off by a hedge. The wildness is in the view of the broad Columbia in all its moods, with its shipping lanes, eagles, and mounts St. Helens and Adams beyond.

Sand Island Marine Park, St. Helens. In summer the free Sand Island Shuttle (503-366-6272) runs Thurs.–Sun. from the St. Helens docks to Sand Island, 42.4 acres of cottonwoods, field, and beach where kids can run and others can stroll, picnic, and even camp in the middle of the river. Pit toilets, picnic tables, and campsites; free.

Trojan PGE Park (503-556-7076), 71760 Columbia River Highway (US 30), Rainier. Talk about transformation. From 1970 to 2006 this was the site of the Trojan Nuclear Facility, a Portland General Electric power plant shut down in 1993 due to environmental and safety concerns. PGE finally imploded the cooling tower in 2006 and changed the site to a 500-acre wooded park, complete with lakes, ponds, walking paths, and picnic shelters (with electric stoves no less). The largest lake is open to fishing and nonmotorized boating.

WILDLIFE REFUGES **Jewell Meadows Wildlife Area** (503-755-2264). From US 26 take OR 103 to Jewell, turn left on OR 202, and go 1.5 miles to parking area. Elk winter in these roadside meadows set in the rough-and-tumble Coast Range between Portland and Seaside. Large herds are visible Nov.–Apr., when driving conditions are often far from ideal (check at www.tripcheck.com). Spring and summer bring abundant songbirds and wildflowers.

Lewis and Clark National Wildlife Refuge (360-795-3915), in the Columbia River estuary between Oregon and Washington. Accessible only by boat, the refuge can be viewed from the overlook at Twilight Creek Eagle Sanctuary.

Twilight Creek Eagle Sanctuary, on Burnside Loop 7 miles east of Astoria via US 30. Part of the Lewis and Clark National Wildlife Refuge, it provides habitat for thousands of wintering waterfowl as well as nesting eagles. A viewing platform on Burnside Loop overlooks 35,000 acres of wetlands, islands, mudflats, and the great river.

✷ Lodging

BED & BREAKFASTS

Clatskanie

✐ **Clatskanie River Hideaway** (503-369-6502), 80 NW Fourth Street. The single suite on the river has its own canoe and kayak docks—you don't have to be a river rat to stay there, but it's great if you are—and sleeps three. It comes with deck, sauna, hot tub, and in-room breakfast, all for $79. The same folks own the **Shirley Suite** (503-728-2051), 203a North Nehalem Street, Clatskanie. This one is downtown and is handy for couples or families, with a queen bed and a fold-down Murphy, kitchen, and bath; $85.

St. Helens

Nob Hill Bed and Breakfast (503-396-5555; www.nobhillbb.com), 285 S. Second Street. A commanding house with a commanding view over the St. Helens waterfront to Mount St. Helens, the finely appointed place was built for a doctor in 1900. Down comforters, luxurious bedding, and fireplaces make any of the three suites a special-occasion treat. $159–189, with full breakfast.

Seawright House (503-366-3044; www.seawrighthouse.com), 134 N. Second Street. *Sybaritic* is the word that comes to mind. Only one party at a time may occupy the 1,700-square-foot luxury suite inside this deceptively sober 1910 frame house, complete with kitchen, deck, sunroom, fireplace, pillow-top beds, and art deco decor. On top of that you can get a massage or even a personal chef. Doubles $225.

Scappoose

♿ **Scappoose Creek Inn** (1-888-875-1670; www.scappoosecreekinn.com), 53758 W. Lane Road. Where the crawl of urban growth meets the edge of rural Oregon, just 0.5 mile off US 30, you'll find a long red barn beside a solid farmhouse. This was the 400-acre Scappoose Creek Dairy right through the Depression (and home of a massive still during Prohibition, which was probably more lucrative). Only 4 acres are left—you're free to stroll around and greet the chickens and llamas—but the farmhouse is now divided into 10 comfortable, unfussy rooms, each with a quilt on the bed and the simple but nice furnishings that might have graced a farmhouse 60 years ago. Plus peace, quiet, and a hearty welcome from innkeeper Sherrie. Rooms, $69–150, with private bath and breakfast. A separate, wheelchair-accessible cottage sleeps six; $150.

Vernonia

Old Mill House Inn (503-429-0952), 487 Arkansas Avenue. When Brooke and David Van Meter turned their former mill house into a bed & breakfast, they conserved all the molding and traditional touches of the 1925 home (but added modern plumbing, TV, and even Wi-Fi). Three rooms in a quiet neighborhood (well, all Vernonia neighborhoods seem quiet) come with a heaping breakfast. From $85.

Rock Creek Bed and Breakfast (503-429-2503; www.rockcreekbb.com), 1162 State Avenue. A quiet 1922 cottage with a fenced garden on a quiet street offers lots of privacy for one party at a time. You're in walking distance of shops, trails, and eateries. Doubles $110, with full breakfast.

MOTELS

Clatskanie

Clatskanie River Inn (503-728-9000; www.clatskanie.com/riverinn), 600 E. Columbia River Highway. Large motel rooms and suites, some with river views. Rates from $89, with continental breakfast.

Northwoods Inn (503-728-4311; www.northwoodsinn.biz), 945 E. Columbia River Highway. Clean rooms and suites with free Wi-Fi, and some with kitchens. Rates from $59.

Westport

Westport Motel (503-455-2212), 49238 OR 30. "It's been here forever," says the innkeeper—quite possibly since US 30 came through. Simple and low-key, but snug, the seven units, mostly with kitchens, are a budget option. From $50.

✷ Where to Eat

EATING OUT

St. Helens

Houlton Bakery (503-366-2648), 2155 Columbia Boulevard. Tues.–Sat. 9–4. Homemade and homestyle breads, rolls, cakes, and pastries make this a stop for a light breakfast. Add one of their salads, soups, or sandwiches, and you have lunch.

Klondike Restaurant and Bar (503-366-2634; www.klondikerestaurant.com), 71 Cowlitz Street. Tues.–Sat. 11–9. Everyone at the Klondike seems to know everyone else, and in short order they know you, too. No short orders here though; steaks and seafood are grilled to order, with generous side dishes, and to boot you get the atmosphere of St. Helens's heyday here in the town's historic hotel.

Plantation House Pizza (503-366-0165), 298 First Street. Daily for lunch and dinner, Thurs.–Mon. for breakfast. The pizzas and home-brewed beers have made this a popular casual spot for all ages. It doubles as local entertainment on Fri. nights, which feature stand-up comedians.

✷ Events

June–September: **13 Nights on the River** (503-397-0685), Thurs. nights, Columbia View Park, St. Helens. Free music in the park.

PORTLAND METROPOLITAN AREA

Gresham schools, Canby, Boring . . .

—OPB radio announcer

I did a double take over the breakfast my children would fail to eat before catching the 6:30 school bus. A winter storm had swept across the state during the night, and I was listening for the school closures. Was this the mischief of some joker in the OPB newsroom? Gresham, Canby, and even Boring are all suburbs of Portland, but there are plenty more. Such a sequence hardly seemed accidental. Chalk it up to the environment that produced Matt Groening, creator of *The Simpsons.*

Settled in 1843, Portland soon earned the unlovely sobriquet "Stumptown" as its abundant, massive cedars and Douglas firs were felled and transformed into astronomical numbers of board feet for markets near and far. Soon the surrounding countryside settled up, providing the nascent city with food. As the long Willamette Valley filled, lumber and produce made their way to the city, whose situation at the confluence of the Willamette and Columbia made it an inevitable hub of local and international trade.

If Portland gleefully razed its primeval forest, it also remade itself as a "green" city before greenness became fashionable. An extensive bus, streetcar, and light-rail system (free downtown) makes it relatively easy to get about. Parks and gardens, including 5,000-acre Forest Park, keep the place clean and green; urban growth boundaries attempt to preserve surrounding farmland. In short, it's ahead of the environmental curve. It does rain a lot, which may be why it's home to the nation's largest independent bookstore . . .

The metro area was shut down with a few inches of snow. Out on the High Desert, with considerably more, it was business as usual, and my sons ran out into the subfreezing dark to await the bus.

GUIDANCE **I-205 State Welcome Center Oregon City** (1-800-404-3002), 1726 Washington Street (exit 10 from I-205), Oregon City 97045.

PIONEER COURTHOUSE SQUARE, THE HUB OF DOWNTOWN PORTLAND

Beaverton Area Chamber of Commerce (503-644-0123; www.beaverton.org), 12655 SW Center, Suite 140, Beaverton 97005.

Cornelius Chamber of Commerce Visitors Center (503-359-4037), 120 N. 13th Street, Cornelius 97113.

Forest Grove Chamber of Commerce (503-357-3006; www.fgchamber.org), 2417 Pacific Avenue, Forest Grove 97116.

Greater Hillsboro Area Chamber of Commerce (503-648-1102; www.hillchamber.org), 5193 NW Elam Young Parkway, Suite A, Hillsboro 97124.

Gresham Area Chamber of Commerce Visitor Center (503-665-1131; www.greshamchamber.org), 701 NE Hood Avenue, Gresham 97030.

Jantzen Beach State Welcome Center (1-800-424-3002), 12348 N. Center Avenue, Portland 97217.

Lake Oswego Chamber of Commerce (503-636-3634; www.lake-oswego.com), 242 B Avenue, Lake Oswego 97034.

North Clackamas County Chamber of Commerce (503-654-7777; www.yourchamber.com), 7740 SE Harmony Road, Milwaukie 97222.

Oregon City Regional Visitor Information Center (1-800-424-3002), 1726 Washington Street, Oregon City 97045.

Oregon's Mount Hood Territory/Clackamas County Tourism and Cultural Affairs (503-655-0490; www.mthoodterritory.com), 2051 Kaen Road, Suite 427, Oregon City 97045.

Portland Oregon Information Center (1-877-678-5263; www.travelportland.com), 701 SW Sixth Avenue, Portland 97205.

Portland Parks and Recreation (503-823-PLAY; www.portlandonline.com), 1120 SW Fifth Avenue #1302, Portland 97204.

Sandy Area Chamber of Commerce (503-668-4006; www.sandyoregonchamber.org), 38775 Pioneer Boulevard, Sandy 97055.

Sherwood Chamber of Commerce (503-625-4207; www.sherwoodchamber.org), 16191 SW Railroad Street, Sherwood 97140.

South Columbia County Chamber of Commerce (503-397-0685; www.scc chamber.org), 2194 Columbia Boulevard, St. Helens 97051.

Tualatin Chamber of Commerce (503-692-0780; www.tualatinchamber.org), 18791 SW Martinazzi Avenue, Suite C, Tualatin 97062.

Vernonia Area Chamber of Commerce (503-429-6081; www.vernonia chamber.org), 1001 Bridge Street, Vernonia 97064.

Washington County Visitors Association (1-800-537-3149; www.wcva.org), 11000 SW Stratus Street, Beaverton 97008.

West Linn Chamber of Commerce (503-655-6744; www.westlinnchamber.com), 2020 SW Eighth Avenue, West Linn 97068.

GETTING THERE *By air:* **Portland International Airport (PDX)** (1-877-739-4636; www.flypdx.com) is served by all major carriers and some minor ones. It's about a 20-minute drive from downtown at exit 24A off I-20; or you can take the convenient **MAX Light Rail** running every 5 to 15 minutes from 4:30 AM till midnight.

By car: **I-5** runs through the city north–south, while **I-84** traverses it east to west. **US 26** comes in from nearby Mount Hood and takes off for the northern coast; **US 30** follows the lower Columbia from Portland to Astoria.

By rail/bus: **Union Station** (503-273-4866), 800 NW Sixth Avenue, is **AMTRAK**'s Portland base (1-800-USA-RAIL; www.amtrak.com), served by two north–south and one east–west routes. Right next door at 550 NW Sixth Avenue is the **Greyhound** station (1-800-231-2222; www.greyhound.com).

GETTING AROUND TriMet (503-238-7433; www.trimet.org), 701 Sixth Avenue, Portland. Portland's user-friendly public transportation network of bus, streetcar, light rail, and commuter rail makes it easy to get around town, to the airport, and to some of the suburbs. Travel within the Fareless Square, which includes most of downtown, is free. Buses and streetcars are equipped to transport bikes.

THE MAIN CONCOURSE AT PORTLAND INTERNATIONAL AIRPORT

MEDICAL EMERGENCY Adventist Medical Center (503-257-2500), 10123 SE Market Street, Portland.

Legacy Emanuel Hospital and Health Center (503-413-2200), 2801 N. Gantenbein Avenue, Portland.

Legacy Good Samaritan Hospital and Medical Center (1-800-733-9959), 1015 NW 22nd Avenue, Portland.

Legacy Meridian Park Hospital (503-692-1212), 19300 SW 65th Avenue, Tualatin.

Legacy Mount Hood Medical Center (503-674-1122), 24800 SE Stark Street, Gresham.

Oregon Health and Science University (503-4948311), 3181 SW Sam Jackson Park Road, Portland.

Providence Child Center (503-251-2400), 830 NE 47th Avenue, Portland.

Providence Milwaukie Hospital (503-513-8300), 10150 SE 32nd Avenue, Milwaukie.

Providence Portland Medical Center (503-215-1111), 4805 NW Glisan Street, Portland.

Providence St. Vincent Medical Center (503-216-1234), 9205 SW Barnes Road, Portland.

Portland Veterans' Affairs Medical Center (1-800-949-1004), 3710 SW US Veterans' Hospital Road, Portland.

Willamette Falls Hospital (503-657-6702), 1500 Division Street, Oregon City.

✷ To See

BOAT TOURS ***Portland Spirit*** (503-224-3900; www.portlandspirit.com), 110 SE Caruthers, Portland. No traffic, no hassle; leave the driving, or rather the navigation, to them. Four vessels, including a stern-wheeler like those that served the Territory before trains, ply the Willamette and Columbia rivers, offering narrated two-hour city cruises or daylong excursions up and down the scenic Columbia Gorge. Cruises depart from Salmon Street Springs in Waterfront Park; buy tickets at that box office, at the Caruthers Street office, by phone, or online. Tours on the sheltered Willamette operate year-round, while Columbia cruises run spring to fall. Adults $24–94, children $17–84 (depending on cruise length and meal options). ***Sternwheeler Rose*** (503-286-76673; www.sternwheelerrose.com) is a paddle-wheel replica offering brunch or dinner cruises on the Willamette. Tours board at the OMSI parking lot at 1945 SE Water Avenue.

FARMERS' MARKETS With all that greenery and Oregonians' insistence on fresh foods, there is a plethora of markets where farmers and consumers meet in happy symbiosis. Here are a few; for more choices check www.oregonfarmers markets.org.

Portland Farmers' Market (503-241-0032; www.portlandfarmersmarket.org). Naturally, Portland's green orientation extends to the edible kind of green. From humble beginnings in 1992, it has mushroomed, so to speak, into a Portland institution of more than two hundred vendors. The area's delightfully long growing season means you can find fresh produce (and eggs, and cheese, and meat) nine months of the year; buy lunch from one of the hot-food stands and make a day of it. The market is held four days a week at four locations: Sat. 8:30–2, Apr.–Oct. and Sat. 9–2, Nov.–Dec., at Portland State University, between SW Harrison and Montgomery; Wed. 10–2, May–Oct., in Shemanski Park on SW Park between Salmon and Main; Thurs. 3:30–7:30, mid-May–Sept., at Hinson Church, SE Salmon and 20th; and Sun. 10–2, May–Oct., at NE Seventh and Wygant.

Hillsboro Farmers' Market (503-844-6685), in Courthouse Square at Second and East Main. Sat. 8–1:30, May–Dec.

Lake Oswego Farmers' Market (503-697-6590), Millenium Park, First and Evegreen, Lake Oswego. Sat. 8:30–1:30, mid-May–mid-Oct.

Tigard Area Farmers' Market (503-244-2479), 11831 SW Pacific Highway, Tigard. Sun. 9–2, mid-May–Oct.

FOR FAMILIES **Oregon Museum of Science and Industry** (503-797-4000; www.omsi.org), 1945 SE Water Avenue, Portland. Tues.–-Sun. 9:30–5:30. General admission $11, seniors and kids 3–13 $9, plus $2 parking. Here's where your kids can do the chemistry or experiments you'd rather they didn't do at home, plus fool around with optics, robots, fossils, creepy-crawlies, and anything science oriented. Browse the five exhibit halls for a more contemplative approach, or tour an actual submarine, see the stars at the planetarium (each $5.50 extra), visit a volcano's insides or time-travel via the Motion Simulator ($4.75), or immerse yourself in an IMAX movie ($8.50).

Oregon Zoo (503-226-1561; www.oregonzoo.org), 4001 SW Canyon Road, Portland. Daily 8–7 in summer, daily 9–4 in winter; closed Christmas. General admission $9.75, seniors and kids 3–11 $6.75 (but you can get a dollar off for arriving via MAX, and on the second Tues. of each month, you can get in for $2); parking $2. Begun with a sailor's private animal collection, the zoo has blossomed to habitat exhibits ranging from the Serengeti to the Amazon, and the tundra to the Northwest, including underwater views of polar bears and sea otters. Portland's elephants have been beloved since they began breeding here—nearly 30 babies since the 1960s—and spearheaded the zoo's conservation programs, which now include a California condor breeding program. An aviary, a seasonal bug house, and several themed gardens make it heaven for zoophiliacs.

End of the Oregon Trail Interpretive Center (503-657-9936; www.endoftheoregontrail.org), 1726 Washington Street, Oregon City. Mon.–Sat. 9:30–5, Sun. 10:30–5; closed Jan. General admission $7, children over five $5; includes admission to the **Museum of the Oregon Territory** and the **Stevens-Crawford House.** Several cities vie for the title (see The Dalles), but Oregon City was seat of government for the entire Oregon Territory; if you wanted to file a land claim, you filed it here, even if you settled in faraway Jacksonville or Eugene. Besides, it was a natural gateway to the fabled Willamette Valley. So right here on Abernethy Green was the official trail's end where those who had survived could take their rest—there's a marker in the Pioneer Garden. The center, built to suggest a gigantic covered wagon train, displays artifacts and explanatory plaques on the vicissitudes of the trail and changing exhibits on pioneer life and skills, complete with hands-on activities for kids (such as packing and unpacking a wagon); unfortunately these indoor exhibits are currently inaccessible due to budget cuts. Docents in period costume offer lively talks on trail history in the replica "mission school."

GARDENS **Crystal Springs Rhododendron Garden** (503-771-8386), SE 28th Avenue at Woodstock Boulevard, Portland. Daily 6 AM–10 PM, Apr.–Sept. and daily 6–6, Oct.–Mar. Admission free following Labor Day–Feb.; otherwise $3 Thurs.–Mon 10–6. Children under 12 always free. Seven acres of rhodies and azaleas are a riot of color through spring, and a tranquil, lakeside oasis is complete with waterfalls and fountains all year-round.

The Grotto (503-254-7371; www.thegrotto.org), Sandy Boulevard at NE 85th Avenue, Portland. The Grotto is a Catholic shrine complete with conference center, a small monastic complex, and a replica of Michangelo's *Pietà*. It also includes an award-winning rose garden, near the cloister, and a rosary-themed Peace Garden comprising tree-shaded paths, lawns, and ponds.

♿ **Hoyt Arboretum** (503-865-8733; www.hoytarboretum.org), 4000 SW Fairview Boulevard, Portland. Daily 6 AM–10 PM; visitors center open Mon.–Fri. 9–4, Sat. 9–3. Free. Here's a Northwest forest with a difference: 187 acres of native and exotic species landscaped for your viewing pleasure, as well as for study, research, and conservation of endangered species. If you like trees, you'll like the miles of paths, visitors center, and browsing library. The center and 2 miles of trails are wheelchair accessible.

International Rose Test Garden (503-823-3636), 400 SW Kingston, Portland. Daily 7 AM–10 PM. Free. Not for nothing is Portland known as the City of Roses. With its mild, moist climate, it's the perfect habitat, and enthusiasts had virtually paved (or at least lined) the streets with roses by the early 1900s. In 1915, fearful that World War I would forever destroy precious European hybrids, Portland's rose hobbyists established this garden, stocking it with slips sent from overseas. In 1940 it became a site for testing new varieties and now displays more than seven thousand bushes of varieties old and new, on grounds landscaped with fountains and footpaths. It has a nice view of the city, too.

Leach Botanical Garden (503-823-9503; www.leachgarden.org), 6704 SE 122nd Avenue, Portland. Tues.–Sat. 9–4, Sun. 1–4. Free; guided tour, suggested $5 donation. Off the beaten path in southeast Portland, this acreage preserves the collection of John and Lilla Leach. Their enthusiastically eclectic plantings mix native species with exotics for an impression of overwhelming variety. The operation includes a nursery producing garden plants for sale.

Portland Classical Chinese Garden (503-228-8131; www.portlandchinese garden.org), 239 NW Everett Street, Portland. Daily 9–6, Apr. 1–Oct. 31 and daily 10–5, Nov. 1–Mar. 31. General admission $8.50, seniors $7.50, students 6–10 $6.50. What to do with an abandoned parking lot occupying a block of prime city real estate? Why, put in a garden, of course. In this case, one typical of a retired Ming dynasty bureaucrat/scholar in Suzhou, Portland's sister city, where the retiree would have spent his time on cultural pursuits and entertaining friends. The jewel box garden creates miniature landscapes with a "lake," highly symbolic rocks and plants, and an amazing number of elegant buildings—including an authentic teahouse where you can sip (expensive) Chinese tea and pretend you're in *Crouching Tiger, Hidden Dragon.* Speaking of beasts, only assistance animals are allowed.

Portland Japanese Garden (503-223-1321; www.japanesegarden.com), 611 SW Kingston Avenue, Portland. Mon. noon–7 and Tues.–Sun. 10–7 in summer, Mon. noon–4 and Tues.–Sun. 10–4 in winter; closed Thanksgiving, Christmas, and New Year's Day. General admission $8, seniors and college students $6.25, kids 6–17 $5.25. Set just above the Rose Garden in Washington Park (so you can spend all day humming amid the flowers), the Japanese Garden was described by former ambassador Nobuo Matsunaga as the most authentic outside Japan. A later envoy, Kunihiki Saito, went him one better and declared it "the most authentic Japanese garden, including those in Japan." A bit of hyberbole, perhaps. But its 5.5 acres seem to enclose a whole world. Designer Takuma Tono provided five gardens cleverly linked by trails, bridges, or stairs: the Strolling Pond Garden, Natural Garden, Flat Garden, the Zen-like Sand and Stone Garden, and the Tea Garden, all artfully designed so that a glance in any direction, in any season, frames a masterpiece. Japanese iris, mountain camellia, pink maple, and a myriad of other species harmonize with carefully placed sculpture—like the pagoda lantern from Sapporo, another sister city—to create the atmosphere of rest and serenity for which Japanese gardens are famous. And it is serene, even in the midst of summer crowds. The garden also hosts lectures and exhibits on Japanese culture, and occasional formal tea ceremonies in the Tea House. Due to the hilly terrain, the garden is only partly wheelchair accessible. Pets are excluded, except assistance animals.

HERITAGE TREES **Dawn Redwood,** Hoyt Arboretum (see *Gardens*). A mere stripling by redwood standards, this tree is a miracle because the species has been extinct in the Americas since the dinosaur era. In fact, it was thought to have been extinct worldwide till specimens were discovered in 1941 in a remote part of China. Seeds were collected and planted in 1948 by various arboreta, including the Hoyt; this, one of the saplings, became the first of its kind to produce cones in this hemisphere in 60 million years.

Nyberg Chestnut. Between exit 289 southbound and I-5, this chestnut was part of an orchard planted in 1903 by immigrant John Nyberg, who managed to save it when the rest of the trees were destroyed by I-5. His son Clayton saved it again when I-205 was being built.

Pow-wow Tree, on West Clackamas Boulevard between Bellevue and Beatrice, Gladstone. At 70 feet high and about 230 years old, this bigleaf maple has seen a lot. It's thought to have been a meeting place for local tribes and was the site of the first Oregon State Fair in 1861.

HISTORIC HOMES **Pittock Mansion** (503-823-3623; www.pittockmansion.org), 3229 NW Pittock Drive, Portland. Daily 11–4 in winter, daily 10–4 in summer; closed Thanksgiving, Christmas, and Jan. 7–31. General admission $7, seniors $6, children 6–18 $4. You could say the Pittocks grew up with the country. Henry Pittock came west on the Oregon Trail as a nearly destitute teenager in 1853 and found a job with the young city's weekly newspaper. Six years later he'd taken the paper over; changed it to the daily *Oregonian,* which remains the state's principal newspaper; and (having made good) married Georgiana, another emigrant and daughter of a flour mill owner. Henry went on to make fortunes in all the Western enterprises—land, wood, banking, mining, the lot—and the couple became pillars of the community. The mansion was a retirement project. Is it a French château or an English manor? Its gray stone bulk, red-tiled turrets, and 22 opulent rooms are definitely imposing and the style eclectic. Finished in 1914, it housed the couple only till their deaths in 1918 and 1919. Georgiana was an avid gardener and is credited with founding the Portland Rose Festival; the lush grounds are open daily 5 AM–9 PM.

Ermatinger House (503-615-1851), 619 Sixth Street, Oregon City. Open occasionally for tea; call for hours and admission. This 1845 house is the oldest in Clackamas County. It was built by John McLoughlin even before he built his own house for Francis Ermatinger, a fellow Hudson's Bay Company employee who married McLoughlin's granddaughter. A plain clapboard house with a pillared porch, it's considered to be the site of a legendary coin toss. Asa Lovejoy and Francis Pettygrove, owners of the original Portland claim, needed a proper name for their ambitious settlement and had to decide whether "Stumptown" should be named after Lovejoy's hometown (Boston) or Pettygrove's (Portland, Maine). Pettygrove won.

McLoughlin House (503-656-5146; www.historicoregoncity.com), 713 Center Street, Oregon City. Wed.–Sat. 10–4, Sun. 1–4. Free. A towering figure in Northwest history (and at 6 feet, 4 inches), Dr. John McLoughlin established Fort Vancouver for the Hudson's Bay Company in 1825 and guided it to prosperity as a fur-trading and farming center. His superiors hoped the outpost would keep the territory British. However, he failed to obey orders to discourage American settlers, sending them instead south of the Columbia, where they proceeded to increase and multiply. So after 20 years' service he was persuaded to retire and built this large home on a claim he had bought from the company. And a majestic home it was for the frontier district Oregon City then was. Many of the elegant pieces on view are family originals, including a piano brought via Cape Horn, a Chinese sewing cabinet for McLoughlin's Cree-Swiss wife, and an impressive set of English dinnerware. Visits are by guided tour under the auspices of the National Park Service, starting at the Barclay House next door.

Rose Farm (503-656-5146), Holmes Lane at Rilance Street, Oregon City. Sat. noon–4, July–Aug. Admission $3, seniors and children 6–17 $2. Louisa Holmes loved roses. She and her husand, William, emigrated in the banner Oregon Trail year 1843 and built a log cabin. In 1847 they finished and moved into this house, which became something of a political center. Joseph Lane, first governor of the Oregon Territory, gave his inaugural address from its balcony in 1849.

Stevens-Crawford House (503-655-2866), 603 Sixth Street, Oregon City. Wed.–Sat. noon–4; closed Jan. This 1908 Foursquare house was built by descendants of Oregon Trail wagonmaster Medorum Crawford and remained in the family until 1963. It still contains most of the original furniture.

HISTORIC SITES The **End of the Oregon Trail** is commemorated with a marker on the grounds of the **End of the Oregon Trail Interpretive Center** (see *For Families*).

Oregon City Walking Tour. A self-guided walk to many of the sites that follow, and then some, is available at the **Barclay House,** 719 Center Street.

Oregon City Municipal Elevator and Promenade, 300 Seventh Street, Oregon City. The 1954 elevator from the bluffs to the literal downtown replaces a 1915 hydraulic one. Rides are free. It's a nice way to access the historic homes, most of which were relocated to the higher ground, and there's a fine view of the falls from the promenade.

Pioneer cemeteries. Pioneers and homesteaders died early and often of accident, disease, or disaster, so individuals often donated land or family burial plots to the community for cemeteries. The Metropolitan Regional Government maintains 14 pioneer cemeteries in the metro area dating back to 1848. **Lone Fir Cemetery,** at SE 20th Avenue and Morrison Street in Portland, is the resting place of Asa Lovejoy, one of the city's founders, and twenty-five thousand others—of whom ten thousand are unknown due to early neglect. **Powell Grove Cemetery,** at NE 122nd Avenue and Sandy Boulevard in Portland, was founded in 1848 but has headstones dating from 1837, the era of explorers and fur trappers. A list of pioneer cemeteries with directions is available at www.oregonmetro.gov. These are still active cemeteries, so tact and sensitivity are in order.

MUSEUMS **3D Center of Art and Photography** (503-227-6667; www.3dcenter.us), 1928 NW Lovejoy Street, Portland. Thurs.–Sat. 11–5, Sun. 1–5. Admission $5; children under 15 free. Dedicated to the ages-old effort to render three dimensions with only two at your disposal, the center displays and explains the hows and whys of stereocards, Viewmaster, and high-tech 3D imaging. Bring some depth to your view of the world!

Canby Depot Museum (503-266-6712), 888 NE Fourth Avenue, Canby. Thurs.–Sun. 1–4; closed Jan. and Feb. Admission by donation. A few blocks from its original site, this "depot" of Oregon history is the oldest remaining train station in Oregon, dating from about 1873, and is devoted to the interlocked agricultural and railway history of the region. Imagine these 'burbs as fields of flax, cutting flowers, and dairy cattle,.and the train comes whistling through.

Museum of Contemporary Craft (503-223-2654; www.museumofcontemporarycraft.org), 724 NW Davis Street, Portland. Tues.–Sun. 11–6 (until 8 on Thurs.). Free. Part museum, part gallery, this is the place to see (and even buy, if so inclined) crafts in all media, from glass to embroidery and beyond. Its philosophy is interactive, so bring your creativity or your kids to a free crafts workshop; check for schedule.

Museum of the Oregon Territory (503-655-5574; www.historicoregoncity.com), 211 Tumwater Drive, Oregon City. Open for events. The museum focuses on the first administrative, commercial, and industrial center in the Oregon Territory: Oregon City, on the strategic Willamette Falls. Logically, it begins with indigenous trade and goes on to detail mill development on the falls and the concomitant business and cultural development. It also houses a number of historic documents, such as San Francisco's first city plat, filed in Oregon City in 1850.

Oregon Historical Society Museum (503-222-1741; www.ohs.org), 1200 Park Avenue, Portland. Tues.–Sat. 10–5, Sun. noon–5. General admission $10, students and seniors $8, kids 6–18 $5. The march of Oregon history starts with a pair of nine-thousand-year-old sage-fiber sandals unearthed at Fort Rock. But these aren't the first shoes you see. Rather, you are greeted at the entrance to the main permanent exhibit with a showcase of extremely varied shoes and hats, from a shipyard worker's hard hat to a blue, black, and red number worn by the first Chinese consul in the Pacific Northwest. The society aims to trace Oregon's evolution with a focus on the ordinary person. Everyday-life displays include an Indian plank house, a replica Hudson's Bay Company ship, a pioneer wagon, and more, with plentiful original and replica artifacts. But the museum also addresses some of the cracks in the facade, inviting the visitor to consider the links between contemporary controversies like the animosity surrounding the spotted owl or the conflicted role of immigrants, and currents present since Oregon's inception.

Oregon Jewish Museum (503-226-3600; www.ojm.org), 310 NW Davis Street, Portland. Tues.–Fri. 10:30–3, Sun. 1–4. Admission $3. The only Jewish museum in the Northwest documents Jewish experience in the region and houses collections of Jewish memorabilia from around the world. Special exhibits through the year highlight facets of Jewish art and history, global and local.

Oregon Maritime Center and Museum (503-224-7724; www.oregonmaritime museum.org), on the stern-wheeler *Portland,* at the sea wall at the foot of Pine Street, Portland. Wed.–Sat. 11–4, Sun. 12:30–4. General admission $5, seniors $4, kids 6–17 $3, under six free. Exhibits on Oregon's shipping and marine history fill the stern-wheeler, which was unfortunately damaged in 2008. Repairs have been completed.

Oregon Nikkei Legacy Center (503-224-1458; www.oregonnikkei.org), 121 NW Second Avenue, Portland. Tues.–Sat. 11–3, Sun. noon–3. Admission $3. Set in what was till 1942 the middle of Portland's "Japantown," this center is dedicated to the story of Japanese immigrants in the Pacific Northwest—the bitter and the sweet. The collection of historic photographs and archives documents the early successes of the Nikkei, who started arriving in the late 1800s to work on the railroads and soon diversified, building truck farms and small businesses; their overnight degradation and deportation to internment camps in 1942; and their postwar recovery in the face of humiliating discrimination. Visit, then reread *Snow Falling on Cedars.*

Portland Art Museum (503-226-2811; www.portlandartmuseum.org), 1219 SW Park Avenue, Portland. Tues.–Wed. and Sat.–Sun. 10–5, Thurs.–Fri. 10–8; closed Mon. General admission $10, students and seniors $9, children under 17 free. Come for an art fix and stay for the afternoon. This museum has amassed quite a trove since its 1892 inception. If nothing else, you should see the stellar collection of Native American art and artifacts from all over North America, including superb coastal Northwest pieces. But it would be a pity to miss the extensive Asian holdings, or the American rooms, or the European galleries, not to mention photography and the decorative arts. Heck, stay for the day; there's a perfectly good café.

Portland Children's Museum (503-223-6500; www.portlandcm.org), 4015 SW Canyon Road, Portland. Daily 9–5, Mar.–Sept. and Tues.–Sun. 9–5 in winter. Ages 1–54 $8, ages 55 and over $7; parking $2. From a toddler-friendly magic forest to a "construction site" for older kids, the studios aim to reach the imaginations of kids ages 1 to 10. Just the place for a child who wants to run the neighborhood hospital or become the next Leonardo, or maybe do both.

Wells Fargo History Museum (503-886-1102; www.wellsfargohistory.com), 1300 SW Fifth Avenue, Portland. Mon.–Fri. 9–6. Free. How the West was won, at least financially, by stage, riverboat, and contemporary banking.

World Forestry Center Discovery Museum (503-228-1367; www.world forestrycenter.org), 4033 SW Canyon Road, Portland. Daily 10–5. General admission $8, seniors $7, children 3–18 $5; parking $2. You can see the forests *and* the trees. Take virtual visits to jungles and boreal forests, then check out life in a fallen log or a tree's root system, and even try your hand at logging (well, this is the World *Forestry* Center). How trees rule the world, and how people rule the trees.

NATURAL WONDERS Willamette Falls, Oregon City. There's a reason why the Falls were settled long before Portland. Fourteen miles upstream of Portland, the river drops 40 feet down a horseshoe-shaped basalt terrace, creating a downsized Niagara. Salmon runs found the valley tribes congregated around the falls to trade and procure their season's food supply. Encroaching civilization, though, showed a sharp eye for other potential. In 1829 the Hudson's Bay Company built a millrace and permanent settlement here that later became Oregon City. Soon flour and lumber mills were roaring away, making the city a commercial hub and the logical first capital of the Oregon Territory (several paper mills still operate). In 1888 the falls were tapped for electricity. Oregon City was illuminated, and, in 1889, power from the falls lit street lamps in downtown Portland—the first long-distance transmission of electricity in the United States. In 1890 came long-distance transmission of alternating current, possibly the first in the world. On the west side of the river, in West Linn, you can visit the **Willamette Falls Locks,** built in 1873 to permit navigation around the falls—the oldest continuously operated multilock and canal system in the United States—and small museum (503-656-3381). The falls can be viewed from the bluff promenade in Oregon City or from a marked viewpoint on OR 99E just north of Oregon City.

TROLLEY TOURS **Oregon City Historic Trolley** (503-496-1571), downtown Oregon City. Free. Hop on and off the trolley to explore the town's several historic sites and museum, or just to shop. It runs all summer. A route map available at www.orcity.org.

Willamette Shore Trolley (503-697-7436; www.oerhs.org), 311 N. State Street, Lake Oswego. Round-trip fares $10, seniors and kids 3–12 $6. Portland has preserved a number of disused railways for light-rail use. This 6-mile segment was opened in 1887 as a narrow-gauge used by antique trolley cars for a relaxing scenic ride along the Willamette River; check Web site for schedule. In fall and winter special excursions focus on fall foliage or illuminated Christmas boats (see *Events*).

WALKING TOURS **Portland Walking Tours** (503-774-4522; www.portlandwalkingtours.com) offers themed, leisurely walks about town Apr.–Nov. Choose among tours of Portland's best (architecture, brewpubs, food, etc.), or discover its seamy side, or even its ghosts. Times and meeting places are posted online. Tickets start at $19 (seniors and youth, $15) and can be purchased online or by phone.

THE PERENNIAL COMMUTER AT PORTLAND'S PIONEER COURTHOUSE SQUARE

WINE Situated between two of the state's prime wine-growing areas—the Willamette Valley and the Columbia Gorge—Portland has a number of bars showing off the local wines. Try **Oregon Wines on Broadway** (503-228-4655; www.oregonwinesonbroadway), 515 SW Broadway, or **Urban Wine Works** (503-226-9797; www.urbanwineworks.com), 407 NW 16th Street.

✷ To Do

BICYCLING Portland is almost obsessively bike friendly, with 200 miles of bike lanes and paths. Bikes can be taken on all public transportation.

Many Portlanders commute by bike, and they are not deterred by rain (drivers, look out). Road cyclists must obey traffic rules and wear bright front and rear lights at night. **Pedal Bike Tours** (503-916-9704; www.pedalbiketours.com), 2249 N. Williams, leads two-hour guided bike tours of the metro area year-round for $49 including bike (bring your own and get $10 off). They also rent bikes at $9/hour. **Waterfront Bicycles** (503-227-1719; www.waterfrontbikes.net), 10 SW Ash Street, services and rents bikes ($9/hour). The city, too, offers **Portland by Cycle,** a series of free guided rides, in summer; see www.portlandonline.com/tranportation. Some favorite rides:

The paved, 12-mile **Waterfront Bike Loop** from the Sellwood Bridge north along the river, across the Steel Bridge, and south along the other side, runs through parks and the historic waterfront for nice river and city views.

A 12-mile loop around **Sauvie Island** is a nice respite from city riding; take US 30 north across the Sauvie Island Bridge and park in the gravel lot. Citywide and suburban bike maps are available from the **City of Portland Bicycle Program** (503-823-2925; www.portlandonline.com), 1120 SW Fifth Avenue, Portland.

The **Springwater Corridor** is a paved former railroad right-of-way connecting Waterfront Park to the suburb of Boring via a series of parks and wildlife refuges; about 16 miles.

Forest Park, with an entrance at NW 29th, offers miles of mountain bike trails, some shared with horses and hikers (please respect hiker- or equestrian-only trails); trail information is available from the Forest Park Conservancy (503-223-5449), 1507 SW 23rd Avenue, Portland.

In the suburbs, the **Clackamas County Bicycle Coordinator** (503-752-4500) publishes an extensive map of bike tour routes, mostly on back roads, from loops in the city's outskirts to a 70-mile excursion to Mount Hood.

CAMPING **Milo McIver State Park** (503-630-7150), off Springwater Road 1.2 miles north of S. Hayden Road, Estacada. Open mid-Mar.–Oct. You actually can camp in the metro area, here along the Clackamas River. Forty-four full hookup sites ($13–17), nine walk-in tent sites ($11–15), and one hiker-biker site.

CANOEING AND KAYAKING **eNRG Kayaking** (503-772-1122; www.enrgkayaking.com) offers kayaking tours and classes in Portland and nearby waters for all levels and nearly all ages.

GOLF **Colwood National Golf Club** (503-254-5515), 7313 NE Columbia Boulevard, Portland. Eighteen holes.

Eastmoreland Golf Course (503-775-2900), 2425 SE Bybee Boulevard, Portland. Eighteen holes.

Gresham Golf Course (503-665-3352), 2155 NE Division Street, Gresham. Eighteen holes.

Heron Lakes Golf Course (503-289-1818), 3500 N. Victory Boulevard, Portland. Two 18-hole courses.

King City Golf Course (503-639-7986), 15355 SW Royalty Parkway, King City. Nine holes.

Lake Oswego Golf Course (503-636-8228), 17525 SW Stafford Road, Lake Oswego. Eighteen holes.

Meriwether National Golf Club (503-648-4143), 5200 Rood Bridge Road, Hillsboro. Twenty-seven holes.

Redtail Golf Course (503-646-5166), 8200 SW Scholl's Ferry Road, Beaverton. Eighteen holes.

Rose City Golf Course (503-253-4744), 2200 NE 71st Avenue. Eighteen holes.

HIKING Portland is a walkable city. Strolling the neighborhoods is fun, but for a brisk stretch of the legs, take the **Westside Riverwalk** through **Tom McCall Waterfront Park,** 1.5 miles from Hawthorne Bridge to Steel Bridge. Return the same way or cross the bridge and walk back on the **Eastside Riverwalk.** Five-thousand-acre **Forest Park** contains almost 70 miles of trails (maps are available from the Friends of Forest Park, www.forestparkconservancy.org); the 30-mile **Wildwood Trail** through the park connects to the **40-Mile Loop** linking several regional greenways. In **Washington Park** trails meander through tall firs to link the Oregon Zoo, the Japanese Garden, and other attractions. **Powell Butte Nature Park** offers several miles of trails through meadows, cedar groves, and wetlands. For many further ideas, check www.explorepdx.com.

✷ Wilder Places

PARKS ✐ **Blue Lake Regional Park** (503-665-4995; www.oregonmetro.gov); take exit 14 off I-84 in Gresham and proceed north on 207th Avenue; turn right on Sandy Boulevard and left on 223rd Avenue. Daily 8 AM–sunset; parking $4. Enfolding a spring-fed lake, this park has something for everyone, from picnic shelters to rowboat and canoe rentals to swimming, games, playgrounds, and a natural garden. On hot, muggy summer days children and adults can cool off in the "spray ground," 3,500 square feet of spurting, climbable water features.

Howell Territorial Park (503-797-1700; www.oregonmetro.gov); take US 30 to the Sauvie Island Bridge, cross and go on a mile, and turn right onto Howell Park Road. Daily sunrise–sunset. A former farm with a restored 1850s farmhouse (not open to visitors), this is a rural spot to enjoy a picnic or stroll the trails.

Milo McIver State Park (503-630-7150), off Springwater Road 1.2 miles north of S. Hayden Road, Estacada. Open mid-Mar.–Oct. This is the only overnight state park in the greater Portland area, with 54 campsites, play areas, trails, and canoeing on the Clackamas River.

♿ **Tryon Creek State Natural Area** (503-636-9886), SW Terwilliger Boulevard, Portland. Free. Tryon Creek still harbors a steelhead run, and its square mile of green ravine minutes from downtown offers nature walks, a paved bike path, and an ADA-compliant trail.

♿ **Tualatin Hills Nature Park** (503-629-6350), 15655 SW Millikan Way, Beaverton. Daily sunrise–sunset. More than 200 acres of mixed forest, ponds, and meadows include an interpretive center and wheelchair-accessible nature trails.

Portland Parks and Recreation (503-823-PLAY; www.portlandonline.com/parks), 1120 SW Fifth Avenue, Portland. The city counts more than 10,000 acres of city parks, some small urban oases with graceful trees and benches, some larger, multipurpose parks, all adding up to plentiful open space and urban forest. A few favorites are:

Forest Park (503-823-4492), NW 29th and Upshur. Daily 5 AM–10 PM. This is the city's largest park, a native forest more than 7 seven miles long sprawling over 5,000 acres of Portland's northwest hills. Lewis and Clark reported Douglas firs with trunks 5 to 8 feet thick. Few of those giants remain, though there are some remarkable specimens, but as the largest forested city park in the United States, it is a precious urban wildland, harboring some rarer plants such as the Pacific yew and a multitude of animals, from songbirds to eagles and deer and squirrels to the occasional bear or bobcat. Two creeks and 70 miles of hiking, bicycle, and equestrian trails wind through it.

Laurelhurst Park, SE 39th Avenue and Stark Street. Until it was purchased by the city in 1909, this land was part of a dairy farm. Now in the middle of the city's busy east side, its 27 acres have a little of everything—shady walks, lawns, play areas, an off-leash dog area, and the original spring-fed pond.

Tom McCall Waterfront Park runs 1.5 miles along the west bank of the Willamette from SW Harrison Street to the Steel Bridge. Runners, walkers, and cyclists enjoy its paved path and close-up river views in all weather. Named for the feisty former governor who enacted the nation's first bottle bill and famously encouraged non-Oregonians to visit but not stay, it embodies some of Oregon's contradictions: the 185 jets of the fountain **Salmon Street Springs** create a merry, constantly shifting water display, while just downriver a plaza set off by a hundred cherry trees commemorates the deportation of Japanese Americans during the Second World War. The stern-wheeler *Portland,* docked at the seawall, houses the **Oregon Maritime Museum. *Portland Spirit*** offers Willamette River cruises from its dock below the fountain (see *Boat Tours*).

Washington Park (503-823-2525), SW Park Place. Daily 5 AM–10 PM. This father of all Portland parks is literally a people's park, being home to the **Oregon Zoo,** the **Japanese Garden,** the **International Rose Test Garden, Hoyt Arboretum,** the **Children's Museum,** and the **World Forestry Center,** connected by several miles of trails. Playgrounds, picnic tables, tennis, and archery areas dot the 130 acres. Founded in the West Hills in 1871 when that was still a wilderness, its earliest access was by cable car. It's still reachable by public transportation. This of all parks can be called Portland's backyard, where people go to enjoy nature, improve themselves, or just stretch out on a lawn and relax.

Butterfly Park, 7720 SW Macadam. This 1-acre park is part of a project to restore southern Portland's riverbanks. Its wet soil, shrubs, natural wildflowers, and grasses create habitat for various butterfly species and songbirds.

Cathedral Park, N. Edison Street and Pittsburgh Avenue. The "cathedral" here refers not to a place of worship, but to the Gothic-arched piers of the St. John's Bridge, under which the 23-acre park is nestled. Long a garbage-strewn eyesore, the spot found a champion in local resident Howard Galbraith, who in the 1970s raised millions to make a park of it. Today the grounds are green and pleasant, with a boat ramp, picnic tables, and an off-leash dog area. It's also thought to be the spot where William Clark camped with a party from the Corps of Discovery on Apr. 2, 1806, to reconnoiter the Willamette's mouth on Lewis and Clark's return voyage.

Mill Ends Park, SW Naito Parkway and Taylor Street. This is said to be the world's smallest park, and it may well be. At 24 inches across, it was intended to house a light pole in the median of Front Street (now Naito Parkway) back in 1946. But no light pole materialized. Dick Fagan, a reporter for the *Oregon Journal,* had an office overlooking the road. The weed-filled hole must have irritated him, for he soon pulled out the weeds, planted flowers, and began including fanciful pieces about the "park" in his column, *Mill Ends.* According to Fagan, the park was home to a colony of leprechauns whose pranks he duly reported. The spot became an official park on St. Patrick's Day, 1976, and is still a site (or at least a focal point) of St Patrick's Day festivities, picnics, concerts, and occasional bagpipers. (There is a bumper sticker reading KEEP PORTLAND WEIRD. Now you know why.)

♿ 🐾 **Mount Tabor Park,** SE 60th and Salmon Street, is draped over an extinct volcano. It includes lots of game areas, disabled access to play and picnic areas, walkways, and an off-leash dog area. Daily 5 AM–midnight.

Peninsula Park and Rose Garden, 700 N. Rosa Parks Way. This is a full-service family park complete with horseshoe pitch, tennis courts, playgrounds, and wading pool. It's also home to a formal rose garden, Portland's first—a sensation when it opened in 1913 and site of Portland's first rose festivals. The festivities later moved to the International Rose Test Garden, but this one remains the only sunken rose garden in Oregon and is arguably more artistic than the Test Garden, which is primarily experimental.

WILDLIFE REFUGES **Audubon Society of Portland** (503-292-6855; www.audubonportland.org), 5151 NW Cornell Road, Portland. Daily dawn–dusk. Free. The local Audubon Society chapter sits on a 150-acre sanctuary adjoining Forest Park. Four miles of trails wind through the moist mixed conifer forest and along Balch Creek, with its population of cutthroat trout and its stand of old-growth Douglas fir (recalling prelogging days in the Pacific Northwest). In spring trillium and other wildflowers dot the forest floor. And, of course, a variety of wild creatures inhabit the woods, such as the moisture-loving Pacific giant salamander. Four miles of trails and a pond pavilion allow for a leisurely appreciation. You may want to visit some of the "educational birds" in the 70-year-old Wildlife Care Center (open daily 9–5); the center treats and rehabilitates more than three thousand injured animals a year and is home to some who could no longer survive in the wild. A small nature store is open Mon.–Sat. 10–6 and Sun. 10–5.

Beggars-tick Wildlife Refuge (503-797-1850; www.metro-region.org), 111 SE 111th Avenue, just north of Foster Road, Portland. Daily 8 AM–sunset. Free. The name may not be prepossessing (it refers to a native sunflower), but the little 20-acre refuge is a wetland magnet for waterfowl in winter and a dry meadow in summer. Near the Springwater Corridor, it's also accessible by foot or bike.

Camassia Natural Area, at the end of Walnut Street in West Linn. Blue camas, a Native American staple, blooms abundantly here among rock outcrops exposed by the Missoula floods twelve thousand to nineteen thousand years ago. The Nature Conservancy works to conserve rare plants such as the white rock larkspur and maintains trails (muddy in spring) and interpretive signs on its 26-acre preserve.

Little Rock Island (503-802-8100), in the Willamette River just upstream of West Linn. Another Nature Conservancy protectorate, this 32-acre island with both forested and bare, rocky ground is famous for its wildflowers, including some rare species. If you have a boat, you can get there from the boat launch at Willamette Falls Park in West Linn.

Mount Talbert Nature Park (503-794-8041), 10695 SE Mather Road, Clackamas. Two characteristic but increasingly rare Willamette Valley habitats are conserved on Mount Talbert, an old lava dome: an oak savanna and a wet native prairie. Camas lily blooms in season. Songbirds, deer, and even coyotes roam the 144 acres, while picnic tables and trails welcome human visitors.

Oaks Bottom Wildlife Refuge (503-823-6131), SE Seventh Avenue and Sellwood Boulevard, Portland. Daily 5 AM–midnight. Right in the middle of the city, this refuge is 140 acres of wetland on the east bank of the Willamette. Part of it covers an old landfill, but now it's favored by ducks, songbirds, and great blue heron. The Springwater Corridor bike trail runs through it, as do walking paths and a railroad.

Sauvie Island Wildlife Area (503-621-3488), 18330 NW Sauvie Island Road, Portland. Between the Willamette and the Columbia just northwest of Portland, Sauvie Island was a plentiful hunting and gathering ground for several hundred Multnomah Indians when Lewis and Clark stopped by in the fall of 1805. Its waters blanketed by wintering ducks and geese (Clark complains of their "horid noise"), and rich in wapato, a native tuber, this indeed must have been a happy hunting ground. Today it's mostly farmland, but 12,000 acres have been set aside for wildlife. They are a prime bird-watching area with thousands of migratory waterfowl in fall and winter, and bald eagles, cranes, and 250 other species present at one season or another. Several beaches line the Columbia River side, of which one, Collins Beach, is clothing optional. Trails, fishing in the rivers or lakes, a picnic area, and a boat ramp all beckon. Some areas are closed Oct.–mid-Apr., except to hunters holding a special permit from the Oregon Department of Fish and Wildlife. Parking permit $3.50, available at the store just over the bridge.

Smith and Bybee Wetlands Natural Area (503-797-1850; www.metro-region.org); leave I-5 at exit 307 and take N. Marine Drive west for 2.2 miles. Daily sunrise–sunset. Free. In the midst of warehouse and port structures, the natural skein of slough, forest, and waterways where the Willamette flows into the Columbia has been restored—at least 2,000 acres of it, forming the largest protected wetland in any American city. Trails, lakes, guided nature walks, viewing platforms, and a new canoe launch allow you to observe nature from land or water. Otter cavort and osprey soar in the wild zone that is much as Lewis and Clark might have seen it.

Tualatin River National Wildlife Refuge (503-625-5944), 19255 SW Pacific Highway, Sherwood; off US 99W about 15 miles southwest of Portland. Refuge open dawn–dusk; wildlife center open Tues.–Sun. 10–4. Free. Nature trails, a wildlife center, and wildlife-viewing platforms open a window to the creatures now squeezed among urban sprawl. Three thousand acres of Tualatin River floodplain habitat were designated in 1992 to protect waterfowl, salmon, and steelhead habitat. No pets or bicycles.

✷ Lodging

BED & BREAKFASTS

Gresham

Forest Springs Bed and Breakfast (1-877-674-9282; www.forestspring.com), 3680 SW Towle Avenue. The hundred-year-old house sits above the street on an 1885 land grant amid trees and terraced gardens. Luckily this is one B&B that takes kids—two of the three rooms can be connected to form a suite. From $95, with full breakfast.

Milwaukie

Historic Broetje House (503-659-8860; www.thebroetjehouse.com), 3101 SE Courtney Road. When the sprawling Victorian was built, Milwaukie was the country. Today it's a short drive from downtown, and the 1889 house welcomes the tired visitor with three comfy rooms and an acre of gardens. $65–115, including full breakfast. Children welcome.

Portland

A Painted Lady Inn (503-335-0070; www.apaintedladyinn.com), 1927 NE 16th Avenue. In a neighborhood of fine older homes, A Painted Lady dates from 1894 and comes complete with porch swing, living-room fireplace, garden patio, and five guest rooms (some with shared bath). Owner Judy Runge serves up the daily *Oregonian* and a hearty breakfast. $109–179.

Blue Plum Inn (1-877-288-3844; www.bluepluminn.com), 2026 NE 15th Avenue. The trim, two-gabled house offers four cozy guest rooms and a copious breakfast, and sits on a public transportation line. From $114.

The Georgian House (1-888-282-2250; www.thegeorgianhouse.com), 1828 NE Siskiyou. This handsome brick home would fit right into the Georgian neighborhoods of New York or Washington, D.C., though it was only built in 1922. Calm and elegant without being overwhelming, it invites you to decompress by the fireplace or in the sunroom before retiring. Four historically themed rooms sleep two to four. Take a walk around the lush rose and lavender gardens—they've been featured in *Better Homes and Gardens*. $85–125.

Heron Haus (503-274-1846; www.heronhaus.com), 2545 NW Westover Road. Okay, this one's a splurge, but consider: you're getting a 10,000-square-foot, ivy-covered 1904 Tudor-style mansion in Portland's West Hills. Not all to yourself, of course; there are six rooms, but you have the run of all the common areas (parlor, sunroom, library, patio, and garden), and you're close to the rose garden, zoo, Forest Park, and much more. A faithful renovation has combined the solid Tudor with contemporary appointments for a graceful, comfortable stay. Doubles $145–195, singles from $95; with breakfast.

♿ **Hostess House** (1-800-760-7799; www.hostesshouse.com), 5758 NE Emerson Street. Just a regular house in a regular Portland neighborhood, but one owned by a former schoolteacher with an urge for hospitality. Milli Laughlin makes two guest rooms available, each with private bath (one handicapped accessible), and you'll wake up to a hearty homemade breakfast—and yes, Milli does share recipes. She'll also accommodate special diets with advance notice. Supervised children are welcome. Doubles $85, singles $75.

Inn at Marquam Hill (503-223-6617; www.innatmarquamhill.com), 3412 SW 13th Avenue. In the hills overlooking Oregon Health Sciences University and Portland's medical complex, the inn offers seven comfortable rooms (some with shared bath), sitting rooms, and common living and dining room. Owners Mike and Leslie Watson host medical residents, researchers, and relatives of patients at the several hospitals, as well as recreational travelers, and dispense local wisdom to all. Nearby is Marquam Park, with access to Portland's 40-mile Loop Trail. Doubles $89–105, with Mike's famous breakfast; long-term rates available.

Lion and Rose (503-287-9245; www.lionrose.com), 1810 NE 15th Avenue. Weddings can and do take place in this particularly flamboyant 1906 Queen Anne, but it's equally appropriate for any special weekend. Six guest rooms in full Victorian regalia all come with private bath and lavish breakfast, not to mention such updates as free Internet. It's in a historic neighborhood a few blocks from shopping and restaurants. Supervised children over 10 are welcome. Doubles from $124, but check for specials.

Portland's White House (1-800-272-7131; www.portlandswhitehouse.com), 1914 NE 22nd Avenue. It does look a lot like *the* White House, only slightly smaller. This was the summer home of lumber baron Robert Lytle, built in 1911 to his exacting specifications—inlaid oak floors, grand columns, manicured grounds, and all. Five large rooms in the main house are adorned with four-poster beds, elegant antiques, Persian rugs, and all modern conveniences, and the three in the carriage house are only slightly more restrained. Doubles $135–235, with full breakfast.

GUEST HOUSES

Portland

✐ **Bluebird Guesthouse** (1-866-717-4333; www.bluebirdguesthouse.com), 3517 SE Division. This is your budget choice if you don't care for hostels. Near the relaxed Hawthorne neighborhood, with cafés and restaurants as good as downtown's but easier to get into, the Bluebird is a straightforward 1910 frame house with a friendly front porch, free Wi-Fi, and (not to be sneezed at) free on-street parking. Seven simply furnished rooms, mostly with shared bath, are named for contemporary authors, plus you have the run of the spacious kitchen and living room. From $55, with self-serve continental breakfast; children over four welcome.

Everett Street Guesthouse (503-230-0211; www.everettstreetguesthouse.com), 2306 NW Everett Street. As owner Terry Rusinow says, there are no frilly curtains, teddy bears, or potpourri. This is a straightforward 1907 Craftsman in and out (Terry used to have a crafts gallery himself, so he should know). Two guest rooms and two living rooms are warmly and comfortably decorated with pieces from Terry's art collection, and a short walk will take you to bakeries, restaurants, nearby Laurelhurst Park, and a $3 movie theater. Doubles $65–80 with shared bath, including large continental breakfast. The new adjacent cottage goes for $100 ($650/week), without breakfast.

Northwest Portland Hostel and Guesthouse (1-888-777-0067; www.nwportlandhostel.com), 425 NW 18th Avenue. Partly a hostel and partly a guest house, this budget alternative is in walking distance of most downtown attractions. The international staff is friendly, the rooms are clean, and the dowager Portland house makes you feel right at home (there's even free Wi-Fi). Dorm rooms hold four to eight beds, while guest house rooms range from small bed-and-chair arrangements to a comfortable bed-sitting room with bay window. Linens are provided, but baths are shared. Dorm beds $20–25, guest house rooms $28–74; add $3 if you're not a Hostelling International member.

HOSTELS

Portland

Northwest Portland Hostel and Guesthouse (see *Guest Houses*), in the Pearl District, is in walking distance of all downtown attractions.

Portland Hawthorne Hostel (1-866-447-3031; www.portlandhostel.org), 3031 SW Hawthorne Avenue. The semibohemian Hawthorne district lies east of downtown and across the river. The hostel occupies a 1909 house and is clean, friendly, and safe, with both dorm and fairly spartan private rooms. It's just steps from interesting little shops and the historic Bagdad Theatre, and a short bus ride from downtown. Linens are provided, and you get free pastries in the morning. Free Wi-Fi. Dorm beds $19–23, private/family rooms $48–55 (children under 19 stay free in private rooms). Add $3 if you're not a member of Hostelling International. Arriving independently by bike gets you $5 off.

HOTELS

Portland

The Heathman Hotel (1-800-551-0011; www.portland.heathmanhotel.com), 1001 SW Broadway. The Heathman was the last built of Portland's grand hotels, finished in 1927. It was propitiously located in the middle of the arts and theater district, and still is—the street's not named Broadway for nothing. Sumptuously restored and updated in the 1980s, it's a luxury hotel that manages to feel hometown friendly, even offering child care. Its more uncommon amenities include a library consisting of signed copies of books by author-guests, and a mezzanine passageway to the adjacent Arlene Schnitzer Concert Hall. And, of course, a slew of environmentally friendly practices. Parking is $29/night, but the fee is waived if you buy a theater or art package—or show up in an ecofriendly vehicle! Doubles $189–325.

Inn@Northrup Station (1-800-224-1180; www.northrupstation.com), 2025 NW Northrup Street. At first blush it looks as if it could have been a station, but no—the brick and industrial materials are intentional (the streetcar does stop just down the street). The retro-hip decor seems to look back at the early 1960s through a haze, but the rooms are spacious, with kitchens, sofas, balconies or patios, and wireless. What's more, you're in the middle of the vibrant Pearl District, with its gamut of restaurants and boutiques. From $114, including breakfast and a streetcar pass.

Jupiter Hotel (1-877-800-0004; www.jupiterhotel.com), 800 E. Burnside. This former motel has metamorphosed into a boutiquey hot spot aimed mainly at the young and hip, with minimalist-chic rooms, a courtyard fire pit, and the attached Doug Fir Lounge, featuring local indie music. You can get a room for $59 if you check in after midnight—not a bad deal for night owls and heavy sleepers. Doubles, normally, from $89.

Mark Spencer Hotel (1-800-548-3934; www.markspencer.com), 409 SW 11th Avenue. This old favorite has been around forever, or at least since 1907, when it was called the Nortonia. With comfortably traditional furnishings, friendly service, and a location right smack in the Arts District, it's been the choice for generations of gallery- and theatergoers. Doubles from $99, including breakfast and afternoon tea and cookies.

McMenamins White Eagle (1-866-271-3377; www.mcmenamins.com), 836 N. Russell Street. The White Eagle advertises itself as a café, saloon, and rock 'n' roll hotel. Which is sort of an unusual combination, but apparently successful. Begun in 1905 by two Poles to cater to the motley waterfront crowd, it's still long, narrow, and dark, full of polished wood (including the magnificently carved mahogany bar) and atmosphere. There are stories of ghosts, customers shanghaied to waiting ships, an opium den in the basement, and other clandestine activities, some of which are undoubtedly true. The staff maintain that the Eagle really deserves the title of the oldest saloon in Portland because it kept serving (quietly) right through Prohibition, while its competitor, Henry's, didn't open until repeal. There's live music every night till the wee hours (till 11 PM Sun.), which doesn't stop the 11 rooms upstairs from filling up most nights. Bunk beds $40, doubles $45–50; baths are shared.

The Nines (1-877-229-9995; www.thenines.com), 525 SW Morrison. The Nines opened in 2008 as Portland's newest luxury hotel, just before the economy spiraled—not so good for its investors, but as of this writing, it meant deals were to be had. Situated on the top three floors of one of the city's oldest department stores, it commands a nice view as well as a central location on Pioneer Square. Sleek without being cold (in fact, some rooms have fireplaces), it offers all the luxury necessities, like pillow-top beds, a fitness center, marble bathrooms, and no fewer than three restaurants. Doubles normally from $249, but check those discounts.

University Place Hotel (1-866-845-4647; www.cegs.pdx.edu), 310 SW Lincoln Street. On the campus of Portland State University, this offers all the amenities of a higher-end motel with a convenient downtown location. Doubles $129, including breakfast; $12 parking.

✷ Where to Eat

DINING OUT

Portland

Andina (503-228-9535; www.andinarestaurant.com), 1314 NW Glisan. Daily for lunch and dinner. With Peruvian chefs and ownership, Andina's mission is to revitalize and re-present pre-Columbian and colonial ingredients, recombining them with decidedly foreign elements—Peruvian home cooking gone haute cuisine (quinoa appears in several intriguing forms, but I didn't see any guinea pig on the menu). A burst of creativity has produced several vegetarian and even gluten-free dishes. Not cheap, but there is a daily happy hour.

Castagna (503-231-7373; www.castagnarestaurant.com), 1752 SE Hawthorne Boulevard. Open Wed.–Sat. for dinner. European regional cuisines with a Northwest accent vary seasonally here, featuring dishes seldom found in Portland, or elsewhere in Oregon for that matter: Nettle-and-spinach cannelloni! Lamb sausage with buckwheat polenta! I never did find out about the Purgatorio bean puree. Most food is fresh and local, and the delicatessen—sopressata, mortadella, pâté, etc.—are actually made in-house. If the prices seem high, check **Café Castagna** next door (503-239-9939; serves lunch and dinner), where you can find some (though not all) of the same dishes. Reservations recommended.

The Heathman Hotel (503-790-7752; www.heathmanrestaurantandbar.com), 1001 SW Broadway. The Heathman is not only a great Portland hotel, it's a great Portland restaurant featuring the best of seasonally adjusted, creative "nouvelle Northwest" cuisine at breakfast, lunch, and dinner. Oregon berries with goat cheese? Sturgeon in Calvados sauce? Yes, please. If your budget is tight, the bar serves smaller portions of many of the same dishes at much reduced prices during the daily happy hour (4–6 PM).

Plainfields (503-223-2995; www.plainfields.com), 852 SW 21st Avenue. Daily for dinner. Plainfields has been pleasing critics and regular people continuously since 1977 with fine Indian cuisine, kept authentic by the Pune branch of the family. And every so often chef Craig Plainfield will have a "whimsy night" where he pairs dishes of other cuisines with fine wines. The wine list, by the way, has earned plaudits from *Wine Spectator* for length, breadth, and quality.

Wildwood Restaurant (503-248-9663; www.wildwoodrestaurant.com), 1221 NW 21st Avenue. Daily for dinner, Mon.–Sat. for lunch. Nowadays you'd call him a locavore, but that just means you buy good and fresh. When Cory Schreiber founded Wildwood in the mid-1990s, he bought from the multitude of small farms surrounding Portland and based dishes on all they had to offer: Hood River fruits, Northwest mussels, Willamette Valley berries, wines, and more. Cory recently moved on to the state Department of Agriculture to promote healthful school lunches, but chef Dustin Clark continues the Wildwood tradition, scouring the mountains for fresh mushrooms and chasing down lettuce and lambs from regional farms (preferably, of course, organic and sustainable). It seems to work; the restaurant has earned accolades all round. Not inexpensive, but there's a bar menu. Reservations suggested.

EATING OUT

Milwaukie

Bob's Red Mill Whole Grain Store and Visitors Center (503-607-6455; www.bobsredmill.com), 5000 SE International Way. Mon.–Fri. 6–6, Sat. 7–5. Bob Moore sure keeps his nose to the grindstone. In the 1960s, like some others, he became obsessed with stone-ground grains; unlike others, he actually bought some old millstones and started milling in California. Ten years later, he and his wife retired to Oregon but couldn't resist buying an old mill and producing all sorts of stone-ground flours and cereals. Today he markets nationwide; you've probably seen the little plastic sacks with the rustic red label in your local store. You can breakfast or lunch here on various wholesome cereals, pastries, and breads, and buy that particular flour (soy, oat, barley, semolina . . .) or muesli you've been looking for. Tours of the actual mill are offered daily.

Portland

Food carts (www.foodcartsportland.com) are the way to get a quick and interesting snack. The choices range from Belgian frites to Vietnamese pho by way of bento, burritos, goulash, curry, and about every cuisine Portland has to offer, including just plain quirky. For listings, partial menus, and maps, check the Web site.

Bambuza Vietnam Bistro (503-206-6330; www.bambuza.com), 3682 SW Bond Avenue. Open for lunch and dinner. Brightly painted walls and silk lanterns are the setting; traditional Vietnamese cuisine is the gem. The fare here is modern Vietnamese/Northwestern, where the crab may be Dungeness and the produce aims for the fresh and local (well, maybe not the papaya). You'll find reliable Vietnamese specialties with generous outreach to vegetarians (they even offer a vegetarian pho). And the price is right.

Bridgeport Brewing Company (503-241-3612; www.bridgeportbrew.com), 1313 NW Marshall Street. Daily for lunch and dinner. Bridgeport was the first microbrewery in a town that is now, so to speak, crawling with them. In 1984 a couple of winemakers hired a brewer and set up shop in an abandoned rope factory, and, well, the rest is history. Here you can imbibe the original Portland pub culture with a bottle, a pub lunch, or dinner, complete with breads and pastries made on-site as traditionally as the beer.

Cha Cha Cha Taqueria (503-295-4077; www.chaportland.com), 305 NW 21st. Open for lunch and dinner. With eight locations around Portland, Cha has made a name for itself with healthy, sustainable, low-cholesterol, and probably even fair-trade Mexican food at reasonable prices. All your favorites, and good for you, too. And it must be kid friendly, because my granddaughters loved it.

Kells Irish Restaurant and Pub (503-227-4057; www.kellsirish.com), 112 SW Second Avenue. Daily for lunch and dinner, weekends for breakfast. Kells is renowned throughout the Northwest, not only for its Guinness and Harp (which, after all, you can get elsewhere), but for its rousing atmosphere and nightly live Irish music by groups both regional and international. The fare is billed as New World Irish, with dishes like lamb stew, shepherd's pie, and corned beef rubbing shoulders with crabcakes and oyster shooters. A lot of the cooking seems to involve Guinness. A must-visit if you're even slightly drawn to things Irish.

Ken's Artisan Bakery (503-248-2022; www.kensartisan.com), 338 NW 21st Avenue. Mon.–Sat. 7–6, Sun. 8–5. In the lively Pearl District (and conveniently close to the International Guesthouse and Hostel), Ken's is just the place to sit with a cup and a croissant or pick up your baguette for dinner. Ken has painstakingly acquired the knowledge and craft of French bakers and bakes a variety of loaves and pastries according to daily inspiration. This is as good as it gets west of the Atlantic.

Laughing Planet Café (503-235-6472; www.laughingplanetcafe.com), 3320 SE Belmont Street. Open for lunch and dinner. In its own words, Laughing Planet is "dedicated to making wholesome food accessible to regular folks with time constraints," going so far as to make a burrito that will fit in a bike's water bottle carrier. Truly affordable (I didn't find an item over $6.50) and determinedly ecofriendly, the café's smoothies, salads, soups, and burritos are made mostly of local, unprocessed ingredients. The decor is often quirky—that's the "laughing" part—and the several branches are set in vibrant, often regenerating parts of town: 922 NW 21st Avenue, 3765 N. Mississippi Street, 4110 SE Woodstock Boulevard, and 4405 SW Vermont Street.

Nicholas Restaurant (503-235-5123; www.nicholasrestaurant.com), 318 SE Grand. Daily for lunch and dinner. You might be elbow to elbow with your neighbor at this cheerfully noisy eatery, but the Lebanese soul food is so satisfying (and so quickly served) that it just seems cozy. Try the tender, triangular spinach pie, a light distant cousin to the phyllo-wrapped Greek version, or the fresh, light tabouleh, or—need I continue? Many dishes can be made vegetarian or vegan upon request.

Noble Rot (503-233-1999; www.noblerotpdx.com), 1111 E. Burnside. Mon.–Thurs. 5–11 PM, Fri.–Sat. 5–midnight. I'm sorry, but that's what it's called. This is because it's a wine bar. You can go to taste wines from Oregon to Australia, and/or to eat from a short but respectable menu of soups, salads, and main dishes with a Continental flavor.

✐ **Old Wives' Tales** (503-238-0470; www.oldwivestalesrestaurant.com), 1300 E. Burnside. For 30 years Old Wives' Tales has sat on this untrendy corner, serving breakfast, lunch, and dinner from an international variety of cuisines. Numerous vegetarian, vegan, gluten-free, and lactose-free choices also adorn the menu, making this a place to go if your group has varied dietary requirements .Prices are moderate and—get this—in addition to three dining rooms, there is a kids' playroom, so parents (and nonparents) can eat in peace.

Rimsky-Korsakoffeehouse (503-232-2640), 707 SE 12th Street. Serving coffees, teas, and homemade desserts evenings only; closed Mon. The lights are low and the music classical (and often live) as you sip espresso over a chocolate torte. The remodel of the old Victorian home preserved the polished woodwork and floors but left room for quirky new art in odd places.

St. Honoré Boulangerie (503-445-4342; www.sainthonorebakery.com), 2335 NW Thurman Street and 315 First Street, Lake Oswego. Open daily. St. Honoré being the patron saint of bakers, this is the place to go for a little bit of France and enjoy a croissant, brioche, or croque monsieur. Dominique Guelin serves up traditional breads, cakes, and sandwiches.

Stumptown Coffee Roasters (503-230-7702; www.stumptowncoffee.com), 4525 SE Division Street. Open daily. Stumptown is Portland's answer to Starbucks. Since 1999 they have traveled to the far coffee-growing corners of the world to find and foster fine beans cultivated sustainably—ecologically and economically. At this, the original location, you can buy any of their selected beans or blends, or come in out of the rain and enjoy a cup. Other locations are: 3352 and 3356 SE Belmont; 128 SW Third Street; and 1026 SW Stark, in the Ace Hotel. (They've even dared to invade Seattle, but that's another story.)

Townshend's Tea (503-445-6699; www.townshendstea.com), 2223 NE Alberta Street. Open daily. Named ambiguously for the author of the 1767 Townshend Acts, which taxed tea imports to the colonies and were the catalyst for the Boston Tea Party, its pudgy sofas and the daily paper make this a place to come out of the rain and kick back with a high-quality tea. Then go out and peruse the shopfronts of the renascent Alberta neighborhood.

Trébol (503-517-9347; www.trebolpdx.com), 4835 N. Albina Avenue. Daily for dinner and Sun. brunch. Wild boar tacos? Hamburger on a caramelized leek bun, with jalapeño aioli? This is a Mexican restaurant with a difference. On Portland's evolving north side, its emphasis is on fresh seasonal ingredients. You can get your huevos rancheros and enchiladas, but don't look for bell peppers in Jan. And it happily follows that Portland institution, the happy hour.

✷ Entertainment

Check out ***Willamette Week,*** Portland's free "alternative" news weekly, for happenings of all sorts. Here are some venues to count on:

Crystal Ballroom (503-225-0047), 1332 W. Burnside, Portland. This place has been famous since 1914 for its floating dance floor, now fully restored. Now it hosts regional and national progressive rock groups, folk, reggae, and the Left Coast Eisteddfodd.

Oregon Symphony (503-228-1353; www.orsymphony.org), 1037 SW Broadway, Portland, in the Arlene Schnitzer Concert Hall.

Portland Baroque Orchestra (503-222-6000; www.pbo.org) plays at the First Baptist Church and at Kaul Auditorium of Reed College.

Portland Center for the Performing Arts (503-248-4335; www.pcpa.com), 1111 SW Broadway, Portland, is a clearinghouse for many of the major and minor area companies.

Portland Center Stage (503-445-3700; www.pcs.org), 128 NW 11th Avenue, Portland. Originally a "sister" to Ashland's Oregon Shakespeare Festival, Portland Center Stage has been presenting live theater by playwrights new and old for more than 20 years with about 10 productions per season. Tickets start at about $15.

Portland Opera (503-241-1802; www.portlandopera.org), 211 SE Caruthers Street, Portland.

White Eagle Saloon (503-282-6810), 836 N. Russell Street, Portland. Folk, rock, and undefinable; also open-mike nights.

✷ Shopping

Portland Saturday Market (503-222-6072; www.portlandsaturdaymarket.com), under the Burnside Bridge on SW Naito Boulevard and in adjoining Ankeny Park. Sat. 10–5 and Sun. 11–4:30, Mar.–Dec. 24. Rain or shine, you'll find work by all kinds of local artisans, plus a food court offering fare from the Northwest to Kathmandu.

Powell's Books (1-800-878-7323; www.powells.com), 1005 W. Burnside, Portland. Daily 9 AM–11 PM. Powell's is the biggest independent bookstore in the United States, if not the world, and is practically Portland's living room. A bibliophilic labyrinth, its main store takes up a whole city block, and with several other locations around town, it stocks over a million new, used, and rare books. Sit in the store café to peruse your latest acquisition.

✷ Events

February: **Portland Jazz Festival** (1-888-828-5299; www.pdxjazz.com/festival), second week, at various venues around Portland. Some concerts are free.

April: **Faux Film Festival** (www.fauxfilm.com), the weekend closest to April Fools' Day, Hollywood Theatre, Portland. Mockumentaries, satires, spoofs, and parodies of films that may or may not exist.

May: **Cinco de Mayo** (503-232-7550; www.cincodemayo.org), first weekend, Tom McCall Waterfront Park. All things Mexican, including performers from Portland's sister city, Guadalajara.

June: **Lake Oswego Festival of the Arts** (503-636-1060; www.lakewood-center.org), last weekend, Lake Oswego. Juried exhibits in various media by local and international artists.

Portland Rose Festival (503-227-2681; www.rosefestival.org), first two weeks, downtown Portland. An elaborate parade, a queen, concerts, races, and roses galore—it's been going on for a hundred years.

June–July: **Chamber Music Northwest** (503-223-3202; www.cmnw.org), at Reed College and Catlin Gable School, Portland. Preconcert picnics on the lawn have become a staple of this festival.

July: **Oregon Brewers' Festival** (503-778-5917; www.oregonbrewfest.com), last full weekend, Tom McCall Waterfront Park, Portland. Craft beers, exhibits, and entertainment. Minors and designated drivers get free root beer.

Waterfront Blues Festival (503-973-FEST; www.waterfrontbluesfest.com), first weekend, various venues around Portland. Performances and workshops.

August: **Bite of Oregon** (1-800-452-0600; www.biteoforegon.com), early in the month, Waterfront Park, Portland. Food, beer, and wine from around the city as far as the eye can see.

Mount Hood Jazz Festival (503-661-2700; www.mthoodjazz.org), mid-month, Mount Hood Community College, Gresham. Jazz, wine tasting, kids' activities, and more.

Tualatin Crawfish Festival (503-692-0780; www.tualatincrawfishfestival.com), Tualatin. Music, contests, food, and cookoffs, all celebrating the crawfish.

December: **Parade of Christmas Ships** (www.christmasships.org), Columbia and Willamette rivers. For 10 evenings in Dec., an illuminated flotilla parades Portland's waterways; check Web site for routes and times.

NORTHERN WILLAMETTE VALLEY

The lower reaches of the Willamette River can fairly be called the historic cradle of Oregon. Here's where a handful of farmers and artisans voted for territorial self-government; where Oregon Trail emigrants shortly afterward poured in; where the utopian Aurora Colony was founded and foundered; in short, where motley crowds came to do what Americans do best, that is, reinvent themselves. The first Oregon missions took root here, and the first Oregon universities. The first peoples, though, suffered the same tragedies as elsewhere: disease, attack, and confinement on the Grande Ronde reservation (now very visible from the highway with its huge casino complex).

Sure, you can challenge Oregon's rugged expanses. But the frontier was right here. And what better way to absorb it than by gently touring its pioneer towns and cemeteries, its fields and farms, and, oh yes, its vineyards and eateries?

GUIDANCE **Albany Convention and Visitors' Association** (541-928-0911; www.albanyvisitors.com), 250 Broadalbin Street SW #110, Albany 97321.

Aurora Colony Visitors' Association (503-939-0312; www.auroracolony.com), P.O. Box 86, Aurora 97002.

Brownsville Chamber of Commerce (541-466-3470; www.brownsvilleoregon.org), P.O. Box 148, Brownsville 97327.

Chehalem Valley Chamber of Commerce (503-538-2014; www.chehalemvalley.org), 415 E. Sheridan Street, Newberg 97132.

Clackamas Valley Regional Visitor Information at Clackamas Chamber of Commerce (503-682-3411; www.wilsonvillechamber.com), 29600 SW Park Place, Wilsonville 97070.

Corvallis Tourism (1-800-334-8118; www.visitcorvallis.com), 553 NW Harrison Boulevard, Corvallis 97330.

Keizer Chamber of Commerce Visitors Center (1-888-218-4747; www.keizerchamber.com), 980 Chemawa Road NE, Keizer 97303.

McMinnville Chamber of Commerce (503-472-6196; www.mcminnville.org), 417 NW Adams Street, McMinnville 97128.

Molalla Area Chamber of Commerce (503-829-6941; www.molallachamber.com), 101 N. Molalla Avenue, Molalla 97038.

Mount Angel Chamber of Commerce (503-845-9440; www.oktoberfest.org), 5 N. Garfield Street, Mount Angel 97362.

Oregon Parks and Recreation (503-986-0707 or 1-800-551-6949; www.oregon.gov), 725 Summer Street NE, Salem 97301.

Philomath Area Chamber of Commerce (541-929-2454; www.philomathchamber.org), 2395 Main Street, Philomath 97370.

Salem Convention and Visitors'Association (1-800-874-7012; www.travelsalem.com), 1313 Mill Street SE, Salem 97301.

Silverton Area Chamber of Commerce (503-873-5615; www.silvertonchamber.org), 426 S. Water Street, Silverton 97381.

Stayton/Sublimity Chamber of Commerce (503-769-3464; www.staytonsublimitychamber.org), 266 N. Third Avenue, Stayton 97383.

Sweet Home Chamber of Commerce (541-367-6186; www.sweethomechamber.org), 1575 Main Street, Sweet Home 97386.

West Valley Chamber of Commerce (503-843-4443), 142 NW Yamhill, Sheridan 97378.

Willamette National Forest (541-225-6300), 3106 Pierce Parkway, Suite D, Springfield 97477.

Willamette Valley Visitors Association (1-866-548-5018; www.oregonwinecountry.org), 250 Broadalbin Street SW #110, Albany 97321.

Woodburn Area Chamber of Commerce (503-982-8221; www.woodburnchamber.org), 2241 Country Club Road, Woodburn 97071.

GETTING THERE *By bus:* **Greyhound** (1-800-231-2222; www.greyhound.com) serves several valley cities, including Salem, Albany, Newberg, and Corvallis.

By car: **I-5** is the north–south artery, while **OR 22** and **US 20** cross the valley east–west, through Salem and Corvallis respectively.

By rail: **AMTRAK** (1-800-USA-RAIL) stops in Salem and Albany on its Coast Starlight and AMTRAK Cascades routes.

GETTING AROUND *By bus:* **Cherriots** (503-588-2877; www.cherriots.org) is the local bus system serving the Salem-Keizer metropolitan area. You'll want a car to visit wineries and the bucolic valley countryside.

MEDICAL EMERGENCY **Good Samaritan Regional Medical Center** (541-768-5111), 3600 NW Samaritan Drive, Corvallis.

Providence Newberg Medical Center (503-537-1555), 1001 Providence Drive, Newberg.

Salem Hospital (503-561-5200), 665 Winter Street SE, Salem.

Samaritan Albany General Hospital (541-812-4000), 1046 Sixth Avenue SW, Albany.

Silverton Hospital (1-888-573-1500), 342 Fairview, Silverton.

West Valley Hospital (503-623-8301), 525 SE Washington Street, Dallas.

✷ To See

COVERED BRIDGES In the old days, when Silverton was dry, residents could go to the **Gallon House Bridge** about a mile northwest of town and inconspicuously pick up a gallon jug of hooch left by their kindly neighbors in wet Mount Angel. Numerous, more law-abiding covered bridges still dot the valley, some of the easiest to visit being: **Irish Bend Bridge,** relocated to the OSU campus in Corvallis from Irish Bend Road; the **Stayton-Jordan Bridge** in Stayton, destroyed by fire in 1988 and rebuilt; the **Weddle Bridge** in Sankey Park in Sweet Home; and **Short Bridge,** a mile east of Cascadia State Park, formerly called Whiskey Butte Bridge for reasons one can only guess. A complete list of covered bridges with a map is available from Corvallis Tourism (see *Guidance*) or from www.covered-bridges.org.

FARMERS' MARKETS **Albany Farmers' Market** (541-752-1510; www.locallygrown.org), City Hall parking lot at Fourth and Ellsworth, Albany. Sat. 9–1, Apr.–Nov.

Calapooia Food Alliance (541-868-4822), 260 N. Main Street, Brownsville. Sat. 9–1, May–Oct.

Corvallis Farmers' Market (541-752-1510), two Corvallis locations: First and Jackson, Sat. 9–1; and Second and B streets, Wed. 3–7; mid-Apr.–late Nov.

Dundee Farmers' Market (503-201-2916), Seventh Street and US 99, Dundee. Sun. 10–2, late May–Sept.

Kings Valley Farmers' Market (541-929-5910), corner of Kings Valley Highway and Maxwell Creek Road, Philomath. Sun. 1–4, mid-June–mid-Oct.

McMinnville Farmers' Market (503-434-0651), Cowls Street between Second and Third, McMinnville. Thurs. 1:30–6, late May–mid-Oct.

Newberg Farmers' and Artisan Market (503-537-7190), School Street between First and Hancock streets, Newberg. Sat. 10–2, early June–Sept.

ONE OF OREGON'S REMAINING COVERED BRIDGES, SHORT BRIDGE, CROSSES THE SOUTH FORK OF THE SANTIAM RIVER.

Salem Public Market (503-623-6605), 1240 Rural Avenue SE, Salem. Sat. 8:30–1, year-round. This is an indoor, heated market.

Salem Saturday Market and **Wednesday Farmers' Market** (503-585-8264), two Salem locations: Summer and Marion streets NE, Sat. 9–3, Apr.–Oct.; and Chemeketa Street NE between Liberty and High streets NE, Wed. 10–2, May–Oct.

Silverton Farmers' Market (503-816-5046), Town Square Park at Main and Fiske, Silverton. Sat. 9–1, mid-May–mid-Oct.

Sweet Home Farmers' Market (541-401-2678), 621 Main Street, Sweet Home. Sat. 10–2, May–Oct.

FARMS AND FARM STANDS **Farmer John's Produce and Nursery** (503-474-3514; www.farmerjohnsproduce.com), 15000 Oldsville Road, McMinnville. Open daily in the fall; closed Tues. in spring and Sun. in summer. Fruits, berries, corn, tomatoes, and the full gamut of Willamette Valley bounty can be found at this 120-year-old family farm.

Gathering Together Farm (541-929-4270; www.gatheringtogetherfarm.com), 25259 Grange Hall Road, Philomath. This 65-acre organic truck farm sells to local and Portland restaurants, at farmer's markets, and at their own farm stand, where you'll also find homemade doughnuts. Buy your own or taste the produce at their Garden Room café, serving breakfast and lunch. Check for seasonal hours.

Hazelnut Hill (541-754-5657; www.hazelnuthill.com), 27681 Nutcracker Lane, Corvallis—milepost 95 on US 99W. Weekends 10–5. Oregon is a major world supplier of hazelnuts, and here you can both see and enjoy the, er, nuts and bolts of it. The Hilles invite you to stop by their 225 acres of groves and watch the toasting and candy-making processes, and maybe buy some hazelnut goodies for the road.

FERRIES From the earliest days of settlement in Oregon well into the train era, ferries were the way to transport people and goods across the territory's considerable number of rivers. Highways and bridges made most of them obsolete, but three historic ferries still carry commuters over the Willamette:

Buena Vista Ferry (503-588-7979), Buena Vista Road, 6 miles south of Independence. Runs Wed.–Sun., mid-Apr.–Oct.

Canby Ferry (503-650-3030), Mountain Road, 3 miles north of Canby. Runs daily "whenever there is a vehicle to transport."

Wheatland Ferry (503-588-7979), Wheatland Road, 13 miles north of Salem. Runs daily except Thanksgiving and Christmas.

FOR FAMILIES ✐ **A. C. Gilbert Discovery Village** (503-371-3631; www.acgilbert.org), 116 Marion Street NE, Salem. Mon.–Sat. 10–5, Sun. noon–5. General admission $5.75, seniors $4.25, toddlers and those on public assistance $2.75. Housed in a row of five historic homes on Riverfront Park, the Discovery Village embodies A. C. Gilbert's principle of learning through play. In his case this was not an empty slogan. Gilbert invented the Erector set and pioneered other 20th-century toy-chest necessities, like magic kits and home chemistry sets (thanks). These and other household inventions are on display, but the fun for kids is in the many total-immersion playrooms—touring the human body, exploring bubbles, walking through a rain forest—all artfully designed with adults as well as kids in mind. Outside, climb on the Giant Erector Set, crawl through a giant animal cell, and have fun on other imaginative creations of Gilbert's spiritual heirs.

Enchanted Forest (503-371-4242; www.enchantedforest.com), 8462 Enchanted Way SE, Turner (exit 248 from I-5). Daily May–Aug., weekends in Apr. and Sept. General admission $9.95, children and seniors $8.95; ride tickets extra. Choruses of "are we there yet?" may be quelled by a stop at the Enchanted Forest. A labor of love, it was constructed bit by bit by Roger Tofte, a state highways employee who found there wasn't much family entertainment in the area in the 1960s and so built his own theme park. It comes complete with bumper cars, flume ride, haunted house, and much more for kids of all ages, though the most charming and personal attraction is also the oldest: Storybook Lane, where your child can run through the Old Lady's Shoe, Gingerbread House, and Alice's rabbit hole, hand built by Roger and family.

Riverfront Carousel (503-540-0274; www.salemcarousel.org), 101 Front Street NE, Salem. Open daily; $1.50 a ride. A herd of hand-carved horses awaits your kids—and you—in Salem Riverfront Park.

GARDENS **Avery Park Rose Garden** (541-757-6918), 1320 SW Avery Park Drive, Corvallis. Daily dawn–dusk. Free. The garden fills the northwestern corner of Avery Park with 250 varieties of roses. Bloom peaks in June, but in this mild climate it may start in May and end as late as Oct.

Bush's Pasture Park, 890 Mission Street SE, Salem. This large urban park contains several areas of botanic interest: a century-old apple orchard at the corner of Mission and High streets, interplanted with plum and crabapple in the 1920s; a two-thousand-plant rose garden; and the formal tulip beds and conservatory next to the **Asahel Bush House** (see *Historic Homes*).

♿ **Cooley's Gardens** (503-873-5463; www.cooleysgardens.com), 11553 Silverton Road NE, Silverton. Mon.–Fri. 8–4:30 (8:30–4 in winter). Free. Irises thrive in this corner of the Willamette Valley, and Cooley's grows and develops more than five hundred varieties. The display gardens are wheelchair accessible, and you can even park your RV overnight.

Delbert Hunter Arboretum and Botanic Garden (503-623-7359; www.delberthunterarboretum.org), Dallas; from Main Street in Dallas, take Ellendale Drive to Westwood Drive to Park Street. Open year-round. Free. An old logging flume cuts through this now-quiet park along Rickreall Creek. Devoted to the study and preservation of native plants, it embraces the varied habitats of Oregon and now includes a rock garden.

Greengable Gardens (541-929-4444; www.greengable.com), 24689 Grange Hall Road, Philomath. Mon.–Sat. 10–5. General admission $5, seniors $4. Just a few miles west of Corvallis is this 10-acre commercial flower farm, devoted mostly to daffodils and tulips. Luxuriant gardens around the farmhouse show off plantings of wisteria, rhododendron, irises, roses, and ornamental trees. The public is welcome to stroll.

Historic Deepwood Estate (503-363-1825; www.historicdeepwoodestate.org), 1116 Mission Street SE, Salem. Four acres of formal gardens surround the stately 1894 home, built by Luke Port (see *Historic Homes*). Designed in the 1930s by the

Salem firm of Elizabeth Lord and Edith Schryver, their "natural" English style presents changing views as paths wind from one garden to the next among boxwood hedges, ornamental trees, and fragrant plantings, and a nature trail leads into adjacent Bush Pasture Park.

♿ **The Oregon Garden** (1-877-674-2733; www.oregongarden.org), 879 W. Main Street, Silverton. Daily Nov.–Sept. General admission (depending on season) $5–10, seniors $4–9, students $4–8; children under eight free. What better place to put Oregon's emblematic garden than the loamy, well-watered Willamette Valley? Especially since the town of Silverton had plenty of reclaimed water looking for a place to go. Dedicated in 2000, the garden now showcases Oregon's botanic diversity, from its four-hundred-year-old oak grove to its water garden, rose garden, conifer grove, children's garden, and other specialized designs—and, of course, many water features. Wheelchairs may be borrowed at the visitors center, and a tram for those with limited mobility tours the garden spring through fall. The Gordon House, the only Frank Lloyd Wright creation in Oregon, sits near the oak grove and may be toured by reservation (503-874-6006).

Peavy Arboretum (541-737-4452), 8 miles north of Corvallis off US 99W. Set within OSU's McDonald Research Forest, the arboretum offers trails amid hundreds of tree and shrub species, both native and exotic.

Schreiner's Iris Gardens (1-800-525-2367; www.schreinersgardens.com), 3625 Quinaby Road NE, Salem. Free. Irises in all possible shades make a fine 200-acre show in spring. Most are for Schreiner's retail business, but in peak season you can walk or picnic amid the 10 acres of display gardens, deciding how many rhizomes you need to take home.

The Thyme Garden (541-487-8671; www.thymegarden.com), 20546 Alsea Highway, Alsea. Daily 10–5, mid-Apr.–June, and Thurs.–Mon. 10–5, June–mid-Aug. Hidden in the foothills of the Coast Range are 80 acres of organically grown herbs. The project started as an addendum to Rolfe and Janet's restaurant and eventually took over, as plants tend to do. The restaurant went by the board, and now they grow more than seven hundred varieties of herbs—medicinal, aromatic, culinary, and just plain curious—including themed display gardens, one consisting solely of 60 kinds of thyme. Ponds, plants, and brooks make for a soothing stroll on your own, or reserve a guided tour and lunch ($25). And, of course, you can buy plants and seeds.

🐾 **Wooden Shoe Bulb Company** (1-800-711-2006; www.woodenshoe.com), 33814 S. Meridian Road, Woodburn. Spring brings riotous color to these acres of tulips and daffodils, drawing lots of admirers. The fields are open for viewing through Apr., with food, games, pony rides, and wine tasting adding to the festive mood. Leashed dogs are welcome. Parking is $5 weekdays and $10 weekends, but you can also enjoy the colors from the road.

HERITAGE TREES **Benedictine Sisters' Giant Sequoia,** 130 feet tall. Queen of Angels Monastery, 840 S. Main Street, Mount Angel. Nuns plan for the long haul—longer than they thought, in this case. Sister Protasia didn't know what sort of sapling she'd found by the railroad tracks running behind the nuns' property. In 1893 the foundation was just six years old and in need of some landscaping, so she planted it in front of the newly built cloister. Turned out the tree was a giant sequoia, dropped apparently from a California train. Now it brushes the windows and dwarfs the imposing stone structure.

Hager Grove Pear Tree, about 160 years old. This single tree is what remains of an orchard planted by the Munkre family, who came to Oregon in 1847. It still blooms in lonely splendor in the spring. Drive-by viewing only, since it's in the northeast corner of the busy OR 22/I-5 intersection.

"Moon Tree," in Wilson Park, just west of the capitol in Salem. There's nothing particularly unusual about this young 65-foot Douglas fir except that it germinated from a seed taken to the moon and back by astronaut Douglas Roosa in 1971. It was planted here in 1976 to celebrate the nation's bicentennial.

Signature Oak, 100 feet tall and about four hundred years old. This is the largest of an Oregon white oak grove that well predates European settlement and now graces the **Oregon Garden** at 875 W. Main Street, Silverton.

"Star Trees," averaging 100 feet, on the front lawn of Willamette University across from the State Capitol in Salem. This cluster of five giant sequoias was planted in 1942 on the university's hundredth birthday. From mid-Dec. to Jan. they are decorated with Christmas lights, making an impressive display.

Willamette Mission Cottonwood, 160 feet tall and about 270 years old. This tree sits near the site of Oregon's first Methodist mission, founded by Jason Lee in 1834. It's also a Champion Tree, being the biggest black cottonwood in the nation. Take exit 263 from I-5 to Willamette Mission State Park, off Wheatland Ferry Road.

HISTORIC HOMES **Albany Historic Walking Tours** introduce you to the city's more than six hundred historic homes and businesses, from the sober 1849 Monteith House to 20th-century bungalows and Craftsman homes. Guides can be downloaded from www.albanyvisitors.com or obtained at the visitors' association at 250 Broadalbin Street, Albany.

Asahel Bush House (503-363-4714), 600 Mission Street SE, Salem. Tues.–Sun. noon–5, May–Sept. and Tues.–Sun 2–5, Oct.–Apr. General admission $4, seniors and students $3, kids 6–12 $2. This Victorian home was built by newspaper and banking magnate Asahel Bush in 1877 on his farm, much of which is now Bush's Pasture Park. Neither enormous nor ostentatious despite its owner's huge fortune, its exterior is pleasantly free of the flamboyance favored by some of the era's tycoons. But he did not stint on furnishings—the 10 fireplaces are cut Italian marble, all bedrooms had hot and cold running water, and much of the wallpaper was imported from France. And there was central heating in addition to all those fireplaces. It remained in the family until Bush's son, Asahel Bush III, died in 1953, having willed that the house and grounds should pass to the city.

Brownsville Historic Homes Walk (541-466-3390), available at the **Linn County Historical Museum,** Brownsville (see *Museums*). Settled in 1846 and bypassed by highway and railroad, Brownsville has remained much as it was 50 years ago, with many buildings dating from the turn of the last century. Easy to visit; Brownsville is small.

Historic Deepwood Estate (503-363-1825; www.historicdeepwoodestate.org), 1116 Mission Street SE, Salem. Sun.–Fri. noon–4, May 15–Sept. 15 and Wed.–Sat. 11–3, Sept. 16–May 14. General admission $4, students and seniors $3, children over six $2. The grounds are free and open dawn–dusk. Built nearly 20 years after the Bush House, this Queen Anne shows the evolution in taste in a brief period. Luke Port was a doctor and commissioned the house in 1894. It's far grander than the banker's house, with turrets, bay windows, multiple gables, and a carriage house; tragically, the Ports never moved in. Their son died in a shipwreck on his way to university in Germany, and in their grief they left Oregon. The house passed to the Bingham family, then the Browns, who put in the formal gardens. The home is in magnificent repair, with original stained glass, beveled woodwork, and original electric lights.

Historic Homes Trolley Tour (503-757-1544), Corvallis. Sat. in summer. You can catch a free trolley ride past the city's numerous older homes while listening to stories about their original owners. Reserve by calling the number above.

Historical Walking Tours (1-800-334-8118), Corvallis. Self-guiding brochures are available for walks around Corvallis's several historic districts. You may download them from www.visitcorvallis.com or pick them up at the visitors center, 553 NW Harrison Boulevard. Also at the visitors center, you can, for a $20 deposit, discover Corvallis's history on an MP3-guided tour.

Hoover-Minthorn House (503-538-6629), 115 S. River Street, Newberg. Wed.–Sun. 1–4, Mar.–Nov. and Sat.–Sun. 1–4, Dec. and Feb. Admission by donation. The house was built in 1881 by Quaker entrepreneur Jesse Edwards and reflects comfortable rural tastes. But its claim to fame is having been the home of 31st president Herbert Hoover, also a Quaker, who lived here from 1885 to 1891 with his uncle and aunt, John and Laura Minthorn. Who knew?

Monteith House Museum (1-800-526-2256), 518 Second Avenue SW, Albany. Wed.–Sun. noon–4, mid-June–mid-Sept., otherwise by appointment. Walter and Thomas Monteith came to Oregon from New York in 1847 with the express purpose of founding a new city. They weren't the first to arrive at the confluence of the Willamette and Calapooia rivers, but they may have been the most enterprising: they bought two adjacent 320-acre claims and built a house straddling the property line, thus fulfilling the requirement that a claim's owner sleep on the claim, and platted their town site. They named it, not very originally, Albany (Oregon is full of such toponyms). Their 1849 home was the first frame house in town. With a railroad and a navigable river, Albany prospered, and so did the Monteiths. Both married. Walter and his wife built their own home, and Thomas stayed on, hosting Free State meetings that eventually led to Oregon's admission to the Union as a nonslavery state. The house has been faithfully restored to portray the Monteith's living quarters and store.

Moyer House (541-466-3390), 204 N. Main Street, Brownsville. Mon.–Sat. 11–4 and Sun. 1–5. Free (donations accepted). A skilled carpenter could do well on the frontier, and the Moyer House is a fine example of that. John Moyer crossed the prairie from Ohio in 1852 and put his skills to work in the growing Calapooia Valley. One thing led to another, and he ended up running a sawmill and a woolen mill, and ultimately built this Italianate villa—a very comfortable house indeed, with 12-foot ceilings and interior murals. The Moyers lived in it till their deaths—his in 1904, and hers in 1921.

Newell House Museum (503-678-5537; www.newellhouse.com), 8089 Champoeg Road NE, St. Paul. Fri.–Sun. 1–5, Mar.–Oct. General admission $4, seniors and

Daughters of the American Revolution (DAR) members $3, children $2. Robert Newell was one of the generation of "mountain men"—trappers and freelance explorers—who ended up guiding settlers and becoming, in their idiosyncratic way, pillars of their new communities. With his friend Joseph Meek he guided the first emigrant train along the Oregon Trail and drifted down the valley, where in 1852 he found a congenial spot to build his trim, gabled farmhouse and plat the town of Champoeg. Rescued from ruin by the DAR and furnished with donated items from pioneer families, the house's ground floor reproduces the home life of a respectable pioneer, while 19th-century quilts, Indian baskets, and other memorabilia are displayed upstairs. On the grounds nearby are the 1849 Butteville Jail and the 1858 Butteville Schoolhouse.

Settlemier House (503-982-1897; www.settlemierhouse.com), 355 Settlemier Avenue, Woodburn. First Sun. of the month 1–4. General admission $5, children 12–18 $3, children under 12 free with adult. Porches, balconies, a tower, and plenty of gingerbread adorn the 14-room home of Jesse Settlemier, founder of Woodburn. Restored to its Victorian glory inside and out, it's often used for weddings and looks not unlike a wedding cake itself; if your visit doesn't coincide with its single open day a month, it's pretty impressive from the outside.

HISTORIC SITES **Benton County Courthouse,** 120 NW Fourth Street, Corvallis. Open to the public Mon.–Fri. 8–5; tours available. In 1888 the residents clearly had ambitions for Benton County. The imposing Italianate courthouse with its clock tower and carillon dominates all of downtown and then some, denoting that this was an Important Place. Local lore has it that when it was dedicated in 1889, the enthusiastic cannon salute blew out windows. But even if the county didn't produce the next Chicago or even Portland, perseverance counts for something: this is the oldest functioning courthouse in the state.

Champoeg State Heritage Area (503-678-1251), 8239 Champoeg Road NE, St. Paul; exit 278 from I-5 toward Newberg and follow the signs. Daily year-round; visitors center Mon.–Fri. 11–4, Sat.–Sun. 10–5. State park parking fee applies. By the 1830s, the area called French Prairie was already a polyglot little community. It was home or hunting ground to the Calapooyas. French-Canadian trappers had retired here, often with Indian wives, to grow wheat for shipment to the Hudson's Bay Company up at Fort Vancouver, and they had been so successful that the company built a warehouse and store. Father François Blanchet's mission at St. Paul ministered to them, and Jason Lee's Methodist outpost was not far off. American farmers were trickling in. Bob Newell's new town, Champoeg, was just a logical extension of the population increase and HBC trade potential. But there was no government, and no law except for the Company, which found the growing melting pot increasingly complicated. Champoeg is considered, symbolically at least, the birthplace of Oregon, for in an HBC granary here on May 2, 1843, 102 males of the community gathered and voted on an America-style provisional government. This led, eventually, to territorial status and statehood. It was close, though—52–50. What if? The visitors center in today's green, rolling park outlines the history, and you can walk down to the where Champoeg stood before it was washed away by the floods of 1861. A few steps away is a pioneer cabin run by the Daughters of the American Revolution (separate entrance fee). After a visit, stop by the old Butteville Store just outside the park for homemade sausage and a root beer float.

PIONEER CABIN AT CHAMPOEG STATE HERITAGE AREA

Elsinore Theatre (503-375-3574; www.elsinoretheatre.com), 170 High Street SE, Salem. Tours $3. Fancifully designed to suggest Hamlet's castle, the Elsinore opened in 1926. Audiences over the years were treated to vaudeville, movies silent and not so silent, and local performers in the ornate hall till neglect took its toll. Slowly the building degraded, and even its Wurlitzer organ was sold for parts. Now completely renovated, the place has hosted the likes of Wynton Marsalis and Itzhak Perlman. Much of the original plasterwork, iron ornamentation, and wallpaper remains, now cleaned of decades of grime, to delight audiences; miraculously, another Wurlitzer organ was donated. Take a tour or take in a show.

♿ **Fort Yamhill State Heritage Area** (503-393-1172), OR 22, 1 mile north of Valley Junction. The 1850s, when settlers poured in in seemingly endless numbers, saw the removal of many Oregon tribes to reservations. Animosity toward the Indians ran so high that Joel Palmer, Indian agent for Oregon, wrote apprehensively of "the threatening attitude of the community" portending a "general and combined attack on the camp of friendly Indians" at Grande Ronde. When the Grande Ronde reservation was established, Fort Yamhill was built to guard its eastern edge—mostly against attack from the outside. Only a blockhouse and officers' quarters still stand, the latter having been discovered under the exterior of a 1915 farmhouse, though the locations of many others can be seen. A handicapped-accessible trail and restroom are on the grounds.

Fox Valley Pioneer Cemetery (503-859-2167), exit OR 22 at Stayton, then take OR 222 at Lyons and drive 1.3 miles. The first burial here was that of five-year-old Frances Berry in 1859, followed shortly afterward by a sibling—a reminder of life's particular brevity for settler children. Their parents later donated the land as a community cemetery. Today it's a hedged, quiet spot, generally open daylight hours except during funerals.

Hull-Oakes Lumber Company (541-424-3110), 23847 Dawson Road, Dawson. It's not exactly a tourist site, being a working sawmill, but as it's one of the last steam-powered mills in the country, people will come by; tours are by appointment. The mill specializes in large logs, used today in historic restoration of ships, houses, or railroad trestles as well as more mundane projects.

McMinnville Walking Tour (503-472-6196). Settled in 1844 and incorporated in 1876, McMinnville became a thriving little market town. Its downtown is still small and friendly; most of its commercial buildings went up between 1885 and 1912. A self-guiding tour can be picked up at the chamber of commerce, 417 NW Adams Street, McMinnville.

Mount Angel Abbey (503-845-3030), 1 Abbey Drive, St. Benedict, and **Queen of Angels Monastery** (503-845-6141), 840 S. Main Street, Mount Angel. When determined German and Swiss immigrants settled this corner of the valley in the late 1800s, they brought their monks with them. The Benedictine brothers settled on a wooded hilltop and eventually founded a seminary, while the sisters made a home in the town (not before spending a season lodged above a tavern), teaching and caring for the sick. Abbey architecture ranges from neo-Romanesque to a modern library by Aarvo Aalto; the sisters' imposing 19th-century stone cloister contrasts with a very new chapel, built to replace one that was damaged in a 1993 earthquake. Tours may be available by request.

Old Aurora Colony (503-678-5754), 15008 Second Street, Aurora. Tues.–Sat. 11–4, Sun. noon–4; closed Jan. and major holidays. General admission $6, seniors $5, students $2. It was utopian while it lasted. The dozen or so clapboard houses and barns are all that remain of a Christian communitarian settlement founded in 1856 by an enthusiastic Prussian immigrant, Dr. William Keil. Keil preached a simple creed based on the Golden Rule and the earliest Christians described in Acts: "All who believed were together and had all things in common." By contemporary accounts, the community was a happy one, composed mainly of industrious German immigrants who enjoyed good food and music. All 18,000 acres of land and goods were held in common, though each family dwelt in a separate house. The farm throve. Keil, who was no fool, saw to it that the railroad came through the

BEN FRANKLIN TAKES A BREAK IN DOWNTOWN MCMINNVILLE.

LEARN ABOUT LIFE IN AURORA, A 19TH-CENTURY UTOPIAN COLONY.

settlement—not only did the farm's produce get to market faster, but the colony opened a hotel and restaurant that became renowned for its hearty German meals. But when Keil died in 1877 the colony floundered. He had always made the decisions, and there was no designated successor or decision-making process in place. The community divided, distributing its assets among the members, and thus ended another hopeful New World experiment. Wandering among the exhibits in the restored houses, gardens, and barns brings back a flavor of the hard but happy communal life.

Salem historic buildings are concentrated around the **Mission Mill** (see *Museums*), where the 1841 home of missionary Jason Lee, an 1841 parsonage, and the 1847 house of John Boon, Oregon's first treasurer, have been placed. Others, such as the neo-Gothic 1878 Methodist church, the **Elsinore Theatre,** and the Old First National Bank are scattered downtown. A list with addresses is available at www.salem.com.

Silverton Walking Tour (503-873-7070), Silverton. A self-guiding brochure from the Silverton Museum at 428 Water Street takes you through Silverton's 150-year history, from the site of the early mills on Silver Creek to the historic depot.

State Capitol (503-986-1388), 900 Court Street, Salem. The current capitol building is Oregon's third, the first two having been destroyed by fire in 1855 (before Oregon was even a state) and 1935. It is adorned inside and out with marble from Vermont, Missouri, and Montana, while murals in the rotunda depict themes from Oregon history: Captain Gray entering the Columbia, Lewis and Clark, the first

THE STATE CAPITOL, SALEM

wagon train, and Dr. McLoughlin of Fort Vancouver welcoming missionaries Narcissa Whitman and Eliza Spalding. On the grounds are Capitol Park and Willson Park, studded with fountains, flower beds, flowering trees, redwoods, and other ornamentals. Call for guided tours.

Willamette Mission State Park (503-393-1172), 8 miles north of Salem on Wheatland Road. It was not easy being a missionary in the Oregon country. For one thing, the inhabitants were not terribly interested. For another, the landscape was unruly and tended to blow down or wash away what you put up. This is what happened to Jason Lee. Arriving in 1834 in the sparsely settled Willamette Valley, he built a small mission on an admittedly lovely site by the river, which flooded in 1841. He relocated upstream to what is now Salem, where his mission was scarcely more successful but had the consolation of founding Willamette University and in helping to draft the Provisional Government. His first mission site is marked by a monument in the park near the **Willamette Mission Cottonwood,** which was already old when Jason came by.

Willamette University (503-370-6300), 900 State Street, Salem. As befits the first university established west of the Mississippi, Willamette was a pioneering institution, graduating women in its first class and admitting females to its medical school as early as 1877. First an Indian school founded by missionary Jason Lee, it became a school for settlers' children, then hosted the first U.S. court in the Oregon Territory and the first Salem session of the legislature before being fully given over to higher education. Its location across from the capitol and its trees and gardens make the campus a pleasant place to stroll.

MUSEUMS Albany Regional History Museum (541-967-7122; www.armuseum.com), 136 Lyon Street S., Albany. Mon.–Fri. noon–4, Sat. 10–2. Free. Photographs and early town plats detail the history and development of Albany, as well as the daily life of its citizens over the years. The building itself dates from 1887 and was moved 3 blocks to its present location by horsepower in 1912, a process that took 26 days.

Benton County Historical Museum (541-929-6230; www.bentoncountymuseum.org), 1101 Main Street, Philomath. Tues.–Sat. 10–4:30. Free (donations accepted.) Located in the former Philomath College, the museum houses an eclectic collection of local historical documents and artifacts, from a mammoth bone to a Civil War military cap, and a collection of antique quilts dating back to the American Revolution.

THE "STAR SEQUOIAS" IN THE WILLAMETTE UNIVERSITY CAMPUS WERE PLANTED TO HONOR THE UNIVERSITY'S CENTENNIAL IN 1941.

Albany Historic Carousel and Museum (503-928-2469), 503 First Avenue W., Albany. Mon.–Sat. 10–4 (till 9 on Wed.). Free. What better addition to a Victorian downtown than an old-fashioned carousel? Albany has come together over its project to build one, by hand, from scratch. The space at present is a sort of combination studio and display area, where volunteers appear daily to carve and paint, while a number of spirited 1895 ponies prance around the display area. Supervised children are invited to seat-test the newly created menagerie, which includes (of course) a lively salmon and a startlingly large, though naturalistic, jackrabbit. When completed, the animals will be mounted on a donated 1909 Dentzel mechanism, and we can all take a spin. Meanwhile it's fascinating to watch it all come to life under hand tools and volunteer power.

Antique Powerland Museums (503-393-2424; www.antiquepowerland.com), 3995 Brooklake Road NE, Brooks (8 miles north of Salem). Tues.–Sun. 9–5, Mar.–Oct. Admission $5. This complex of several museums is devoted to the history, development, and love of power machines and vehicles, from antique Caterpillar machinery to vintage motorcycles, trucks, tractors, firefighting apparatus, and more. Every summer (call for dates) they put on the Great Oregon Steam-Up, getting the machines up and running, even to the steam-powered sawmill. Bring the mechanical buffs in the family; just be prepared to pry them away.

Evergreen Aviation Museum (503-434-4180; www.sprucegoose.org), 500 NE Captain Michael King Smith Way, McMinnville, just off OR 18, 2.5 miles east of McMinnville. Daily 9–5. Admission: one museum, $11–13; two museums, $20–24; two museums and IMAX movie, $26–30. The complex looks like three glass hangars set back from the highway. The first is where the *Spruce Goose* came home to roost—the monster eight-engine plane commissioned in 1942 as a personnel and materiel transport. The war ended before the plane, plagued with cost overruns and technical constraints, was ready, and it flew only once: a test flight lasting about one minute. At Evergreen it occupies an entire hangar, with smaller planes of various stages of aviation history nestling under its wings. A second "hangar" contains the new Space Museum, with original and replica rockets, space capsules, space gear, and flight simulators for your inner astronaut. And the third building contains the IMAX theater, just in case all this flight was not real enough for you.

ONE OF THE MENAGERIE AT ALBANY HISTORIC CAROUSEL AND MUSEUM

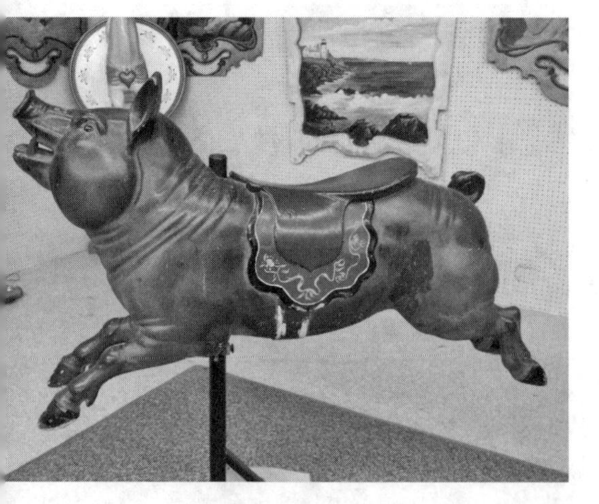

Hallie Ford Museum of Art (503-370-685), on the Willamette University campus at the corner of State and Cottage streets, Salem. Tues.–Sat. 10–5, Sun. 1–5; closed Dec. 24–Jan. 1. General admission $3, student and seniors $2, children 12 and under free. Though the university was founded in 1842, its art museum came into being in 1998. Permanent exhibits focus, naturally enough, on art of the Pacific Northwest, with a collection of historic and contemporary Indian baskets as well as paintings by regional artists from the 1800s to the present, though donations include works in many media from around the world.

Jensen Arctic Museum (503-838-8468), 590 W. Church Street, Monmouth. Wed.–Sat. 10–4. Admission by donation. This is the only West Coast museum dedicated to the life and cultures of the Arctic, and it's right here on the campus of Western Oregon University. Though the Danish-born Paul Jensen settled in Oregon, his work developing educational materials in native languages took him north, where he fell in love with the Arctic. The museum is based on the collection he acquired over decades of travel and provides a fascinating glimpse of indigenous arctic life, including kayak frames, bone spear points, arctic clothing, art, and quite a number of stuffed animals.

Keizer Heritage Museum (503-393-9660; www.keizerheritage.org), 980 Chemawa Road NE, Keizer. Tues. and Thurs. 2–4, Sat. 1–4. Free. This local collection is housed in an unusual Craftsman-style school. Naturally the displays include school history, with many Keizer families having contributed school photos and memorabilia. Changing exhibits every other month focus on specific historic facets, such as the Chemawa Indian School, the Keizer Volunteer Fire Department, or whatever creative idea seizes the curators.

Linn County Historical Museum (541-466-3390), 101 Park Avenue, Brownsville. Mon.–Sat. 11-4, Sun. 1–5. Free (donations accepted.) A genial collection of donated memorabilia fills the old Brownsville Depot, tracing county history from tribal times through agricultural development to today. An actual Oregon Trail covered wagon stands out front.

Mission Mill Museum (503-588-9902; www.missionmill.com), 1313 Mill Street SE, Salem. Mon.–Sat. 10–5. General admission $6, seniors $5, students $4, kids 6–17 $3. The museum interprets the history of Thomas Kay Woolen Mill, one of Salem's major early industries, which produced woolen fabric and blankets from 1889 to 1962. The main buildings have been restored, and you can trace operations through the washing and carding process to dying, weaving, and cutting, learning something about the workers' lives in the process (what stuck in my mind was how children playing in the millrace downstream rushed out of the water to avoid turning blue or green when a vat of used dye was emptied). Also on the property are early buildings of the Jason Lee mission, open to guided tours. Changing exhibits highlight aspects of Oregon or textile history. There's a lot to see, and you can refresh yourself at the tasty **Mission Mill Café,** featuring homemade soups, sandwiches, quiche, and specials.

Santiam Historic Museum (503-769-1406), 260 N. Second Avenue, Stayton. Sat. 1–4, Mar.–Nov. Free. Photos, newspaper clippings, clothing, and other memorabilia recall pioneer life in this quiet valley.

Thompson's Mills State Heritage Site (541-491-3612), 32655 Boston Mills Road, Shedd, 1.5 miles east of US 99E. Open daily; guided tours available. A year older than Oregon, the mill was built in 1858 so settlers wouldn't have to go all the way to Oregon City to grind their grain, and it kept grinding till the 1980s. In 2007 it opened as a state park where visitors can admire the antique milling equipment and the miller's house.

NATURAL WONDERS **Erratic rock,** on Oldsville Road off OR 18, 6 miles east of Sheridan. One doesn't think of rocks as wandering around, but geologists determined that this boulder was clearly out of place, being of a type normally found in northern Canada. Like others scattered around the valley, it's thought to have been pushed down to Montana by glaciers during the Ice Age, then carried here

MELTING GLACIERS CARRIED THIS ERRATIC ROCK HUNDRED OF MILES TO DUMP IT ON MCMINNVILLE FARMLAND.

on icebergs swept down the Columbia River by the Missoula Floods of fifteen thousand to twelve thousand years ago. A 0.25-mile paved trail leads up to the rock and a picnic table, where you have a nice view of surrounding vineyards.

SCENIC DRIVES **Over the Rivers and Through the Woods Scenic Byway** runs from the junction of OR 126 and US 20, high in the Cascades, to quiet Brownsville in the valley farmland; 66 miles. The winding road includes points of interest such as old-growth stands, the old Santiam Wagon Road, fall foliage, covered bridges, and historic Brownsville itself. Avoid the higher elevations in winter, as conditions can be extreme.

Silver Falls Tour Route, Woodburn to Aumsville along OR 214; 55 miles. Not so far from the madding I-5 crowd, the road loops away east through farm and forest to take in the Oregon Garden, gorgeous Silver Falls State Park, and little towns that time forgot: with names like Sublimity, Mount Angel, and Silverton, what's not to like? And there are pleasant places to eat or sleep along the way, should the mood strike you.

Winery tours. All the back roads from Corvallis to the Columbia seem to be dotted with vineyards. This area was Oregon's first venture into wine—a gamble that paid off, what with the mild climate, rich soil, and abundant water. Forty years and six appellations later, winery tours are a favorite visitor activity. For a list of vineyards, check **Willamette Valley Wineries Association** (503-646-2985; www.willamettewines.com), P.O. Box 25162, Portland 97298. In addition to van tours, tasting tours by bike are offered in summer through www.oregonbiketours.org.

✷ To Do

BICYCLING Corvallis has been designated a "bike-friendly city," which it certainly is given its relatively flat terrain, urban bike lanes, and low traffic. The 12-mile **Corvallis Bike Path** circles the city via its numerous parks and riverside trails.

Then there is a plethora of scenic area road tours for all skill levels; contact the **Mid-Valley Bicycle Club** (www.mvbc.com), P.O. Box 1373, Corvallis 97339, for a list and map. Mountain bikers cycle to the **McDonald Research Forest,** 8 miles north of Corvallis, for 60 miles of trails over varied terrain. **Mary's Peak,** 25 miles west of Corvallis in the Coast Range, offers more rugged trails. **Silver Falls State Park** (see *Parks*), near Silverton, has a 4-mile bike path. **Champoeg State Park** (see *Parks*) offers paved trails suitable for families, as do **Minto-Brown Park** and **Riverfront Park** in Salem. Bike rentals are available at **Peak Sports** (541-754-6444), 129 NW Second Street, Corvallis.

BIRD-WATCHING With its rivers, woodlands, and wetlands, and elevation gradients, the valley offers some prime birding, especially in spring. You may check out the **Jackson-Frazier Wetland,** 3580 NE Lancaster Street, Corvallis; **Willamette Park and Kendall Natural Area,** between Fisher Lane and Goodnight Avenue, Corvallis; the **Riverfront parks** in Salem and Corvallis; and **Champoeg State Heritage Area,** which has a bluebird nest box program. See also the locations listed under *Wilder Places.*

CAMPING Area state parks with campgrounds: **Cascadia State Park,** open May–Sept., 25 primitive sites, no reservations, ADA restroom. **Champoeg State Park** has a full-service campground including 6 yurts, 6 cabins, 6 walk-in tent sites, 67 partial hookup and 12 full hookup sites, and a hiker-biker camp; ADA facilities. **Detroit Lake Recreation Area** has several campgrounds open May–Sept., with 133 tent sites, 106 full hookup and 72 electrical hookup sites, and 82 boat slips, plus ADA restroom; call 1-800-452-5687 to reserve. **Silver Falls State Park** has three public campgrounds with 52 electrical hookup sites, 45 tent sites (closed in winter), a horse camp, 14 cabins, and ADA facilities; call 1-800-452-5687 to reserve.

Forest Service campgrounds dot the Cascade foothills. In the North Santiam corridor: off OR 22 east of Mill City you'll find **Cove Creek Campground** (63 sites) and **Southshore Campground** (30 sites) on the south side of Detroit Reservoir, with toilets and drinking water, and **Piety Island Campground** (22 tent sites) actually in the lake, accessible by boat, with pit toilets and no water; these are open Apr.–Sept., no reservations. The **Shady Cove Campground,** 19 miles north of Mehama, has 12 tent sites and toilets but no water; open year-round, no reservations. **Hoover** and **Santiam Flats,** at the eastern end of the reservoir, have respectively 37 and 32 sites, with water and toilets; no reservations. Farther east on OR 22, **Whispering Falls** offers 16 sites with toilets and water; no reservations. **Riverside Campground,** 14 miles east of Detroit, has 37 sites with water and toilets; no reservations. **Marion Forks Campground,** 16 miles southeast of Detroit, presents 16 sites with toilets but no water; no reservations. Northeast of Detroit along FR 46 are **Humbug Campground,** 5 miles from Detroit, open May–Sept., with 22 sites, toilets, and drinking water, no reservations; **Cleator Bend,** 10 miles from Detroit, with nine sites, toilets, and water, no reservations; and **Breitenbush,** with 30 sites open May–Sept., toilets and water, no reservations. For fees and information contact the **Willamette National Forest, Detroit Ranger District** (503-854-3366), on OR 22 in Mill City.

South Santiam corridor: Eighteen miles east of Sweet Home on US 20, **Longbow Organization Camp,** open May–Sept., has six three-sided cabins sleeping up to

50 people, toilets, and water, but no electricity; call 1-877-444-6777 to reserve. **Trout Creek Campground,** 1 mile to the east, offers 24 sites (no RVs) with water and toilets; open May–Sept., no reservations. **Yukwah,** right next door, has 20 sites, water, and toilets; open May–Oct., no reservations. **Fernview Campground,** 23 miles east of Sweet Home, has 11 sites, two tent-only, toilet, and water; open May–Oct., no reservations. **House Rock,** 26 miles east of Sweet Home, offers 17 sites (five tent-only) with water and toilets; open May–Oct., no reservations. **Sevenmile Horse Camp,** 32 miles east of Sweet Home, comes with four tent sites, a toilet, corrals, and water for stock only; no reservations. **Lost Prairie Campground,** open May–Oct., 37 miles east of Sweet Home, has 10 sites, of which eight are walk-in tent sites only, water, toilets, and is near several trailheads; no reservations. **Big Lake Campground,** 4 miles south of the Santiam Pass on OR 126 (and at 4,600 feet elevation), is open May–Oct. depending on snow levels and offers 49 sites with water and toilets; call 1-877-444-6777 to reserve. A couple of miles east is **Big Lake West,** with 11 tent-only sites; no reservations. For fees and information call the **Sweet Home Ranger District** (541-367-5168), 4431 US 20, Sweet Home.

Several county parks are sprinkled around **Foster** and **Green Peter reservoirs,** just east of Sweet Home: **Whitcomb Creek,** open mid-Apr.–mid-Sept., with 39 sites (no hookups) on 328 forested acres, toilets; **Sunnyside,** 138 sites; and **River Bend,** with 35 full hookup and 10 basic sites.

CANOEING AND KAYAKING You can enjoy quiet boating in the Cascades at **Clear Lake,** on OR 126, 18 miles east of McKenzie Bridge; and the **McKenzie River,** with plenty of whitewater, originating at Clear Lake. Down in the valley, the **Yamhill River** near Sheridan offers a peaceful paddle. The **Willamette** is the nation's 13th-longest river and has something for everyone: access points at **Irish Bend County Park** in Corvallis and nearby **Crystal Lake** present mostly flat water in the river's pools and back channels. The **Willamette Kayak and Canoe Club** (www.wkcc.org), P.O. Box 1062, Corvallis 97339, organizes trips and supplies regular river reports.

GOLF **Bayou Golf Club** (503-472-4651), 9301 SW Bayou Drive, McMinnville. Nine holes.

Cross Creek Golf Course (503-623-6666), 13935 OR 22, Dallas. Eighteen holes.

Evergreen Golf Course (503-845-9911), 11694 W. Church Road NE, Mount Angel. Nine holes.

Golf City (541-753-6213), 2115 NE US 20, Corvallis. Nine holes.

The Golf Club of Oregon (541-928-8338), 905 NW Springhill Drive, Albany. Eighteen holes.

Marysville Golf Club (541-753-3421), 2020 SW Allen Street, Corvallis. Nine holes.

McNary Golf Club (503-393-4693), 6255 River Road N., Salem. Eighteen holes.

Salem Golf Club (503-363-6652), 2025 Golf Course Road S., Salem. Eighteen holes.

Trysting Tree Golf Club (541-752-3332), 34028 NW Electric Road, Corvallis. Eighteen holes.

SILVER FALLS AT SILVER FALLS STATE PARK

HIKING The 8.7-mile **Trail of Ten Falls** winds through misty, green **Silver Falls State Park** (see *Parks*). This is a great, somewhat strenuous hike passing, you guessed it, 10 waterfalls, as Silver Creek and its tributaries tumble down the West Cascade foothills. The constant spray, tall trees, and big ferns make it a fairyland. Tie-in trails allow you to loop back if you don't want to go the whole 9 yards, er, miles.

In and around Corvallis are trails long and short, easy and hard. The **Old Growth Trail** in McDonald Research Forest (see *Bicycling*) is a short descent, then an easy mile among tall ancient trees. Also in McDonald Forest is the **560 Loop,** a 5-mile loop with an 800-foot elevation gain; start from the sign marked ADAIR ORANGE GATE across from the Camp Adair store on US 99W, 6 miles north of Corvallis. On the OSU campus, the **OSU Covered Bridge Trail** is 2.2 paved miles, round-trip, through some of the research fields and past the Irish Bend covered bridge; park at the barn off 35th Street. At the **Peavy Arboretum** (see *Gardens*) there's the **Calloway Intensive Loop,** 3 miles with a 560-foot rise, a nature trail with interpretive signs, and old and new growth.

The gravel path from the parking lot to the top of **Mary's Peak,** west of Corvallis, is only 1.5 miles round-trip but leads to great views. Also at Mary's Peak, but the other end of the spectrum, is the **East Ridge Trail,** 9.25 miles up the mountain for a 2,250-foot elevation gain; start 5.5 miles from OR 34 on Mary's Peak Road (closed in winter). Intrepid hikers can confront **Corvallis to the Coast,** 66 miles from Corvallis to Newport on back roads, logging roads, and trails; start from Oak Creek Road at the Dimple Hill parking lot. Check with the **Mary's Peak Group** (541-929-6272) for conditions and information.

Higher in the West Cascades are a multitude of trails. Several trails meander along the streams and forests of the wild **Opal Creek Scenic Area** (see *Wilderness Areas*), among them: the **Opal Creek Trail,** 5 miles round-trip; from Salem take OR 22 east for 21 miles; turn off opposite the Swiss Village restaurant onto Little North Fork Road (FR 2209) and continue 21 miles. Park at trailhead. For a longer trek, take the **Little North Santiam Trail,** a 9-mile round-trip past waterfalls, pools, and a deep gorge. Eight "rustic log footbridges" must be crossed. Trailhead at **Shady Cove Campground.** In the **Menagerie Wilderness,** 20 miles east of Sweet Home on US 20, the 6-mile round-trip **Trout Creek Trail** rises 2,000 feet ("smoothly graded," though) through forest regenerated after a fire a hundred years ago, ending at the base of Rooster Rock. If this seems a bit much, take the 0.5-mile **Walton Ranch Interpretive Trail** from the same trailhead. This leads to two viewing platforms with views of meadows and the river canyon and, in winter, a herd of elk. Trail and platforms are wheelchair accessible. The old **Santiam Wagon Road** runs parallel to and sometimes across US 20, starting 23.4 miles east of Sweet Home. The 19.5-mile segment open to recreation can be walked in sections of 3 to 7 miles, traversing thick old forest and numerous streams, and giving you some idea of what Oregon travel meant in the mid-1800s. Off OR 22 between US 20 and FR 11 you'll see two access points to the new **Old Cascades Crest Trails,** a system linking peaks of the Old Cascades (as opposed to the High Cascades, which are the sharp, snowy, and geologically young peaks you see around you); for day hikes or serious backpacking. The **Upper McKenzie Trail Area** includes the 26-mile **McKenzie River National Recreational Trail,** a glorious mountain river walk conveniently divvied up into manageable segments such as the 3-mile **Waterfall Loop Trail,** accessible from Sahalie Falls or Koosah Falls on OR 126, 15.5 miles east of the McKenzie Ranger Station, or the 5-mile **Clear Lake Loop** that takes in the headwaters of the McKenzie River, 2 miles farther east. For information on these and other trails, contact the **Willamette National Forest Detroit Ranger District** (503-854-3366), the **Sweet Home Ranger District** (541-367-5168), or the **McKenzie River Ranger District** (541-822-3381).

✷ Wilder Places

PARKS **Corvallis Department of Parks and Recreation** (541-766-6918), 1310 Avery Park Drive, Corvallis. Corvallis offers several pleasant, green city parks. Here is a selection: **Central Park,** between Sixth and Eighth streets and Monroe and Madison, with lovely perennial beds, walkways, and a playground; **Bald Hill Park,** on the western edge of town, with 284 acres of prairie, oak savanna, and walking trails; **Riverfront Commemorative Park,** stretching along nearly a mile of downtown riverfront and adorned with ornamentals, sculpture, and a paved hike-bike trail; and **Woodland Meadow Park,** at the intersection of Circle Boulevard and Witham Hill Drive, with 33 acres of meadows, including a dog off-leash area. See also *Gardens.*

TRILLIUM AND WOOD SORREL IN CASCADIA STATE PARK, ON THE WESTERN SLOPES OF THE CASCADES

Cascadia State Park (541-367-6021), US 20, 14 miles east of Sweet Home. Site of a mineral spring resort in the late 1800s, the park is now a quiet mountain escape with a few camp and picnic sites shaded with cedar, hemlock, and Douglas fir. Trails run down to the river and to Soda Creek Falls. Wildflowers abound in spring.

Champoeg State Park (503-678-1251), 8239 Champoeg Road NE, St. Paul; exit 278 from I-5 toward Newberg and follow the signs. Besides being the "birthplace of Oregon" (see *Historic Sites*), Champoeg is a great place for a picnic by the river, with rolling meadows, tall cottonwoods, picnic areas and campgrounds, and historic and educational programs.

ONE OF OREGON'S OLDEST BARNS, CHAMPOEG STATE PARK

Detroit Lake State Recreation Area (503-854-3346), OR 22, 50 miles east of Salem. Open mid-Mar.–Sept. Nine-mile-long Detroit Lake was created in 1953 by the Detroit Dam, which raised the water level 400 feet. It's a big area for water sports, camping, and fishing, complete with store and visitors center. One and a half miles to the west is **Mongold Day Use Area,** also on the lake, with a grassy beach.

Ellmaker State Wayside, on US 20, 31 miles east of Newport. It's just a wayside, but it boasts old fruit trees from some previous incarnation and four picnic tables. A stream runs through it.

North Santiam State Recreation Area (1-800-452-5687), OR 22, 4 miles west of Mill City. No fee. Set along the rushing North Santiam River, this is a spot for walking, fishing, or just contemplating the river.

Mary's Peak, just 25 miles west of Corvallis off OR 34. The highest mountain in the Coast Range at just over 4,000 feet, its "island habitat" preserves quite a number of odd plant and insect species seemingly left over from the Ice Age. On a clear day you can see to the coast. Locals optimistically drive up here to observe eclipses and meteor showers and confront some challenging hiking and biking trails. There are even a few campsites (first come, first served). A 9-mile road winds up to a parking lot where a gravel trail leads to the summit.

Maud Williamson State Recreation Area (1-800-551-6949), OR 221, 12 miles north of Salem. A level playing field (for horseshoes and volleyball) overlooks farmland. Picnic tables and Douglas firs make it a nice rest stop. Trilliums bloom here in spring.

Minto-Brown Island Park, 2200 Minto Island Road SE, Salem. Nearly a thousand acres of park with trails, woodlands, meadows, and a dog off-leash area—formerly two islands settled by a Mr. Minto and Mr. Brown, before the river rearranged things. Wetlands provide winter habitat for waterfowl.

River Bend County Park, 45931 Santiam Highway (US 20), Foster. Ninety acres along the South Santiam River to walk along, camp in, swim, or tube.

GOVERNOR TOM MCCALL IS MEMORIALIZED IN SALEM'S RIVERFRONT PARK.

Riverfront Park, 116 Marion Street NE, Salem, is Salem's front yard—23 acres along the Willamette River, bought by the city from Boise Cascade when the plant closed. A leftover pressure tank was transformed into an "Eco Earth Globe" with hundreds of colored tiles. Other attractions include a carousel, amphitheater, jogging paths, and outdoor events.

Sarah Helmick State Recreation Site, US 99W, 6 miles south of Monmouth. No fee. Individual and group picnic sites are set along the Luckiamute River among bigleaf maple, cedar, and cottonwood. Groups sites must be reserved (fee).

♿ **Silver Falls State Park** (1-800-4542-5687 reservations, 503-873-8681 information); from OR 22 take exit 7 onto OR 214 and continue east about 17 miles. The Silver Creek drainage was still wild country when the park was dedicated back in 1933. The creek and its tributaries had pretty well dissected these Cascade foothills, leaving steep slopes covered in temperate rain forest—discouraging to ox or pioneer—so the series of 10 waterfalls ranging from 27 to 178 feet high remained practically a secret till the park opened. An 8-mile trail connects the falls, part of a 25-mile hiking, equestrian, and biking trail system. Though this is a

SILVER CREEK, SILVER FALLS STATE PARK

popular park offering guided walks and nature talks, it's easy to escape into the deep ferny forest, and when you stand in the mist behind a hundred feet of falling water, everything else seems to fall away. Other attractions include the South Falls Lodge, built by the Civilian Conservation Corps in the 1930s, with a snack bar and activity room, picnic tables, campgrounds, and an unsupervised swimming hole. Some ADA-compliant trails, campsites, and restrooms. Day use $3; tent or RV camping, $12–20; cabins from $35.

Washburne State Wayside, on US 99W, 4 miles northwest of Junction City. This deeply shaded rest area has a nature trail and signs explaining the Applegate Trail, an Oregon Trail alternative that avoided the Columbia River and approached the Willamette Valley from the south.

Willamette Mission State Park (503-393-1172), 8 miles north of Salem on Wheatland Road. This park was the site of Jason Lee's 1834 Methodist mission, the first in Oregon. But it's also a large recreation area, with 1,680 acres of meadow and woodland with picnic and camping areas, plentiful wildlife, boating and fishing on the Willamette River and Mission Lake, as well as hazelnut and walnut orchards.

WILDERNESS AREAS **Menagerie Wilderness.** Access by trail from US 20 at milepost 48.8 or 51.5. The draw of this remote, 5,000-acre forested wilderness is a jumble of strange rock pinnacles that attract climbers to climb and day hikers to gaze. Partially closed Jan. 15–July 31.

Middle Santiam Wilderness. Reached by taking FR 11 from OR 20 and continuing on FR 1142 or 1152 to the McQuade Creek or Gordon Peak trailheads. This is a rugged, low-use area, with elevations ranging from 1,600 to 5,000 feet. Some of the thick forest is old growth. The Santiam River and Donaca Lake abound with native fish.

Opal Creek Wilderness, FR 2209—turn north onto North Fork Road off OR 22 at the Swiss Village Restaurant (11 miles west of Gates) and continue for 20 miles. Deep in the West Cascades, and I mean deep, are nearly 35,000 acres of old-growth Douglas fir, western hemlock, and cedar—the biggest forest primeval at low elevation remaining in Oregon. Protection of these huge, ancient trees came about through a decades-long, contentious process, but accommodation was reached in 1996 whereby 20,827 acres

BEHIND SILVER FALLS, SILVER FALLS STATE PARK

of the upper Opal Creek drainage received wilderness status, and the lower reaches were designated the **Opal Creek Scenic Recreation Area,** with 13,538 acres. Trails thread through the wilderness of old boles, pristine streams, and myriad waterfalls. Rustic accommodations at the old mining site called Jawbone Flats (there was gold in these hills) are available by reservation through **Friends of Opal Creek** (503-892-2782).

Table Rock Wilderness, off OR 211 and S. Molalla Road, 20 miles southeast of Molalla. Five and a half thousand acres of steep, old lava flow in the western Cascades foothills culminate in a 4,881-foot plateau. Four trails wind into the wilderness, offering a good workout and fine views—but carry water. Though the surrounding forest has been logged, the rugged terrain here protected the old growth, and it's now administered by the Bureau of Land Management (503-375-5646). The slopes are a riot of blooming rhododendron in spring.

WILDLIFE REFUGES **Ankeny National Wildlife Refuge** (503-588-2701), 2301 Wintel Road, Jefferson; take exit 243 from I-5 and proceed west on Wintel Road. Open sunrise–sunset. Before the Oregon Trail, the Willamette Valley was a wildlife paradise of forest, stream, meadow, and wetland. By the 1960s much of it had been altered by draining and plowing, not to mention urban development, so Ankeny, **Baskett Slough,** and **Finley** (see below) were created in the 1960s to preserve at least some of this habitat. The primary beneficiaries have been the dusky Canada geese, who apparently are more selective in their choice of surroundings than their larger cousins. But naturally many other waterfowl love it and come to rest or winter as their ancestors have for millennia, drawing eagles and peregrine falcons. Also protected is the Fender's blue butterfly. Observation blinds and several miles of trails offer easy wildlife viewing. Pets are allowed only in parking areas, on leash.

Baskett Slough National Wildlife Refuge (503-623-2749), on OR 22, 2.5 miles west of its intersection with US 99W, Dallas. Open year-round. Nearly 2,500 acres of oak groves, croplands, and marsh provide wintering grounds for thousands of ducks and geese, while songbirds dominate the summer. Five miles of trails wander between observation blinds for your viewing pleasure.

E. E. Wilson Wildlife Area (541-745-5334), 29555 Camp Adair Road, Monmouth; about 9 miles north of Corvallis on US 99W.

Willliam L. Finley National Wildlife Refuge (541-757-7236), 26208 Finley Refuge Road, Corvallis. Besides the waterfowl frequenting such places, the Finley refuge is home to a sizable herd of highly visible Roosevelt elk. The largest of the three national refuges here, it allows hunting and fishing (check for seasons) and retains some historic buildings: the 1855 Fiechter house, on the original donation claim of German immigrant John Fiechter, and several farm buildings dating from the early 1900s. An auto tour route and 12 miles of trails run through the varied habitats, presenting nice views of wildlife and the nearby Coast Range.

Kingston Prairie Preserve (503-802-8100), 3 miles southeast of Stayton. The Nature Conservancy has protected this 152-acre tract of native prairie, saved from the plow originally by its shallow soils. Just a fragment of the great oak-savanna-prairie habitat that dominated the Willamette till the 1800s, it can give you an idea of what the pioneers saw.

✷ Lodging

BED & BREAKFASTS

Albany

✐ **Pfeiffer Cottage Inn** (541-971-9557; www.thepfeiffercottageinn.com), 530 Ferry Street SW. One room and two suites, all with private bath, welcome travelers to this two-story, 1908 bungalow. So do Debbie and Ray Lusk, who opened the bed & breakfast in 2008. They will spoil you with fresh, hearty breakfasts and evening wine, and hope you enjoy Albany as much as they do. Well-behaved children welcome. Doubles $105–135.

Alsea

Alsea Valley Bed and Breakfast (541-487-4526; www.alseavalley.com), 19237 Alsea Highway. Hiking and fishing are the draws in the Alsea River Valley, and here are two guest rooms for when you want to get indoors. Both have private baths, and there's a common room with Wi-Fi. Rooms $75, with continental breakfast.

Aurora

Feller House Bed and Breakfast (503-678-0268; www.thefellerhouse.com), 21625 Butteville Road NE. Two guest rooms in the 1865 Feller House give you a base for exploring historic Aurora, St. Paul, and Champoeg State Park. They go for $100, including a hearty breakfast.

Carlton

Lobenhaus Bed and Breakfast and Vineyard (1-888-339-3375; www.lobenhaus.com), 6975 NE Abbey Road. Lobenhaus has its own little vineyard, so if you come to the wine country, you need go no further. In fact, you may well want to stay put and luxuriate in your elegantly modern room and bucolic view. Built more like a lodge than a traditional B&B, its six rooms all give onto a deck or patio, and a bountiful breakfast is included. $160–180.

R. R. Thompson House (503-852-6236; www.rrthompsonhouse.com), 517 N. Kutch Street. This grandiose house was built in 1936 by the grandson and heir of the R. R. Thompson who founded the Oregon Steam Navigation Company in the heady days of Oregon's development. The woodwork is mahogany, the gardens roses and wisteria, and the accommodations follow suit: two suites and three rooms with all the luxuries. This is for a gala weekend, perhaps of wine tasting; several wineries are within walking distance in little Carlton. $150–245.

Corvallis

✐ 🐾 **Hanson Country Inn** (541-752-2919), 795 SW Hanson Street. Here's a 1928 Dutch Colonial sitting on 5 acres that actually takes kids and pets. The house has five guest rooms, and there's a two-room cottage out back. $125–175.

Harrison House (1-800-233-6248; www.corvallis-lodging.com), 2310 NW Harrison Boulevard. A comfortable hip-roofed, column-porched 1930s house, the Harrison draws parents visiting kids at OSU, wine-country travelers, and business visitors. The original owners lived in it for more than 50 years, and though it's been remodeled to give each bedroom a private bath, it retains the feeling of a home with its cozy fireplace, warm rugs, and polished wood. Owners Allen Goodman and Hilarie Phelps returned to innkeeping just to take care of this place, and the care shines from Hilarie's warm welcome to Allen's inspired breakfasts to the complimentary Oregon wines served in the afternoons. Relax in the patio, sunroom, or comfy living room, or just retire to your own well-appointed room. Four rooms and a suite all have high-speed Internet, and a guest computer is at your service downstairs. Doubles from $129.

Foster

✐ **Foster Lake Bed and Breakfast** (541-367-3331; www.fosterlakebandb.com), 6281 US 20. This family-run place is on the shores of Foster Lake, with its boating and swimming opportunities. The kid-friendly white frame house offers four rooms (some with shared bath), and breakfast is continental. $69–109. There's also a lodge for large families or groups; check for rates.

Independence

Independence House (503-838-0612; www.independencehousebb.com), 615 Monmouth Street. Independence is a quiet sort of town, and this is a quiet sort of place, ideally located for wine country tours or small-town sight-seeing. The solid 1895 house offers a homey front porch, and three comfortably furnished guest rooms share a large common bathroom. Doubles $95, with full breakfast and afternoon snacks.

Lafayette

Kelty Estate Bed and Breakfast (1-800-867-3740), 675 Third Street. Right in downtown Lafayette (but then what part of Lafayette is not downtown?), this 1872 white house is set among lawns and tall oaks. How its clean lines avoided Victorian excrescences I don't know; maybe because the substantial home was just the Keltys' summer place. Now it caters to winery visitors and wedding groups with five handsomely furnished rooms and suites, all named after Oregon lakes. You get all the amenities and then some, plus, for a fee you can get a limo and driver for your wine-tasting tour. $129–179, including breakfast and afternoon wine.

Lebanon

Peggy's Alaskan Cabbage Patch (541-258-1774; www.cabbage-patch-b-and-b.com), 194 S. Second Street. Peggy moved down from Alaska, where she ran a B&B and grew quantities of cabbages, both edible and ornamental (cabbages being one thing that will grow there). Now in tamer Oregon, she offers guests two rooms, one with rustic log furniture and the other with delicately turned "gold rush–style" pieces. She still makes a hearty Alaskan (or Icelandic or Spanish, depending on her mood) breakfast. Doubles $75 with shared bath, $125 with private bath.

Lyons

✐ **Elkhorn Valley Inn** (503-897-3033), 33016 N. Fork Road. Down a remote country road in a fold of the Cascade foothills, the Elkhorn is for those who like a bit of isolation—for quality time with family, spouse, or friends, or just to rejuvenate. Waterfalls and endless hiking trails are within a short walk or drive, or you can watch the wildlife from your window—hostess Robin Goucher will point the way. You may want to plan for meals: after Robin's breakfast, you might not need lunch, but the closest dinner is in Mill City or Gates, which have a few small restaurants. Well-behaved children are welcome. Five rooms and a cottage rent for $85–145.

McMinnville

Baker Street Inn (503-472-5575; www.bakerstreetinn.com), 129 SE Baker Street. One of McMinnville's solid Craftsman houses offers three rooms, each with its individual decor, a big front porch, a deck in the back, and plenty of welcoming common space. And, they will prepare breakfast for virtually any dietary restrictions! $139–179.

Steiger House Bed and Breakfast (503-472-0821), 360 SE Wilson Street. The tall, pointed cedar house near downtown looks down upon rhododendron-filled grounds and, unlike some other wine-country hostelries, offers a range of accommodation from expansive suites to the twin-bedded "rooftop room" (under the roof, not on it)—all very pleasantly appointed and with private baths. $95–150, with full breakfast.

Salem

Andrea Bed and Breakfast (503-365-7788; www.andreabedandbreakfast.com), 4430 Andrea Drive NW. A rambling art deco house in the hills west of Salem receives guests in three large rooms furnished with antiques or modern pieces and art. You can spend plenty of time exploring the library, living room, dining room, and solarium—there's even an elegant media room complete with movies and popcorn! Then head outside to more than 6 acres of gardens complete with gazebo, koi pond, and hidden nooks. Popular for weddings and similar occasions. Double occupancy starts at $180.

Betty's Bed and Breakfast (503-399-7848), 965 D Street NE. Two rooms with private bath in a 1922 Craftsman house come with hearty homemade breakfasts and Betty Dehaven, whose avowed favorite hobby is cooking. Since she's also lived in Salem for 50 years, she can tell you a thing or two about what to see and where to go. Doubles from $110.

Bookmark Bed and Breakfast (503-399-2013), 975 D Street NE. The Bookmark has two suites, each with private bath, and welcomes families. Double occupancy $80, with full breakfast.

Silverton

Wild Rose Inn (503-873-8183; www.wildroseinnbnb.com), 16284 S. Abiqua Road. The Wild Rose sits on an acre in the bucolic countryside north of Silverton, where the lawns invite you to play croquet and the gardens invite a stroll. Five themed rooms each have a private bath. Doubles $90–110, with full breakfast.

COTTAGES

Alsea

Leaping Lamb Farm Stay (1-877-820-6132; www.leapinglambfarm.com), 20368 Honey Grove Road. As the name suggests, Scottie and Greg Jones raise lambs, but they also keep chickens, turkeys, horses, and geese—a diversified small operation 25 miles west of Corvallis. Their airy guest cabin has two bedrooms, kitchen, bath, living room, and deck, and sleeps up to six—so bring your kids to feed the hens and gambol about the farm. Breakfast materials are provided. Double occupancy $125; discounts for longer stays.

Brownsville

The Nest (541-466-5913; www.thenestbb.com), 308 Averill. A cozy one-room cottage on the old Brownsville Woolen Mills millrace makes a perfect little hideaway set in a garden with a pasture view. You can watch the birds from the porch or take your (two) wheels onto the new Oregon State Scenic Bikeway. $115 with breakfast or $100 without.

Corvallis

Brooklane Cottage (541-754-0258; www.brooklanecottage.com), 1923 SW Brooklane Drive. A simple one-bedroom cottage on the green edge of town, it yet has all the amenities: a full kitchen and bathroom, living/dining room, lush garden and sunny porch, and even a gas fireplace. Hop on your bike and hit the trails, or drive downtown in five minutes (or walk in 20). The price is right, too: double occupancy $55–115, with children under 12 free.

Donovan Guest Houses (541-758-6237; www.donovanplace.com), 5720

SW Donovan Place. Escape with your family or friends to the Donovans' Christmas tree farm. A cozy, four-bedroom 1880s farmhouse awaits you with amenities they didn't have in the 1880s, such as Wi-Fi and a hot tub. Or choose the modern apartment—its two bedrooms and sleeper sofa sleep up to six. Either way, you'll have a full kitchen and more comforts than at home. Relax—or maybe you'd like a pottery class? Dale, whose pottery display room is on the premises, offers lessons and occasional pottery parties. Inquire! Pets allowed on approval. Double occupancy rates for either accommodation $150 daily, $800 weekly.

Philomath

The Granny Flat (541-602-1538), 206 S. 15th Street. A large one-room cottage with a full kitchen can be your home away from home—it's walking distance to local shops and 5 miles from Corvallis. $75–150; no credit cards.

FOREST SERVICE LOOKOUTS AND CABINS **Gold Butte Lookout,** about 10 miles north of Detroit on FR 46, sleeps four and rents for $65. The access road is steep and involves a steep walk of almost a mile, furnishings are simple, and you must bring your own bedding and water. Looking out on a 360-degree view over the national forest beside a crackling woodstove is an experience hard to duplicate, however. Reservations available through www.recreation.gov or by calling 1-877-444-6777.

HOTELS

McMinnville

Hotel Oregon (1-888-472-8427; www.mcmenamins.com), 310 NE Evans Street. If you can't afford or don't need fancy digs in the wine country, try the historic Hotel Oregon in downtown McMinnville. The McMenamin brothers, as they so often do, bought up the 1905 hotel and restored it to their particular brand of quirky glory. This means you get impish artwork throughout, odd murals in the halls, and a friendly pub downstairs—and, in this establishment, a rooftop bar with panoramic views. So you have access to McMenamins's own microbrews, as well as all the Oregon wines you could wish. $50–$135; some rooms with shared bath.

RESORTS

Detroit

Breitenbush Hot Springs (503-854-3320; www.breitenbush.com), P.O. Box 578, Detroit 97342; from OR 22 turn north onto FR 46 at Detroit and follow signs (better yet, download directions). Back in the nooks and crannies of the Cascades rain forest, hot water comes bubbling out of the ground. Named for a one-armed hunter encountered by an early expedition, the springs were developed, abandoned, then reborn in 1977 as a countercultural community and retreat center. The main draw is the springs—comprising outdoor pools, tubs, and cedar-shingle steam sauna (all clothing optional)—but the yoga retreats, well-being programs, and so forth are a natural spin-off; check their schedule for activities throughout the year. Rustic cabins are geothermally heated, and meals are generous and vegetarian; if you prefer to skip organized activities, there are 154 acres to stroll, and forest trails radiate from the property. Accommodations range from dorm beds ($50–72 per adult) and lodge rooms ($53–76 per adult) to cabins, some with bath and some without ($68–115). You can also pitch your own tent in summer ($54–61). Kids' rates $26–38. No pets except service animals, and you have to bring your own bedding.

✷ Where to Eat

DINING OUT

Corvallis

Big River Restaurant and Bar (541-757-0694; www.bigriverrest.com), 101 NW Jackson Street. Open for lunch, dinner, and happy hour. Big River prides itself on locally grown, often organic ingredients, and its menu is a salt-and-pepper of Italian and Northwestern cuisine with pizza, polenta, and pan-fired halibut vying for your attention.

Le Bistro Corvallis (541-754-6680; www.lebistrocorvallis.com), 150 SW Madison Avenue. Daily for dinner (except Super Bowl Sun.). On the ground floor of what used to be the Hotel Corvallis, the bistro's subtitle is "country French cuisine"—though the menu has a distinct Northwestern accent (I have not yet seen wild salmon with balsamic cherry confit on a menu in France but would certainly like to try it). You'll find your escargots, chèvre salad, and onion soup, not to mention filet mignon; also grilled ahi and pork tenderloin à la marocaine (now there's a crossover dish). Imaginative—and oh, check the dessert menu.

Dayton

Joel Palmer House (503-864-2995; www.joelpalmerhouse.com), 600 Ferry Street. Tues.–Sat. 5–9. Jack and Heidi Czarnecki are crazy about mushrooms. That's why they live and cook in this part of the world, where those who know can find wild chanterelles, morels, and more in the nearby mountains and draws. So almost any dish you order comes with some kind of mushroom, wild or tame (even some desserts). Jack will even make a five-course dinner showcasing mushrooms based on your choice of entrée. This all doesn't come cheap, but it is unique; and you're in the mansion built by Joel Palmer, pioneer and Superintendent of Indian Affairs for the Oregon Territory, 1853–1857 (the same who tried to forestall settler attacks on the Grande Ronde Reservation).

McMinnville

Bistro Maison (503-474-1888; www.bistromaison.com), 729 NE Third Street. Dinner Wed.–Sat.; lunch/brunch Wed.–Fri. 11:30–2, Sun. noon–3. On McMinnville's quintessential Main Street, USA (actually Third Street), there's a little bit of France: Bistro Maison, serving up French home cooking from the kitchen of chef Jean-Jacques Chatelard, from bouillabaisse to pot-au-feu. Casual, friendly, and everything *maison*—homemade.

La Rambla (503-435-2126; www.laramblaonthird.com), 238 NE Third Street. Mon.–Fri. 11:30–2:30 and 5–closing; Sat.–Sun. all day. McMinnville is getting quite adventurous: first fine Italian, then French, and now Spanish specialties prepared, as often as not, with fresh Northwest ingredients—the oysters with aioli come from Willapa Bay. Paella, ham-wrapped trout, and fabada jostle some more familiar menu items (hamburguesa de búfalo, anyone?) for a dining experience that's still unusual around here. If it seems a bit spendy, you can try the Rapido Lunch, though you could also do quite well on a couple of tapas for a light supper.

Nick's Italian Café (503-434-4471; www.nicksitaliancafe.com), 521 NE Third Street. Mon.–Sat. 11:30–2:30 and 5–closing, Sun. 12–8. Nick Peirano has been dishing up Italian menus from his wood-fired oven for more than 30 years, complementing famous food with a shining Oregon wine list, to become a wine-country "must." His dinners are five courses, prix-fixe (though you can order à la carte if you want). The pasta, of course, is handmade.

Salem

Bentley's Grill (503-779-1660; www.bentleysgrill.com), 291 Liberty Street SE. Mon.–Sat. for lunch and dinner, Sun. dinner only. With a fire pit in the middle, a wine bar off to the side, and a free-ranging Northwest menu, the grill's dining is fine and convivial, though it can get a tad noisy. Special events like the monthlong wild game and wine festival expand an already varied menu, and lunch offers the same quality for smaller stomachs (or purses).

Prudence Uncorked (503-362-0888; www.jjamesrestaurant.com), 325 High Street SE. Mon.–Fri. for lunch and Mon.–Sat. for dinner. The energetic Jeff Tomaino has taken over the former j. james restaurant *con brio,* whipping up traditional and innovative dishes (duck confit, brined pork, tender seafood). There's an array of smaller plates for the smaller appetite. The menu changes seasonally.

Silverton

Silver Grille Café (503-873-4035; www.silvergrille.com), 206 E. Main Street. Open for dinner and Sun. brunch. Fine dining in little old Silverton means the Silver Grille, whether your preference is duck confit or homestyle meat loaf. Menus vary seasonally, even the desserts (hm, chocolate mousse with cassis center—you don't see that every day).

EATING OUT

Albany

Novak's Hungarian Restaurant (541-967-9488; www.novakshungarian.com), 2306 Heritage Way. Daily for breakfast, lunch, and dinner. You don't expect to find a Hungarian restaurant in small-town Oregon, and certainly not one tucked improbably into the mammoth Heritage Shopping Mall. But there it is. The Novaks immigrated in 1957 and introduced Albany to Hungarian cuisine in 1984, from their signature chicken paprikas to the strudel. The homemade spaetzle, I can assure you, would not be sneezed at in Budapest. Even the breakfast has a Hungarian accent.

Amity

Blue Raeven Bakery and Produce (503-835-0740), 20650 South US 99W. This roadside store just south of Amity sells Blue Raeven Farm's fresh produce in season, but also heavenly pies and other goodies baked on-site. Hard to resist getting breakfast for the road here, or a snack or dessert to go.

Corvallis

The Broken Yolk (541-738-9655; www.broken-yolk.com), 119 SW Third Street. Daily 7–3. Specializing, obviously, in eggs, the Broken Yolk is a downtown breakfast and lunch hot spot where virtually every dish comes from the hen, with a remarkable assortment of additions and permutations. Not for the HDL-challenged.

Crystals Cuisine and Café (541-752-6403), 1425 NW Monroe Avenue. Daily for lunch, Mon.–Sat. for dinner. *Really* generous portions of hummus, falafel, and other Middle Eastern specialties, at prices to beat the band. Right across from the university, of course.

Le Patissier (541-752-1785; www.lepatissier.net), 956 NW Circle Boulevard. Wed.–Fri. 6:30–3, Sat. 7–3, Sun. 8–2. Hidden in a strip mall on the north edge of town, Didier Tholognat whips up éclairs, Napoleons, and fine pastries to bring you back to that Left Bank patisserie. Take some home or sit and enjoy over coffee.

Nearly Normal's (541-753-0791; www.nearlynormals.com), 109 NW 15th Street. Mon.–Fri. 8 AM–9 PM and Sat. 9–9, Apr.–Sept. and Mon.–Wed. 8–8, Thurs.–Fri. 8 AM–9 PM, and Sat. 9–9, Oct.–Mar. All vegetarian, all day, but that doesn't mean boring. With recipes borrowed from global cuisines, you have plenty of choice whether your preference runs to curries, savory tofus, or south of the border. And then there are the owners' original creations. Eat in the cozy dining room or out on the patio.

Old Europe Deli (541-752-8549), 341 SW Second Street. Mon.–Sat. 8 AM–10 PM, Sun. 11–5. Not particularly European, but it's a fun place—a brick-floored downtown building also home to Oregon Trail Brewery, with a café serving soups, sandwiches, lasagna, chili, and other comfort food. The space is big enough for evening entertainment, usually free (you don't even have to buy anything). When I visited, a 20-piece accordion band was playing to a clapping, dancing audience of all ages.

Shogun Bowl (54-757-7356), 2461 NW Monroe Avenue. Mon.–Fri. 11–8:30, Sat. noon–8. Another university-area favorite, and not only among students; most entrées under $10.

Idanha

✐ **Marion Forks Restaurant** (503-854-3669), milepost 66 on OR 22. Daily 8–8 in winter, daily 6 AM–9 PM in summer. This fixture along Marion Creek, where the road gathers itself for a leap over the Cascade crest, sadly closed in 2008 but reopened in Jan. 2010, to the relief of those regularly crossing the pass. Hearty breakfasts, sandwiches, steaks, burgers, and seafood—including some prizewinning clam chowder—refresh the weary traveler. There's a kids' menu and a "lite" menu, too (meaning you don't have to be over 65 to enjoy a light meal).

McMinnville

Harvest Fresh Grocery and Deli (503-472-5740), 251 NE Third Street. Okay, it's a little more expensive than Safeway (though not much), but it's right in historic downtown McMinnville, and you can grab a yogurt or soda and sit down at a window table to watch the world go by. Or get something from the deli. And I'm not talking corn dogs or deep-fried burritos here, but rather quiche, stuffed grape leaves, and the like. Plus coffee.

Red Fox Bakery and Café (503-434-5098; www.redfoxbakery.net), 328 NW Evans Street. Tues.–Sat. 7–4, Sun. 7–1. Get your croissants, scones, Danish, and fresh bread here, but come early—they sell out fast. On the other hand, you can have a soup or salad for lunch.

Sage Restaurant (503-472-4445), 406 NE Third Street. Mon–Fri. 10:30–3:30, Sat. 10:30–3. This is a popular, inexpensive lunch spot on McMinnville's pleasant main drag, featuring homemade bread and hearty soups.

3rd Street Pizza Company (503-434-5800; www.3rdstreetpizza.com), 433 NE Third Street. Mon.–Thurs. 11–9, Fri.–Sat. 11–10. Handmade New York–style pizza together with some creative sandwiches and salads, plus an in-house movie theater—kick back! They'll also deliver.

Wildwood Café (503-435-1454), 319 NE Baker Street. Daily 7–2:30. This is the town's favorite breakfast spot, so get there bright and early—it's a tiny place, and people line up for their pancakes, omelets, and French toast. The bread and jam are homemade, too.

Mill City

Rosie's Mountain Coffee House (503-897-2378), 647 NE Santiam Boulevard. Daily for breakfast and lunch. On the western slope of the Cascades near Detroit Lake, Rosie's is the spot for locals and campers alike to come in from the cold and enjoy coffee and pastry or a hot soup and sandwich. Free Wi-Fi, too.

Salem

Blue Pepper Gallery, Framing and Internet Café (503-371-4600; www.thebluepepper.com), 241 Commercial Street NE. Mon.–Fri. 6–3. It's hard to categorize the Blue Pepper. It's a gallery, frame studio, and Internet café—accent on the café, which serves a variety of espressos, loose teas, and a decent snack menu—with live music and occasional poetry readings. Oh, and a wine bar. Mostly it's a nice place to hang out on sofas with friends or a book and sip, or check your e-mail.

Croissant and Company (503-362-7323; www.croissantandco.com), 190 High Street SE. Get 'em while they're hot—the place opens at 6 AM weekdays (8 on Sat.). Croissants, Danish, and sundry delicacies fresh from the oven, plus soups, salads, and sandwiches at midday.

Kwan's (503-362-7711; www.kwanscuisine.com), 835 Commercial Street SE. Daily for lunch and dinner. Mr. Kwan started cooking at the age of 11 in China, and it shows. The decor may be unpretentiously Sino-American, but Kwan allows you to taste every ingredient in a dish—no smothering with MSG. The menu is extensive, with a lengthy vegetarian section and several varieties of whole-grain rice, but the staff will also make the effort to accommodate special needs (no sugar, wheat, etc.—even no soy!). Friendly, and seemingly always open.

✐ **Sybil's Omelettes Unlimited** (503-581-7724), 2323 State Street. Mon.–Sat. 6–2, Sun. 7–2:30. For people who love to eat, especially breakfast. Is a hundred varieties of omelet unlimited enough? Not just your common-or-garden, cheese-and-mushroom, or spinach-and-feta; among 98 other choices, you can have your omelet with linguica, chicken livers, or oysters (there's an ethnic spread for you)—supplemented by a list of waffles, pancakes, and lunch sandwiches. They have a kids' menu and a seniors' menu, and the waitress is just as friendly to you as to the regulars.

✷ Entertainment

Elsinore Theatre (503-375-3564; www.elsinoretheatre.com), 170 High Street SE, Salem (see *Historic Sites*).

Pentacle Theatre (503-485-4300; www.pentacletheatre.org), 324 52nd Avenue, Salem. Pentacle is community theater in the woods—just beyond the edge of town, in a grove of oaks and firs. The company has been staging works solemn and sweet for more than 50 years, first in a barn and now in an intimate hemicircle structure that blends into the forest. Tickets start at $17, with discounts for students and seniors.

✷ Shopping

ANTIQUES **Aurora,** home of the historic **Aurora Colony,** bills itself as the antiques capital of Oregon. For a small town it does offer quite a concentration of antiques shops, which you can investigate with a leisurely stroll up and down the main street. And more than a hundred dealers sell their wares at the **Lafayette Schoolhouse Antiques Mall** (503-864-2720), 748 US 99W, Lafayette.

CANDY **Pacific Hazelnut Candy Factory** (1-800-634-7344; www.pacifichazelnut.com), 14673 Ottaway Avenue,

Aurora. Here you can indulge in the Willamette Valley's other (and earlier) specialty: Oregon hazelnuts, plain and fancy.

MUSIC There is something about the area that attracts those who love handcrafted instruments. Jonathan Franke makes his violins by hand, like Stradivarius, in his small-town studio (actually some are modeled on specific Stradivari instruments), **Franke Violin Studios** (541-847-6021), 1381 Commercial Street, Monroe. Kindred spirit Dave Thormalen crafts exquisite harps at **Thormalen Harps** (541-753-4334; www.thorharp.com), 1876 SW Brooklane, Corvallis. Also guitars and mandolins. Rob Gándara, of **Pipe Makers' Union** (541-829-3016; www .carbonycom), produces flutes, bagpipe chanters, and the like out of nonfolky carbon fiber (and what is wood but carbon fiber, may I ask?).

✷ Events

May: **UFO Festival** (503-472-8427; www.ufofest.com), midmonth, McMinnville Community Center, 600 NE Evans Street, McMinnville. A tongue-in-cheek commemoration of a purported 1950 UFO sighting and now the biggest UFO festival after the one in Roswell, New Mexico.

June: **Linn County Pioneer Picnic** (541-466-5709), third weekend, Brownsville. It started in 1887 as a reunion of Oregon Trail pioneers and has been running ever since. Games, food, a logging jamboree, and more.

July: **Hubbard Hop Festival** (503-981-9454), third Sat., Hubbard. Hops were big in this district before wine grapes, so why not? The volunteer fire department puts on the event, which of course includes a beer garden, parade, kids' games, square dance, and barbecue.

St. Paul Rodeo (1-800-237-5920; www.stpaulrodeo.com), Fourth of July weekend, St. Paul. It's been happening since 1935—a full-scale rodeo complete with bull riding, roping, and all, plus pony and carnival rides. Tickets $14–18.

International Pinot Noir Celebration 1-800-775-4762; www.ipnc.org), last Sun., Linfield College, McMinnville. Pinot Noir being a highly prized wine, it's always fun to see how the Willamette Valley vintages stack up. Sixty international Pinot Noir vintners attend this combo of tastings, seminars, and tours.

August: **Oregon Covered Bridge Festival** (541-942-2411; www.covered-bridge.org), first weekend, various locations around the Willamette Valley. Bridge tours, demonstrations, food, and music.

August–September: **Oregon State Fair** (1-800-833-0011; www.oregonstatefair.org), 10 days spanning Labor Day Weekend, State Fairgrounds, Salem. Oregon's premier agricultural fair—critters, giant vegetables, preserves, the whole bit—together with music, rides, food, and wine. Tickets $3–10 (concerts extra).

September: ✐ **Oktoberfest** (503-845-9440; www.oktoberfest.org), third weekend, Mount Angel. Never mind that it takes place in Sept. (the weather's better, anyway)—Mount Angel was founded by German pioneers, and the town's family-friendly Oktoberfest embraces the heritage of beer, oompah, yodeling, and wurst.

Shrewsbury Renaissance Faire (541-929-4897; www.shrewfaire.com), third weekend, on Grant Road off OR 223 in Kings Valley. Adults $9, seniors and kids 6–12 $5, under five free. Arts, crafts, music, theater, and lots of costumed Renaissance mania.

SOUTHERN WILLAMETTE VALLEY

Despite the decline of the lumber industry, Springfield's massive pulp mill still runs day and night—you can't miss it, visually or olfactorily. The rail lines running south still bring in quantities of logs. But the biggest single employer is the University of Oregon, next door in Eugene, home of the Ducks. Eugene also gained brief notoriety as the home of "anarchists" protesting at the 2000 WTO meetings in Seattle. As a big university town, it spawns both culture and counterculture: opera and ballet, folk music, and the requisite number of health food stores and yoga centers. And you're still in the Willamette Valley, so there are plenty of good foods, wineries, and mushrooms for those in the know.

GUIDANCE **City of Eugene Parks and Open Space** (541-682-5010), 777 Pearl Street, Eugene 97401.

Coburg Chamber of Commerce (541-682-7850; www.coburgoregon.org), P.O. Box 8275, Coberg 97408.

Cottage Grove Chamber of Commerce (541-942-2411; www.cgchamber.com), 700 E. Gibbs, Suite E, Cottage Grove 97424.

Creswell Visitor Center (541-895-5161; www.creswell-or.com), 55 N. Fifth Street, Creswell 97426.

Eugene Convention and Visitors Center of Lane County (1-800-547-5307; www.visitlanecounty.org), 754 Olive Street, Eugene 97440.

Fern Ridge Chamber of Commerce (541-935-3950; www.ci.veneta.or.us), 24967 OR 126, Veneta 97487.

Junction City/Harrisburg Chamber of Commerce (541-998-6154; www.jch-chamber.org), 585 Greenwood Street, Junction City 97448.

Lane County Parks (541-682-2000; www.lanecounty.org/parks), 3050 N. Delta Highway, Eugene 97408.

Oakridge/Westfir Chamber of Commerce (541-782-4146; www.oakridgechamber.com), P.O. Box 217, Oakridge 97463.

Siuslaw National Forest (541-750-7000; www.fs.fed.us/r6/siuslaw), 4077 SW Research Way, Corvallis 97339.

Umpqua National Forest (541-672-6601; www.fs.fed.us/r6/umpqua), 2100 NW Stewart Parkway, Roseburg 97471.

Willamette National Forest (541-225-6300; www.fs.fed.us/r6/willamette), 3106 Pierce Parkway, Suite D, Springfield 97477.

GETTING THERE *By air:* **Eugene Airport** (541-682-5544; www.flyeug.com), 28801 Douglas Drive, Eugene, 7 miles north of town, connects the valley to world via Horizon Air, United Express, Delta, and Allegiant Air.

By bus: **Greyhound** (1-800-231-2222) stops in Eugene at 987 Pearl Street.

By car: **I-5** and **US 99W** serve the southern valley north to south, and **OR 126** crosses it east to west. **OR 58** runs from the Willamette Pass down to Eugene. Farther south, **OR 138** runs from the Cascades crest down to Roseburg.

By rail: **AMTRAK** (1-800-USA-RAIL) stops in Eugene at 433 Willamette Street.

GETTING AROUND *By bus:* **Lane Transit District** (541-687-5555; www.ltd.org) covers the county from mountains to coast with bus service, with its hub in Eugene between 10th and 11th avenues and Olive and Willamette streets.

MEDICAL EMERGENCY **Cottage Grove Community Hospital** (541-942-0511), 1515 Village Drive, Cottage Grove.

McKenzie-Willamette Medical Center (541-726-4400), 1460 G Street, Springfield.

Sacred Heart Medical Center Riverbend (541-222-6929), 3333 RiverBend Drive, Springfield.

Sacred Heart Medical Center University District (541-686-6931), 1255 Hilyard Street, Eugene.

✷ To See

COVERED BRIDGES **Cottage Grove** calls itself the covered bridge capital of Oregon, and it does have seven of the structures within a small radius of town: **Dorena Bridge, Stewart Bridge, Mosby Creek Bridge, Currin Bridge, Chambers Railroad Bridge, Centennial Bridge,** and **Swinging Bridge.** Most were built between 1920 and 1949. Only the oldest, Mosby Creek, is still open to traffic. A brochure guide to the pleasant **Covered Bridge Scenic Byway** is available from the chamber of commerce (see *Guidance*).

FARMERS' MARKETS **Creswell Farmers' Market** (541-895-2096), 64 W. Oregon Street, Creswell. Tues. 4–7, May–Sept.

Eugene has four farmer's markets (541-431-4923). Three meet at E. Eighth and Oak streets: one Sat. 9–4, Apr.–mid-Nov.; one Tues. 10–3, May–Oct.; and one Thurs. noon–7, June–Sept. The fourth, a holiday farmer's market, meets at the fairgrounds, W. 13th and Monroe streets, Sat.–Sun. 10–6, mid-Nov.–late Dec.

Springfield Farmers' Market (541-345-7106) is held Fri. 9–2, early May–early Oct., on Main Street between Fifth and Sixth. A **Farmers' and Artists' Market** (503-407-3404) is held at the Gateway Mall Tues. 4–8, May–Oct.

Veneta's Downtown Farmers' Market (541-463-7565) takes place Fri. 2–6, June–Sept., at Territorial Highway and W. Broadway Avenue.

FARMS AND FARM STANDS **Hansen's Coast Fork Farms** (541-895-3082), 82735 Sears Road, Creswell. Fruits, berries, corn, and pumpkins. Mon.–Sat. 9–6, June–Sept.

Herrick Farms (541-741-1046), 88088 Millican Road, Springfield. Vegetables, fruits, and pumpkin patch. Daily 9–6, May–Dec.

J&M Farms (541-747-0065), 34435 Seavey Loop, Eugene. U-pick strawberries. Mon.–Sat. 8–5, June.

Johnson Vegetable Farms (541-343-9594), 89733 Armitage Road, Eugene. Berries, fruits, flowers, vegetables. Daily 9–6, June–Nov.

Saginaw Vineyard (541-942-1364), 80247 Delight Valley School Road, Cottage Grove. Blueberries (u-pick), vineyard, and winery (u don't pick). Call for hours.

Wet Rock Gardens (541-746-4444; www.wetrock.com), 2877 N. 19th Street, Springfield. U-pick fruits, berries, and nuts Sun., Wed., and Fri., Mar.–Oct.; and open daily 5–10 PM year-round.

FOR FAMILIES **Saturday Market** (541-686-8885; www.eugenesaturdaymarket.org), at Eighth and Oak streets, Eugene, Apr.–Nov., and indoors at the Lane Events Center Nov.–Dec. Two hundred arts and crafts booths, food, live music, and general merriment.

The Science Factory (541-682-7888; www.sciencefactory.org), 2300 Leo Harris Parkway, Eugene. Daily 10–4, planetarium shows Sat.–Sun. at 1 and 2. General admission $7; exhibits only or planetarium only, $4; seniors $4 or $6; children two and under free. Closed holidays. The Factory aims to thrill kids about science with frequently changing hands-on games and exhibits. And who can resist the mystery of a planetarium? Shows cover constellations, space travel, and more.

GARDENS **Hendricks Park** (541-682-4800), 2200 Summit Avenue, Eugene. The moist, temperate climate of western Oregon is prime habitat for rhodedendrons, wild and domestic, and Hendricks Park has a world-class collection. Twelve acres of rhodies and relatives bloom under a canopy of native oaks, peaking in Apr. and May. The park also boasts a new native plants garden.

Mount Pisgah Arboretum (541-747-3817), 34901 Frank Parrish Road, Eugene. Open dawn–dusk. Free. Draped on the side of Mount Pisgah, the arboretum offers 209 acres of trails and wildflowers, but it's the trees people come for. Dedicated to the preservation and appreciation of Pacific Northwest plant communities, miniecosystems show off trees of the oak savanna, water meadows, montane forests, and others. You may see deer or coyotes, as well. A visitors center contains native animal displays and a gift shop.

Owen Memorial Rose Garden (541-692-4824), 300 N. Jefferson, Eugene. Four hundred varieties of roses grace these few riverside acres, wound around with paved and graveled paths. Benches and picnic tables invite you to slow down and smell the climbing, tree, and bush roses, all labeled for your convenience. The garden also contains a Black Tartarian cherry tree, thought to be the nation's oldest, at about one hundred years.

HISTORIC HOMES **Belshaw-Condon House,** 1272 Jackson Street, Eugene. Thomas Belshaw was a musician and pharmacist who bucked the Victorian trend and built himself a French-style home complete with mansards, which, however, has a distinctly frontier look, being built with local materials and tools. Built in 1872, it was sold in 1882 to the famous missionary and geologist Thomas Condon, who excavated the John Day Fossil Beds and taught at the University of Oregon.

Christian House, 170 E. 12th Avenue, Eugene. This may be the oldest extant house in Eugene, having been built in 1855 as a farmhouse for Daniel Christian.

Collier House, 1170 E. 13th Avenue, Eugene. This vaguely Italianate 1885 building was originally the home of a physics professor, then housed several University of Oregon presidents before being given over to the music department.

Eugene Skinner's Replica Cabin, Skinner Park, Eugene. In the winter of 1846 Eugene Skinner came up the Willamette with an exploring party and selected a building site at the base of what is now Skinner Butte. Luckily a few Indians happened by who knew the river's proclivity for flooding and advised him to build higher, which he did, and next spring brought his wife down. Exhausted Applegate trail emigrants sheltered in it over the winter. Other settlers drifted down. The Skinners farmed and ran a ferry, and a few years later he and Judge Risdon platted out the town, which Mrs. Skinner named for her husband. As the settlement grew, Skinner turned to practicing law, but he died after catching a chill in the flood of 1861. This replica has been placed in a park by the river.

Mims House, 330 High Street, Eugene. Oregon had stringent Jim Crow laws, de facto and de jure, before the Civil Rights era. Among other restrictions, black people could not own land within the Eugene city limits. The Mims family managed to purchase this property with the help of C. B. Mims employer Joe Earley, who posed as a buyer and financed the purchase. The Mims were hospitable to black UO students and other visitors who couldn't get rooms elsewhere, and they turned part of their property into a boardinghouse (336 High Street). Luminaries like Ella Fitzgerald and Paul Robeson, who were good enough to entertain the city but not to stay in its hotels, lodged at the Mims'. The guest house, rather more upscale, still exists as the Annie D. Guesthouse, named for C. B.'s wife, Annie.

Shelton-McMurphey-Johnson House (541-484-0808; www.smjhouse.org), 303 Willamette Street, Eugene. Tues.–Fri. 10–1, Sat.–Sun. 1–4. General admission $5, children 12 and under $2. Named for the three families who lived in it, the house is a florid 1888 Queen Anne Victorian rife with arches, gables, carved capitals, and the obligatory tower. The intermarried families were instrumental in the creation of such essential entities as newspapers, the library, and the Eugene Water Company. Three times a year, a tea and tour are offered (call to reserve).

Some lovely old homes cluster in **Cottage Grove,** such as the 1896 **Dr. Snapp House,** now used for community celebrations and events.

HISTORIC SITES **County Clerk Building,** 740 W. 13th Street, Eugene. Small but dignified, it resembles a miniature Parthenon designed for home use. The county's first jury trials were held here from 1853 to 1855, but since the jury often had to sit outside under an oak tree, a larger building was soon commissioned. This relic is just south of the **Lane County Historical Society Museum.**

Deady Hall, opened in 1876, was the original University of Oregon building, known for a time simply as the Building. It had a student body of 177, of whom 98 were in the "preparatory department" as Eugene had no high school. Later it was named for Matthew Deady, a judge of the Territorial Supreme Court and district judge for Oregon. Like the Belshaw House, but considerably more imposing, it's another example of French Second Empire–style architecture.

Dorris Ranch Living History Farm (541-736-4544), 205 Dorris Street, Springfield. The Dorrises settled here in 1892 and started the first commercial hazelnut orchard in the United States. It's still a working orchard of more than nine thousand trees, now owned by the Park and Recreation District, and open for self-guided tours, interpretive history events, and strolls along 2 miles of trails.

Lane Hotel, 488 Willamette Street, Eugene. Originally the Gross Hotel, it went through a few name changes and now houses some local businesses. Built in 1903, it is one of just a few wooden buildings remaining in downtown Eugene.

Pioneer Cemetery, University Street between 15th and 18th avenues, Eugene. Many of the first owners of Eugene's historic homes are buried here, together with local Civil War veterans.

MUSEUMS **Bohemia Gold Mining Museum** (541-942-9044), 737 E. Main Street, Cottage Grove. Wed., Thurs., and Sat. 1–4. Free. Gold was discovered in the Bohemia Mountains just east of Cottage Grove in 1858, which was a boon for the town as it became a convenient supply site. The rush lasted longer than most as mining operations continued to the 1920s. The museum brings together rocks, tools, and equipment to explain the town's mining heritage; ask for a lesson on panning for gold.

Conger Street Clock Museum (541-344-6359; www.museum-of-time.com), 730 Conger Street, Eugene. Mon.–Sat. 10–5:30. If you need to make the most of time, this is certainly the place to do it. You can buy a clock here or have one fixed, or you can fixate on the eclectic collection. Did you know you could by an alarm clock in the 1850s that, at the appointed time, would strike a match that would then rotate over an oil lamp to light it? At least that was the idea. Most of these clocks burned up. Chockablock with antique clocks, this is a sort of, er, time warp.

Cottage Grove Museum (541-942-3962), Birch and H streets, Cottage Grove. Wed.–Sun. 1–4, mid-June–Labor Day and Sat.–Sun. 1–4 after Labor Day. Formerly St. Mary's Catholic Church, the museum displays memorabilia and industrial equipment of the town's early days, especially the heyday of the Bohemia Mines. The structure itself is of interest: why would parishioners have built an octagonal church in 1897? Such churches were not uncommon in the fifth-century Mediterranean and enjoyed a small renaissance in medieval Europe, but here?

THE COTTAGE GROVE MUSEUM WAS ONE OF THE VERY FEW OCTAGONAL CHURCHES IN THE UNITED STATES.

Creswell Historical Museum (541-895-5464), 55 S. Fifth Street, Creswell.

THE NEO-MOORISH FACADE OF THE JORDAN SCHNITZER MUSEUM OF ART AT THE UNIVERSITY OF OREGON

Sat.–Sun. 1–4. Free. The history of Creswell, along the Applegate Trail, is present in changing exhibits in an 1889 Methodist church.

Jordan Schnitzer Museum of Art (541-346-3027; www.uoma.uoregon.edu), 1430 Johnson Lane, Eugene. Tues. and Thurs.–Sun. 11–5, Wed. 11–8. General admission $5, seniors $3, children and students free. All free on first Fri. A vaguely Moorish brick building houses the University of Oregon's art collection, with a mixture of permanent and changing exhibits. It's recognized particularly for its Asian collection, from textiles to ceramics to prints, but also displays European and American works. On any given visit you might see ornate kimonos, a hall of Russian icons, a French impressionist series, Coptic illuminated gospels—or something completely different, depending on what's out there.

Lane County Historical Society and Museum (541-682-4242; www.lanecountyhistoricalsociety.org), 740 W. 13th Avenue, Eugene. Tues.–Sat. 10–4. General admission $3, seniors $2, students 15–17 $0.75. Since the Lane County area was the destination of many who came out on the Oregon Trail, the museum has a lot to preserve and commemorate in the way of artifacts, early photos, and tools of the great migration and of pioneer life. A collection of vehicles shows how people got around—across the prairie or to market—and a series of period rooms brings you into daily life in the growing state (the newest is an 1880s kitchen). Kids have their own space to explore pioneer history with puppets and antique clothes.

Oakridge Pioneer Museum (541-782-2402; www.oakridgemuseum.com), 76433 Pine Street, Oakridge. Tues. and Thurs. 9–noon, Sat. 1–4. Free. In the 1850s several attempts were made to find and clear a workable settlers' road across Oregon, to avoid both the perilous Columbia River and the arduous Applegate route over the Siskiyous. Oakridge lies in the hills along what became the Free Emigrant Trail connecting the Deschutes River with Eugene, now known as OR 58—free as opposed to the Barlow Road around Mount Hood, which charged a toll. It, too, was a hard route, crossing Willamette Pass, and the early parties suffered snow, hunger, and thirst—in the end only a couple of thousand settlers used it. The museum details the trail's history and the lives of the folks who settled here.

Oregon Air and Space Museum (541-461-1101), 90377 Boeing Drive, Eugene. Wed.–Sun. 10–4 (call to confirm). General admission $5, seniors $4, youth 13–18 $3, kids 6–12 $2. At the south end of Eugene Airport, this collection presents a brief history of aviation. Aircraft on display include fighters from a Fokker triplane to a Soviet MiG 17; a set of nine hundred scale models built by a very focused enthusiast trace plane history from its beginnings at Kitty Hawk to the present.

Springfield Museum (541-726-2300; www.springfieldmuseum.com), 590 Main Street, Springfield. A 1911 transformer station doesn't sound like a very hopeful home for a museum, but the Oregon Power Company was instrumental in the development of the southern Willamette Valley, so in a way it's a kind of exhibit in itself; in fact, it's on the National Register of Historic Places. Though Springfield has always been in Eugene's shadow—Eugene got the railroad first—it has had its own importance as a farming and timber center. The museum traces daily life from the original inhabitants, the Kalapuyas, to the farmers and lumbermen who came to define the region. It has even come into the present with a temporary exhibit of the Simpsons' couch—yes, this is Springfield.

University of Oregon Museum of Natural and Cultural History (541-346-3024; www.uoregon.edu/~mnh), 1680 E. 15th Avenue, Eugene. Wed.–Sun. 11–5. General admission $3, youth and seniors $2, families $8. As the intellectual home of anthropologist Luther Cressman, the university houses some of the very ten-thousand-year-old sagebrush sandals he discovered in the 1930s at Fort Rock, together with a whole series of footwear and other fiber items spanning the millennia (I always wondered how those sandals worked in cold weather and was relieved to see one lined with rabbit fur). Many more artifacts illuminate the daily life of the precontact Kalapuyas, complementing the natural history displays of modern Oregon species as well as some of Thomas Condon's famous fossil finds from central Oregon.

NATURAL WONDERS ♿ **Delta Old Growth Nature Trail,** 0.25 mile off OR 126 on FR 19. This grove of 650-year-old Douglas firs escaped the ax and rise over 200 feet high. A 0.5-mile, wheelchair-accessible trail winds through it.

Sahalie Falls and **Koosah Falls,** 100 and 120 feet tall, are about a mile apart along OR 126, 22 miles northeast of McKenzie Bridge. Thundering waters can be viewed from a short (but sometimes slippery) trail.

SCENIC DRIVES **Aufderheide Memorial Scenic Byway,** otherwise known as Forest Road 19, is 58 miles winding through the Willamette National Forest between OR 126, near Blue River, and Westfir on OR 58. Part of its length runs along the edge of the Three Sisters Wilderness, and most of the time you'll be paralleling the McKenzie or the Willamette River. At milepost 27 there is a stand of more than two hundred ancient Douglas firs called Constitution Grove.

Oregon Country Trails (1-877-276-8636; www.longtomtrail.com) will supply you with maps for several agricultural tours around the Willamette Valley (they'll also supply a limousine if you prefer). Download a tour guide and discover alpaca farms, herb gardens, petting farms, wineries, and all the fertile valley can offer.

WALKING TOURS A downloadable walking tour of **Eugene** takes you to points of historical or cultural interest, as well as favorite local markets. A similar tour takes in downtown **Springfield,** its series of murals, and historic millrace. Download these from www.discovereugene.com.

WINE A dozen or so vineyards dot the hills surrounding Eugene, notably **King Estate** (1-800-884-4441), 80854 Territorial Way, specializing in organic Pinot Noir and Pinot Gris, and **Territorial Vineyards** (541-684-9463), with a tasting room at 907 W. Third Avenue, Eugene, with Pinot Noir and Gris, Riesling, and Chardonnay. **The Wineries of Lane County** (541-345-1945; www.wineriesoflanecounty.com), P.O. Box 147, Creswell 97426, organizes tours and offers a downloadable map.

✷ To Do

BICYCLING Eugene prides itself on being bicycle friendly—after all, it's a green city—with 89 miles of bike lanes and 30 miles of paths. And that's just in the city limits. The 8-mile **Riverbank Path System** runs along both banks of the Willamette River, linking several parks. It is part of the **Willamette River Trail,** a 100-mile system connecting with Springfield's 29 miles of bike trails. Farther afield, the **Brice Creek Trail** is 11 miles of single-track along Brice Creek in Cottage Grove, moderately strenuous; for directions call 541-767-5000. Oakridge is something of a cycling mecca: the **Middle Fork Trail** (541-782-2283) starts level and then climbs upriver; 27 miles of flowers and waterfalls. Starting south of Eugene at Lane Community College, the **Rattlesnake Butte Trail** runs 43 miles on country roads with views of farms, meadows, and woods. The **City of Eugene Bicycling Program** (541-682-5471), 858 Pear Street, Eugene, has maps and information on these and many other trails.

BIRD-WATCHING The **Willamalane Birding Trail** takes in several parks around Springfield for a variety of songbirds and waterfowl; download a guide from www.willamalane.org (where you can also get checklists for the various birding areas). The **Fern Ridge Wildlife Area,** along OR 126 between Eugene and Veneta, with its marshes and reservoir, attracts 250 species of birds during the year, including osprey, herons, and migratory waterfowl. In Eugene, **Mount Pisgah Arboretum** (see *Gardens*) is a lovely habitat for songbirds. **Willow Creek,** a Nature Conservancy property south of W. 18th Avenue, is a fragment of native wet prairie with black terns, phalaropes, stilts, and other wetland birds. In the Cascades toward Oakridge, **Salt Creek Falls** is good in summer for warblers, woodpeckers, and black swifts.

CAMPING These **Lane County Parks** have campgrounds with RV and tent sites, and amenities like drinking water, showers, restrooms, and wheelchair access; to reserve call 541-682-2000. **Baker Bay Campground,** 35635 Shoreview Drive, Dorena, has 49 sites, no hookups, no reservations; open Apr.–Oct. **Richardson Park,** 25950 Richardson Park Road, Junction City, is on Fern Ridge Lake, with 88 hookup sites and play areas; reservations available. Open mid-Apr.–mid-Oct.

Fall Creek State Recreation Area, off OR 58, 27 miles southeast of Eugene, has 42 tent and five primitive campsites on Fall Creek Reservoir, with a swimming area, boat ramp, and toilets; open May–Sept., no reservations.

A wealth of campgrounds dot the **Willamette National Forest** in the mountains to the east. In the McKenzie River Ranger District (for fee and reservation information, call the district office at 541-822-3381): **Delta Campground,** 5 miles east of Blue River off OR 126 on FR 400, with 38 tent/trailer sites, drinking water, ADA sites, toilets, and nature trail; no reservations, open May–Oct. **Mona Campground,** 7 miles east of Blue River via OR 126 and FR 15, with 23 tent/trailer sites, toilets, and swimming; open Apr.–Sept., no water or reservations. **Lookout Campground,** 6 miles east of Blue River by OR 126 and FR 15, with 20 tent/trailer sites, water, and toilets; open Apr.–Sept., no reservations. **McKenzie Bridge Campground,** 1 mile west of McKenzie Bridge on OR 126, with 20 tent/trailer sites (eight reservable), water, and toilets; open Apr.–Sept. **Paradise Campground,** 4 miles east of McKenzie Bridge on OR 126, with 64 tent/trailer sites (23 reservable), water, toilets, and boat launch; open Apr.–Sept. **Olallie Campground,** 11 miles east of McKenzie Bridge on OR 126, with 17 tent/trailer sites (all reservable), toilets, and water; open Apr.–Sept. **Trail Bridge Campground,** 13 miles east of McKenzie Bridge on OR 126, with 19 RV sites and 27 walk-in or tent sites, water, toilet, and boat launch; open Apr.–Sept., no reservations. **Lakes End Campground,** boat access only from across Smith Reservoir (from OR 126, 12 miles northeast of McKenzie Bridge take FRs 732 and 730, then paddle), with 17 tent-only sites and toilet; no water, no reservations; open May–Oct. **Ice Cap Creek Campground,** 17 miles northeast of McKenzie Bridge, just off OR 126, with eight tent-only sites and 14 tent/trailer sites, water, toilets, and nonmotorized boating; open May–Sept. (snow permitting), no reservations. **Coldwater Cove Campground,** 18 miles northeast of McKenzie Bridge on OR 126, with 35 tent/trailer sites (12 reservable), toilets, water, and trail; open May–Oct. **Lost Lake Campground,** 28 miles northeast of McKenzie Bridge, near junction of OR 126 and US 20, with 15 sites and toilets; no water, no reservations; open May–Nov. (weather permitting). **Limberlost Campground,** on OR 242, 5 miles east of McKenzie Bridge, with 10 tent/trailer and two tent-only sites, toilet; no water, no reservations; open May–Oct. **Alder Srongs Campground,** on OR 242, 12 miles east of McKenzie Bridge, with six tent-only sites, toilet, and trails; no water, no fee, no reservations; open June–Sept. (weather permitting). **Scott Lake Campground,** on OR 242, 17 miles east of McKenzie Bridge, with 20 tent-only, walk-in sites, toilet, nonmotorized boating, close access to Mount Washington Wilderness; no water, no reservations; open July–Oct. Along FR 19, which branches off OR 126 4 miles east of McKenzie Bridge, are several campgrounds: **Slide Creek Campground,** off FR 19 on FR 1900-500, with 16 tent/trailer sites, toilets, water nearby, swimming, boating; open June–Sept., no reservations. **Cougar Crossing Campground,** on FR 19, 9 miles south of OR 126, with 12 tent/trailer sites, toilets, swimming, trails; no water, no reservations; open May–Sept. **Sunnyside Campground,** 0.25 mile beyond Cougar Crossing on FR 1900-500, with 13 tent/auto sites (trailers discouraged due to steep entrance road), toilet, swimming, hiking; no water, no reservations; open May–Sept. **French Pete Campground,** on FR 19 about 11 miles south of OR 126, with 17 tent/trailer sites, water, toilets, hiking, deep shade; open May–Sept., no reservations. **Red Diamond Campground,** 15 miles south of OR 126 on FR 19, with three tent/trailer sites, portable toilet; no water, reservable. **Roaring River Campground,** 22 miles south of OR 126 on FR 19, with five sites, toilet; no water, reservations allowed. **Frissell Crossing Campground,** 21 miles south of OR 126 on FR 19, with 12 tent/trailer sites, water, toilets, streamside forest; open

May–Sept., no reservations. **Box Canyon Horse Camp,** 33 miles south of OR 126 on FR 19, with 13 tent/trailer sites, corrals, toilets, water for livestock only; open June–Nov. (snow permitting), no reservations.

In the Middle Fork Ranger District (OR 58 corridor), call 541-782-2283 for fee and reservation information: **Hampton Campground,** 9 miles west of Oakridge on OR 58, with four tent/trailer sites, toilet, water, boat launch, on reservoir; open Apr.–Sept., no reservations. **Black Canyon Campground,** 6 miles west of Oakridge on OR 58, with 59 tent/trailer sites and 13 tent-only sites, water, toilets, boat ramp, nature trail, ADA restrooms and campsites; open Apr.–Sept., reservations allowed. **Blue Pool Campground,** 10 miles east of Oakridge on OR 58, with 24 tent/trailer sites, toilets, water, near McCredie Hot Springs; open May–Sept., no reservations. **Salmon Creek Falls Campground,** 6 miles from Oakridge along Salmon Creek Road, with 15 tent/trailer sites (some ADA), water, ADA toilets, hiking, cycling; open Apr.–mid-Sept., no reservations. **Kiahanie Campground,** 20 miles northeast of Westfir on OR 58, with 19 tent/trailer sites (some ADA), quiet old growth, water, ADA toilets; open May–Sept., no reservations. **Packard Creek Campground,** 9 miles southeast of Oakridge via OR 58, Kitson Springs Road, and FR 21, with 35 tent/trailer sites (13 reservable), water, ADA restrooms, swimming, waterskiing; open Apr.–Sept., reservations advised. **Secret Campground,** 21 miles south of Oakridge via OR 58, Kitson Springs Road, and FR 21, with six tent/trailer sites, toilets, open Apr.–Sept.; no water, no reservations. **Camper's Flat Campground,** 2 miles beyond Secret Campground, with five tent/trailer sites, toilet, water, cycling, hiking; open Apr.–Oct., no reservations. **Sacandaga Campground,** 26 miles southeast of Oakridge via OR 58, Kitson Road, and FR 21, with 17 tent/trailer sites, water, toilets, trails, riverside; open July–Oct., no reservations. **Indigo Springs Campground,** 3 miles beyond Sacandaga on FR 21, with three tent-only sites, toilet; open Apr.–Oct.; no water, no fee, no reservations. **Gold Lake Campground,** take OR 58 for 28 miles east to Gold Lake Road, and continue 2 miles to the campground; 21 tent/trailer sites, water, toilets, huckleberries, canoeing; open June–Oct., no reservations. Several campgrounds edge Waldo Lake high in the Cascades: **Shadow Bay Campground,** take Waldo Lake Road from OR 58 for 6 miles and follow signs; 92 tent/trailer sites (57 reservable), water, ADA toilets, trails, swimming, boating; open July–Sept. **Islet Campground,** leave OR 58 and take Waldo Lake Road for 11 miles to FR 5898, and follow that to campground; 55 tent/trailer sites, water, ADA toilets, beaches, mosquitoes; open July–Sept., no reservations. **North Waldo Campground,** from Waldo Lake Road take FR 5898 to FR 5895 to campground; 58 tent/trailer sites, ADA toilets, water, swimming, mosquitoes, trails; open July–Oct., no reservations.

CANOEING, KAYAKING, AND RAFTING **Willamette Water Trail** (503-223-6418; www.willamettewatertrail.org) is a paddling trail down the Willamette River from Eugene to Portland—the aorta, if you will, of the valley's agricultural heartland. Guides can be downloaded from the above Web site or ordered by phone. The **McKenzie River** is a rafting mecca with thrilling rapids; do it yourself or hire an outfitter like **A. Helfrich** (541-726-5039), 2605 Harvest Lane, Springfield, or **High Country Expeditions** (1-888-461-7238), Belknap Hot Springs, McKenzie Bridge. For quieter waters try some of the mountain lakes, like **Gold Lake** or **Scott Lake** (see *Camping*).

GOLF **Emerald Valley Golf Club** (541-895-2174; www.emeraldvalleygolf.com), 8301 Dale Kuni Road, Creswell. Eighteen holes.

Fiddler's Green Golf Center (1-800-548-5500), 91292 OR 99, Eugene. Eighteen holes.

Laurelwood Golf Course (541-484-4653; www.golflaurelwood.com), 2700 Columbia Street, Eugene. Nine holes.

Tokatee Golf Club (1-800-452-6376), 54947 McKenzie Highway (OR 126), Blue River. Eighteen holes.

HIKING The **Riverbank Path System** (see *Bicycling*) is a Eugene favorite for walkers as well as cyclists. Also in Eugene, a series of short, easy loops make **Mount Pisgah** a place for family walks; the adjacent **Howard Buford Recreation Area** offers longer trails. The 1-mile **Skinner Butte Trail** at the north end of High Street rewards the walker with views over town, and the steeper **Spencer Butte Trail** leads to an all-around panorama. Near Cottage Grove, the **Brice Creek Trail** is a moderate 6-mile path beside small waterfalls, open to bikes as well and hikers (see *Bicycling*). For the dedicated walker, the **Row River Trail** is a rails-to-trails achievement: 15 fairly level miles from downtown Cottage Grove (541-942-2411) to Culp Creek, with a trailhead in town and one at Mosby Creek, and restrooms at several points.

Naturally many trails crisscross the **Willamette National Forest.** A selection from the McKenzie River District (541-822-3381): the **Sahalie-Koosah Falls Loop** is 2.5 miles, often bathed in mist of some very impressive waterfalls, 19 miles east of McKenzie Bridge on OR 126. A 0.5-mile link trail (or you can drive) takes you to a 5.5-mile loop around **Clear Lake,** formed when a lava flow dammed the McKenzie three millennia ago; it is clear and a hundred feet deep. **French Pete Creek,** near **French Pete Campground** (see *Camping*), offers two choices: an easy 3.4-mile round-trip, or a 10-mile trip involving a thousand-foot climb and two unbridged creek crossings. Then there's the challenging **McKenzie River Trail,** 26 miles along the rushing McKenzie River, but a child could walk the first 4 miles (round-trip) through old forest to view the river disappear underground and reappear from a turquoise pool; turn right off OR 126 onto FR 655, 14 miles east of McKenzie Bridge and park at the trailhead 0.5 mile on.

In the **Middle Fork District** (541-782-2283): **Elijah Bristow State Park,** 7 miles east of Oakridge on OR 58, presents two restful loops of 1 and 3 miles among maples and blackberries. Fifteen miles east of Springfield via Marcola Road, you can turn left to **Shotgun Creek Park** for another family-friendly, 3.5-mile loop among the woods of Shotgun Creek. **Fall Creek** is a popular trail, especially for mushroom hunters, 28 miles from Oakridge by OR 58, Jasper-Lowell Road, and a series of signed turns; 6 miles round-trip through old growth and woodland wildflowers. **Larison Creek Trail,** on FR 21 east of Oakridge, is an easy 6-mile round-trip, good for spring wildflowers and fall colors; open year-round.

HOT SPRINGS The nice thing about a volcanic heritage is hot running water. **Belknap Hot Springs** (541-822-3512; www.belknaphotsprings.com), 59296 Belknap Springs Road, McKenzie Bridge, is a developed but down-to-earth resort built on the springs lining the river 60 miles east of Eugene. Bathing is in two swim-

MUSIC-INSPIRED SCULPTURE AT BELKNAP HOT SPRINGS

ming pools; the grounds, set in deep forest, are nicely landscaped, too. **McCredie Hot Springs,** just past Blue Pool Campground on OR 58 near Oakridge, is rustic and clothing optional; campgrounds nearby. **Terwilliger Hot Springs** (541-822-3799), also known as **Cougar Hot Springs,** lies on FR 19 about 8 miles south of OR 126 and is a series of clothing-optional small pools; small fee, no alcohol.

WINTER SPORTS Several sno-parks near **Santiam Pass** and **Willamette Pass** are starting points for snowmobiling, cross-country skiing, snowshoeing, etc. (sticker required); check with Willamette National Forest for fees and directions. For downhill skiing at **Willamette Pass Ski Area,** see "Klamath Basin–Crater Lake Area."

✷ Wilder Places

PARKS Eugene prides itself on being green, and so it is, with plenty of open space. Some city parks: **Alton Baker Park,** the city's largest park, extends along the river from the Ferry Street Bridge east to Aspen Street and is a haven of shady bowers, paths, and footbridges. You'll also find an off-leash dog area, community garden, and the Hays Tree Garden—in short, it's where the city goes to relax. **Hendricks Park,** at the corner of Summit and Skyline Drive, contains trails, old forest, a native plant garden, and a renowned rhododendron garden within its 78 acres. **Skinner Butte Park,** from Ferry Street to Lincoln along Cheshire, takes in 100 acres of the butte Eugene Skinner homesteaded and includes a replica of his cabin as well as trails and a rock-climbing area.

Lane County has quite an extensive park system, including some camping parks. A $3 day-use parking fee applies. Campsites must reserved in advance (541-682-2000): **Armitage Park,** 90064 Coburg Road, Eugene. Play horseshoes or volleyball, picnic, run your dog, or launch your boat at this 57-acre park. There's a year-round campground with 37 sites at $25 each.

Baker Bay Park, 35635 Shoreview Drive, Dorena. On Dorena Lake, the park has play areas, boating, swimming, a marina, and a 49-site campground (open mid-Apr.–mid-Oct.).

Howard Buford Recreation Area, south of Springfield, is a 2,363-acre park sprawling over much of Mount Pisgah, including the arboretum. Hike a thousand feet to the top for views of the Willamette flowing around its base, or just stroll.

Perkins Peninsula Park, 26647 OR 126, Veneta, is open for day use May–Sept. This is a quiet location on Fern Ridge Reservoir with picnic tables, unsupervised swimming, and a nature trail.

Richardson Park, 25950 Richardson Park Road, Junction City. Also on Fern Ridge Reservoir, this is a busy park with a marina, food concessions, play areas, and an 88-site campground (open mid-Apr.–mid-Oct.).

Area state parks (for state park information call 1-800-551-6949):

Cascadia State Park, in the Cascade foothills 14 miles east of Eugene on US 20. A hundred years ago, a resort stood here to draw visitors to the mineral springs. And they did come, by wagon and then by car, but little remains of it now except the Soda Springs themselves. It's a peaceful spot seemingly a world away from the highway, with short trails to a swimming hole and to Soda Creek Falls. A 25-site primitive campground is not too primitive to have restrooms; to reserve, call 1-800-551-6949.

Dexter State Recreation Site, 16 miles east of Eugene on OR 58, sits on the edge of Dexter Reservoir and is a recreational site for boating and fishing, with equestrian and walking trails besides (no water though). No fee. Foot trails lead to nearby **Elijah Bristow State Park.** Bristow was one of the earliest settlers in Lane County and is honored with an 837-acre park along a stretch of the Willamette that still enjoys salmon and steelhead runs. No fee to play in this lush, green park with picnic tables, water, and restrooms.

Fall Creek State Recreation Area, 31 miles southeast of Eugene; from OR 58 turn left on Jasper-Lowell Road, right on Winberry Creek Road, and right on Peninsula Road. Where Fall Creek flows into a reservoir, you'll find a park among venerable Douglas firs with five day-use areas (mostly for boaters) and a campground with vault toilets, 42 tent sites, and five "primitive" sites (no reservations). The campground is open May 1–Sept. 30.

Jasper State Recreation Site, 12 miles southeast of Eugene on Jasper Park Road, off OR 58. Open May–Sept. This riverside park gets busy in the summer with several reservable group picnic shelters, but it has plenty of bird- and wildlife viewing in its quieter moments.

Lowell State Recreation Site, 17 miles southeast of Eugene on Old Pengara Road, off OR 58. On the north side of Dexter Reservoir, the day-use park is used for boating, picnicking, and general relaxation.

Washburne State Wayside, 4 miles northwest of Junction City on US 99W. This is just a wayside, but it's nicely shaded, and a series of interpretive signs explains the Applegate Trail that passed here on its way from southern Oregon to the northern Willamette Valley.

WILDERNESS AREAS **Waldo Lake Wilderness,** high in the Cascades, embraces a chain of mountain lakes; Waldo Lake (named for pioneering conservationist Judge Waldo), the second deepest in Oregon, actually lies just outside the wilderness area. Trails connect meadows and lakes, with a 22-mile loop circumambulating Waldo Lake. Hiking, fishing, and camping are the primary activities, but mosquitoes can be thick, especially in July. Access is via FRs 24, 19, and 5897, off OR 58.

WILDLIFE REFUGES ♿ **Buckhead Wildlife Area,** 5 miles north of Oakridge off OR 58, consists of 250 acres of woods and wetlands along the Middle Fork of the Willamette River. A 1-mile, wheelchair-accessible trail allows viewing of osprey, waterfowl, and songbirds.

Fern Ridge Wildlife Area (541-935-2591), 5 miles west of Eugene on OR 126. Run by the Oregon Department of Fish and Wildlife, Fern Ridge is a popular bird-watching spot, attracting eagles, osprey, shorebirds, and migrating waterfowl. Several parks adjoin the refuge, providing camping, picnicking, swimming, and canoe launching, while paths and boardwalks take you close to the wildlife. Maps and bird checklists are available at headquarters. Some seasonal restrictions are in place to protect waterfowl and during hunting season; check with headquarters.

West Eugene Wetlands (541-683-6494; www.wewetlands.org), 751 S. Danebo Road, Eugene. Daily 6 AM–11 PM. Just west of Eugene, this tract protects some of the 1 percent of Willamette Valley wetland habitat that has survived draining, homesteading, agriculture, and urban sprawl. Along the bike path or walking trails you might spot a beaver or an otter, or some of the plant species endemic to the valley. Maps are available online or at the Project Office.

✷ Lodging

BED & BREAKFASTS

Blue River

Drift Inn (541-822-3822; www.carolyngabriel.com), 51592 McKenzie Highway. Three rooms welcome guests year-round at Carolyn Gabriel's home on the river. This one is convenient for fishing, hiking, and horseback riding, and Carolyn makes a hearty breakfast and evening snacks. Doubles $100, with breakfast; shared baths.

Cottage Grove

Apple Inn (1-800-942-2393; www.appleinnbb.com), 30697 Kenady Lane. Out in the country, you can rest on Harry and Kathe's 180-acre tree farm in one of two snug, quilt-decorated rooms. And even though they supply your room with a refrigerator and microwave, they still fix a full breakfast and serve a snack tray in the evening! Better hit the bike trail or at least stroll among the trees. $119–139, double occupancy.

🐾 **Gray Cat Inn** (541-942-1900; www.graycatinn.com), 337 N. Ninth Street. Two bedrooms, one down and one up, welcome guests to Celia Weimer's 1920s Craftsman. She does have cats but welcomes other small pets with prior notice—and she'll accommodate virtually any dietary restrictions if you let her know ahead of time. $75–95, including full breakfast, double occupancy.

Eugene

♿ **A Secret Garden Bed and Breakfast** (1-888-484-7655; www.secretgardenbbinn.com), 1910 University Street. Tucked away on a side street near the university, this rather imposing, dormered house is in fact screened from the street by hedged gardens. The 12 rooms and one apartment offer all you could wish in the way of puffy comforters and quiet ease; one room is wheelchair accessible. Doubles $115–160, with breakfast.

♿ **The Campbell House** (1-800-264-2519; www.campbellhouse.com), 252 Pearl Street. This massive Victorian house boasts a mind-boggling 20 guest rooms. It was the retirement "dream home" of John Cogswell, who came west on the Oregon Trail, made a fortune in the California gold rush (not to mention timber and sheep), and built the house in 1892 for his daughter Idaho. Today the house is luxuriously furnished with all the amenities you could want, and close to downtown besides. But if you don't feel like going out, the on-premises restaurant will take care of you. Ground-floor rooms are wheelchair accessible. $129–349, with breakfast.

C'est la Vie Inn (1-866-302-3014; www.cestlavieinn.com), 1006 Taylor Street. The flamboyant Queen Anne made quite a stir when it was built, and it still does, though many of the details had to be restored or replaced over the years: scrollwork, sunbursts, shingle patterns, turret, and more (it's on the National Register of Historic Places and worth a look even if you don't stay). The interior decor, though, is distinctly modern and uncluttered, which is probably just as well. Four rooms run $125–$250, with all the amenities, including breakfast.

The Oval Door (1-800-882-3160; www.ovaldoor.com), 988 Lawrence Street. Five large, contemporary rooms named for flowers fill the house with the oval door, and chef/owners Nicole Craig and Melissa McGuire will fill you with their imaginative breakfasts. Each room has, of course, its own bath, clean-lined furniture, and Wi-Fi. Doubles $85–195; children 12 and over welcome.

River Walk Inn (1-800-621-2904; www.ariverwalkinn.com), 250 N. Adams Street. Just steps from the Owen Rose Garden, the B&B is also a stone's throw from the Willamette walking and biking paths (bicycles available). The restful 1930s house offers three rooms to guests, each with designated bath, and a library with books for all ages. Children welcome. $100–120, double occupancy.

CABINS AND COTTAGES

McKenzie Bridge

Loloma Lodge (541-822-6231; www.lolomalodge.com), 56687 McKenzie Highway. Auto travel over the Cascades had just become feasible when the log house and cabin were built in the 1930s, and the solid old buildings give a sense of snug independence. Several newer cabins date from the 1960s. The three-bedroom house comes with a fireplace and porches to enjoy the view, while the cabins all have a kitchen and bath (the newer ones have radiant floor heating). House $500, cabins $175.

Vida

Heaven's Gate River Cottages (541-896-3855; www.heavensgateriver cottages.com), milepost 50018, McKenzie River Highway. Studio and one-bedroom cottages sleep two to four along the McKenzie River. All have decks over the water, fireplaces, full kitchens, and bathrooms. $105–120, double occupancy.

FOREST SERVICE RENTALS To reserve these, call 1-877-444-6777 or go to www.recreation.gov.

Box Canyon Guard Station, on FR 19 about 75 miles southeast of Eugene, can sleep up to four and has a small propane stove and an outhouse. Bring bedding and water. Open mid-June–mid-Oct.; $60

Indian Ridge Lookout, about 65 miles southeast of Eugene on FR

1980-247, has two twin beds but no heat or cooking facilites. An outhouse is 50 feet from the tower. Bring bedding, water, and cooking materials. Open mid-June–mid-Oct.; $55.

Timber Butte Cabin, 19 miles from Lowell off OR 58 (call Middle Fork Ranger District at 541-782-2283 for directions). With windows on all sides and a catwalk, the small cabin sleeps two to four and has a propane cookstove and heating stove. A vault toilet is 300 feet from the cabin. Bring bedding and water. Open mid-May–Oct.; $65.

Timpanogas Shelter, 85 miles southeast of Eugene via OR 58, FR 21, and FR 2154, is a rustic cabin sleeping six to eight, with a woodstove and an outdoor fire ring. There's an outhouse, but bring water and bedding. Open June–Oct., but mosquitoes can be fierce till Aug.; $50.

HOSTELS

Eugene

Eugene being a youthful town, there is some youthful budget accommodation:

Eugene Whiteaker Hostel (541-343-3335), 970 W. Third Avenue. Renovated in 2006, this little house offers five private rooms and dorm rooms sleeping two to five, close to the river and parks. Dorm beds $22–27, private rooms $22.50–35.

HOTELS AND MOTELS

Eugene

Excelsior Inn (1-800-321-6963; www.excelsiorinn.com), 754 E. 13th Avenue. One of Eugene's more elegant hotels, it used to be a University of Oregon sorority house, though you wouldn't know it to look at it. The overused phrase "old-world charm" actually seems to mean something here, where stained glass, wrought iron, and polished cherrywood join in harmony to make you feel at home rather than impressed. Fourteen rooms range from $99 to $270 and include a full breakfast; the **Excelsior Ristorante** (see *Dining Out*) is right downstairs.

RESORTS

McKenzie Bridge

🐾 **Belknap Hot Springs** (541-822-3512; www.belknaphotsprings.com), 59296 Belknap Springs Road. The water at Belknap Hot Springs is *really* hot, coming out of the ground at 185–195 degrees across the river from the lodge. There it's mixed with cooler water and piped for bathing—the attraction here since one R. S. Belknap opened the resort in the 1870s. People would take the 16-hour stagecoach ride from Eugene to spend time here, soak, and hike into the mountains. The

NATURE-INSPIRED SCULPTURE ALONG THE MCKENZIE RIVER AT BELKNAP HOT SPRINGS

current lodge and premises date from the 1970s, as the previous structures were washed out in the floods of 1962 and 1964. Today you can choose a lodge room or cabin, or bring your own RV or tent. But don't just soak in the mineral-laden hot water; the gardens are lovely, and there is access to miles of hiking and biking trails. Pets allowed in a few cabins; check with management. Lodge rooms $100–125, cabins $65–130 (no linens in the pet-friendly cabins), RV sites $35, tent sites $20–25; a house sleeping 12 runs $400.

✷ Where to Eat

DINING OUT

Eugene

Ambrosia (541-342-4141; www.ambrosiarestaurant.com), 174 E. Broadway. Open for lunch and dinner. Regional Italian cuisine with Northwest ingredients—pasta, seafood, and, of course, pizza from a wood-fired stove.

Excelsior Inn (see *Lodging*). Daily for breakfast, lunch, and dinner, and Sun. brunch. The Excelsior Ristorante, at the inn, prides itself on seasonal, fresh ingredients for their Italian menu—the pasta is made in-house, from raw materials, and all the rest follows from that—elegant food, elegantly served. Reservations recommended.

Ring of Fire (541-344-6475; www.ringoffirerestaurant.com), 1099 Chambers Street. Daily for lunch and dinner. Pornwadee Gardner prepares the top-notch Thai cuisine she learned at her grandma's knee, and dishes from all round the Pacific Rim—hence the name Ring of Fire (speaking of which, you can, of course, choose mild, medium, or hot). The restaurant's Lava Lounge is known for its creative drinks.

Veneta

Our Daily Bread (541-935-4921; www.ourdailybreadrestaurant.com), 88170 Territorial Road. Daily for breakfast (or brunch), lunch, and dinner. In the heart of wine country, Our Daily Bread serves fine meals in a former church. In fact, all breads, pastries, and dessert goodies are made by pastry chef Catharine Perkins, and just about everything else is homemade with fresh, local ingredients as well. The cuisine is Northwestern and so are the wines, and the prices are right. Local art hangs on the walls, and a local harpist-pianist duo plays on weekends. Kids eat free on Sat.!

EATING OUT

Cottage Grove

Fleur de Lis Patisserie and Café (541-767-0700; www.fleurdeliscafe.net), 616 Main Street. Tues.–Sat. 7–3. French pastries by French pastry chef Eric Jegat, who took a Pascal-like bet in leaving his Monterey bakery to open one in small Cottage Grove. Bravo! Real croissants, fruit tarts, and fancy cakes, plus soups, quiches, and sandwiches at lunchtime.

Eugene

Café Siena (541-344-0300), 853 E. 13th Street. Mon.–Fri. 8–7, Sat.–Sun. 9–4. Small and scrappy, this is where Eugene wakes up, especially college Eugene. Crêpes, huevos rancheros, pancakes—it's quick, and it's tasty.

Mezza Luna Pizzeria (541-684-8900; www.mezzalunapizzeria.com), 933 Pearl Street. Daily for lunch and dinner. Eighteen varieties of some of Eugene's best, and half of them are vegetarian. Even better, you can get most of them by the slice.

Newman's Fish Company (541-344-2371; www.newmansfish.com), 1545 Willamette Street. Closed Sun. Buy your fresh fish (it doesn't come much fresher), Pacific salmon, halibut, crab, whatever's in season; or buy some fish-and-chips made with same at the walk-up window. Another location is at 485 Coburg Road. Newman's has been around for more than a hundred years.

Red Agave (541-683-2206; http://redagave.net), 454 Willamette Street. Open for dinner from 5 PM; closed Sun. Not your usual Mexican-American fare. Summer-squash pupusas and oysters with tomatillo-habanero sauce are just a couple of the Northwest/south of the border flavors you can expect, and the ingredients come from local and regional sources whenever possible. They're just combined differently.

Sweet Basil Thai Cuisine (541-284-2944; www.sweetbasileug.com), 941 Pearl Street. Daily for dinner; Mon–Sat. for lunch. This one stands out in a city with no lack of Thai restaurants. The food is authentic, delicious, and graciously served. A favorite.

Sweet Life Patisserie (541-683-5676; www.sweetlifedesserts.com), 755 Monroe Street. Open daily. Cakes, cookies, tarts, tartlets, croissants, and many more goodies adorn the display counters here; to be enjoyed with a cup of organic coffee or tea, or spirited away.

✷ Entertainment

Hult Center for the Performing Arts (541-682-5000; www.hultcenter.org), Seventh and Willamette, Eugene. Home of the Eugene Ballet, Opera, Symphony, Mozart Players, and Concert Choir, and venue for a panoply of visiting performers.

The Shedd Institute (541-687-6526; www.ofam.org), 868 High Street, Eugene. Musicals, jazz, folk, and anything musical.

✷ Shopping

Fifth Street Public Market, corner of Fifth Avenue and High Street, has food courts, musicians, galleries, crafts stores, and an array of small shops.

✷ Events

January–February: **Oregon Truffle Festival** (503-296-5929; www.oregontrufflefestival.com), end of Jan.–beginning of Feb., Eugene. Yes, Oregon has truffles, too; learn, taste, eat. Admission.

June: **Black Sheep Gathering** (541-935-1744; www.blacksheepgathering.org), third weekend, Lane Events Center, 796 W. 13th Avenue, Eugene. Everything to do with sheep and goat wool; this is one of the biggest expositions of its kind in the United States, with workshops, spinning circles, and animals.

July: **Bohemia Mining Days** (541-942-2411), second full week, Coiner Park, Cottage Grove. Cottage Grove celebrates its mining heritage with a week of parades, tours, mining equipment displays, food, and crafts, culminating with a breakfast in the nearby gold-bearing hills.

Oregon Country Fair (541-935-3247; www.oregoncountryfair.org), 24550 Chickadee Lane, Veneta. The woods outside Veneta have been the setting for this festival of the counterculture for the past 40 years. And even though counterculture isn't what it used to be (for one thing, it's now officially a drug- and alcohol-free event), it produces a lot of quirky art, entertainment, food, and practical stuff.

June–July: **Oregon Bach Festival** (1-800-457-1486; www.oregonbachfestival.com). Nearly a month of Bach-themed concerts at Eugene's Hult Center and around the state.

Mount Hood and the Columbia River Gorge

4

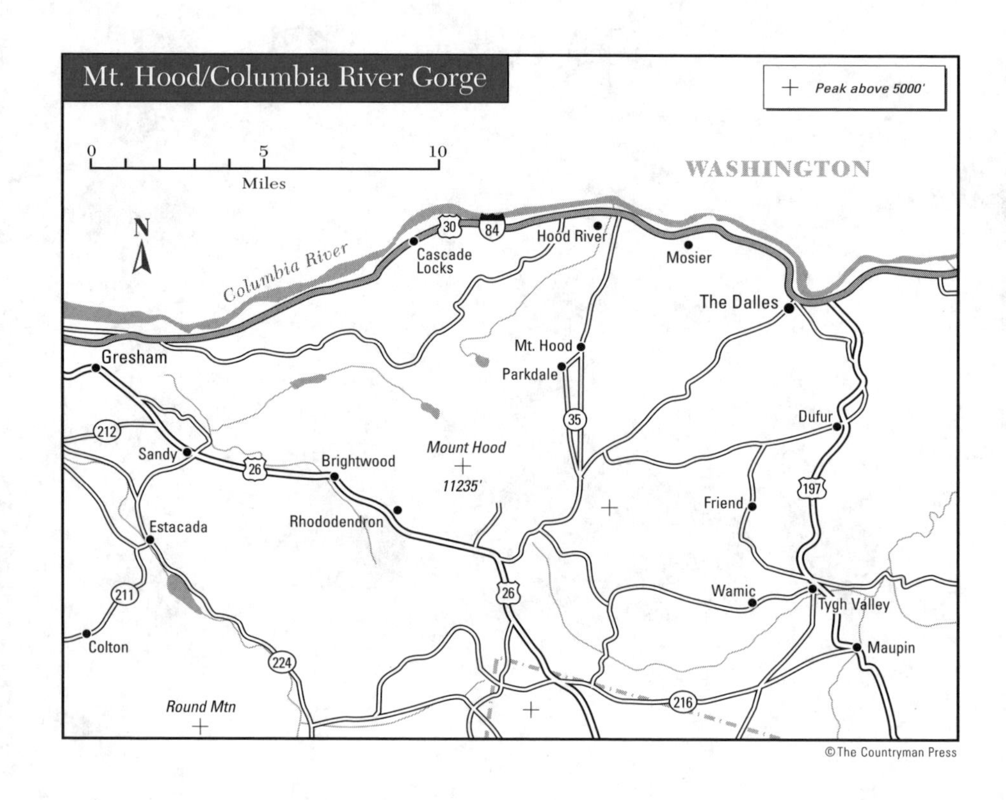
Mt. Hood/Columbia River Gorge
Peak above 5000'
0
5
10
Miles
N
WASHINGTON
Columbia River
30
84
Cascade Locks
Hood River
Mosier
The Dalles
Mt. Hood
Parkdale
Gresham
35
Dufur
212
Sandy
Mount Hood
11235'
26
Brightwood
197
Friend
Rhododendron
Estacada
26
Wamic
Tygh Valley
211
Colton
224
Maupin
216
Round Mtn
©The Countryman Press

MOUNT HOOD AND THE COLUMBIA RIVER GORGE

Standing here I realize the magnitude of my task . . . that we might have sense enough to do the right thing in the right way . . . so as not to mar what God has put there.

—Samuel Lancaster, Historic Columbia River Highway engineer

An admirable aspiration, in which Lancaster and his crews largely, and surprisingly, succeeded—creating road access to an extremely rugged, but extremely beautiful area without ruining it is a rare accomplishment, then or now. Yet you can drive his road today and admire the sinuous grading and stonework almost as much as the waterfalls. Since his time, of course, the gorge has been irremediably altered. The great dams that indundated beaches, villages, and historic sites, turning the mammoth river into a series of long flowing lakes, and the roar of I-84, would probably make Lancaster cry. Yet it may have been his impetus that finally kept the 70 miles of towering basalt cliffs fir-clad and high-rise-free. The 1987 act creating the Columbia River Gorge National Scenic Area means growth and development must be compatible with its natural, rural, and aesthetic value.

Oregonians are deeply ambivalent about the river. Most of us use electricity derived from the Columbia or its tributaries. We even use I-84 when we have to, though we might wish it had been routed behind the gorge rather than through it. But we desperately want, need, to commune with the 4,000-foot canyon, its forests, waterfalls, and small towns, its altered river. Like Lancaster, we see the stupendous phenomenon and want to preserve it. And now that we understand how it came to be (see *Natural Wonders*), the awe factor is even greater.

Though less than a hundred miles long, the Columbia River Gorge is a study in contrasts. From the western end, you drive through thick forest, damp with high rainfall and waterfall spray (77 falls just on the Oregon side). You are edging around the massive base of Mount Hood, and as you pass Hood River you enter the mountain's rain shadow to find yourself amid high, barren plateaus in a completely different ecosystem—from rain forest to High Desert in one afternoon. In fact, if you start earlier and add the Mount Hood Loop to your day, you can take in alpine meadows and montane forest as well (or better, put in a whole additional day to experience the mountain). Mountain and gorge come together at the only sea-level crossing of the entire Cascade Range. They make up only a small part of the state, but a uniquely varied and spectacular one.

GUIDANCE **Columbia Gorge National Scenic Area** (541-308-1700; www.fs.fed.us/r6/columbia/forest), 907 Wasco Avenune, Hood River 97031.

Columbia River Gorge Visitors Association (1-800-984-6743; www.crgva.org), 404 W. Second Street, The Dalles 97058.

The Dalles Area Chamber of Commerce (1-800-255-3385; www.thedalleschamber.com), 404 W. Second Street, The Dalles 97058.

Hood River County Chamber of Commerce and Visitor Center (1-800-366-3530; www.hoodriver.org), 405 Portway Avenue, Hood River 97031.

Mount Hood National Forest (503-688-1700; www.fs.fed.us/r6/mthood), 16400 Champion Way, Sandy 97055.

Oregon's Mount Hood Territory (1-800-424-3002; www.mthoodterritory.com), 2051 Kaen Road, Oregon City 97045.

Sandy Area Chamber of Commerce (1-800-424-3002; www.sandyoregonchamber.org), 39345 Pioneer Boulevard, Sandy 97055.

West Columbia Gorge Chamber of Commerce (503-669-7473; www.westcolumbiagorgechamber.com), 226 W. Historic Columbia River Highway, Troutdale 97060.

GETTING THERE *By car:* From Portland, **I-84** east will take you through the gorge, but it will be more scenic to get on **US 30** at Troutdale for the **Historic Columbia River Highway.** Mount Hood is accessible via **US 26** from Portland, or **OR 35** from Hood River.

GETTING AROUND Public transport in these areas is infrequent at best, so you'll need a car.

MEDICAL EMERGENCY **Legacy Mount Hood Medical Center** (503-674-1122), 24800 SE Stark Street, Gresham.

Mid-Columbia Medical Center (541-296-1111), 1700 E. 19th Street, The Dalles.

Providence Hood River Memorial Hospital (1-800-955-3911), 811 13th Street, Hood River.

TOWNS **Troutdale.** Now a suburb of Portland, Troutdale was once a welcome center for pioneers finally entering the Promised Land, especially those who had taken the arduous Barlow Road around Mount Hood. Today it's the gateway to the Columbia Gorge. Capt. John Harlow, a businessman and town booster, raised trout on his farm and convinced the railroad to build a depot for his convenience; hence the town and the name.

Cascade Locks. Early Oregon Trail emigrants, and later traders along the river, were obliged to portage around the river's worst rapids, some of which were right here. The town began as a portaging point where goods were carried first by foot, then by mule rail, and finally by the *Oregon Pony,* a steam engine. In 1896 locks were built at this point, ushering in the era of Columbia River steamers. Now locks and rapids have been covered by the dams, but you can still ride a steamer and hark back to the old days.

Hood River. Just to leeward of Mount Hood, Hood River gets enough rain to keep things green but not enough to dampen the spirits. The town started life as a lumber and fruit-shipping point. Its fortunes declined with the lumber industry, but it has been delightfully reborn—windsurfers discovered it, and other travelers followed, so now you find vintage hotels cheek by jowl with high-end restaurants, brewpubs, and a varied music and arts scene, surrounded by miles of spreading orchards. People even started to move there again.

The Dalles. Like several other towns, The Dalles credits itself with being the end of the Oregon Trail, as here the emigrants had to take to the river or the Barlow Road to complete their journey. Some actually did settle here, figuring they might as well trade with the soldiers at Fort Dalles and the emigrants as toil on to farm the Willamette Valley. *Dalles* is French for flagstones—before the dams, large, flat-topped rock formations punctuated the river here, creating the "Great Narrows" that struck fear into the hearts of Indian and emigrant navigators alike.

✷ To See

FARMERS' MARKETS AND FARM STANDS The western Columbia Gorge, with its mild climate and volcanic soils, is famous for fruit and one of the biggest apple-producing areas in the country. In addition to the markets listed here, see *Scenic Drives.*

Boring Farmers' Market (503-989-4452), 28051 SE Wally Road, Boring. Sun. 10–3, mid-May–mid-Sept.

Canby Saturday Market (503-263-5151), NW First Avenue between Ivy and Holly, Canby. Second Sat. of May to second Sat. of Oct., 9–1.

Clackamas Farmers' and Artists' Market (503-407-3403), 12000 SE 82nd Avenue, Clackamas Town Center. Wed. 4–8, May–Oct.

The Dalles Farmers' Market, E. Fifth Street and Union, The Dalles. Sat. 8–1, June–mid-Oct.

Don Smith Blueberries (503-631-2915), 22509 S. Stormer Road, Estacada. Pick your own blueberries in early July, but call ahead. Closed Sun.

Estacada Growers' Market (503-630-4490), Third and Broadway, Estacada. Sat. 10–3, May–Oct.

Glover's Century Farm (503-637-3820), 29177 SE OR 224, Estacada. Daily 8–8, July for u-pick berries; bring containers and call ahead for availability.

Hood River Saturday Market (541-387-8349), Fifth and Cascade, Hood River. Sat. 9–3. Produce, crafts, and music.

Sandy Farms (503-668-4525), 34500 SE OR 211, Boring. Pick your own raspberries, blueberries, marionberries, and more, or buy them ready-picked. June–Sept. for berries (call for hours), and weekends before Christmas 9–4 for Christmas trees.

Sandy Saturday Market (503-668-4006), corner of Hoffman Avenue and Pioneer Boulevard, Sandy. Sat., mid-May–Sept.

Sunnyside Grange Farmers' and Artists' Market (503-407-3403), 13100 SE Sunnyside Road, Happy Valley. Sun. 11:30–3:30, Apr.–Oct.

Wilsonville Farmer's Market (503-241-3834), 11422 SW Barber Street, Wilsonville. Sun. 10–2, May–Oct.

FOR FAMILIES **Bonneville Dam Visitor Centers** (541-374-8820), exit 40 on I-84, about 40 miles east of Portland. Two visitors centers display dam history and technology: the Bradford Island Visitor Center, open daily 9–5, and the smaller Navigation Lock Visitor Center, open daily 1–4. Admission to either is free. Coming online in 1938, Bonneville was the first of the giant Columbia River dams, built to provide electricity for regional homes and industry, water for irrigation and flood protection. Gaze on the huge turbines on a self-guided or guided tour and learn how hydropower works; also observe salmon as they climb fish ladders and sturgeon in the outdoor pools, where a hatchery tries to boost populations of this ancient fish. Interpretive programs take place throughout the day.

Columbia Gorge Sternwheeler (1-800-224-3901; www.portlandspirit.com), Cascade Locks Marion Park, 355 Wa-Na-Pa Street, Cascade Locks. Before the dams, before even trains came to the gorge, steam-run stern-wheelers ferried people and cargo between falls along the mercurial river; the pilots had to have nerves of steel. Your trip today will be a lot more placid, so you can enjoy narrated, iconic views of the rugged gorge, possibly even with dinner. Cruises run May–Oct.; general fares $26–82, seniors $26–63, children $16–63.

Mount Hood Railroad (1-800-872-4661; www.mthoodrr.com), 110 Railroad Avenue, Hood River. The railway started running fruit and lumber down to the port at Hood River in 1906. These are still economic staples of the Hood River Valley, but you can now ride the vintage train to view the fruit trees in bloom, stunning views of Mount Hood, and the forests and orchards that first drew settlers to these hills. Trains run Apr.–Dec. and offer simple excursions to Odell or Parkdale at the valley's head, dinner trains, and murder-mystery trips; kids may enjoy the Polar Express in winter or traveling with Thomas the Tank Engine. Rates start at $25 for adults, $18 for kids.

HERITAGE TREES **Foster Lilac,** 29912 SE OR 211, Eagle Creek. Unlike most settlers, Mary and Phillip Foster came to Oregon City via Cape Horn and planted the lilac as soon as they arrived in 1843. They moved five times, transplanting the lilac each time, till settling here at the **Philip Foster Farm** (see *Historic Sites*) in 1847.

HISTORIC SITES **The Dalles Historic Walking Tour,** available from **The Dalles Area Chamber of Commerce** (see *Guidance*), leads you to numerous historic buildings and homes, including the 1891 **Vogt Opera House** and the 1857 **Chinese Building,** dating to the year of the city's incorporation. Also of interest are **Old St. Peter's Church** downtown, built in 1897, open to the public; the **Rorick House,** at 300 W. 13th Street, built in 1850 by an office at Fort Dalles and the oldest home in the city, open weekends 10–4 in summer; and the **Pulpit Rock** at 12th and Court streets, where missionaries like Jason Lee and his nephew

Daniel used to preach to the Indians before there was even a road, let alone a city. Except for the last three sites, most of the historic buildings are private property; please respect the owners.

Barlow Road. Most Oregon Trail emigrants took the Columbia River route from The Dalles to present-day Portland—an experience that involved negotiating terrifying rapids that not infrequently swallowed boats and passengers. It didn't take long for enterprising pioneers to search for alternatives, of which the Barlow Road was one. Scouted and blazed by Samuel Barlow and his partner Philip Foster, it led from The Dalles over the southern flank of Mount Hood: a route that avoided the river but involved excruciatingly steep climbs and descents where pioneers had to lower wagons and beasts by rope. Not all emigrants appreciated paying a substantial toll for the experience, which, if safer, was a good deal longer and more arduous than the river. "The slopes were almost impassible for man or beast . . . It seemed we must all perish, but weak, faint and starving we went on. I weighed less than eighty pounds." So wrote emigrant Sarah Cummins. Barlow Road tolls were collected until 1919! A CD driving route approximating the Barlow Road route is available at the **Mount Hood Cultural Center and Museum** (see *Museums*). Sites along US 26 that can be visited with or without the CD are a replica of the **toll gate,** between mileposts 45 and 46, and **Laurel Hill Chute,** between mileposts 50 and 51—the word *chute* is telling. Barlow Road **ruts** and a **pioneer woman's grave** can be seen on FR 3531, off OR 35 a short distance from its junction with US 26. Finally, a segment of the road is open to hiking or biking from the east end of Government Camp to Still Creek Campground, 0.7 mile. You may continue to Summit Meadow, where a pioneer cemetery testifies to the perils of the way.

Celilo Falls, about 10 miles east of The Dalles. The falls are no longer there, having been drowned by The Dalles dam in 1957, but there are those who can still remember the constant thundering of those waters. The greatest concentrations of salmon on the Columbia occurred here during the runs, as the fish strove to jump up the falls, making it the prime gathering place for plateau tribes who met here from time immemorial right up to 1957, to trade and socialize as well as fish. (Seals and sea lions would follow the fish, too, as they still do, except now they can only get as far as Bonneville Dam, where they risk being shot.) The loss of the falls was a body blow to tribal culture. **Celilo Park** is as close as you can get now to the site; here architect Maya Lin is creating a ramp over the water to recall Indian fishing platforms, scheduled for completion in 2010. Film footage of the falls prior to the dam can be viewed at the **Columbia Gorge Discovery Center** (see *Museums*).

Multnomah Falls Lodge (503-695-2376; www.multnomahfallslodge.com), 50000 Historic Columbia River Highway, Bridal Veil (exit 31 from I-84). Built in 1925 to accommodate the multitudes who flocked to beautiful Multnomah Falls as soon as the Columbia River Highway let them, the gray stone lodge is a solemn foil to the ethereal falls. Originally its several guest rooms and a dormitory offered a snug haven from the nearly constant precipitation (notice the steep roof pitch); today there are no accommodations, but it's a fine example of western lodge architecture, and the restaurant serves breakfast, lunch, and dinner with views of the falls. Every sort of stone present in the gorge was incorporated into the structure. A Forest Service information center is located on the lower level.

MULTNOMAH FALLS AND THE HISTORIC LODGE

Philip Foster Farm (503-637-6324; www.philipfosterfarm.com), 29912 SE OR 211, Eagle Creek. Grounds open daily dawn–dusk, buildings daily 11–4 Father's Day–Labor Day; suggested donation of $3. Philip and Mary Foster arrived in Oregon by sea in 1843, just as the Oregon Trail was getting under way. They moved to this claim in 1847, and their growing farm promptly became an important way station for emigrants coming in along the Barlow Road, which Mr. Foster had coincidentally helped to build and promote. Today it's a National Historic Site offering seasonal events like the fall cider squeeze and a summer garden party, as well as daily tours of the 1847 store, an 1860s barn, and the 1883 farmhouse.

Pioneer Cemetery, 400 E. Scenic Drive, The Dalles. More than two hundred graves of early settlers to The Dalles occupy this burial ground, the earliest dating from 1860.

Timberline Lodge (1-800-547-1406; www.timberlinelodge.com), about 6 miles from Government Camp on Timberline Road. Open year-round. It seems much longer than 6 miles as you wind up and up into the forest, till you round a bend and come upon the enormous lodge, looking almost like an outgrowth of the mountain itself, with its two huge wings outspread in welcome. Behind it rises the foreshortened cone of Mount Hood. The project was a brainchild of Emerson Griffith, a Portland businessman who had tried in vain to promote a resort on the mountain and then was suddenly, serendipitously made Oregon's WPA director. Work began in 1935 and continued for three frenetic seasons—the season is short at 6,000 feet—and the lodge opened in 1938. Built of wood and rock with an eye to harmonizing with its setting, the accomplishment is even more impressive when you consider that it was built entirely by hand, mostly by young workers under the direction of expert artisans. A fire roars in the center of the hexagonal lobby, and the entire decor is vintage Northwest—from the carved beaver, eagle, or owl topping the newel posts to interior designer Margery Hoffman Smith's handmade textiles (which have been twice replaced, with meticulous replicas). The guest rooms are much as they originally were. Even if you can't stay (it's hardly a budget stop), you're welcome to go in, look around, and admire the fine craftsmanship.

Lewis and Clark sites. Having reached the Great River of the West, the Corps of Discovery rapidly made its way downstream while making detailed observations. On Oct. 22 and 23, 1805, they camped at **Celilo Falls** (see above) and noted stacks of dried salmon; contemplate the site from **Celilo Park,** about 10 miles east of The Dalles (exit 97 from I-84). They then shot the life-threatening Long Narrows of The Dalles in canoes, and Oct. 25–27 found them repairing their boats at **Rock Fort** on what is now the **Lewis and Clark Riverfront Trail** in The Dalles; a plaque where First Street meets the trail commemorates the event (they must have liked it, for they camped there again in 1806). They also noted **Memaloose Island,** one of the few remaining Indian burial grounds in the region. On Nov. 2 they slept at what is now **Rooster Rock State Park,** just below Vista House, and on their return trip they camped near **Bradford Island Visitor Center** (see *For Families*) at the Bonneville Dam, where there are interpretive displays. Leaving the gorge, they noted heavy and apparently recent sand deposits at the mouth of the **Sandy River,** now in **Lewis and Clark State Park;** it's now thought the sand was a result of volcanic activity on Mount Hood in 1800.

Vista House (503-695-2230), about 24 miles east of Portland at Corbett. Daily 9–6 in summer; check for winter hours. Crown Point is a basalt promontory towering 733 feet above the Columbia River, and Vista House sits on top of Crown Point. Gray sandstone on the outside and Alaskan marble within, the octagonal house must have been conceived to suggest a jewel in a fantastic setting. Opened in 1918, it was a place for motorists to rest and gape at the view, and still is. Indoors you'll find a gift shop, information on the gorge, and marble and mahogany restrooms.

MUSEUMS **Cascade Locks Historical Museum** (541-374-8535), 1 Portage Road, Cascade Locks. Daily noon–5, May–Sept. Free. The locks were built so river traffic could bypass some of the Columbia's notorious rapids and saw plenty of use from 1896 to 1914. Now they have been mostly drowned by the Bonneville Dam, but the little museum in one of the original lock tender's houses explains the

THE ATRIUM AT TIMBERLINE LODGE

history with artifacts and photographs. Outside is the *Oregon Pony,* a small, specialized steam locomotive built in 1862 that brought passengers around the falls even before the locks were built.

✐ **Columbia Gorge Discovery Center** (541-296-8600; www.gorgediscovery.org), 5000 Discovery Drive, The Dalles. Daily 9–5. General admission $8, seniors $7, kids 6–16 $4, children five and under free. How did Lewis and Clark manage to pack 30 tons of equipment into their flat-bottomed riverboat? An entire hall here is devoted to displaying and interpreting the things they carried—period items and replicas—and your kids can try loading a model boat in the Explorer room. In this expansive museum on the banks of the Columbia you can learn virtually everything about the Columbia Gorge, from its cataclysmic origins to its inhabitants, human and wild. Galleries are devoted to a fine collection of Native American baskets, Ice Age wildlife, exploration, and history. Under the same roof, the **Wasco County Historical Museum** features displays on the huge salmon canneries that flourished a hundred years ago, early Columbia River steamers, and the entire modern history of the gorge; highlights are a 1916 film produced by Henry Ford to promote the Columbia River Highway and another on "The Singing Waters," a portrait of Celilo Falls before the dams. You can easily spend the better part of a day here, then move on the see gorge of today with new eyes.

Fort Dalles Museum (541-296-4547; www.historicthedalles.org), 500 W. 15th Street, The Dalles. Daily 10–5 in summer; call for winter hours. General admission $5, seniors $4, children 7–17 $1, under seven free. Established after the Whitman massacre in nearby Walla Walla, Fort Dalles was intended to help and protect Oregon Trail emigrants and enforce reservations policy. It boasted its own lumber mill, quarries, and several impressive officers' houses, but cost overruns brought government disapproval, and it was abandoned after most of the houses burned down in 1867. Today only the surgeon's house remains. The modest Frontier Gothic home has been restored to give a picture of an Army doctor's daily life on the frontier, with period furnishings, tools, photos, and maps. Outdoors, visit the 1895 **Anderson Homestead,** originally on the plateau near Dufur, and a collection of early local vehicles, including a city omnibus.

Harlow House Museum and **Barn Museum** (503-661-2164; www.troutdale history.org), 726 E. Columbia River Highway, Troutdale. The 1900 pioneer house was home to two generations of Harlows—a Maine sea captain and his son—and the Evanses, another pioneer family. The senior Harlow has the distinction of (a) bringing the depot to town, and (b) giving the town its current name, due to the fishponds he installed on the property. Formerly it was called Sandy, after the Sandy River; that honor is now held by the current town of Sandy, a few miles off. The house holds Harlow and Evans household goods and other residents' donations, while the Barn holds donated farming artifacts and changing exhibitions on local history. Both are run by the Troutdale Historical Society and are open when a volunteer is available; call for hours.

Hood River County Museum (541-386-6772; www.co.hood-river.or.us/museum), 300 E. Port Marina Drive, Hood River. Wed.–Sat. 10–4 and Sun. noon–4, Apr.–Aug. and daily noon–4, Sept.–Oct. Free. The Hood River Valley is the heart of Oregon's fruit industry, and the museum showcases the area's agricultural and logging history as well as the heritage of the Finnish, Japanese, and Hispanic workers who successively made them succeed.

Mount Hood Cultural Center and Museum (503-272-3301; www.mthood museum.org), 88900 E. US 26, Government Camp. Daily 10–5. Free. Where the Oregon Trail meets serious skiing, the center explains the Barlow Road, the natural history of Mount Hood, forestry, and more. It also doubles as an arts center and gallery.

Troutdale Depot Museum (503-661-2164; www.troutdalehistory.org), 473 E. Columbia River Highway, Troutdale. Tues.–Fri. 10–4. Troutdale grew up with the railroad. In 1882 the line came through, and Troutdale's founder, John Harlow, thought the new settlement, on the Sandy River just before it flows into the Columbia, was a natural for a depot. The railway men thought otherwise (it isn't called the Sandy for nothing). So Harlow got into his little boat during spring flood, sailed it up the river, and declared the Sandy navigable. It would obviously require a drawbridge to accommodate river commerce. The railway hastily offered a depot after all in exchange for his withdrawing the drawbridge demand, and Troutdale prospered for a time. Its most exciting moment came in the depression year of 1894, when a band of the unemployed tried to hijack a train for a march on Washington; a quixotic venture soon ended by federal troops. The present depot dates from 1907 and contains railroad artifacts and memorablia.

Sandy Area Historical Museum (503-668-3378; www.sandyhistorical.org), 39345 Pioneer Boulevard, Sandy. Daily 10–4. This new museum focuses on the development of the Sandy-Boring-Estacada area along the Barlow Road, an Oregon Trail cutoff avoiding the frightful rapids at The Dalles by a steep climb over the southern flanks of Mount Hood. Logging and homestead artifacts are on display alongside historic photos—my favorite was one entitled "The Original Boring School," a one-room schoolhouse founded and funded by pioneer W. H. Boring.

Western Antique Aeroplane and Automobile Museum (541-308-1600; www.waaamuseum.org), 1600 Air Museum Road, Hood River. Daily 9–5. General admission $12, seniors and veterans $10, children 5–18 $6, children under five free. These antique planes don't just sit around looking pretty, they actually fly, at least from time to time. The true enthusiast may want to come for the annual fly-in, in mid-Sept., when vintage aircraft from around the country come to visit. For the earthbound there is a large collection of antique cars going back to early Model T Fords, also still in operation.

NATURAL WONDERS **Beacon Rock,** about 35 miles east of Portland, is actually on the Washington side of the river, but standing 848 feet above the water, it is observable for miles around. The ancient, basalt volcanic core is thought to be the second-largest monolith in the world, after the Rock of Gibraltar. It was here that Lewis and Clark first noted tidal influence on their descent of the Columbia on Oct. 31, 1805.

Bridge of the Gods, Cascade Locks. The current Bridge of the Gods is a spidery metal-truss affair connecting Cascade Locks to the Washington side of the river, but Indian legends tell of an earlier bridge: long ago the Great Spirit built a stone bridge so the people could cross from one side of the river to the other. However, his two sons, Klickitat and Wy'east (Mount Adams and Mount Hood), got into a fight over a woman, Squaw Mountain (or Loowit—Mount Saint Helens—in some versions). They hurled fire and rock at each other, and their projectiles fell and broke the bridge. Their father was angry and created great rapids where the bridge had been. Geologists think a landslide occurred three hundred to nine hundred years ago, blocking the river for a time with a bridge of rubble that eventually was washed away. If you look up at the northern side, you can see where part of Table Mountain has slid toward the river. Meanwhile, Klickitat's and Wy'east's shenanigans sound like typical volcano behavior, similar to the dueling of Mazama and Shasta that created Crater Lake (see "Southern Cascades and Siskiyous").

Columbia River Gorge, extending from Portland's eastern suburbs upriver about 100 miles. The majestic basalt canyon has captivated the public since the post–Civil War era, when photographer Carleton Watkins began packing his camera and portable darkroom into its nearly inaccessible reaches (the early Oregon emigrants, bouncing down the boulder-strewn river on their rafts, had probably been less entranced). Soon steamers were plying the navigable stretches, followed by a railway and eventually, wonder of wonders, a veritable parade of Model Ts along a new scenic highway (see *Scenic Drives*)! So, what did those drivers go out to the wilderness to see? Fir-clad basalt cliffs rising thousands of feet festooned with a multitude of waterfalls, transformed to brooding bare precipices upstream of Mount Hood; the biggest, most untamed river of the West, punctuated by impassable cascades; vast runs of salmon and the native fishing platforms over the falls; in short, a wonder of the Wild West. Its story was pieced together by geologists over the better part of a century: 17 or so million years ago lava began pouring out of the ground to the north and east, covering the primeval Northwest under layers of basalt thousands of feet thick and changing the course of the ancient Columbia. Ice came and went. The Cascade Range rose, and the river began to cut its way through. Much later—twelve thousand to ten thousand years ago—warming trends melted ice dams holding back massive, prehistoric Ice Age Lake Missoula, far upstream. The resulting floods were the stuff of nightmares: walls of water hundreds of feet high charging downstream at 60 miles an hour, churning with rocks, mud, and the debris of a 300,000-square-mile watershed. Leaving the plateaus, it plunged precipitously down, scouring out the gorge and leaving its tributaries hanging where they still remain, lovely threads of silk on the chasm walls. Though the river has been stilled by a series of dams, from the Bonneville up to Grand Coulee, its dramatic walls and the sheer volume of water rival any canyon for grandeur.

Waterfalls. A plethora of falls tumble down the mossy Columbia Gorge cliffs, some of them forming subsidiary chasms of their own. At 620 feet, the granddaddy is **Multomah Falls,** exit 31 from I-84 or 15 miles east of Troutdale on the Historic Columbia River Highway, with a graceful two-tier drop; a viewing platform behind Multnomah Lodge is accessible to wheelchairs and strollers. Equally lovely are nearby **Latourell, Shepperd's Dell, Bridal Veil, Wahkeenah, Horsetail,** and **Elowah falls,** all within a 15-mile stretch of the old highway. Short hikes into the green gloom reward with more isolated cascades (see *Hiking*).

Mount Hood. On a clear day Oregon's tallest mountain can be seen from as far away as Bend in central Oregon, floating above its surroundings like a gigantic ice cream cone. Named for a British admiral by the Vancouver expedition of 1792, the sight of it a hundred miles off excited Lewis and Clark as they approached from the east in 1805—if they could see Mount Hood, the Pacific couldn't be far. A stratovolcano like most of the High Cascades, it's thought to be about 730,000 years old and still active: pyroclastic flows occurred shortly before Lewis and Clark's visit, and there are reports of red glows from the mid-1800s. Fumaroles and earthquake swarms show that the mountain's sleep is uneasy. But this doesn't bother most Portlanders, whose 11,239-foot backyard volcano provides a scenic backdrop to their lives and a year-round playground.

SCENIC DRIVES **Hood River Fruit Loop** (541-386-7697; www.hoodriverfruitloop.com), a 35-mile loop up and down the Hood River Valley via OR 35 and Dee Highway. Pleasing the to eye as well as the palate, the drive runs through the heart of the orchard country, now supplemented by wineries, herb and alpaca farms. Summer and early fall are the best times to take advantage of the many farms stands and U-pick farms—fruit doesn't get any fresher than this—but spring brings clouds of cherry, apple and pear blossoms offset by frosty Mount Hood. A sef-guiding tour map can be downloaded from the above Web site, or picked up at the **Hood River Chamber of Commerce.**

Historic Columbia River Highway, from Troutdale to Multnomah Falls and Mosier to The Dalles. Before I-84, before even US 30, there was the Columbia River Highway. Designed in 1913 to provide access to the gorge's waterfalls and other scenic wonders, it was a major engineering feat in its time, finding its way up, down, and along the high basalt cliffs. It was particularly impressive as its engineer, Samuel Lancaster, "did not want to mar what God had put there"—his guiding principle was to enhance, not ruin, the view, and in this he largely succeeded, helped by teams of Italian stonemasons. Parts of the original 70-mile road have been abandoned, but this leaves a leisurely drive with plenty of time to admire wildflowers, views, and the myriad waterfalls before picking up the road again at the dry eastern end of the gorge (you'll need to take I-84 between the two sections). Though an adventurous ordeal for early drivers, today it's an easily accessible scenic byway three seasons out of four, and not to be missed.

Mount Hood Loop, 105 miles Troutdale to Hood River, or vice versa. The route follows US 26 up the south flank of Mount Hood, through moist forest communites with names like Rhododendron and Zigzag, then down the wilder eastern slope along OR 35. You'll rise from near sea level to over 4,000 feet and descend again along the rushing Hood River, with views of forest, wildflowers, and the towering volcanic cone; if you feel like it, you can check out the farm stands of the Hood River Valley. Not recommended in winter, when OR 35 is often closed.

WINE The Columbia Gorge is one of the newer vine-growing areas in the Northwest. The cool, damp soils of the western gorge and the sunny, dry east allow for a lot of experimentation here. Wineries dot both sides of the river, and traces of old vineyards found near Bingen, Washington, suggest that that town's German founders were on to something. You could spend a day sampling, from **Edgefield Vineyards** near Troutdale to **The Pines Estate** near The Dalles, not to mention the various tasting rooms there and in Hood River. For details, check with the **Columbia Gorge Wine Growers' Association** (1-866-413-WINE; www.columbiagorgewine.com).

✷ To Do

BICYCLING More of the **Historic Columbia River Highway** is open to bikes than to cars: the 5-mile **Twin Tunnels** segment between Hood River and Mosier and a 3.5-mile bit from Cascade Locks to the Bonneville Dam are pieces of the original highway that fell into disuse and were restored for nonmotorized recreation. The trailheads require a day-use state parks pass if you park there. The rest of the 80-mile highway is bikeable, but caution should be used as it is often narrow and winding, with virtually no shoulder.

A 17-mile mountain bike trail starts at the **Deschutes River State Recreation Area** (see *Camping*) and follows the river upstream; it can be extremely hot in summer.

For the myriad mountain biking opportunities in the Columbia River Gorge and Mount Hood National Forest, contact the Forest Service (503-688-1700) or the **Columbia Gorge National Scenic Area** (541-308-1700).

CAMPING Columbia Gorge area: **Ainsworth State Park,** 17 miles east of Troutdale on the Historic Columbia River Highway, with 45 full hookup and six walk-in, primitive sites, restrooms, water, showers, interpretive programs. No reservations; open mid-Mar.–Oct.

Deschutes River State Recreation Area (1-800-452-5687), off OR 206, 17 miles east of The Dalles, just south of I-84, with 25 primitive and 34 electric hookup sites, restrooms, but no showers. Reservations taken; open year-round.

Memaloose State Park (1-800-452-5687), 11 miles west of The Dalles off I-84, with 66 tent and 44 full hookup sites with restrooms, showers, and water; reservations taken. Open mid-Mar.–Oct.

Viento State Park (541-374-8811), 8 miles west of Hood River at exit 56 from I-84, with 18 tent and 56 electrical hookup sites, restrooms, water, showers; no reservations. The park is between the highway and an active railway. Open mid-Mar.–Oct.

Forest Service campgrounds: **Eagle Creek,** exit 40 or 41 from I-84, with 20 sites, no hookups, restrooms, and water; no reservations; open late Apr.–Sept. This was the first Forest Service campground built in the United States. **Eagle Creek Overlook** (take directions as for Eagle Creek and follow signs) has a group campground with 40 sites, no hookups, water, restrooms, and ADA facilities. Open late May–Sept. **Herman Creek Horse Camp** (from Cascade Locks take Forest Lane east to the Herman Creek Work Center), with seven sites, water, restrooms, hitching posts; no reservations; open late Apr.–Sept. **Wyeth** (exit 51 from I-84 and take Herman Creek Road for 0.25 mile), with 40 tent or vehicle sites, no hookups, restrooms; no water, no reservations; secluded. The secluded site was formerly a CCC and conscientious objector camp. Open late Apr.–Sept.

Mount Hood National Forest campgrounds generally include vault or flush toilets and variable fees; for maps contact the ranger districts. Barlow Ranger District (541-467-2291): **Badger Lake,** on FR 4860-140; no water, high-clearance vehicles. **Bear Springs,** on OR 216, with 21 sites, water. **Bonney Crossing,** on FR 2710, with eight sites, no water. **Bonney Meadow,** on FR 4891, with six sites, no water. **Camp Windy,** FR 4550, with three sites, no water, no fee. **Eightmile Crossing,** FR 4430, with 21 sites, no water. **Forest Creek,** FR 4885, with eight sites, no water. **Knebal Springs,** FR 1720, with eight sites, no water. **McCubbins Gulch,** FR 2110, with 15 sites, no water. **Rock Creek Reservoir,** FR 4820, with 33 sites, water, boat launch (electric motors only); reserve at www.recreation.gov.

White River Station, FR 43 or 48, with five sites, no water. All generally open summer only.

Clackamas Ranger District (503-630-6861): **Armstrong,** access via OR 224, with 12 sites, water; wheelchair accessible; reserve at www.recreation.gov. **Camp Ten,** FR 4220 near Olallie Lake, with 10 sites, no water. **Carter Bridge,** access via OR 224, with 15 sites, no water; wheelchair accessible; reserve at www.recreation.gov. **Fish Creek,** OR 224, with 24 sites, water; wheelchair accessible; reserve at www.recreation.gov. **Indian Henry,** FR 4620, with 86 sites, water; wheelchair accessible; reserve at www.recreation.gov. **Kingfisher,** FR 70, with 23 sites, water; reserve at www.recreation.gov. **Lake Harriet,** FR 4630, with 13 sites, water; wheelchair accessible. **Lazy Bend,** OR 224, with 21 sites, water; reserve at www.recreation.gov. **Lockaby,** OR 224, and **Riverside,** FR 46, with 16 sites, water; reserve at www.recreation.gov. **Roaring River,** OR 224, with 14 sites, water; reserve at www.recreation.gov.

Hood River Ranger District (541-352-6002): **Clear Lake,** FR 2630, with 26 sites, water; wheelchair accessible; reserve at www.recreation.gov. **Frog Lake,** FR 2610, with 33 sites, water; wheelchair accessible, reserve at www.recreation.gov. **Kinnikinnick,** walk-in only, nearest access from FR 2840, with 20 sites, no water. **Lost Lake**, FR 1340, with 125 sites, water; wheelchair accessible; horse facilities. **Nottingham,** on OR 35, with 23 sites, no water; wheelchair accessible.

Zigzag Ranger District (503-622-3191): **Alpine,** FR 173, with 16 sites, water; wheelchair accessible. **Camp Creek,** access via US 26, with 25 sites, water; wheelchair accessible; reserve at www.recreation.gov. **Clackamas Lake,** FR 4270, with 46 sites, water, horse facilities; wheelchair accessible; reserve at www.recreation.gov. **Gone Creek,** FR 57, with 50 sites, water; wheelchair accessible; reserve at www.recreation.gov. **Green Canyon,** FR 2618, with 15 sites; no water or other services. **Hoodview,** FR 57, with 43 sites, water; wheelchair accessible, reserve at www.recreation.gov. **Joe Graham Horse Camp,** FR 42, with 14 sites, water, wheelchair access, horse facilities; reserve at www.recreation.gov. **Little Crater Lake,** with 16 sites, water, wheelchair access; reserve at www.recreation.gov. **Lost Creek,** FR 1825, with 16 sites; reserve at www.recreation.gov. **Oak Fork,** FR 57, with 47 sites, water, wheelchair access; reserve at www.recreation.gov. **Pine Point,** FR 57, with 25 sites, water, wheelchair access; reserve at www.recreation.gov. **Still Creek,** US 26, with 27 sites, water, wheelchair access; reserve at www.recreation.gov. **Tollgate,** US 26, with 15 sites, water, wheelchair access; reserve at www.recreation.gov. **Trillium Lake,** FR 2656 (3 miles east of Government Camp on US 26), with 57 sites, water, wheelchair access; reserve at www.recreation.gov.

CANOEING AND KAYAKING **Trillium Lake, Clear Lake,** and **Frog Lake** are motor-free lakes near US 26. **Lost Lake,** on the eastern flank of Mount Hood, also forbids motors, and the resort rents out rowboats, canoes, and kayaks.

GOLF **Hood River Golf Course** (541-386-3009; www.hoodrivergolf.com), 1850 Country Club Road, Hood River. Eighteen holes.

Indian Creek Golf Course (541-386-7770; www.indiancreekgolf.com), 3605 Brookside Drive, Hood River. Eighteen holes.

HIKING Between the Mount Hood National Forest and the Columbia Gorge National Scenic Area, there are literally hundreds of miles of trails for your hiking pleasure. *Note:* It's really, really smart to bring rain gear for hiking the gorge; even if it doesn't rain, there is a lot of spray from the ubiquitous waterfalls. Here is a selection:

Columbia Gorge area: A network of waterfall-viewing trails is easily accessed from **Multnomah Falls.** A trail from **Multnomah Lodge** rises to the top of the falls, 2.2 miles round-trip with a 700-foot elevation gain; very scenic but slippery with spray, not for small children. If you continue up the trail rather than coming back down, you will meet the **Wahkeena Trail,** which winds back down 2.6 miles to **Wahkeena Falls;** or you can start from the **Wahkeena Falls Trailhead** about a mile west of Multnomah Lodge and do it backwards. Both these trails meet the **Larch Mountain Trail** (13.6 miles round-trip from Multnomah Falls), a challenging but spectacular hike. Just 2 miles east of Multnomah Falls is the **Oneonta Trail,** a less-frequented but fairylike path rising up narrow Oneonta Gorge to 60-foot Oneonta Falls through misty firs and ferns; you can continue a mile up to Triple Falls, or loop left to take in gushing **Horsetail** and **Ponytail falls,** which look just like their names. You'll then have to walk 0.5 mile of road back to your car, for a total loop of 3 miles (not including Triple Falls).

Farther east, the nonmotorized sections of the **Historic Columbia River Trail** are open to hikers as well as bikers (see *Bicycling*). The nearby **Tom McCall Preserve,** a Nature Conservancy property, offers two trails through the savanna-like plateau: a 2.2-mile round-trip stroll down to small ponds, and a 3.4-mile round-trip to Tom McCall Point, with a climb of 1,100 feet. Wildflowers are riotous in spring, but watch for poison oak. Take sunscreen and a hat: this is not the cool rain forest of the western gorge. Take exit 69 from I-84 and drive 6.6 miles to the parking area at Rowena Crest.

Mount Hood Area: A 2-mile, wheelchair-accessible gravel trail loops around **Trillium Lake** (see *Camping*) for terrific views of Mount Hood and ADA-accessible fishing platforms and picnic tables. Another wheelchair-friendly option is the **Wildwood Area,** on the mountain's lower reaches. A paved 1-mile loop winds along Salmon River, and a boardwalk takes in a wetland. The Wildwood Recreation Site is 0.2 mile east of milepost 39 on US 26. For a higher-altitude experience, try the trails from **Timberline Lodge** (see *Historic Sites*). A 4.5-mile round-trip takes you across the mountain's flank, with some ups and downs, to Zigzag Canyon and back to the lodge for some refreshment. A 2.2-mile loop leads straight up to Silcox Hut, containing a hiker's refuge and small café; or choose the challenging 12.2-mile loop to Paradise Park, rightly named for its summer wildflowers, which uses the Pacific Crest Trail as its return leg. And, the 40-mile **Timberline Trail** encircles Mount Hood at tree line—a several days' jaunt (parts may be closed due to washouts, so check with the district office).

Martin's Hike and Bike (1-877-290-8687; www.martinshikeandbike.com), P.O. Box 18177, Portland 97218. Martin will take you to his favorite spots in the beautiful Columbia River Gorge, whether you want to take in waterfalls, wildflowers, or wine. Regularly scheduled hikes (call or check Web site) are 1 to 3 miles, and transportation to and from Portland or Cascade Locks is provided, along with water and snacks. Bike tours are by request. Trips start at $50.

For many other hikes of all levels, check with the **Mount Hood National Forest** (see *Guidance*), the **Columbia Gorge Vistors Association** (see *Guidance*), or look at William Sullivan's excellent book, *100 Hikes in Northwest Oregon and Southwest Washington.*

HOT SPRINGS **Bagby Hot Springs,** 40 miles southeast of Estacada via OR 224 and FRs 46, 63, and 70—plus a 1.5-mile hike to the springs. These secluded springs along the Clackamas River are rustic, with log tubs and cedar piping, sheltered by tall firs. Commune with nature; just remember, clothing is not optional here at this Forest Service site, and alcohol is out. A recreation pass is required for parking.

WINDSURFING **Hood River** has become the windsurfing capital of the United States, if not the world, thanks to the strong, constant Columbia Gorge winds. For lessons and rentals, contact **Brian's Windsurfing** (541-386-1423; www.brianswindsurfing.com), 100 Marina Way, Hood River, or **Hood River WaterPlay** (541-386-9463; www.hoodriverwaterplay.com), Port Marina Park, Hood River. Or if you're already an expert, just bring your board and find out about beach access from the **Columbia Board Windsurfing Association** (541-386-9225; www.cgwa.net), 202 Oak Street, Hood River.

WINTER SPORTS **Mount Hood** is home to three ski resorts: **Timberline** (503-272-3158; www.timberlinelodge.com), where the lifts radiate from **Timberline Lodge,** is Oregon's only year-round ski station with a drop of 3,690 feet and trails descending from 8,500; **Mount Hood Meadows** (1-800-754-4663; www.skihood.com), 10 miles east of Government Camp on OR 35, occupies a large and varied slab of mountain with 11 lifts, 2,150 acres, night skiing, and cross-country trails; and **Mount Hood Ski Bowl** (1-800-SKIBOWL; www.skibowl.com), at Government Camp, has eight lifts and a drop of 1,500 feet rising from the eateries and brewpubs of the resurgent village.

THE SNOW ENTRANCE AT TIMBERLINE LODGE

✷ Wilder Places

PARKS **Columbia River Gorge National Scenic Area** (541-308-1700; www.fs.fed.us/r6/columbia), 902 Wasco Street, Hood River. Stretching from Troutdale through The Dalles, the 292,500-acre area flanking the Columbia was created in 1986. Formed almost literally by fire and ice (see *Natural Wonders*), the gorge has two distinct zones: the western one, receiving 75 inches of rain a year, thick with tall Douglas fir and crashing cascades, and moist underfoot; and the eastern, in the rain shadow of Mount Hood, getting only one-fifth the rainfall, composed of bare rock backed by grassy plateaus. Miles of hiking trails meander past the **waterfalls,** many of which are also accessible from the **Historic Columbia River Highway** (see *Scenic Drives*), as are **Vista House** at Crown Point, an octagonal Art Nouveau viewing station completed in 1918; **Multnomah Falls;** and **Multnomah Lodge** (see *Historic Sites*). Wildflowers are gorgeous in spring, including some relict species left over from the Ice Age. The gorge is also a wind tunnel, fueled by the gradient between hot, dry desert and cool, moist forest winds funneled through thousand-foot crags, making it a windsurfers' mecca. Visitors shouldn't miss the **Columbia Gorge Discovery Center** (see *Museums*), detailing culture as well as nature, or the **pictographs** at Columbia Hills State Park on the Washington side.

Tom McCall Preserve, 11 miles east of Hood River on US 30; park at the Rowena Crest viewpoint. Right at the ecotone between the moist western gorge and the high, dry plateaus to the east, the 271-acre Nature Conservancy preserve presents impressive spring wildflower displays and is home to four plant species unique to the Columbia Gorge. Three miles of trails offer expansive river views, botanizing, and bird-watching. To protect sensitive species, dogs and horses are asked to remain in vehicles.

✐ **Wildwood Recreation Site** (503-375-5646), milestone 39 on US 26, 40 miles east of Portland. This BLM-run site features interpretive wetland trails, varied wildlife, and an education in salmon and steelhead—the Wild and Scenic Salmon River runs through it, with an underground fish-viewing chamber. Plus, you can play and picnic. Parking $5; open mid-Mar.–Nov.

Oxbow Regional Park, 10 miles east of Troutdale via 257th Street, Division Street, and Oxbow Parkway, is where suburbia meets the wilderness. Twelve hundred acres in the Sandy River gorge take in old-growth forest, 15 miles of trails, wild creatures from songbirds to cougars, and a section of the river for swimming, rafting, or kayaking. And in fall you can see the wild salmon returning upstream to spawn. If you find it hard to leave, there's a campground, too, with 67 tent sites, restrooms, showers, and water (no reservations).

For more information on the parks that follow, call 503-986-0707 or log onto www.oregonstateparks.org.

Ainsworth State Park, 17 miles east of Troutdale on the Historic Columbia River Highway. With a full-service campground, creek, and hiking trails, the park is a convenient base for exploring the many nearby waterfalls or the surrounding forest. Open mid-Mar.–Oct.

Benson State Recreation Area, 1 mile east of Multnomah Falls off I-84. This day-use site has picnic tables and a fishable, swimmable lake.

Bridal Veil Falls State Park, milepost 28 on the Historic Columbia River Highway, is a viewpoint for beautiful Bridal Veil Falls with grassy lawns, tall trees, a picnic area, and two scenic trails. No fee.

Guy W. Talbot State Park, 12 miles east of Troutdale on the Historic Columbia River Highway. Mr. Talbot donated his summer estate to the state in 1929. Now it is a quiet retreat with treed lawns and a picnic area. A trail from the park leads to Latourelle Falls and on to the **George Joseph Natural Area,** a dim forest of firs, mosses, and ferns. Continuing the trail leads you to secluded Upper Latourelle Falls. No fee for either park.

John B. Yeon State Corridor, exit 35 from I-84, where the interstate meets the historic highway. A trail from this park leads to two seldom-visited waterfalls: Elowah Falls and McCord Creek Falls. It offers fine views of the gorge, too.

Lewis and Clark State Recreation Site, just east of Troutdale at the mouth of the Sandy River. Lewis and Clark camped here, remarking on the sand-choked river (now it runs clear). The park commemorates the visit with a plaque and a Confluence Project installation by Maya Lin honoring the meeting (or clash) of cultures. Swim at the beach or picnic in the park.

Mayer State Park, 10 miles west of The Dalles. At the dry eastern end of the gorge, Mayer includes Rowena Point and a rare lake for swimming and boating—also multitudes of spring wildflowers.

Rooster Rock State Park, 10 miles east of Portland off I-84. Summer crowds flock to the 3 miles of Columbia River beaches, and somewhat fewer to one of Oregon's two nude bathing beaches to the east end of the park (separated from the other park beaches). Then there's picnicking, disc golf, camping—in short, a full-service park.

Seneca Fouts, Wygant, and **Vinzenz Lausmann** are conjoined state parks 6 miles west of Hood River. The terrain is rugged, full of rock formations, trees, and canyons, and there's not much else but some hiking trails. If you are an experienced backpacker, this is a place to get away from it all.

Shepperd's Dell State Natural Area, 14 miles east of Troutdale, was given to the state by a dairy farmer as a memorial to his wife. Luckily for the state, the tract included a two-tiered waterfall tumbling 90 feet down to the river. Stop and admire.

Starvation Creek State Park, 10 miles west of Hood River off I-84, is small but offers access to the trail system of the adjacent national forest. It also allows viewing of the Starvation Creek waterfall.

Deschutes River State Recreation Area (see *Camping*). This rugged park lies beside the lower reaches of the Wild and Scenic Deschutes. Trails welcome hikers, mountain bikers, and equestrians (the latter must preregister), and there are rafting, fishing, and camping. The sheltered canyon warms up early, making this park attractive as early as late winter. In summer beware of high heat and rattlesnakes.

WILDERNESS AREAS In 2009, Congress felicitously added 124,000 acres to existing wilderness within the **Mount Hood National Forest** (see *Guidance*). Wilderness areas now include:

Badger Creek, on the eastern slopes of Mount Hood, has terrain ranging from subalpine forest to open woods and grasslands, most of it rugged. Three creeks and 55 miles of trails cross the wilderness, accessed from OR 35.

Bull of the Woods is a sprawling, highly dissected wilderness, full of cliffs and rushing streams, home to spotted (and other) owls and other shy forest creatures. Accessible by trail from forest roads; contact the Forest Service for directions.

Mark O. Hatfield, just south of the Columbia River Gorge, is the destination of many trails starting in the gorge itself; its protection has preserved the river's priceless wild hinterland of rough plateau and mountain peaks—a recreational paradise.

Mount Hood Wilderness protects the peak and upper slopes of Mount Hood, with many trails and views.

Salmon-Huckleberry Wilderness, accessible by forest road from Welches, protects the Salmon River Basin, prime habitat for steelhead, coho, and chinook salmon. The drainage is shrouded in thick rain forest and includes 70 miles of trails. Although beautiful, it's little used (it *is* rain forest). Just south of it is the new **Roaring River Wilderness,** named for a tributary of the Clackamas River and another spawning area for salmon and steelhead. Five trails, lakes, alpine meadows, and abundant large wildlife await the intrepid visitor. To the west is the **Clackamas Wilderness,** another newly designated area consisting of five separate tracts of roadless area along the Clackamas River.

✷ Lodging

BED & BREAKFASTS

Bridal Veil

Bridal Veil Lodge (503-695-2333; www.bridalveillodge.com), about 25 miles east of Portland on the Historic Columbia River Highway, across from Bridal Veil Falls State Park. In the old days a motorist could pull into the lodge, get a hot meal, and pitch a tent out back if he couldn't afford a room. Built in 1927 of local lumber and simply furnished, it became a way station for the new species called "motorists," much like Multnomah Lodge down the road. Still owned and operated by its founding family, the Amends, it offers a quiet rest beside one of the gorge's more spectacular falls. They don't serve dinner anymore, but you do get breakfast at the original plank table. $135, with breakfast.

Hood River

Gorge View Bed and Breakfast (541-386-5770; www.gorgeview.com), 1009 Columbia Street. Hood River hostelries tend to cater to sports lovers, and Gorge View is no exception. The dignified 1917 house offers room to keep your gear and a number of rooming options, from a single private to a bunkroom. $39–130, with full breakfast.

Hood River Bed and Breakfast (541-387-2997; www.hoodriverbnb.com), 918 Oak Street. Simple but comfortably furnished rooms overlook the marina or the mountains, and the house offers common areas to relax and others for storing your sailboard, etc. Breakfast is served at three different times to accommodate your sporting schedule. $85–135.

Panorama Lodge (1-888-403-2687; www.panoramalodge.com), 2290 Old Dalles Drive. The rustic, shingled house sits on a ridge 4 miles east of

Hood River; hence the panorama including, but not limilted to, Oregon's highest peak. Guests can enjoy the deck and surrounding flowers, and a choice of five guest rooms. $80–235, with full breakfast.

Sakura Ridge Bed and Breakfast (541-386-2636; www.sakuraridge.com), 5601 York Hill Drive. *Sakura* is Japanese for cherry blossoms, and there are plenty of those here in season. It's fine if you miss the season, though, because then you can enjoy the harvest of ripe black cherries—and pears—all from orchards on the property. The decor is a delicate blend of Japanese and Western (uncluttered polished wood, Pendleton blankets), and breakfast is straight from the farm. $150–225.

Seven Oaks Bed and Breakfast (541-386-7622; www.sevenoaksbb.com), 1373 Barker Road. In the hills overlooking the town, this large Craftsman house was built in 1928 by a French, er, craftsman who had found his way to Hood River. At the time it was surrounded by orchards in farms; now it sits on 2 acres of gardens. The two rooms each adjoin additional rooms, which can be rented as add-ons. Rooms $85–140; a cottage is also available for $140.

Villa Columbia Bed and Breakfast (1-800-708-6217; www.villacolumbia.com), 902 Oak Street. A 1911 Craftsman right in downtown Hood River ratchets the bar up a bit with organic breakfasts, Jacuzzis, and "rain showers" in every room (hey, this is Oregon—do I want rain showers in the room, too?), equipment storage rooms, warm colors, and nice views. $139–169.

Vineyardview Bed and Breakfast (1-866-588-8466; www.vineyardviewbnb.com), 4240 Post Canyon Drive. Leave Hood River and wind westward up the ridge, and you'll enter wine country. So there are plenty of vineyards to view, and a choice of five room configurations to suit families, friends, or honeymooners. And, of course, breakfast features homegrown fruit. $95–175.

Parkdale

Mount Hood Bed and Breakfast (1-800-557-8885; www.mthoodbnb.com), 8885 Cooper Spur Road. At the head of the Hood River Valley, the B&B sits on a small ranch looking over its shoulder at Mount Hood. The farmhouse has four large, wood-paneled rooms with electric or wood-burning fireplace, all conveniences, and spectacular views. From $140.

🐾 **Old Parkdale Inn** (1-877-687-4669), 4932 Baseline Drive. Two suites and a guest room named for Monet, Gauguin, and Georgia O'Keeffe fill this fine old house appropriately surrounded by gardens in the middle of Parkdale. Elegant appointments, including fireplaces in all rooms, don't prevent this inn from being pet friendly, though you should call and consult ahead of time. Doubles $130–162, with full breakfast.

Sandy

Brookside Bed and Breakfast (503-668-4766; www.brooksidebandb.com), 45232 SE Paha Loop. Three miles east of Sandy, Brookside is "country" enough to have its own brook, chickens, geese, goats, and enviable views of Mount Hood, yet it is close to shops and restaurants. The house is a post-war home with a huge deck and five very reasonable guest rooms. $50–75, with breakfast.

Sandy Salmon Bed and Breakfast Lodge (503-622-6699; www.sandysalmon.com), 61661 E. US 26. Situated at the confluence of the Sandy and Salmon rivers, this spreading contemporary log home gives you the feeling of being at the edge of wilderness, which you are: Mount Hood National Forest and the Mount Hood Wilderness are at your doorstep. Owners Maggie and Jerry Emmert have made the most of the setting, with a huge stone fireplace, twisted-juniper furniture, and carefully framed views. This is a place to celebrate a special occasion. Four guest rooms all have private baths and Wi-Fi. $195–245, with breakfast.

CABINS

Brightwood

Brightwood Guest House (503-622-5783), 64725 E. Barlow Trail Road. The single, cedar-paneled cabin affords lots of privacy on 2 acres with flourishing gardens screened by evergreens. It comes with hot tubs, a fireplace, and kitchenette, and a hearty breakfast delivered when you want it. $135–150.

Salmon River Inn (503-704-2882), 20550 E. Country Club Road. Tucked under Mount Hood along the Salmon River, this elegant "cabin" has two bedrooms, two bathrooms, a deck over the river, and a hot tub—a getaway for a family or close friends. $135.

Sandy

Hidden Woods Bed and Breakfast (503-622-5754; www.thehiddenwoods.com), 19380 E. Summertime Drive. The 1929 log cabin sits in the woods halfway between Sandy and Welches. Rented to one party at a time, it comes complete with kitchen, hot tub, fireplace, a cozy living room, and two bedrooms. $130, with breakfast.

GUEST HOUSES

The Dalles

Columbia Windrider Inn (541-296-2607; www.windriderinn.com), 200 W. Fourth Street. This budget option caters to the "windriders" flocking to the gorge beyond Hood River, though you don't have to be one to stay here. Four rooms in a vintage home sleep two to six people, and a swimming pool and Ping-Pong table help you relax after a hard day on the river (or elsewhere). $45–59.

HOSTELS

Cascade Locks

Mount Hood Hostel (1-888-865-4597; www.mthoodhostel.com), next to the Skibowl East parking lot, Government Camp. The young or budget minded can bunk down here for $20 a night. It helps to be agile; the beds come in tiers of three. You get a common room, kitchen area, and Wi-Fi, and proximity to the slopes.

HOTELS AND MOTELS

Government Camp

Cascade Motel (541-374-8750), 300 Forest Lane. A vintage motor court offers 12 clean and quiet cottages. From $77, double occupancy.

The Dalles

♿ 🐾 **Cousins Country Inn** (1-800-848-9378; www.cousinscountryinn.com), 2114 W. Sixth Street. Fundamentally a motel, it's at least a change from the chains dominating The Dalles. Ninety-seven rooms, a swimming pool, and an on-site restaurant make it convenient for families, and ADA or pet-friendly rooms are available upon request. Doubles from $80.

Hood River

Hood River Hotel (541-386-1900; www.hoodriverhotel.com), 102 Oak Street. Once upon a time, about the 1880s, the railroad came to Hood River. A large and impressive hotel sprang up to accommodate the large number of businesspeople, magnates, and late Oregon Trail emigrants flocking to the frontier. The present hotel was originally an annex; the rest of the building has disappeared. But the remainder is a charmingly restored boutique hotel with 13 rooms, nine suites, and its own restaurant. Doubles $89–129.

Oak Street Hotel (1-866-386-3845; www.oakstreethotel.com), 610 Oak Street. The large old home on Hood River's main drag is now a hotel with nine artfully simple rooms and handcrafted furniture in walking distance of shops and restaurants. From $129, including a buffet breakfast of homebaked pastries and fruits.

Troutdale

Edgefield McMenamins (1-800-669-8610; www.mcmenamins.com), 2126 SW Halsey Street. Formerly known as the "poor farm," the imposing redbrick structure actually did house indigent residents from 1911 to 1962, when it became a nursing home. The McMenamin brothers have renovated and put their irrepressible stamp on it, complete with their signature whimsical artwork. Pubs, art studios, a brewery, and even a distillery fill the former outbuildings, often graced by live music. Gardens supply greens and herbs for the restaurant (see *Dining Out*), and a soaking pool steams into the open air. Many of the cozy, vintage-furnished rooms are "European-style," which seems to mean shared bathrooms; but even the shared baths are subdivided into individual, lockable bathroomlets comprising shower, sink, and toilet. Doubles $75–105; dorm beds $40.

LODGES

Mount Hood

Timberline Lodge (1-800-547-1406; www.timberlinelodge.com), 6 miles from Government Camp up Timberline Road. Huddled against 11,239-foot Mount Hood at the 6,000-foot level, Timberline makes an impression whether swathed in snowdrifts or outspread in the sun. The massive wood and stone lodge was built by hand in three short years during the Depression, to create both jobs and a lasting Oregon legacy, which came about: Timberline is one of the great lodges of the West (see *Historic Sites*). While rooms have been updated to include private baths, the decor is otherwise as it was, handcrafted and unique. $120–290.

✷ Where to Eat

DINING OUT

Hood River

Celilo Restaurant and Bar (541-386-5710; www.celilorestaurant.com), 16 Oak Street. Open for lunch, dinner, and Sun. brunch. As it focuses on local and seasonal foods, the menu constantly changes, but you can be sure of getting something creative and fresh. Naturally it includes Northwest seafood and meats, but it also makes an effort in the noncarnivore category. (French lentil cakes with morels? Sounds good. Smoked Idaho trout salad? Likewise.) And reasonable withal.

FIREPLACE AT TIMBERLINE LODGE

Cornerstone (541-386-1900; www.hoodhotel.com), 102 Oak Avenue. Open for breakfast, lunch, and dinner. In the old Hood River Hotel, Cornerstone leans subtly toward Pacific-Asian fusion but doesn't forgo American favorites like rib-eye steak or seared wild salmon—with just a dash, perhaps, of truffle butter or basil aioli. And the ingredients strive to remain chemical-free.

Sixth Street Bistro and Loft (541-386-5737; www.sixthstreetbistro.com), Sixth and Cascade streets. Daily for lunch and dinner. With 12 microbrews, a wine list densely populated with Northwest wines, and the earnest effort to serve local, organic, sustainable food, the Bistro is a sort of microcosm of current Oregon food culture. It's also democratic: you can order fish-and-chips or rib-eye steak, depending on your tastes and pocketbook, a curry, satay, or one of the vegetarian options. One of the first restaurants in town to offer more than meat and potatoes, it became one of the most popular, offering fare that's both satisfying and interesting.

Stonehedge Gardens (541-386-3940), 3405 Cascade Avenue. Open for dinner only. Six acres of lush gardens, as much as the menu, make this a venue for weddings and other special occasions. The cuisine is basically Northwestern with a nod to the continent: Wiener schnitzel, crêpes, and other occasional exotica. Reservations recommended.

Mount Hood

Cascade Dining Room (503-272-3311), at Timberline Lodge. Daily for breakfast, lunch, and dinner. It's not cheap—you're paying for the location as well as the menu—but it is high cuisine, literally and figuratively. Executive chef Leif Eric Benson (a lucky name, to be sure) puts interesting accents on classic dishes, such as roast breast of pheasant with Pinot Blanc sauce and swordfish grilled with miso, and brings on some that would frankly startle the early guests, like smoked duckling enchiladas. Whichever dish you choose from the eclectic menu will have been carefully thought out and prepared, and likely to make you a memorable meal.

Troutdale

Black Rabbit Restaurant (503-492-3086; www.mcmenamins.com), 2126 SW Halsey Street. **Edgefield McMenamins** (see *Hotels and Motels*) has several pubs on-site, but this is their fine-dining restaurant, where you can get a fine breakfast, lunch, or dinner without spending a fortune. The menu varies daily and comprises a mix of traditional and "creative" Northwest cuisine: from roast chicken to succulent swordfish on polenta by way of smoked salmon and ricotta ravioli, for example. Some of the produce even comes from the Edgefield McMenamins's "poor farm" garden (see *Hotels and Motels*). An attentive staff rounds out the experience. Reservations recommended on weekends or holidays.

EATING OUT

The Dalles

ANZAC Tea Parlour (541-296-5877; www.anzactea.com), 218 W. Fourth Street. Tues.–Sat. 11–4. The Dalles may seem an improbable place to find a tea parlor honoring the Australia–New Zealand Army Corps, or indeed any tea parlor at all. But owner Bev Eagy imbibed Down Under culture during 20 years in Sydney, came back to the United States, bought the 1865 home of cattle baron Ben Snipes, and began serving tea to unsuspecting Americans. Also cakes, high tea, and lunches including meat pies and sausage rolls.

Baldwin's Saloon (541-296-5666; www.baldwinsaloon.com), 201 Court Street. Mon.–Thurs. 11–9, Fri.–Sat. 11–10. The place has had a chequered history. In 1876, near the riverfront and the train station, it was the perfect place for a saloon. A house of questionable repute was later added on, with the madam conveniently married to the saloonkeeper. The place was later converted to other purposes before being restored as a saloon and restaurant once again (now quite respectable). Some of the early furnishings are still in use, notably an 1894 mahogany piano and an antique cash register. Seafood occupies pride of place on the menu, with ample choices in the steak, pasta, and salad departments.

La Petite Provence (541-506-0037), 408 E. Second Street. Daily for breakfast and lunch. Quite a discovery at the dusty edge of the Palouse, this is a plucky offshoot of the little Portland chain owned by brothers Alain, Pascal, and Didier. The pastries are as authentic as they come, and the blend of French baking with American-sized breakfasts and sandwiches has gone over well in this wheat-and-cattle town.

Hood River

North Oak Brasserie (541-387-2310), 113 Third Street. Daily for lunch and dinner. Owned by the same couple who have **Stonehedge Gardens** (see *Dining Out*), the Brasserie offers a more intimate setting for relaxed dining and specializes in Italian cuisine. Though wouldn't that make it a trattoria, really? Anyway, you can find favorites like eggplant alla parmigiana or venture slightly further afield—Italy isn't all tomato sauce, and neither is this menu.

Troutdale

Tad's Chicken 'n Dumplings (503-666-5337; www.tadschicdump.com), 1325 E. Historic Columbia River Highway. Daily for dinner. Tad Johnson set up his roadhouse here in the 1920s, when the highway came in and motorists went out. Being on the banks of the Sandy River, Tad's served mainly fish and beer. Later owners instituted the hearty chicken and dumplings dinner, which is still served—and plenty of other items on the menu as well, including a children's menu (with a kid-sized version of the chicken dinner).

THE BARLOW TRAIL ROADHOUSE HAS BEEN SERVING TRAVELERS SINCE 1926.

Welches

Backyard Bistro (503-622-6302), 67898 E. US 26. Open for lunch and dinner; breakfast on Sun. Tucked into the back of a crafts shop, this is a cozy spot; it's particularly pleasant to sit on the tiny outdoor patio on a summer afternoon. Choose among burgers, huge and varied salads, and some inventive dishes such as white chili (with white beans and chicken broth base) or zucchini patties (intended as a vegetarian crabcake, but in my opinion much better). Relax, as service can be leisurely.

Barlow Trail Roadhouse (503-622-1662), 69580 E. US 26. Daily for breakfast, lunch, and dinner. This rustic cabin has been a local favorite since 1926, when it was practically the only eatery between the Portland suburbs and Mount Hood. It has served grateful generations of loggers, road workers, and Timberline building crews and still doesn't lack for devotees, mostly drawn by word of mouth. The cooking is unpretentiously American, featuring such dishes as chicken and dumplings, steaks, and such, but here when they say "home cooking," they really mean it. Look for some great specials—three-course meals can pop up at about $10.

✷ Entertainment

Columbia Center for the Arts (541-387-8877; www.columbiaarts.org), 215 Cascade Street, Hood River. The gorge's place for live theater, music, and lectures.

Edgefield McMenamins (see *Hotels and Motels*), in Troutdale, offers eclectic live music several nights a week in its several pubs, from jazz to Celtic to blues to . . . well, check out www.mcmenamins.com.

✷ Shopping

Artifacts (541-387-2482), 202 Cascade Avenue, Hood River. A quirky used-book store also selling pins, badges, bumper stickers, and other opinion-expressers.

Spirit of the Woods Flutes (1-800-236-0406), 3785 Acree Drive, Hood River. Handcrafted Native American–style flutes.

✷ Events

April: **Hood River Blossom Festival** (1-800-366-3530), midmonth, Hood River Fruit Loop. A celebration of orchards in flower.

June: **Sternwheeler Day,** last weekend, Marina Park Cascade Locks. Crafts, a regatta, games, and quilts celebrating the days of the steamers.

July: **Sandy Mountain Festival,** weekend after July Fourth, Meinig Memorial Park, Sandy. Parade, races, games, music, artisans, and food celebrate the community under the mountain.

August: **Gravenstein Apple Days,** third weekend, at Rasmussen Farms, Hood River. Pies, cider, recipes, music, and a corn maze.

September: **Hood River Pear Celebration,** third weekend, occurs at the pear harvest season and includes pear dessert sampling, pear art, and wine-and-cheese "pearing" along the Hood River Fruit Loop.

October: **Hood River Valley Harvest Fest,** midmonth, Hood River Waterfront. Fruits and vegetables from the cornucopia that is the Hood River Valley, music, food court, kids' activities, and more.

North Central Oregon

5

BEND–SISTERS–LA PINE AREA

REDMOND–MADRAS–PRINEVILLE AREA

COLUMBIA PLATEAU

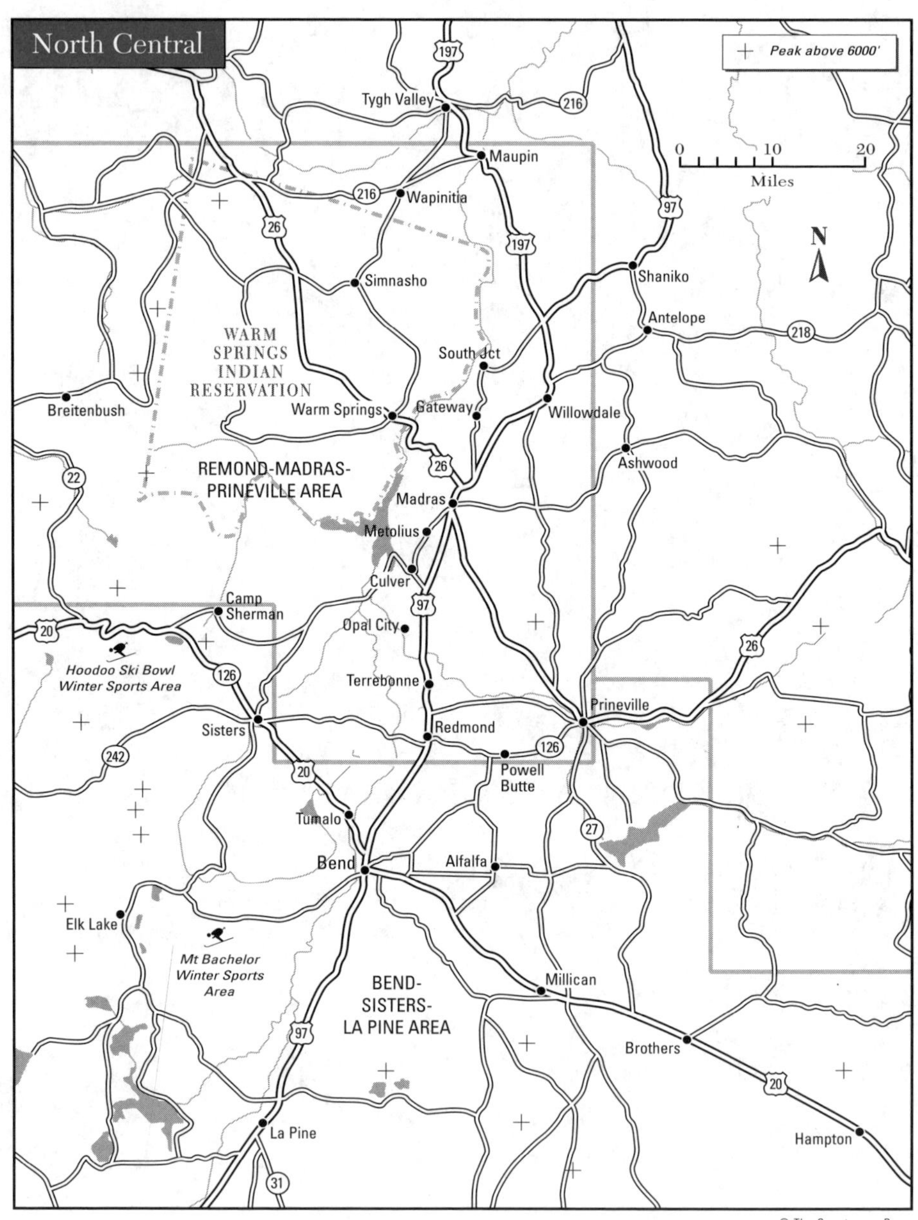

© The Countryman Press

NORTH CENTRAL OREGON

Stretching from the northern edge of the Great Basin to the Columbia River and from the verdant slopes of the Cascades to the foothills of the Wallowas, this vast swath of land must have seemed even vaster to those crossing it on foot or by wagon. Which wasn't so long ago. Livery stables starting morphing into gas stations about the 1920s, and it was a long time before paved roads really made motoring practical. Even today the wheat fields and scabbed basalt hills can seem endless.

Most trappers stuck to the edges and few riverbeds, and the native inhabitants—Teninos, Tyghs, Bannocks, and others—were left more or less in peace until the great westward migration picked up steam in the mid-1840s. An unhappy period of wars and reservation confinement ensued, and settlement was discouraged for a time. But eventually the Willamette Valley filled, and a backflow brought sheep and cattle, and finally wheat, to the volcanic soils of the Columbia Plateau. To the south and west, timber became king and remained so well into the 20th century.

These goods, and the grazing rights and railroad land grants that fostered them, brought prosperity. But as you drive around, you'll see ghost towns and abandoned homesteads, or maybe just a marker where a even a ghost town has disappeared, succumbing to the vagaries of shifting train lines, the marketplace, and (not least) a harsh environment. Kinzua, Wetmore, Mikkalo, Monkland, McDonald, are gone or nearly so. But amber waves of grain remain, complemented increasingly by wind farms, and the rougher country invites outdoorspersons to the wild sparkling rivers and hills. And anyone would gape at the region's unique treasure: its huge fossil beds set in multicolored clay hills.

BEND–SISTERS–LA PINE AREA

Bend, Sisters, and La Pine germinated where the pines meet the junipers. On the frontier between mountains and desert, northbound travelers paused at a river meander before parting ways with the Deschutes River; the "farewell bend" became Bend. Sisters was named for the neighboring Three Sisters peaks. And La Pine was apparently not named by French trappers, but by early resident Alfred Aya for its abundant pines. Pines (and fir, and Douglas fir) drove the area's economy for decades: timber cut at La Pine could be floated down to Bend and milled with the wood from Bend's own far-reaching operations, and shipped on. Times change. Bend's last lumber mill closed in 1994 and now anchors the upmarket Old Mill Shopping District, with REI occupying its belly. But they don't change that much: wood is the mainstay of construction, which with tourism was Deschutes County's economic mainstay till the crash of 2008.

Its genesis as a tourism mecca began in 1958 when the first ski lifts opened at Mount Bachelor. Those who came to ski heard that there was plenty to do in summer as well: trout fishing, backpacking, riding the range, and generally reveling in the mighty rivers and mountains edging the sagebrush steppe. Cultural interests have grown with the population, so you can browse art galleries or take in a play. Summer brings outdoor concerts in all genres. The local symphony is no slouch, though composed entirely of amateurs. And you can almost always count on sunshine. That explains why Portlanders vacation here.

GUIDANCE **Bend Chamber of Commerce** (541-382-3221; www.bendchamber.org), 777 NW Wall Street, Bend 97701.

Bend Oregon Visitor and Convention Bureau (541-382-8048 or 1-877-245-8484; www.visitbend.com), 927 NW Harriman, Bend 97701.

Central Oregon Visitors Association (1-800-800-8334; www.visitcentraloregon.com), 661 SW Powerhouse Drive, Bend 97702.

Deschutes National Forest (541-383-5300), 1001 SW Emkay Drive, Bend 97702.

La Pine Chamber of Commerce (541-536-9771; www.lapine.org), 54125 US 97, La Pine 97739.

Sisters Area Chamber of Commerce (541-549-0251 or 1-866-549-0525; www.sisterschamber.com), 291 E. Main Avenue, Sisters 97759.

THE THREE SISTERS

Sunriver Area Chamber of Commerce and Visitors Center (541-593-8149; www.sunriverchamber.com), Building 5, Sunriver Village Mall, Sunriver 97707.

GETTING THERE *By air:* **Redmond Airport (RDM)** is about 16 miles north of Bend and is served by United, Delta, and Horizon Airlines.

By bus: **Porter Stage Lines** (541-382-2151) runs a minibus between the coast and eastern Oregon, with stops in Sisters and Bend. The shuttle service **Central Oregon Breeze** (541-389-7469 or 1-800-847-0157; www.cobreeze.com) runs twice daily from Bend to Portland, with a stop at **Portland International Airport (PDX),** a trip that takes four and a half to five and a half hours.

By car: Bend is accessible from north or south via **US 97,** and from east or west via **US 20,** which also passes through Sisters. La Pine lies 30 miles south of Bend on **US 97.**

By rail: Central Oregon is full of retired train stations. Alas, the closest **AMTRAK** (1-800-USA-RAIL; www.amtrak.com) passenger stop is in Chemult, about 65 miles south of Bend.

GETTING AROUND Much of the above is irrelevant, as you will need a car to get around.

By bus: **Bend Area Transport** (541-322-5870), Bend's embryonic bus system, operates on the city's north–south and east–west axes, but not after 6 PM.

By car: At Redmond Airport you'll find car rentals at **Avis** (541-523-3750), **Hertz** (541-923-1411), **Budget** (541-923-0699), and **Enterprise** (541-504-9226); in Bend itself you may rent from **Enterprise** (541-383-1717).

MEDICAL EMERGENCY **Bend Memorial Clinic** (541-382-2811), 2600 NE Neff Road, Bend; and 231 E. Cascade Avenue, Sisters.

St. Charles Medical Center (541-382-4321), 2500 NE Neff Road, Bend.

✱ To See

FARMERS' MARKETS **Bend Farmers' Market** (541-408-4998) offers fresh produce at two locations: downtown Bend off Franklin Street above Mirror Pond, Wed. 3–7, early June–mid-Oct.; and at St. Charles Medical Center, 2500 NE Neff Road, Bend, Fri. 2–6, June–Sept.

Sisters Country Local Market (541-549-0251), 291 E. Main Avenue, Sisters. Tues. 11–3, May–Sept.

FOR FAMILIES ✐ **Wizard Falls Fish Hatchery** (541-595-6611), off US 20 on FR 41 northwest of Sisters. Kokanee, rainbow trout, and Atlantic salmon fill the viewing ponds at this hatchery in the woods. Visitors are welcome to stroll the parklike grounds, and tours can be arranged upon request. It's also a rewarding bird-watching spot.

✐ **Working Wonders Children's Museum** (541-389-4500; www.workingwonders .org), 520 SW Powerhouse Drive, Bend. Wed.–Sat. 10–5 and Sun. 11–5. General admission $6, seniors $5. If it's cold or nasty out, or if your kid just needs kid time, let him or her into the hands-on exhibits here. Your child can, of course, paint and draw and sing and dance, but can also create his or her own TV news and weather report, learn building skill with life-sized Lincoln Logs, play veterinarian, and even learn to throw pizza dough. You can learn, too.

HERITAGE TREES A **ponderosa pine** in La Pine State Park, 27 miles south of Bend off US 97, is the state champion of the species at 191 feet tall with a circumference of nearly 30 feet.

HISTORIC HOMES Pick up a walking-tour brochure at **Deschutes County Historical Society** (541-389-1813), 129 NW Idaho Avenue, and discover Bend's stately homes, mostly dating from the early 1900s, between Drake Park and Wall Street. Of interest is the 1911 **G. P. Putnam House,** 606 NW Congress Street. Putnam was heir to the Putnam publishing fortune and came to what was still a frontier town to seek his own fortune. He managed to become owner of the *Bend Bulletin* and mayor of Bend in short order, but eventually he moved back to New York. The **McCann House,** 440 NW Congress Street, is an imposing Dutch Colonial structure built in 1916 by the first manager of the Shevlin-Hixon lumber company, one of prime movers behind Bend's existence. The house contained servants' quarters and a central vacuum system (but no central heating).

HISTORIC SITES **Camp Polk,** 3.5 miles northeast of Sisters on Camp Polk Road. Today it's a natural preserve, but in 1865 it was the site of a military camp set up to protect traffic along the new Santiam Wagon Road from Indian attack. No such attacks materialized, and the camp was abandoned within a year. The only old structure visible today is the frame of a barn built in 1871 by the Hindmans, who homesteaded after the army left.

Old Mill, Ponderosa Drive, Bend. In the beginning two titans ruled the timber industry in central Oregon: competitors Shevlin-Hixon and Brooks-Scanlon. They both built mill complexes on the Deschutes River and became two of the largest pine milling operations in the world. Gradually available timber declined, and the mills finally shut down in the 1990s. The three smokestacks you see today sit on a restored Brooks-Scanlon mill now housing an REI store. The rest of the complex has evolved from production to consumption and is called the Old Mill Shopping District.

Reid School, 129 NW Idaho Street, Bend. The three-story school built of volcanic tuff now houses the Des Chutes Historical Museum (see Museums), but it functioned as a school from 1914 to 1979. Ruth Reid was a revered principal.

MUSEUMS Des Chutes Historical Museum (541-389-1813; www.deschutes history.org), 129 NW Idaho Avenue, Bend. Tues.–Sat. 10–4:30. General admission $5, youth $2, children under 12 with adult, free. The French trappers called it the *rivière des Chutes*, the River of the Falls that drains the high Cascades and was so rich in lovely fur-bearing beaver and otter (now recovering after being nearly trapped out). Set in the solid 1914 Reid School, the museum enthusiastically traces Deschutes County history from fine obsidian points through the Fremont expedition to the logging rush to coming of the railway (1911), electricity (1914), and irrigation (a long while). What would you wear to work outdoors in subfreezing temperatures half the year but a pair of bearskin gloves? Did every cowboy own angora chaps? My favorite object is a boulder inscribed "1813," found a mile south of Bend, predating by 12 years any documented non-Indian incursion (the earliest known was a Hudson's Bay party that probed the area in 1825). Local historians guess that trappers from Astoria, founded 1811, may have come this way, but who knows? And that juniper log cryptically reading LOST MEEKS is the desperate, anonymous cry of emigrants following Stephen Meek, who thought cutting across the desert would be a faster way to the Willamette Valley. He led two hundred families into the Oregon desert, where many perished, and was lucky to escape assassination himself.

The High Desert Museum (541-382-4754; www.highdesertmuseum.org), 59800 S. US 97, Bend. Daily 9–5, except Thanksgiving, Christmas, and New Year's Day. Admission (for two days): adults $15, seniors $12, students $9, May–Oct.; adults $10, seniors $9, students $6, Nov.–Apr. Children four and under free. Otters and bobcats and lynx, oh my—and that's just to mention some of the outdoor exhibits. Beautifully designed using local materials, the museum showcases the nature, history, and development of the High Desert via exquisite dioramas, reconstructions, wildlife habitat, and a priceless collection (including the stagecoach Mark Twain rode while writing *Roughing It*). Stroll through the Spirit of the West gallery, from a cool, presettlement desert morning, to high noon on the thirsty Oregon Trail, to a burgeoning frontier town, to a lonely ranch at twilight complete with yipping coyotes. Learn about the lives of Columbia Plateau tribes and immigrant Basque sheepherders—then stroll outside to see eagles, otters, and other High Desert neighbors, and experience some living history at the reconstructed pioneer homestead. Children's and adult events, including demonstrations of some of the museum's one hundred wildlife species, take place daily; check the schedule at the entrance.

Sunriver Nature Center and Observatory (541-593-4394; www.sunriver naturecenter.org), River Road, Sunriver (take US 97 to the Sunriver exit and follow the signs). The nature center is open daily 9–5; the observatory is open daily 10–2 and Tues.–Sun. 9–11 PM in summer (call for winter hours). Adults $3, children 2–12 $2; adults $6 and children $4 for evenings at the observatory.The small but

Patrick Roberts

THE THREE SISTERS FROM THE HIGH DESERT

friendly nature center offers displays on local flora, fauna, and geology—the latter including a curious collection of meteorites. A pleasant 0.25-mile nature trail winds along the river. Botany buffs will enjoy the outdoor garden featuring native plants and their traditional uses. The observatory has 20-inch telescopes for its popular evening programs and special lenses for safely viewing the sun.

NATURAL WONDERS High Cascades. Once upon a time, about 35 million years ago, a row of volcanoes plopped up from the ocean, giving Oregon a coastline a hundred or so miles farther west than before. They blocked much of the rain that had blown in from the Pacific, so that the land east of it slowly dried up; over time they eroded, losing much of their height. They are now known as the Western Cascades. Much later, new volcanic activity caused by subduction of the Juan de Fuca tectonic plate created the sharp, high peaks we see today running from British Columbia to Mount Lassen in California. The iconic Three Sisters, averaging 10,000 feet, preside over central Oregon, flanked by the 9,000-foot cone of Mount Bachelor and majestic Mount Jefferson (10,500 feet). Some of these mountains are quite young. Mount Bachelor is only about fourteen thousand years old, and if you walk between its looming cone and the even younger flows of Lava Butte you sense an unsettled landscape. In fact, the ground is slowly rising in an area just west of South Sister, which is considered the volcano most likely to reawaken.

FALL CREEK, IN THE HIGH CASCADES NEAR BEND

Newberry Crater. Looming on Bend's southern horizon like a whale is the forested rim of Newberry Crater. Rising slowly but inexorably from the surrounding plain, and some 30 miles east of the Cascade chain, Newberry's broad flanks are studded with cinder cones—evidence of long and barely stoked volcanic activity. In fact, hot springs underlying the chilly lakes within the caldera are periodically considered for geothermal energy development. Like Crater Lake, Newberry is the remains of a collapsed volcano, but older and bigger: built of multiple magma eruptions starting six hundred thousand years ago, Newberry Volcano reached 9,000 feet high, averages 25 miles in diameter, and covers 500 square miles. Eruptions a hundred thousand years later depleted the magma chamber beneath, and subsidence left today's crater, now occupied by Paulina and East lakes. Activity continued, however, creating the massive **Obsidian Flow** a mere 1,300 years back, and the numerous cinder cones of which **Lava Butte,** just south of Bend, is one of the most recent (about seven thousand years old). In the **Lava Cast Forest** on the northwestern slopes you can see basalt "trees"—casts of actual trees engulfed in a lava flow seven thousand years ago. The **Lava River Cave** near US 97 south of Lava Butte was formed by lava cooling from the outside as it flowed, creating a stone tunnel. All these geologic features are part of **Newberry National Volcanic Monument** and can be visited seasonally (see *Parks*). A magma chamber is thought to lie about 2 miles beneath the caldera.

Headwaters of the Metolius, 10 miles west of Sisters by US 20 and FR 14, near Camp Sherman. The 29-mile-long, Wild and Scenic Metolius River springs nearly full grown from the ground here. The spot is almost postcard perfect, amid tall ponderosas leading the eye to views of Mount Jefferson. A short, wheelchair-accessible trail leads from the parking area to the springs. As impressive, but much less well known, are the springs where **Fall River** emerges from the ground south of Sunriver; from Bend take US 97 south 17 miles to FR 42, turn right, drive 12 miles, and park at the Fall River trailhead.

SCENIC DRIVES **The Cascades Lakes Scenic Byway** and **Century Drive** run concurrently from Bend up OR 372 to Mount Bachelor, then along FR 46, looping among the high lakes of the Cascades. After 83 miles, the Scenic Byway continues south to OR 58, which crosses the Cascade Range, while the Century Drive loop turns east on FR 42, taking you back to US 97 via Sunriver and thus north to Bend. Along the way are ample opportunities for viewing the Cascades's flamboyant geology in the form of pumice fields, obsidian flows, and looming volcanic peaks. You'll pass 11 of the hundred-odd pristine Cascade lakes, some of which warm up enough to swim in along about Aug.; plenty of trailheads leading into the wilderness (see *Hiking*); and campgrounds on several of the lakes (see *Camping*). You can even take a ski lift to the top of Mount Bachelor and see nearly forever. Burgers and such are available at **Elk Lake Resort, Cultus Lake Resort,** and **Crane Prairie Resort.** Take a day or take three; it's spectacular. The route is closed from about Thanksgiving till Memorial Day between Mount Bachelor and Crane Prairie, though Elk Lake Resort is open in winter and accessible by snowmobile.

McKenzie/Santiam Pass Scenic Byway, an 80-mile loop starting in Sisters, takes in two mountain passes and some of the area's best scenery. From Sisters take OR 242 up to McKenzie Pass (5,325 feet) and stop at the Dee Wright Observatory. Here you can see a long line of Cascade peaks and take a wheelchair-friendly

CASCADES SKYLINE FROM THE TOP OF TUMALO PEAK, NEAR BEND

interpretive trail through extensive lava fields only about 1,500 years old. Continue past waterfalls along OR 242 to OR 126, 22 miles from Sisters, and turn right to reach US 20 after 19 miles. Turn right again to return to Sisters via the Santiam Pass (4,817 feet). *Caution:* Skip this drive in winter conditions. McKenzie Pass is closed from fall to late May or June; the Santiam Pass is usually open but is dangerous in ice or snow.

✷ To Do

BICYCLING Biking is practical only in summer at the higher elevations, spring through fall lower down. The **Deschutes River Trail** (see *Hiking*) in Bend is a relaxing ride on a trail shared with hikers. **Shevlin Park,** 3 miles west of Bend, welcomes bikes along its paved central road and on side trails.

Many trails and old logging roads in the **Deschutes National Forest** (541-383-5300) are open to bikers. Near Bend: **Tangent Loop,** from Virginia Meissner Sno-Park, 14 miles west of Bend on Cascade Lakes Highway; 6 miles. Combine with the **Swampy Lakes Trail** for another 2.5 miles, or park at Swampy Lakes Sno-Park for a short ride. The **Inn Loop,** 7 miles west of Bend, starts just past the Seventh Mountain Resort at the junction of Cascade Lakes Highway and FR 41; 13 miles of dirt road and lodgepole pine. **Phil's Trail,** 2 miles west of Bend on Skyliner Road, is the entrance to a network of bike trails looping through secondary pine forest. Four miles of flat dirt road invite you from **Sunriver to Benham Falls** along the Deschutes; start from FR 600 at traffic circle No. 7 in Sunriver. The more challenging **Crane Prairie Loop** follows FRs 42, 182, 200, 400, 440, and 4270 around Crane Prairie Reservoir for 10 miles of rough double-track.

In the Sisters area, the **Camp Sherman H Trail** is a family-friendly, 2.5-mile ride starting at Camp Sherman. The 15-mile **Sisters Mountain Bike Trail** starts at Sisters City Park and runs on old, closed roads. The 3.2-mile **Suttle Lake Loop,** about 15 miles west of Sisters off US 20, follows the lake's shoreline through various recreation areas, handy if you're staying or picnicking by the lake; Forest Pass required.

The 21-mile **Crater Rim Trail** is a challenging, high-country trail around **Newberry Crater** (see *Natural Wonders*), tying in to several shorter trails in the caldera. Forest Pass required.

BIRD-WATCHING The **First Street** section of the **Deschutes River Trail** in Bend (see *Hiking*) makes for a simple but productive bird stroll, with resident trumpeter swans and transient ducks on the river, swallows above, and towhees, thrushes, and hummingbirds in the streamside brush. **Sawyer Park,** 62999 O.B. Riley Road in Bend, is a convenient favorite with local birders. In its river, riparian, and upland pine forest habitats you're likely to spot a great variety of songbirds—migrating warblers, nesting tanagers, and bluebirds, to mention some of the most colorful—as well as wood ducks, herons, resident osprey, and perhaps the occasional bald eagle. Northwest of Sisters on US 20, **Cold Spring Campground** and **Indian Ford Campground** are good sites for woodpeckers and songbirds in summer. **Crane Prairie Reservoir,** about 55 miles southeast of Bend via US 97 and Century Drive, is great for osprey, bald eagles, and flocks of waterfowl during migration.

CAMPING 🐾 **La Pine State Park,** about 30 miles south of Bend via US 97 and State Park Road, sits along the Deschutes River in high pine forest. Five rustic cabins, five deluxe cabins (some pet friendly), 80 full hookup, and 48 electrical hookup sites fill the campground, with restrooms, water, and showers. Reservations taken; call 1-800-452-5687.

♿ **Tumalo State Park,** 6 miles north of Bend on US 20, offers 54 tent and 23 full hookup sites along the Deschutes River, with all amenities. Open year-round; call 1-800-452-5687 for reservations.

A wealth of campgrounds dot the **Deschutes National Forest** (541-383-5300), most requiring a daily fee. A selection in the Bend area, off Century Drive: **Cultus Lake,** 40 miles west of Bend, 55 sites, vault toilets, water; no reservations; open May–late Sept. **Little Cultus Lake,** 46 miles west of Bend and follow signs, 10 sites, vault toilets, water; no reservations; open May–Oct. **Big River,** 25 miles south of Bend via US 97 and Century Drive, 11 sites, vault toilet, boat launch; no water; open Apr.–Oct.; no reservations. **Deschutes Bridge,** 41 miles southwest of Bend off Century Drive, 12 sites, vault toilets, water; open Aug.–Oct.; no reservations. **Elk Lake, Little Fawn,** and **Point,** around Elk Lake 36 miles from Bend, have a total of 53 sites, water, vault toilets; open June–Sept.; reservations for Little Fawn only via www.recreation.gov. **Fall River,** 31 miles southwest of Bend via US 97 and FR 42, 10 sites, vault toilets; no water; open Apr.–Oct.; no reservations. **Mallard Marsh** and **South** at Hosmer Lake, 35 miles southwest of Bend via Century Drive and FR 4625, total of 38 sites, vault toilets; no water; open May–Oct.; no reservations. **Soda Creek,** 26 miles west of Bend, 10 sites, vault toilets; no water, no fee; open June–Oct.; no reservations. **Todd Lake,** 24 miles west of Bend, 11 walk-in sites (0.5 mile), vault toilet; no water, no reservations.

Newberry Crater area: **Cinder Hill,** at East Lake, 110 sites, toilets, water; open May–Oct.; reservations through www.recreation.gov. **East Lake,** at East Lake, 29 sites, toilets, water; open May–Oct.; no reservations. **Hot Springs,** at East Lake, 50 sites, toilets, water; open July–Sept.; no reservations. **Little Crater,** at Paulina Lake, 50 sites, toilets, water; open May–Oct.; no reservations. **Paulina Lake,** at

Paulina Lake, 69 sites, toilets, water; open May–Oct., reservations through www.recreation.gov.

Sisters area: **Camp Sherman,** 15 miles northwest of Sisters by US 20 and FRs 14 and 1419, 15 sites, toilets, water; open year-round; no reservations. **Lower Bridge,** 7 miles north of Camp Sherman store, 12 sites, toilets, water; open May–Oct.; no reservations. At Suttle Lake, **Blue Bay, Link Creek,** and **South Shore** have a total of 97 sites, toilets, water; open Apr.–Sept.; some reservations through www.recreation.gov. **Driftwood** and **Three Creeks Lake,** 17 miles south of Sisters on FR 16, have a total of 27 sites, toilets; no water; open July–Sept.; no reservations. **Three Creek Meadow,** 15 miles south of Sisters on FR 16, 11 sites, toilets; no water; open June–Sept.; no reservations. **Cold Springs,** 4 miles west of Sisters on OR 242, 23 sites, toilets, water; open Apr.–Sept.; no reservations. **Indian Ford,** 5 miles northwest of Sisters on US 20, 25 sites, toilets; no water; no reservations.

CANOEING, KAYAKING, AND RAFTING Whether you like flat water or whitewater, there are plenty of choices here. **Hosmer Lake,** 35 miles west of Bend off Century Drive, is a quiet mountain lake that allows electric motors only. **Irish Lake, Lucky Lake, Taylor Lake,** and **North Twin Lake,** off FR 600, allow no motors at all. **Todd Lake** (see *Camping*) also excludes motors, as does **Three Creeks Lake** south of Sisters. Larger lakes such as **Elk Lake, Cultus, Sparks, Lava** and **Little Lava lakes** restrict motorized boat speed to 10 mph. White-water enthusiasts shoot sections of the **Deschutes River;** for guidance contact **Sun Country Raft Tours** (1-800-770-2161; www.suncountrytours.com), 531 SW 13th Street, Bend. The truly devoted should consider the **Deschutes Paddle Trail,** 120 miles of the Deschutes and Little Deschutes rivers and several Cascade lakes; information and maps can be downloaded from www.deschutespaddletrail.info.

DIVING **The Central Oregon Diving Connection** (541-388-3660; www.codiving.com), 157 NE Greenwood Avenue. Diving may not seem an obvious pastime so far from the sea and so close to the desert, but some of the high Cascade lakes are gaining a following for their crystal-clear (though chilly) water and submarine geology. Central Oregon's diving enthusiast Walt Bolton guides divers in Waldo and Crater lakes and teaches PADI certification classes.

GOLF **Aspen Lakes Golf Course** (541-549-4653), 16900 Aspen Lakes Drive, Sisters. Eighteen holes.

Black Butte Ranch: Big Meadow and **Glaze Meadow** (541-595-1500), 8 miles west of Sisters on US 20. Each 18 holes.

Lost Tracks Golf Club (541-385-1818), 60205 Sunset View Drive, Bend. Eighteen holes.

Sunriver Resort: Crosswater, Meadows, Woodlands, and **Caldera Links** (1-800-737-1034), 17600 Center Drive, Sunriver. Caldera Links nine holes, the others 18 each.

Quail Run Golf Course (541-536-1303), 16725 Northridge Road, La Pine. Eighteen holes.

SOUTH, MIDDLE, AND NORTH SISTERS FROM BROKEN TOP

River's Edge Golf Course (541-389-2828), 3075 N. US 97, Bend. Eighteen holes.

HIKING Bend area: The **Deschutes River Trail** follows the river through town: the 4-mile stretch downstream from NW First Street is popular with joggers, bikers, walkers, and baby strollers, while the 3 miles upstream from access at the Old Mill District starts paved and soon becomes a near-wilderness path. **Shevlin Park,** 3 miles west of Bend on Shevlin Park Road, offers a paved road in the Tumalo Creek Canyon and several miles of dirt trails on the ridges above. Just southwest of Bend, unpaved forest roads off Century Drive access miles of riverside trails to **Dillon Falls, Benham Falls,** and numerous lovely picnic areas. Higher in the mountain, the **Green Lakes Trail,** 27 miles west of Bend on Cascade Lakes Drive, rises 4 miles through forest to end at alpine lakes but can be very busy. From the same trailhead, the **Soda Creek Trail** is less frequented, meandering through old-growth forest to end in alpine meadows under Broken Top; 4.5 miles one-way, but it can tie in with Green Lakes or Todd Lake trails. **Todd Lake** is a trailhead for a 2-mile loop around the shoreline, a 3-mile loop on the surrounding ridge, and the **Upper Todd Trail,** which rises about 3 miles to meet the Soda Creek Trail. These trails enter the **Three Sisters Wilderness** and enjoy fine wildflowers and mountain views. Or, walk miles of desert trails in the **Badlands** through sagebrush and

ANCIENT JUNIPER IN THE OREGON BADLANDS

ancient junipers; parking on the left at milepost 16 on US 20 east of Bend. No water or restrooms. **Tumalo Falls,** a day-use area 14 miles west of Bend in the Deschutes National Forest, has access to the network of forest trails and a 2-mile interpretive trail with impressive views of the falls. From Bend drive west on Galveston; after 12 miles turn onto FR 4603. May not be accessible in winter.

Sisters area: A level 3-mile trail loops around **Suttle Lake.** Another level trail runs 10 miles along the **Metolius River** (no fee), accessible from several points, including the Wizard Falls fish hatchery and **Camp Sherman** campground (see *Camping*). A more strenuous hike involving a 2,300-foot elevation gain leads 4 miles to **Black Crater,** from a trailhead 11 miles west of Sisters on OR 242. The **Tam McArthur Rim Trail** rises steeply from a trailhead 16 miles south of Sister on FR 16, then levels out to majestic views of the entire central Cascade range; 5 miles round-trip. A 2-mile trail climbs to the top of **Black Butte;** 6 miles north of Sisters on US 20, turn right on FR 11, drive 4 miles to FR 1110, and continue 3 miles west, then park at the end of FR 1110. The **Park Meadow Trail** starts 15 miles south of Sisters on FR 16 (no fee) and joins the **Green Lakes Trail** after 6 miles.

La Pine area: In **Newberry Crater,** the **Crater Rim Trail** is a rugged 21-mile path around the caldera. Shorter trails include the **Paulina Lakeshore Trail** (7 miles around Paulina Lake), the 1.5-mile **Little Crater Lake Trail**—both accessed from Little Crater Campground—and the 10-mile **Peter Skene Ogden Trail** along Paulina Creek (no fee at Ogden trailhead).

The **Pacific Crest Trail** runs through the entire area; for details check www.pcta .org.

UNIQUE ADVENTURES ✐ **Pine Mountain Observatory,** 32 miles southeast of Bend; take US 20 east 24 miles to Pine Mountain Road and turn right to drive up the mountain. Fri. and Sat. nights, late May–late Sept. Admission free, but a $3 donation is suggested. It's a bit of a field trip, but a breathtaking experience for older children and adults. The University of Oregon research facility is set at 6,300 feet in the High Desert for atmospheric clarity—and *you* can search the universe. A visit starts with a presentation on the telescopes and basic astronomy, then moves on to viewing of galaxies, planets, or whatever is visible that night through the 15-inch or 24-inch telescopes and CCD camera. A particularly enthusiastic group may stay up watching till the wee hours. A primitive Forest Service campground is adjacent and free.

WINTER SPORTS **Hoodoo Ski Area** (541-822-3799; www.hoodoo.com), US 20 at Santiam Pass. This is the low-key ski area of the central Cascades: five lifts, 20 runs, and 10 miles of groomed cross-country trails.

Mount Bachelor Ski Resort (1-800-829-2442; www.mtbachelor.com), about 20 miles southwest of Bend on the Cascade Lakes Highway. At 9,000 feet, Mount Bachelor (formerly known as Bachelor Butte, but the promoters didn't like that) looks like a miniature Mount Fuji: smoothly conical, with a nice crater on top and lava flanks. Ideal for skiing if you get a lot of snow, which is the case. Local skiers praise the powder, disparaging the competition's "Portland cement." Ten lifts, trails for all levels, several terrain parks, snow play areas, and groomed cross-country trails make it a major resort.

MOUNT BACHELOR

✷ Wilder Places

PARKS Bend City parks: **Drake Park**'s long, ponderosa-studded greensward is a favorite spot for picnics or leisurely strolls right in the middle of Bend. Watch the resident mute swans on Mirror Pond, created by the small dam on the Deschutes that first brought electricity to town, or enjoy an evening concert. **Shevlin Park** (541-389-7275), 18920 Shevlin Park Road, just 3 miles west of Bend, is 652 acres of mostly forested ravine, through which tumbles Tumalo Creek. Three picnic areas, an events hall, and a bucolic setting make it a popular afternoon escape. A paved road (closed to cars during fire season) is an easy surface for strollers or wheelchairs, while dirt paths among the ponderosas provide access to the adjacent Deschutes National Forest. Fremont Meadow, at the far end of the road, is named for explorer John Fremont, who reportedly camped here with a party while exploring Oregon's far reaches in 1843. With luck you may spot a deer or coyote or, rarely, a cougar. **Sawyer Park,** 62999 O.B. Riley Road, straddles the Deschutes River with 45 acres of willow, pine, and juniper and grassy picnic areas.

Newberry National Volcanic Monument (see *Natural Wonders*). Access at Lava Butte, 11 miles south of Bend on US 97, at FR 9720 3 miles farther south, and 10 miles farther south yet where FR 21 meets the highway. This sprawling 55,500-acre site, designated in 1990, includes several impressive reminders of Oregon's volcanic roots. The best way to see it is to visit first **Lava Lands Visitor Center** (541-593-2421), open daily 9–5, July–Sept. and Wed.–Sun. 9–5, May–June and Labor Day–Oct. 15. Located just below **Lava Butte,** its exhibits explain the geological cataclysms that shaped the region. You can take a short walk in the lava field, then walk or drive to the top of the butte and see the 9-square-mile flow that extruded from the cone seven thousand years ago and changed the course of the nearby Deschutes. Then drive a mile south to **Lava River Cave.** This is a stone tube that formed when a rivulet of lava cooled on the outside while the inside was still liquid. The molten lava flowed out of its hardened shell like toothpaste from a tube, leaving a mile-long tunnel. Hours as for Lava Lands; lantern rentals are $4.

The cave is cold (42 degrees); wear warm clothes and comfortable shoes. Two miles farther south, you may turn left on FR 9720 and follow signs for a 9-mile drive to the **Lava Cast Forest.** Here lava flows from a rift on Newberry Volcano are punctuated with standing stone cylinders—casts where trees enveloped by lava burned, leaving a stone shell. A 1-mile interpretive trail is wheelchair accessible. Return to US 97 and drive 10 miles south to FR 21 to enter the crater itself, view the two lakes and the huge, 1,300-year-old obsidian flow, and take in the panorama from 7,984-foot Paulina Peak: crater, lakes, Cascades, High Desert, and five hundred or so cinder cones dotting the volcano's flanks.

Pilot Butte State Scenic Viewpoint, east US 20; from downtown take Greenwood Avenue about 2 miles due east. This red cinder cone rising 500 feet from the plain used to define Bend's eastern edge. It's now engulfed by development but is still popular with daily joggers and power walkers for its trails to the top (about 1 mile each way) and panoramic views of the Cascades and High Desert. Deer and the occasional cougar, too, roam its slopes. Try to ignore Costco and the car dealerships below. A paved road up is open to cars in summer.

La Pine State Park (541-536-2071 or 1-800-551-6949), 27 miles southwest of Bend via US 97 and State Park Road. In high-country forest along the Deschutes River, this is a place to camp, fish, hike, or loll about. It's also incidentally home to Big Red, the tallest ponderosa pine in Oregon (see *Heritage Trees*).

Tumalo State Park (541-382-3586 or 1-800-551-6949), 5 miles northwest of Bend off US 20, is a family park where the pines meet the sagebrush, offering camping, a riverside trail, wading in the river, and general relaxation.

WILDERNESS AREAS **Mount Jefferson Wilderness** (503-854-3366; www.fs.fed.us/r6/willamette), accessible from US 20 from the Pacific Crest and Summit trailheads. This sprawling wilderness covers 111,177 acres—much of Mount Jefferson's western slopes—and rises from a moderate 3,000 feet to the very peak of the mountain, over 10,000 feet. It greets all kinds of wilderness lovers with 190 miles

SUNSET OVER THE DESERT

of trails (including 40 miles of the Pacific Crest Trail), lakes, streams, conifer forest, glaciers, and alpine meadows. Unfortunately, mosquitoes can be thick in places all summer.

Mount Washington Wilderness (541-822-3381; www.fs.fed.us/r6/willamette) is accessible by the Pacific Crest Trail at the Dee Wright Observatory on OR 242. This smaller wilderness (52,516 acres) between US 20 and OR 242 is less frequented than the bordering **Three Sisters** or **Mount Jefferson** wildernesses. You've got to be a bit rugged to enjoy the lava plains—75 square miles of them—that surround Mount Washington's eroded cone and wear out your shoes. But it's a place for close encounters with geology, including Belknap Crater, source of some of the most recent lava flows, and the lava is edged with lodgepole-hemlock forest. The Pacific Crest Trail and several shorter trails provide access.

ENTERING THE THREE SISTERS WILDERNESS

Three Sisters Wilderness (541-822-3381; www.fs.fed.us/r6/willamette), the area's biggest wilderness at 285,192 acres, can be entered from many trailheads along **Cascade Lakes Highway, McKenzie Highway,** and various forest roads. This is a playground for central Oregonians, encompassing four major peaks (the Three Sisters and Broken Top), many lakes, trails, streams, wildflowers—in short, everything a wilderness is supposed to be. In consequence, some areas see high use, particularly **Green Lakes.** But the wilderness is huge; you'll never feel crowded.

✷ Lodging

BED & BREAKFASTS

Bend

Cabin Creek Bed and Breakfast (541-318-4798; www.cabincreekbandb.com), 22035 OR 20 E. Melody and Dave Spice wanted to create a B&B that avoided Victorian clichés, so they built this Western log home on 14 acres about 8 miles east of Bend—like a small lodge or a large log cabin. All three guest rooms have fireplaces and private baths, there are free snacks and soft drinks in the fridge, there are home-baked cookies in the afternoon, and there is a copious breakfast in the morning. $145–165.

Cricketwood Country Bed and Breakfast (1-877-330-0747; www.cricketwood.com), 63520 Cricketwood Road. Cricketwood welcomes guests into three suites, two with massage tables and Jacuzzis, and breakfasts made to order. On 10 acres at Bend's eastern edge, this is a good place to view the stars. $105–145.

Juniper Acres Bed and Breakfast (541-389-2193; www.juniperacres.com), 65220 Smokey Ridge Road. The large log home faces seven Cascades peaks and has two guest rooms, just beyond Bend's agglomeration. $95–125.

Lara House Lodge (1-800-766-4064; www.larahouse.com), 640 Congress Street. This huge 1910 Craftsman house encourages lazy vacationing, being a couple of blocks from Drake Park in one direction and Bend's downtown in the other. All you need is within reach, really, and you can just sit in front of the fire or lounge in the sunroom. Six rooms come with private baths, high-thread-count linens, and all the amenities that go with the price range, plus evening wine and a large breakfast. $189–299.

La Pine

DiamondStone Guest Lodges (1-866-626-9887; www.diamondstone.com), 16693 Sprague Loop. Doug and Gloria Watt have been cultivating this out-of-the-way haven for 20 years. First, the large house became a bed & breakfast with three bedrooms (or two suites), huge deck, and plenty of common space. Then they branched out to embrace a log cabin across the way and have just opened a huge guest house—*stunning* is really the word—built by Doug himself. He calls it the Grange, and it's designed to recall those pillars of American agriculture (albeit a sight more comfortable). Two soaring pine stories tapping solar energy for hot water and heating; a clean, warm decor; a full kitchen; and five bedrooms—well, I've seen churches that are less pretty. Amid the pines and a stone's throw from the Little Deschutes River, it harbors plenty of wildlife, and Mount Bachelor beckons the skier. Bed & breakfast rooms start at $99, including full breakfast; Mahulia log cabin at $175; call to check Grange rates and availability.

Sisters

Blue Spruce Bed and Breakfast (1-888-328-9644; www.blue-spruce.biz), 444 Spruce Street. A comfortable house, a quiet neighborhood, and spreading gardens just a couple of blocks from downtown Sisters—it couldn't be much more convenient for summer or winter adventures, family reunions, or just a peaceful escape. Have one of owner Sandy Affonso's hearty breakfasts in the cheery dining room; afterward check out the common-room library or relax in the garden, where the guests may include resting fawns or other forest denizens. Four spacious rooms and a master suite with pillow-top, king-sized beds and private jetted baths. $129–189; groups or multi-night individual stays only..

COTTAGES AND CABINS

Camp Sherman

Metolius River Lodges (1-800-595-6290; www.metoliusriverlodges.com), Camp Sherman. The hamlet of Camp Sherman has been a summer retreat since the 1920s, quiet and unpretentious, hidden in the Deschutes National Forest far from the madding crowds of Bend or anywhere else. Rustic cabins, duplexes, and fourplexes line up along the wooded banks of the Metolius, mostly with kitchens and fireplaces, but no TVs or phones; this is a place to get back to such basics as hiking, biking, fishing, and maybe even talking with your family. Cottages sleep three to eight and run $99–265.

FOREST SERVICE RENTALS

Green Ridge Lookout (541-549-7700) lies on a ridge in the forest about 20 miles north of Sisters. There are fine views of the Cascades from the 14-by-14 cabin. Up to four guests are allowed (bring pads and sleeping bags; there's only one bed), and there are basic cooking facilities and utensils. Toilets are outdoors. Call the Forest Service for directions, and be careful with children; the cabin is on a two-story-high tower. $40.

THE BACK OF MOUNT BACHELOR IN SUMMER

HOTELS AND MOTELS

Bend

Entrada Lodge (541-382-4080; www.entradalodge.com), 19221 Century Drive. Three miles from Bend on the road to Mount Bachelor, the Entrada's rooms are standard but comfortable one- and two-bedroom units with fridge and microwave; shared amenities are a swimming pool, hot tub, and ski equipment lockers. The attraction is a reasonable, quiet location backing onto the Deschutes National Forest, with its network of trails to access the Deschutes River. $79–129.

McMenamins Old St. Francis School (541-382-5174; www.mcmenamins.com), 700 NW Bond Street. Formerly a parochial school and parish center, this version of McMenamins features a hammam-style bath, as well as such amenities as two pubs, a restaurant (see *Eating Out*), a movie house, and live music. Oh, and comfy rooms, too. McMenamins's signature quirky art is much in evidence, as is a photo history of St. Francis from its early days as a pioneer mission parish. Rooms $104–175; cottages $175–395; dorm $40.

Mill Inn (1-877-748-1200), 642 NW Colorado Avenue. Just off the old industrial area (pardon me, the Old Mill District), this 10-room inn is likely considerably more comfy than it was when it served as a boardinghouse for mill workers. But it's still among Bend's more affordable options, with rooms ranging from $60 with shared bath to $80–100 with a private bath. The only inconvenience is the high traffic along Colorado Avenue, mostly during daylight hours.

The Riverhouse (541-389-3111 or 1-866-453-4479; www.riverhouse.com), 3075 N. US 97. With its back to the river and its face to US 97, the Riverhouse anchors a resort community that includes a golf course, restaurants, and access to Sawyer Park and the **Deschutes River Trail** (see *Hiking*). The 220 units run from simple queen-bedded rooms to large suites, with all the grand motel amenities: pool, sauna, spa, and complimentary hot buffet breakfast. Doubles from $115.

LODGES

Sisters

🐾 **FivePine Lodge and Conference Center** (1-866-974-5900; www.fivepinelodge.com), 1021 Desperado Trail. Opened in 2007, FivePine, on the edge of town, is the newest upscale getaway in the area. Everything is at your fingertips: besides the 26 cottages and eight lodge rooms, the property includes an on-site spa, fine dining (see *Dining Out*), and brewpub, with the Sisters cinema right next door. With abundant wood and stone and dignified, Amish-made furniture, the decor harks back to traditional Western lodges, but with two-story lodge rooms, pillow-top beds, plasma TVs, oversize "waterfall" bathtubs, and tile showers—barely understated luxury. The self-contained concept seems a bit at odds with the small, inviting town and vast recreational opportunities, but for a family reunion or pampered weekend it could be just the ticket. Lodge suites $149–209; cottages $159–199. Pets allowed in certain cottages for a $20/day fee.

RESORTS

Bend

Seventh Mountain Resort (1-800-452-6810; www.seventhmountain.com), 18575 SW Century Drive. Formerly the Inn of the Seventh Mountain, this is a full-service resort and the last lodging on the way to Mount Bachelor. Children's activities and excursions parallel the adult offerings of rafting, horseback riding, mountain biking, and tennis (all for a fee). Included are the pool, skating rink, and a free shuttle bus to the ski area in winter, and of course dining is on premises, too. Accommodations vary from studios to houses, and rates vary seasonally. $99–369.

✱ Where to Eat

DINING OUT

Bend

Ariana (541-330-5539; www.arianarestaurantbend.com), 1304 NW Galveston. Tues.–Sat. for dinner. Unlike several of Bend's top restaurants, Ariana has so far weathered the current economic storm. Founded in 2004 by enthusiastic young chefs Ariana and Andrés Fernández, it quickly became an extended-family operation with a seasonally variable menu concentrating on authentic Spanish, Italian, and (of course) Northwestern cuisine. The pasta is homemade, the cheeses are imported, and the wine list marries the Pacific Northwest to Spain, Italy, Chile, France, and Germany.

Cork (541-382-6881; www.corkbend.com), 150 NW Oregon Avenue. Tues.–Sat. for dinner. Flowers and candlelight in a elegantly pared-down setting: Cork makes for a special night out. Locally grown greens and cheeses complement a menu distributed between seafood and fine meats, with an experimental touch—lavender-injected pork with mission figs?—but whatever you order will come as a pleasant surprise. A vegetarian dish is usually available.

Camp Sherman

Kokanee Café (541-595-6420; www.kokaneecafe.com), 25545 SW FR 1419. Daily, May–Dec.; call as hours may vary. Deep in the woods 18 miles northwest of Sisters, off US 20, the rustic Kokanee regales the little resort community of Camp Sherman with fine dishes ranging from venison and duck breast to rib eye and trout. Eat indoors or out overlooking the Metolius River, and take a predinner stroll to observe the huge fish under the bridge. Reservations recommended.

Sisters

The Boathouse Restaurant (541-549-2628; www.thelodgeatsuttlelake.com), the Lodge at Suttle Lake, 14 miles west of Sisters on US 20. Daily for lunch and dinner. You can enjoy a meal overlooking the lake and surrounding forest in the pine-paneled, log-beamed restaurant of the Lodge at Suttle Lake. A choice of small or large plates allows you to tailor the experience to your pocketbook or appetite without sacrificing quality; the entrées run from tenderloin to fish to lobster-stuffed salmon fillet, with creative side dishes.

Chloe (541-588-6151; www.chloefivepine.com), 1021 Desperado Trail. Tues.–Sat. for dinner. Attached to the **FivePine Resort** (see *Lodging*), Chloe is Sisters's most upscale restaurant, with a corresponding price tag. Chef Jerry Phaisanath blends French technique with American ingredients to produce an appealing menu balanced among meat, fish, and vegetarian choices. The decor seems to hark back to an unspecified era of circular alcove seating for all in tones of black, brown, and beige, the better, presumably, to set off the starry ceiling.

Sunriver

The Trout House (541-593-8880; www.trouthouserestaurant.com), 57235 River Road. Daily for breakfast, lunch, and dinner. Situated on the riverbank at the far reaches of Sunriver Resort, the Trout House has been a fixture for years, with people driving out from Bend for a fine meal at the edge of wilderness. Seafood, steaks, elk burgers, wild boar, and, of course, trout jump out from the menu; breakfasts are hearty, and the views over meadow and mountain are fine.

EATING OUT

Bend

Anthony's (541-389-8998; www.anthonys.com), 475 SW Powerhouse Drive. Open for lunch and dinner (dinner only on Sun.). A homegrown Northwestern chain, Anthony's is reliable for decently prepared fresh fish and water views; family friendly, too.

Deschutes Brewery and Public House (541-382-9242), 1044 Bend Street. Daily for lunch and dinner. "Brew" is Oregon's lifeblood. Today the actual brewery is a mile or so away near the Old Mill (you can take a tour), but this was its original home. Its Black Butte Porter and Mirror Pond Pale Ale are now known around the world, and you can get them right here, plus their entire line of new and old ales. A fairly extensive pub menu is also on tap, featuring such things as burgers from beef fed on the brewery's spent grain. **Bend Brewing Company** (541-383-1599), 1019 NW Brooks Street, is the "new" brewery in town (1995), and it's also well appreciated by local beer lovers. Mon.–Sat. for lunch and dinner.

McKay Cottage (541-383-2697; www.themckaycottage.com), 62910 O.B. Riley Road. Daily 7–2. A stone's throw from Sawyer Park, the 1916 Craftsman cottage is worth venturing beyond downtown for a quiet, relaxed breakfast or lunch. Originally on Bend's Mirror Pond, it belonged to Bend pioneers Olive and Clyde McKay. Enjoy nouvelle or traditional American cuisine—homemade in either case—on the porch for a view of the river or, cozily, indoors.

McMenamins Old St. Francis School (541-382-5174; www.mcmenamins.com), 700 NW Bond Street. Daily for breakfast, lunch, and dinner. Fundamentally it's pub food for families, but it's good, especially the trademark fish-and-chips. You can enjoy it in the restaurant, a Catholic school artfully redecorated to bring Bend's early logging days to mind; in one of the two pubs (where smoking is actually allowed); or order dinner to be brought to the movie theater, where tables punctuate rows of upholstered seats, and you can have dinner and a movie simultaneously. McMenamins is also famous for its home brews with names like Terminator and Hammerhead. Weekend evenings can get noisy.

Pine Tavern (541-382-5581; www.pinetavern.com), 967 NW Brooks Street. Daily for dinner and Mon.–Sat. for lunch. The Pine Tavern has seen a lot of changes since it opened its doors in 1936. Back then "downtown" was the entire town and certainly wasn't filled with boutique shops. The menu has expanded a bit: they probably didn't have pan-seared ahi back then, much less hazelnut Brie, but cowboy favorites like prime rib and rib-eye steak are still there. The quality can be a bit uneven, but it's worth a visit—where else do you see a mature pine tree growing right up through the floor and roof?

Sparrow Bakery (541-330-6321), 50 SE Scott Street. Mon.–Sat. 7–2. Tiny Sparrow seats 10 and serves improbably authentic European pastries, sandwiches, and salads from its industrial-zone location between the railroad tracks and the parkway—not just croissants, but things you seldom see even in the big city (ever tried canelé de Bordeaux)? And the only croque monsieur I know of in central Oregon.

Taj Palace (541-330-0774; www.tajpalacebend.com), 917 NW Wall Street. Daily for lunch and dinner. Bend's only Indian restaurant stands up well to any Indian food in the country. Both meat and vegetarian selections are scrumptious, and with a daily lunch buffet at $7.95 and a very reasonable dinner menu, it's one of the city's deals.

Taquería Los Jalapeños (541-383-1402), 601 NE Greenwood. Mon.–Sat. for lunch and dinner. A hole in the wall that has nonetheless done a roaring business for a decade now, this is where you'll find Bendites out for a quick taste of Mexico, high-schoolers on lunch break, and everyone who knows this place has the best cost-benefit ratio in town. Tacos, burritos, mole, chile verde, or chile rojo—all the taco-stand standbys, made by and for those who appreciate them.

Thai food: Bend has no fewer than four Thai restaurants, all good: **Toomie's Thai** (541-388-5590), 119 NW Minnesota, is the oldest and most genteel, with white tablecloths, attentive service, and satisfying curries and noodle dishes. Weekdays for lunch and Mon.–Sat. for dinner. **Angel's Thai** (541-388-5177), 1900 NE Division Street, has beat the odds at an obscure location by offering quality Thai dishes at affordable prices. You feel like you're visiting someone's kitchen. Weekdays for lunch and Mon.–Sat. for dinner. The newest is **Typhoon!** (541-385-8885), 550 NW Franklin Street, the latest of six Typhoons that Thai chef Bo Kline has opened around the Northwest. It is, if you'll pardon the expression, a perfect storm. The menu is ample for vegetarians and carnivores alike, and then there's the wine list and the tea menu, which, you can be sure, does not include Stash or Tazo. The only downside is that the noise level can be fairly high due to the brick walls of this refurbished downtown building. Mon.–Fri. 11–2 and Sat.–Sun. noon–3; Sun.–Thurs. 4:30–10 and Fri.–Sat. 4:30–11. Finally, there is **A Taste of Thailand** (541-815-0180), 696 NE Greenwood Avenue. It's not really a restaurant; locals call it Thai on the Fly—a Thai drive-through where the menu changes daily. Four choices a day run $5–7 each. Mon.–Sat. 11–8.

Sisters

Depot Deli (541-549-2572), 250 W. Cascade Avenue. Daily for breakfast and lunch. Get your fresh soups, salads, and hot and cold sandwiches here, as the locals do. It's been a Sisters standby for years.

Sisters Bakery (541-549-0361), 251 E. Cascades Avenue. Daily 5–5. Serving doughnuts, breads, cakes, knishes, and more in downtown Sisters for a generation.

✷ Entertainment

McMenamins offers free live music on Wed. nights; check their Web site for specifics. Very devoted amateur theater companies perform at **Cascades Theatrical Company** (541-389-0803; www.cascadestheatrical.org), 148 NW Greenwood, Bend, and **2nd Street Theater** (541-312-9626; www.2ndstreettheater.com), 220 NE Lafayette Avenue, Bend. The **Tower Theater** (541-317-0700; www.towertheater.org), 835 NW Wall Street, Bend, hosts everything from belly dance to musicals to nationally known performers. The **Central Oregon Symphony** (541-317-3941; www.cosymphony.com) is an amateur orchestra growing yearly in professionalism; three free concerts a year at the Bend High School auditorium. Check Web sites for playbills.

✷ Shopping

Bend has consciously preserved a viable **downtown,** roughly 9 blocks along Bond and Wall streets—though now trendy restaurants and shops shoulder small bookstores, businesses, and even the timeworn D&D Bar. Browse original jewelry designs by local and regional jewelers at **Silverado** (541-322-8792), 1001 NW Wall Street, or check one of the galleries for art in many media: **Mockingbird** (541-388-2107), 869 NW Wall Street, or **Tumalo Art Company** (541-385-9144), 540 SW Powerhouse Drive, in the nearby Old Mill District.

In **Sisters, The Stitchin' Post** (541-549-6061), 311 W. Cascade Avenue, caters to quilters, which is only natural as Sisters hosts and impressive annual quilt festival (see *Events*).

✷ Events

May: **Pole-Pedal-Paddle** (541-388-0002), third Sat. Skiers, cyclists, runners, and paddlers compete in a pentathlon from Mount Bachelor to the Les Schwab Amphitheater in Bend. This has been going on for more than 30 years and has evolved from a local race to an event drawing competitors from afar. But it's still for amateurs and enthusiasts of all ages and is celebrated amid music and food booths.

June: ✐ **Balloons over Bend** (541-323-0964; www.balloonsoverbend.com), first weekend, Old Mill District, Bend. Balloon launches, street art, food, music, and kids' activities welcome summer to Bend.

July: **Cascade Cycling Classic** (541-388-0002), fourth week. Five days of road races and time trials linking mountains and desert; draws top cyclists from across the country.

Sisters Outdoor Quilt Show (541-549-0989), the weekend after July Fourth, Sisters. Storefronts, homes, and businesses are bedecked with handcrafted quilts, complemented by workshops, classes, and entertainment.

August: **Sunriver Music Festival** (541-593-1084; www.sunrivermusic.org), second weekend. Three days of classical music at the Great Hall in Sunriver and the Tower Theater in Bend.

September: **Sisters Folk Festival** (541-549-4979; www.sistersfolkfestival.org), weekend after Labor Day, Sisters. Six stages of nonstop music, with a free, high-powered gospel choir concert Sun. morning.

REDMOND–MADRAS–PRINEVILLE AREA

This is cattle and alfalfa country—well, it is now. A hundred years ago there were multitudes of sheep, and some of the sharpest conflicts between ranchers and sheepmen took place here, with a few men ending up suspended from the Steel Bridge at Prineville. Cattle won. Such crops as there are can be seen near Madras and Prineville, thanks to irrigation—mainly alfalfa, strawberries, and onions. In a region that has tended toward human monoculture, Madras is the most diverse town of the area, with a large Hispanic population and Native American families from the nearby Warm Springs reservation; although you can hear more languages at Smith Rock, where rock climbers from around the world gather to challenge the fantastic tuff formations. And speaking of scenery, it's hard to beat the sight of the Deschutes, Metolius, and Crooked rivers flowing together from the south and east through spectacular gorges to join in basalt canyons a thousand feet deep.

GUIDANCE **Crooked River National Grassland** (541-475-9272), 813 SW US 97, Madras 97741.

Madras–Jefferson County Chamber of Commerce (541-475-2350 or 1-800-967-3564; www.madraschamber.com), 274 SW Fourth Street, Madras 97741.

Ochoco National Forest (541-416-6500), 3160 NE Third Street, Prineville 97754.

Prineville–Crook County Chamber of Commerce (541-447-6304; www.visitprineville.com), 390 NE Fairview, Prineville 97754.

Redmond Chamber of Commerce and CVB (541-923-5191; www.visitredmondoregon.com), 446 SW Seventh Street, Redmond 97756.

GETTING THERE *By air:* Redmond is served by **Redmond Airport (RDM)** by Delta, United, Horizon, and Allegiant airlines.

By car: **US 97** and **OR 126** are the principal arteries.

GETTING AROUND There is no public transportation, which makes a car necessary.

MEDICAL EMERGENCY Bend Memorial Clinic (541-322-3560), 1541 NE Canal Boulevard, Redmond.

Mountain View Hospital (541-475-3882), 470 NE A Street, Madras.

Pioneer Memorial Hospital (541-447-6234), 1201 NE Elm Street, Prineville.

St. Charles Medical Center (541-548-8131), 1253 NW Canal Boulevard, Redmond.

TOWNS Redmond. Named for settler Frank T. Redmond, the town was platted in 1906 and became a supply and shipping center for cattle ranchers. Its relative isolation was shattered during World War II when the U.S. Air Force established a base at the municipal airport. Electricity arrived at the same time. Nevertheless it remained a small, ranch-oriented town till the real estate boom of the 1190s.

Madras. No one knows why it's called Madras—whether after the Indian city, or (as legend has it) a bolt of madras cloth in a local dry goods store. As the town has an elevation a little lower than surrounding areas, and due to the advent of deep well irrigation, local farms are able to cultivate a few hardy crops. Migrant labor came to harvest, and many laborers stayed on, giving Madras a significant number of Mexican groceries, bakeries, and so on.

Prineville is situated in the geographic center of Oregon and is the namesake of Barney Prine, the town's first merchant. It's also one of central Oregon's oldest towns, designated the seat of Crook County when the county was established in 1882. Cattle and lumber remain the primary industries; it's also the birthplace of Les Schwab Tires, a company with branches around the Northwest.

Terrebonne. The name Terrebonne (good land) may refer to the fact that gardeners can grow tomatoes there—outdoors, even—unlike in most parts of central Oregon. At least that's my theory. In fact, the original name was Hillman, after Jim Hill and E. Harriman, who raced to finish their respective train lines to Bend (yes, the town did get a depot).

Warm Springs Reservation. North and west of Madras, the 640,000-acre Warm Springs Reservation became home to three tribes: the Wascos, who had lived along the Columbia and the Warm Springs, were relocated there in 1855. In 1879 they were joined by Northern Paiutes, who were exiled to Warm Springs after the Bannock War. These groups had different languages and cultures, especially the Paiutes, who had come from the southeastern part of the state. Together they formed the Confederated Tribes of Warm Springs and operate a sawmill, resort, and the **Museum at Warm Springs** (see *Museums*), and they invite members of the public to various celebrations and dances.

* To See

FARMERS' MARKETS Madras Saturday Market (541-546-6350), in Sahalee Park at Seventh and C streets. Sat. 9–2, June–Sept.

Prineville Farmers' Market (541-280-4097), on Third Street across from the courthouse. Sat. 9–2, June–mid-Oct.

Redmond Farmers' Market (541-504-7862), at St. Charles Medical Center off Kingwood Avenue. Mon. 2–6, Memorial Day–Labor Day.

FOR FAMILIES ✐ **Operation Santa Claus Reindeer** (541-548-8910), 4355 W. OR 126, Redmond. Daily dawn–dusk. Free. Forget about eight tiny reindeer (and miniature sleighs). A herd of 50 reindeer lives right here in Redmond, and you can see them any time of year; just park in the lot and follow the signs.

✐ **Petersen's Rock Garden** (541-382-5574), 7930 SW 77th Street, Redmond. Daily 9–5. General admission $4.50, seniors $3, children 12 and over $3, kids 6–11 $1, kids under six free. Rasmus Petersen must have been fascinated by Oregon's colorful volcanic rocks. Coming from Denmark in 1900 at age 17, he settled this property near Redmond and lived quietly till 1935, when he began collecting rocks from all over central Oregon and building things with them. Not useful pioneer things like root cellars and such, but fanciful castles, forts, and bridges inspired by his native Denmark. Then he went on to American themes like the Statue of Liberty and the American flag, continuing till his death in 1952. Rasmus's elfin projects are set in gardens covering 4 acres run by his family. Picnicking is allowed on the grounds, but you may have to compete with the resident peacocks.

HISTORIC SITES **City of Prineville Railway** (541-447-6251), 185 NE 10th Street, Prineville. A hundred years ago, small western towns were desperate to get a train depot or, better yet, a terminus, to ship their cattle, timber, grain, and what have you to eastern markets. Prineville was as desperate as any. But when the Union Pacific and Oregon Trunk Railroad completed their lines in 1911, both bypassed it in favor of Bend. So the citizens of Prineville voted to fund a spur line connecting themselves to the outside world. It was completed in 1918 and has been carrying freight between Prineville and Prineville Junction (3 miles north of Redmond), a distance of 18 miles, ever since—it's the oldest continuously operating short line in the United States. Until 1939 it carried passengers as well. It shares its tracks with the **Crooked River Dinner Train** (see *Unique Adventures*).

Crook County Courthouse, 300 E. Third Street, Prineville. The 1909 courthouse looks much bigger than the county's population warrants, but back then it seemed logical enough. Prineville was in the exact physical center of the state and should surely have become a hub, but it never did. The venerable brick and stone structure, now covered with ivy, still presides over the main street and still conducts the county's business.

Jefferson County Courthouse, Sixth and D streets, Madras. The brick courthouse and city hall served from 1917 to 1961, when a new one was built. Behind it, the former jailhouse with its barred windows is reminiscent of an old Western movie.

MUSEUMS **A. R. Bowman Memorial Museum** (541-477-3715; www.bowmanmuseum.org), 246 N. Main Street, Prineville. Tues.–Fri. 10–5, Sat. 11–4, and additionally Sun. 11–4 and Mon. 10–5 in summer. Closed Jan. Free. The story of Crook County, from pioneer Mr. Prine, for whom Prineville is named, through its sheepherding heyday to the coming of the train. Well, it never did come, so the citizens had to build one. This is can-do country, after all.

Farrell Homestead, Jefferson County Fairgrounds, Madras. A 1903 homestead, originally some 10 miles northeast of Madras, now stands on the Country Fairgrounds. The four-member Farrell family dwelt in the 14-by-18 shack till they enlarged it with a (doubtless much appreciated) two-story wing. A one-room pioneer schoolhouse stands alongside. While neither building is open, you can look from the outside.

Jefferson County Museum (541-475-3808), 34 SE D Street, Madras. Mon.–Fri. 1–5, May–Oct. Admission $2. The development of Madras and surroundings by sheepherding, cattle ranching, and dry-land farming is told through clothes, photos, and memorabilia assembled in a 1917 courthouse.

Museum at Warm Springs (541-553-3331; www.museumatwarmsprings.org), 14 miles north of Madras on US 97, P.O. Box 909, Warm Springs 97761. Tues.–Sun. 9–5 in summer and Wed.–Sun. 9–5 in winter. Closed Thanksgiving, Christmas, and New Year's Day. General admission $7, seniors $6, students and members of non-local tribes $4.50, children 5–12 $3, children under five free. The building itself is striking: opened in 1993, it is intended to suggest a creekside encampment, harmoniously incorporating shapes of tepees and longhouse into a brick facade adorned with basket-weaving designs. A nature trail wanders the grounds, passing a memorial at the spot where the 1855 treaty was signed—the treaty by which most of northern central Oregon was ceded in exchange for the 1,000-square-mile Warm Springs Reservation. Three different languages and cultures had to make a go of living together in a place not entirely of the people's choosing: the Wasco, Warm Springs (Sahaptin), and Northern Paiutes. The museum was conceived to preserve and promote their history and traditions in today's world. Its collection of woven bags, baskets, parfleches, beaded apparel, and other household goods, most in excellent condition and many donated by reservation families, is prodigious, and you can see not only heirloom garments and tools, but takes on traditional styles—cradleboards that incorporate fleece bedding, for instance. It's a beautiful introduction to the Plateau and Great Basin cultures, and in summer there are live demonstrations of crafts, dance, and more.

Redmond Museum (541-504-3038), 529 SW Seventh Street, Redmond. Thurs.–Sat. noon–4. Suggested donation $2. This brand-new (2009) museum houses exhibits on potato farming, an antique musical instrument collection, clothing, a replica 1930s farmhouse kitchen, and other exhibits tracing Redmond's history from its hardscrabble early days to the present.

THE MUSEUM AT WARM SPRINGS

NATURAL WONDERS **Crooked River Gorge, Peter Skene Ogden Scenic Viewpoint,** 9 miles north of Redmond on US 97. You don't see it till you're on top of it, literally—the Crooked River has cut such a gash in the plain that you have to drive up to the rim to see down into it. The narrow canyon drops 300 feet between vertical basalt cliffs to the river below. The viewpoint on the west side of the highway allows you to stop and look down.

Cove Palisades, 8 miles southeast of Madras; turn off US 97 4 miles south of Madras and follow the signs another 4 miles. A chasm in the sagebrush plains marks the confluence of the Deschutes, Crooked, and Metolius rivers nearly a thousand feet below (lower yet before a dam backed up the waters in 1964). The neatly sliced basalt cliffs lay out the geologic history: massive Columbia basalt flows 10 to 13 million years ago, lava and tuff from local volcanoes about 3 million years ago, and occasional deposits of river rock in between. The rivers, converging fast from nearby mountains, cut the rock like cake, leaving some interesting chunks of plateau: the Island, nearly untouched by livestock- and seed-bearing settlers, and thus a preserve for disappearing native plants; and the Peninsula, similar but less isolated. Now encompassed by **Cove Palisades State Park,** the Island is now open only to researchers or for occasional tours, but the Peninsula is accessible by a moderately strenuous trail from the water's edge.

The spires and fins of **Smith Rock,** 9 miles northeast of Redmond, look more like something out of the Southwest than the Pacific Northwest. They are composed of volcanic tuff and rhyolite in pleasing shades of tan, red, maroon, and buff. The lighter shades are tuff, formed during explosive eruptions of steam and ash about 14 million years ago, while the darker ones are intrusions of thicker rhyolite from later activity. Today the vertical columns attract scads of climbers as well as nesting eagles, hawks, and ravens.

THE ISLAND AT COVE PALISADES, WHERE THREE RIVERS MEET

✱ To Do

BICYCLING Mountain bikers use the **Gray Butte Trail,** with trailheads at **Smith Rock State Park** and FR 57, 18 miles south of Madras via US 97 and Lone Pine Road; 6.5 miles each way, with views of buttes and volcanic formations. Road bikes frequent the straight, flat roads of **Crook County** south and west of Prineville.

BIRD-WATCHING Birders gravitate to the several reservoirs that concentrate birdlife in this dry zone: **Haystack, Prineville,** and **Ochoco reservoirs** (the latter just east of Prineville on US 26), where they may see white pelicans, shorebirds, waterfowl, and raptors. **Smith Rock** is also a prime spot for raptors and songbirds.

CAMPING **Cove Palisades State Park** (1-800-551-4969), 7300 Jordan Road, Culver, has two campgrounds: **Crooked River** is open year-round with 91 full hookup sites, and is open May–Sept. with 82 hookup sites, 92 tent sites, and 3 cabins. **Smith Rock State Park,** east of Terrebonne, has a small walk-in (a few hundred feet) campground; no reservations. **Prineville Reservoir,** 14 miles southeast of Prineville, has 22 full hookup, 22 electric hookup, 23 tent sites, and 5 cabins, with all amenities; open year-round; reserve at 1-800-452-5687. **Jasper Point,** in the same park, has 30 electric hookup sites, open in summer; no reservations.

For a small fee, there's plenty of summer and fall camping in the **Ochoco National Forest** (541-416-6500), 3160 NE Third Street, Prineville. **Haystack Campground,** at Haystack Reservoir, 23 miles from Prineville via US 26 and FR 96, has 24 sites, toilets, water, and a boat ramp; no reservations. **Dry Creek Horse Camp,** 17 miles east of Prineville by US 26, Mill Creek Road, and FRs 3370 and 3370-200 (road not suitable for RVs), has Five primitive sites with horse stalls, toilets, a 12-mile loop trail; water for stock only; no fee, no reservations. **Wildcat Campground,** southwest edge of **Mill Creek Wilderness** (see *Wilderness Areas*), has 17 sites, water, toilets, old growth, and trails; no reservations. **Deep Creek Campground,** 48 miles from Prineville via US 26 and various forest roads (contact district office for directions), has six sites, trout, water, and toilets; no reservations. **Ochoco Campground,** 25 miles east of Prineville along US 26 and County Road 23, has six sites, toilets, water, a creek, and trails; no reservations. **Ochoco Divide Campground,** 30 miles east of Prineville on US 26 at Ochoco Pass, has 28 sites, toilets, old growth, and a creek; no water, no reservations. **Walton Lake Campground,** 25 miles east of Prineville on US 26, then north 9 miles on FR 22, has 30 sites, water, toilets, a beach, and a boat launch; no reservations. **Wildwood Campground,** off FR 2210 north of Walton Lake, has five sites and toilets; no water, no fee, no reservations. **Lone Pine** (541-416-6700), a BLM campground about 15 miles south of Prineville on OR 27, has eight sites, toilets, swimming, and fishing; no water, no reservations.

CANOEING, KAYAKING, AND RAFTING For a quiet paddle try **Walton Lake** (see *Camping*), where only electric motors are allowed. Rafting is popular on the **Crooked River,** with put-ins at Lone Pine Bridge and Crooked River Ranch; for maps, equipment, and information, contact **Cascade Outfitters** (1-800-223-RAFT; www.cascadeoutfitters.com).

CLIMBING **Smith Rock State Park** (see *Parks*) draws climbers to its fantastic spires nearly year-round. For a directory to route guides, instruction, and more, call 541-923-0702 or log onto www.smithrock.com.

GOLF **Crooked River Ranch Golf Course** (1-800-833-3197), 5135 Clubhouse Road, Crooked River Ranch. Eighteen holes.

Eagle Crest Resort: Ridge Course, Resort Course, and **The Challenge** (1-877-818-0286), 1522 Cline Falls Road, Redmond. Each 18 holes.

Meadow Lakes Golf Course (541-447-7113), 300 SW Meadow Lakes Drive, Prineville. Eighteen holes.

HIKING You can choose your terrain: sagebrush steppe or forest, mountain or plateau. The **Tam-a-lau Trail** at **Cove Palisades State Park** (see *Parks*) rises steeply from water level to circle the rim of a plateau called "the Peninsula"—a promontory overlooking the confluence of three rivers into Lake Billy Chinook—for a total of about 8 miles. **Alder Springs,** a short but lovely trail on the **Crooked River Grasslands,** descends 300 feet from the surrounding plateau to cross Whychus Creek, which is usually calf-deep but possibly deeper in spring, and continues along the fairyland creek bottom to a small rapids; about 2.7 miles each way. From OR 126, 4.5 miles east of Sisters take Goodrich Road, turn left on Road 6360, and follow signs. Closed Dec.–Mar.; watch for rattlesnakes in summer. The **Gray Butte Trail** (see *Bicycling*) is open to bikes and horses as well as hikers; 13 miles round-trip.

In the **Ochoco National Forest,** the **Walton Lake Trail,** on FR 2220 7 miles from the old Ochoco Ranger Station 25 miles east of Prineville, a 1-mile trail around Walton Lake, is barrier-free and open spring to fall; no fee. From the **Wildcat Campground** at the edge of the **Mill Creek Wilderness** (see *Camping*), the **Twin Pillars Trail** winds along wooded Mill Creek for 8 miles for views of two volcanic plugs; no fee. The **Steins Pillar Trail** runs for 2 steep miles through forest and meadow to the pillar, another volcanic formation; from Prineville take US 26 east 9 miles to Mill Creek Road, go northeast for 6.5 miles, and take FR 3300-500. No fee. **Lookout Mountain Trail** starts at the old Ochoco Ranger Station 25 miles east of Prineville and ascends Lookout Mountain for 8 miles with Cascades views and possible sightings of elk and wild horses. Avoid the old mines and tailings, and carry water.

A WILD LILY PUSHES UP THROUGH THE COARSE SOIL OF THE HIGH DESERT PLATEAU, COVE PALISADES

UNIQUE ADVENTURES **Crooked River Dinner Train** (541-678-3230; www.crookedriverdinnertrain.com), NE 10th and Main streets, Prineville. The three-hour train tour runs along the **City of Prineville**

Railway (see *Historic Sites*), serving dinner or brunch, dinner theater, murder mysteries, and special events. General fares \$79, seniors \$69, kids \$39.

✷ Wilder Places

PARKS **Cline Falls State Park** (1-800-551-6949), 4 miles west of Redmond on OR 126. A shaded picnic spot by the river with paths wandering along the banks, and a swimming hole. No fee, and no alcohol.

Cove Palisades State Park (541-546-3412), 7300 Jordan Road, Culver. This is canyon country—deep canyon country. Where the Deschutes, Crooked, and Metolius rivers join, basalt columns tower nearly a thousand feet above three-pronged Lake Billy Chinook. It makes you wonder how deep the canyons were before the Round Butte Dam created the reservoir in 1964. With a 4,000-acre lake and 5,200 acres of shore and high plateau, there's something for everyone: a marina, 14 miles of trails, spring wildflowers, camping, even a petroglyph. Kayak tours are offered in summer, while the third weekend in Feb. brings Eagle Watch, a festival celebrating the great birds that congregate in these cliffs.

Prineville Reservoir State Park (541-477-4363), 14 miles southeast of Prineville via OR 126, Combs Flat Road, and Juniper Canyon Road. Where the Crooked River backs up behind the Bowman Dam, it pools up into former tributaries and canyons among the brown juniper-pocked hills into a 3,000-acre lake. Mostly it's a year-round fishing spot with boat ramp and a large campground—the Parks Department allows ice fishing if the lake freezes. The desert skies also make it a good place for stargazing.

Smith Rock State Park (541-548-7501 or 1-800-551-6949), 9 miles northeast of Redmond; take US 97 and follow signs from Terrebonne. This spectacular park in the Crooked River Gorge is lined with red rock formations that draw rock climbers from all over the world, so it can get crowded on summer weekends. But it's also a

THE ISLAND AND BASALT CLIFFS AT COVE PALISADES

favorite of hikers, with trails along the river or up among the rocks, and birdwatchers—eagles nest in the cliffs, and migrating songbirds love the riparian greenery. A walk-in primitive campground allows climbers (and others) to get an early start.

WILDERNESS AREAS **Mill Creek Wilderness** (541-416-6500), 17 miles northeast of Prineville; from Prineville take US 26 east, turn left after 9 miles, and continue north to **Wildcat Campground.** You can come here and hardly see a soul. Hike along quiet Mill Creek or choose some of the more demanding trails; the terrain includes canyons, ridges, and riverbottoms, seldom visited except in hunting season. Another smaller, more primitive campground is at the northern edge of the wilderness.

WILDLIFE AREAS **Crooked River National Grassland** (541-475-9272), office at 813 S. US 97, Madras. Homesteaders didn't survive on this plateau, though they tried from the 1880s to the 1930s; like the Fort Rock area, it was just too dry and extreme. So the government acquired 155,000 acres of the rough country, smoothed over the attempts at ploughing and grazing, and planted it with crested wheatgrass, a native plant. Now the original aspect of the country is more or less restored. Wildlife includes deer, elk, cougar, and many birds. Recreational sites within the grassland include **Cove Palisades** (see *Natural Wonders*), **Round Butte Dam,** and **Haystack Reservoir,** and activities include camping, wildlife viewing, hiking, rockhounding, and fishing. A map is available at the Madras office.

Rimrock Springs Wildlife Management Area (541-475-9272). From US 97 take US 26 for 9 miles to the parking area. Two short trails and two viewing platforms let you observe shorebirds, waterfowl, songbirds, and wildflowers, depending on the season. A natural seep pools up behind a small dam, creating a wetland in the desert.

* Lodging

BED & BREAKFASTS

Metolius

Sweet Virginia's Bed and Breakfast (541-546-3031; www.sweetvirginiasbedandbreakfast.com), 407 Sixth Street, 4 miles southwest of Madras. If a small-town stay sounds good to you, the little frame house with the picket fence may do the trick. Near the recreation at Cove Palisades, in a formerly buzzing railroad town, Virginia's offers three rooms, one with a queen bed and two with full-sized beds (two rooms share a bath). Nothing fancy, but comfy. And you won't have to leave your well-behaved pet home. $55–95, with continental breakfast; full breakfast by request ($20/couple).

FOREST SERVICE RENTALS

Cold Springs Cabin, 47 miles from Prineville by US 26, CR 23, FR 42, and FR 30; near Big Summit Prairie. The former guard station has three bedrooms, two bathrooms, and a propane-powered kitchen, and it's near hiking trails among sagebrush and ponderosa woods with plentiful wildlife. Reserve at www.recreation.gov or by calling 1-877-444-6777. Open June–Sept. $75.

HOTELS

Madras

♿ **Inn at Cross Keys Station** (1-877-475-5802), 66 NW Cedar Street. This brash, upwardly mobile chain materialized like an apparition above dusty

Madras in 2008, startling residents and US 97 commuters alike. It has tried to soften its impression with some stone facing and a grand gas-fired lobby, and it certainly has the most comfort you'll find in town—big rooms, pillow-top mattresses, wide-screen TV, continental breakfast, and even a swimming pool. In case you're wondering what a 72-room hotel is doing in a town of five thousand, its intent is to house folks boating the lake to the west and climbing the rocks to the east, as well as business travelers. Doubles from $99.

RANCHES

Sisters

Long Hollow Ranch (541-877-923-1901; www.lhranch.com), 71105 Holmes Road. Run as a guest ranch in the summer and a bed & breakfast in winter, Long Hollow is a working ranch where you can indulge your cowboy dreams. Help out on the ranch, take trail rides, fish the ponds, and enjoy the Wild West—halfway between Sisters and Madras, you are in the wide-open spaces. Five guest rooms have private baths and all conveniences. Six-day ranch stays run $1,410 double occupancy, including all meals, horseback riding, rafting, fishing, and more. Off-season, activities are extra, and bed & breakfast rates are $115, or $159 for or a freestanding cottage.

RESORTS

Warm Springs

♿ **Kah-Nee-Ta Resort and Casino** (1-800-554-4786; www.kahneeta.com), P.O. Box 1240, Warm Springs 97761. You might think this is one more case of a casino rescuing a reservation, but the Warms Springs reservation started pulling itself up by the bootstraps with its lumber mill during World War II. Then they reasonably decided to capitalize on the hot springs, building Kah-Nee-Ta Village—pool, motel, and tepee complex. The long, luxurious lodge that echoes the surrounding rimrock came in 1972, and the casino—admittedly the economic capstone—opened in 1995. Since it's a full-service resort, you can also eat, raft the river, ride a horse, hike, play golf, or go to the spa, using the shuttle to get around. Lodge rooms and suites are spacious, decorated in earth tones, and all have views; summer rates are from $173 to $293. Down at the village, motel rooms are $153–179; tepees sleep up to 10 for $69–75, and a two-bedroom cottage is $365. RV hookups are available at $53. Check for low-season rates and midweek specials, which can save you as much as 50 percent.

✷ Where to Eat

DINING OUT

Warm Springs

The Juniper Room (541-533-1112), Kah-Nee-Ta Resort. Fri.–Sat. for dinner; reservations recommended. This is Kah-Nee-Ta's fine-dining venue, and the menu ranges from Pacific salmon and Black Angus steaks to an adaptation of the Native American "bird in clay"—fowl packed in clay and slowly baked. Fine views, too.

EATING OUT

Redmond

One Street Down Café (541-647-2341; www.onestreetdowncafe.com), 124 SW Seventh Street. Daily 7–3. Just a block from Redmond's downtown, the little red house where the neighborhood goes for breakfast or lunch is encircled by shaded front yards and homes. You'll find pancakes and omelets, soups and sandwiches, all made in-house, served with crusty bread from a local Italian bakery. One Street Down is a family project, and it shows.

Santiago's Maté Company (541-504-8870), 528 SW Sixth Street. Mon.–Fri. 8–6. Not exactly an eatery, it's a tea shop of a special kind: the beverage sold here is yerba maté, the national drink of Argentina, made from the leaf of a tree in the holly family. If you've never tried it, try it here; if you have, choose here from several house blends, to buy or drink on the spot. The friendly café setting also welcomes occasional poetry readings and discussion groups.

Terrebonne

Terrebonne Depot (541-548-5030; www.terrebonnedepot.com), 400 NW Smith Rock Way. Three miles north of Redmond on the turnoff for Smith Rock State Park, the square 100-year-old depot has been made over to an airy though sparsely decorated restaurant serving a variety of homemade pizzas, soups, and salads with a Mediterranean twist, and full-course meals. All emphasize local ingredients, including buffalo.

Warm Springs

Eagle Crossing (541-553-3123), 2198 US 26, Warm Springs. Open for breakfast, lunch and dinner. On the long, lonely stretch of road between Mount Hood and Bend, Eagle Crossing sits on the southern edge of the Warm Springs reservation. If you've worked up an appetite, you'll appreciate the huge portions of elk steak, huckleberry pie, fry bread and other Indian specialties, as well as more familiar fare. Kids' and seniors' menus, too..

✷ Events

February: **Eagle Watch** (541-923-7551), Presidents' Day weekend, Round Butte Dam, Lake Billy Chinook. Eagle populations swell here in winter, so you have a good chance of seeing some. Field tours, raptor presentations, Native American programs, and more.

August: **Deschutes County Fair,** first weekend, Deschutes County Fairgrounds, Redmond. Four days of prize livestock and rodeo, jams and pies, cotton candy and carnival rides, food and music. Day passes $5–9.

COLUMBIA PLATEAU

From Madras the Columbia Plateau rolls north to the Great River and east as far as a person can think (technically, to the Wallowas in the far northeast), composed partly of ancient volcanic outcroppings and partly of rolling wheat fields. Towns are few and far between; some that grew up around sheep or hopeful mining claims are ghosts of their former selves. It makes for a fine drive on a spring day, with the fields greening up and wildflowers blooming, with a stop maybe to raft the Deschutes—wild and scenic from here to the Columbia—or to take in the cultural heritage at Warm Springs. Just make sure you have a full tank.

GUIDANCE **Boardman Chamber of Commerce** (541-481-3014; www.visitboardman.com), 206 N. Main Street, Boardman 97818.

Condon Chamber of Commerce (541-384-7777; www.discovercondon.com), 234 Main Street, Condon 97823.

Gilliam County Tourism (541-384-3758), P.O. Box 466, Condon 97823.

Grant County Chamber of Commerce (1-800-769-5664; www.grantcounty.cc), 301 W. Main Street, John Day 97845.

Heppner Chamber of Commerce (541-676-5536; www.heppnerchamber.com), P.O. Box 1232, Heppner 97836.

Sherman County Visitors Association (541-565-3232), P.O. Box 173, Moro 97039.

Wheeler County (541-763-4328), P.O. Box 86, Fossil 97830.

GETTING THERE *By car:* **US 395** traverses this vast area north–south at its eastern edge, **US 97** at its west, and **OR 19** in the middle. **OR 74** runs from Heppner to the Columbia. **US 26** and **OR 7** ramble across the southern section.

GETTING AROUND A car is the only thing that will get you around out here.

MEDICAL EMERGENCY **Blue Mountain Hospital** (541-575-1311), 170 Ford Road, John Day.

Pioneer Memorial Hospital (541-676-9133), 564 E. Pioneer Drive, Heppner.

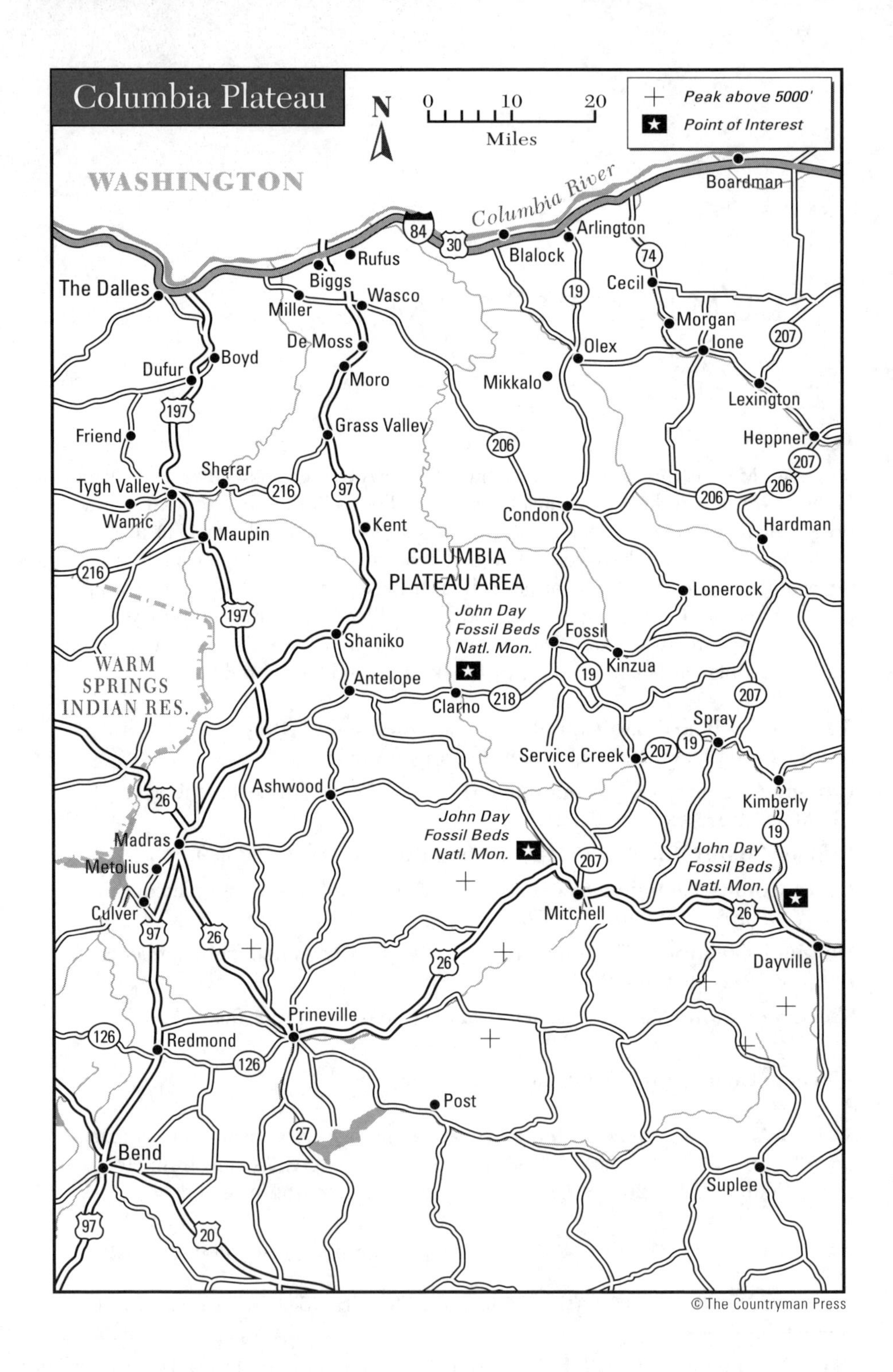

© The Countryman Press

THE WOOLLY MAMMOTH ROAMS AGAIN IN FOSSIL—AS A LARGER-THAN-LIFE IRON SCULPTURE DOWNTOWN.

TOWNS **Condon.** Originally called Summit Springs, for the springs that greeted thirsty travelers on an Oregon Trail variant, it was renamed for its first postmaster, Harry Condon. Sheep soon gave way to wheat, and the small settlement became a major wheat growing and shipping center in the early 1900s. It's still a small town surrounded by wheat fields, with a nearby wind farm adding some relief to the scenery, and has the distinction of counting two Nobel laureates among its former citizens: William Murphy, who won the prize for medicine in 1934, and Linus Pauling, who took the prize for chemistry in 1954 and the Nobel Peace Prize in 1962.

Antelope and **Mitchell** were stage stops on the The Dalles–Canyon City line during the latter's gold rush days. Today Mitchell sits quietly in a cleft between sandy hills, and Antelope is a scattering of streets around a central green. Antelope's main event since the gold rush was the rise and fall of the Baghwan Shree Rajneesh, a self-styled Indian guru who built a commune on a nearby ranch. His red-clad followers were something of an oddity in rural central Oregon. Mutual distrust turned to animosity when the commune was found to be stockpiling weapons and tried to take over the county by vote manipulation. When the leadership was implicated in a food-poisoning episode and an attempt to assassinate the lieutenant governor, the Baghwan was deported and the ranch abandoned.

Fossil is at the center of Oregon's fossil country (no surprise there), so named for some mammoth remains found when the town was under construction. It's also at the midpoint of the **Journey through Time Scenic Byway.** A tranquil place of about five hundred friendly inhabitants, it's a pleasant place to stroll, dig some fossils, even spend the night.

Heppner. Twenty miles north of the Blue Mountains, Heppner is a base for exploring those mountains as well as a solid farming community. It was solid farmland back in 1903, too, when a freak flash flood barreled down a creek, drowning more than two hundred people and all but two buildings. Two young men heroically raced the flood waters to warn neighboring Lexington and Ione; thanks to them, lives and livestock were saved. Today a dam and reservoir protect the town from further flooding.

WINDFARM NEAR CONDON

OFFICIALLY A GHOST TOWN, SHANIKO STILL SUPPORTS SOME LIFE.

Shaniko. A hundred years ago, much of central Oregon was sheep range, and the only port for shipping all that wool and mutton was The Dalles, on the Columbia. Shaniko was a planned community, designated the terminus for a railroad moving those goods from the High Desert down to the river. From 1900 to 1911 Shaniko was a boomtown with a population of six hundred, boasting several saloons, a hotel, school, city hall, and water system, shipping the largest volume of wool in the American west—indeed, it called itself the Wool Capital of the World. You can still see the wool sheds and other relevant buildings (see *Historic Sites*). Then change set in. A competing train line diverted traffic, cattle began to displace sheep, the advent of synthetics reduced the demand for wool, and Shaniko shrank to the point of becoming a near ghost town. A renascence took place in the 1980s and 1990s, with the opening of several shops and the reopening of the hotel; but as of this writing the hotel is closed, the town is quiet, and the population of twenty or so listens to the desert wind.

✷ To See

FARMERS' MARKETS **Condon Community Farmers' Market** (541-225-3345), Condon. First Sat. of July, Aug., Sept., and Oct.

FOR FAMILIES ✐ **Fossil Digging Beds,** Wheeler High School, Fossil. Admission $3 to benefit the school system. Thirty-three million years ago, lush broad-leaved forests stood here, bordering shallow lakes—not exactly what you see today. Behind the high school the crumbly rock is full of fossil leaves and branches that fell into the lake and were covered by eons' worth of silt, and you can forage to your heart's content. You can even take some home. Ancient roses, sycamore, and metasequoia (dawn redwood, Oregon's state fossil) are among the species you're likely to find. An interpreter is usually on hand to provide tools and identify fossils.

✐ **Oregon Paleolands Institute** (541-763-4480; www.paleolands.org), 333 W. Fourth Street, Fossil. Tues.–Fri. 9–4:30, Sat. 9–3. Field Center free; call for program and field trip rates. You are in the midst of fossil beds, painted hills, weird formations, and geological mayhem. Where better to learn about central Oregon's brontotheres, oreodonts, and cataclysmic past than from experts inspired with the area and a burning desire to share it? Hands-on children's and family programs, field trips and lectures, and exhibits at the new Field Center give you a glimpse of what this landscape is all about. And if you prefer to go about on your own, they will design a trip for you at no charge.

HISTORIC SITES Oregon Trail sites. As wagon trains moved west from the agency near Umatilla, many chose an inland route to The Dalles rather than the longer path along the shores of the Columbia. It was shorter, but hot, dusty, and, above all, dry. Travelers covered 15 to 25 miles a day to spend the night at one of the few water sources—sometimes the John Day or Deschutes River, but sometimes springs that soon grew muddy from overuse. At **Well Spring,** 14 miles east of Cecil on a gravel road, you can find wagon wheel ruts and interpretive panels put up by the National Park Service. It happens to be on the Boardman Bombing Range, so you should call the navy (541-481-2565) before hiking the 5-mile trail. **Four Mile Canyon** lies just 6 miles west of Cecil off Four Mile Canyon Road. "Over rocks, gravel and sand we plod along all day. Nothing indicates life except an occasional Juniper tree . . . to cook with a fire made of green sagebrush with the sand driving into your eyes, ears and mouth, being mixed in our dough . . . is a task we seldom want repeated" observed Harriet Loughary near this point in 1864. Where the trail crossed OR 19, 7 miles south of Arlington, a tall log holds a commemorative plaque honoring W. W. Weatherford, who made the crossing at age 17—you can't miss it. From there pioneers would have gone to camp at Cedar Springs, then on to **MacDonald Ford,** where the wagon trails crossed the **John Day River.** This was the first watercourse of any consequence the emigrants had seen since the Umatilla River, but the country was barren for all that. To get there, take Cedar Springs Road from OR 19, then Lower Rock Creek Lane; about 20 miles. After the crossing, emigrants arrived at a fork in the road, now 12 miles west of Wasco: should they turn north toward The Dalles and the Columbia River

SHANIKO'S SCHOOL

THE WOOL SHED AT SHANIKO, ONCE THE NORTHWEST'S BIGGEST WOOL-SHIPPING POINT

descent, or south and west on the cutoff to the Barlow Road over Mount Hood? Either way, they would still have to cross the **Deschutes River,** either at its fearsome mouth on the Columbia or its equally ominous rapids farther south.

Shaniko, on US 197 about 57 miles south of Biggs Junction. A few people still live in Shaniko, and in summer a tiny museum displays photos and old newpaper clippings from the town's glory days as a wool-shipping point. Buildings still standing from that era include the huge wool sheds (some filled with antique farm equipment), a wooden water tower, the old school that closed in 1946 but has been renovated as a community center, the first city hall, and a bell to be rung in case of fire. The historic Shaniko Hotel is now closed. A few antiques shops open in the summer.

Sherar's Falls, about 12 miles east of Tygh Valley by OR 216 and Deschutes River Road. In the late 1800s, pioneer John Sherar built a bridge and hotel at these falls, where the Dalles-California Highway crossed the Deschutes River. The frothing whitewater now draws rafters and fishermen, including Indians dip-netting from platforms built out over the water.

Morrow County Courthouse (541-676-9061), 100 S. Court Street, Heppner. Eastern Oregon went through a courthouse-building frenzy around the turn of the 20th century as new counties were carved from old ones and (sometimes) older courthouses burned down. This one replaced a previous wooden structure that succumbed to a fire and was solidly built of local blue basalt. The inside, however, shone with fine woodwork, of which the oak staircase is the centerpiece (the 3-foot tall candelabra topping the newel posts are, however, missing). Call for a guided tour.

Wheeler County Courthouse, Fossil. Fossil won a county-wide election for county seat in 1900 (the other candidates being Spray and Twickenham), and the courthouse was built in 1902. The square brick building is adorned with two turrets, and its expansive lawn is the site of the annual **Bluegrass Festival** (see *Events*).

MUSEUMS **Fossil Museum and Pine Creek Schoolhouse** (541-763-4440), 501 First Street, Fossil. Daily 10–2, Memorial Day–Labor Day. Free. Sitting in a handkerchief-sized park on the street corner, the log schoolhouse and sheepherder's wagon summarize Wheeler County history with photos, tools, and other artifacts.

Gilliam County Depot Museum (541-384-4233), OR 19 at Burns Park, Condon. Wed.–Sun. 1–5, May–Oct. By donation. Set in the wheat country just outside Condon is a collection of historic buildings and artifacts, many donated by citizens anxious to recall the times before so many towns emptied out. Visit the Rice cabin, built in 1884 by pioneer Silas Rice; he had to haul the logs from 20 miles away, because there were no trees closer by, and raised a large family in the 15-by-30-by-11 house. Take a look at the old barber shop and the city hall, the aisles of farm machinery filling a large barn, and the photos of harvesting and threshing in not-so-old Condon. And, of course, the 1905 railroad depot, responsible in large part for the town's existence. There's more than enough here to keep a history buff occupied all afternoon.

Morrow County Museum (541-676-5524), 444 N. Main Street, Heppner. Tues.–Fri. 1–5 and Sat. 11–3, Mar.–Oct. Admission $3. Furniture, apparel, saddles, tools, and crafts document the county's pioneer days and development.

Sherman County Museum (541-565-3232; www.shermanmuseum.org), 200 Dewey Street, Moro. Daily 10–5, May–Oct. It's a big museum for a small town—16,000 square feet, organized around the themes of wheat, roads, the coming of electricity, and rural life. The collection includes items used by local Indians, Oregon Trail emigrants, and farming households, but also grain research equipment, and a hall dedicated to local veterans—even those of the Civil War. Here is a volunteer-run microcosm of rural pioneer life on one of the last frontiers.

NATURAL WONDERS The **John Day Fossil Beds National Monument** (541-987-2333; www.nps.gov/joda) contains some of the richest, most spectacular fossil beds in North America (besides being a treasure trove for paleontologists, the beds are set in multicolored rock and soil formations, making them beautiful as well as useful). Imagine a tropical forest. Shallow lakes lap at the forest's edge, fed by meandering streams. The breeze is punctured by screams of tropical birds, weird animal cries, and the occasional belch of a nearby volcano. Fifty million years ago this land of bare hills and bunchgrass was a jungle. Slowly, with the rise of the Cascades and global cooling, the landscape changed to warm, then temperate hardwood forests, to savanna, to grasslands. The youngest deposits in the formations are about 7 million years old. And over all that time immense quantities of fossils were laid down, helped by the frequent floods, mudflows, and eruptions. The formations extend over large parts of central and eastern Oregon, but Congress elected to preserve three unique areas: the Clarno, Painted Hills, and Sheep Rock units. Remember, collecting fossils (or anything else) on these lands is prohibited, but you can dig quite happily and legally in the hillside behind Wheeler High School in Fossil (see *For Families*).

The **Clarno Unit,** 18 miles west of Fossil off OR 218, contains fossils of the oldest species preserved in the John Day beds: fierce creodonts, crocodiles, small precursors of horses, and banana trees; also lots of nuts and twigs. The most visible feature is a high cliff, formed of an ancient mudflow that solidified over time. You can see fossils close up along two short trails below the cliff. An interpretive trail connects the trailheads with the picnic area.

The **Painted Hills Unit,** 9 miles northwest of Mitchell (follow signs from US 26), consists of more than 3,000 acres of rounded, rolling hills banded with layers of white, buff, red, green, gold, and black, all varying with the time of day and atmospheric conditions. The formation dates back about 33 million years and was created by wind-blown ash from a series of volcanic eruptions. Explanatory plaques will point you to likely fossil-bearing sites (mostly leaves), but even if you find no fossils, a walk through these multicolored clay hills is wondrous enough; especially if you come during wildflower season. A series of short trails, some wheelchair friendly, afford fine views; so does the picnic area.

The **Sheep Rock Unit,** on OR 19, 2 miles north of its junction with US 26, is perhaps the showiest of all, with pointy Sheep Rock descending in bands of buff and bright blue to the weird formations of "Blue Basin" and the flowing John Day River. Made of claystone and tuff, these formations too are the result of ashfall and contain a fascinating record of mammal life here 30 to 18 million years ago—beardogs, three-toed horses, sheep-sized oreodonts, and the first canids. Seven trails ranging from 0.25 mile to 3 miles lead you into the formations or above them for terrific views. The historic **Cant Ranch** (Mon.–Thurs. 9–4) at the entrance to the site has become a museum of human history in the region, including that of the Cant family who ranched here in the early 20th century. Across the highway, the new **Thomas Condon Paleontology Center** (541-987-2333) is both a research facility and a spellbinding tour of prehistoric John Day, where the various epochs are brought to life by murals, sound tracks, and fossil displays. Condon, by the way, was a missionary who visited the John Day country in 1865 and was so enthralled with its story in stone that he wrote treatises and went on to chair the University of Oregon's geology department till his death in 1907. Rangers lead hikes and museum tours in spring, summer, and fall. The center is open daily 9–4 in winter, 9–5 spring and fall, and 9–5:30 in summer. Like all parts of this national monument, it is entirely free.

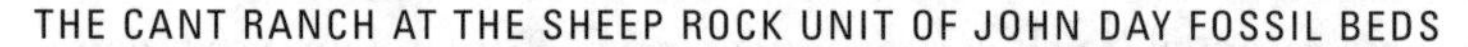
THE CANT RANCH AT THE SHEEP ROCK UNIT OF JOHN DAY FOSSIL BEDS

SCENIC DRIVES The northern segment of the **Blue Mountains Scenic Byway** runs along OR 74 from Heppner to I-84 at the Columbia River, a distance of about 46 miles. This part of the byway links small towns of the rolling wheat country and should remind you how much easier you have it than the Oregon Trail emigrants did.

The **Journey through Time Scenic Byway,** at 286 miles, merits a day or two at least. Starting at Biggs on the Columbia, it follows US 97 south to Shaniko, through the Kimberly orchards, past the John Day Fossil Beds, and through the town of John Day up to Sumpter in the Wallowas. It's a journey through a very long time indeed, as some of the fossil beds go back to the days of the dinosaurs, and it covers Oregon's history by way of ghost towns, abandoned mines, hopeful grand hotels, the rise of a few fortunes, and the fall of many.

✷ To Do

BICYCLING A 17-mile mountain bike trail leads from **Mack's Canyon** (see *Camping*) along the lower Deschutes River to Deschutes River State Park; from Maupin take Deschutes River Access Road to the trailhead.

The **Heppner Chamber of Commerce** (541-676-5536; www.heppner.net) posts a list of road cycling routes around Morrow and surrounding counties (they do caution that most of the roads have little or no shoulder).

Oregon Paleo Lands (541-763-4480; www.paleolands.org) knows all the best back roads in the John Day country and will help you plan your fat-tire trip or take you there: every year they sponsor spring and fall rides supported by sag wagons, meals, and staff. Register by phone or online.

CAMPING The **Bureau of Land Management** (541-416-6700) maintains a series of primitive campsites along the Deschutes River from Pelton Dam to the Columbia, mostly used by rafters and anglers. Those with vehicle access usually require a fee: **Whiskey Dick,** 78 miles upstream of the river's mouth, with seven campsites, toilet, no water; **Oasis** and **Grey Eagle,** 50 and 49 miles upstream of the river's mouth, with toilets; **Jones Canyon,** 34 miles upstream, with toilets but no water; **Beavertail,** 31 miles upstream, with toilets, water, and trailer parking; **Rattlesnake Canyon,** 30 miles upstream, has toilets, but no water; **Mack's Canyon,** 23 miles upstream, has water, toilets, trailhead, and nearby historic site. "Vehicle access" in this area can be rough and winding. For maps and a comprehensive listing, visit www.boaterpass.com.

In the Mitchell-Paulina area, **Ochoco National Forest** (541-416-6500): **Allen Creek Horse Camp,** on FR 22 near the northeastern corner of Big Summit Prairie, with four campsites, horse stalls, toilets; no water except for stock, no fee, no reservations. **Barnhouse,** 5 miles south of US 26 off FR 12, with six sites, toilet; no water, no fee, no reservations. **Big Springs,** 26 miles southwest of Mitchell via US 26, FR 12, and FR 4270, with five sites, toilet; no water, no fee, no reservations. **Biggs Springs,** south of Summit Prairie off FR 4215, with three sites, toilet; no water, no fee, no reservations. **Deep Creek,** with six sites, water, toilet; no reservations. **Scotts,** near junction of FRs 22 and 3010 northeast of Big Summit Prairie, with three sites, toilet; no water, no fee, no reservations.

In the Heppner area, the **Umatilla National Forest** (541-278-3716) campgrounds are: **Bull Prairie,** 36 miles south of Heppner by OR 207 and FR 2039, with 28 tent sites, water, restrooms, trails, lake (no motorboats). **Fairview Campground,** 34 miles south of Heppner on OR 207, with five sites; no water or toilets, no fee. **Penland Lake Campground,** 28 miles from Heppner via OR 207, FR 21, and FR 2103, with five to seven sites; no water, no fee.

Cutsforth Park, a county park off Willow Creek Road 22 miles south of Heppner, has a large family campground with full, partial, or no hookup sites and all amenities.

CANOEING, KAYAKING, AND RAFTING The two great Wild and Scenic Rivers in this area are the **Deschutes** and the **John Day,** both wildly popular with rafters and paddlers. **Maupin** is the center for running the Deschutes, with plenty of whitewater and outfitters ready to meet your needs, such as **High Desert River Outfitters** (1-800-461-5823), P.O. Box 264, Maupin 97037; **River Trails Deschutes** (1-888-324-8837; www.rivertrails.com), 301 Bakeoven Road, Maupin; and **Sage Canyon River Company** (1-800-538-RAFT), 502 Deschutes Avenue, Maupin. Resorts like **Imperial River Company** and **Oasis** also offer guide services and rentals. Rates start at about $80 for a day trip; it can get crowded on summer weekends.

The **John Day** has more elbow room (280 miles of free-flowing river), with both rapids and calm stretches and many possible put-in points. For guide service or just guidance, contact **Oregon River Experiences** (1-800-827-1358); **Ouzel Outfitters** (1-800-788-7238), P.O. Box 817, Bend 97709; **Arrowhead River Adventures** (1-877-21-RIVER); or **Service Creek Lodge** (541-468-3331), Service Creek.

GOLF **Condon Golf Course** (541-384-4266), N. Lincoln Street, Condon. Nine holes.

John Day Golf Club (541-575-0170), W. US 26, John Day. Nine holes with dual tees.

Kinzua Hills Golf Club (541-763-3287), Fossil. Take OR 19 for 3 miles south of Fossil, then turn east on the Kinzua town site road and go 5 miles. This calm green was the bustling site of Kinzua Corporation, a lumber mill and company town, for 50 years. Now the town is gone and the old millpond and sorting area are under turf, with the distinction of being the shortest course in Oregon: six holes, with triple tees so you can get 18.

Willow Creek Country Club (541-676-5437), OR 74, Heppner. Nine holes, with dual tees to make 18.

HIKING When God created Sheep Rock, He must have squeezed the **Blue Basin** formations from a giant frosting tube. Well, maybe not. But the Dali-esque ziggurats with their gloppy columns obviously originated as mud, solidified and eroded. The 1-mile **Island in Time Trail** at the Sheep Rock Unit of the **John Day Fossil Beds** winds among the bright blue mounds still embedded with fossils. The 3-mile **Blue Basin Overlook Loop** is more strenuous but brings you to a panoramic view of the John Day valley (not recommended when wet).

In the northeast corner of the **Ochoco National Forest,** a network of trails is accessed from forest roads: the **Black Canyon Trail,** 12 fairly rugged miles up Black Canyon Creek; **Cottonwood,** 3.2 miles, joins the 5-mile **Back Trail;** the **South Prong Trail,** 5.5 rugged miles across the **Black Canyon Wilderness.**

Shorter trails link some of these; those outside the wilderness are open to bikes as well as hikers and horses. Distances are one-way. The area is remote, accessed from county and forest roads south of Dayville; contact the Forest Service (541-416-6500) for maps and directions.

The Heppner District of **Umatilla National Forest** (541-676-9187) has a small trail network: **Bald Mountain,** 23 miles south of Heppner off Willow creek Road, 2.5 miles one-way, or a 7.5-mile loop by continuing on the **Hell's Half Acre Trail** and the **Willow Creek Trail,** all connected. A 0.5-mile trail circles **Bull Prairie Lake** at **Bull Prairie Recreation Area,** about 37 miles south of Heppner by OR 207 and FR 2039. The **Copple Butte Trail,** about 30 miles south of Heppner on FR 53-5350, 6 miles, offers mountain views and connects to other trails. **Madison Butte Trail,** off FR 21 about 8 miles from Anson Wright County Park, is a 3-mile trail up the butte with panoramic views.

UNIQUE ADVENTURES **Richardson's Rock Ranch** (1-800-433-2680; www.richardsonrockranch.com), 6683 NE Haycreek Road, Madras. Leave US 97 at mile 81, about 11 miles north of Madras, and follow signs another 3 miles. Open Apr.–Oct. Rock hounds, listen up. Richardson's happens to be a working cattle ranch, but it's situated on what is possibly the world's largest deposit of thundereggs, Oregon's state rock, and masses of agate. So besides ranching, the Richardsons will also let you dig for rocks to your heart's content, even providing free camping and showers (taking your rocks home, though, will cost a dollar a pound). You can also get them cut or polished for a fee, or even just buy ready-cut and polished jasper, agates, and more. Take hats and drinking water, for it's likely to be hot, and call ahead; the digging grounds are 8 miles from the office on dirt roads, impassable if wet. Oh—what's a thunderegg? It's a hollow blob of lava that has been ejected by an ancient volcano, buried after cooling, and infiltrated by mineral-laden water, so that after millions of years the cavity is filled with crystalline silica and other minerals. No two are alike.

✷ Wilder Places

PARKS **White River Falls State Park** (1-800-551-6949), on OR 216, 4 miles east of Tygh Valley. Where the White River falls 90 feet over a basalt shelf, the park offers scenic viewpoints and a steep 0.25-mile trail to the canyon below. Here a power plant harnessed the river's energy from 1910 to 1960 (the plant is still visible). Open spring through fall.

WILDERNESS AREAS **Bridge Creek.** At just a bit over 5,000 acres, this is one of the smallest wilderness areas in Oregon (all states should be so lucky), but it's wild. Only 3 miles of unmaintained trails—abandoned roads, really—are there for the hiking. Otherwise you bushwhack across the plateau and creek canyon that constitute this wilderness, some of it bare and some forested. Few people come, but it's a habitation of elk, cougar, peregrine falcon, and goshawk.

WILDLIFE AREAS **White River Wildlife Area** (541-544-2126), 78430 Dodson Road, Tygh Valley. From Tygh Valley turn west on Wamic Market Road, continue on Dodson Road, and follow signs. This rather remote tract of mixed forest offers views of elk at feeding stations in winter and concentrations of introduced wild turkeys. Spring brings wildflowers and songbirds.

✷ Lodging

BED & BREAKFASTS

Fossil

Bridge Creek Flora Inn (541-763-2355; www.fossilinn.com), 828 Main Street. **Fossil Lodge,** 808 Main Street. Choose between the historic three-story bed & breakfast or the more rustic lodge next door, with rough beams and a stone fireplace, for a total of 12 rooms; both are under the same ownership. You are steps away from the town center and incidentally share a lawn with Woolly Willy, a life-sized, metal-strip sculpture of a woolly mammoth. Willy is on loan from an Alaskan sculptor who heard that Fossil was named for a mammoth bone found on the town site, which is true. $75–95, with full breakfast; some rooms share baths.

Wilson Ranches Retreat (1-866-763-2227; www.wilsonranchesretreat.com), 16555 Butte Creek Lane, 2 miles northwest of Fossil off OR 19. Phil and Nancy are lifetime ranchers who can take you out on a cattle drive or tour of their 9,000-acre ranch or point you to hiking trails and fishing holes; though you may just want to relax on the deck. The spaces are wide open, and you may well observe some deer and antelope playing. Seven guest rooms accommodate one to six people. Doubles from $79, with full "cowboy" breakfast.

CABINS

Maupin

🐾 **The Oasis Resort** (541-395-2611; www.deschutesriveroasis.com), 609 US 1997 South. Guided fishing, river rafting, and 11 cabins are on offer here beside the wild Deschutes. The simple units have one or two beds and run $65–85, while two bunkhouses rent for $40 each and share a restroom. Come in winter and get two nights for the price of one (though the cabins don't have kitchens, and few Maupin restaurants are open on winter weekdays). The on-site **Oasis Café** has served fishermen (and fish, presumably) since 1928 with big breakfasts, burgers, ribs, and full dinners, and is open mid-Apr.–Oct. Pets okay.

FOREST SERVICE RENTALS

Ditch Creek Guard Station, in Umatilla National Forest, is a 1935 CCC-built cabin on a tributary of the North Fork John Day River. It has a bedroom with two bunk beds, living room, bathroom, and kitchen; water may not always be available. Six occupants are allowed. From Heppner take Willow Creek Road 23 miles and turn right on FR 21, continuing 3.5 miles to the site. $50. Open year-round, but access is by skis or snowmobile in winter; reserve at www.recreation.gov or by calling 1-877-444-6777.

HOTELS

Condon

Hotel Condon (1-800-201-6706; www.hotelcondon.com), 202 S. Main Street. Condon is in wheat country and was formerly a railroad hub for shipping grain. So it was entirely logical to build a 42-room hotel in 1920, complete with a fine dining room. But the railroad gradually declined, and so did the hotel, changing functions and closing completely in 1997. Rather than see it go under the wrecker's ball, residents managed to preserve and restore it, with much of the work done by local craftsmen and some of it as donated labor. Now, instead of 42 rooms, the hotel has 18 (the difference being made up by private bathrooms, not a feature of the original hotel), with all comforts, each decorated slightly differently, an atrium lounge, and an in-house restaurant (see *Eating Out*). $100–199.

Maupin

✐ 🐾 **Imperial River Company** (1-800-395-3903; www.deschutesriver.com), 304 Bakeoven Road. No phones or TV in the rooms, but Wi-Fi access almost everywhere: this is seclusion in the 21st century. Down in the Deschutes River Canyon, Maupin is a haven for rafters and other river types, and the Imperial sits right on the riverbank. Arrange a guided raft trip down the Deschutes whitewater or a tour of the Imperial Stock Ranch, an 1871 outfit that once covered 100 square miles and is still going strong; or fish, raft, bike, or hike on your own. About half the rooms have balconies and river views; all have private baths. $59–279; children under 12 free.

Mitchell

Oregon Hotel (541- 462-3027; www.theoregonhotel.com), 104 E. Main Street. The present white frame house is the third hotel on the site. The original idea was to be a grand commercial hotel, perhaps in view of the region's mineral resources, but the first was destroyed by a flood in 1906, and the second by fire in 1936—and Oregon's middle never did become a great business center anyway. So today you can find rustic, old-fashioned rooms at very reasonable rates. The place is popular during hunting season and is a find for frugal travelers at any time. Of 12 rooms, two have kitchenettes and seven have shared bathrooms; there's even a dorm room with bunk beds. Bunks $15, doubles $39–89, including continental breakfast.

LODGES

Mitchell

Service Creek Lodge (541-468-3331; www.servicecreek.com), Service Creek, 20 miles south of Fossil on OR 19. Service Creek is for when you really want to get away from it all. The population of the "town" is two—Kate and Dave, owners and operators of the historic lodge since 2007. The lodge has been there alongside the John Day River since the 1920s, as a stage stop and rooming house for early tourists, and comprises six cozy rooms (some family sized), six bathrooms, porches, rocking chairs, and lots of relaxation. Rafts and kayaks are for rent, and Kate and Dave will even shuttle you to your put-in or take-out. Next door, the site of the old post office is occupied by a deli, store, and the **Service Creek Restaurant** (see *Eating Out*), the latter open seasonally (three meals on weekends and lunch and dinner Wed.–Thurs., May–Aug.; lunch and dinner Fri. and three meals on weekends, Apr. Sept.) for hearty country meals concentrating on local, organic ingredients.

✷ Where to Eat

EATING OUT

Antelope

Antelope Store and Café (541-489-3413), just across from the park. Mon. and Wed.–Sat. 8–8, Sun. 8–5. You can't miss it. A tiny place in a tiny town, its owners are also the cooks, servers, and dishwashers. It's appreciated for its home cooking, including natural burgers and lamb from the nearby Imperial Stock ranch, but especially for its marionberry cobbler.

Condon

Sage Restaurant and Lounge (541-384-4624; www.hotelcondon.com), 202 E. Main Street. Wed.–Sat. for lunch and dinner. At the **Hotel Condon** (see *Hotels*), the Sage harks back to the genteel dining room of 1920 and caters to hearty appetites with steaks, seafood, and down-home favorites like pot roast and fried chicken. It's also the only place for miles around where you're likely to find after-dinner liqueurs.

Maupin

Imperial River Company (1-800-395-3903; www.deschutesriver.com), 304 Bakeoven Road. Lunch and dinner daily, late Apr.–Oct., and weekends (including Fri. dinner) Nov.–Apr. Eat inside or out at this riverside hotel—either way you enjoy river views and rustic twisted-juniper furniture. Local range-fed beef anchors the menu, but you'll also find venison, Northwest fish, and the occasional vegetarian option—in portions calculated to satisfy the clients of this river runners' mecca.

Mitchell

Bridge Creek Café (541-462-3434), 208 US 26. Sun.–Tues. and Thurs.–Fri. for breakfast and lunch. You might almost miss it on entering or leaving town—if fact, you might miss the town—but here's the spot for soups, sandwiches, burgers, and ice cream, or a country breakfast.

Service Creek Restaurant (see *Lodges*) serves hearty riverside meals to the intrepid explorer willing to go off the beaten track. Wed.–Sun. in summer, weekends Apr. and Sept.

✷ Events

March: **St. Patrick's Day Celebration** (541-676-5536), midmonth, Heppner. Many of the wheat country's settlers came from Ireland, and it shows. Ceili, sheepdog trials, theater.

July: **Bluegrass Festival,** July Fourth weekend, Fossil. Nonstop bluegrass performances on the courthouse lawn draw audiences from a hundred miles around. Workshops, too.

August: **Dufur Threshing Bee** (541-467-2205; www.dufurthreshingbee.com), second weekend, Dufur. Founded in the 1970s to keep wheat country traditions alive, the bee holds a threshing show with horse-drawn equipment, an antique car show, steak feed, and parade.

South Central Oregon

6

FORT ROCK–CHRISTMAS VALLEY–SILVER LAKE AREA

PAISLEY–LAKEVIEW–BLY AREA

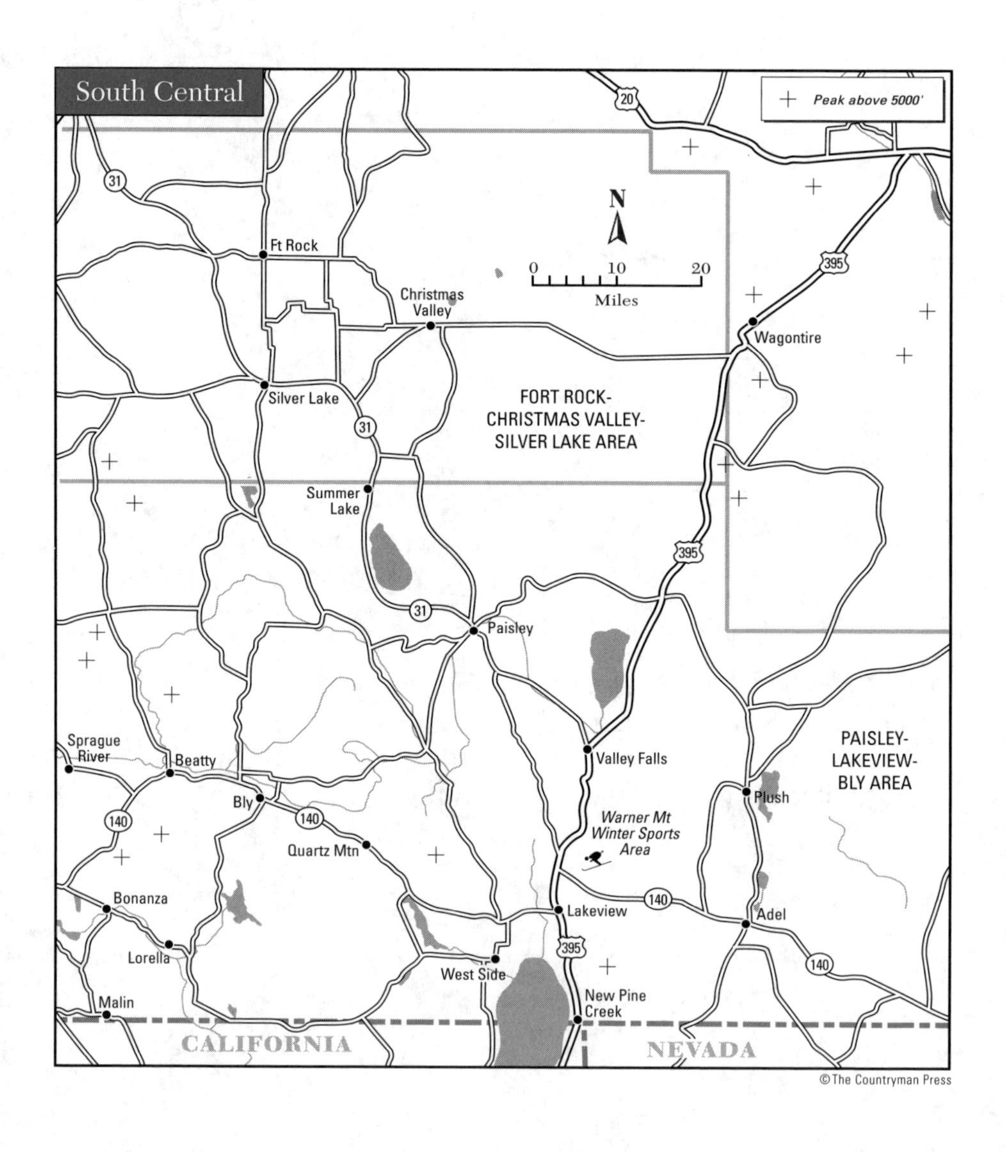
South Central
Peak above 5000'
N
0
10
20
Miles
Ft Rock
Christmas Valley
Silver Lake
Summer Lake
Wagontire
FORT ROCK-CHRISTMAS VALLEY-SILVER LAKE AREA
Paisley
Valley Falls
PAISLEY-LAKEVIEW-BLY AREA
Plush
Sprague River
Beatty
Bly
Quartz Mtn
Warner Mt Winter Sports Area
Bonanza
Lorella
Lakeview
Adel
West Side
New Pine Creek
Malin
CALIFORNIA
NEVADA
20
31
395
140
©The Countryman Press

SOUTH CENTRAL OREGON

The brochures call this stretch of desert "Oregon's Outback." Fair enough. In the immediate rain shadow of the Cascades and the northwesternmost corner of the Great Basin, it's a country of dust and sage, long tilted mountains separating flat valleys, and geological formations that look as if they had come out of a pastry tube. There aren't a lot of people, and apparently there never have been.

Ten or twelve thousand years ago it looked different. The few valley-bottom lakes now struggling for survival were big and deep, fed by melting glaciers, and the buttes and tuff rings that rose above water level housed—sporadically, at least—small bands of people who followed the game. The earliest evidence of human habitation in Oregon has been found here: a cache of woven, 10,000-year-old sagebrush sandals near Fort Rock, and human feces dated to 14,400 years ago in Paisley Caves. Pictographs of whose age and meaning no one is quite sure remain scattered about the desert.

But it was one of the last parts of the country to "settle up." Remote and rugged, with valley floors starting at 4,000 feet above sea level, it wasn't what the land-hungry farmers of the Oregon Trail had in mind. In the 1860s cattlemen began drifting up from California, taking advantage of grasses around the seasonal lakes, and livestock spread thin became the region's industry; though *industry* may be too strong a word. When boosters started promoting cheap land with fantastic agricultural potential—and *fantastic* is probably the right word—about 1912, homesteaders poured in from as far as Europe, confounding the ranchers who knew by then what the land would support. The era of hopeful farms dotting the sea of sage vanished almost as quickly as it had come, like the desert lakes that rise suddenly in spring and shortly evaporate; though a few settlements survive today, buoyed by deep-well irrigation and surrounded by alfalfa. Here and there, in the lonelier reaches of the desert, you can still find an ancient windmill or tumble-down cabin.

The land is spectacular and austere, with thousand-foot escarpments rising from dusty lake beds. Check your gas gauge. Carry water. Watch the deer and antelope play, and if you're lucky, maybe some bighorn.

FORT ROCK–CHRISTMAS VALLEY–SILVER LAKE AREA

Leaving US 97 south of La Pine for OR 31 32 miles south of Bend, the road rises through the high pine country to cross the southern flank of Newberry Crater, then drops rather suddenly through an ecotone where the trees thin out and disappear. Before you spreads the flat sagebrush country of the Great Basin, punctuated by the rim of Fort Rock and other volcanic residue. The roads are long and straight, and the utility poles are topped with hawks and eagles. Pull off nowhere in particular, get out of your car, and stop the engine. The only assault on your senses is likely to be the wind and the smell of sagebrush.

GUIDANCE **Bureau of Land Management** (541-947-2177; www.blm.gov), 1301 S. G Street, Lakeview 97630.

Christmas Valley Chamber of Commerce (541-576-3838; www.christmas valley.org), P.O. Box 65, 87541-B Christmas Valley Highway, Christmas Valley 97641.

Fremont-Winema National Forests Headquarters (541-947-2151; www.fs .fed.us/r6/frewin), 1301 S. G Street, Lakeview 97630; ranger district office also on OR 31 in Silver Lake (541-576-2107).

GETTING THERE *By car:* **OR 31** is the only artery serving this area.

GETTING AROUND A car is essential.

MEDICAL EMERGENCY **North Lake Health Center** (541-576-2343), 87520 Bay Street, Christmas Valley. Minor emergencies only.

TOWNS **Silver Lake.** Unlike some of the "lakes" hereabouts, Silver Lake actually persisted into historic times. Irrigation in the homesteading years tapped it beyond its powers to recharge. Today after a heavy rain, which is infrequent, or when snow melts off the nearby ridges, it may briefly sparkle again. The hamlet itself boasts a gas station, saddlery, general store, diner, and scattered residences. The disastrous Christmas Eve fire of 1894, when flames from a fallen oil lamp consumed 43 men, women, and children gathered from the surrounding desert to celebrate, is still engraved in local memory.

Fort Rock. A mile south of the great ring (see *Natural Wonders*), the town of Fort Rock served the multitude of homesteaders who were lured to the High Desert by tall tales of tall grass in the early 1900s. Well, there were a few "wet" years. Most, it's said, took three years to go broke: one to build and attempt to plow; two to fight gophers, jackrabbits, and dust; and three to get tired of eating jackrabbit stew and leave. Local cowboy philosopher Reub Long said the land was only fit for running horses and cattle, and he was probably right. A few of the early families remain as ranchers or hay farmers.

Christmas Valley. Here, too, homesteaders tried to eke a living from the miserly soil and mostly failed. The town itself never existed until deep-well irrigation became feasible in 1961, at which point much land was bought up by an enterprising Californian and resold. Now the community thrives on hay—and kitty litter, made from a local volcanic clay.

✷ To See

HISTORIC SITES **Fort Rock Cave.** In 1938, in a rocky outcrop 0.5 mile from Fort Rock, Dr. Luther Cressman of the University of Oregon made a block-busting discovery: a cache of sagebrush-fiber sandals carbon dated at nine or ten thousand years old. Till 2008 they were the oldest evidence of human habitation in Oregon (see **Paisley Caves** under *Historic Sites* in "Paisley–Lakeview–Bly Area"). The dry climate and layers of Mount Mazama ash sifting into the cave had done a fine job of preserving them. The site is accessible only by guided tours arranged in advance; to reserve call 541-388-6055.

MUSEUMS **Fort Rock Valley Historical Homestead Museum** (541-576-2207), County Road 5-10, Fort Rock. Fri.–Sun. 10–4, Memorial Day–Labor Day. Admission $2; kids under 12 free. The homesteading epoch out here wasn't so very long ago. Promoted a hundred years ago by local boosters and the Homestead Act, the dusty sagebrush plains drew settlers from the East Coast, Germany, and especially Ireland (you wonder what natives of the Emerald Isle felt when they arrived). Rainfall was above average for a few years, and advertisers praised the "grasslands," admonishing starry-eyed would-be farmers that "rain follows the plow." It doesn't. Most settlers gave up after a few years, and the valley that had briefly twinkled with homesteaders' lamps emptied out but for a few. The museum "village" brings together some of their abandoned homesteads, as well as St. Rose's Catholic Church—the only one in the valley for quite some time—and the office of the revered Dr. Thom, who had the vast valley under his care during the influenza epidemic of 1918.

THE FORT ROCK VALLEY HISTORICAL HOMESTEAD MUSEUM GATHERS PIONEER HOUSES FROM THE SURROUNDING DESERT.

Wandering through these nearly windowless plank cabins (glass was dear) gives you but an inkling of the hardships endured by these hopefuls in a land of little water or wood, extreme temperatures, and constant wind.

NATURAL WONDERS **Crack in the Ground,** 8 miles north of Christmas Valley off County Road 5-14 C. No fancy names here, just a simple descriptor for a chasm 2 miles long and up to 70 feet deep. The ground is a basalt flow. When a nearby later eruption occurred a few miles off, it left the ground unsupported, and so it cracked. This is thought to have happened just a thousand or so years ago—the blink of an eye—but even so, normally such a crack would have filled in with eroded debris by now. In this dry climate that happens more slowly. The crack is accessible to walkers, though going all the way through entails some serious squeezes and scrambling over boulders. At the bottom the sun seldom shines, and sometimes in summer you find ice from the previous winter. The settlers knew this and would sometimes resort there in the torrid season to cool off and make ice cream.

Fort Rock. Turn off OR 31 and follow the signs, about 7 miles. Looming above the desert, the formation resembles nothing so much as a Celtic ring fort, till you get up close. Solid walls of red rock rise 200 feet in a circle nearly a mile across, unhewn and mortared only by nature. It's thought to have formed 50,000 to 100,000 years ago (previous estimates ranged to about 2 million years ago) when magma erupted under the lake that then covered the basin. The contact of hot magma with cool water made the magma explode into tiny frothy bits, which then settled around the eruption site and welded together into a ring. The lake lasted long enough to erode the south side, and you can trace wave terraces at several different levels on the rock face. A 0.5-mile trail leads into the crater.

FORT ROCK LOOMS OVER THE DESERT OUTBACK.

Fossil Lake, 12 miles north of Christmas Valley off County Roads 5-14 and 5-14 D. Like other lakes around here, this one was part of a huge Ice Age lake that dried up thousands of years ago. This particular one is one of the premier Pleistocene fossil sites in North America, with remains of creatures ranging from flamingoes and giant sloths down to snails and chipmunks. It has also linked humans with some animals that are now extinct. The public is welcome to walk in the fenced area (vehicles are excluded), but please do not remove any fossil or archaeological remains.

Hole in the Ground, about 2.6 miles off OR 31 near milepost 25 via forest roads; contact the forest ranger at Silver Lake (541-576-2107) for details. Another down-to-earth High Desert feature, this hole in the ground is a "maar"—a crater formed when rising magma comes into contact with groundwater and explodes, making the ground subside at the point of contact. Most maars fill with rainwater and become lakes, but not here in the desert, obviously. Like Fort Rock, Hole in the Ground is nearly a mile across, but its floor is nearly 500 feet below the original ground level while its rim is over 100 feet above. A primitive road circles the rim.

Lost Forest, 22 miles east of Christmas Valley via CR 5-14 D. As you approach over the featureless sagebrush plain, a dark line on the horizon resolves itself into tall trees, like a tropical island rising from the sea. This is a relict forest of ponderosa pines and junipers, 40 miles from any other ponderosa forest (or from any forest at all, really). The theory is that these 9,000 acres are all that remains of a great forest that stood here thousands of years ago, when the area was much cooler and watered with numerous lakes. As the climate warmed and dried, the forest shrank. Why did this bit survive—on 10 inches of rainfall a year, when ponderosas normally need 14? One theory is that the **sand dunes** (see below) on which the forest stands, being made of fine pumice, are very porous and hold water, besides sitting not far above a convenient layer of hardpan. However, these same dunes occupy more than 15,000 acres, mostly south and west of the forest, and are constantly shifting—often into the forest, sometimes killing trees. Whether the trees or the sands eventually win remains to be seen. *Caution:* Access is via BLM roads that are mostly unimproved and often impassable due to mud in wet weather and sand when dry. For road conditions, call 541-947-2177.

Sand dunes, entrance 16 miles east of Christmas Valley. In the desert you expect to find sand, but the 16,000 acres composing the Christmas Valley sand dunes call to mind the Sahara more than Oregon. Formed by ash blown from the eruption of Mount Mazama (now Crater Lake) some seven thousand years ago and dust from ancient lake beds, they shift constantly like beach dunes. Sagebrush has gained a foothold on some. Administered with the Lost Forest by the BLM, the complex is an eerie place but unlikely to be still: OHV use is permitted without restriction on the unvegetated dunes and on marked trails elsewhere, though it was designated a Wilderness Study Area in 1982. Primitive camping is allowed, but there are no facilities. And the same road restrictions apply here as in the Lost Forest.

SCENIC DRIVES **Christmas Valley Backcountry Byway.** This tour of the desolate sagebrush country starts at the Fort Rock turnoff on OR 31 and loops to end back on OR 31, 10 miles east of Silver Lake. The 68-mile drive takes you past lava flows and odd geological formations (see *Natural Wonders*), the few remaining pioneer hamlets, and the **Fort Rock Valley Homestead Museum** (see *Museums*), with an optional 23-mile detour to the Lost Forest and sand dunes—

and lots of big sky. Most roads are paved or graveled, but some are unimproved; in this case there's usually a paved alternate route. You do want a map, which is available from the Bureau of Land Management (541-947-2177).

Oregon Outback Scenic Byway. *Outback* is the right word—there's not much out here but sand, sagebrush, rock, cattle range, and hayfields, the latter made possible only by deep-well irrigation. Oh, and desert lakes, high scarps, petroglyphs, coyotes, and eagles. And lots of stillness. It's forbidding or spectacular, depending how you look at it—maybe both. Starting at La Pine, OR 31 angles south and east from the forest to the plain, past Summer Lake, through tiny High Desert settlements, to meet US 395 and continue to the high town of Lakeview and the California border. Total: 157 miles, all on paved roads.

✷ To Do

BICYCLING Many of the Fremont-Winema National Forest trails are open to mountain bikes; check with the ranger station (541-576-2107) for restrictions and trail conditions.

BIRD-WATCHING Despite the extreme climate, the outback boasts huge numbers of waterfowl and cranes during migration, exciting raptors in winter, and desert songbirds. A guide to the Basin and Range Birding Trail is available from the Lakeview Chamber of Commerce (541-947-6090). Some highlights:

Cabin Lake, where the desert meets the pines, has been dry for millennia, but the Forest Service provides two wildlife guzzlers (water sources) that draw songbirds from both habitats. They also thoughtfully put up two blinds for observation. From Fort Rock take graveled FR 18 north for 9.5 miles, then turn left for 0.25 mile.

Fort Rock State Park. The massive rock walls of this formation are favored nesting spots for golden eagles and prairie falcons; in winter they are joined by bald eagles, ferruginous hawks, and many other raptors. From OR 31 take CR 5-10 to the hamlet of Fort Rock, then turn north on County Road 5-11 for a mile.

Oatman Flat (see *Wildlife Refuges*). This can be hit or miss, but I have seen thousands of staging sandhill cranes feeding while eagles and falcons soared overhead.

CAMPING **Fremont National Forest, Silver Lake District** (541-576-2107). These are high-altitude sites, generally maintained May–mid-Nov.; check for fire restrictions.

Thompson Reservoir, about 13 miles south of Silver Lake on FR 27, offers several campgrounds: **Alder Spring,** three campsites, outhouse; no water. **East Bay,** with 17 sites, some handicapped accessible, water, and outhouses (bring firewood); $8. **Thompson Reservoir,** 19 sites, water, and outhouses. **Silver Creek Marsh,** eight sites, water, and outhouses, also corrals and water troughs; the campground is on the Fremont National Recreation Trail. Near Silver Lake: **Upper** and **Lower Buck Creek** (good for wildlife viewing), nine sites, outhouses; no water. **Bunyard Crossing,** three sites, outhouses; no water. **Trapper Spring,** northeast of Silver Lake, nice wildflowers, two sites, outhouse; no water.

GOLF **Christmas Valley Golf Course** (541-576-2216), 1 Christmas Tree Lane, Christmas Valley. Nine holes.

HIKING Most of the **Fremont National Recreation Trail** runs through the mountains above OR 31. This new path runs nearly 175 miles to connect the **Pacific Crest Trail** with the **Warner Mountains Trail System**—that is, from the High Cascades through meadows and mixed forest to the rainshadow hills. Take it in a gulp or in small bites: access points occur at intervals, sometimes even with restrooms and water. For details contact the **Fremont National Forest** (541-576-2107). Other hikes:

From the **Farm Well Trailhead,** 12 miles southeast of Silver Lake by County Road 4-12 and FR 2916, a 5-mile trail leads to the top of **Hager Mountain** and its fire lookout. A hike around **Fort Rock** (see *Natural Wonders*), 3 miles in circumference, is a big-sky, High Desert experience.

* Wilder Places

WILDLIFE REFUGES **Oatman Flat,** milepost 39 on OR 31. This one isn't really a refuge; it's somebody's farm. But if you time it just right in spring—near Easter, usually, despite that feast's mobility—you may see hundreds of sandhill cranes in the newly turned alfalfa field stuffing themselves with small invertebrates before continuing their trek north. In winter, mule deer show up here en masse for similar reasons. A wildlife-viewing sign alerts you to a small turnout.

Sycan Marsh Preserve, 22 miles south of Silver Lake on FR 27, is a 30,000-acre Nature Conservancy preserve protecting tens of thousands of cranes, pelicans, and waterfowl during migration. A self-guided driving tour brochure is available from the the Nature Conservancy (541-273-0789), 226 Pine Street, Klamath Falls 97601.

* Lodging

BED & BREAKFASTS

Christmas Valley

Outback Bed and Breakfast (541-420-5229; www.outbackbedandbreakfast.com), 92946 Christmas Valley Highway. Outback is right—12 miles east of Christmas Valley, population nearly 1,000, and 30 miles west of US 395. But there's satellite TV for those who need it, and plenty of fresh air and star-studded nights for those who don't. One twin-bedded and one queen room sport homemade quilts. $95, with full breakfast; no credit cards.

FOREST SERVICE LOOKOUTS

Hager Mountain Lookout, about 10 miles south of Silver Lake by CR 4-12 and FR 28; then a 4-mile ski or snowshoe, uphill. This one is for the hard core. Since it's still manned in summer, it's only available for rent in the winter. A woodstove and firewood are (luckily) provided, as are a cookstove, cots, and an outhouse. Bring water or hope there's lots of snow. $25 for up to four occupants.

MOTELS

Christmas Valley

Desert Inn Motel (541-576-2262), P.O. Box 148, Christmas Valley 97641. Sixteen modest but tidy units on Christmas Valley's main drag. From $35.

* Where to Eat

EATING OUT

Silver Lake

Cowboy Dinner Tree (541-5762426; http://cowboydinnertree.homestead.com), 4.5 miles south of Silver Lake on East Bay Road (CR 4-12). Open for dinner Thurs.–Sun in summer, Fri.–Sun. in winter. Reservations are required. Suppose you've been riding the range all day and forgot to pack a lunch, or maybe you've spent a week hiking the Fremont Trail with nary a McDonald's in sight. This is the time to head for the Cowboy Dinner Tree, down a slightly paved road 4 miles south of Silver Lake. You may choose a 26- to 30-ounce steak or a whole chicken, with all the trimmings in either case. Splitting plates is not allowed.

PAISLEY–LAKEVIEW–BLY AREA

Watching dust devils rise hundreds of feet in the air from the flats across Summer Lake is a quintessential Great Basin experience. It was here, or rather from Winter Ridge above the lake, that explorer John C. Fremont was sure that he had indeed traced the western edge of the Great Basin—a personal project he had embarked on without permission from his superiors late in 1843. (Evidently it meant a lot to him, as he himself remarked on the risks of setting out with winter coming on and a polyglot company of 25 very young explorers.) He then set off eastward, coming to the great ridges of Abert Rim—named in honor of his commanding officer—and Hart Mountain. You will have a much easier time following the highway south to Lakeview, where steam rises from several hot springs, than driving northeast on US 395 to majestic Abert Rim. Besides which, you can rustle up refreshment in the small roadside towns rather than having to shoot jackrabbits for your supper.

GUIDANCE **Bureau of Land Management** (541-947-2177; www.blm.gov), 1301 S. G Street, Lakeview 97630.

Fremont-Winema National Forests (541-947-2151; www.fs.fed.us/r6/frewin), 1301 S. G Street, Lakeview 97630. Ranger district offices also on OR 140 in Bly and OR 31 in Paisley.

Lake County Chamber of Commerce (1-877-947-6040; www.lakecountychamber.org), 126 N. E Street, Lakeview 97630.

GETTING THERE *By car:* The area is served by **OR 31** (northwest to southeast), **US 395** (northeast to southwest), and **OR 140** (east–west).

GETTING AROUND A car is essential.

MEDICAL EMERGENCY **Lake District Hospital** (1-866-543-4325), 7000 S. J Street, Lakeview.

TOWNS **Lakeview.** The "lake" is not much in evidence nowadays, but at one time Goose Lake—now receded to 10 miles south of town—was visible from the settlement. Lying in basin and range country, Lakeview is still very much a cattle and timber town and boasts several hot springs, a geyser, and a geothermally heated swimming pool. At 4,820 feet, it's the "tallest town in Oregon." And if you climb the hill behind Safeway on a clear day, you may still glimpse the edge of Goose Lake.

Bly. A tiny town built on timber and livestock, Bly mostly minds its own business, so it's ironic that the only American mainland casualties of World War II occurred here: on May 5, 1945, a balloon bomb from Japan killed a woman and six children. More recently Bly made the news when terrorists allegedly tried to set up a training camp on a nearby ranch. Other than that, it's a quiet place, really.

New Pine Creek. Founded in 1869, this is the oldest town in the Goose Lake Valley, though the word *town* is a bit hyperbolic. A couple of antiques shops and a general store constitute the business district. Nestled between placid Goose Lake and the high ridges of the Warner Mountains, and straddling the California border, it's a bit of the Old West, with the Lake Valley Railroad chugging through once a week, hauling local timber down to California. Why *New* Pine Creek? In 1876, when postal service came, there was already a Pine Creek post office elsewhere in Oregon, so this disgruntled community had to add *New* to its name.

Paisley. An early Scots settler is thought to have given the town its name. Home to some three hundred souls, its surrounding steppe watered by the Sycan and Chewaucan rivers drew cattlemen about 1870. Ranching is still the principal occupation; this is the headquarters of the ZX Ranch, the biggest in Oregon, plus several that have been in the same ranching families for a century. Paisley came on the map again in 2008 when evidence of human occupation in Oregon was pushed back over fourteen thousand years by discoveries in nearby Paisley Caves (see *Historic Sites*).

Summer Lake. With its back to Winter Ridge and its face to the broad marshes, the settlement today consists mainly of the wildlife area and supporting services (see *Wildlife Areas*), a few ranchers, and a few retirees, all of whom gravitate to the lodge (see *Motels*) for a friendly word and a hearty meal.

THE HARRIS SCHOOLHOUSE AT SUMMER LAKE

✷ To See

FARMERS' MARKETS Lakeview Saturday Market (541-947-5300), north Second Street between D and E streets. Sat. 9–1, June–mid-Oct.

HISTORIC HOMES Heryford House, 108 S. F Street, Lakeview. Built in 1913 by William P. Heryford, a pioneer cattleman, this two-story gabled house with a semicircular porch was occupied by the family till the 1960s and is on the National Register of Historic Places. Private.

HISTORIC SITES Fremont Memorial, just north of the entrance to the Summer Lake Wildlife Area on OR 31. In Dec. 1843 an exploratory expedition led by John C. Fremont was struggling from The Dalles, on the Columbia, to Sacramento—a journey that was to give rise to one of history's great mass migrations, the trek to Oregon Country. For some reason they were proceeding along the ridges despite the season. Fremont's journal describes standing in 3 feet of snow and descrying, below, a lake spread out in the sun. He immediately named the features "Winter Ridge" and, rather optimistically, "Summer Lake." The names have stuck, and the plaque marks the spot where the party came to rest after descending the gully directly across the road. A small parking and picnic area make a nice pause for the motorized explorer.

General Crock "Pioneer Buggy Horse" Memorial, southwest corner of courthouse yard, Lakeview. The sign is weathered and gives little detail but the date July 30, 1906, indicating that someone cared for General Crock, the horse buried here.

Mitchell Monument, 10 miles north of Bly via OR 140 and FR 1259. In spring of 1945, the Japanese launched thousands of hydrogen balloons in an attempt to attack the U.S. mainland. Made of paper, they were intended to float on the jet stream and arrive in the United States in a matter of days, raining fire and death—each carried incendiary and antipersonnel bombs. Many, in fact, came down in the Northwest but did little damage in Oregon's remote, damp forests. But in May 1945, pastor Archie Mitchell chose this spot for a picnic with his wife and five local children. One child picked up a strange object—the cargo of one balloon that happened to land here, far inland—which detonated, killing Mrs. Mitchell and all the children. A modest plaque and pleasant picnic site mark the spot where the only mainland U.S. deaths of World War II occurred.

Paisley Caves. A low black hill near the south end of Summer Lake is the site of a stunning archaeological find. Already excavated in the 1930s by Luther Cressman, the caves in the hill drew a University of Oregon archaeological team led by Dennis Jenkins back in 2002–2003 for another look. They turned up horse and camel bones—no great surprise there—but also bits of cordage, wooden pegs, and, wonder of wonders, some coprolites. That's a polite word for preserved ancient feces. Now, your gut is continually sloughing off cells, so of course the team immediately thought to test the samples for DNA. They found some, and it turned out to be human. What's more, radiocarbon dating showed it was more than fourteen thousand years old, making it the oldest human DNA to be discovered in the Americas and pushing confirmed human habitation in the Americas back a good thousand years earlier than had been previously verified.

Petroglyphs. Prehistoric rock carvings and paintings dot the Great Basin. Among the most accessible is an image of people and animals a short walk from Picture Rock Pass, just north of Summer Lake on OR 31. Another, at **Hart Mountain National Antelope Refuge,** clearly depicts the bighorn sheep that have recently been reintroduced; for directions consult the refuge office (541-947-2731).

MUSEUMS **Lake County Museum** (541-947-2200; www.lakecountymuseum.com), 118 S. E Street, Lakeview. Tues.–Sat. 1–4:30 in summer, otherwise Wed.–Fri.1–4:30 and Sat. 1–4; closed Jan. and Feb. Admission by donation. In the 1927 Kent House, donated artifacts, mementos, documents, and photographs trace the history of this Old West county. Some of the nine-thousand-year-old sandals discovered at Fort Rock are on display here.

Schmink Museum (541-947-3134), 128 S. E Street, Lakeview. Tues.–Sat. 11–4, Feb.–Oct. General admission $4, seniors $3, children $2. A hundred years after her parents had crossed the country on the Oregon Trail, Lula Schmink willed her house and considerable collection of pioneer and native artifacts to the Oregon chapter of the Daughters of the American Revolution, as a museum.

NATURAL WONDERS **Abert Lake** and **Abert Rim,** about 17 miles north of Lakeview on US 395. At 30 miles long, Abert is one of Oregon's largest lakes. It's certainly one of the briniest. Like Summer Lake, it was once part of Pleistocene Lake Chewaucan and has been evaporating ever since; its concentration of salts is considerable. In fact, it's inadvisable to swim in it, but the brine shrimp love it, and so do shrimp-loving waterfowl. Abert Rim, a 30-mile-long massive fault block, towers nearly vertically 2,000 feet above it; if you're lucky, you may see bighorn sheep picking their way along the rock face.

Old Perpetual Geyser, 1 mile north of Lakevew on US 395. The geyser was "discovered" in 1923, when well drillers for the new Hunter Hot Springs resort hit a vein and 200-degree water came shooting out of the ground. Three geysers were eventually struck. The developers were not slow to recognize the potential, and when two died out, a casing was placed in the third. It spouted every 90 seconds (less often in summer), sending a plume 60 feet into the air, until it mysteriously stopped in fall of 2009. No one knows why..

ABERT LAKE, A RELIC OF THE VAST ICE AGE LAKES

Slide Mountain, visible from OR 31, 21 miles south of Summer Lake. This is the mountain with its north face missing. Although the slide took place several thousand years back, it could have happened yesterday—the scar is too deep and steep for vegetation to grow back.

SCENIC DRIVES **Oregon Outback Scenic Byway** (see "Fort Rock–Christmas Valley–Silver Lake Area").

THE HIGH ESCARPMENT OF ABERT RIM IS A FAULT BLOCK OVERLOOKING ABERT LAKE.

Abert Lake Drive. North of Lakeview, US 395 runs between the lake's edge and Abert Rim, one of the most spectacular though least known spots in the state (see *Natural Wonders*). Turnouts allow you to stop, listen to the silence, and contemplate the vast lake stretching away under 2,000-foot crags. Once past the lake, sagebrush flats take over, and it's a long way to anywhere; you may want to continue to Alkali Lake Station (40 miles from Lakeview) to get an idea of the huge amount of empty space out here. Or, just turn and head back to Lakeview.

Lakeview to Steens Backcountry Byway. Between this byway and US 50 in Nevada ("the loneliest road"), this is definitely the road less traveled. Ninety-one miles wind over basin and range, through sagebrush and past desert wetlands, from Lakeview to OR 205 south of Frenchglen. The escarpments of Hart and the Warner Mountains, and the broad deserts between, are superb. More than half the byway is gravel or dirt, and there are some steep grades; a high-clearance, four-wheel-drive vehicle is recommended. Winter travel is discouraged or simply impossible.

WALKING TOURS The self-guided **Historical Lakeview Walking Tour** offers a glimpse of frontier life that's not so far removed, with homes and commercial buildings dating from the 1880s to the 1920s. Available from the **Lake County Chamber of Commerce** (see *Guidance*).

✱ To Do

BICYCLING The 36-mile **Crane Mountain National Recreation Trail** (see *Hiking*) is open to mountain bikes and offers magnificent views and wildflowers.

Summer Lake Wildlife Area (OR 31 at Summer Lake) offers miles of level, graveled trails; closed during hunting season.

BIRD-WATCHING The **Basin and Range Birdwatching Trail** extends to southern Lake County and includes these stellar sighting areas:

BIRDS LIKE BRINY ABERT LAKE.

Goose Lake State Park, in New Pine Creek (see *Parks*). Thousands of waterfowl and shorebirds stop here during migration, and songbirds like orioles, warblers, and lazuli buntings nest in the willow and cottonwoods lining the shore.

Abert Lake (see *Natural Wonders*) is saline enough to breeds millions of brine shrimp, which apparently are as irresistible to ducks, geese, ibis, and stilts as potato chips are to kids. Snowy plover nest near milepost 68 on the alkali flats north of the lake.

Hart Mountain (see *Wildlife Refuges*) is home to sage grouse; they can be found near water or, in summer, near the campground. Also present are ravens, raptors, sage thrashers, and many songbirds. The campground hot springs are an added perk. *Caution:* The access road is rough; a high-clearance, four-wheel-drive vehicle is advised.

Warner Wetlands, 5 miles east of Plush on County Road 3-12. At the base of Hart Mountain, these shallow lakes fluctuate a lot; in good years they, like the desert lakes above, host multitudes of migrating waterfowl and nesting shorebirds.

CAMPING Lakeview area: **Goose Lake State Park** (541-947-3111), State Line Road, New Pine Creek; 48 sites, water, showers, toilets. Closed winter.

Fremont National Forest, Lakeview District (541-947-2151). High-elevation forest campgrounds here are maintained June–mid-Oct. **Crane Mountain,** some 20 miles southeast of Lakeview via OR 140 and FR 3915, has two rustic campgrounds: **Dismal Creek,** with three sites and an outhouse, no water; and **Deep Creek,** four sties plus two tent-only sites, ADA-accessible outhouse, no water. Nearby **Twin Springs** has three sites with outhouse and water, and **Willow Creek** has eight sites and an outhouse but no water. **Cottonwood Recreation Area,** about 32 miles west of Lakeview via OR 140 and FR 3870, has 12 sites plus nine tent-only sites, outhouse, water, boat ramps, and trail access. **Dog Lake,** some 30 miles west of Lakeview via OR 140, County Roads 1-13 and 1-11 D and FR 4017, has eight sites, water, outhouses, a boat ramp, bird-watching, and fishing. **Drews Creek** has five sites with outhouse and water, and access to Drews Reservoir. Far to the east, in the Warner Mountains, is **Can Springs,** with three sites and an outhouse but no water.

Bly area: **Fremont National Forest, Bly District** (541-353-2427). Campground usually open June–Oct. **Lofton Reservoir,** about 26 miles east of Bly by OR 140, FR 3715, and FR 013; 26 sites with outhouses, water, boat ramp (electric motors only), and fishing pier. **Horseglade Trailhead,** 17 miles north of Bly via Ivory Pine Road and FR 27; two sites and an ADA outhouse.

Paisley area: **Fremont National Forest, Paisley District** (541-943-3114). Campgrounds generally open mid-May–Oct. **Campbell Lake,** 35 miles southwest of

Paisley via FR 33, FR 28, and FR 033; 16 sites with water and outhouses, boat launch (electric motors only). Very popular. Just beyond is **Dairy Creek,** also very popular, four sites with water and outhouses. **Happy Camp,** nearby on FR 047, has nine sites, an outhouse, and water nearby at Clear Creek. **Deadhorse Creek,** also on FR 047, has four sites and an outhouse; water is at Clear Creek. **Jones Crossing,** just 9 miles from Paisley on FR 33, offers eight sites with no water but an ADA-compliant outhouse. **Lee Thomas,** about 25 miles southwest of Paisley by FR 3315 and FR 3411; seven sites with water and outhouse. **Marster Spring,** 7 miles south of Paisley on FR 33, has 10 campsites with ADA-accessible outhouse and water. **Rock Creek,** 24 miles from Paisley via FR 29 and FR 28, has six sites and an outhouse; fills in hunting season. **Sandhill Crossing,** about 27 miles west of Paisley via FR 3315, FR 28, and FR 3411; five sites with water and ADA-accessible outhouse. **Slide Lake,** 15 miles west of Paisley by FR 3315 and FR 3360, has three campsites but no water or outhouse. **Upper Jones,** 9 miles south of Paisley on FR 33, has two sites, no water, and no outhouse, but offers fishing along the Chewaucan River. **Chewaucan Crossing Trailhead,** 8 miles south of Paisley on FR 33; five sites with handicapped-accessible outhouse and access to the **Fremont National Recreation Trail** (see *Hiking*).

GOLF **Lakeridge Golf Course** (541-947-3855), OR 140 and Klamath Highway. Nine holes.

HANG GLIDING Not all views are from mountaintops. With its flat basins and steep scarps creating ideal thermals for hang gliders and paragliders, Lake County claims to be the **hang-gliding capital of the West** and even hosts an annual festival to prove it. For information on launch sites, safety, and etiquette, contact the **Lake County Chamber of Commerce** (see *Guidance*).

HIKING Lakeview District: The **Cottonwood Trail System** is 12 miles of forest trails accessible from the **Cottonwood Recreation Area** (see *Camping*).

The **Crane Mountain Recreation Trail,** in the **Warner Mountains** east of Lakeview, affords 36 miles of mountain hiking with splendid views over Goose Lake and as far as Mount Shasta in California. The southern 8 miles are open to ATVs, but the rest is motor-free. Accessible from the Rogger Meadow Trailhead on FR 3915, off OR 140.

The 175-mile **Fremont National Recreation Trail** connects the **Crane Mountain Trail** to the **Pacific Crest Trail** and enjoys magnificent views and wildflowers. This approximately 18-mile segment is cut off from the rest by an undeveloped stretch; you can pick it up at the Mill Trailhead by taking US 395 north of Lakeview for 9 miles, exiting at County Road 2-13/FR 012, and driving 2 more miles.

Bly-Paisley area: **Gearhart Mountain Wilderness Area** (see *Wilderness Areas*) lies in rugged mountains between Bly and Paisley. Few amenities, but 17 miles of trails above and below tree line, mountain streams, and a pristine lake. The **Campbell and Dead Horse Lake Trail System** offers 25 miles of trails open to hikers, cyclists, and horses, accessible from the Lee Thomas trailhead on FR 3411, 24 miles southeast of Paisley. The **Hanan Trail System** is reached from the Hanan-Coffeepot Trailhead 18 miles west of Paisley on FR 3315; an 8-mile trail marked with cairns leads to the headwaters of the Sycan River and follows an early transportation route into that wild area.

HOT SPRINGS The Great Basin's stretching crust gives rise to hot springs large and small, some just steaming away in roadside fields. Some of the more accessible are:

Hunter's Hot Springs (1-800-858-8266; www.huntersresort.com), 2 miles north of Lakeview on US 395 at the Hunter's Hot Springs Resort. Pool 102–104 degrees.

Hart Mountain Hot Springs, Hart Mountain National Antelope Refuge campground. One semienclosed and one open pool, virtually undeveloped. Free.

Summer Lake Hot Springs (1-877-492-8554; www.summerlakehotsprings), 5 miles north of Paisley on OR 31. The centerpiece of Summer Lake Hot Springs Resort, the 101-degree pool is in a 1928 corrugated metal enclosure. Drop-ins $10.

UNIQUE ADVENTURES **Oregon Sunstone Collecting Site,** north of Plush; take County Road 3-10 from US 395, turn left on BLM Road 6165, right on 6115, and left on 6195 for a total of about 22 miles. The opaque, yellow sunstone is Oregon's state gem, and you can dig some yourself right here in the High Desert—hand tools only, and fill in your holes. Camp anywhere you like but bring what you need; there are no facilities other than a picnic table and vault toilet. *Caution:* BLM roads are remote, unimproved, and impassable when wet. For road conditions, call 541-947-2177.

WINTER SPORTS **Warner Canyon Ski Area.** From Lakeview take US 395 north 2.5 miles, then go east 4.5 miles on OR 140. Open weekends, Christmas break, and spring break. It's not one of the big-name ski resorts—it's a semiremote 200 acres of downhill skiing with a 1,000-foot drop, ungroomed cross-country and snowshoe trails, and no lift lines. And at $30 for a day's lift pass, it's probably the cheapest ski deal in the state.

SUMMER LAKE HOT SPRINGS

✷ Wilder Places

PARKS Chandler State Wayside, off US 395, 16 miles north of Lakeview. Free. If you're coming from the north or east, this is where you start to see trees again, as the hills rise into ponderosa forests. The Chandler family, who owned ranchland all over the area, thought it would make a nice rest stop for travelers and donated this 85-acre parcel, where you can enjoy a picnic by the creek under tall pines.

Goose Lake State Park (1-800-551-6949), 14 miles south of Lakeview, State Line Road, New Pine Creek. A quiet green park on the edge of placid Goose Lake includes a full-service campground (summer only), boat ramp, walking trails, and an old homestead's overgrown orchard. The long, shallow lake straddling the California-Oregon line draws multitudes of geese in spring. Between the lake and piney hills, it's a lovely peaceful spot with an easy stroll to the hamlet of New Pine Creek.

WILDERNESS AREAS Gearhart Mountain Wilderness, about 15 miles northeast of Bly; not accessible in winter. Nearly 40 square miles of pine forest, streams, meadows, and craggy rock formations are open to primitive recreation. Remote and pristine, it offers 17 miles of trails, fishing, horse trekking, and camping (no water or facilities). The average altitude is 7,500 feet; be prepared for any weather.

WILDLIFE REFUGES Hart Mountain National Antelope Refuge (541-947-2731), 65 miles northeast of Lakeview; take US 395 and OR 140 through Plush, then turn right at refuge entrance. You could call this the outer part of the outback. Coming from Plush, you drive gingerly up the jagged face of a massive fault block, arriving finally at a rolling plateau that slopes gently away eastward. This is Hart Mountain, 278,000 acres at an altitude of about 7,000 feet, with higher peaks. Designated in 1936 to protect dwindling pronghorn herds (which are now doing just fine), the refuge is habitat for deer, bighorn sheep, sage grouse, and about three hundred other wildlife species. Its high grasslands and rugged canyons are the kind of scene you expect to see in glossy photos in *Audubon Magazine,* or *Nature. Caution:* None of the few roads is paved, and most are minimally maintained. Access in spring or winter is virtually impossible, and even in summer a brief rain makes driving risky. Don't expect speedy rescue services. But if you're reasonably prudent, enjoy primitive camping and equally primitive hot springs, and love wilderness, this one's for you.

Summer Lake Wildlife Area (541-943-3152), 53447 OR 31, Summer Lake. Summer Lake is one of those 20-mile-long, fluctuating lakes left over from the huge Pleistocene lakes that covered much of the Great Basin. The marshy area at its northern end is administered by the state for fall hunting and is a prime bird-watching spot the rest of the time, attracting thousands of migrating waterfowl and shorebirds. To quote the Oregon Department of Fish and Wildlife, "viewing is not recommended during hunting seasons," which unfortunately include much of fall migration—in fact, the auto tour route closes. But swans and geese may be observed in the small lake across the highway. Self-contained camping is available; no facilities.

Warner Wetlands, about 40 miles northeast of Lakeview. This series of ephemeral desert lakes at the base of Hart Mountain gets a lot of attention from wildlife, especially migrating birds, though much depends on water levels, which can vary wildly; check ahead with the BLM office (541-947-2177). Their remoteness ensures you won't have a lot of competition except for hunters in season. Picnic tables and a restroom are available. Bring a canoe, bring a tent. There's no official campground, but plenty of wilderness. Be discreet and leave no trace.

✷ Lodging

COTTAGES

New Pine Creek

Pine Creek Cabin (530-946-4184), 675 State Line Road. Cozy, self-contained cabins surrounded by gardens and wild birds in tiny New Pine Creek, steps away from Goose Lake and miles of mountain trails—you couldn't ask for much more than accessible wilderness and the comforts of home. Owners Anita and Jim Spence will point you up the canyon, down to the lake, or across the border to the winery, depending on your interests, and even cook if you don't feel like using the cabin kitchen. Check your bird sightings against their list: the town is on the **Great Basin Birding Trail.** Enjoy the woodstove in the evening. Cabins sleep eight and start at $95 for a couple. Children and pets are welcome.

Paisley

Summer Lake Hot Springs (541-943-3931; www.summerlakehotsprings.com), milepost 92 on OR 31. Two simple but cozy mosaic-decorated, geothermally heated cabins; a larger house; RV slots; and a tent camping area are the eclectic lodgings surrounding the historic mineral springs. Historic on two scales: in nearby Paisley Caves, visible from the property, archaeologists recently discovered human coprolites (look it up) more than fourteen thousand years old. Very likely those people knew and enjoyed the waters. In the late 1800s settlers began to develop the springs, putting up the current corrugated metal enclosure in the 1920s. Additional cabins and conference space are in the works, and the setting, overlooking the lake and two mountain ranges, is spectacular. From $75.

FOREST SERVICE LOOKOUTS AND CABINS The CCC built many fire lookouts and guard stations during the Depression, many of which are now used only seasonally if at all. Several are available for a wilderness experience. The facilities are very basic, but the price is right and the surroundings fairly unbeatable. Smoking is forbidden and pets generally allowed, with some restrictions. To reserve, log onto www.recreation.gov or call 1-877-444-6777.

Aspen Cabin, 18 miles west of Lakeview via US 395, OR 140, and FR 3615, all paved. A log cabin furnished with four cots, a table, and chairs, Aspen sits in the Warner Mountains 3 miles from the **Crane Mountain Trail.** There is an outhouse, but drinking water is at Mud Creek Campground, 1.5 miles away. Pets are allowed. Open June 15–Oct. 15. $25/night, up to four occupants.

Currier Guard Station Cabin, about 30 miles west of Paisley via FR 29 and FR 30; rough road but okay for regular vehicles. At the edge of forest and meadow, Currier sleeps four and boasts a kitchen and bedroom, corrals, a propane stove, propane heater, and outhouse, but no water. Open June 15–Oct. 15. $30.

HOTELS

Lakeview

♿ **Fremont Inn** (541-947-2060), 524 N. G Street. Owned by the adjacent Best Western, this imposing building used to be an assisted-living facility, which accounts for the handrails in the showers. Consequently the 31 rooms and suites are fairly spacious and include at least a refrigerator and microwave. They've also been redecorated with warm wood furniture and queen beds to accommodate both families and business travelers. Doubles from $88, including continental breakfast.

Paisley

Sage Rooms (541-943-3145), OR 31, center of town. Three simple rooms with pine wainscoting are your base for exploring Paisley, whether you want to fish the Chewaucan River, watch birds in the marshes, or hike the surrounding hills. Doubles from $79, including tax.

LODGES

Bly

Aspen Ridge Resort (1-800-393-3323; www.aspenrr.com), P.O. Box 2, Bly 97622; turn south on Fishhole Creek Road 1 mile east of Bly and continue 17 miles. How does a high-altitude, working ranch sound? A hard-scrabble livestock-and-lumber town once stood on this site and, like so many in the county, drifted away in the 1930s; the entire settlement was sold and became the 14,000-acre Fishhole Creek Ranch, where today cattle, buffalo, and visitors roam. Four lodge rooms; five large, self-contained cabins; and a restaurant make up the resort, all overlooking a broad meadow surrounded by national forest. That makes plenty of room to hike, bike, fish, ride horseback, or just plain lounge, which many guests seem to prefer. Open May–Oct. Lodge rooms from $90, cabins from $150; horse rentals, guided rides, meals, etc., are extra.

MOTELS

Lakeview

Hunter's Hot Springs Resort (1-800-858-8266; www.huntersresort.com), 18088 US 395. Founded in 1925 as a therapeutic resort, Hunter's has drawn visitors for more than 80 years. You don't have to be sick to enjoy hot springs, and today's guests generally are just looking for a nice warm soak, dinner, and a bed. The rooms are motel style, with some RV parking, and the whole place is geothermally heated. Doubles from $65; pool use alone, $5/day.

Summer Lake

🖉 🐾 **The Lodge at Summer Lake** (1-866-943-3993; www.thelodgeatsummerlake.com), 53460 OR 31. In fall and winter it belongs to the hunters, in spring and summer to the birders. Owners Gary, Jan, Marie, and Gil cater gracefully to all and can produce a wealth of local information on demand. Just across the street from the entrance to Summer Lake Wildlife Area, it began in the 1940s with two barracks moved down from the army base at Sunriver. They still form the skeleton of the restaurant and kitchen, while a seven-unit motel and three cabins overlooking a bass pond were added more recently. All rooms are simple but cozy with log furniture. A woodstove heats the restaurant, which draws locals and visitors alike with three hearty and reasonable meals a day. Motel rooms start at $56, and cabins, with kitchen or kitchenette, at $77.

Lakeview

Willow Springs Guest Ranch (541-947-5499; www.willowspringsguestranch.com), 34064 Clover Flat Road. On their 2,500-acre working high-country ranch, Patty and Keith Barnhart welcome you to ride the range, hike, mountain bike, or sit on your front porch staring at the view. A ranch horse will take time off to give you a ride, or you can bring your own (boarding and rental extra)—guided rides are also available. Ask for a boxed lunch and come back for a ranch dinner. The rustic cabins each have a queen bed, fireplace, private bath, and porch. There's a wood-fired hot tub and hurricane lamps to use after lights out—all electricity here is home-generated. Cabin doubles from $115, with full breakfast.

✷ Where to Eat

DINING OUT

Bly

Aspen Ridge Resort (1-800-393-3323; www.aspenrr.com), P.O. Box 2, Bly 97622; turn south on Fishhole Creek Road 1 mile east of Bly and continue 17 miles. Definitely off the beaten track, Aspen Ridge serves three hearties a day, specializing in mesquite-barbecued ribs, beef, and chicken, in portions to match a rancher's appetite, plus homemade desserts if you have room. Open May–Oct. and for Thanksgiving. Dinner reservations are recommended.

EATING OUT

Paisley

The Homestead Restaurant (541-943-3187), 331 OR 31. This site has fed hungry cowboys and passersby since 1880. Today's building is a bit newer, but you'll still find heaping portions of home cookin' served up daily at breakfast, lunch, and dinner.

Summer Lake

✐ **The Lodge at Summer Lake** (1-866-943-3993; www.thelodgeatsummerlake.com), 53460 OR 31. Besides being a place to stay, the lodge is also the only restaurant for miles around. Luckily, it's good. Breakfast can be as hearty or as continental as you like, from an array of pancakes and omelets to a bowl of oatmeal or an English muffin. Lunch is an equally substantial sandwich or burger, while dinner reaches out to the rancher and the urban visitor alike with steaks, herbed breast of chicken, seafood, and more, and three generous courses (oh, I get soup *and* salad?), lovingly prepared by chief chef Gary or sous chefs Marie and Jan, who wear several hats. Reasonable, too.

✷ Events

March: **Irish Days** (541-947-6040), nearest weekend to St. Patrick's Day, Lakeview. A corned beef and cabbage dinner, parade, and other shenanigans salute Lake County's many Irish pioneers.

July: **Festival of Free Flight** (1-877-947-6040), July Fourth weekend, Lakeview. Hang-gliding pilots from around the country descend, as it were, on the area's many launch sites for flying and festivities.

Mosquito Festival (541-943-0801), last weekend, Paisley. This event was born in 1984 as a way to raise funds for mosquito control (a word to the wise). Today proceeds go to various charities, and the festivities include a barbecue, a parade featuring Miss and Mr. Quito, music, and cowboy events.

September: **Lake County Fair and Roundup** (541-947-2125), Labor Day weekend, at the County Fairgrounds, 1900 N. Fourth Street, Lakeview. Rodeos, 4-H competitions, a greased-pig contest for kids—all you expect from a celebration of Western agriculture.

Southern Cascades and Siskiyous

7

KLAMATH BASIN–CRATER LAKE AREA

ASHLAND–MEDFORD–ROGUE VALLEY AREA

ILLINOIS VALLEY AREA

ROSEBURG–MYRTLE CREEK–CANYONVILLE AREA

SOUTHERN CASCADES AND SISKIYOUS

I was used to waking in bear tracks by this time; it was instructive to find that a bear could also walk in mine.

—*David Rains Wallace,* The Klamath Knot

While tooling around southwestern Oregon, you may encounter the State of Jefferson. You won't find it on any map, much less on a highway marker, and you won't be required to declare your fruits and vegetables—but it's there.

In 1941, residents of northern California and southwestern Oregon were fed up with their respective legislatures' unfulfilled promises to improve roads (which were indeed abysmal) through the area. The mineral and timber resources were useless without transport. So they decided to protest by forming the State of Jefferson, comprising most of southwestern Oregon and California as far as Redding and Mendocino—a region that shares similar topography and independent attitudes. Every Thursday they would "secede" from the Union. Border controls were set up in Yreka, where motorists received pamphlets about the movement. It was a tongue-in-check demonstration (though the guys manning the checkpoints did carry rifles), not without its Hollywood film crews, but it was sidelined by the bombing of Pearl Harbor and withered away. Something of it lives on, though, in a certain contrarian spirit. Jefferson Public Radio, not National Public Radio, broadcasts from Southern Oregon University in Ashland.

The first settlers, though, were neither miners nor lumbermen, but Oregon Trail emigrants. The Oregon Trail "shortcut" blazed by Jesse and Charles Applegate in 1846 was hardly that. Today you can drive the stretch between Klamath Falls and Ashland in a leisurely two hours (in summer, anyway). But to drive an ox team over the endless tangled Siskiyous is nearly unimaginable—especially considering the emigrants had already crossed the Great Plains, the Rockies, and the High Desert. It did avoid the perilous Columbia River descent, which was the whole point, but had plenty of river crossings of its own. Not to mention steep mountainsides, cliffs, and dense forest. No longer virgin forest and not completely impenetrable—old logging roads run through it, and even in the further reaches

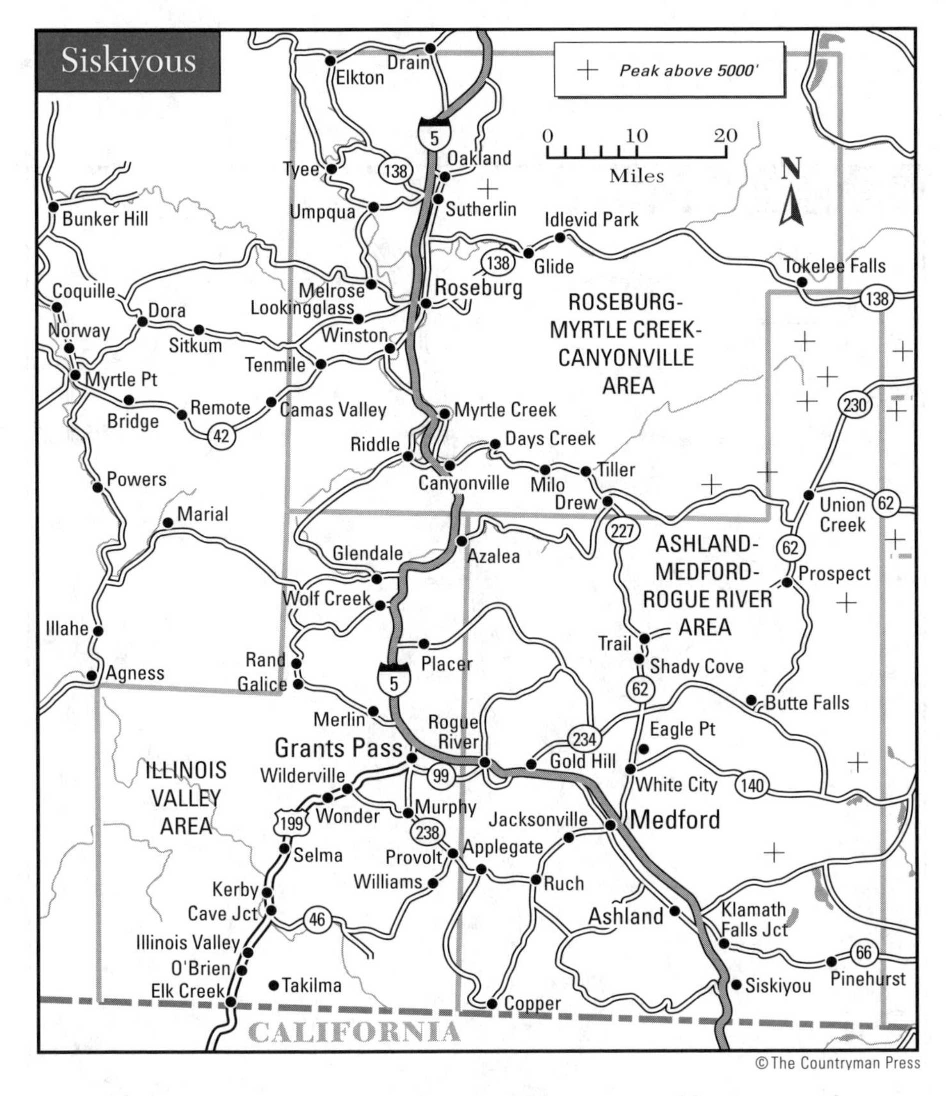

©The Countryman Press

you might stumble on an abandoned mining claim—it's a giddying piece of scenery, and no wonder the anomalous Oregon Vortex is here and not in, say, Lakeview. It's a real challenge to backpackers and a haven for the shyer forms of wildlife.

Of course, the edges and lower reaches have been civilized, but in a civilized way. Orchards and vineyards dot the bucolic Applegate and Rogue valleys. Every year thousands of visitors attend Ashland's Oregon Shakespeare Festival. The boisterous prospectors who rushed to the goldfields of the 1840s and the 1850s have given way to more sedate but proud descendants, some still inhabiting the solid homes built by their forebears.

The area has also seen some of the saddest in a sad litany of Indian wars: the Rogue River War of 1855–1856, and the Modoc War of 1872–1873. The former was opposed by regional Indian agents but pushed by vigilantes and state officials; the latter a bloody debacle for the U.S. Army. Both ended as usual in forced relocations, though most Indian lands had already been ceded by then.

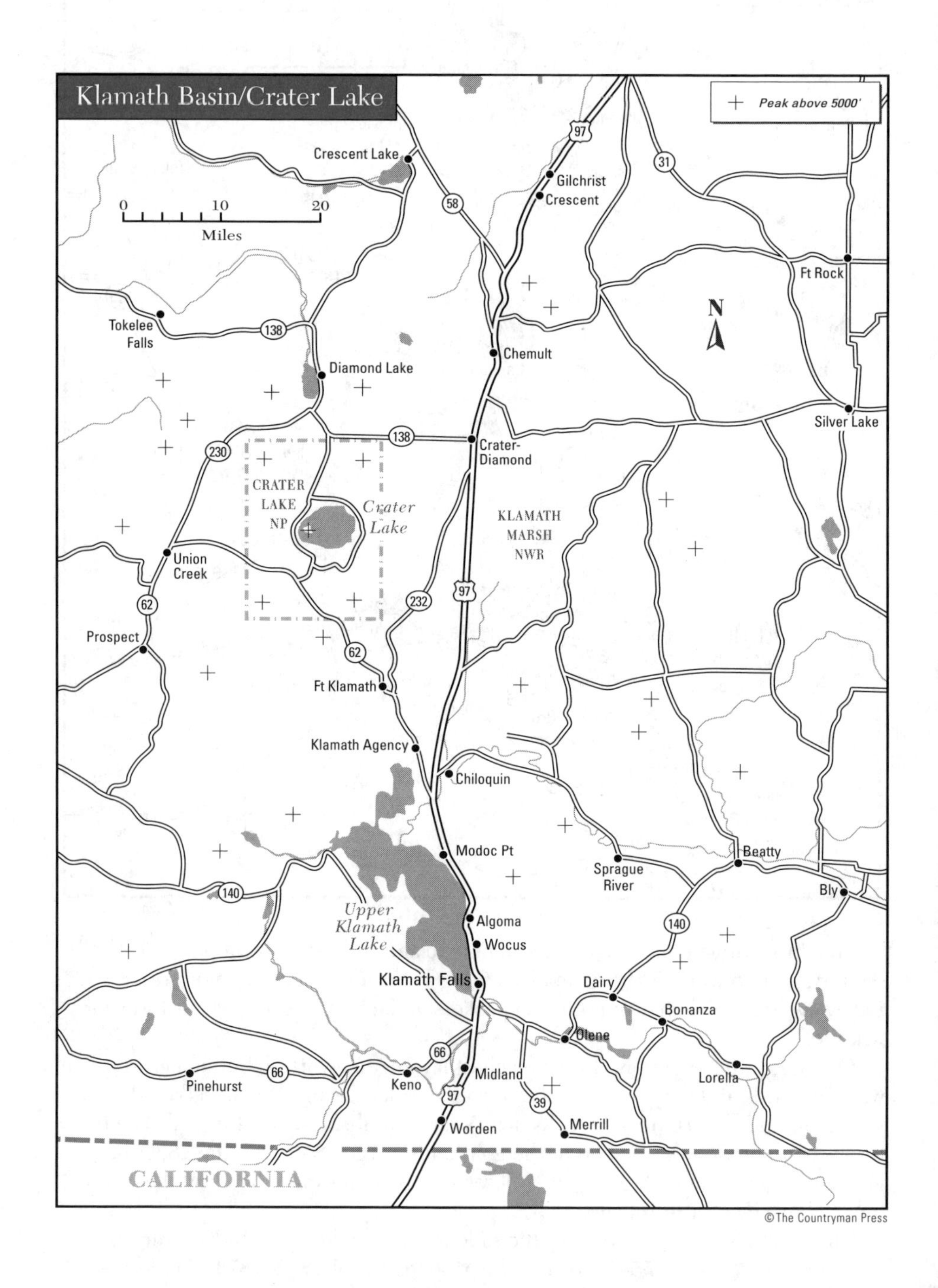

©The Countryman Press

KLAMATH BASIN–CRATER LAKE AREA

Four score and seven thousand years ago, give or take, a great mountain imploded, leaving a caldera that slowly filled to become Crater Lake. The sapphire lake is a jewel in the crown of the National Park System; but smaller lakes are scattered around its forested flanks, laced with cabins and campgrounds, not to mention expansive Upper Klamath Lake in the lee of the mountains, where forest grades into desert. The only real town here is Klamath Falls, where you can discover exquisite Indian artifacts at the Favell Museum and view the faded art deco downtown. Along the back roads, a few bed & breakfasts dot the lonely shores of Upper Klamath, and the skies show a million stars.

GUIDANCE **Discover Klamath** (1-800-445-6728; www.discoverklamath.com), 205 Riverside Drive, Klamath Falls 97601.

Fremont-Winema National Forest: Chemult Ranger District (541-365-7001), Chemult; **Chiloquin Ranger District** (541-783-4001), 38500 US 97 N., Chiloquin 97624; **Klamath Falls Ranger District** (541-883-6714), 2819 Dahlia Street, Klamath Falls 97601.

Klamath County Chamber of Commerce (1-877-552-6284; www.klamath.org), 203 Riverside Drive, Klamath Falls 97601.

Klamath Welcome Center (541-882-7330), 11001 US 97 S., Klamath Falls 97603. Open May–Oct.

Northern Klamath County Visitor Center (541-433-2348; www.klamathcounty.net), 138351 US 97 N., Gilchrist 97737.

ITALIAN-INSPIRED BUT WESTERN-THEMED ARCHITECTURAL DETAIL IN KLAMATH FALLS ART DECO DISTRICT

Umpqua National Forest: Diamond Lake Ranger District (541-498-2531), 2020 Toketee Ranger Station Road, Idleyld 97447.

GETTING THERE *By air:* **Klamath Falls Airport** (541-883-5372), 6775 Arnold Avenue, Klamath Falls, offers connections to Portland and San Francisco.

By bus: **AMTRAK**'s Coast Starlight stops at 1600 Oak Avenue, Klamath Falls, and in the center of Chemult.

By car: **US 97** traverses the Klamath Basin north to south. **OR 140** and **70** reach Klamath Falls from the east, and **OR 66** comes in from the west.

GETTING AROUND *By bus:* You will want a car to get around the area, but **Basin Transit** (541-883-2877; www.basintransit.com) offers service within Klamath Falls six days a week.

MEDICAL EMERGENCY **Sky Lakes Medical Center** (541-882-6311), 2865 Daggett Avenue, Klamath Falls.

✷ To See

FARMERS' MARKETS **Klamath Falls Farmers' Market,** Ninth Street between Klamath Avenue and Main Street. Sat. 9–1, June–Oct.

FOR FAMILIES ✐ **Klamath Ice Sports** (541-850-5758; www.klamathicesports.org), 5075 Fox Sparrow Lane, Klamath Falls. If you happen to be in Klamath Falls between early Nov. and late Mar., why not go skating on the community rink? A lightweight cover allows it to be open in all weathers. Lessons are available, too, in case you've forgotten how.

✐ **Train Mountain Miniature Railroad** (541-783-3030; www.trainmountain.org), 36941 S. Chiloquin Road, Chiloquin. Sun. 10–3 in summer. With 25 miles of track, this is the longest miniature hobby railroad in the world—the *Guinness Book of Records* even says so. And for a small donation you can actually ride the model heritage trains through the pine woods, piloted by the enthusiasts of the Klamath and Western Railroad.

HERITAGE TREES **Waldo Tree.** In 1888 Judge John Waldo and his friends carved their names on this mountain hemlock deep in the forest. Why? Well, Waldo is a big name in Oregon conservation history—there's a lake named after him as well—and they were on a fact-finding trip to support the establishment of the Cascade Forest Reserve, a precursor of the Forest Service.

HISTORIC HOMES **Baldwin House,** 142 Riverside Drive, Klamath Falls. This 8,000-square-foot mansion with its corner tower and two-story porch must have wowed the town when it was built in 1900.

Goeller House, 234 Riverside Drive, Klamath Falls. Mr. Goeller was a carpenter and planing mill owner. At some point he got hold of a pattern book and evidently got carried away, for his 1905 house has more pirouettes and curlicues than a fancy wedding cake. It's open only for certain events, but it's hard to think how the inside could be more fun to look at than the outside.

Moore House, 128 Riverside Drive. Modest compared to its neighbors on the next block, the Moore House belonged to the family who built the town's first sawmill. And though it's only one and a half floors, it has two levels of porches and nicely turned gingerbread. Private home.

HISTORIC SITES **Fort Klamath** (541-381-2230), 51400 OR 62, Fort Klamath. Thurs.–Mon. 10–6, June–Labor Day. At the lonely north end of Upper Klamath Lake is the site of Fort Klamath, built in the uneasy decade leading up to the Modoc War. It functioned until 1890. None of the buildings here is original, but a modest frame museum and gift shop houses photos and relics of the period. Here, too, are the gravesites of Modoc leader Captain Jack and three of his warriors, who were executed here at the end of the war. The 8 acres of grounds are open for strolling, reflection, and picnicking.

The ***Klamath Falls Old Town Tour Guide,*** available from the chamber of commerce (see *Guidance*), highlights the city's pioneer and art deco buildings, among them:

The **Oregon Bank Building,** 905 Main Street, dating from 1929—a mixture of styles with some glazed terra-cotta detail, oak and mahogany woodwork, and an actual elevator operator.

The **Williams Building,** 724 Main Street, built about 1927 by a cattleman who enlivened his functional building with arches and terra-cotta friezes depicting cow skulls and twining Douglas fir branches.

MUSEUMS **Collier Memorial State Park Logging Museum** (1-800-551-6949), 46000 US 97 N., Chiloquin. On the west side of the highway is a collection of logging equipment spanning a century of central Oregon's timber boom. Huge wheels for skidding logs, drag saws, "steam donkeys," and early locomotives lead up to the heavy gas, diesel, and computerized equipment of the late 20th century.

SKULL AND FIR FRIEZE IN KLAMATH FALLS

The exhibits occupy several acres and are complemented by a blacksmith shop and pioneer village; a must for mechanical, history, and railroad buffs.

Baldwin Hotel Museum (541-883-4207), 31 Main Street, Klamath Falls. Wed.–Sat. 10–4, summer only. George Baldwin was state senator who put up a hardware store in 1906, then converted it to a hotel for all the California tourists who would surely flock to Oregon's great outdoors on the new train line. Tour guides tell stories amid the original furnishings, including the photography studio of George's daughter Maud, who photographed widely in the Klamath Basin.

Favell Museum (541-882-9996; www.favellmuseum.org), 125 W. Main Street, Klamath Falls. Tues.–Sat. 10–5. General admission $7, children 6–16 $4, under six free; families $20. Gene Favell started collecting Native American artifacts as a boy back in the 1930s. In those days you could wander the desert and pick up what struck your fancy—arrowheads, mortars, pestles, and so forth—and there was quite a bit out there. You can't do that anymore—in fact, it could get you arrested—but it became Gene's passion. He amassed a truly astounding collection. Literally thousands of arrowheads and spear points, some so beautiful as to take your breath away, are arranged in geometric patterns alongside now-priceless and unique items, like the mortar carved in the shape of a beaver. Added to this is an assortment of quirky Westerniana running from paintings by the likes of John Clymer and Charles Russell to a series of humorous dioramas by Ray Anderson (Paiute women with a baby mammoth three thousand years ago? Really?) I don't know if Favell kept proper archaeological records, but he did share his vision with the public, and it's definitely not boring.

Klamath County Museum (541-883-4208), 1451 Main Street, Klamath Falls. Mon.–Sat. 9–5:30 in summer and Mon.–Sat. 9–4:30 in winter. If you can't find the native birds outside, you can find them in here, disposed in naturalistic dioramas. You'll also find artifacts and documents from the region's Native and pioneer history, and displays on the fierce Modoc War that took place in 1872–1873 on both sides of the Oregon-California border.

NATURAL WONDERS **Crater Lake.** Today's deep blue lake set in its crater seems an eye gazing calmly at heaven. Five miles across, surrounded by 2,000-foot cliffs, and at 1,943 feet the deepest lake in the nation, it was taboo to the tribes and became known to the public only when gold prospectors stumbled on it in 1853. And its geology tells a tale:

It used to be a mountain. Geologists call it Mount Mazama, and it was still young when it collapsed. Only half a million years ago it began building its cone rapidly through massive eruptions till it grew to 12,000 feet—higher than Mount Hood, Oregon's highest, is today. But the massive magma pressure from below also created many side channels. They undermined the mountain as termites undermine a house. So when it erupted powerfully only 7,700 years ago, its insides were blown into the air to rain down on the landscape for miles around, and the cone collapsed into what is now the caldera. Thick ash deposits from this eruption can be seen in nearby road cuts and for miles into the desert—in fact, Mount Mazama ash is found in eight states and into Canada (150 times more ash than was released by Mount St. Helens in 1980). Legends of the Klamath tribe seem to possess a memory of the cataclysm, adding that for a long time the caldera floor was too hot to approach. We can certainly believe that; in fact, for a time any water touching it would have boiled off. But eventually it cooled, and slowly the rains and snows created the lake. Later eruptions created Wizard Island and the Phantom Ship that seems to float on the waters. There is no outlet; what comes in is balanced only by evaporation and seepage, and the lake is still one of the purest in the world—it never even had fish till it was stocked (a practice that has been discontinued). If you can see only one Oregon sight, this should be it; you won't find its like elsewhere.

SCENIC DRIVES The **Volcanic Legacy Scenic Byway** is 500 miles of volcanism. From Crater Lake, the volcano that blew its top, the byway winds along Upper Klamath Lake's western shore, past Klamath Falls and into California, passing Lava Beds National Monument and Mount Shasta (a volcano that hasn't yet blown its top, but residents are prepared), and ending up at Lassen Peak. But you don't have to drive the whole thing; the Oregon section is only 110 miles, and beautiful. The Crater Lake segment is passable only in summer.

* To Do

BICYCLING Between the country roads and the national forests there is plenty of opportunity. Below are a few suggestions; for more, contact the Klamath Ranger District (541-885-3400), or **Hutch's Bicycles** (541-850-2453) in Klamath Falls—they rent bikes, too.

Rim Road around **Crater Lake** is a challenging 33 miles at an altitude of 7,000 feet; spectacular, but beware of cars on the winding road. The loop road around **Diamond Lake,** 15 miles north of Crater Lake on OR 138, is a gentle 11 miles.

At **Fort Klamath** you can take a 10-mile spin through level, bucolic terrain; or take the Westside Road down to Rocky Point, 24 miles of quiet road, lake views, and pine forest.

Hard-core cyclists can circle **Upper Klamath Lake** in a day; others might prefer to break the 85-mile trip at one of the campgrounds near the upper end. Fairly level roads and great views.

MOUNT SHASTA, 60 MILES AWAY, LOOMS OVER THE KLAMATH RIVER.

The **O, C & E Woods Line State Trail** is 100 miles of the former Oregon, California and Eastern Railroad right-of-way. Starting in Klamath Falls, the trail extends to Bly with a spur to Sycan Marsh, through ponderosa, sagebrush, and farmland, under the gaze of Mount Shasta. Only the first 7 miles are paved, and the trail may be shared with hikers and equestrians. Camping is allowed only on designated sites.

The graveled **High Lakes Trail** runs to Fish Lake from Lake of the Woods Recreation Area, 33 miles northwest of Klamath Falls on OR 140.

Mount Bailey is a challenging 5-mile forest trail near Diamond Lake; access from OR 138, FR 4795, and FR 4795-300. And the nearby **North Crater Trail** runs 9 miles through gently rolling forest and meadow; access from FR 4799, 1 mile east of the north entrance to Crater Lake off OR 138. Both these trails are shared with hikers.

BIRD-WATCHING The **Klamath Basin Birding Trail** (1-800-445-6728; www.klamathbirdingtrails.com) takes in some of Oregon's best bets—and some of the most spectacular. Bald eagles, ducks, geese, swans, grebes, pelicans, and shorebirds flock to the lakes and marshes composing the several national wildlife refuges (see *Wildlife Refuges*), while songbirds cavort in the brush. Many good viewing points are in Klamath Falls itself, including the Link River Trail and Lake Ewauna. Then drive up to Crater Lake for woodpeckers, goshawks, and other mountain species. For maps, events, and a list of sites, call or check the Web site.

CAMPING The **Fremont-Winema National Forest** (541-947-2151) has many developed and primitive campgrounds. In the Klamath District: **Aspen Point,** at Lake of the Woods, 33 miles northwest of Klamath Falls on OR 140, then south 1 mile on FR 370 at Lake of the Woods, with 60 sites, water, toilets, ADA restrooms; few reservations. **Fourmile Lake,** below Mount McLoughlin, 35 miles northwest of Klamath Falls on OR 140 and 6 miles north on FR 3661, with 25 sites, water, and toilets; no reservations. **Malone Springs,** on Westside Road 5 miles north of OR 140, with two primitive sites, launch for canoe trail; no reservations. **Odessa,** 22 miles from Klamath Falls on OR 140, then 1 mile north on FR 3639, with five sites; no water, no reservations. **Sunset,** at Lake of the Woods, 32 miles northwest of Klamath Falls on OR 140 and 2 miles south on Dead Indian Road, with 67 sites, water, and toilets; some reservations. In the Chemult District: **Corral Springs,** 2 miles north of Chemult on US 97 and 2 miles west on FR 9774, with six rustic campsites, horse stalls, and toilets; no water, no reservations. **Digit Point,** on FR 9772, 12 miles west of Chemult from US 97, with 64 sites, toilets, water; no reservations. **Jackson Creek,** 25 miles south of Chemult on US 97, then 22 miles northeast on FR 676, with 12 sites; no water, no reservations. **Scott Creek,** 24 miles south of Chemult on US 97, then west and north on FR 66, Sun Pass Road, and FR 2310, with six rustic sites; no water, no reservations. In the Chiloquin District: **Head of the River,** from Chiloquin 5 miles east on Sprague River Road, 20 miles northeast on Williamson River Road, and 0.5 mile north on FR 4648, with five rustic sites; no water, no reservations. **Williamson River,** from Collier State Park 1 mile northeast on FR 9730, with seven sites, water, and ADA restrooms; no reservations.

In the **Umpqua National Forest** (541-498-2531), **Diamond Lake Campground** is at a full-service resort on the eastern shore of Diamond Lake, with 238 sites, water, toilets, showers, boating, and restaurant. Some reservations; open mid-May–Oct. From US 97 take OR 138 east and follow it for 22 miles. **Thielsen View Campground,** on the western shore of Diamond Lake, has 60 sites with water and toilets; no reservations; open mid-May–mid-Oct. At the south end of the lake, **Broken Arrow Campground,** with 147 sites, has water, toilets, and showers; open mid-May–Labor Day; reservations for groups only.

In **Deschutes National Forest** (541-383-5300) you'll find four campgrounds around **Crescent Lake** with a total of 145 sites, all with restrooms and some with drinking water; no reservations except at **Whitefish Horse Camp;** 26 miles northwest of Crescent via FR 61, OR 58, and FR 60. **Crescent Creek Campground,** 9 miles west of Crescent on FR61, has 10 sites, vault toilets, and pumped water; no reservations. On **Odell Lake,** 2 miles east of Willamette Pass on OR 58, there are three campgrounds: **Princess Creek,** 46 sites, toilets, no reservations; **Sunset Cove,** 20 sites, water, toilets, no reservations; and **Trapper Creek,** 32 sites, water, toilets, reservations.

At **Crater Lake National Park,** the **Mazama Village Campground** (1-888-774-2728) has 212 tent and RV sites, a few with hookups, water and restrooms, and shower for an extra charge; half the sites are reservable. **Lost Creek Campground** (541-594-3100) has 16 tent sites.

Topsy Recreation Site (541-883-6916), 20 miles southwest of Klamath Falls on OR 66, has 13 campsites beside the Klamath River and reservoir with access to fishing, boat launch, and hiking; restrooms and some sites handicapped accessible; water and toilets, but no showers.

Collier Memorial State Park (1-800-551-6949), 30 miles north of Klamath Falls on US 97, has 50 full hookup and 18 tent sites, corrals, laundry facilities, showers, and ADA restrooms; open Apr.–Oct.; no reservations.

Jackson F. Kimball State Recreation Site offers 10 primitive sites with no water; open mid-Apr.–Oct.; no reservations.

CANOEING AND KAYAKING **Upper Klamath Canoe Trail,** access from the Rocky Springs or Malone Springs launches on Westside Road, at the northwest corner of Upper Klamath Lake. The only real access to the Upper Klamath Wildlife Refuge is by this 9.5-mile marked water trail through marsh and open lake, with views of mountain and forest. It's also a great way to see some of the million or so courting waterfowl that pass through in spring—being careful, of course, not to disturb them. Boats can be rented at the Rocky Springs Resort (541-356-2287). The clear waters of the **Williamson River** flowing through **Collier Memorial State Park, Wood River** near Fort Klamath, and the canoe trail at **Klamath Marsh National Wildlife Refuge** are paddlers' heaven. **Roe Outfitters** (541-884-3825) in Klamath Falls will provide rentals and/or guided tours.

GOLF **Harbor Links Golf Course** (541-882-7430), 601 Harbor Isles Boulevard, Klamath Falls. Eighteen holes.

Round Lake Golf and RV Resort (541-884-2520), 4000 Round Lake Road, Klamath Falls. Nine holes.

Running Y Ranch Resort Golf Course (1-877-866-1266), 5500 Running Y Road, Klamath Falls. Eighteen holes.

Shield Crest Golf Course (541-884-5305), 3151 Shield Crest Drive, Klamath Falls. Eighteen holes.

HIKING In Klamath Falls: the **Link River Trail** runs along the short Link River to Upper Klamath Lake, 1.5 miles, with riparian and desert habitat. South from the park, the 1-mile, wheelchair-accessible **Lake Ewauna Interpretive Trail** follows the western shore of Lake Ewauna. Park in Veteran's Park and cross the bridge. The **O, C & E Woods Line Trail** is a 100-mile rail trail starting downtown; it's shared with bikes, and the first 7 miles are paved.

Northwest of Klamath Falls: The **Seven-Mile Creek Trail,** 49 miles north of Klamath Falls via OR 140, FR 3300, and FR 3334, travels along a marsh, past the source of the Rogue River's middle fork and several lakes, 10.5 miles round-trip. **Varney Creek Trail,** 25 miles west of Klamath Falls via OR 140 and FRs 3637 and 3664, offers a climb of 2,200 feet through evergreen forest and meadow on a round-trip of 8.5 miles. Thirty-six miles west of Klamath Falls via OR 140 and FR 3650 you can really stretch your legs on a hike up 9,495-foot **Mount McLoughlin**—a fairly rugged 11 miles round-trip.

Chemult-Chiloquin area: If you just want a historic stroll, try the **Desert Forest Journeys,** three tiny loop trails and a short forest drive taking in traces of former logging railroads and dry forest ecology. Leave US 97 for OR 138 63 miles north of Klamath Falls, then turn south on FR 70. At **Collier Memorial State Park** there is a 1.5-mile nature trail beside the Williamson River. Several trails circumambulate **Lake of the Woods,** 33 miles west of Klamath Falls off OR 140. The 11-mile paved **John Dellenback Trail** winds around Diamond Lake, at the junction of OR 138 and OR 230.

Then, of course, there's the **Pacific Crest Trail,** accessible at the foot of Mount McLoughlin, Miller Lake, Fourmile Lake, and Lake of the Woods. For more trails, see *Wilder Areas* and inquire at the various national forests.

WINTER SPORTS **Crater Lake** (see *Parks*) attracts the hardy for cross-country skiing and snowshoeing, but don't expect groomed trails or warming huts. This is more of a wilderness experience.

Willamette Pass Resort (541-345-7669; www.willamettepass.com), on OR 58 about 20 miles northwest of its junction with US 97. This low-key ski center with a drop of 1,563 feet, 29 runs, and 20 kilometers of cross-country trails is generally open Thurs.–Sun., late Nov.–early Apr., and daily during Christmas break.

✷ Wilder Places

PARKS **Crater Lake National Park** (541-594-3000; www.nps.gov/crla), 57 miles north of Klamath Falls. South and west entrance off OR 62 and north entrance off OR 138. Neither the public nor the discoverers themselves made much of the lake at the time (the Klamaths had known it, of course, and tried to steer people away). "This is the bluest lake we've ever seen," reported the three prospectors in 1853, then wandered off in the perennial search for gold. Blue it is—sunlight absorbed in its depths turns it cobalt—and looking down on it from the 7,000-foot rim tends to reorder our petty concerns rather quickly. But 249 square miles of vast, largely undisturbed forest surrounding the spectacular caldera became a national park in

CRATER LAKE

1902 (see *Natural Wonders*) through the zeal and tireless labor of William Gladstone Steel, on whom the place had cast a spell and who did much of the early surveying. It's Oregon's only national park and a jewel in the system's crown. Contemplate it from the majestic lodge or drive the 30-mile Rim Road to take in all the views. Several hiking trails will take you into the backcountry, or down to the shore where you can swim in the remarkably pure waters. Guided snowshoe walks are offered in winter. In summer you can take a boat tour around the lake or to Wizard Island, a volcanic cone rising from the depths. Two visitors centers provide orientation, and cultural and scientific information about the park. And, as at all such parks, friendly rangers give talks and tours on everything you want to know. Stay at **Crater Lake Lodge** (see *Lodges*) or at one of the cabins, tent sites, or RV sites at Mazama Village Campground (www.craterlakelodges.com). Lost Creek Campground (541-594-3100), smaller and more remote, is run by the Park Service for tents only. Several motels and bed & breakfasts outside the park are within reasonable driving distance. Restaurants are at the lodge and Mazama Village. In winter only the park's south entrance and the Steel Visitor Center are open, as the rest is blocked by snow, of which the place gets about 40 feet a year.

Collier Memorial State Park (1-800-551-6949), on US 97, 30 miles north of Klamath Falls. Besides the **Logging Museum** (see *Museums*), you can enjoy clear mountain streams, reservable picnic shelters, trails, and camping.

Jackson F. Kimball State Recreation Site (541-783-2471 or 1-800)-551-6949), 3 miles north of Fort Klamath on OR 232. This is where a spring bursts from the hillside to become the Wood River. The park encompasses its headwaters; with pine forests behind you, the meadows of Klamath Marsh before, and the nearest "city" 40 miles away, this is the place to feel the spirit of the Old West. Ten primitive campsites are there for you.

WILDERNESS AREAS **Diamond Peak Wilderness** (541-782-2283), just south of OR 58 at the Willamette Pass; access via forest roads and trails. Diamond Peak is one of the High Cascade volcanoes, with snowfields near the top and lakes around its base. Most terrain is coniferous forest traversed by several trails, notably a 38-mile segment of the Pacific Crest Trail and the Diamond Peak Trail.

Mount Thielsen Wilderness (541-498-2531), on the north side of OR 138 just across from Crater Lake National Park. Partly rolling and partly rugged, it's all high country—55,000 acres of it, with about 70 miles of trails, including a 34-mile segment of the Pacific Crest Trail.

WILDLIFE REFUGES **Mountain Lakes Wilderness,** a counterintuitively perfect square of wilderness, lies south of Rocky Point and can be accessed only by trail. The terrain varies from steep slopes to broad valleys and is thought to be the result of a volcanic cone collapse, much like Crater Lake except for the lake. For access information contact the **Fremont-Winema National Forest** (see *Guidance*).

The **Klamath Basin National Wildlife Refuges Complex** (530-667-2231; www.fws.gov/klamathlakerefuges) preserve remnants of the wetlands scattered along the boundary between mountains and desert. These marshes used to draw Pleistocene-sized flocks of geese and ducks during spring and fall migration, and still bring in flocks in their thousands although the lakes have shrunk, some considerably, since the onset of irrigation. Pelicans, cranes, and shorebirds also abound seasonally, and eagles can be seen anytime.

Klamath Marsh Refuge lies off US 97 north of Chiloquin, accessible by Silver Lake Road or Military Crossing. Its meadows and marshes are backed by majestic views of Mount Thielsen and has an auto tour route, a canoeing area, and a visitor station. **Upper Klamath Refuge,** at the northwestern edge of Upper Klamath Lake, borders OR 140 and OR 62; it's mostly marsh and open water and is best seen by canoe. **Lower Klamath Refuge** straddles the Oregon-California line and can be reached by US 97 and CR 161. Here a mix of pasture, open water, marsh, uplands, and croplands promotes a multitude of species, and you'll find a visitors center, driving tour routes, and photography blinds. **Bear Valley Refuge,** just west of US 97 and just north of the state line, by contrast, is forest, mostly old-growth ponderosa, incense cedar, white fir, and Douglas fir. It was set aside to protect a winter roost site of bald eagles, who congregate there in their hundreds. The public may not enter, but from outside the refuge observers can watch impressive numbers of eagles and other raptors fly out in early morning for the day's hunt. **Tule Lake Refuge,** where headquarters is located, and **Clear Lake Refuge** lie completely within California.

Klamath Wildlife Area (541-883-5734), 4 miles south of Klamath Falls off US 97, is run by the Oregon Department of Fish and Wildlife. Part of the Klamath Basin biome, its meadows, marshes, and open water offer shelter to nesting and migratory birds under looming Mount Shasta, 80 miles to the south. Hunting is allowed in season.

✷ Lodging

BED & BREAKFASTS

Fort Klamath

Crater Lake Bed and Breakfast (1-866-517-9560; www.craterlakebandb.com), 52395 Weed Road. This relatively new B&B in the shadow of Crater Lake has three rooms, all with private baths. $129, including taxes, with full breakfast.

Klamath Falls

Thompson's Bed and Breakfast (541-882-7938; www.thompsonsbandb.com), 1420 Wild Plum Court. This large home overlooking the lake offers four rooms with private baths, and a private entrance and common room for guests. You're also within walking distance of a park, marina, and hiking trail. $115–125, with full breakfast.

COTTAGES

Fort Klamath

Wilson Cottages (541-381-2209), P.O. Box 488, Fort Klamath 97626. Just a mile outside Crater Lake National Park, these rustic but homey cottages along Annie Creek were hand built in 1937. All are self-contained with kitchen and bathroom (though you have to ask for dinnerware) and sleep anywhere from two to seven people. $75–110, no credit cards.

HOTELS AND MOTELS

Chemult

🐾 **Feather Bed Inn** (541-365-2235; www.thefeatherbedinn.com), 108915 US 97 N. The standard motel rooms come with feather beds (don't laugh—at an altitude of 4,800 feet, even summer nights are cool). Pets stay free, even horses, though a horse stall is extra. $45–70.

Fort Klamath

🐾 **Aspen Inn Motel** (541-381-2321; www.theaspeninn.com), 52250 OR 62. Five regular motel rooms, three suites, four A-frame cabins, and two vacation houses can be your base for exploring the Upper Klamath's big skies and Crater Lake National Park. Open Apr.–Sept. Pet-friendly; rooms from $67, cabins from $125, but ask about seasonal and senior discounts.

Klamath Falls

🐾 **Golden West Motel** (541-882-1758), 6402 S. Sixth Street. It's a modest but friendly mom-and-pop motel, quiet and clean, and is a good budget option; the only downside being that the walls are a little thin. From $46.

LODGES

Crater Lake National Park

✐ **Crater Lake Lodge** (541-594-2255; www.craterlakelodges.com), Rim Village. One of the great national park lodges, this wood and stone hotel stands grandly just behind the crater rim, offering tremendous views in a historic atmosphere. From the fire-

CRATER LAKE LODGE

place in the Great Hall to the Exhibit Room off the lobby, immerse yourself in the joys and ideals behind our National Park System, then go out and enjoy the park. The dining room serves breakfast, lunch, and dinner. $151–282; children under 12 free.

RESORTS

Chiloquin

Agency Lake Resort (541-783-2489; www.agencylakeresort.net), 37000 Modoc Point Road. Just west of Chiloquin, Agency Lake and its attendant marsh empty into Upper Klamath Lake, with much of the same wildlife. At the lakefront resort you can have a cabin with partial or shared bath, park your RV, or pitch a tent. Bring your boat or rent one; the place is popular with fishermen and hunters in season. Cabins from $45, RV sites $14–20, tent sites $12–13.

Crescent

Crescent Lake Resort (541-433-2505; www.crescentlakeresort.com), P.O. Box 223, Crescent 97733. From US 97b take OR 58 west 12 miles, then turn south on FR 5814 for 1.5 miles. Cool air, mountain views, fishing, and swimming—like several resorts that grew up among the Cascade Lakes in the 1920s, this is a family place with cabins, boats, and access to miles of Forest Service hiking and mountain biking trails. Cabins $75–225.

Diamond Lake

Diamond Lake Resort (1-800-733-7593; www.diamondlake.net), 350 Resort Drive. Just north of Crater Lake is teardrop-shaped Diamond Lake, surrounded by forest under the spire of Mount Thielsen—a location destined for resorthood. The fishing lodge that went in in the 1920s gradually grew into a year-round family destination with 38 motel rooms, 42 cabins, 10 housekeeping studios, and a luxury suite. Now you can rent canoes, pedal boats, mountain bikes, or a horse and guide for a mountain ride, fish, and hike. In winter people come for snow sports. Motel rooms $79–99, cabins $189–559, studios $89–109.

Fort Klamath

Crater Lake Resort (541-381-2349; www.craterlakeresort.com), 50711 OR 62, 2 miles south of Fort Klamath. Probably your quintessential Western stay—six cabins on the banks of Fort Creek on the Upper Klamath plain, with the Cascades as backdrop. Most units have kitchens, and all have TV and VCR or DVD if you get tired of looking at the stars. There's also an RV area with full hookups and a small store. Cabins $60–100, RV sites $25.

Klamath Falls

♿ **Lake of the Woods Resort** (1-866-201-4194; www.lakeofthewoods resort.com), 950 Harriman Route. "Discovered" in 1870, the mountain lake soon drew rustic forest camps and fishing retreats. It was one of these favored fishing spots that gradually became this family, summer resort. In keeping with the aesthetic of the times, buildings were designed and sited to interfere as little as possible with the views, so the place still has a woodsy, harmonious aspect despite extensive modernization. All your resort needs are on-site, from the lodge restaurant serving three meals a day to the marina, pizza parlor, and summer vintage movie showings. The 26 cozy cabins all include bathrooms, and many come with kitchenettes and fireplaces; two are handicapped accessible. Pets allowed in some cabins. Cabins $139–325 (weekly rates available), RV sites $28–35.

Rocky Point Resort (541-356-2287; www.rockypointoregon.com), 28121 Rocky Point Road. Contrary to the postal address, Rocky Point is not in Klamath Falls but 25 miles to the northwest on the far forested shore of Upper Klamath Lake. That said, it's a rustic resort in a humdinger of a location, in a tiny community dedicated to fishing and other outdoor pursuits (the Upper Klamath Canoe Trailhead is just down the road). Campsites, cabins, and lodge rooms should cover your needs, with a restaurant to provide dinner (reservations are recommended—it's the only place around). Guest rooms $85, cabins $140–160, tent sites $22, RV sites $28–30. Open Apr.–Nov.

✷ Where to Eat

EATING OUT

Klamath Falls

Mia and Pia's Pizzeria and Brewhouse (541-884-4880; www.miapia.com), 3545 Summers Lane. Daily for lunch and dinner. Pizzerias and brewpubs seem to be a natural combination, at least in the Northwest, and this was the first in K-Falls. Get your thick- or thin-crust pizza here in 27 varieties along with a mug of their finest, produced by brewmeister and former bull rider Rod Kucera, who used some of the fittings from the building's previous incarnation as a dairy to create the brewery. Video games and TVs provide entertainment for kids and others so inclined.

Rocky Point Resort (541-356-2242), 28121 Rocky Point Road; 25 miles northwest of Klamath Falls on Upper Klamath Lake. Open for dinner only, Wed.–Sun. in summer and weekends spring and fall. Reservations required. The resort restaurant offers the most sought-after and indeed the only fare for miles around—fresh fish, of course, and the best of the West.

✷ Events

May: **International Migratory Bird Day** (541-883-7131), second weekend, Veterans Park, Klamath Falls. Bird walks, historic tours, kids' activities, live bird demonstrations, food, and music. Free.

Captain Jack Memorial Day Rodeo and Powwow (541-783-7545), Memorial Day weekend, Klamath County Fairgrounds, Klamath Falls. Leader of the Modocs in the Modoc Wars, Captain Jack was executed and buried at Fort Klamath. This powwow in his honor includes competitions, arts and crafts, and a rodeo.

August: **Klamath Blues Festival** (541-331-3939; www.klamathblues.org), last weekend, Veterans Park, Klamath Falls. Blues artists from around the region.

Klamath Tribes Restoration Celebration (1-800-524-9787), fourth weekend, Chiloquin Rodeo Grounds. In 1986 the federal government decided that they would once again recognize the Klamath tribes. This festival celebrates that recognition with a parade, a princess, drumming, races, and more.

September: **Loggers' Breakfast** (541-783-2471), second weekend, Collier State Park. Come on an empty stomach for a hearty breakfast cooked on an antique logging camp stove at this outdoor logging museum.

October: **Klamath Basin Potato Festival** (541-798-5808), second weekend, Merrill. Celebrating the humble tuber with a barbecue, games, music, a parade, and oh, yes—potatoes.

ASHLAND–MEDFORD–ROGUE VALLEY AREA

It's a little disconcerting, on driving over the crazy Siskiyous or descending from otherworldly Crater Lake, to enter Ashland with its genteel Victorian homes, fine dining, and theater hub. This is the little town that could—starting with a few claims and mills, it quickly added a cultural life not always found on the frontier, and voilà—a major arts scene cupped in a Siskiyou valley. It's a gateway, too, to the pear orchards and vineyards of the lower river valleys. It's worth some slow, lazy drives to check out farm stands, or, for more exertion, a hike to a swimming hole or a spin in a raft on the Rogue.

GUIDANCE **Ashland Chamber of Commerce** (541-482-3486; www.ashland chamber.com), 110 E. Main Street, Ashland 97520.

Central Point Chamber of Commerce Visitor Center (541-664-5301; www.centralpointchamber.org), 27 S. Seventh Street, Central Point 97502.

Jackson County Parks (541-774-8183; www.jacksoncountyparks.com), 7520 Table Rock Road, Central Point 97502.

Jacksonville Chamber of Commerce (541-899-8118; www.jacksonvilleoregon .org), 185 N. Oregon Street, Jacksonville 97530.

Medford Visitor Information Center (1-800-469-6307), 1314 Center Drive, Medford 97501.

Medford Visitors Convention Bureau (1-800-469-6307; www.visitmedford.org), 101 E. Eighth Street, Medford 97501.

Phoenix Chamber of Commerce (541-535-6956; www.phoenixoregon.net), 205 Fern Valley Road, Phoenix 97535.

Rogue River Chamber of Commerce (541-582-0242; www.rrchamber.cc), 8898 Rogue River Highway, Rogue River 97537.

Rogue River–Siskiyou National Forest (541-618-2200), 3020 Biddle Road, Medford 97504; **High Cascades Ranger District,** 47201 OR 62, Prospect 97536; **Siskiyou Mountains Ranger District,** 6941 Upper Applegate Road, Jacksonville 97530, and 645 Washington Street, Ashland 97520.

Siskiyou State Welcome Center (541-488-1805), 60 Lowe Road, Ashland 97520.

Southern Oregon Visitors Association (1-800-488-4856; www.southernoregon.org), P.O. Box 1645, Medford 97501.

GETTING THERE *By bus and rail:* **AMTRAK** and **Greyhound** have stations at 200 and 220 S. Front Street, respectively, in Medford.

By car: **I-5** is the main artery here, with interchanges to **OR 66** at Ashland, **OR 238** at Medford, and **OR 99** at Grants Pass.

GETTING AROUND *By bus:* **Rogue Valley Transportation District** (541-779-2877; www.RVTD.org), 3200 Crater Lake Avenue, Medford, links the small towns from Ashland to Medford by bus.

MEDICAL EMERGENCY **Ashland Community Hospital** (541-201-4000), 280 Maple Street, Ashland.

Providence Medford Medical Center (541-732-5000), 1111 Crater Lake Avenue, Medford.

Rogue Valley Medical Center (541-789-7000), 2825 Barnett Road, Medford.

✷ To See

COVERED BRIDGES **Antelope Creek,** at the corner of Main Street and Royal Avenue in Eagle Point. The 1922 bridge originally crossed Antelope Creek, 10 miles from here, but was moved in 1987.

Lost Creek, 4 miles south of Lake Creek; take OR 140 east to Lake Creek Loop Road, South Fork Little Butte Creek Road, and Lost Creek Road. This bridge's official date is 1919, though some local old-timers insist it was built about 1880. Which is not impossible; the builder is also known to have roofed another nearby bridge in the 1880s. So maybe the plank reading LOST CREEK BRIDGE, BUILT ABOUT 1881 is right. In any case, it's in its original location and is the shortest covered bridge in Oregon, 39 feet long. A small park beside the bridge honors early pioneer John Walch with gardens, a bandstand, and a 1900s outhouse.

McKee Bridge, 8.5 miles south of Ruch on Applegate Road. This substantial bridge over the Applegate River served as a rest stop for mining traffic between Jacksonville and the Blue Ledge mine in California. It was named for the landowner who donated the land on which the bridge is supported.

Wimer Bridge, Covered Bridge Road, Wimer. This is actually a new bridge, built in 2008 to replace a 1927 bridge that disintegrated in 2003. It's thought a bridge might have stood on this site in 1892.

FARMERS' MARKETS The **Rogue Valley Growers and Crafters Market** is held Tues. 8:30–1:30 at the Ashland National Guard Armory; Thurs. 8:30–1:30, mid-Mar.–mid-Nov. at the Medford National Guard Armory; and Sat. 9–1, May–Oct. at Lithia Way and First Street in Ashland.

Talent Evening Market, 110 E. Main Street, Talent. Fri. 5:30–8:30, mid-June–mid-Sept.

FARMS AND FARM STANDS **Fox Run Farm** (541-608-7886), 3842 W. Main Street, Medford. Daily 10–6, mid-May–Nov. Sells berries, asparagus, fruit, cider, and other goodies.

Hillcrest Orchard (541-608-3898; www.hillcrestorchard.com), 3285 Hillcrest Road, Medford. Reginald Parsons bought the orchard in 1908, when the pear industry was taking off in the Rogue Valley, and his family has owned and run it ever since. Like some other valley orchards, though, it's been partly converted to wine grapes; you can buy pears in season and taste their Bordeaux varietals anytime.

Southern Oregon Sales (541-772-6244; www.sosales.com), 18 Stewart Avenue, Medford. Open year-round with seasonal produce, meats, microbrews, and more.

Valley View Orchard (541-488-2840), 1800 N. Valley View Road, Ashland. Organic cherries, apples, nectarines, peaches, apricots, and pears; pick them yourself or buy ready-picked.

FOR FAMILIES ✐ **Crater Rock Museum** (541-664-6081; www.craterrock.com), 2002 Scenic Avenue, Central Point. Tues.–Sat. 10–4. General admission $4, seniors, students, and children $2. Petrified wood, fluorescent rocks, dinosaur eggs, and plenty of Oregon's state stone, the thunderegg—there's everything here to tempt your inner rock hound, plus one of the famous pairs of prehistoric sandals, this one dated at more than twelve thousand years old.

✐ ♿ **Dogs for the Deaf** (541-826-9220; www.dogsforthedeaf.org), 10175 Wheeler Road, Central Point. Free. The world's oldest Hearing Dog training center is right here in Central Point. Amazingly, these are not dogs with fancy pedigrees or backgrounds, but animals rescued from shelters all along the West Coast. Here they are trained to aid not only the deaf, but autistic children and others in need of, in their words, a "helping paw." Learn the history of the place and see how the dogs are trained; four tours a day are offered in summer and two in winter, weekdays only.

✐ **Oregon Vortex House of Mystery** (541-855-1543; www.oregonvortex.com), 4303 Sardine Creek L Fork Road, Gold Hill. Daily 9–5, June–Aug. and daily 9–4 Mar.–May and Sept.–Oct. General admission $9, seniors $8, kids 6–11 $7, under five free. Balls rolling uphill, people shrinking as they move toward you, vertigo—is there some strange force at work here, or is it optical illusion? The main building is a 1904 assay office that long ago slid from its foundation, accounting perhaps for some of the off-kilter feeling. Whatever the case, this is a classic American roadside attraction that's been reeling in visitors since the 1930s.

✐ **ScienceWorks Hands-On Museum** (541-482-6767; www.scienceworksmuseum.org), 1500 E. Main Street, Ashland. Wed.–Sat. 10–4, Sun. noon–4. General admission $7.50, seniors and children 2–12 $5. Like its cousin OMSI in Portland, ScienceWorks gets kids of all ages involved in the wonders of natural phenomena and technology. Propel a train by pedaling a bike, draw in 3-D, or get inside a bubble—hands-on (or feet-on) exhibits concretize principles of energy production, flight, anatomy, and perception—then catch one of the events for adults. Ever wonder about the physiology of climbing Mount Everest, or the science of wine?

GARDENS **Beekman House Garden,** 106 N. Central Avenue, Jacksonville. Behind the 1876 home of the self-made C. C. Beekman is a pleasant 19th-century-style kitchen garden whose paths lead into the Jacksonville walking trail system.

Britt Gardens (1-800-882-7488; www.brittfest.com), downtown Jacksonville. Peter Britt's house burned down after a hundred years, but the Swiss immigrant was an avid gardener, and his gardens are still lovingly tended. Four and a half acres of native and introduced trees and flowering plants flow down a gentle slope, whose upper reaches host thousands of music fans at the summer-long **Britt Festival** (see *Events*). The giant sequoia, planted at the birth of Peter's son Emil in 1862, is a Heritage Tree.

Lithia Park, in the center of Ashland, winds along Ashland Creek, enfolding a Japanese garden and a formal rose garden within its 93 acres.

North Mountain Park Nature Center (541-488-6606; www.northmountainpark.org), 620 N. Mountain Avenue, Ashland. Behind the nature center are several lovely gardens to browse: gardens for butterflies, birds, herbs medicinal and culinary, native plants, and heirloom plants, germinating inspiration for your own gardens. Farther back are nature trails, a restored wetland, and a replica Shasta Indian dwelling.

Siskiyou Rare Plant Nursery (541-535-7103; www.siskiyourareplantnursery.com), 2115 Talent Avenue, Talent. Thurs.–Sun. 9–4. This little nursery specializes in alpine plants, especially those of the Northwest. Visitors are welcome to stroll the rock and scree gardens.

HERITAGE TREES **Britt Sequoia,** Britt Gardens, Jacksonville. A mere stripling as sequoias go, this one was planted by Peter Britt when his son Emil was born in Mar. 1862.

Lonesome Hickory, a mile south of Shady Cove just east of OR 62. The only shagbark hickory in the area, and possibly in Oregon, this one grew from a nut brought over the Oregon Trail by Mary Louisa Black in 1866.

THE GARDENS AT NORTH MOUNTAIN PARK NATURE CENTER, ASHLAND

HISTORIC HOMES **Beekman House,** California and Laurelwood streets, Jacksonville. Sat.–Sun. 11–4, Memorial Day–Labor Day. General admission $5, children and seniors $3. Living history takes place here as volunteers play the roles of the prominent Beekman family. C. C. Beekman, banker, Wells Fargo agent, and gold freighter, built this comfortable home in 1876, and it's been kept pretty much as the family left it in the 1920s, with its furniture, kitchenware, photos, and decorations. You might even speak to Mr. Beekman himself.

HISTORIC SITES OR 66 from Klamath Falls to Ashland follows, approximately, the **Applegate Trail**'s route across the Siskiyous (after which it turned north as far as Dallas and is more or less buried under I-5). The Applegate family had lost two children to the treacherous Columbia River on their 1843 Oregon Trail odyssey. They weren't the only ones; that last segment was among the riskiest of the trail. Brothers Jesse and Lindsey, therefore, sought a route to the Willamette Valley that would avoid the river. The trail they blazed in 1846 left the main thoroughfare at Fort Hall, Idaho, turning south into Nevada to follow the Humboldt River and the California Trail, trending northwest toward Oregon, looping south again into California to go around Lower Klamath Lake, and over the Siskiyous to approach the Promised Land from the south. Though it avoided the river transit, it was extremely rugged, had far less forage for the livestock than the original trail, and less water. Emigrants died just as readily of typhus and the other trail hazards. Some pioneers said the Applegates had actually made the journey harder. (The trail seems to have had another, seldom-mentioned purpose: to provide settlers an escape route in case Britain and the United States came to blows over the Oregon Country. If so, it seems a circuitous one.) Nonetheless, emigrants continued to use it, possibly into the 1870s, and it has been designated a National Historic Trail.

Buncom (www.buncom.org), 6 miles southeast of Ruch via Upper Applegate and Little Applegate roads. First a gold camp, then a stage stop and market town for farmers along the Little Applegate, Buncom gave up the ghost when cars made it obsolete. Abandoned by the 1920s, its post office, cookhouse, and bunkhouse are

THE 1876 BEEKMAN HOUSE IN JACKSONVILLE

all that remain amid the trees and meadows of the former town site, preserved by the Buncom Historical Society.

PRESBYTERIAN CHURCH, JACKSONVILLE

Butte Creek Mill (541-826-3531), 402 Royal Avenue N., Eagle Point. This 1872 water-powered gristmill produces stone-ground flours plus waffle, pancake, and muffin mixes; not run-of-the-mill. Next door, the Eagle Point Historical Museum tells the history of the town.

All of **Jacksonville** is a National Historic District. When gold was struck at Daisy Creek here in 1851, gold diggers predictably flocked to the Rogue Valley, and by late 1852 a complete and typically rowdy mining town had sprung up. As the only economically lively town in the area, it became the county seat and business hub till the 1880s, when the gold had played out and the railroad bypassed the town in favor of Medford. Today agriculture dominates the valley, and Jacksonville is a quiet town of 2,700 with a startling concentration of homes, churches, and commercial building dating from the 1850s to the 1920s. A walking tour brochure, available from the visitors center at 185 N. Oregon Street, will take you to one hundred sites, including the spot where gold was first struck. Among them are the **Beekman House** (see *Historic Homes*). The **Beekman Bank,** corner of California and Third streets, was probably the most important place in this gold rush town next to the assay office, and this was the first one in Oregon. Mr. C. C. Beekman opened it in 1863—one of his hats was that of a Wells Fargo agent—and today it holds a walk-through exhibit of period bank artifacts. Daily 1–5 in summer; free. The **United States Hotel** (1880), at California and Third streets, hosted President Rutherford B. Hayes soon after it opened and contains some exhibits. The 1855 **J. W. McCully Building,** at the corner of Fifth Street and S. Oregon, opened as a general store and housed a synagogue upstairs, till it was sold to the Odd Fellows in 1860.

UNITED STATES HOTEL, JACKSONVILLE

Living-history activities take place at several locations in the summer. The actors remain strictly in character. In summer you can see it all by trolley or Segway; call 541-899-5269 for schedules.

Tub Springs, OR 66, 18 miles east of Ashland (see *Parks*). From 1846 to the 1930s thirsty travelers stopped here for a rest and a drink, and you can, too.

MUSEUMS **Ashland Historic Railroad Museum** (541-261-6605; www.ashlandrrmuseum.org), 258 A Street (upstairs), Ashland. The railway came to Ashland in 1888, and 120 years later the museum opened. Sadly, the town's rail connection had by then become history, having been rerouted through Klamath Falls. But it fueled Ashland's growth for decades and is commemorated here with artifacts and photographs. Call for hours.

✐ **Hanley Farm** (541-899-8123), 1053 Hanley Road (OR 238), between Jacksonville and Central Point. First Sat. of the month 11–4, June–Sept. General admission $5, children and seniors $3. This 1850s farmhouse and its outbuildings demonstrate 19th-century farm life in the Rogue Valley.

Jacksonville Museum of Southern Oregon History (541-899-8123), Fifth and C streets, Jacksonville. Wed.–Sun. 11–4. General admission $5, children and seniors $3. Since Jacksonville had the gold rush, it was obviously destined to be the county seat, and this imposing building was its courthouse. Today it's a repository of local history, including, of course, gold rush artifacts, but also a collection of Peter Britt's photographs (he of the gardens and music festival) and basketry of the Takelma, a tribe that has sadly disappeared. With the same admission ticket you can visit the **Children's Museum,** right there on the same grounds (if your kids are restive, remind them that this used to be the county jail). Here you can get your hands on history in a 1920s kitchen, set up camp along the Oregon Trail, work in the general store, and try on old-time clothes.

Trail Creek Museum (541-621-4462), 144 Old Highway 62, Trail. Wed.–Sun. 11:30–4:30, Apr.–Oct. and Sat.–Sun. 11:30–3:30, Nov.–Mar. Free. It was formerly a tavern, and it looks the part. Now it displays photos, stories, and memorabilia of life as it was along the Upper Rogue River not so long ago.

NATURAL WONDERS **Siskiyou Mountains.** A subrange of the Klamaths, these mountains straddling the Oregon-California border are accretions of twisted, deformed seafloor, pushed up by the scraping together of tectonic plates. Some of the formations are highly unusual peridotite and serpentinite that break down into soils unfriendly to most plants, being high in heavy metals and low in calcium—so some have evolved to adapt to the harsh soils, like the Darlingtonia or California pitcher plant, which eats bugs, and ceanothus, which fixes nitrogen from the air. Botanists gravitate to the high plant diversity here, and so do butterflies—there's even a scenic botanical drive (see "Illinois Valley Area"). Strangely, the Oregon Siskiyous trend east–west while the nearby Cascades and Coast Ranges trend north–south; and even more strangely, the range is crossed by the Klamath River that flows from Upper Klamath Lake at an altitude of 4,105 feet and snakes among the valleys to finds the path of least resistance, reaching the Pacific 263 miles later. These mountains are altogether less straightforward than their neighbors: their thick forests and deeply dissected contours have kept many of their corners remote, leaving room to roam for large mammals like elk, bear, cougar, and maybe even Sasquatch.

Table Rocks, north of Central Point; leave I-5 at exit 33 and drive 1 mile to Table Rock Road, 7.6 miles to Wheeler Road, and another mile to park at the trailhead. Towering 800 feet above the Rogue River Valley, these mesas are actually lava flows that filled the primordial river valley 7 million years ago. The river kept running, though, and eventually cut its way through the andesite flow, so that by now 90 percent of the lava has gone to sea, leaving only these formations. They are now a protected area administered by the Nature Conservancy and the Bureau of Land Management. A 2-mile trail leads to the plateau, where you'll find an isolated ecosystem of oak savanna, chaparral, and prairie, and fantastic spring wildflower displays.

SCENIC DRIVES The **Applegate Trail** (see *Historic Sites*) crosses the Siskiyous between Klamath Falls and Ashland along 64-mile-long OR 66. A leisurely drive will allow you to enjoy mountain views and fir and cedar forest while negotiating hairpin bends. Rest by one of the lakes or eat lunch at **Green Springs Inn** (see *Inns and Lodges*), and stop at **Tub Springs** (see *Parks*) to see where pioneer, stage, and auto travelers stopped to refresh themselves. Do not attempt this drive in winter.

The 40-mile stretch of OR 238 from Medford to US 199 south of Grants Pass winds through the **Applegate Valley,** as pretty a stretch of scenery as you're likely to find in Oregon or anywhere. It parallels the rushing Applegate River between steep hills and century-old farms, pear orchards, wineries, and farms. Stop in historic **Jacksonville** for living gold-rush history or for a riverside lunch or dinner at the **Applegate River Lodge** (see *Dining Out*), or really anywhere just to admire the view. The 1917 **McKee Covered Bridge** (see *Covered Bridges*) crosses the river about 8 miles south of Ruch.

Rogue-Umpqua Scenic Byway, 172 miles. You can't get much more scenic than this—farmlands giving way to forest, wild rivers, waterfalls, and sapphire Diamond Lake, then the same in reverse as the loop descends once more to the lowlands. Leave I-5 for OR 234 at Gold Hill; it soon becomes OR 62, then OR 230, and finally OR 138 as it heads to its terminus at Roseburg. Summer allows a side trip to Crater Lake.

The **Siskiyou Loop** is 85 miles running from Ashland, Medford, and Jacksonville through Applegate farmland and up over the rugged Siskiyou Crest. The surface varies from interstate to graveled forest roads, so allow time. Do not attempt in winter.

The **South Cascades Loop** starts by taking OR 140 east from Medford and climbing to several mountain lakes before descending to OR 62 along the western shore of Upper Klamath Lake, then turning west to Ashland on OR 66. This 140-mile route can take all day or more, as you have options for canoeing, fishing, or camping.

WALKING TOURS A walking tour of downtown **Medford,** including a 1911 Carnegie library and turn-of-the-20th-century commercial buildings, can be picked up at the visitors center, 1314 Center Drive, or the Southern Oregon Historical Society at Sixth and Central. See also **Jacksonville** under *Historic Sites.*

WINE The Rogue River and Applegate valleys have become Oregon's latest up-and-coming wine-growing areas due to their mild, sunny climate and varied exposures. The same characteristics built the area's still-vital pear industry a century ago, but some orchard acreage is slowly going under vines. Places to taste the vintages are:

Del Rio Vineyards Tasting Room (541-855-2062; www.delriovineyards.com), 52 N. River Road, Gold Hill. Open daily. The **Fiasco Winery** at **Jacksonville**

Vineyards (541-899-6923; www.jacksonvillevineyards.com) is open Thurs.–Mon. 11–5. **Eden Valley Orchards** (541-512-2955; www.edenvalleyorchards.com), 2310 Voorhees Road, Medford, catalyzed the Medford-area pear industry back in the 1880s and remained a major producer for decades. That, and the stately home built by founder Joseph Stewart, have put the property on the National Register of Historic Places. In the waning years of the 20th century its acres were converted to wine grapes, especially tempranillo and granache. Open daily. You can, of course, leave the driving to others, such as **Rogue Valley Wine Tours** (541-482-6737), Four Beach Avenue, Ashland; **Ashland Wine Tours** (541-552-9463), 35 S. Second Street, Ashland; or **Jules of the Valley** (1-877-215-7676), P.O. Box 464, Grants Pass 97528.

✷ To Do

BICYCLING The new, 21-mile **Bear Creek Greenway** (www.bearcreekgreenway.com) connects Ashland to Central Point via Phoenix, Talent, and Medford; it starts at Oak Street in Ashland.

The **Ashland Watershed Loop** is for experienced cyclists: a grueling 25-mile ride, mostly on dirt road but with some single-track, and a 3,000-foot elevation gain, starting from Lithia Park in the center of Ashland.

The **Lost Creek Lake Loop** starts at Casey State Park near Shady Cove, north of Medford on OR 62, and is 26 miles of mostly single-track with some steep climbs; shared with horses.

Rent your wheels at **Siskiyou Cyclery** (541-482-1997; www.siskiyoucyclery.com), 1729 Siskiyou Boulevard, Ashland, or **Bear Creek Bicycle** (541-488-4270), 1988 US 99 North, Ashland. And ask them for more trail information, or consult the **Ranger District** at 645 Washington Street, Ashland.

BIRD-WATCHING Southern Oregon's dissected topography, orchards, and coniferous and deciduous forests make almost all of it a lively songbird zone. A few likely spots are **Britt Gardens,** in Jacksonville, and its adjacent trail system; around the bridge at the **Applegate Restaurant and Inn,** Applegate; **Lithia Park,** in Ashland; and **North Mountain Park,** in Ashland.

CAMPING ♿ **Emigrant Lake** (541-774-8183), 6 miles southeast of Ashland on OR 66, with 42 tent sites and 32 RV sites in a full-service county park with 12 miles of lakeshore and ADA facilities. Reservations for RV sites only. Open Apr. 15–Oct. 15.

♿ 🐾 **Howard Prairie Lake Recreational Area** (541-482-1979), 22 miles east of Ashland; from OR 66 take Dead Indian Memorial Road 17 miles to Hyatt Prairie Road and turn right. Has 167 tent sites and 183 RV hookups amid tall trees along the lake, plus fully equipped trailers for rent; some ADA facilities. Managed in conjunction with Howard Prairie Resort, which offers a marina, boat rentals, and restaurant. Open mid-Apr.–Oct.; no reservations. Controlled pets allowed.

♿ **Cantrall-Buckley Park** (541-774-8183), off OR 238 just south of Ruch, with 50 campsites above the Applegate River. Handicapped-accessible restroom and shower. Campground open mid-Apr.–mid-Oct.; no reservations.

Fish Lake Resort (541-949-8500; www.fishlakeresort.net), P.O. Box 990, Eagle Point 97524. From Medford take OR 62 and OR 140 and turn right at sign for Fish Lake; 30 miles. Has 46 RV sites, 11 cabins, wooded tent sites, shower, café, laundry, and boat rentals.

Joseph H. Stewart State Recreation Area (1-800-452-5687), about 35 miles northeast of Medford on OR 62, has 151 electrical hookup sites and 50 tent sites with water, restrooms, showers, trail access, and reservoir beachfront. Open Mar.–Oct.; some reservations.

♿ **Rogue Elk Park** (541-774-8183), 27301 OR 62, Trail. Fifteen hookup sites along the Rogue with showers, ADA-accessible campsites, and parking.

🐾 **Willow Lake** (541-560-3900; www.roguerec.com), 37 miles northeast of Medford via OR 62, OR 140, and side roads. Has 29 tent sites, 37 hookup sites, 4 cabins sleeping six, showers, and toilets. Swimming and hiking available at the foot of Mount McLoughlin. Open Apr.–Oct.; reservations accepted.

♿ **Valley of the Rogue State Park** (1-800-452-5687), 12 miles east of Grants Pass off I-5. This tends to be a populous park, especially in summer, but it does have over a mile of riverfront and 6 yurts, 21 tent sites, 59 partial and 88 full hookup sites, plus picnic areas, interpretive programs, and a rustic meeting hall. Open all year; call to reserve.

Rogue River–Siskiyou National Forest campgrounds (541-618-2200): **Doe Point,** 30 sites on Fish Lake, toilets; **Fish Lake,** 19 sites, toilets; **Fourbit Ford,** seven sites, toilets; **Whiskey Springs,** 34 sites, toilets; **Hamaker,** 10 sites, toilets; **Union Creek,** junction of OR 62 and OR 230, 78 sites, toilets; **Farewell Bend,** 61 sites, toilets. **North Fork,** 30 miles east of Ashland by Dead Indian Memorial Road and FR 37, has six tent and three trailer sites, water, and toilet; open May–mid-Nov. Around Applegate Lake, **Hart-Tish,** 16 miles south of Ruch on Upper Applegate Road, has seven RV and five walk-in tent sites, water, and toilets; closed fall and winter. **Watkins,** 18 miles south of Ruch on Upper Applegate Road, has 14 tent sites, toilets, ADA facilites; no water. **Carberry,** 19 miles south of Ruch via County Roads 859 and 777, has 10 tent sites, toilets; no water. **Jackson,** 7 miles south of Ruch on Upper Applegate Road, has four tent sites and eight car sites (trailers not recommended), toilets, and water.

CANOEING, KAYAKING, AND RAFTING The **Rogue River** was one of the original streams protected under the Wild and Scenic Rivers Act, and it is both of those. Its steep canyons and rapids attract enthusiasts from around the world, to the extent that a permit is now required to float the river in season. Equally attractive are the **Umpqua** and **Klamath rivers,** also Wild and Scenic for part of their lengths. Tackling any one of these requires advanced skills. You can find rentals, guides, and organized trips through outfitters like **Noah's River Adventure** (1-800-858-2811; www.noahsrafting.com), 53 N. Main Street, Ashland; **Rogue Klamath River Adventures** (541-779-3708; www.rogueklamath.com), 13430 OR 234, Gold Hill; **Raft the Rogue** (1-800-797-7238; www.rafttherogue.com), 21171 OR 62, Shady Cove; or **Momentum River Expeditions** (541-488-2525; www.momentumriverexpeditions.com), 3195 E. Main Street, Ashland. Half-day trips tend to run $70–80, full days from $139.

For calmer paddling, try **Squaw Lakes,** 6 miles from Applegate Lake on FR 1075. **Agate Lake,** 14 miles northeast of Medford on OR 140, is quiet, with motorboats restricted to electric motors.

GOLF **Bear Creek Golf Course** (541-773-1822), 2355 S. Pacific Highway, Medford. Nine holes.

Cedar Links Golf Club (541-773-4373), 3155 Cedar Links Drive, Medford. Nine holes.

Oak Knoll Golf Course (541-482-4311), 3070 OR 66, Ashland. Nine holes.

Centennial Golf Club (541-773-4653), 1900 N. Phoenix Road, Medford. Eighteen holes.

Eagle Point Golf Course (541-826-8225), 100 Eagle Point Drive, Eagle Point. Eighteen holes.

Quail Point Golf Course (541-857-7000), 200 Mira Mar, Medford. Nine holes.

HIKING Paths wind along Lithia Creek in 93-acre **Lithia Park,** right in the middle of Ashland. Stroll the woodlands or formal gardens before dinner and a play.

Jacksonville's Woodland Trail System meanders through the wooded hills surrounding the historic district. Eight miles of looping paths, accessible from **Britt Gardens** or the gardens behind the **Beekman House,** allow you to choose easy or strenuous walks amid leafy trees and, in spring, abundant wildflowers including Gentner's fritillary, the town's official flower.

Two trails, 1.25 and 1.75 miles one-way, rise to the top of **Upper** and **Lower Table rocks** respectively (see *Natural Wonders*). Once there, you can wander the unique mounded prairie and vernal pools that support a multitude of wildflowers, including the endemic dwarf woolly meadowfoam. There is no drinking water.

The **Pacific Crest Trail** crosses OR 66 within the **Cascade-Siskiyou National Monument** (see *Parks*). A hike up **Grizzly Peak** is about 5 miles round-trip with expansive views; from OR 66 out of Ashland take Dead Indian Highway 7 miles to Shale City Road, turn left, and continue for 3 miles, turning left on road 38-2E-9.2, for a total of about 12 miles.

The **Rogue River–Siskiyou National Forest** (541-618-2200) offers a plethora of trails; for example: the **High Lakes Trail,** a 19-mile trek over the Cascade Crest from **Fish Lake** to **Lake of the Woods**—do part or all! Four trailheads allow short or long hikes. Mostly graveled, the path is shared with cyclists and, for one segment, equestrians. Carry water. If you prefer a more leisurely walk, try the creekside **Beaver Trail,** 4 round-trip miles among firs, pines, and Pacific yew, where you may, in fact, spot a beaver. Access from Beaver Dam Campground on FR 37, 23 miles east of Ashland off Dead Indian Road. An easy 3.5-mile takes you to the impressive Rogue River Gorge, where the river churns through a narrow basalt channel. Park at the Natural Bridge viewpoint off OR 62, just south of the **Union Creek Resort** (see *Ranches and Resorts*).

HORSEBACK RIDING **Howlin' Acres Trail Rides** (541-326-9046; www.howlinacrestrailrides.com), 16061 OR 66, Greensprings (21 miles east of Ashland). Joe and Tia Johnson board and train horses on their ranch, an inholding inside Cascade-Siskiyou National Monument. They'll also take you out on the trail, meaning you get an insider's view of the Siskiyou Mountains's wide-open spaces. Ride an hour or a day; first hour $40.

WINTER SPORTS **Mount Ashland Ski Resort** (541-482-2897; www.mtashland.com), 8 miles west of Ashland; take exit 6 from I-5 and follow the signs. Fri.–Sun. Nov. and Apr. and Wed.–Mon. Dec.–Mar., but daily during holiday season. At 7,500 feet, it's not Oregon's most spectacular mountain, but it's a nice cone with about 300 inches of snow annually and is the highest peak in the Siskiyous. Four chairlifts, 23 trails, and a bowl accommodate all levels of skiers on some challenging terrain; plus, lift tickets are a lot more reasonable than at the big-name areas. Open to mountain bikers in summer.

✷ Wilder Places

PARKS **Cascade-Siskiyou National Monument** (541-618-2245), trailhead access along OR 66, 15–20 miles east of Ashland. Signed into existence in 2000, this 53,000-acre national monument was the first to be set aside specifically to protect biodiversity. Two great mountain ranges intersect here: the Cascades, a young and generally orderly north–south row of high volcanic peaks, and the Siskiyous, a much older hodgepodge of rock cast up from the ocean bed and twisted into steep slopes with unusual mineral formations. The geological crossroads has given rise to an astonishing number of plant and butterfly species within a limited area, including endemics and rarities. Day hikers, cyclists, and backpackers can enjoy old-growth forest, wildflower meadows, and streams along the Pacific Crest Trail, open to hikers and horses; cross-country skiing is popular in winter. It's rugged, but with an elevation generally below 7,000 feet, the snow tends to be out by May, making it a jewel for anyone who loves views, botany, clear streams, and untrammeled nature. An information kiosk next to Green Spring Inn contains maps and brochures.

♿ **Cantrall-Buckley Park** (541-774-8183), off OR 238 just south of Ruch. Camp along the Applegate River or just picnic and relax. Nearly 2 miles of riverfront and 88 acres of shaded lawns and woods in the lovely Applegate Valley make it a low-cost base for exploring the area or for just relaxing. Handicapped-accessible bathrooms and showers are available.

🖍 ♿ **Emigrant Lake Recreation Area** (541-774-8183), 5505 OR 66, 6 miles east of Ashland. A busy park with a water slide, fishing, swimming, and camping, this is a handy play area in easy reach of Ashland. And there are ADA facilities throughout. Day use $4.

🖍 **Lithia Park,** in the middle of Ashland, began as 8 acres designated in 1892. By that time the town was nearly three thousand strong and a need for cultured entertainment was felt, so they built a hall for Chautauqua presentations, which, in the course of time, gave rise to the Oregon Shakespeare Festival. More property was acquired, and John McLaren, who designed Golden Gate Park in San Francisco, was brought in to create a worthy park. Which he did. Ninety-three acres flank Ashland Creek. Paths wind through woodlands, lawns invite repose, playgrounds invite children, and formal gardens (rose and Japanese) delight the eye. And at the fountain on the entrance plaza you can drink what was supposed to make Ashland famous (but I don't advise it)—lithium-rich springwater. Tastes like rotten eggs.

Casey State Recreation Site (1-800-551-6949), 29 miles northeast of Medford on OR 62. This is a small riverside park for picnicking or trout fishing, with shaded lawns. No fee.

Prospect State Scenic Viewpoint (1-800-551-6949), OR 62, 1 mile south of Prospect. Trails lead to three waterfalls on the wild Rogue River. No fee.

TouVelle State Park (541-582-1118), 9 miles north of Medford on OR 62. Where the Rogue River flows below the huge plateau of **Table Rocks** (see *Natural Wonders*), you can picnic, swim, fish, or hike. Salmon and steelhead use the river, and the park is next to **Denman Wildlife Refuge** (see *Wildlife Areas*), allowing for lots of migratory flyovers. A large picnic shelter with kitchen is available by reservation.

Tub Springs State Wayside (1-800-551-6949), on OR 66, 18 miles east of Ashland. Route 66 follows the Applegate Trail, blazed by Jesse Applegate for Oregon Trail emigrants in 1846 as an alternative to the terrifying descent of the Columbia River (the Applegate was no picnic either). In the 1930s, after the road came in, travelers still stopped to use the springs, and tubs were installed for their convenience; these have been restored and still work! No fee.

♿ **Valley of the Rogue State Park** (1-800-452-5687), off I-5, 12 miles east of Grants Pass. This park sprawls along 3 miles of the Rogue River, with picnic grounds, nature programs, a large campground, reservable meeting and day-use areas, and ADA restrooms. Open year-round.

♿ **Upper Rogue Regional Park** is an 8-acre day use park on the Rogue River just north of Shady Cove, with a boat ramp, picnic tables, restrooms, and a wheelchair-accessible fishing platform.

WILDERNESS AREAS **Rogue-Umpqua Divide Wilderness** (541-825-3201), 10 miles west of Crater Lake National Park. As the name implies, the wilderness is on the divide between the Rogue and Umpqua River watersheds and is densely forested at the lower elevations, while higher up you'll find alpine meadows with an abundance of wildflowers. A hundred miles of trails crisscross the terrain.

Sky Lakes Wilderness (541-947-2151) is a long, narrow tract of more than 100,000 acres stretching south from Crater Lake to Mount McLoughlin near OR 140. With more than two hundred lakes and forested ridges, it is popular for camping and hiking.

WILDLIFE AREAS **Agate Desert Preserve** (541-770-7933), 8 miles north of Medford on Antelope Road, just off Table Rock Road. The Nature Conservancy happily acquired this 53-acre site to protect and restore a bit of remaining native prairie. The gravelly river plain supports grasses and endemic wildflowers, while its seasonal wetlands attract migratory birds. Open to the public, but there are no signs or trails.

Ken Denman Wildlife Area (541-826-8774), 1495 E. Gregory Road, Central Point. Both waterfowl and upland birds gravitate to this state-managed area. A self-guided interpretive trail allows wildlife viewing. Hunting and fishing are permitted in season.

✷ Lodging

BED & BREAKFASTS

Ashland

♿ **Albion Inn** (1-888-246-8310; www.albion-inn.com), 34 Union Street. In a city of gardens, the Albion is distinguished for its rose and meditation gardens around a perfumed courtyard. Five rooms focus on light and comfort, all with private baths and views either of the Siskiyous or the flowered patio, and one has wheelchair access. $124–164, with full breakfast.

A Midsummer's Dream (1-877-376-8800; www.amidsummer.com), 496 Beach Street. This is the higher end of the spectrum, but all rooms are very elegantly furnished suites with marble or granite fireplaces in a tall Victorian a mile from downtown. $190–230 in summer; check for off-season rates.

Anne Hathaway's Cottage (541-488-1050), 586 E. Main Street. As a former boardinghouse, the "cottage" has plenty of rooms—seven at last count, with more amenities than its original lodgers dreamt of in their philosophies, not to mention fine antique furniture and a library. On the next block, seven suites offer even more space with decks, garden, and kitchenettes. $110–210, with breakfast and afternoon tea (continental breakfast in suites).

Barking Raven Inn (1-888-870-2688; www.barkingraveninn.com), 900 Iowa Street. Not one of Ashland's stately homes, but a regular person's 1937 Cape Cod—a college professor's, to be exact, respectably and comfortably furnished. Two upstairs rooms $120–170, with full breakfast.

Blue Moon Bed and Breakfast (1-800-460-5453; www.bluemoonbandb.com), 312 Helman Street. It's blue all right—you can't miss it. A farmhouse in the 1890s, the place is now just a few blocks from downtown with five pleasant, clean-lined rooms and a "cottage" (attached apartment) for your Ashland stay. A front porch and garden deck invite you to enjoy the sunny weather, which in summer is most of the time. Rooms sleeping two or three, $100–180; cottage sleeping four, $150–225; with full breakfast. Pets allowed in the cottage with advance approval.

Chanticleer Inn (1-800-898-1950; www.ashlandbnb.com), 120 Gresham Street. Chanticleer has been hosting theatergoers for nearly 30 years now, so it must be doing something right. Six quietly luxurious rooms in a renovated 1920 Craftsman house either have Cascade views or open onto a rock garden. All, of course, have their own bathrooms, TV, DVD, and Wi-Fi, plus little extras like bathrobes and the *New York Times.* $135–199, with full breakfast. Children 10 and over are welcome. Pets in some rooms by prior approval.

Coolidge House Bed and Breakfast (1-800-655-5522; www.coolidgehouse.com), 137 N. Main Street. Dating from 1875, this is one of Ashland's oldest houses, and its "Italianate-Victorian" style indicates that Mr. Coolidge was a man of substance. In fact, he was a nurseryman, supplying the Rogue Valley's burgeoning fruit and nut operations. Five rooms and suites offer quiet, floral comfort. A separate cottage has its own kitchenette and patio. Rooms and suites $95–195, cottage $130–185.

Cowslip's Belle Bed and Breakfast (1-800-888-6819; www.cowslip.com), 159 N. Main Street. Open Mar.–mid-Oct. It's a good thing Shakespeare was so prolific; otherwise the Ashland hostelries would run out of names. In this case the rooms are named for Shakespearean flowers, which is only fitting. Cowslip's Belle is one of the town's cohort of Craftsman homes with comforts old-fashioned and modern (think afternoon sherry, a Japanese-style garden, plush furniture, and high-speed Internet, and of course private bathrooms). Two suites in the carriage house run $150–175. Rooms in the big house sleep up to three for $145-185, and studio suites with fireplace, kitchen, and sitting area go for $215–245.

Hersey House (1-888-3-HERSEY; www.herseyhouse.com), 451 N. Main Street. The large 1904 house was inhabited by five generations of the Hersey family and became a bed & breakfast in 1984. Elegant gardens and an equally elegant interior make it a place to relax before seeing a show. The four rooms are Shakespeare themed (of course "Romeo and Juliet" has a balcony), while the Olde Globe Cottage, refurbished in 2005, is self-contained with two bedrooms and full kitchen. Rooms $99–169, with full breakfast; cottage $150–225, with a basket of fresh pastries and fruit delivered to your door in the morning. Children and pets are welcome in the cottage, and children 12 and over in the main house.

Iris Inn (1-800-460-7650; www.irisinnbb.com), 59 Manzanita Street. Homemade breakfast in the morning and port, sherry, and chocolates in the evening—your hosts make sure the service matches the elegant decor of the 1905 home. Antiques and strong color themes distinguish the guest rooms, together with bathrobes and other comforts. $95–175.

McCall House (1-800-808-9749; www.mccallhouse.com), 153 Oak Street. John McCall was a gold prospector who actually struck it rich and became one of the pillars of Ashland society, serving eventually in the state legislature. After seven years of marriage, he and his wife, Elizabeth, built this rather dazzling house—an eminent Victorian complete with bow windows and ornate carved details, but wisely omitting the turrets and gingerbread that would have turned it to parody. The house was intended to match their station in life, and, in fact, they did host such luminaries as Rutherford B. Hayes and General Sherman (yes, the Civil War Sherman). Restored and beautifully painted to showcase the fine workmanship, it contains 10 very comfortably appointed guest rooms (this is a big house) with period furnishings nad private bath. $105–250, with full breakfast. Closed Jan.

Oak Street Station (1-800-482-1726; www.oakstreetstation.com), 239 Oak Street. This sensible 1888 exterior does not show off like some of the painted ladies along the street, but the four rooms are certainly decorated to compete, with floral spreads and filmy curtains. All come with private bath and a copious breakfast. $130–150.

♿ **Tudor House** (1-800-760-4428; www.ashlandbb.com), 271 Beach Street. Here's a real family B&B—three generations of family, to be exact: the 1940s house is the home of friendly hosts Raliegh Grantham, his wife, Julie, and daughter Roxanne, while Raliegh's mother, Jan, created the quilts and watercolors and runs the garden. Five homey rooms come with private bath (and beautiful quilts) and Raliegh's creative breakfast. One new room is wheelchair accessible with its own entrance and kitchenette. According to the season, you can spend your downtime in the exuberant gardens or in the reading room; in a quiet neighborhood 0.5 mile from downtown, it's perfect for a relaxed stay. And, if you want to feel a bit closer to the stage than you can normally get, Julie is an actress who appears not infrequently on Ashland's (and other) stages. $93–155.

Jacksonville

♿ 🐾 **Jacksonville's Magnolia Inn** (541-899-0255; www.mag-inn.com), 245 N. Fifth Street. The inn is in the middle of historic Jacksonville with nine old-fashioned, cozy rooms—that's not too unusual in this town. But owners Robert and Susan Roos do offer some unusual perks, like free nationwide phone calls and up to two dogs in a pet-friendly room. $95–165, with extensive continental breakfast.

TouVelle House (1-800-846-8422; www.touvellehouse.com), 455 N. Oregon Street. Frank Touvelle was a judge who became prominent enough to have a park named in his honor (see *Parks*) and build this substantial three-story home in 1916 (actually, his wife is said to have designed it). Filled with Arts and Crafts furniture and plenty of common space, it sits on more than an acre of lawns and garden with its own swimming pool and sauna. Five rooms are decorated in sumptuous style. $129–189, with full breakfast in summer, continental breakfast in winter.

Medford

Under the Greenwood Tree (541-776-0000; www.greenwoodtree.com), 3045 Bellinger Lane. The location gives you the best of both worlds—southern Oregon's cultural and culinary offerings, 10 or 20 minutes away by car, and rural beauty. Ten acres of gardens and mature trees where the hand-hewn 1860s building still stands might make you just want to stay put, though. The stately home's four guest rooms are named after pear varieties (since pears put this region on the map) and, of course, come with all comforts, even complimentary bicycles. $120–140.

COTTAGES

Ashland

🖍 ♿ 🐾 **Oak Street Cottages** (541-488-3778; www.oakstreetcottages.com), 171 Oak Street. Four cottages lined up along Oak Street date to the late 1800s. All are self-contained and family friendly, with full kitchens, porches, yards, even TV and phone, and sleep six to 11—not a bad deal. And just a couple of leafy blocks from downtown.

HISTORIC DOWNTOWN JACKSONVILLE

One cottage is handicapped accessible; pets must be cleared with proprietor. $235–300, but check for specials and extended stays.

Jacksonville

✐ **Duncan Cottage** (541-899-1360; www.duncancottage.com), 120 W. C Street. A cozy 1930s cottage steps from the Britt Gardens can be your Jacksonville home away from home. A queen bedroom, a twin bedroom, kitchen, living room, and game chest makes it family friendly. Double occupancy $125; ask about weekly rates.

Several other cottages are available by the week in Jacksonville, with rates running $450–1,770, through **Ramsay Realty** (541-951-0165).

FOREST SERVICE CABINS AND LOOKOUTS The **Rogue River–Siskiyou National Forest** rents out former fire stations or lookouts. For $35–40, they usually have basic amenities, except water, and sleep several people. Contact the national forest for directions, but reserve through www.recreation.gov or by calling 1-877-444-6777. No smoking, of course.

🐾 **Imnaha Guard Station** is a rather luxurious guard station cabin near Imnaha Springs with a stone fireplace, running water (hot, too), flush toilet, and cookstove but no cookware or utensils. Open spring, summer, and fall. About 10 miles from Butte Falls.

🐾 **Willow Prairie Cabin** is a 1924 log cabin adjacent to Willow Prairie Horse Camp and in the middle of a network of trails, so it is popular with equestrians. Just one room at the base of Mount McLaughlin, it has a woodstove and very rustic furnishings; visitors must bring their own cookware and utensils. Outside is a fire ring and vault toilet. Pets must be leashed.

GUEST HOUSES

Ashland

Delaunay House (541-621-5409; www.delaunayhouse.com), 185 N. Pioneer Avenue. Ashland is full of handsome Victorians and Craftsman bungalows, and this is one of the latter—a solid, roomy residence 1 block from the theaters. Made over in 2002, it now consists of four luxury suites, each with a kitchenette and private bath, and has kept its broad wraparound porch. Like a top-of-the-line bed & breakfast without the breakfast. $135–250.

HOSTELS

Ashland

The Ashland Hostel (541-482-9217; www.theashlandhostel.com), 150 N. Main Street. Friendly and clean, this Craftsman house welcomes the impecunious or the merely frugal to Ashland's cultural amenities. It's a 10-minute walk at most from the theaters and downtown shops and restaurants, and offers a full kitchen and free Wi-Fi. Dorm beds $28, small private rooms $40–59, and $84 for a family room with private bath. Bedding is provided. Reservations are advisable.

HOTELS AND MOTELS

Ashland

✐ **Ashland Springs Hotel** (1-888-795-4545; www.ashlandspringshotel.com), 212 E. Main Street. Not so long ago, this was the Mark Antony, where school groups from all over Oregon stayed while getting acquainted with Shakespeare. Time was not kind to the old hotel, and it closed in 1997, but it was quickly snapped up by Doug and Becky Neuman, who carried out a complete renovation, restoring it to the dignity of its first incarnation—built in 1925, it was the tallest building between Portland and San Francisco, a luxury stop for wealthy travelers or those "taking the waters" for which Ashland was known. They were able to retain the great lobby fireplace, some of the ballroom chandeliers, and stained-glass windows and much of the original flavor while wiring the place for the 21st century. Like a proper grand hotel, it has a ballroom, conservatory, large lobby, and courtyard garden, so if the weather isn't fine, you can explore indoors. Room rates include continental breakfast, served in the mezzanine, and children under 12 stay free. Lark's, the hotel restaurant, is open daily for lunch and dinner, and brunch on weekends. Doubles from $109 low season, $139 high.

Columbia Hotel (1-800-718-2530; www.columbiahotel.com), 262½ E. Main Street. You might easily miss it, squeezed in as it is between downtown storefronts, but that would be a pity. It's probably the most bang for the buck you'll find in Ashland outside the (quite respectable) hostel. Enter the 1910 building and go upstairs, and you'll find 24 clean, comfortable, homelike rooms done up with simple antiques. Some even have private baths. Doubles $56–115, suites $79–155.

The Palm (1-800-691-2360; www.palmcottages.com), 1065 Siskiyou Boulevard. Not just any old motel, the Palm is reminiscent of a 1950s California motel with a well-tended garden, pool, and retro-decorated rooms (but not so retro as to exclude Wi-Fi, flat-screen TV, or high-thread-count sheets). It's three minutes' drive from downtown and just across from the campus of Southern Oregon University—different, affordable, and easy parking. Doubles $64–139, suites $89–169.

Peerless Hotel (1-800-460-8758; www.peerlesshotel.com), 243 Fourth Street. Considerably more luxurious now than when it opened as a railroad workers' boardinghouse in the early 1900s, its six rooms are spacious with private baths, antique carved bedsteads, and flowing drapes. (Originally there were 14 10-by-10 rooms and one bath.) Not coincidentally, its next-door restaurant has a pricy menu to match, but you can enjoy the same quality filet mignon or oysters on their list of small plates. $83–269, with breakfast; children 14 and over welcome.

Prospect

Prospect Historic Hotel-Motel (541-560-3664; www.prospecthotel.com), 391 Mill Creek Drive. It's a simple frame lodging in the woods halfway between Rogue River and Crater Lake, founded as a stage stop in 1888 (the lake was already an attraction). Zane Grey slept here, as did Teddy Roosevelt, Jack London, and other eminent outdoors enthusiasts. Naturally the travelers brought their appetites, and the Dinner House still satisfies them with Western specialties—pork loin or prime rib in Jack Daniel's sauce, for instance. The 10 historic rooms come with handmade quilts, antique beds, and private baths. In 1991 a modern 14-unit motel was built behind the house, fortunately in a harmonious style, convenient for families, pets, and wheelchairs. Use it as a base for visiting the lake or enjoying the Rogue River and surrounding forests, like T.R. did. Hotel rooms $110–195, motel units $90–120.

Shady Cove

Maple Leaf Motel (541-878-2169; www.mapleleafmotel.org), 20717 OR 62. This small, tidy motor court can be your base for exploring the river and surroundings. Fifteen rooms offer the usual motel amenities, plus complimentary rafting shuttle, at reasonable rates. Doubles $54–91.

Applegate

🐾 **Applegate River Lodge** (541-846-6082; www.applegateriverlodge.com), 15100 OR 238. The new log inn has already become popular for weddings, and you can see why: its impossibly bucolic setting right on the clear Applegate River, with lawns shaded by tall trees and spring birds singing, could hardly be more welcoming. Each of the seven Western-themed rooms has its own deck overlooking the river and a private bath with Jacuzzi, there's a common-room fireplace, and it's pet friendly. $130–150, with breakfast, but ask about specials.

Ashland

Ashland Creek Inn (541-482-3315; www.ashlandcreekinn.com), 70 Water Street. This low, stuccoed inn tucked into a side street puts one in mind of a Spanish Colonial hacienda. The illusion is carried indoors, though each suite is individually decorated with antiques and authentic furnishings evoking homes in the Mediterranean, China, Scotland, and farther afield. All units are suites, with decks overlooking the creek, some with several rooms. The experience is one of understated luxury, which extends to the full breakfast. Doubles $130–350.

♿ 🐾 **Green Springs Inn** (541-482-0614; www.greenspringsinn.com), 11470 Greensprings Highway (OR 66). On the edge of **Cascade-Siskiyou National Monument** (see *Parks*), the inn offers a comfortable base for exploring the great outdoors. Eight pine-paneled lodge rooms fit right into the forest; in fact, some of them have private decks with Jacuzzis, to get even closer to the wild. And in 2008, owner Diarmuid McGuire put five spanking-new, green-technology cabins farther back in the woods. These are not rustic, but glow with polished fir cut on the property, double-glazed windows, and decks. Inside you have a full kitchen, Jacuzzi, woodstove, and all the comforts of home (and considerably more than some). Designed and built by Diarmuid and son, they are a labor of love. As if this weren't enough, the lodge restaurant serves three home-style meals a day (closed Wed. and Thurs. in winter)—locals from Ashland and beyond drive up here to eat. Well-behaved, supervised dogs are welcome. Lodge rooms $79–119, cabins $159–199, but ask about specials and weekly rates. Most cabins sleep six. One lodge room is handicapped accessible.

Mount Ashland Inn (1-800-830-8707; www.mtashlandinn.com), 550 Mount Ashland Road. Fifteen miles from Ashland, but several thousand feet higher, the inn sits on the Siskiyou Crest and is the place to go if you want to play on the Pacific Crest Trail, yet come back to luxury accommodations in the evening. Conversely, in winter you can could ski Mount Ashland, or just grab a pair of the inn's complimentary snowshoes and head into the woods. The contemporary log structure has five rooms, each with spa tub, fireplace, and sleek-antique decor. $175, with full breakfast.

The Pinehurst Inn (541-488-1002; www.thepinehurstinn.com), 17250 Greensprings Highway (OR 66). No telephone, no TV, no Wi-Fi—sound good? Don and Denise Rowlett think so. They think their guests should be romantic, or at least interactive, and how can you be with all sorts of electronic umbilical cords? You're much better off without, especially if you want to get the flavor of the inn. Back in 1915, the DeCarlo family ran a farm and stage stop just about here. The stage took two days to get from Ashland to Klamath Falls along the Applegate Trail route, so you can imagine the convenience of a place to eat and sleep. Then the paved road came in, bringing the horseless carriage! The DeCarlos saw an opportunity and built a real inn—it looks like a scaled-down great lodge à la Crater Lake or Timberline, with huge timbers, fine paneling, stonework, and a long porch—opening it in the late 1920s (the earliest extant register dates to 1929). But autos could make the trip in one day, and business dwindled. Fast forward to 1985, when Don's parents bought the place and lovingly restored it. There have been a few alterations: for instance, while the original hotel had 10 rooms and one bathroom, the current arrangement is six rooms, each with its private bath. Otherwise it retains the atmosphere of a slower, warmer era, when folks actually talked to each other. In person. Denise runs the restaurant, open to guests every night and to the general public on weekends; reservations recommended. $85–125, with continental breakfast, though you can also order from a full breakfast menu.

Winchester Inn (1-800-972-4991; www.winchesterinn.com), 35 S. Second Street. Okay, this is where you get to pretend you're Queen Elizabeth (the first, that is), only with central heating. She would have been quite happy with the afternoon pastries delivered to her chambers, and indeed with the chambers themselves, complete with feather beds, French toiletries, and—what's this? Indoor plumbing fit for a queen? Three cottages disposed around the main house mean 10 guest rooms and eight even more luxurious suites, amid lush gardens. There's always a choice of breakfast menus. The Winchester also happens to be a fine-dining restaurant serving dinner daily (reservations recommended). Offerings include such un-Elizabethan fare as grilled antelope burger alongside the salmon and rack of lamb that Queen Bess might have recognized. Rooms $140–195, suites $190–295.

Jacksonville

Jacksonville Inn (1-800-321-9344; www.jacksonvilleinn.com), 175 E. California Street. The brick-and-sandstone inn stands on the same corner as it has since the gold-rush days. They say you can still see flecks of gold in the mortar. Though the outside looks much as it always has, the juxtaposition of four-poster beds with Jacuzzis and free-standing gas fireplaces might startle any prospectors' ghosts haunting the place—the rooms have been made over with high style in mind. Today it is one of the town's most recherché hostelries, with a restaurant to match. The inn also owns several appropriately appointed "honeymoon cottages" down the street. Rooms $159–199, cottages $270–465.

THE PINEHURST INN, IN THE SISKIYOUS EAST OF ASHLAND

Ashland

Buckhorn Springs (541-488-2200; www.buckhornsprings.org), 2200 Buckhorn Springs Road. Buckhorn is a historic mineral spring resort inside the **Cascade-Siskiyou National Monument** (see *Parks*), homesteaded in the 1860s and expanded for guest use in the 1890s. Today their focus is primarily group retreats and events, but individuals or families are welcome as space permits. The lodge has eight bedrooms, most with private bath, and six cabins that sleep two to four people—all rustic, in keeping with the character of the place. $80–300, including hearty vegetarian meals.

Lithia Springs Resort (1-800-482-7128; www.lithiaspringsresort.com), 2165 W. Jackson Road. Four acres of English gardens surrounding a small complex of elegant cottages, suites, and garden rooms would probably have been enough to make this a favored getaway. With the added fillip of hot-spring-fed whirlpools in all suites and cottages, it couldn't miss (though, apparently, owner Duane Smith had to convince the banks of that back in 1990). Halfway between Ashland and Talent, its splendid isolation is only minutes from either town. $179–299; add $10 for breakfast and evening wine tasting.

Willow-Witt Ranch (541-890-1998; www.willowwittranch.com), 6658 Shale City Road. Up in the hills 10 miles north of Ashland, Suzanne Willow and Lanita Witt invite you to the farm they've been working for 25 years now, raising goats, hogs, and free-range chickens while restoring the property's woodlands and wetlands. A studio apartment enables you to enjoy the fresh mountain air while participating (or not) in the daily round. Double occupancy $99.

Prospect

Union Creek Resort (541-560-3565; www.unioncreekoregon.com), 56484 OR 62. This resort has been here since before the national forest was a national forest. A rustic lodge and equally rustic cabins cluster under the tall Douglas firs; across the street, Beckie's Café serves meals and famous pies with ice cream from the Ice Cream Shop. It has always catered to lovers of the Rogue River, like Zane Grey and Jack London, and is still the closest accommodation to Crater Lake's west entrance (about 23 miles). The nine lodge rooms contain one or two beds and gleaming fir paneling; cabins come with linens and sleep two to 10. Lodge rooms with shared bath, $54–64; cabins (most with kitchens) $80–235.

✷ Where to Eat

DINING OUT

Applegate

Applegate River Ranch House (541-846-6082), 15100 OR 238. Wed.–Sun. for dinner and weekends for lunch. Adjacent to the **Applegate River Lodge** (see *Inns and Lodges*), the Ranch House serves seafood, steaks, chicken, and breast of duck grilled over oak, with pastoral views over the Applegate River.

Ashland

Châteaulin (541-482-2264; www.chateaulin.com), 50 E. Main Street. Wed.–Sat. for lunch and dinner. When you think "dinner and a play," this may be the kind of dinner you think of—braised duck in cherry sauce, or maybe just French onion soup for after the show. Order à la carte or the three-course prix-fixe menu at $30, or from the bar menu if you don't want to go, er, whole hog. Local and organic ingredients are used as much as possible, and the wine list runs into the hundreds of labels. Chef David Taub immigrated from New York 20 years ago, bringing a love of French cuisine, and his restaurant has become a much-appreciated fixture.

Jacksonville

Jacksonville Inn (1-800-321-9344; www.jacksonvilleinn.com), 175 E. California Street. Serves breakfast, lunch and dinner; dinner reservations advisable. In the 1860s, gold-rush tycoons ate here. The inn's brick-and-stone dining room preserves an ambience of those days, though the menu has opened up to include some creative vegetarian choices alongside the trusty rib eye and filet mignon.

Shady Cove

Bel Di's on the Rogue (541-878-2010; www.beldisrestaurant.com), 21900 Crater Lake Highway (OR 62). Fri.–Sat. at 5 PM for dinner in winter; call for other seasons' hours. Reservations recommended. Right on the Rogue River, Shady Cove is a favorite spot for rafting, fishing, and just enjoying the river. Bel Di's is a three-bedroom home made over into an intimate restaurant in 1977, where you can enjoy the river view and your favorite steak or seafood dish.

For more fine-dining options, see **Peerless Hotel, Prospect Hotel,** and **Winchester Inn** under *Lodging.*

EATING OUT

Ashland

Ashland Bistro Café (541-482-2117; www.ashlandbistrocafe.com), 38 E. Main Street. Panini and wraps for lunch, huge breakfasts, and dinner with a continental-Northwest flavor—and homemade breads and fine pastries, in a fine-dining ambience yet with moderate prices.

The Black Sheep Pub and Restaurant (541-482-6414; www.theblacksheep.com), 51 N. Main Street. Daily 11:30 AM–1 AM for lunch and dinner. Another bit of Anglomania on the plaza, but not particularly Elizabethan—a pub featuring grub like beans on toast, Welsh rarebit, and Cornish pasties, but also (this being 21st-century Oregon) Pacific salmon, chicken in blackberry sauce, and several vegetarian options. There's a functioning English phone box inside and a dartboard on the wall. And the brews hail from all beer-loving lands, including, of course, microbrew country.

Firefly (541-488-3212), 15 N. First Street. International cuisine, traditional and experimental, attracts the theater crowd (and others) nightly.

Greenleaf (541-482-2808; www.greenleafrestaurant.com), 49 N. Main Street. Serves three meals a day. Greenleaf is a perennial favorite, as well it might be with an eclectic menu and seating right over Ashland Creek. From Northwest standbys to cannelloni to tofu burgers, you should be able to satisfy everyone in your party.

Grilla Bites (541-488-0889), 47 N. Main Street. Homemade soups and healthful sandwiches and salads on Ashland's plaza make this a convenient and affordable place for lunch or a light supper. Families and students, take note!

Mix Sweet Shop (541-488-9885), 57 N. Main Street. Gelato pre- or post-show, pastries, and chocolates—a favorite for years.

Morning Glory (541-488-8636; www.morninggloryrestaurant.com), 1149 Siskiyou Boulevard. Snuggled in a humble bungalow, Morning Glory appropriately specializes in breakfast and lunch, wooing customers with wholesome ingredients (they even smoke their own salmon) and meals for appetites large and small. Go early on weekends; it gets crowded!

Tabú (541-512-3900; www.tabu restaurant.com), 76 N. Pioneer Street. Daily 11:30–9. Tabú advertises its cuisine as "nuevo latino fusion." This means you'll meet dishes from around the Spanish-speaking world: Spanish tapas, guava ribs, Cuban black bean soup, and creative combinations. In late evening it becomes a destination for the post-theater crowd, especially on the two nights a week when music takes over and dancers take the floor. With dance lessons, too, for us staid Northwesterners.

Taj Indian Cuisine (541-488-5900; www.taj-indiancuisine.com), 31 Water Street. Daily 11–3 for lunch and 5–9:30 for dinner. If you don't need another cutting-edge nouvelle-cuisine-fusion meal, sit down at the Taj for unfused, reliable Indian food. It's reasonable, tasty, and the service is attentive.

Jacksonville

MacLevin's Whole Foods Deli (541-899-1251; www.maclevinsonline.com), 150 W. California Street. Open for breakfast, lunch, and dinner; closed Tues. and Wed. Here's what you don't expect to find in small-town southern Oregon: home-corned beef, home-made pastrami, knishes, smoked white-fish . . . you get the picture. Mostly natural or organic, too (the Oregon touch).

Medford

Porters Dining at the Depot (541-857-1910; www.porterstrainstation .com), 147 N. Front Street. Dinner nightly from 5 PM; bar open nightly from 4 PM. Medford's old train depot now serves seafood, steaks, and pastas, with an emphasis on Oregon and Northwest foodstuffs—halibut! Oysters!—and a respectable array of desserts. Named for those who carried our bags, and coincidentally for cofounder Brian Porter.

✷ Entertainment

Craterian Ginger Rogers Theater (541-779-3000; http://craterian.org), 23 S. Central Avenue, Medford. Song and dance from flamenco to ballet, to comedy to symphony to children's theater.

Oregon Cabaret Theatre (541-488-2902; www.oregoncabaret.com), P.O. Box 1149, corner of First and Hargardine streets, Ashland 97520. Originally a Baptist church, it was renovated and outfitted with a magnificent movie palace chandelier, and presto! A cabaret theater offering musical entertainment since 1986. And you can enjoy dinner or brunch with the show. Tickets $19–32, not including meal; student ticket with ID $10 half an hour before show.

Oregon Shakespeare Festival (541-482-0940; www.orshakes.org), 15 S. Pioneer Street, Ashland. From humble beginnings, the Shakespeare Festival has practically become Ashland's reason for being ("everything turned Elizabethan," said one former resident, not entirely happily). The circular Chautauqua building that early Ashlandites had built eventually crumbled, but its ruins inspired young Angus Bowmer in 1935 to stage some Shakespeare plays—after all, Will's Globe Theatre had been circular, too. And a festival was born. Today the open-air Elizabethan Stage stands within the old walls, and three theaters stage not only Shakespeare but Tom Stoppard, Wole Soyinka, playwrights old and new, and plays famous and obscure. The season lasts Feb.–Oct. Tickets run $20–91 depending on the day, the play, and seating (but $10 for student rush half an hour before performance). Backstage tours take you behind the scenes ($9–12), and festivities often include free music in the plaza, lectures, concerts, and discussions.

✷ Shopping

Bloomsbury Books (541-488-0029), 290 E. Main Street, Ashland. Browse or buy; there's a café upstairs.

Cripple Creek Music (541-482-9141; www.cripplecreekmusic.com), 353 Main Street, Ashland. Acoustic guitar or bowed psaltery? Here is a great variety of instruments for a tiny store, and very helpful staff.

Harry and David's Country Village (541-864-2277), 1314 Center Drive, Medford. If you've ever wondered where Harry and David's cheeses, fruits, and other goodies come from, look no further. Tours are available at $5 a head.

Unicorn Toys and Gifts (541-488-5943; www.unicornstore.com), 53 N. Second Street, Ashland. Things you don't find at Toys R Us.

✷ Events

April: **Pear Blossom Festival** (541-772-6295; www.pearblossomparade.org), second weekend, downtown Medford. Floats, races, square dances, and a street fair, in honor of the fruit that underpins the Rogue Valley.

Summer: **Britt Festival** (1-800-882-7488; www.brittfest.org), Britt Gardens, Jacksonville. All music, all summer, all kinds, since 1963.

November–December: **Festival of Light,** Ashland. A million lights light up the town from Thanksgiving Fri. to Christmas, with parades and music on the plaza.

ILLINOIS VALLEY AREA

Rugged and inimical to agriculture, save for the occasional pot grower, the Illinois River Valley was one of the last corners of Oregon to be "settled up." If *settled up* is the right term; much of it is national forest or national monument. You might find the ruins of a mining operation in some remote valley, and countercultural enclaves off US 199, but otherwise the attractions are natural—marble formations in Oregon Caves, unique botanical areas, and three wild, scenic rivers.

GUIDANCE **Grants Pass Josephine County Chamber of Commerce** (1-800-547-5927; www.grantspasschamber.org), 1995 NW Vine Street, Grants Pass 97528.

Grants Pass Visitors and Convention Bureau (1-800-547-5927; www.visitgrantspass.org), 1995 NW Vine Street, Grants Pass 97528.

Illinois Valley Chamber of Commerce Visitor Center (541-592-3326; www.cavejunctionoregon.com), 201 Caves Highway, Cave Junction 97523.

Josephine County Parks (541-474-5285), 125 Ringuette Street, Grants Pass 97527.

Oregon Caves Information Station (541-592-2100), 19000 Caves Highway, Cave Junction 97523.

Rogue River–Siskiyou National Forest (541-618-2200; www.fs.fed.us/r6/rogue-siskiyou), 3040 Biddle Road, Medford 97504; **Wild Rivers Ranger District,** 2164 NE Spalding Avenue, Grants Pass 97526, and 26568 Redwood Highway, Cave Junction 97523.

GETTING THERE *By bus:* **Greyhound** (1-800-231-2222; www.greyhound.com) can bring you as far as the Grants Pass Greyhound Station, 460 NE Agness Avenue.

By car: **US 199** brings you to the Illinois River Valley, whether from California or Grants Pass.

GETTING AROUND You will need a car.

MEDICAL EMERGENCY **Three Rivers Hospital** (541-472-7000), 500 SW Ramsey Avenue, Grants Pass.

✷ To See

COVERED BRIDGES Grave Creek, so named for 16-year-old Martha Crowley, who died in 1846 of typhoid fever along the **Applegate Trail** and was buried here, is spanned by a 1920 covered bridge 0.5 mile east of I-5 on Sunny Valley Road. The **Don Porter** covered bridge across Limpy Creek, 17 miles west of Grants Pass, dates only from 1980.

FARMERS' MARKETS Growers' Market Grants Pass (541-476-5375), First and F streets, Sat. 9–1, Mar.–Nov., and in Riverside Park, Wed. 9–1, June–Sept.

FARMS AND FARM STANDS Cron Produce (541-660-7902), 22995 Redwood Highway, Kerby. Daily 9 AM–dusk, late July–Nov. Produce, flowers, and a fall hay maze.

Kerbyville Farm (541-592-2638), 23790 Redwood Highway, Kerby. Daily 10–6, May–Oct. Berries, tomatoes, sweet corn, and everything you look for at a farm stand.

FOR FAMILIES ✐ **Great Cats World Park** (541-592-2957; www.greatcatsworldpark.com), 27919 Redwood Highway, Cave Junction. Daily mid-Mar.–Oct., weekends Nov. and Feb. General admission $12, seniors $11, children 4–12 $9. Visit snow leopards, ocelots, Bengal tigers, and other rarities in this wildlife park focusing on magnificent felines. Many of the cats are actually working animals—they appear on TV and in the movies, magazines, and calendars. Owner Craig Wagner works with them constantly to keep them in training (translation: they'll cooperate without mauling him) and now welcomes you to visit.

✐ **Siskiyou Field Institute** (541-597-8530; www.thesfi.org), 1241 Illinois River Road, Selma. Naturalist-led classes, field trips, and nature walks cover all aspects of astonishingly varied natural history of the Siskiyous. Snorkel the streams with salmon, learn about edible mushrooms, or hike a wild or historic trail. Many of the offerings are child appropriate; call for age limits.

✐ ♿ **Wildlife Images** (541-476-0222; www.wildlifeimages.org), 11845 Lower River Road, Grants Pass (actually 12 miles west of Grants Pass, just southwest of Merlin). Open daily. Free. This is where the wild things come to be healed and rehabilitated, back in the Oregon woods. Most of the patients are released back into the wild. Those who can't stay on to delight visitors, who can view wolves, mountain lions, eagles, and more creatures great and small while learning about treating injured animals. Visits by guided tour only; call a day ahead to reserve.

HISTORIC HOMES Schmidt House Museum (541-479-7827), 512 SW Fifth Street, Grants Pass. Tues.–Fri. 10–4. Claus and Hannchen Schmidt homesteaded near Grants Pass in the 1880s. After 10 years, tired of lumbering, prospecting, and farming, he opened a grocery store in town and prospered. The house was begun in 1901 and grew piecemeal as the family did, finally becoming the handsome Craftsman dwelling visible today, and two surviving Schmidt daughters donated it in 1978. Many of the furnishings the women lived with are still there, including the wood-burning stove and quilts they had made. Children and adults will enjoy the antique toys. Visits are by guided tour.

HISTORIC SITES A weatherbeaten house, store, shed, and church are all that remain of **Golden,** off I-5 3 miles east of Wolf Creek. A mining town in the 1850s (and tiny even then), it oddly had no saloons, but it had two churches. The site is on the National Register of Historic Places.

Wolf Creek Inn (541-866-2474; www.wolfcreekinn.com), 100 Front Street, Wolf Creek (20 miles north of Grants Pass off I-5). It took 16 days by stage to get from San Francisco to Portland in the 1880s, and there was enough traffic to make a stage stop profitable. The Wolf Creek Tavern was one of those, with a room and a meal going for 75 cents. It has been going ever since, making the oldest continuously operating hotel in the Northwest, and its guest roster looks like a who's who of the West Coast: Jack London, Clark Gable, Orson Welles . . . well, why not? You can join their illustrious company, though I fear the price has gone up.

MUSEUMS **Applegate Trail Interpretive Center** (1-888-411-1846), 500 Sunny Valley Loop, Sunny Valley (14 miles north of Grants Pass). Daily 10–5, June–Oct.; Thurs.–Sun. 10–5, Nov.; weekends only in Dec. General admission $5.95, seniors and teens $4.95, children 12 and under free. The trail Jesse Applegate blazed through the Oregon desert looped down into California and through the tortuous Siskiyou range before arrowing north to the Promised Land—that is, the Willamette Valley. It never did become as busy as the main "trunk" trail, as it added both time and distance, but it still brought thousands of pioneers to the state. Built to look like the old stage stop that was once here, the interpretive center shows and tells the stories of life on the trail (a poor girl who died of typhus is buried nearby) as well as the development of the road through the gold rush and the coming of the railroad.

Kerbyville Museum (541-592-5252), 24195 Redwood Highway, Kerby. Daily 11–3, Apr.–Oct.; closed Wed. Adults $4, seniors $3, kids over five $2; family $10. Pioneer, mining, and Native American artifacts trace the life and times of the Illinois Valley inside a hundred-year-old house.

NATURAL WONDERS **Oregon Caves National Monument** (541-592-2100; www.nps.gov/orca), 19000 Caves Highway, Cave Junction. Cave tours start on the hour or half-hour Memorial Day–Nov. Caves and visitors center are closed Dec.–Mar., though the monument is open year-round. Monument admission free, no reservations; tours $8.50 for those 17 and over, $6 for youth under 17. Children must be 42 inches tall to take a cave tour. Do you dream that you dwelt in marble halls? Leave US 199 at Kerby and wind 20 miles up into the mountains, and you'll find the 3.5-mile marble cave that was discovered in 1874. Formed during the creation of the Siskiyous, the marble was subjected to the slow work of carbon dioxide and seeping water that, over the eons, sculpted the rock into the columns, stalactites, and flows visible today. The cave tour lasts one and a half hours and is fairly strenuous—only 0.5 mile, but more than five hundred stairs and some tight squeezes. Bring a jacket, as temperatures in the caves are a constant 44 degrees. Only the first chamber of the cave is handicapped accessible, and service animals are not allowed at all. If all this seems a bit much, there are plenty of hiking trails aboveground, as well as four CCC buildings from the 1930s, including **The Chateau at Oregon Caves** (see *Inns, Lodges, and Ranches*), one of the West's great lodges.

♿ **Rough & Ready Wildflower Area,** US 199 about 4.5 miles south of Cave Junction. For a place that gets 60 inches of rain a year, it sure looks barren. Sparse, spindly trees rise from low scrub. The flat lies on an alluvial fan, meaning the ground is basically gravel and thin soil. So the rain percolates through and leaves a virtual desert—a desert where the nutrient-poor, metal-rich rock common in the Siskiyous makes plant life even harder. A 1-mile wheelchair-accessible trail and a longer hiking trail wind among dwarf versions of common plants and rarer wildflowers that have adapted to the harsh environment. Blooming peaks in May and June.

SCENIC DRIVES **T. J. Howell Botanical Road.** This 15-mile tour, also known as Eight-Dollar Mountain Road, leaves US 199 near milepost 24 and takes you through or near several areas of botanical interest, contrasting the deep evergreen forest on "normal" soils with the serpentine-influenced vegetation. Near the end of the drive you'll find a trailhead for **Babyfoot Lake** (2 miles round-trip), home to rare plants—badly burned in the 2002 Biscuit Fire, but recovering. There are also some good viewpoints of the Illinois River canyon. Most of the road is gravel, so take a sturdy car. And much of it is inaccessible in winter. A guide is available at www.highway199.org.

✷ To Do

BICYCLING There's a little something for everyone here—for a complete listing check with the **Rogue River–Siskiyou National Forest** (541-618-2200).

Bear Camp Ridge is a 6-mile ridge trail with great views and wildflowers; from I-5 take exit 61 onto the Merlin-Galice Road and take access road 34-8-36 for 21 miles to FR 2308.

Onion Way is a 2-mile trail good for families with children. Take I-5 to the Merlin-Galice Road and turn left on FR 2500, continuing to Secret Creek Campground. This can be combined with the 3-mile, somewhat more difficult **Secret Way Trail.**

The 11-mile **Taylor Creek Trail** connects several other trails and recreation sites; from the Merlin-Galice Road turn left on FR 2500 and go 3 miles to the trailhead.

BIRD-WATCHING Songbirds abound at **Lake Selmac** and **Illinois River State Park,** and raptors like bald eagles are not uncommon. The woods above **Oregon Caves** harbor highland species.

CAMPING Inexpensive campgrounds dot the **Rogue River–Siskiyou National Forest** (541-618-2200): **Big Pine,** 18 miles northwest of Grants Pass by Merlin-Galice Road and FR 25; 12 campsites, restrooms, a champion ponderosa with interpretive loop trail; no drinking water; open May–Oct. **Bolan Lake,** 7 miles east of O'Brien via County Roads 5560 and 55, and FR 4812; 12 sites, nonmotorized boating, toilets; no water; summer only. **Cave Creek,** 16 miles east of Cave Junction on OR 46; 18 primitive sites, toilets, water; summer only. **Grayback,** 12 miles east of Cave Junction on OR 46; 39 tent sites and one RV hookup, toilets, water, 1-mile loop trail; summer only. **Meyers Camp,** 18 miles northwest of Grants Pass by the Merlin-Galice Road and FR 25; a primitive forested campground with just two sites, pit toilet; no water; nearby trails are open to motorcycles; open spring–fall. **Sam Brown** and **Sam Brown Horse Camp,** meadowy locations with 29 campsites and ADA-compliant toilets; no water; elk come despite nearby motorbike trails; open May–Oct. **Secret Creek,** 1.5 miles south of Big Pine (see above) on FR 25; four primitive creekside sites, ADA toilet; no water; open spring–fall. **Spalding Pond,** 22 miles southeast of Grants Pass by US 199, FR 25, and FR 2524; four rustic campsites near a stocked trout pond and historic mill site, toilets; no water; open May–Oct. **Tin Can,** 3 miles up FR 25 from the Merlin-Galice Road; four rustic sites, toilets; no water; open year-round.

Josephine County Parks: Lake Selmac, 52 tent sites, 33 full hookups, 3 partial hookups, 2 yurts, all facilities. **Indian Mary,** 34 tent sites, 44 full hookups, 14 partial hookups, 2 yurts, restrooms, and water. **Whitehorse,** 34 tent sites, 8 full hookups, 1 yurt. **Wolf Creek,** 32 sites, all facilities. **Griffin,** 4 tent sites, 15 full hookups, 1 yurt, all facilities. **Schroeder,** 22 tent sites, 29 full hookups, 2 yurts. **Almeda,** 34 tent sites, 1 yurt, restrooms. Reserve by calling 1-800-452-5687 or logging onto www.reserveamerica.com. Tent sites $7–19, partial hookups $20, full hookups $22.

Valley of the Rogue State Park (1-800-452-5687), 21 tent sites ($12–16), 88 full hookups ($16–20), 59 partial hookups ($16–20), 6 yurts ($27), all facilities.

CANOEING, KAYAKING, AND RAFTING The **Illinois River** is remote and wild and offers some very challenging rapids for experienced river runners. So does the **Lower Rogue,** which, however, has steadier water levels regulated by dams upstream. There are plenty of river guides to take you on a float, such as: **Rogue Wilderness Inc.** (1-800-336-1647), P.O. Box 1110, Merlin 97532; **Orange Torpedo Trips** (1-800-635-2925), 210 Merlin Road, Merlin; and **O'Brien's Rogue River Rafting** (1-800-957-7238), 5556 Lower River Road, Grants Pass.

GOLF **Applegate Golf Course** (541-955-0480), 7350 New Hope Road, Grants Pass. Nine holes.

Dutcher Creek Golf Course (541-474-2188), 4611 Upper River Road, Grants Pass. Eighteen holes.

Illinois Valley Golf Course (541-592-3151), 25320 Redwood Highway, Cave Junction. Eighteen holes.

Red Mountain Golf Course (541-479-2297), 324 Mountain Greens Lane, Grants Pass. Eighteen holes.

HIKING More than 60 national forest trails stitch through these wild, spectacular hills, among them: **Dutchy Creek,** a fairly strenuous 8-mile (each way) horse and foot trail over a divide; accessible from **Sam Brown Horse Camp** (see *Camping*). **Bear Camp Ridge Trail,** a moderately strenuous 6-mile ridge trail offering wildflowers and great views; take Merlin-Galice Road from Merlin to Galice Creek access road and continue 21 miles. **Bolan Lake Trail,** a moderately strenuous 3.6-mile round-trip from **Bolan Lake Campground** (see *Camping*) to the Bolan Mountain Lookout; access from campground. **Burned Timber Interpretive Trail,** an easy 1.8-mile loop through meadows and forest; access from spur road 045 off FR 25. **Grayback Interpretive Trail,** 1 easy mile from the **Grayback Campground** (see *Camping*) to an old CCC camp. **Osgood Ditch Trail** runs 1.8

easy miles along an 1850s mining ditch to connect with the East Fork Illinois River Trail (which is 10 difficult but beautiful river miles); from Takilma take FR 4904 to FR 011.

Illinois River Trail is a rugged 28-mile hike along the remote, wild, and scenic Illinois River from Briggs Creek to Agness, famous for its old-growth forests and wildflowers. Unfortunately, much of it was affected by the 2002 Biscuit Fire; trail and bridge rehabilitation is ongoing. But you don't have to slog along the whole trail to enjoy a wild panorama: a 5-mile round-trip hike to Buzzards Roost gets you a terrific wilderness view. Campsites exist along the trail and at trailheads. From Selma take Illinois River Road west, preferably in a high-clearance vehicle, to the trailhead. Contact the Forest Service district office in Cave Junction or Grants Pass (see *Guidance*) for maps.

For information on the above and other forest trails, contact the **Rogue River–Siskiyou National Forest** (541-618-2200).

Four trails wander around outside the **Oregon Caves** (541-592-2100). Three are under 1.5 miles and take in marble outcrops, old-growth forest, and views, while the **Big Tree Trail** is a steep 3.3 miles to the widest-girthed Douglas fir in Oregon.

Rogue River Trail. This is a 40-mile wilderness experience along one of our most spectacular wild rivers, leading from Grave Creek, 30 river miles from Grants Pass, to Foster Bar, just 30 miles shy of the Pacific town of Gold Beach. Begin at either end or in the middle, where Marial Road provides access. Primitive camping is available along the trail; so are more expensive lodges, if you reserve ahead. Average trail time is four or five days, though high water and downed trees can slow you up. Shuttle service can be arranged. For information and maps contact the **Bureau of Land Management** (541-471-6500).

UNIQUE ADVENTURES **Hellgate Jetboat Excursions** (1-800-648-4874; www.hellgate.com), 966 SW Sixth Street, Grants Pass. Trips run two to five hours and cost $37–62; May–Sept. only. It is not the policy of this guide to encourage noisy wilderness intrusions. But these jetboat excursions stay clear (just) of the protected area and afford a close-up river experience for those who prefer both speed and control.

Howling Acres Wolf Sanctuary (541-846-8962; www.howlingacres.org), 555 Davidson Road, Williams (about half an hour south of Grants Pass). Thurs.–Mon. 10–5 in summer, Thurs.–Mon. 10–4 in winter. General admission $8, seniors and kids 6–11 $5, children five and under free. One day a friend sent Charles and Sherrie LaBat a wolf cub he could no longer care for. He wasn't the only one to discover that wolves aren't cuddly for long. Thus began Howling Acres, a sanctuary set in one of southern Oregon's remoter areas to care for abandoned, orphaned, or injured wolves and wolf-dog hybrids, and to educate people about wolves by a direct connection. You can visit the facility's 15 wolves and five wolf-dogs by guided tour (call ahead to reserve). Or, you can even spend the night and hear the wolves howl. Don't bring your pet, though.

WINTER SPORTS **Page Mountain Snow Park** (541-592-4000), half an hour's drive south of Cave Junction via Waldo Road, offers informal sledding and 8 miles of ungroomed cross-country ski trails.

✱ Wilder Places

PARKS **Illinois River Forks State Park (1-800-551-6949)**, 1 mile south of Cave Junction on US 199. Situated where the North and South forks of the Illinois River flow together, this is a spot to have a quiet picnic, stroll, and contemplate the wild, scenic river. No fee.

Josephine County (541-474-5285) has quite a collection of scenic parks, many of which include camping and river access. A day use fee of $2 applies unless you arrive by foot, bike, or horse. For campsite reservations call 1-800-452-5687. Some are:

♿ **Indian Mary Park,** 7100 Merlin-Galice Road, Merlin. "Indian Mary" was the eldest daughter of Umpqua Joe. In the turbulent period of Indian wars and imposed treaties, Joe warned local settlers of an impending 1855 attack, and in gratitude they granted him this allotment, where he ran a ferry for miners; it became for a time the country's smallest Indian reservation. Mary took the ferry over after his death, but eventually she leased the property to the stage line, and in 1958 the county bought it to create a gemlike park. Sixty-one acres in the gorge of the wild river offer camping and picnicking, swimming, hiking, and great scenery.

♿ **Lake Selmac County Park,** 500 Reeves Creek Road, Selma. A beaver cuts a wedge across serene Lake Selmac as the stars come out. With seven campgrounds plus picnic areas, playgrounds, and beaches, you might think it crowded and busy, but the park's 300 acres allow these facilities to be disposed prettily around the long lakeshore with private, quiet campsites and room for all. Some features are wheelchair accessible. Privately owned **Lake Selmac Resort** (541-597-2277; www.lakeselmac.com), also on the lake, offers boat rentals, cabins, a store, and other diversions.

♿ **Schroeder Park,** 605 Schroeder Lane, Grants Pass. This riverside park offers camping and picnic sites (some ADA accessible), a boat ramp and dog park, and a wheelchair-accessible fishing platform.

Tom Pearce Park, 3700 Pearce Park Road, Grants Pass. This extensive (108-acre) park is for day use only, with a nature trail, game areas, and picnic sites. And, on Fri. evenings, in Aug., free movies! Bring your own blanket or lawn chair.

Whitehorse, 7613 Lower River Road, Grants Pass. Twenty-four riverside acres include a bird sanctuary and nature trail, boat ramp, picnicking, and playground.

Wolf Creek Park, near Wolf Creek Inn (see *Historic Sites*) is a creekside spot to camp, picnic, or hike through tall trees to the top of London Peak.

WILDERNESS AREAS **Kalmiopsis Wilderness (541-247-3600)**, about 20 miles west of Grants Pass via US 199 and FR 4201 or 4203. This huge, geologically and botanically diverse wilderness was named for *Kalmiopsis leachiana,* a kind of laurel discovered here in 1930 that turned out to be the oldest surviving member of the heath family—a relic from before the last ice age. Its 180,000 acres were dramatically altered in 2002 when it was almost completely consumed in the Biscuit Fire. The landscape of deep canyons and elevations ranging from 500 to 5,000 feet is now mostly bare snags, but it does clarify why some folks call this the Red Rocks wilderness—much of the rock is red, raw ocean floor metamorphics. You can see, too, how the forest is regenerating. The terrain is rugged, but intrepid outdoorsfolk will find rewards in the headwaters of the Wild and Scenic Chetco, Illinois, and Smith rivers; huge salmon; and wilderness solitude. The forest around Babyfoot Lake escaped the fire and is part of the **Babyfoot Lake Botanical Area,** protecting rare endemic species.

Red Buttes Wilderness is in a remote corner of the Rogue–Siskiyou National Forest almost due south of the Oregon Caves National Monument. Straddling both the Oregon-California border and the divide between the Applegate and Klamath rivers, it shares the jumbled geology of the Siskiyous that gives rise to some unusual species—even, according to some, Sasquatch. You should have a lot of solitude among the old growth, tarns, rushing streams, and canyons. Access is by trail from the national monument or a very circuitous system of forest roads (call 541-618-4200 for directions).

✷ Lodging

BED & BREAKFASTS

Grants Pass

The Restful Nest (541-582-8259; www.restfulnestbandb.com), 6015 Rogue River Highway. Three miles west of the little town of Rogue River, the Restful Nest offers two rooms vacated by owner Carolyn Arguijo's two daughters. Each has a fine view of the river, and guests have the run of the gardens, living room, and deck—even the paddleboat. Carolyn is a pioneer descendant and has some tales to tell. $75–105.

Merlin

Rogue Forest Bed and Breakfast and River Company (541-472-1052; www.rogueforest.com), 12035 Galice Road. Just two private suites in the woods above the Rogue River make this a pretty getaway—the redwood decks, private balconies, and rock fireplaces don't hurt, either. Your hosts will happily arrange a float trip for you down the river or help you find a rental; or you can hike some of the canyon trails. Then again, you might just want to sleep off a hearty breakfast. Doubles $165–195, with full breakfast.

Rogue Glen Lodge (541-474-1888; www.rogueglen.com), 10526 Galice Road. Three guest rooms on the scenic section of the Rogue River are there for lovers of the river, whether you prefer to raft, fish, hike, or watch the eagles and herons. Doubles $125, including full breakfast, with discounts for several-night stays.

FOREST SERVICE RENTALS 🐾

Bolan Mountain Lookout is a cupola-style structure with wraparound windows. There is no kitchen and just a single bed, so this is a spot for solitary communion with nature—which isn't bad, being on top of Siskiyou Crest. Open summer and fall. About 30 miles from Cave Junction via US 199, Happy Camp Road, and FRs 4812, 4812-040, and 535.

HOTELS AND MOTELS

Cave Junction

🖍 🐾 **Country Hills Resort** (1-888-592-3406; www.countryhillsresort.com), 7901 Caves Highway. How about this: an actual, affordable homey place to stay with creekfront, trails, woods, and a choice of cabin, motel room, or campsite? This is the kind of old-fashioned, nearly rustic motor court/resort that sprang up in the 1940s and '50s, when families began to be able to hit the road in numbers. Motel rooms are individually decorated, and the cabins are paneled entirely in mellow wood. Cabins come with full kitchens and daily maid service, and motel rooms come with continental breakfast. And, there's an ice cream parlor on the premises! Children and pets are welcome; it's expected that they'll be well supervised—this *is* the edge of wilderness. Tent sites $16, RV sites $20–28, motel rooms $54–58, cabins $75–89; ask about weekly rates in winter.

Grants Pass

Buona Sera Inn (1-877-286-7756; www.buonaserainn.com), 1001 NE Sixth Street. New owners Irene and Peter saw a mission and chose to accept it: to buy an old motel and remake it as an Italian lodging. You still wouldn't mistake it for an *agriturismo* in Tuscany, but the cascading flower baskets and ochre walls are certainly warm and welcoming, and the 14 rooms cleverly disguise standard motel layouts with pastel paint, frescoes, arched partitions, and varied bedsteads. Doubles $44–125.

Motel del Rogue (541-479-2111; www.moteldelrogue.com), 2600 Rogue River Highway. This two-story 1930s motel has 15 units, some rustic and some updated, running from simple rooms to suites, and most have decks over the river. Child friendly and pet friendly, though it's expected that both be well behaved. $85–135; weekly rates available.

INNS, LODGES, AND RANCHES

Cave Junction

The Chateau at Oregon Caves (1-877-245-9022), 20000 Caves Highway, P.O. Box 1824, Cave Junction 97523. One of Oregon's three "great lodges" (with Timberline and Crater Lake), the six-story, gabled lodge stands straddling a ravine with a stream running through its dining room. Despite its size, its adaptation to the land's contours and its siding of Port Orford cedar bark make it harmonize with its wild surroundings (if they could do that during the Depression, why can't they do it now?). Indoors a fire blazes in the hearth, and rooms are still decorated as in the 1930s; due to National Historic Landmark status, there are no elevators, and rooms are not handicapped accessible. Dine on Northwest specialties like buffalo meat loaf in the dining room or take a coffee break in the 1930s Caves Café. Doubles $90–140. Open May 1–Oct. 15.

Grants Pass

Weasku Inn (1-800-493-2758; www.weasku.com), 5560 Rogue River Highway. Clark Gable slept here, and so did other Hollywood luminaries seeking, presumably, an escape from themselves along the pristine forested banks of the Rogue River. Built in 1924, the fine log inn underwent an interior renovation in 1998, so that today the flavor is one of understated rustic luxury. Lodge rooms $199–299, cabins from $225, and a large group house (sleeps 10) $395.

Merlin

Doubletree Ranch (541-476-0120; www.doubletree-ranch.com), 6000 Abegg Road. Doubletree was homesteaded in 1891 by Mary Tyler, a circuit-riding nurse who likely had a lot of riding to do back in 1891. It's still a 160-acre, family-owned spread with nearly a mile of riverfront; Rogue River Trail hikers stop over here, and so do vacationing families. Four self-contained cabins sleep one to six for $95–145. There's even a guest laundry room.

RESORTS

Cave Junction

Out 'n' About Treehouse Treesort (541-592-2208; www.treehouses.com), 300 Page Creek Road. In the land of tree-sitters, it was only a matter of time before someone thought of lodging guests in trees. If you're willing to go out on a limb (their phrase, not mine), you can enjoy a very solid and comfortable tree house, with real beds and sometimes even kitchen and bath facilities. The 18 units are all different; some sleep two, some sleep up to six, and some even have plumbing; others share bathrooms on the ground. Located on 36 wooded acres about 10 miles from Cave Junction in the hamlet of Takilma, it's billed as a summer family camp complete with evening campfires, creek-fed swimming pool, and a full breakfast in summer. What with ziplines, platforms, stairs, and swinging bridges, you could spend all day reverting to our arboreal primate phase. If you're not sure, take a tour; just call ahead. Open year-round. Summer doubles $120–240, but ask about off-season or special rates.

Merlin

Galice Resort (541-476-3818; www.galice.com), 11744 Galice Road. Here's a lodge over the wild Rogue with a choice of rustic cabins in various sizes, a lodge, and a large house. Weekends bring live local bands, and the restaurant is open daily for casual dining and breakfasts—on the deck overlooking the river when the weather's good, which it mostly is. The resort's own river guides will float you down the river or rent a raft or kayak to do-it-yourselfers. Cabins $119–149 for two to six guests; the entire lodge goes for $609 for up to 12 people. River House is rented out by the floor, each of which sleeps 10–16, for $259–579.

✷ Where to Eat

DINING OUT

Grants Pass

Summer Jo's (541-476-6882; www.summerjos.com), 2315 Upper River Road Loop. Thurs.–Sun. for three meals Valentine's Day–New Year's Eve (Fri.–Sun. in winter). Organic farm, dinner theater, music venue—Summer Jo's is all of these, but its main interest to us here is as a restaurant and bakery. They grow practically all of what they put on the table (even the wheat for the bread), and what they can't (like buffalo) they get from reliable local producers. The decor is like that of an old farmhouse, which it probably is; the kitchen is open, and you're welcome to stroll around the gardens—this is organic cuisine without the snobbery. And the prices aren't even that high. There's live music Thurs. nights and, in summer, theater on the lawn.

Merlin

Morrison's Rogue River Lodge (1-800-826-1963; www.morrisonslodge.com), 8500 Galice Road. The 1945 lodge has grown and adapted, but it retains an atmosphere of wild-country leisure. Dine overlooking the canyon three seasons a year, or at long tables indoors; the fare is definitely haute cuisine à la Northwest—bouillabaisse, elk chops, quail—while lunch is more sandwiches and burgers (Angus beef or bison, of course). Reservations required of nonresidential guests.

Wolf Creek

Wolf Creek Inn (541-866-2474; www.thewolfcreekinn.com), 100 Front Street. The 1883 hotel serves lunch and dinner Thurs.–Sun. (brunch on Sun.), mostly American "country cooking" classics—chicken and biscuits, roast turkey—in an elegant historic setting.

Cave Junction

Taylor's Sausage (541-592-4185; www.taylorsausage.com), 525 Watkins Street. Not so much for eating out, but for taking home—Taylor's has been making hot dogs, brockwurst, salami, boudin, and many other kinds of sausage since 1924. And if you do feel like eating at the horse's mouth, so to speak, nearby **Taylor's Country Store** (541-592-5358), 202 Redwood Highway, serves breakfast and lunch daily and dinner Fri. nights in its rustic café, often with live local music.

Grants Pass

Chocolate Affair Bakery (541-476-9016; www.chocolateaffairbakery.com), 404 SW Fifth Street. Mon. and Sat. 10–3, Tues.–Fri. 10–5. Cakes, confections, cookies, and more, all handmade and chocolate based.

Jimmy's Classic Drive-In (541-479-5313), 515 NE E Street. Tues.–Sat. 11–7. The 1950s diner serves 1950s diner fare, meaning milk shakes, burgers, and fries untouched by the fast-food culture. Eat in or out, or drive through!

Laughing Clam (541-479-1110; www.thelaughingclam.com), 121 SW G Street. Mon.–Thurs. 11–9, Fri.–Sat. 11–10. Not only about seafood, the Laughing Clam is an informal family place offering burgers, seafood, pasta, microbrews, and weekend music.

✷ Shopping

It's a Burl (1-800-548-7064; www.itsaburl.com), 24057 Redwood Highway, Kerbyville. Daily 8–5. Talk about the spirit of the wood. Dan Shinerock (who ought to have been named Shinewood) carves furniture, bowls, sculptures, and more in his studio/shop/gallery that looks like Hobbiton by way of Hippiedom. Gnomes and elves peer from boles, and even the tables and chairs have the organic look of living wood. Also, a tree grows through the building. This is an idiosyncratic operation producing really beautiful pieces.

✷ Events

October: **Applegate Wagon Train Reenactment** (1-888-411-1846), Sunny Valley. A wagon train treks a segment of the Applegate Trail, ending at the **Applegate Trail Interpretive Center** (see *Museums*). Children's games, music, and historical presentations.

ROSEBURG–MYRTLE CREEK–CANYONVILLE AREA

Roseburg is the only incorporated Oregon town to be named for a Jewish settler—Aaron Rose, who in 1851 bought a claim at the confluence of Deer Creek and the Umpqua River, built a farm, and platted the town. During the ensuing gold fever, when ore was discovered up the Umpqua, would-be miners stopped there for supplies. Soon the Sacramento–Portland stage came through, and the Roses' farmhouse became a tavern of sorts, sheltering and refreshing the motley travelers.

The mines played out and the area fell back on its rich timber, but it's farming that still underpins the economy here, the rich soil and plentiful water being less subject to booms and busts. Rose farmed, the Applegate brothers farmed, and a leisurely drive around the valley shows interspersed forest and field (some now given over to wine grapes). It has remained a bit of a backwater, which means quiet roads and no crowds, the main tourist draw being the spectacular Umpqua, a rafting and fishing legend, rushing down the western slopes of the Cascades.

GUIDANCE **Canyonville Information Center** (541-839-4258), 250 N. Main Street, Canyonville 97417.

Douglas County Parks (541-957-7001; www.co.douglas.or.us), 6536 Old Highway 99N, Winchester 97495.

Roseburg Visitors and Convention Bureau (1-800-444-9584; www.visitroseburg.com), 410 SE Spruce, Roseburg 97470.

Sutherlin Visitors Information Center (541-459-5829), 1310 W. Central Avenue, Sutherlin 97479.

Umpqua National Forest (541-672-6601; www.fs.fed.us/r6/umpqua), 2900 NW Stewart Parkway, Roseburg 97471.

Winston Visitor Information Center (541-679-0118), 30 NW Glenhart, Winston 97496.

GETTING THERE *By car:* **I-5** is the north–south corridor. **OR 138** links Roseburg to Crater Lake and points east, while **OR 42** runs circuitously west to the coast.

GETTING AROUND A car is necessary.

MEDICAL EMERGENCY **Mercy Medical Center** (541-673-0611), 2700 Stewart Parkway, Roseburg.

Veterans' Administration Roseburg (541-440-1000), 913 NW Garden Valley Boulevard, Roseburg.

✷ To See

COVERED BRIDGES Six covered bridges remain in the greater Roseburg area: **Cavitt Creek,** on Little River Road, 8 miles south of OR 38, built in 1943; **Horse Creek,** built in 1930, was moved from its McKenzie River site to Millsite Park in Myrtle Creek, where it now functions as a footbridge; the 1962 **Milo Academy Bridge,** 18 miles east of Canyonville at the Adventist school in Milo, is a steel replacement for a 1920s timber bridge; **Neal Creek,** about a mile from the town of Myrtle Creek on Days Creek Cutoff Road, dates from 1939 and is the second shortest in Oregon; **Pass Creek,** behind the library in Drain, was rebuilt on the original 1870 plan after collapsing in a heavy snowfall; **Rochester,** on Stearns Lake Road, 3 miles west of I-5 from exit 138, dates from 1933 and has arched side windows, unusual for Oregon.

FARM STANDS AND FARMERS' MARKETS **Brosi's Sugartree Farms** (541-679-1472), 540 Winston Section Road, Winston. Daily June–Oct. Buy your fruits and berries, or pick them yourself.

Kruse's Farm Stand (541-580-6392; www.krusefarms.com), 532 Melrose Road, Roseburg. Daily mid-Apr.–mid-Jan. Berries, fruits, vegetables, pies, and other good country stuff.

Umpqua Valley Farmers' Market (541-530-6200), 2082 Diamond Lake Boulevard, Roseburg. Sat. 9–1, mid-Apr.–Oct.

FOR FAMILIES ✐ **Wildlife Safari** (541-679-6761; www.wildlifesafari.net), 1790 Safari Road, Winston. Daily 9–5, spring break–Oct. 1 and daily 10–4, Oct. 1–spring break. Admission covers two drives through: $14.99 winter, $17.99 summer, seniors $11.99/$14.99, kids 4–12 $8.99/11.99. Going on safari in Oregon means you don't have to lay out airfare to distant lands, and further, that you can take in fauna of several continents in a mere 600 acres. A 4.5-mile park road wends through lion, bear, and cheetah habitat enhanced by numerous other exotic species; you do *not* want to get out of your car, as these animals roam free. You can roam freely in Safari Village, though, where presentations and talks on the various animals vie for your attention with a petting zoo (no predators) and the Safari Café. The facility has recognized breeding programs for cheetah and other endangered creatures.

✐ **Winchester Dam,** at exit 129 from I-5. A viewing window lets you observe steelhead and salmon making their way up the North Umpqua past the dam.

GARDENS Roseburg's **Friendship Garden** stands next to the library as a token of the sister-city relationship with Shobu, Japan. *Shobu* means iris, and the garden includes plenty of those, as well as an intermingled selection of plants native to Oregon and Japan, and many rocks.

The **Butterfly and Hummingbird Gardens** at the Elkton Community Education Center (541-584-2692), 15850 OR 38 W., Elkton, attract beautiful flutterers with colorful plantings from Memorial Day to Labor Day. Also at the center, the **Native Oregon Plant Park** brings together species from Oregon's very varied climate zones.

HERITAGE TREES The **American elm** gracing the grounds of the Douglas County Courthouse, 1036 SE Douglas Street, Roseburg, is more than a hundred years old and was a gift of congressman Binger Hermann.

The **Hinds Walnut Tree** is a curiosity in that it is more than 250 years old, yet it is not a species native to Oregon. No one knows how it got there; it predates the arrival of settlers by a century, and of trappers by a probable 50 or 60 years. You can find it 12 miles northwest of Sutherlin on OR 138.

HISTORIC HOMES **Applegate House** (541-849-3139; www.applegatehouse.com), Yoncalla; from I-5 exit 150, take Eagle Valley Road north to Halo Road, turn right, then left on Old Applegate Road and continue to the end. The house will be familiar to you if you've read Shannon Applegate's *Skookum,* about her Applegate ancestors who trekked west, blazed the Applegate Trail, and settled in this valley to become some of early Oregon's prime movers. (If you haven't read it, you should.) It stands majestically with its two-level porches overlooking the surrounding farmland and is today an arts and educational center directed by the same Shannon Applegate, a descendant of Charles Applegate, who built the house in 1852, conducting events, classes, and workshops on the culture and lifeways of the early settlers and of the native peoples among whom they settled. For scheduled activities, call or check the Web site.

Floed-Lane House, 544 SE Douglas Avenue, Roseburg. Sat.–Sun. 1–4. Free. This was the last home owned by Joseph Lane, an early governor of the Oregon Territory and one of Oregon's first senators after statehood. Lane even had a brief fling with presidential hopes, running for vice president in 1860 on a proslavery platform, which soon ended his political career. He retired to this stately home with the two-tiered porch and died in 1881; the house remained in the family till his great-granddaughter left it to the Douglas County Historical Society.

Parrott House, 1772 SE Jackson Street, Roseburg. Built about 1891, the house is a curious mix of a muted Queen Anne, with octagonal turret, and an otherwise more horizontal, Eastlake-influenced exterior. Private home.

Drain Castle, Main Street, Drain. This was the impressive home of Charles Drain, who bought the claim from Jesse Applegate in 1861 and platted the town site on it (explaining the town's unusual name). He did rather well, judging by the house he built in 1895, all spindles, balustrades, and gingerbread; though the town, after a brief boost from the railroad, declined when the railroad moved to Eugene.

Charles E. Hasard House, W. A Street, Drain. Hasard was a carpenter with the Oregon and California Railroad, which may explain some of the wilder features of this 1902 Queen Anne—turret, gables, porches and balconies, carved decoration—and it's painted in a variety of assertive colors. Please respect the owner's privacy.

HISTORIC SITES The **Applegate Trail** ran along what is now Main Street in Roseburg; a marker stands just north of Douglas Avenue.

SEVERAL QUEEN ANNES ADORN THE HAMLET OF DRAIN.

The town of **Oakland,** whose 2-block downtown looks pretty much as it did in the 1880s, is on the National Register of Historic Places. A walking tour guide to these storefronts and some 90 historic houses can be had at the **Oakland Museum** (see *Museums*) or at **Tolly's Restaurant** (see *Eating Out*). In 1900 Oakland was the epicenter of turkey production in the western United States. A similar tour brochure to **Roseburg** is available at the **Roseburg Visitors and Convention Bureau** (see *Guidance*).

MUSEUMS **Douglas County Museum of History and Natural History** (541-957-7007), 123 Museum Drive, Roseburg. Mon.–Fri. 9–5, Sat. 10–5, and Sun. noon–5, Jan.–Oct.; Tues.–Fri. 9–5 and Sat. 10–5, Nov.–Dec. General admission $4, seniors $3, persons 17 and under free. The scope of this museum is the entire Umpqua watershed ecosystem, from mountain forests to the river valleys to the coast. If you've been confused about the thick vegetation you've been seeing, check out the large herbarium collection, then wander the wildlife dioramas to see who else lives here. The human piece of the landscape is brought to life through Native American tools; pioneer, mining, farming, and logging artifacts; and thousands of photographs dating back to the mid-1800s. Oh, and the Oregon and California Railroad's last remaining depot.

Oakland Museum (541-459-4531), P.O. Box 624, Oakland 97462. Daily 12:30–3:30; closed holidays. Free. The people's history of Oakland through memorabilia, photos, and mock-ups of a pioneer town's doctor's office, post office, bank, and more.

NATURAL WONDERS **Colliding rivers,** off OR 138, Glide. Here the North Umpqua and Little rivers meet head-on, an unusual phenomenon that makes for impressive displays during spring runoff. The rest of the time, they meet and glide together seaward, as the name of the nearest town suggests. Across the road is a 1930s CCC ranger station, now an information kiosk.

SCENIC DRIVES The drive from Roseburg to Diamond Lake along OR 138 is part of the **Rogue-Umpqua Scenic Byway.** This segment runs along the Wild and Scenic North Umpqua River and takes in more than two dozen waterfalls in the course of 76 miles, with several opportunities for short hikes to viewpoints. You rise from Roseburg oak savannas to the High Cascades, so check road conditions.

OR 42 is a startlingly beautiful and practically untraveled drive from just south of Roseburg to Coquille, near the coast. It's only 67 miles, but you should allow a good two hours for careful driving and gawking. The road winds through a deep gorge along the Middle Fork of the Coquille River with forest and rock formations rising on each side—not designated wilderness, but the Coast Range terrain is so rugged, it was never much developed. One of the settlements along the way is named Remote.

WINE The Umpqua Valley is one of Oregon's up-and-coming wine areas, with a good 20 vineyards dotting the valleys west of Roseburg. A self-driving winery tour can be had at the **Roseburg Visitors and Convention Bureau** (see *Guidance*) or its Web site, www.visitroseburg.com. Some of the more established are Henry Estates, Spangler, Palotai, and Abacela (oddly, a stream known as Champagne Creek does not have an eponymous winery), producing grapes as varied as Cabernet, Merlot, Tempranillo, Granache, and more due to its differentiated terrain. The local winegrowers' association calls it Oregon's "most complex wine-growing region." If you don't feel like driving yourself, there are those who will drive you, such as **Oregon Wine Country Tours** (1-800-704-2943; www.oregonwinecountrytours.com), 5043 Melqua Road, Roseburg.

✷ To Do

BICYCLING Sometimes it helps to know someone. The **Umpqua Velo Club** (www.umpquavelo.com), P.O. Box 2538, Roseburg 97470, organizes group rides three times a week in summer and will know all about local routes. A system of bikeways (though not necessarily bike lanes) covers the region from downtown Roseburg to the far reaches of Douglas County, offering pretty rural roads among farms and pastures; maps are available from the **Roseburg Visitors and Convention Bureau** (see *Guidance*). Finally, there is a wealth of mountain biking trails in the **Umpqua National Forest** (see *Guidance*). Here is a selection: the **Brice Creek Trail** runs along scenic, forested Brice Creek for about 20 miles, but there are several trailheads, so you can bike shorter sections; access from Brice Creek Road, about 25 miles southeast of Cottage Grove. The **Crawfish Trail** is a challenging 5 miles with a rise of 3,000 feet through both old-growth and new forest; it was originally a fire watch patrol road. Access is from milepoint 5.8 on Brice Creek Road, about 29 miles from Cottage Grove. It connects with the Brice Creek Trail and the **Knott Trail,** a 5-mile trail through woods and meadows with views and wildflowers (also open to motorcycles). Farther south, the **Donegan Prairie Trail** is a short (4-mile) ride through subalpine meadows (huckleberries in fall!), about 33 miles from Tiller by County Roads 46, 29, 68, and 2925-800. The **Mayflower Loop Trail** is a 7.25-mile loop along an old mining road and passes the remains of some mining operations; access is by Steamboat Creek Road (44 miles east of North Umpqua Ranger Station off OR 138), then along Horse Heaven Road to its end. Then, for the intrepid, there is the **North Umpqua Trail,** 79 miles into the wild with giant trees, wildlife, flowers, and fishing holes (the last 20 miles are actual designated wilderness and closed to bikes).

BIRD-WATCHING **Stewart Park,** in Roseburg, with its oak grove and riverbanks, hosts nesting songbirds and osprey. **Fords Pond,** 1.5 miles from Sutherlin, is a place to spot snipe, swallows, and the occasional bald eagle. Another frequented spot is the ponds behind Fred Meyer's in Roseburg, for its ducks and occasional vagrants.

CAMPING Several Douglas County parks have campgrounds with water, restrooms, and showers. To reserve, call 541-957-7001. **Chief Miwaleta Park,** 8399 Upper Cow Creek Road, Azalea; 20 full hookups (first come, first served), and a cabin with electricity and water at $32; also nonhookup sites. **Pass Creek Park,** 201 Curtain Park Road, Curtain; 30 full hookup and some nonhookup. **Stanton Park,** 1540 Stanton Park Road, Canyonville; 20 full hookup and 20 nonhookup sites; reservable. **Whistler's Bend Park,** 2828 Whistler's Park Road, Roseburg; 23 nonreservable sites plus two reservable yurts in this scenic riverside park; restrooms and showers; closed in winter.

Umpqua National Forest campgrounds (541-672-6601), in the Tiller Creek Ranger District, 27812 Tiller Trail Highway: **Boulder Creek,** 14 miles from Tiller Ranger Station on CR 46 and S. Umpqua Road; seven sites with picnic tables, water, and toilets; open May–Oct. **Camp Comfort,** 12 miles beyond Boulder Creek campground; five sites with toilet but no water, short trail to river; open May–Oct. **Cover,** 18 miles from Tiller via CR 46 and Jackson Creek Road; seven sites, water, and toilet; open May–Oct. **Devil's Flat,** 17 miles from the Azalea exit of I-5 along County Road 36; three sites with toilet, trails; no water; open May–Oct. **Dumont Creek,** 11 miles from Tiller on CR 46 and S. Umpqua Road; three sites (not suitable for trailers), toilet, river beach; no water; open May–Oct. **South Umpqua Falls,** 20 miles from Tiller on CR 46 and S. Umpqua Road; 16 sites, toilets; no water; open May–Oct. **Threehorn,** 13 miles south of Tiller on County Road 1; five sites with toilet; no water; open year-round. **Three C Rock,** 4 miles from Tiller on CR 46; five sites, trail to waterfall; no water, no fee.

North Umpqua Ranger District (541-496-3532), 18782 N. Umpqua Highway, Glide: **Apple Creek,** 28 miles east of the North Umpqua Ranger Station on OR 138; eight sites, toilet; no water; open May 20–Oct. 31. **Bogus Creek,** 19 miles east of the North Umpqua Ranger Station on OR 138; 15 sites, water, toilets, paved, trails, raft launch; handicapped-accessible campsite and toilet; open May 20–Oct. 15. **Boulder Flat,** 36 miles east of the ranger station on OR 138; 11 sites, toilet, trails, great scenery, raft launch; no water; open May 1–Oct. 15. **Coolwater,** 16 miles from ranger station along Little River Road; seven sites, water, toilets, trails, fishing, and swimming; open May 20–Oct. 31. **Eagle Rock,** 34 miles east of ranger station on OR 138; 25 sites, toilets; ADA campsites and toilets; no water; open May 20–Sept. 30. **Hemlock Lake,** 32 miles from ranger station on Little River Road; 13 sites, toilets, trails, swimming, and nonmotorized boating; no water; open June–Oct. **Horseshoe Bend,** 30 miles east of ranger station via OR 138, FR 4750, and FR 4750-001; 22 sites, water, toilets, trails, boat launch; ADA restrooms and campsites; open May 20–Sept. 30. **Island,** 24 miles east of Glide on OR 138; seven sites, toilet, trails; no water; open year-round. **Lake in the Woods,** 27 miles from the ranger station on Little River Road; 11 campsites, water, toilets, wildflowers, trails, nonmotorized boating; open late May–Oct. **Steamboat Falls,** 24 miles east of the ranger station via OR 138, FR 38, and FR 3810; 10 sites, toilet, trails; no water; open May–Dec. **White Creek,** 18 miles from ranger station by Little River Road and Red Butte Road; four sites (no trailers), water, toilets, river beach, trails; open May 20–Sept. 30. **Williams Creek,** 21 miles from ranger station off OR 138 on FR 4710-038; three rustic campsites (tents only), toilet, river access; no water, no fee; open June 1–Sept. 10. **Wolf Creek,** 12 miles from ranger station on Little River Road; eight sites, water, toilets, swimming, play areas, hiking, wildflowers; open May 20–Sept. 30.

Cottage Grove Ranger District (541-767-5000), 78405 Cedar Park Road, Cottage Grove: **Cedar Creek,** 23 miles from exit 174 on I-5 via Row River Road and Road 2470; 10 campsites, toilet, water, trails; open May 20–Sept. 30. **Hobo Camp,** 29 miles from Cottage Grove via Row River Road and Brice Creek Road; five sites, toilet, trails, swimming, gold panning; no water, no fee; open May 25–Sept. 30. **Lund Park,** 28 miles from Cottage Grove by Row River Road and Brice Creek Road; 10 sites, toilet, trails, mineral panning; no water; open year-round. **Mineral Camp,** 25 miles from Cottage Grove by Row River Road and Sharps Creek Road; three sites, toilet, trails; no fee; open Mar. 15–Sept. 15. **Rujada,** 21 miles from Cottage Grove via Row River Road and Road 17; 15 sites, water, toilets, trails, creek; ADA campsite and toilet; open May 25–Sept. 15.

CANOEING, KAYAKING, AND RAFTING The Wild and Scenic section of the **North Umpqua** is a favorite of white-water connoisseurs, what with its multitude of rapids, class II to class V, and arresting scenery. The closest outfitters are **North Umpqua Outfitters** (1-888-454-9696), P.O. Box 158, Idleyld Park 97447. Several Douglas County parks are on lakes or reservoir good for flat-water canoeing or kayaking; see *Wilder Places*.

CLIMBING The **Callahan Mountains,** 25 miles west of Roseburg, are a cluster of sandstone crags with about two hundred rock-climbing routes and fine views over the Flournoy Valley. Contact the **Roseburg Visitors and Convention Bureau** (1-800-444-9584) for directions.

GOLF **Myrtle Creek Golf Course** (1-888-869-7853), 1316 Fairway Drive, Myrtle Creek. Eighteen holes.

Stewart Park Golf Course (541-672-7701), 900 SE Douglas Avenue, Roseburg. Nine holes.

Umpqua Golf Resort (541-459-4422), 1919 Recreation Lane, Sutherlin. Eighteen holes.

HIKING Many trails follow the waterways of the Umpqua drainage, the "trunk trail" being the **North Umpqua Trail.** Beginning near Glide, it rises along the river 79 miles past Boulder Creek Wilderness and up to the Mount Thielsen Wilderness for a concentrated Cascades experience—literally, as you pass dozens of waterfalls. It's divided into 11 segments, each with road access, so you don't have to hike the whole thing. Contact the **Umpqua National Forest** (541-672-6601) for directions and maps.

Also in the North Umpqua District is **Twin Lakes,** a 2.5-mile trail (each way) path to small tranquil lakes with primitive camping and nonmotorized boating; 31 miles from the ranger station via Little River Road, FR 27, FR 2715, and FR 2715-530.

In the Tiller Ranger District: **Acker Divide Trail,** a hearty 7-mile hike to Hershberger Lookout with (in good weather) views as far as Mount Shasta; passes among old timber, meadows, and marshes, and a CCC shelter. From Tiller take CR 46/S. Umpqua Road to Jackson Creek Road to Road 2900-550 to the trailhead, about 31 miles. **Cow Creek Trail,** 6.5 miles through venerable trees and forest glades; some stream fording required. From Azalea take CR 36 to FR 3232, a total of about 19 miles. **Devil's Flat Trail,** 5 miles from a 1915 cabin up to the top of Red Mountain. From Azalea take CR 36 for 17 miles to the Devil's Flat Guard Station. **Sandstone Trail,** 3.5 miles up the Rogue-Umpqua Divide ridge, with a 2,000-foot climb; at the top it meets the **Rogue-Umpqua Divide Trail,** 30 miles of rugged ridgeline hiking. For Sandstone, take CR 46 to Jackson Creek Road to Road 68 and continue to the trailhead, about 31 miles from Tiller.

In the Cottage Grove District: **Adams Mountain Trail,** a strenuous 3.6-mile hike from Lund Park up a ridge, was a miners' trail before it became a "way" trail—the most direct way for forest fire patrols to reach lookout points, and therefore pretty steep—this one rises 2,500 feet. From Cottage Grove take Row River Road and Brice Creek Road and continue to Lund Park. For a more relaxed walk, take the **Brice Creek Trail,** 6 pleasant miles along Brice Creek with several trailheads, so you can do all or some; 25 miles southeast of Cottage Grove by Row River Road and Brice Creek Road. Or the **Swordfern Trail,** lush and ferny as the name implies, a 2-mile loop through an early, regenerated logging area; access from Rujada Campground, 19 miles southeast of Cottage Grove via Row River Road and Layng Creek Road.

✷ Wilder Places

PARKS **Douglas County** (541-957-7001) runs 77 parks, among them several with campsites, boat ramps, and other amenities. Some are:

Cable Crossing Wayside, 5 miles east of Glide on OR 138. This picnic area on the North Umpqua has river access, lovely views, and a popular fly-fishing hole.

Chief Miwaleta Park, 8399 Upper Cow Creek Road, Azalea. Set on Galesville Reservoir, the park offers camping, fishing, boating, picnic areas, and trails.

Mildred Kanipe Park, 6 miles east of Oakland via Oak Street and Driver Valley. These 1,100 acres form a historic ranch complete with ranch buildings and equipment and occasional living-history demonstrations. You can hike or ride your horse; just watch out for the peacocks roaming the premises.

Pass Creek, 201 Curtain Park Road, Curtain. The day-use area surrounds a pond and has picnic and play areas. There's a campground, too, but unfortunately it butts up against I-5.

Whistler's Bend Park, 2828 Whistler's Park Road, 15 miles east of Roseburg on OR 138. An idyllic 147-acre park, Whistler's meadows and groves lie along the North Umpqua, with nonhookup campsites, picnic and play areas, trails, and a boat ramp. Good for an overnight or a day by the river.

The **Umpqua National Forest** (see *Guidance*) covers a lot of territory, from about 20 miles east of I-5 up to the Cascades Crest. Though only a portion of it is formal wilderness, there are plenty of woods, remote canyons, mountains, and streams among which to get lost, voluntarily or not. The vegetation is chiefly moist coniferous forest with an understory of big-leaf maple, with some hardwoods at lower elevations, and in a mountain range dubbed "Cascades," it has an extraordinary number of waterfalls.

WILDERNESS AREAS **Boulder Creek Wilderness** (541-498-2531), about 45 miles east of Roseburg just off OR 138; access via Boulder Creek Trail. This wilderness of more than 19,000 acres was burned twice in recent years, 1996 and 2008, some areas more than others. Wandering through, you can find pockets of fire-resistant ponderosas and areas of intense burn as well as impressive columnar basalt formations. The Boulder Creek Trail runs through the middle of the wilderness along the creek, with a few side trails.

✷ Lodging

BED & BREAKFASTS

North Umpqua Highway

Idleyld Lodge Bed and Breakfast (541-496-0088; www.idleyldlodge.com), 23834 N. Umpqua Highway, Idleyld Park. The lodge has been sitting here for 120 years. You can still huddle around the river-rock fireplace or belly up to the antique bar (now serving breakfast rather than beer), then go out and enjoy all the recreation the North Umpqua has to offer. Three suites and one double sleep three to four people, and come with a continental breakfast. Double occupancy $47–77; a mobile home under the trees sleeps six and goes for $97. Pets allowed on approval. Their **Eatery** serves lunch and dinner all day.

Roseburg

C. H. Bailey House (1-877-322-4539; www.chbaileyhouse.com), 121 Melton Road. The grand house with its columned porch was the happy home of Dr. Clarence Bailey and family, built in 1909. They planted their 50 acres to fruit trees, most of which were eventually eliminated to make way for the current Christmas tree farm, and sorted apples in the barn, where you can now play at darts. Out in the country about 10 miles southeast of Roseburg, it's a restful base for exploring the area or for swinging on the porch. $125–145, including full breakfast (more on holidays). Pets on approval.

Hokanson's Guest House (541-672-2362; www.hokansonsguesthouse.com), 848 SE Jackson Street. The Hokansons got their hands on this modest Victorian in 1987 and rescued it from disintegration at the hands of vandals and time. Now it stands neatly in downtown Roseburg, comfortably traditional without being fussy. Two guest rooms (with possible overflow into a former maid's room) are named for the Howells, who inhabited the house for more than a century; each has a private bath, and one has an original wood-burning fireplace. The Hokansons will make you feel at home and let you choose whether you want a continental or three-course breakfast. $85–105.

FOREST SERVICE LOOKOUTS

Several Forest Service cabins and fire lookouts give a taste of fire watching in the old—well, not that old!—days of the Forest Service. Generally they run $40 a night and can sleep several people. Guests must bring their own bedding and cooking utensils. No smoking, obviously. Reserve through www.recreation.gov (or by calling 1-877-444-6777).

🐾 **Butler Butte Cabin** was built in 1942 as part of the Aircraft Warning System, to detect possible Japanese warplanes and the incendiary balloons launched by the Japanese forces in hopes of setting off huge forest conflagrations in the Northwest (few of which caused any damage). After the war it was converted to fire observation. The cabin is at ground level and sleeps four on a double bed and two singles, and has a heater, cookstove, lights, and refrigerator, and vault toilet, but no water. Open year-round. Pets are welcome, but don't let them roam. High-clearance vehicle recommended, and in winter the road isn't plowed. Contact the Tiller District Office (541-825-3201) for the somewhat complicated directions.

Fairview Peak Lookout stands 53 feet tall on top of a peak in the Bohemia Mountains. The site started out as a fire lookout in the 1920s, then functioned as an Air Force radar station till 1964. The small cabin comes with a futon and kitchenette (without utensils). There's a vault toilet, but no water. Views are great and hiking is fine, but avoid the nearby mining sites, which present hazards and are private property anyway. This lookout isn't recommended for children since access is by a high tower and catwalk. About 42 miles from Cottage Grove by Row River Road, Brice Creek Road, Noonday Road, Sharps Creek Road, and Fairview Lookout Road; high-clearance vehicle recommended. Open summer and fall.

🐾 **Musick Guard Station** is within the Bohemia Mining District, which had a gold boom after ore-bearing quartz was found in 1863. The two-story cabin in the woods was a firefighters' base beginning in the 1930s and has two bedrooms, one up and one down, with platform beds and bunk beds, a woodstove and cookstove, but no utensils, lights, refrigerator, water, or firewood. There are a vault toilet and a fire ring. About 42 miles from Cottage Grove by Row River Road, Brice Creek Road, Noonday Road, and Sharps Creek Road. Pets welcome.

🐾 **Pickett Butte Lookout** seems an unlikely site to homestead, being perched on top of a butte, but that's what William Pickett did in 1898. Apparently he moved or passed on at some point, because a watchtower appeared in 1934 (the current 40-foot tower dates from 1948). The small cabin has a single bed, propane heat, lanterns, cookstove, and outdoor vault toilet, but no water. From Tiller take CR 46 to Pickett Butte Road to Road 3113, then take Road 3113-300 and follow to the lookout, for a total of about 13 miles. Be cautious in taking children, as the railing around the cabin is only 3 feet high and 40 feet off the ground.

🖉 🐾 **Whisky Camp Guard Station** is a cedar, two-room cabin that was set deep in the forest in the 1940s for a solitary fire guard. A double bed and two singles and propane-powered kitchen appliances make this good for families; there's the usual vault toilet and no water. About 22 miles from Tiller by CR 46, Jackson Creek Road, Road 2925, Road 3114-600, and Road 3114-625, where there's a locked gate.

HOTELS AND MOTELS

North Umpqua Highway

Dogwood Motel (541-496-3403; www.dogwoodmotel.com), 28866 N. Umpqua Highway, Idleyld Park. A log-cabin motor court that won't break the bank, the Dogwood is prettily decorated with gardens (including dogwood trees) and a koi pond. And it's right on the bank of the North Umpqua, with all the hiking, fishing, and rafting that entails. Cabins $65–85, double occupancy; long-term rates available.

INNS, LODGES, AND RANCHES

Elkton

Big K Guest Ranch (1-800-390-2445; www.big-k.com), 20029 OR 138 W. Where the Umpqua approaches the Coast Range, the Big K runs cattle as it has for a hundred years, except now it runs tourists, too—on 2,500 hilly acres with 10 miles of riverfront. That's plenty of elbow room for hiking, wildlife-watching, swimming, or fishing the river (with or without a guide), and riding the range. Rates of $399 for lodge suites and $369 for cabins include three ranch-style meals. Activities like horseback riding and float trips involve additional fees.

North Umpqua Highway

♿ 🐾 **Illahee Inn** (541-496-4870; www.illaheeinn.net), 170 Wild Thyme Lane, Glide. Six rooms sit in pleasant gardens in the town of Glide, cheek-by-jowl with the hiking trails, river access, and waterfalls of the Cascade foothills. Doubles $76; pets welcome for a fee; one room is wheelchair accessible. The on-site restaurant (see *Dining Out*) serves breakfast, lunch, and dinner.

Steamboat Inn (1-800-840-8825; www.thesteamboatinn.com), 42705 N. Umpqua Highway, Steamboat. Born of a series of fishing camps along the North Umpqua, the Steamboat got under way in the 1950s with a lodge and a series of cabins. Dinners were rough and ready—lots of freshwater fish—and served half an hour after sunset so the fisherman would lose no prime time. Accommodations have been added and updated for the demands of 21st-century guests, making them rather less rustic than they were then, and dinners likewise (see *Dining Out*). Lovely perennial gardens surround the lodge, screened from the road by rhododendron hedges, and you can get an in-room massage, but people still come for the fly-fishing as well as for an elegant forest getaway. Cabins run $175–215, double occupancy, though some can sleep more; three-bedroom houses $215, double occupancy; and luxurious river suites, $300 (but ask about midweek discounts).

✷ Where to Eat

DINING OUT

North Umpqua Highway

🖍 **Illahee Restaurant and Bakery** (541-496-3338; www.illaheeinn.net), 150 Wild Thyme Road, Glide. Open daily. Along a lonely stretch of road, the Illahee's steaks and Northwest seafood are more than alluring. There are a kids' menu and nightly specials; breakfast and lunch are on offer, too. And with a bakery on the premises, all the breads and pastries are homemade.

Steamboat Inn (1-800-840-8825; www.thesteamboatinn.com), 42705 N. Umpqua Highway, Steamboat. Dinner at the Steamboat takes place in a log dining room at the long sugar-pine table carved in the 1930s. The meals are hearty, as befits a place dedicated to outdoor pursuits, and generally a fixed menu based on Northwestern cuisine and chefs' Patty Lee and Sharon Van Loan's inspirations (though with some notice, they'll accommodate food allergies or special diets). Reservations are required. The restaurant is also open during the day for drop-ins and early-bird specials.

EATING OUT

North Umpqua Highway

Idleyld Lodge Eatery (541-496-0088), 23834 N. Umpqua Highway,

Idleyld Park. Daily for lunch and dinner. In the great room of the lodge, or on the deck in summer, you'll find solid American food cooked to order—or get a brown bag lunch to go.

Oakland

Tolly's Restaurant and Soda Fountain (541-459-3796; www.tollys-restaurant.com), 115 Locust Street. Closed Mon.–Tues.; otherwise open for lunch, dinner, and Sun. brunch (reservations recommended for the latter). Besides being the place for a robust dinner in Oakland (Alaska salmon with crimini and mustard sauce, half a dozen varieties of steak), there's an old-fashioned soda fountain to go with the old-fashioned town, and a bar menu for the economy minded. All in a structure of brick and gleaming wood dating from another era.

Roseburg

Brix 527 (541-440-4901), 527 SE Jackson Street. Daily 7–3 (Fri. till 9 PM). This relatively new restaurant has put a bit of pizzazz in Roseburg's food options, serving Northwestern cuisine prepared attentively.

✷ Events

July: **North Douglas County Fair** (541-836-7776), third weekend, 205 W. A Avenue, Drain. Family picnic, games, animals, food vendors, and live entertainment.

Sutherlin Stampede, Rodeo and Timber Parade (541-459-5829; www.sutherlinstampede.com), second weekend, Sutherlin Festival Grounds; free.

August: **Blackberry Festival** (541-459-4510; www.sutherlinbbfest.org), midmonth, Sutherlin. Lawnmower races, music, belly dancing, a classic car cruise, and, of course, blackberry recipes to benefit local youth and community causes.

Canyonville Pioneer Days (541-839-6966), last weekend, Canyonville. Parade, fiddler's contest, races, and music.

Douglas County Fair (541-440-4396; www.douglasfairgrounds.com), first full week, Douglas County Fairgrounds, Roseburg.

Sheepdog Championships (541-440-9513), third weekend, Seven Springs Ranch, Glide. Sheepdog trials and demonstrations of shearing, weaving, and spinning.

September: **Umpqua Valley Wine, Art and Music Festival** (541-549-5120; www.umpquavalleywineries.org), second Sun., Umpqua Community College, Roseburg. This celebration of regional art and wine has been going on for 40 years.

Tours of area **lumber mills** take place certain summer weekends; call 541-672-9731 for schedule.

Northeast Oregon

8

PENDLETON–HERMISTON–
MILTON FREEWATER AREA

LA GRANDE–UNION–ELGIN AREA

WALLOWA VALLEY–
SNAKE RIVER AREA

POWDER RIVER–SUMPTER
VALLEY–UKIAH AREA

JOHN DAY RIVER AREA

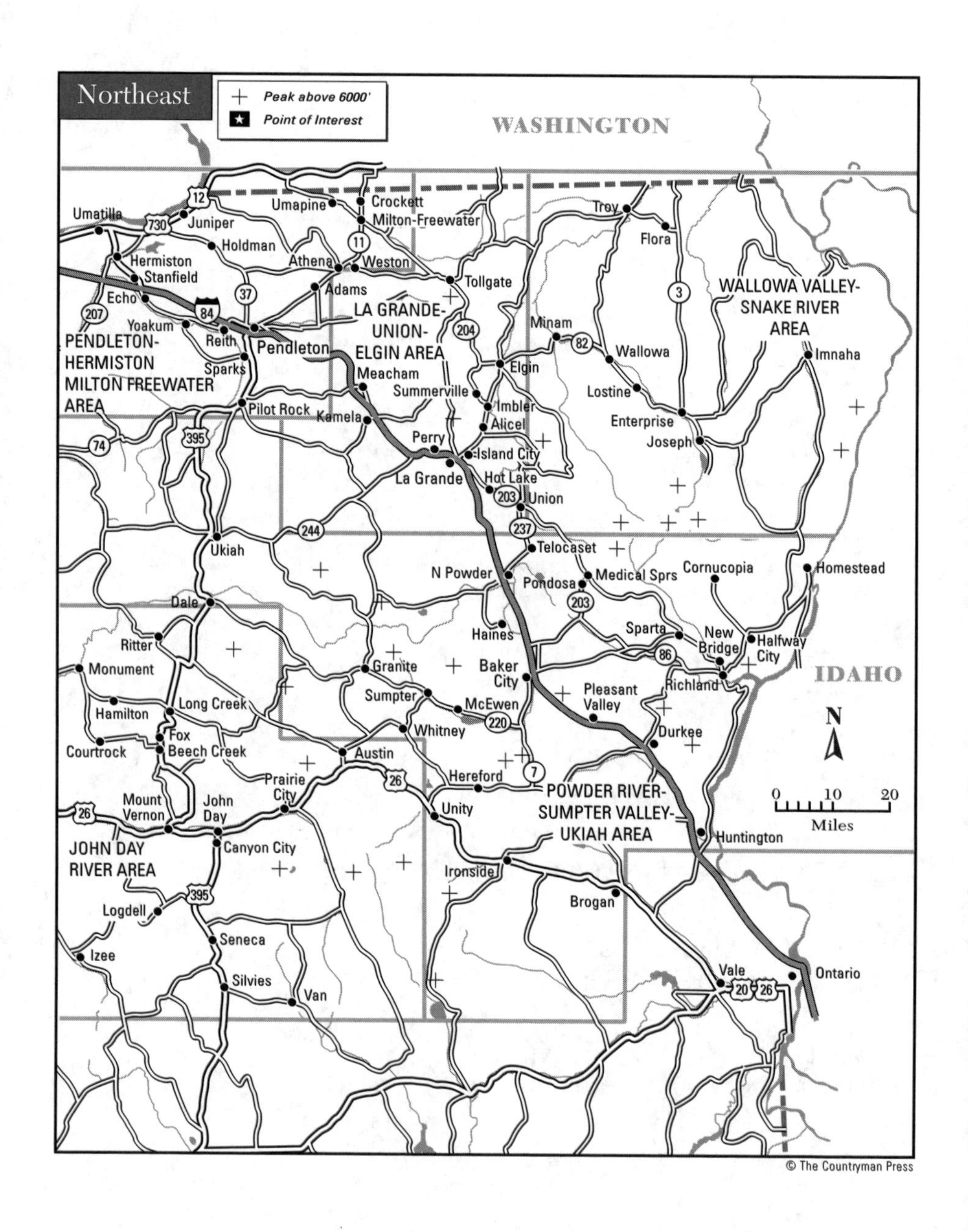

© The Countryman Press

NORTHEAST OREGON

A small string of covered wagons makes its way across the wilderness of eastern Oregon. Stephen Meek, the train's guide, knows a more direct route to the Willamette Valley than the tortuous Applegate Trail or the terrifying Columbia River. At least, he says he does; friends of his have scouted it out. The group actually has no idea where it is, Meek no more than the rest. People will die. At one point they nearly lynch Meek.

On this day, however, some boys of the party chance upon some large nuggets of gold in a streambed. But gold is the last thing on these people's minds at the moment, starved and exhausted as they are, and heavy metals are the last thing they need to add to their loads. Hoping to come back and find the lode someday, but mostly hoping to survive, they take one nugget with them and leave the rest, so numerous the boys say they could have filled a blue bucket (the typical pioneer painted-wood pail) with them. Some version of the story percolated out when they were finally found near the Cascades, and so the legend of the Blue Bucket Mine was born. But they never did find it, and no one ever has.

But it hardly mattered. The 1860s saw gold strikes all over the quadrant, from Canyon City in the John Day country to the Wallowas and the Blue Mountains. Boom towns came and went, some growing to several thousand souls before going bust—most fitting the Wild West stereotype of bordellos and saloon shootouts. There was a war going on, testing whether the nation would long endure, but you'd hardly have known it. Here the wars were different.

There's nothing like gold to tear up a country. In 1855, treaties had settled most Oregon tribes on reservations, some quite extensive. The Wallowa Nez Perce, for example, retained much of their original territory. But just eight years later, when gold was struck in their area, President Grant took away most of it with the stroke of a pen. Skirmishes broke out when the whole country was opened to settlers, and the Nez Perce, who had welcomed Lewis and Clark and lent a hand to some of the early emigrants, were driven from their home.

The Oregon Trail, of course, had kept flowing while all this was going on, cutting across the state's corner from southeast to northwest. You can see many sites and markers recording trail events along I-84. Old mines dot the backwoods, and Native American culture persists in the area, shared with the public at museums and cultural centers. So venture onto the back roads of this huge area. There are riches enough without the gold—wild rivers, Western heritage, pristine mountains, waving wheat fields—and who knows, maybe the Blue Bucket is waiting for you.

PENDLETON–HERMISTON–MILTON FREEWATER AREA

The Pendleton–Hermiston–Umatilla triangle is not writ large in the travel annals of the Great American West. Maybe the endlessly rolling wheat fields of the Palouse are less exciting than some other kinds of topography, but it's a good bet that one or more of those place-names is engraved somewhere on your inner hard drive. Let's do a little free association: Pendleton?—blankets! Yes, this is where they came from. You can visit the mill. Umatilla?—chemical weapons depot! It does make the papers every now and then as the cold-war stock of deadly chemicals is gradually destroyed, and people demonstrate either for or against the incineration, or maybe against the whole idea. Hermiston?—a tougher call. However, a few years ago Hermiston became the first town in the United States to install free Wi-Fi over the whole city. It still has the biggest electronic "cloud" in the nation, if not the world.

Well, you can't visit the chemical weapons depot. But you can drive the back roads and absorb the indigenous, pioneering, ranching, and wheat-farming heritage of the area, and stop in at a few of the sites in this chapter to deepen your appreciation.

GUIDANCE **Greater Hermiston Chamber of Commerce** (541-567-6151; www.hermistonchamber.com), 415 US 395, Hermiston 97838.

Milton-Freewater Area Chamber of Commerce (541-938-5563; www.mfchamber.com), 157 S. Columbia Avenue, Milton-Freewater 97862.

Pendleton Chamber of Commerce (5541-276-7411; www.pendletonchamber.com), 501 S. Main Street, Pendleton 97801.

Umatilla Chamber of Commerce (541-922-4825; www.umatillachamber.com), 611 Sixth Street, Umatilla 97882.

Umatilla National Forest (541-278-3716; www.fs.fed.us/r6/uma), 2517 SW Hailey Avenue, Pendleton 97801; **North Fork John Day Ranger District** (541-427-3231), P.O. Box 158, Ukiah 97880; **Walla Walla Ranger District** (509-522-6290), 1415 W. Rose Street, Walla Walla, WA 99362.

PENDLETON'S HUNDRED-YEAR-OLD WOOLEN MILLS MADE PENDLETON BLANKETS, AMONG OTHER THINGS.

GETTING THERE *By car:* **I-84** traverses the region east to west, while **I-82** and **OR 11** connect Hermiston and Milton-Freewater, respectively, to the main artery.

GETTING AROUND You will need a car.

MEDICAL EMERGENCY Good Shepherd Medical Center (541-667-3405), 610 NW 11th Street, Hermiston.

Saint Anthony Hospital (541-276-5121), 1601 SE Court Avenue, Pendleton.

✱ To See

FARMERS' MARKETS AND FARM STANDS Davis Orchards (541-938-7093), 53285 Appleton Road, Milton-Freewater. Sun.–Fri. 9–5, Sept.–Dec. Apples, pears, peaches, plums, gift baskets.

M&D Farms (541-938-7955), 53012 County Road, Milton-Freewater. Daily 8–6, June 25–Aug. 30. U-pick peaches.

Hermiston Farmers' Market (541-571-1952), at Main Street and Second in downtown Hermiston, Wed. 3–7, mid-May–mid-Oct., and at the Hermiston Community Center parking lot, Sat. 8–noon.

Pendleton Farmers' Market (541-969-9466), Main Street between Emigrant and Dorion, Pendleton. Fri. 4–dusk, mid-May–mid-Oct.

FOR FAMILIES ✐ **Pendleton Underground Tours** (1-800-226-6398; www.pendletonundergroundtours.org), 37 SW Emigrant Avenue, Pendleton. Ninety-minute tours given Mon.–Sat. 9:30–3, Mar.–Oct. and four days a week Nov.–Feb. Admission $15. Pendleton was wild from the beginning—its first ordinances addressed discharging firearms in town, brawling, and public drunkenness. It was the place where sheepherders and cowboys could come to collect their season's pay and spend it at the public baths, saloons, and other, er, conveniences. The Underground Tours explore aboveboard and underground Pendleton businesses—

literally, as subterranean tunnels connected many enterprises of both kinds and attracted more. Tours focus on the rumbustious goings-on in the bars, brothels, gambling houses, and opium dens, and their interface with legal commerce on the frontier. The lower age limit is six.

GARDENS **Oregon Trail Arboretum,** 801 E. Gerone, Echo. A hundred years ago, Echo residents ordered quantities of black locust trees to provide relief from the relentless sun on these treeless plains. The impulse must have been passed down to result in the Oregon Trail Arboretum, whose creation coincided with the sesquicentennial of the trail. A tulip poplar at the entrance? That's not native. No; trees here include those the emigrants left behind as well as those they found in Oregon. Crabapples, oak, even bald cypress coexist here. In fact, more than 130 trees and shrubs occupy this 0.75-acre plot between homes and the school athletic field.

HISTORIC SITES **Lewis and Clark Trail.** On Oct. 19, 1805, Captain Clark noted "a rock . . . resembling a hat just below a rapid." The rapid is now drowned behind McNary Dam, but the rock formation is still quite visible at **Hat Rock State Park** (see *Parks*), 9 miles east of Umatilla on US 730. Eight miles downstream were **Umatilla Rapids,** also disappeared, where Clark noted "banks of Muscle shells banked up in the river in Several places."

Oregon Trail sites. Eighteen miles east of Pendleton on Emigrant Hill Road, pioneers would descend the Blue Mountains at **Emigrant Hill** to cross the Umatilla and proceed down the Columbia.

Several sites near **Echo** preserve wagon wheel ruts: **Corral Springs,** on County Road 1300, 5 miles southeast of Echo, shows two sets of ruts descending a gully and coming up the other side. Property owners allow public access to the ruts, but please respect their property. The trail becomes visible again at **Echo Meadows Ruts,** also on private property just north of OR 320 on Whitehouse Road, 2.7 miles from Echo. Another 3 miles west of Echo, turn north onto a gravel road and drive a mile to the parking area of **Echo Meadows Oregon Trail Site,** 320 acres of BLM land with a mile of visible ruts accessible via a 0.5-mile walking trail. Another trail reaches a hilltop for a panoramic view of the region. A marker on OR 207, about a mile north of OR 320, commemorates an emigrant graveyard near Butter Creek Crossing, which, however, is 3 miles south of here on private property. A driving brochure showing acess to theses sites is available at Echo City Hall, 20 S. Bonanza Street, Echo.

Pendleton walking tour. Pick up a brochure from 501 S. Main Street and stroll the Old West side of downtown Pendleton, board sidewalks and all.

Echo walking tour. Echo is a backwater now, some 20 miles west of Pendleton and a few miles off I-84, but a world away. A hundred years ago Echo bustled with activity as goods moved through it from the interior to the port at Umatilla. The town of a few hundred has managed to preserve some 23 buildings from the late 1880s and early 1900s, from the rustic former saloon (and current restaurant) to the beaux-arts bank and the large Victorian homes of the city fathers and mothers. A brochure from city hall, at 20 S. Bonanza Street, guides you on an easy stroll around town. Also worth seeing is **Fort Henrietta Park,** site of the Utilla Agency (1851). This was one of the first Indian agencies in the area, often mentioned by Oregon Trail emigrants as the first frame building they'd seen since Fort Laramie. The building burned in 1855 and was replaced by Fort Henrietta, also now gone.

St. Peter's Church, now disused and in need of repair, stands at the edge of the park, a large stucco reminder of the town's earlier importance.

MUSEUMS **Echo Historical Museum,** 230 W. Main Street, Echo. Sat.–Sun. 1:30–4:30, May–Sept. The former Bank of Echo looks remarkably like an oversized safe or a miniature Roman basilica—a cube covered in glazed terra-cotta whose entry is flanked by two Corinthian columns. Today it houses artifacts dug up nearby at **Fort Henrietta** and from days when this was an Oregon Trail campsite and, later, when Echo was a major point for shipping cattle, sheep, and wool. The nearby **China House and OR&N Railroad Museum** bunked Chinese railroad workers (ask at city hall for entry) and now holds railroad memorabilia, historic photos, and medicine bottles dug up near the White House (where white railway workers slept).

Frazier Farmstead Museum (541-938-4636), 1403 Chestnut Street, Milton-Freewater. Thurs.–Sat. 11–4, Apr.–Dec.; closed Jan.–Mar. W. S. Frazier homesteaded this site in 1868, and it remained in his family for 115 years. The foursquare house dates from 1892 and is filled with most of the furnishings present when the family willed it to the town in 1983—which in turn date back mostly to the turn of the 20th century. The house and outbuildings represent a typical farm of the time and place, and are on the National Register of Historic Places.

Heritage Station Museum (541-276-0012; www.heritagestationmuseum.org), 108 SW Frazer, Pendleton. Tues.–Sat. 10–4. General admission $6, children $2, families $15. The repository of Umatilla County history is now the renovated 1909 train depot, whose halls display changing exhibits on the area's history, cultures, and economy. Outdoors you can visit a homesteader's cabin, a one-room schoolhouse, and a caboose (all but the caboose moved here from their original sites) and see how life was lived not so long ago.

Tamástslikt Cultural Institute (541-966-9748; www.tamastslikt.org), 72789 OR 331, Pendleton. Daily 9–5, Apr.–Oct. General admission $8, seniors and youth $6, families $17; kids five and under free.
By now you've seen and heard a lot about the Oregon Trail pioneers; now take a look at some of the people on the receiving end of that migration. This region is the home of the Umatilla, Cayuse, and Walla Walla peoples, and the museum beautifully portrays their precontact subsistence culture with dioramas, tools, and the yearly round of hunting, gathering, and ceremonies; the great shift brought by emigrants and missionaries through photographs, artifacts, and treaty copies; and the tribes' hopes for the future. Not only hopes: the tribes work on salmon, economic, and cultural recovery. The exhibits make powerful use of maps to show early trade routes

A LONELY RAILROAD CROSSING AT ECHO, FORMERLY A BUSY TRANSIT TOWN FOR SHEEP AND CATTLE

and progressively diminished reservations. Designed by Jean-Jacques André of Vancouver, the building is itself a work of art, with native wood and stone blending into the dry grassland. Don't miss it.

SCENIC DRIVES **Old Highway 30,** also called Old River Road, is the back road from Pendleton to Echo, following the Umatilla River. You'll traverse wheat fields and rock formations, and can stop at the Corral Springs Oregon Trail Campsite at milepost 7.

✷ To Do

BICYCLING The **Pendleton River Parkway,** also known as the River Walk, is a paved path almost 3 miles along the Umatilla through Pendleton, from the Little League Ball Park to the Babe Ruth Ball Park. **Lake Wallula River Trail** (see *Hiking*) is also open to mountain bikes.

CAMPING **Indian Lake Recreation Area** (541-276-3873), 19 miles east of Pilot Rock on E. Birch Creek Road; 43 tent/trailer sites, pit toilets, seasonal water; open May 15–Sept. 30; reservations possible.

Umatilla National Forest: Woodland, off OR 204; seven tent/trailer sites, toilet; no water. **Umatilla Forks,** 30 miles from Pendleton by OR 11, Blue Mountain Station Road, and Couse Creek Road; 15 sites, toilet; no water.

CANOEING AND KAYAKING **Indian Lake** (541-276-3873), E. Birch Creek Road, 19 miles east of Pilot Rock. Nonmotorized boating on this 80-acre lake, plus fishing and a campground.

GOLF **Echo Hills Golf Course** (541-376-8244), 400 Golf Course Road, Echo. Nine holes.

Milton-Freewater Golf Course (541-938-6411), 301 Catherine Avenue, Milton-Freewater. Eighteen holes.

Umatilla Golf Course (541-992-3006), 705 Willamette Street, Umatilla. Eighteen holes.

Wildhorse Resort Golf Course (541-276-5588), 72777 OR 331, Pendleton. Eighteen holes.

HIKING **Lake Wallula River Trail,** in **Hat Rock State Park** (see *Parks*), is a 9-mile section of the Lewis and Clark Commemorative Trail. Running along the section for the Columbia River now called Lake Wallula, backed up as it is behind McNary Dam, it has some steep bits but offers fine views of the hills, buttes, and water. Open to mountain bikes, too.

✷ Wilder Places

PARKS **Hat Rock State Park** (1-800-551-6949), 9 miles east of Umatilla on US 730, is a welcome bit of shade on a usually parched plain. Just upstream of McNary Dam, it's a place to picnic, launch your boat, or swim; or take a hike on the **Lake Wallula River Trail** (see *Hiking*). Lewis and Clark stopped here to remark upon the rock formation.

WILDLIFE REFUGES **Cold Springs National Wildlife Refuge** (509-546-8300), about 6 miles east of Hermiston on Highland Hills Road. Open 5 AM–sunset. A reservoir set in the sagebrush steppe is bound to attract wildlife, and here beaver, coyotes, elk, and deer may be seen in the streamside brush, while waterfowl and eagles flock to the lake in fall and winter. Hunting allowed in season.

McKay Creek National Wildlife Refuge (509-546-8300), 8 miles south of Pendleton on US 395. Open 5 AM–10 PM; closed Feb. A 1,300-acre lake surrounded by upland habitat where the Blue Mountains meet the plains attracts shorebirds and waterfowl on migration, as well as fishermen and hunters in season.

Umatilla National Wildlife Refuge (509-546-8300), six units scattered around Boardman in Oregon and Washington; call for directions. When the John Day Dam was built at the confluence of the Columbia and John Day rivers, it drowned thousands of acres of riparian habitat used by local wildlife and migratory birds. This refuge was set up in 1969 as mitigation and includes islands, wetlands, croplands, and upland zones. You might see herons, pelicans, curlews, or eagles and are bound to see ducks and geese.

* Lodging

BED & BREAKFASTS

Pendleton

🐾 **Pendleton House Bed and Breakfast** (1-800-700-8581; www.pendletonhousebnb.com), 311 N. Main Street. It's slightly startling to come across a four-floor, pink-stuccoed, Italianate villa in the heart of rough-and-ready Pendleton, but there it is, right on Main Street. The five guest rooms are all on the second floor, with a fifth in the attic; porches, balconies, and gardens invite lounging. $100–145, including full breakfast. Small pets welcome upon approval.

HOTELS AND MOTELS

Pendleton

Rugged Country Lodge (1-877-7RUGGED; www.ruggedcountrylodge.com), 1807 SE Court Avenue. A "boutique motel"—I like the idea. The mom-and-pop owners bought the rundown place in 2004 and gave it a complete makeover, putting in furniture a cut above the usual, tiled bathrooms, and Thomas Moran prints, and planting fragrant herb gardens. Each room is a bit different from the next. $72–82, double occupancy.

* Where to Eat

DINING OUT

Pendleton

Hamley Steak House (541-278-1100; www.hamley.com), 8 SE Court Avenue. Daily for lunch and dinner. Hamley and Co. has been a sadlery for a century and a quarter (entrance around the corner) but has recently expanded its offerings to include other parts of the cow. Six kinds of steak ranging in size from 8 to 16 ounces with all the trimmings are there for carnivores who have been riding the range all day. They're all cut and aged in-house; the menu gives a nod to chicken and fish eaters, too. Waddle next door for your spurs. Higher end.

Raphael's (1-888-944-CHEF; www.raphaelsrestaurant.com), 233 SE Fourth Street. Dinner Tues.–Sat. 5–9, June–mid-Sept.; Tues.–Thurs. 5–8, Fri.–Sat. 5–9, mid-Sept.–May. The house must be Pendleton's stateliest home, built originally in 1876 by a pioneer mother and considerably expanded by subsequent owners (one of whom founded the **Pendleton Round-Up** [see *Events*]). Now it has seven gables, 9,500 square feet, and a remarkable quantity of carved mahogany and oak. The menu takes advantage of Northwestern fish and game (it's not everywhere you'll find smoked rattlesnake and rabbit sausage, but maybe you'd prefer wild salmon with huckleberry puree) but does include some vegetarian options and a children's menu. And the wine list, of course, emphasizes the finest of the Walla Walla Valley. Higher end.

Virgil's at Cimiyotti's (541-276-7711), 137 S. Main Street. Jennifer Keeton moved up from California to buy a venerable and well-loved steak-house, reopening it in July 2009 as a venue for creative cuisine. Steaks are still on the menu, but so are seafood, fowl, and vegetarian dishes. My "appetizer" of stuffed portobello mushroom came full of feta cheese and sautéed veggies, with home-baked bread on the side, and was dinner for me. Service was superattentive (and they didn't know I was a writer), and the historic building doesn't hurt. Maybe it was a speakeasy, maybe something else, but it has a great tin ceiling and romantic nooks and crannies. (The restored bordello wallpaper and red lighting no doubt evoke an era but could be lightened up a bit.) Moderate.

EATING OUT

Pendleton

Cookie Tree Bakery and Café (541-278-0343), 30 SW Emigrant Avenue. Serves breakfast and lunch, and between meals. Cookies galore, even sugar-free, plus quiche, soups, and sandwiches.

✷ Shopping

Blue Mountain Cider Company (541-938-5575; www.bluemountaincider.com), 235 E. Broadway, Milton-Freewater. Mon.–Sat. 11–4. It's not all about beer and wine. Blue Mountain cider makes and produces handcrafted hard ciders—from locally grown apples, of course—and invites you to come and taste, and maybe take home a bottle. Opened in 2003, it's one of fewer than one hundred craft cideries in the United States and Canada combined.

Pendleton Woolen Mills (1-800-568-3156), 1307 SE Court Place, Pendleton. Mon.–Sat. 8-6, Sun. 9–5; tours Mon.–Fri. at 9, 11, 1:30, and 3. Where do Pendleton blankets come from? They come from right here and have since 1909, when huge herds of sheep grazing the Columbia Plateau produced wool for the world. Come and browse, or take a tour to see how the blankets (sweaters, dresses, etc.) are made.

✷ Events

July: ✐ **Athena Caledonian Games** (541-566-3880; www.athenacaledoniangames.org), second weekend, City Park, Athena. Free. Athena has a Caledonian Society going back to 1899, and they're still at their games, with pipes, sheepdog trials, Highland dancing, and children's activities. Camping is allowed on the elementary school grounds.

August: ✐ **Muddy Frogwater Festival,** midmonth, Yantis Park, Milton-Freewater. It used to be the Pea Festival, this being a legume-growing area of the Palouse, but that fell out of favor. Art shows, Kiddie Land, races, games, live entertainment, and a watermelon-eating contest (yes, the last two are separate events).

September: **Pendleton Round-Up** (1-800-45RODEO; www.pendletonroundup.com), second full week, Happy Canyon Arena, Pendleton. Bull riders, bucking broncos, calf roping, and clowns—all the things that make a rodeo, and Pendleton's is one of the oldest and biggest. Tickets $14–17.

LA GRANDE–UNION–ELGIN AREA

This is where the waters come down—the Grande Ronde flowing down from the Blue Mountains, and the Wallowa from the Wallowas, joining the race to the Snake—to form an arable valley. Most Oregon Trail farmers went on to the milder, wider Willamette, but a few came back here and started growing things. The few towns are small (even La Grande is kind of petite), and most have seen better days. Mosey around the city and into the canyons to discover a start-up brewery or nuggets of local history (the other kind of nugget, alas, has become scarce).

GUIDANCE **Elgin Chamber of Commerce** (541-786-1770; http://elginoregon chamber.com), 3 S. Eighth Street, Elgin 97827.

Umatilla National Forest (541-278-3716; www.fs.fed.us/r6/uma), 2517 SW Hailey Avenue, Pendleton 97801; **North Fork John Day Ranger District** (541-427-3231), P.O. Box 158, Ukiah 97880; **Walla Walla Ranger District** (509-522-6290), 1415 W. Rose Street, Walla Walla, WA 99362.

Union County Tourism (1-800-848-9969; www.visitlagrande.com), 102 Elm Street, La Grande 97850.

GETTING THERE *By car:* **I-84** is the main artery, cutting the county northwest to southeast, while **OR 82** and **OR 244** arrive from the northeast and west, respectively.

GETTING AROUND You will need a car.

MEDICAL EMERGENCY **Grande Ronde Hospital** (541-963-8421), 900 Sunset Drive, La Grande.

✷ To See

FARMERS' MARKETS **La Grande Farmers' Market** (541-975-2411), at Fourth and Adams streets. Sat. 9–noon, May 16–Oct. 24 and Tues. 4–6:30, July 7–Sept. 29.

FOR FAMILIES ✐ **La Grande Drive-In** (541-963-3866; www.lagrandemovies .com), 404 20th Street, La Grande. Tired of sight-seeing in the great outdoors?

A COVERED WAGON IS THE SITE OF LIVING-HISTORY EVENTS AT BLUE MOUNTAIN CROSSING.

Take the family to the drive-in, one of very few left in Oregon. Call or check the Web site for titles and hours. (If you prefer air-conditioning, the theater does have some indoor screens.)

HISTORIC HOMES A self-guiding **walking tour** of solid La Grande homes, dating mostly from the early 1900s, is available from the visitors center at 102 Elm Street.

HISTORIC SITES You'll find several **Oregon Trail** commemorative sites as you travel I-84, which, after all, approximates the trail's route through Idaho and Oregon. Approach the **Oregon Trail Interpretive Park** at **Blue Mountain Crossing,** 12 miles west of La Grande off I-84, by a road winding up into the forest; then wander the three trails through the woods, where plaques describe the exhausted emigrants' crossing of the heavily timbered Blue Mountains (one trail is paved and wheelchair accessible). Ruts through the fir forest, now softened by weather and falling needles, show clearly where the wagons used to pass. In summer living-history displays take place by the covered wagon. There are restrooms and a picnic area; Northwest Forest Pass required. From the picnic area, the mile-long **California Gulch Trail** leads to a spring used by the travelers. Interpretive signs explain the logging history in this stretch of forest, and a self-guiding poetry walk pairs poems by William Stafford, Robert Frost, and other greats with appropriate spots in the woods for your contemplation (this last the project of former ranger Deb Barrett).

Emigrant Springs, off I-84 just 26 miles southeast of Pendleton, was another pioneer campsite offering water for them and their animals. A state heritage area, it offers a resting place for today's traveler, too, with a campground (see *Camping*), old-growth forest, nature trail, interpretive programs, and, of course, water.

Hot Lake Springs Resort (541-863-4685; www.hotlakesprings.com), 66172 OR 203, La Grande. This used to be a derelict place. Before that, it was a busy place, where several trains a day from Portland dropped people off to take the waters or receive treatment at the medical center. As in some spots around the desert, hot sulfurous water gushes out of the ground—in such volume, here, as to create a hot lake—almost a natural-born resort. It just took Dr. William Phy to build a hotel in 1908, then a hospital, and people came to enjoy mud baths, soaking in the hot springs, and copious meals of food raised by ancillary farms. But when a fire gutted half the building in 1934, the slumped economy prevented rebuilding, and it limped along until finally being abandoned. Suddenly, in 2003, the bronze artist David Manuel and his extended family bought the property, put in a foundry, and began to rebuild, with the aim of turning it into something like its former glory, with art galleries, guest rooms, gardens, and a restaurant. Call for tours.

Union Public Library (541-562-5811), 185 N. Main Street, Union. There are a number of Carnegie libraries in Oregon, but this is one of the few that still remains a public library. And you can't say it doesn't move with the times: though operating since 1912, it has high-speed wireless Internet access.

Whitman Route Overlook, exit 243 from I-84 and take Road 31 for 9 miles, then FR 3109. Before the Oregon Trail even existed, missionaries Marcus and Narcissa Whitman crossed the Blue Mountains on their way to Fort Vancouver. Their guide was fur trader John McLeod, who as a Hudson's Bay Company employee knew the quickest way to company HQ. The most direct route, though, was hardly the easiest. On Aug. 29, 1836, Narcissa wrote: "Before noon we began to descend one of the most terrible mountains for steepness and length I have yet seen . . . We had no sooner gained the foot of this mountain, when another more steep and dreadful was before us." This from a woman who had already crossed the country from upstate New York. They made it, being on foot and horseback, but wagons never could; the Oregon Trail blazers chose a slightly different route. The Whitman route was lost from disuse but reconstructed in the1960s by ranger Gerald Tucker, based heavily on Narcissa's diaries. As you stand at the overlook, you'll see why the expanse of the Blues, though not terribly high, was so very difficult to cross.

TRACES OF RUTS ON THE OREGON TRAIL AT BLUE MOUNTAIN CROSSING, WEST OF LA GRANDE

MUSEUMS **Eastern Oregon Fire Museum** (541-963-8588), 102 Elm Street, La Grande. Mon.–Fri. 9–5, and Sat. 9–3 in summer. Free. Awaken your dormant firefighter with vintage fire trucks and equipment in a century-old fire hall, and learn about firefighting from ancient Rome to modern Oregon.

Elgin Museum, 104 N. Eighth Street, Elgin. Tues.–Fri. 10–4 and Sat. 9–1, mid-May–mid-Oct. General admission $2, students $1, children under 12 free. Here is the story of Elgin in photos, memorabilia, and a blacksmithing display. Just as interesting is the building itself: a 1912 opera house with pressed tin ceilings.

NATURAL WONDERS More rounded than the Wallowas to the east, the **Blue Mountains** are timbered nearly to the top and cover a remarkable amount of territory: the Strawberry Mountains near John Day and the Ochocos just east of Prineville are considered part of the Blues. But that's because the Blues are thought to be a collection of several Pacific island chains that washed up separately on Columbia's shores (except that there was likely no Columbia that far back). And, they are apparently home to the first breeding pair of wolves to inhabit Oregon in more than 50 years.

SCENIC DRIVES La Grande is one of the endpoints of the **Hells Canyon Scenic Byway** (see "Wallowa Valley–Snake River Area"), 218 paved miles of scenery ranging from lush forest to dry rimrock, with another 200 miles of optional side trips. For details and a route map, check www.hellscanyonbyway.com.

Road 31/Summit Road is a beautiful gravel byway over the Blue Mountains, leading from the **Whitman Overlook** to OR 204 between Elgin and Spout Springs. Summer only; about 30 miles, to be savored slowly.

✷ To Do

BICYCLING Some Umatilla National Forest trails are open to mountain biking: **Martin Prairie Trail** is an easy 1.25-mile meadow ride with good wildlife viewing. It follows a closed road that leads to the **Copple Butte Trail,** a 6.24-mile ridgeline trail with views of the surrounding hills. South of Heppner, take Willow Creek Road 23 miles to FR 21; at the guard station, turn onto FR 21-050 and go 1.5 miles to the ROAD CLOSED sign; total 28 miles.

The **Spring Creek Trail System** is open to mountain bikes, hikers, and horses—two 5- and 7-mile loops through old forest, where you may see springboard cuts in stupms left by loggers in the late 1800s. Even better, it's prime wildlife habitat (see *Wildlife Areas*) where you may spot the elusive great gray owl or calving elk. Dogs must be leashed. From I-84 take Spring Creek exit (248) and continue south about 3 miles to FR 2155 and park.

BIRD-WATCHING **Bird Track Springs Interpretive Trail,** 15 miles west of La Grande. A spring, forest, and river floodplain attract a variety of species here, especially in spring when ducks and colorful songbirds come through. Overhead, osprey and bald eagles check out the buffet. Take I-84 west to Ukiah, then follow OR 244 for 6 miles and park in the campground.

Spring Creek Trail System (see *Bicycling*) runs through deep forest, meadow, and ponds—ideal habitat for the great gray owl, which should be on any birder's must-see list. Several nesting platforms almost guarantee you'll see one, especially in spring. Other raptors also use the area.

Ladd Marsh Wildlife Area (see *Wildlife Areas*), 5 miles south of La Grande on Foothill Road, exit 268 from I-84. Set aside to protect nesting and migratory waterfowl, the marsh allows viewing from certain viewpoints and a 1-mile trail.

CAMPING South of La Grande, several campgrounds invite the camper with clear streams, meadows, forest, and access to trails. The following are nonreservable, **Wallowa-Whitman National Forest** campgrounds requiring a small fee unless otherwise indicated: **Bird Track Springs** (see *Bird-Watching*), 21 tent/trailer sites, ADA toilet and campsite; no water; open spring, summer, early fall. **Moss Springs,** 24 miles east of La Grande via US 82, OR 237, County Road 65, and FR 6220 (this access road is steep); a high-country campground on the edge of Eagle Cap Wilderness, offering trail access to it plus 11 campsites, ADA toilets; no water; open spring–fall. **North Fork Catherine Creek,** 29 miles southeast of La Grande by OR 203 and FR 7785 (gravel last 6 miles); six tent/trailer sites, horse and foot trails, ADA toilets; no water, no fee; open spring–fall. **Spool Cart,** 27 miles southwest of La Grande via I-84, OR 244, and FR 51; fully ADA accessible with nine tent/trailer sites, ADA toilet, nicely treed; no water; open spring–fall. **Two Color,** 49 miles southeast of La Grande via OR 203, FR 67, FR 77, and FR 7755 (last 11 miles gravel); 14 tent/trailer sites along Eagle Creek, all ADA compliant, vault toilet; no water, no fee. **Umapine,** 35 miles southwest of La Grande by I-84, OR 244, and FR 5160; eight ADA tent/trailer sites and ADA toilet; mushroom and berry picking nearby if you know your stuff; no water, no fee. **West Eagle Meadow,** 49 miles southeast of La Grande by OR 203 and FR 77 (gravel last 20 miles); 24 tent-only sites in an alpine meadow just outside **Eagle Cap Wilderness,** ADA toilet, great hiking and horseback riding; no water.

Fees apply in the **Umatilla National Forest: Jubilee Lake,** 12 miles northeast of Tollgate off FR 64; 50 lakeside tent and trailer sites with a 3-mile trail around the lake, ADA toilets, drinking water. **Target Meadows,** 2 miles north of Tollgate by FRs 204 and 6401; 16 tent/trailer sites, four tent-only sites, water, toilets. **Woodward,** 18 tent/trailer sites. **Mottet,** 30 miles northeast of Tollgate by a series of forest roads (call Walla Walla Ranger District for directions); seven tent-trailer sites, wilderness access.

Catherine Creek State Park, 8 miles south of Union on OR 203; 20 primitive sites ($5–8), water, restrooms; no reservations; open mid-Apr.–mid-Oct.

Emigrant Springs State Heritage Area, off I-84, 26 miles southeast of Pendleton, memorializes the Oregon Trail with a covered wagon display but also has a campground with 8 full hookup sites, 1 partial hookup, 15 tent sites, 6 "rustic" cabins sleeping five, and 2 "totem cabins" sleeping seven (bring bedding), water, and restrooms. Hookup sites $16, tent sites $10–14, cabins $20–35. Open Apr.–Oct.

Hilgard Junction State Park, 8 miles west of La Grande off I-84 on the Grande Ronde River; 17 primitive sites ($5–8), water, restrooms; no reservations; open year-round.

Red Bridge State Wayside, 16 miles southwest of La Grande on OR 204; 10 walk-in tent sites and 10 primitive sites ($5–8), water, restrooms; no reservations.

CANOEING, KAYAKING, AND RAFTING The **Wallowa, Grande Ronde,** and **North Fork John Day rivers** are wild, scenic, free-flowing, and popular with rafters. Their relative remoteness means they seldom get crowded; it also means you're pretty much on your own, so it's best to have experienced rafters in your party. A free permit is required to float the Grande Ronde, available at major launch sites and the Baker Resource Area Office (541-523-1256). River levels can fluctuate unpredictably. A printed guide to the rivers is available from the Umatilla National Forest (541-278-3716). A favorite put-in on the **Wallowa** is **Minam** (see *Parks*). For the **John Day,** there are several put-ins near Dale; for directions contact the **North Fork John Day Ranger District** in Ukiah (541-427-3231).

For a nice quiet paddle, **Jubilee Lake** (see *Camping*) is closed to motorized craft and has a campground alongside.

GOLF **Buffalo Peak Golf Course** (541-562-9031; www.buffalopeakgolf.com), 1224 E. Fulton Street, Union. Eighteen holes.

HIKING A 2.7-mile trail circles clear **Jubilee Lake** (see *Camping*) amid evergreen forests. For a longer hike involving either a car shuttle or camping overnight, the **North Fork Umatilla Trail** is a 10-mile path with a 2,700-foot elevation gain inside the **North Fork Umatilla Wilderness;** from Gibbon take Umatilla River Road 11 miles east to the Umatilla Forks day use area and trailhead.

The **Lake Creek Trail** is an 8-mile in-and-out from Lake Creek to the Buck Creek Trail, with little elevation change, open to hikers and horses only. From Weston take OR 204 for 27 miles to FR 31, turning onto FR 3150 after 6 miles. Turn right again and drive about a mile to the trailhead.

HOT SPRINGS **Cove Warm Springs** (541-586-4890), 907 Water Street, Cove. Daily 11–8, Memorial Day–Labor Day. Warm, not hot, but natural. The springs well up into a concrete swimming pool built around them—look down, and you'll see them bubbling up at 300 gallons a minute from the depths of the earth. The property is privately owned, so there's a small fee for swimming.

✷ Wilder Places

PARKS **Gangloff Park,** just off I-84 north of La Grande, is a roadside patch overlooking the city. The native vegetation is being restored, and a reconstructed cabin reminds one of the pioneers who probably gazed on the town site from here as they arrived (or departed). **Riverside Park,** down the hill within town, is a 12-acre expanse of lawns and gardens. **Birnie Park,** at B Street and Gekeler, is in the oldest part of town and was once an Oregon Trail campsite—a logical place to take a breather before tackling the Blue Mountains.

Catherine Creek State Park (**1-800-551-6949**), 8 miles south of Union on OR 203. In the canyon of Catherine Creek and shade by tall pines, the park is a place to relax for a day or three. Camp, play horseshoes, stroll, or paddle in the stream.

✐ **Emigrant Springs State Park** (**541-983-2277 or 1-800-551-6949**), off I-84, 26 miles southeast of Pendleton (see *Historic Sites*). Walk a nature trail through the woods, take in a ranger talk in the amphitheater, and visit the historic Oregon Trail display here. Or camp and imagine yourself on the trail.

Hilgard Junction State Park (1-800-551-6949), 8 miles west of La Grande off I-84. The park sits on the Grande Ronde River, attracting fishermen; also on I-84, which is less fortunate. Nonetheless, the river makes for good wildlife, and there is primitive camping.

Red Bridge State Wayside (1-800-551-6949), 16 miles southwest of La Grande on OR 244. Unfrequented and quiet, this one is also on the river, with camp and picnic sites and shaded by pines and cottonwoods.

WILDERNESS AREAS **North Fork Umatilla Wilderness (509-522-6290)**, a mile south of Tollgate. At "only" 20,144 acres, it nevertheless offers varied terrain, trout streams, and 27 miles of hiking trails for those who like to backpack into the wilds.

The **Wenaha-Tucannon Wilderness (509-843-1891)** straddles northeastern Oregon and southeastern Washington and is a remote area of deep canyons, ridges, and subalpine forest. Bighorn sheep, elk, bobcat, and cougar wander here, as do a few backpackers in summer and hunters in fall. Two hundred miles of trails meander up and down the canyons. Access is by trail, the most easily reached being the one along the Wenaha River from Troy.

WILDLIFE AREAS **Bird Track Springs** (541-963-7186), 15 miles west of La Grande on OR 244. Not only birds, but also beaver and deer are seen in this floodplain of the Grande Ronde. Bird and poetry guides are there to enhance your experience of the 1.5-mile nature trail.

Ladd Marsh Wildlife Area (541-963-4954), 5 miles south of La Grande on Foothill Road, exit 268 from I-84, is managed by the Oregon Department of Fish and Wildlife for waterfowl (see *Bird-Watching*). Spring is the time to observe migratory birds; hunting is allowed in fall.

Spring Creek Trail System (see *Hiking*). From I-84 take the Spring Creek exit (248) and continue south about 3 miles to FR 2155 and park. Two loop trails extend through prime great gray owl nesting habitat and elk calving grounds. Dogs must be leashed, and the trails are open to mountain bikes.

✷ Lodging

BED & BREAKFASTS

La Grande

Stange Manor Bed and Breakfast (541-963-2400; www.stangemanor.com), 1612 Walnut Street. Quite an imposing mansion sporting two tall chimneys, the manor has four guest rooms, each with private bath, and spacious living and dining rooms. August Stange rather daringly built the 9,000-square-foot house in 1923 shortly after building La Grande's biggest sawmill, having left his native Wisconsin, where mills were closing for lack of timber; his family lived in the house for 37 years. $110–145, with full breakfast. Children 12 and over welcome.

Starkey

Grande Ronde Cow Camp Bed and Breakfast (541-428-2199; www.granderondecowcamp.com), 58303 Grande Ronde River Road. Far from the madding crowd, the "cow camp" lies off the tourist track in the middle of the Blue Mountains. You can choose among the log lodge, with bedrooms in the loft and a cozy living room below; a bunkhouse with two twin beds; or a log cabin (perfect for families) with two bed sets, each having a single twin above a queen bed, refrigerator, and microwave. Relax in nature or visit the nearby hot springs. Lodge rooms $80–85, bunkhouse $60, cabin $95, double occupancy. They board horses, too.

Union

Joshua's Country Store and Inn (541-786-1492; www.joshuascountry storeinn.com), 1598 N. Cove Street. Here's your chance to stay in a hundred-year-old farmhouse on an active farm. Seven acres with fruit trees, a creek, and gardens just outside the small town of Union can be your base for exploring, or just staying put while owners Donna and Joshua run the farm and the store and whip up your hearty farm breakfast. $99, double occupancy.

FOREST SERVICE RENTALS Two Color Guard Station, about 23 miles from Medical Springs on FRs 77 and 7755. More of a lodge than a cabin, this station was built as a crew bunkhouse in 1959 to replace one dating from the 1930s. It has beds for 12 and—what luxury—sofas, propane lights and cookstove, cooking utensils, even a flush toilet and shower. Though in winter there is no running water, and you must bring your own and use the outhouse. Near trailheads for the Eagle Cap Wilderness, it even has a corral; and if you want to gaze at the creek from the back porch, that's fine, too. Open June 1–Dec. 31—but remember the caveats about winter, and you may need a snowmobile to get there. $80 a day for up to four, $60 after Oct. 1, and $10 per additional person. Reserve at www.recreation.gov or by calling 1-877-444-6777.

HOTELS AND MOTELS

Union

Historic Union Hotel (1-888-441-8928; www.thehistoricunionhotel .com), 326 N. Main Street. Annie Oakley slept here. So, maybe, did Clark Gable. This 1920s hotel in slow-paced Union has 16 nicely restored rooms and suites, all discreetly decorated with various Western themes, some old-fashioned and some contemporary. To stay in character, there are no phones or TVs in the rooms, though a TV adorns the lobby. But they do have private baths (except the "Original Room"). $39–109. Pets allowed in some rooms. The in-house **Fireside Café and Pub** serves breakfast, lunch, and dinner.

✱ Where to Eat

DINING OUT

La Grande

Foley Station (541-963-7473; www .foleystation.com), 1114 Adams Street. Daily 3–9 for dinner, Fri. 11–3 for lunch, Sun. brunch 9–3. Foley's knows that one size doesn't fit all. You crave a haute cuisine entrée like tournedos Henri IV or Basque spareribs (always with vegetables and fresh sourdough bread) but don't have the stomach capacity or pocketbook for a full serving? Get the "petit" serving for 60 to 70 percent of full price. Likewise for the appetizers—get a "small plate" or a "taster." This is a stroke of genius, especially for a semirural community where they said it couldn't be done (wouldn't be a bad thing for urban dwellers, either). The menu is eclectic: Hawaiian char sui barbecue, scallops with lemongrass sauce—tumbleweed onion rings?—but always fixed with the light touch of chef Merlyn Baker, who has been heading the kitchen here for more than a decade.

EATING OUT

La Grande

Mount Emily Ale House (541-962-7711; www.mtemilyalehouse.com), 1202 Adams Avenue. Tues.–Sat. 4:30–11. Opened early in 2009, Mount Emily (named for a nearby peak) proves that microbrewing has conquered the Great Interior of the state. They make five of their own, well received by the local connoisseurs, accompanied by hearty selection of sandwiches, salads, pizza, and naturally ale-battered fish-and-chips. The most expensive menu item is $11 (excluding pizzas).

Ten Depot Street (541-963-8766; www.tendepotstreet.com), 10 Depot Street. Mon.–Sat. 5–10; bar open Mon.–Thurs. 4–10:30, till 11 Fri.–Sat. It's one of those utilitarian brick buildings put up a hundred or so years ago, whose utility has been changed to dining. The obligatory steaks and chops share menu space with smoked salmon pâté, lamb meatballs, and even lentil-pecan burgers, paired up with a wine list featuring, of course, regional wines.

✱ Events

July: **Elgin Stampede** (1-800-848-9969), second weekend, OR 82 and Hemlock Street, Elgin. Buckaroos and bucking broncos.

North Powder Huckleberry Festival, last Sat., North Powder. A huckleberry dessert contest, parade, barbecue, and games.

Union County Fair (541-534-2683; www.unioncountyfair.org), last weekend, 3604 Second Avenue, La Grande. Food, farm animals, fun, and a fiddle festival.

WALLOWA VALLEY–SNAKE RIVER AREA

Late in life, Chief Joseph of the Wallowa Nez Perce begged the government for a plot in his beloved homeland. But nothing doing. He died on the Colville Reservation in Washington, where he and some survivors of his band were eventually confined after detours to Fort Leavenworth and Oklahoma.

It's easy to understand his longing for the Wallowa country. Not only was it home, it is stunningly beautiful. The Wallowa and Lostine rivers, still sparkling, rush between fir-covered canyons. To the east the grasslands begin, happy feeding grounds no doubt to all those Appaloosas, today mostly farms though partly preserved. Farther east yet is the great canyon of the Snake River; all of this presided over by the granite Wallowa Mountains. Happy hunting grounds, truly.

Interestingly, the little settlement of Silver Lake, or Lake City, at the north end of Wallowa Lake, renamed itself Joseph in 1880, a scant three years after Joseph and his band had been driven out. Whether out of respect or regret, or both, isn't clear, but it seems an independent-minded thing to do for the times. A hundred years later, Joseph rescued itself from the constant boom-and-bust of timber and rose again as an arts town, complete with galleries in all media, a bronze foundry, a writers' colony, and, yes, artists. It took a vision quest of sorts, but there it is.

A BRONCO BUCKS ON JOSEPH'S MAIN DRAG.

GUIDANCE Joseph Chamber of Commerce (541-432-1015), Community Center, Main Street, P.O. Box 13, Joseph 97846.

Wallowa County Chamber of Commerce (1-800-585-4121; www.wallowacountychamber.com), P.O. Box 427, Enterprise 97828.

Wallowa Mountains Visitor Center (541-426-5546), 88401 OR 82, Enterprise 97828.

Wallowa-Whitman National Forest (541-523-6291; www.fs.fed.us/r6/w-w), 1550 Dewey Avenue, Baker City 97814. District offices: **Whitman Ranger District** (541-523-4476), 3285 11th Street, Baker City 97814; **Eagle Cap Ranger District** and **Hells Canyon National Recreation Area** (541-426-5546), 88401 OR 82, Enterprise 97828; **La Grande Ranger District** (541-963-7186), 3502 US 30, La Grande 97850; **Pine Ranger Station** (541-742-7511), 38470 Pine Town Lane, Halfway 97834; **Unity Ranger Station** (541-446-3351), 214 Main Street, Unity 97884.

GETTING THERE *By car:* **OR 82** and **OR 86** link the small towns of the Wallowa Valley/Hells Canyon area with an almost-complete arc around the Wallowa Range, broken, however, by a forest road that is closed in winter (spectacular in summer), when one must take the long way round by **I-84.**

GETTING AROUND A car is essential.

MEDICAL EMERGENCY **Wallowa Memorial Hospital** (541-426-3111), 601 Medical Parkway, Enterprise.

✷ To See

FARMERS' MARKETS **Enterprise Farmers' Market** (541-398-0707), County Courthouse Lawn, Enterprise. Thurs. 4–7, June–mid-Sept.

Joseph Farmers' Market (541-398-0707), Main and Joseph streets, Joseph. Sat. 9–1, June–mid-Oct.

FOR FAMILIES ✐ At the south end of Wallowa Lake, **Scenic Meadows Go Carts,** 59781 Wallowa Lake Highway, puts minigolf, go-carts, and an arcade at your kids' disposal. And at **Joe's Place,** 72662 Marina Lane, they'll find bumper boats, croquet, ice cream, and pizza. **Eagle Cap Wilderness Pack Station** (1-800-681-6222), 59761 Wallowa Lake Highway, offers horse rides into the backcountry for the whole family for an hour, a day, or a week. Rides from $35; reservations recommended. Adjacent **Wallowa Lake State Park** offers children's programs. For information call 1-800-452-5687.

GALLERIES Tiny **Joseph** has been a concentrated arts center since the opening of the bronze foundry in 1982; the modest main drag is lined with galleries showing paintings, photos, sculpture, textiles, bronzes, and more. A stroll up and down Main Street will include **Indigo,** 2 Main Street; **Kelly's,** 103 N. Main Street; the **Sheep Shed,** 207 N. Main Street; and **Valley Bronze,** 307 Alder Street. And that's for starters.

HISTORIC SITES **Nez Perce National Historic Park** (208-843-7001; www.nps.gov/nepe) is scattered about Idaho, Washington, Montana, and Oregon—38 sites, of which one is at the confluence of the **Lostine and Wallowa rivers,** 2 miles south of Wallowa on OR 82. Not a developed site, it was once a summer campsite of the Wallowa band and the place where Old Chief Joseph died in 1871. Other Nez Perce Park sites are:

DOWNTOWN JOSEPH AND THE WALLOWA RANGE

Chief Joseph Gravesite, Wallowa Lake Road about 0.5 mile south of Joseph. This grassy knoll is the final resting place of Old Chief Joseph, father of the Chief Joseph who led his band on a 1,300-mile retreat from the U.S. Army in 1877. The elder Joseph died in 1871 and was buried near the town of Wallowa; as the grave was twice vandalized, his body was removed to this spot in 1926. Offerings are often left at the base of the stone column.

Dug Bar, way up on Imnaha River Road, 27 miles north of Imnaha on a primitive dirt road. Here Young Chief Joseph led some eight hundred men, women, and children across the Snake River, at the direction of Gen. O. O. Howard. They were to go to a reservation in Idaho but soon found themselves fighting the U.S. Army; a few unruly Nez Perce had murdered a number of settlers, and that sealed the fate of the tribe forever.

CHIEF JOSEPH SENIOR RESTS HERE, ABOVE WALLOWA LAKE.

Joseph Canyon Viewpoint, off OR 3, 30 miles north of Enterprise, looks over Joseph Canyon, where some of the Wallowa Nez Perce camped in winter. According to tradition, Joseph was born in a cave along the river.

Several sites in **Hells Canyon** memorialize the native and settlers' history: **Kirkwood Ranch,** on the Snake River near Kirkwood Creek, is open to visitors with exhibits explaining ranching within the harsh canyon environment (there are still a few active ranches, though not this one); access by trail or boat. Mining operations pocked the canyon from the 1860s into the 1900s; **Eureka Bar,** near the mouth of the Imnaha River, is accessible by boat or the **Imnaha River Trail;** it's the site of a very short-lived town (1903–1906) that sprang up when copper was discovered and vanished as quickly, being too remote and difficult of access to be profitable. Near **Dug Bar,** but 4 miles upstream, is the site of a **massacre.** In May 1887 a Chinese mining camp was set upon by thieves, and 31 men were casually shot, dismembered, and thrown into the river. The robbers made off with the miners' gold and got away with murder: though three of them were arrested, others simply escaped, and the three accused were acquitted by a jury (most likely, of their peers).

MUSEUMS Nez Perce Interpretive Center (541-886-3101), 209 E. Second Street, Wallowa. Part of the **Nez Perce National Historic Park** (see *Historic Sites*), the center interprets the culture and history of the Nez Perce in this region.

Wallowa County Museum (541-432-6095), 110 S. Main Street, Joseph. 10–5, Memorial Day–mid-Sept. General admission $2.50, children under 12 free. The Wallowas tell a bittersweet story, being the ancestral home of the Nez Perce, from which they were driven in the tragic chase of 1877. The museum's collection of Native American and settlers' artifacts from the area traces the historic shift.

NATURAL WONDERS Hells Canyon. From the Hells Canyon Overlook you look over the canyon all right, but the Snake River is so far below you can't see it beyond the intervening bars, terraces, and benches. And the overlook isn't even the highest point on the rim. The west rim stands 5,632 feet above the river, and the east rim on the Idaho side 8,043 feet—9,393 if you count He Devil Peak just behind the rim. So it truly is deeper than the Grand Canyon, though not quite as broad. Well, the river has been at it a long time, cutting through layers of basalt 17 million years old. And since it drains a huge area of Wyoming and Idaho before getting to this point, it has a lot of power. So much, in fact, that dams were built to take advantage of it. But the stretch from Hells Canyon Dam to Washington remains wild and free, and the canyon, with its basalt cliffs, maze of side canyons,

FARMING AND RANCHING COUNTRY EAST OF THE WALLOWAS

and climates ranging from Sonoran to alpine, remains wild and remote—a habitation of eagles and a way station of wilderness wanderers.

Wallowa Lake lies brooding under the mountains between two armlike moraines, 5 miles long and 283 feet deep. You can swim in it, but it is, um, glacial—formed by not one but a series of glaciers that ebbed and flowed with the ice ages. As they came down the mountain they pushed rubble ahead of them, dropping it when retreating to leave long, almost undisturbed moraines on either side. The last glacier retreated about seventeen thousand years ago, leaving this clear, still lake.

The **Wallowa Mountains** are sometimes called Oregon's Alps, or little Switzerland, and as a massed, jagged range, they do resemble the Swiss mountains. Unlike most Oregon mountains, many of the peaks are granite; the range is thought to be an "exotic terrane" that rose in the Pacific and then crashed on the former coast of North America as the North American tectonic plate inched westward, whereupon granitic magma welled up, creating the massif. That last episode occurred about 130 million years ago, and now it's full of cirques, spires, and streambed carved out by glaciers to form one of the country's most remote and spectacular ranges.

THE CANDY-COLORED PRESBYTERIAN CHURCH AT HALFWAY, AT THE EDGE OF THE WALLOWAS

SCENIC DRIVES It would be hard to find a nonscenic drive in this region, but here are a few standouts: **Hells Canyon Scenic Byway** follows the arc of OR 82, FR 39, and OR 86 from Baker City to La Grande in a great circle around the Wallowa Mountains—241 miles of rough sagebrush hills, national forest, rushing rivers, and scattered Old West towns and settlements. The canyon itself is only visible from the overlook near Salt Creek Summit (and that's quite a view from over 5,000 feet), but the varied farm country and wilderness, massed wildflowers, mountain views, and historic sites are well worth the drive. Give yourself two or three days, or more to recreate on the way. If you don't have time for the whole byway, try **Halfway to Joseph** (no, that's the town of Halfway): from Halfway take Pine Creek Road, then turn onto FR 39. The narrow Forest Service roads wind up and up through dense fir forest, then meadows of wildflowers, before dropping into the green Wallowa Valley. Halfway along (distance wise) is a turnoff to **Hells Canyon Overlook,** where the Snake River hides deep in a series of gorges. The roads are all paved, but the route is closed by snow in winter.

The Wallowa Valley has many impressive and even unusual barns; the **Wallowa Valley Barn Tour** (541-426-0219) allows many photo-ops of red barns against mountains. A self-guided driving brochure is available at the Bookloft in Enterprise or Second Harvest Bookstore in Joseph.

A BARN SLOWLY CRUMBLES ON THE GRASSLANDS EAST OF THE WALLOWAS.

SCENIC EXCURSIONS **Eagle Cap Excursion Train** (1-800-323-7330; www.eaglecaptrain.com), Alegre Travel, 101 Depot Street, La Grande. Ride the rails along the Wallowa and Grande Ronde rivers for views of ranches, peaks, and meadows. Half-day trips run about $65 (seniors $55, kids $25), including lunch and beverage service. Reservations encouraged.

Hells Canyon Adventures (541-785-3352; www.hellscanyonadventures.com), P.O. Box 87, Council, ID 83612. For those who want to experience the canyon in the fast lane and don't mind some noise, jetboat rides take you in at river level (though not on the designated Wild portion of the river). A half-day trip runs about $65–75, kids under 12 $45–50.

✷ To Do

BICYCLING Several **Wallowa-Whitman National Forest** trails are open to mountain bikes: the **Wagon Road Loop** follows an old wagon trail for 10 miles along single-track and dirt road with scenic views. From Joseph take OR 350 for 7 miles and turn right on Wallowa Mountain Loop Road, then turn right on FR 3920 and park. Adjacent is **Forest Road 3915-025,** a lightly used 8-mile loop with some spectacular panoramas. Near Halfway, the **Sugarloaf-Deadman Trail** is a moderately strenuous 6.5 miles on the edge of **Eagle Cap Wilderness** among alpine meadows and granite peaks. Shared with horses. From Halfway take FR 66 for 20 miles to the trailhead at Fish Lake Campground. The **Mud Lake Trail** follows FRs 4135, 100, and 118 for a challenging 5 miles of high mountain views and remains of the Cornucopia Mine. From Halfway take County Road 413 for 6.5 miles to FR 4135, turn east, and park.

In the **Hells Canyon National Recreation Area** (the wilderness is closed to bikes), the **Imnaha River Trail** (see *Hiking*) is open to mountain bikes. The **Windy Ridge Trail** (open also to hikers and horses) is a moderate 9-mile ride with one steep climb, some steep drop-offs, and panoramic views; from Imnaha take FR 4220 to the Warnock Corral trailhead, and ride 2 miles to the Windy Ridge trailhead. For more trails, check www.fs.fed.us/r6/w-w.

BIRD-WATCHING This is a region where you can spot forest, alpine, grassland, and desert species, and some eastern species' ranges overlap here with those of western species. **Zumwalt Prairie** (see *Wildlife Refuges*) is fantastic for various sparrow species, plus peregrine falcons, golden eagles, and other raptors. **Wallowa Lake** harbors hummingbirds, thrushes, and many other songbirds. **Hells Canyon,** with its great variety of habitats, is home to raptors, grouse, and songbirds of many kinds, as well as waterfowl on the reservoirs.

CAMPING **Minam State Recreation Area,** 15 miles northeast of Elgin, is a raft launch site with 12 primitive campsites and restrooms, somewhat marred by arrays of power pylons.

Wallowa Lake State Park (1-800-452-5687) has a spectacular setting on Wallowa Lake and 89 tent sites, 121 full hookup sites, 2 yurts, showers, restrooms, swimming, and boating. It does fill up in summer (reservations recommended), but you can easily lose the crowd in the surrounding wilderness.

The **Wallowa-Whitman National Forest** offers plenty of camping opportunities. Generally they do not take reservations, and fees range from zero to a few dollars. Near Halfway: **Eagle Forks,** 11 miles northwest of Richland on FR 7735; seven tent/trailer sites, water, toilet; no shower. **Fish Lake,** 29 miles north of Halfway on FR 66; 15 tent/trailer sites, water; no showers. **McBride,** 10 miles from Halfway via OR 86 and FR 37; toilet; no water, no showers, no fee. **Tamarack,** 36 miles northwest of Richland via FRs 7735, 7720, and 77; water, toilet; no shower.

Near Joseph and Enterprise (several of these are in **Hells Canyon National Recreation Area): Blackhorse,** 42 miles southeast of Enterprise by OR 82, OR 350, and FR 39; 16 tent/trailer sites, water, toilets. **Dougherty,** 45 miles northeast of Enterprise by OR 3 and FR 46; eight tent sites and four tent/trailer sites, toilet; no water, no fee. **Hurricane Creek,** 6 miles south of Enterprise by OR 82 and FR 8205 (too rough for trailers); five tent sites and three tent/trailer sites, toilet; no water. **Ollokot,** 43 miles southeast of Enterprise via OR 82, OR 350, and FR 39; 12 tent/trailer sites, toilets, water. **Lick Creek,** 29 miles southeast of Enterprise on OR 82, OR 350, and FR 39; seven tent sites and five tent/trailer sites, toilet; no water. **Williamson,** 20 miles west of Enterprise by OR 82 and FR 8210; five tent sites and four tent/trailer sites, toilet; no water.

CANOEING, KAYAKING, AND RAFTING The **Snake River** is much in demand for rafting by both commercial and private craft. A somewhat complex reservations and permit system is in place; for details check www.fs.fed.us/r6/hellscanyon, or call 509-758-1957. To obviate this process, go with an outfitter such as **Winding Waters River Expeditions** (541-432-0747; www.windingwatersrafting.com), P.O. Box 566, Joseph 97846, or **Canyon Outfitters** (541-742-4110; www.canyonoutfitters.com), P.O. Box 893, Halfway 97834.

GOLF **Alpine Meadows Golf Course** (541-426-3246), 66098 Golf Course Road, Enterprise. Nine holes.

HIKING Needless to say, the wilderness, official and not, is crossed by miles of uncrowded, lovely trails, whether you prefer alpine meadows or dry rimrock, a half-day hike or a trek of several days. Here's a selection; for more trails check www.fs.fed.us/r6/w-w.

In **Hells Canyon:** the **Snake River Trail** runs for 45 miles along the river, from Dug Bar to Saddle Creek—almost the entire protected stretch of the Snake. Great wildflower and wildlife viewing, but very hot in summer; watch for rattlesnakes. The trailhead is 27 miles north of Imnaha on County Road 735 and FR 4260, a rough slippery road not suitable for trailers. For a shorter but historic walk, take the same route to Dug Bar but choose the **Nee-mee-poo National Historic Trail,** 3.7 miles of the route followed by Chief Joseph and his band heading, though they did not yet know it, for their last stand. The **Four Mile Trail** descends from the trailhead 2 miles below Hat Point to the Snake River—very arduous due to the steep descent (and ascent), but fine wildlife and flowers. The **Imnaha River Trail** is 5 miles each way from Cow Creek Bridge to the Snake River, with scenic views of the Imaha canyon and its whitewater. The trail is fairly level, and ruins of the Eureka mining operation are visible where the Imnaha enters the Snake. From Imnaha take CR 735/FR 4260 and continue 40 miles to trailhead (rough road; high-clearance vehicle recommended).

In **Eagle Cap Wilderness:** the **Maxwell Lake Trail** is 4 miles each way, with an elevation gain of 2,400 feet and fir forest interspersed with meadows and fine views. From Lostine take Lostine River Road south and continue 17 mostly graveled miles to trailhead. The **Blue Creek Trail** starts at the site of the old Cornucopia mine and is a little-used, 14-mile round-trip through tall pines and flowing streams; for a shorter walk turn back at one of several trail junctions. From Halfway take Cornucopia Road/FR 4190 about 10 miles to the trailhead. The **East Fork Wallowa Lake Trail** starts at the south end of Wallowa Lake (no Forest Pass required) and rises almost 4,000 feet in the 6 miles to Tenderfoot Pass; but for a short, scenic walk you can turn back after your first great view of Wallow Lake, about 1.5 miles from the trailhead.

UNIQUE ADVENTURES **Valley Bronze Foundry Tour** (541-432-7551), Joseph. Joseph's Main Street is adorned with numerous bronze sculptures reflecting its

PUBLIC ART CELEBRATING THE WILD WEST COMES OUT OF JOSEPH'S FAMOUS FOUNDRY.

Western heritage. If you wonder where they come from, look no further: they came from the foundry. Since 1982 Valley Bronze has been producing works of art, giving an impetus to the town's reorientation as an arts community, and has produced, among other things, frames for the Declaration of Independence at the National Archives. To find out how bronze work is actually made, take a tour of the foundry, offered daily at 10:30 AM in summer; meet at the Valley Bronze Gallery at 18 S. Main Street, Joseph.

Wallowa Lake Tramway (541-432-5331; www.wallowalaketramway.com), 59919 Wallowa Lake Highway, Joseph. Even if you're afraid of heights, the views of glacial Wallowa Lake and he panorama of the jagged Wallowas may be worth it. The four-person gondola rises 3,700 feet from the lake to the top of 8,000-foot Mount Howard, whence a network of trails radiates into the Eagle Cap Wilderness. Or if you just need to catch your breath, you might grab lunch at the Summit Grill. The tram operates through the summer 10–4; a round-trip ticket is $34, seniors $21, students 12–17 $18, children 4–11 $14.

✷ Wilder Places

PARKS **Blue Mountain Forest State Scenic Corridor,** off I-84 about 37 miles southeast of Pendleton. No fee. One of the few stands of mature forest along I-84 in Oregon, the spruce-fir corridor often harbors elk and bursts into wildflower bloom in summer.

Wallowa Lake Highway, Wallowa River and **Minam State Parks** lie along OR 82 between Joseph and La Grande; the first two are no-fee rest areas beside the Wallowa River, while Minam also offers rustic campsites away from the somewhat noisy park entrance.

Wallowa Lake State Park (541-432-4185 or 1-800-551-6949), 6 miles south of Joseph at the south end of Wallowa Lake. Spreading from the lake's edge to the base of the mountains, the park is a place to swim, boat, camp, and watch the wildlife, besides being a place of outstanding natural beauty. It's also an ideal base camp for hikes and horseback rides into the wilderness. Children's programs are offered in summer, and several restaurants and amusements lie just outside the park.

WILDERNESS AREAS **Eagle Cap Wilderness** (541-426-5546). More than 350,000 acres spread over the crests of the Wallowa Mountains, Eagle Cap is a country of granite peaks, alpine lakes, meadows, and an occasional stand of old-growth evergreens—think of the Alps maybe a thousand years ago. It's home to mountain goats and bighorn, bear and cougar, eagles, badgers, and the high-country pika; humans come and go, and (hopefully) leave no trace. Access is by any of several trails from the surrounding areas, with one of the most accessible being trail #8250 from Lake Wallowa.

Hells Canyon Wilderness (541-426-5546) sprawls along both banks of the Snake River from just north of Homestead to **Dug Bar,** taking in not only the roaring Snake but a maze of side canyons. The vast territory comprises arid canyons, cliffs, rimrock, and the lofty peaks that make this the deepest gorge in North America. Though homesteaders tried to tame the canyon, it really is inimical to permanent habitation, leaving it a majestic wilderness threaded with 360 miles of trails and wild rivers. Go for a day or an extensive backpacking trip, but remember the weather is subject to extremes, any mechanized equipment is excluded, and you will be mostly out of cell phone range. A guide or outfitter can smooth the way: call **Tri-State Outfitters** (541-426-4468) in Enterprise, **Wallowa Llamas** (541-742-2961) in Halfway, or any of the long list available from the Forest Service (www.fs.fed.us/hellscanyon). Access is mostly by trail from the surrounding **Hells Canyon Recreation Area,** more than 600,000 acres of the same terrain where you may enjoy fixed campgrounds, mountain biking, and boating the river.

WILDLIFE REFUGES **Zumwalt Prairie** (541-426-3458), about 20 miles from Enterprise. From OR 82, take Cow Creek Road, Zumwalt-Buckhorn Road, and Duckworth Road, and park at gate; all but the first few miles are gravel, but it's nicely graded. Free. Standing at the edge of this 51-square-mile preserve, you can see what drew ranchers to the area more than a century ago: thick bunchgrasses as far as the eye could see, interspersed with grassland wildflowers. Today such a stretch of healthy grassland is a rare thing, which is why the Nature Conservancy bought it in 2000 and 2006. Eagles, hawks, and grassland songbirds are some of the creatures you can expect to see, plus lots of ground squirrels and, if you're lucky, a badger or weasel. And what will you hear? Lots of silence, broken by bird-song and the wind in the grass—not even distant cars or farm machinery, though ranching still occurs on some parts of the range. No camping, and remember your wilderness manners.

* Lodging

BED & BREAKFASTS

Enterprise

Enterprise Historic Bed and Breakfast (1-888-448-8825; www.enterprisehousebnb.com), 508 First South Street. The Warnock family built this respectable farmhouse in 1910, and current owners Jack and Judy Burgoyne (yes, that Burgoyne—Jack is a direct descendant of British general John Burgoyne, who surrendered to the Americans after an unsuccessful attempt to invade New York from the north during the Revolutionary War) enlarged it so that it now has three rooms and two suites, all with private bath and luxurious new-antique furnishings, and a huge living room set around with plump sofas for relaxing in front of the fire. Plus, you hosts will pay to board your pet, as their home is pet-free. Doubles $120–185, with full breakfast and a hearty welcome.

Imnaha

♿ **Imnaha River Inn** (1-866-601-9214; www.imnahariverinn.com), 73946 Rimrock Road. North of the remote town of Imnaha is the even more remote Imnaha River Inn, a new log home in the gorge of the Imnaha River. Seven guest rooms, a rock fireplace, wraparound deck, and hunting trophies here and there remind you that you're in the West—and you're on the edge of Hells Canyon National Recreation Area. Dinner and packed lunch are available for an additional fee. Wheelchair friendly. $70 single, $120 double occupancy; shared bathrooms.

Joseph

Belle Pepper's Bed and Breakfast (1-866-432-0490; www.bellepeppersbnb.com), 101 S. Mill Street. Not your image of a typical Wild West house, this large neoclassical (or is it neo-Georgian?) home sits squarely on its acre lot as if in one of our more upscale suburbs. It was the home of Frank McCully, who came here from Salem in 1880, went into business, made it to the legislature, and became a founder of Wallowa County. Spacious living and dining rooms hint at the dignity of the builder, while three guest rooms are quietly and comfortably furnished. McCully and his wife are the only non-Indians to be honored with a grave in the Nez Perce cemetery where Old Chief Joseph is buried. Doubles $85–150.

Bronze Antler Bed and Breakfast (1-866-520-9769; www.bronzeantler.com), 309 S. Main Street. Within walking distance of Joseph's galleries and restaurants, the 1925 home has its original woodwork and restored Arts and Crafts stencils. Period-style furniture and puffy down comforters grace each of the four rooms for a cozy stay; or you can socialize in the equally comfy living room. Doubles $75–259.

Chandler's Inn (541-432-9765), 700 S. Main Street. A contemporary home within striking distance of "downtown" has three guest rooms with mountain views. $85–160, with full breakfast (but ask about specials).

Whitetail Farm Bed and Breakfast (541-432-1630; www.whitetailfarm.com), P.O. Box 1066, Joseph 97846. Particularly if you have kids (but even if you don't), you might want to stay on this working farm with all the traditional farm animals to get acquainted with. Two farm-style guest rooms look out onto mountains and sunrise or sunset, depending, and a river runs through it—really. It's just a mile from Joseph's attractions. Double occupancy $110, with full breakfast, but ask about multinight stays.

CABINS AND COTTAGES

Enterprise

Arrowhead Ranch Cabins (541-426-6420; www.arrowheadranchcabins.com), 64745 Pine Tree Road. Open May–Oct. Halfway between Joseph and Enterprise is a historic ranch where you can stay in an (updated) 1890s ranch wagon house. The self-contained cabins sleep four, and the view of the barn and mountains is quintessential West. Cabins $110–125.

Joseph

♿ **Eagle Cap Chalets** (541-432-4704; www.eaglecapchalets.com), 59879 Wallowa Lake Highway. At the end of Wallowa Lake and the edge of the Eagle Cap Wilderness, you're well positioned for recreation. The "chalet rooms" are fundamentally motel rooms (one handicapped accessible) and go for $65–120. Cabins may have one to three bedrooms, and most have a kitchen and gas fireplace; $65–185 depending on season.

HOTELS AND MOTELS

Wallowa

Minam Motel and Market (1-877-888-8130; www.minammotel.com), 72601 OR 82. This one's an experiment—a revived 1950s motel next to the train tracks. Sounds like a winner, right? Well, think again. The railroad that once carried logs from Elgin to Wallowa now takes fishing, hiking, and other outdoors enthusiasts into the wilds, while these same enthusiasts get to stay at the motel. It doesn't hurt that there's also a well-used rafting put-in at nearby Minam State Park. Eight units each have doors carved with outdoors scenes; some have kitchenettes. $68–78.

LODGES

Joseph

Wallowa Lake Lodge (541-432-9821; www.wallowalake.com), 60060 Wallowa Lake Highway. Open June–mid-Oct. and on weekends mid-Oct.–Memorial Day. Even in 1923 folks recognized the potential in fresh air, a crystalline lake, and mountain wilderness. So they built this rustic mountain lodge, and people came, by ferry at first. And kept coming. An amusement park entertained them after they'd finished fishing, swimming, or riding for the day. The 22 rooms have comfortable 1920s summer house decor, while the cabins have the original knotty pine walls and stone fireplaces. Breakfast and dinner are served in the dining room (not included in room rate). Rooms $80–170, cabins $100–235.

✷ Where to Eat

DINING OUT

Enterprise

Rimrock Inn (541-828-7769; www.rimrockrestaurant.com), 83471 Lewiston Highway. Thurs.–Sat. 11–8 for lunch and dinner. Quite a view to go with your rib eye or filet mignon; or you may want to venture into the chef's further culinary territory. In either case, you're away from it all on the edge of Joseph Creek Canyon. If you feel like staying the night, there are comfy tepees from $40–60.

Joseph

Calderas (541-432-0585; www.calderasofjoseph.com), 300 N. Lake Street. Dinner Wed.–Mon. 4–9:30, June 3–Sept. 21 and Thurs.–Sat. 4–8, Sept. 25–Jan. 2. This is where Josephites go for an important dinner to enjoy rib-eye steak, scallops, homegrown salads, and a few other chosen dishes—the menu is short but interesting. The place doubles as an art gallery.

EATING OUT

Enterprise

Cloud 9 Bakery (541-426-3790), 105 SE First Street. Your sweet fix in Enterprise—doughnuts, cakes, and other pastries.

Lear's Main Street Pub and Grill (541-426-3300), 111 W. Main Street. Open for breakfast, lunch, and dinner. Not just a pub (though much appreciated by lovers of the brew), Lear's is a place where you'll find biscuits and gravy but crêpes, too, pub sandwiches, and full dinners, whether your taste runs to thick steaks or porcini-crusted halibut. Meats and vegetables are from local sources, and the seafood is flown in from Alaska several times a week.

Terminal Gravity Brewing (541-426-0158), 803 School Street. Wed.–Mon. 11–10. Yes, it is a brew house making at least five unique beers, with a tiny pub attached so you can drink (and eat) indoors, on the porch, or under the aspens. Friendly and informal, its menu is basic American pub with fresh salads, hot sandwiches, pasta, and a kids' menu—and a few pub pastimes like darts and Foosball.

Joseph

The Embers Brewhouse (541-432-2739), 206 N. Main Street. Daily for lunch and dinner. Seven microbrews, hot and cold sandwiches, pizza, and a cheerful, relaxed ambience.

Vali's Alpine Restaurant and Delicatessen (541-432-5691), 59811 Wallowa Lake Highway. Wed.–Sun. for dinner (reservations required) and weekend mornings for homemade doughnuts. Vali and Maggie have been offering Hungarian cuisine by the lake for 25 years! A small but authentic menu keeps them coming.

✷ Shopping

If you have bronze tastes but a clay budget, you might check out some of the ceramic or glass pieces at the galleries lining Joseph's streets. Of course, if you do have the budget for fine arts, the same galleries are there for you (see *Galleries*).

✷ Events

July: **Chief Joseph Days** (541-432-1015; www.chiefjosephdays.com), July 22–26, Joseph. Rodeo, a dance competition, and celebration in honor of Chief Joseph.

TamKaLiks Celebration (541-886-3101; www.wallowanezperce.org), third weekend, Nez Perce celebration grounds at 70956 Whiskey Creek Road, Wallowa. A Nez Perce homecoming celebration, powwow, and feast.

August: **Wallowa County Fair** (541-426-4097), first week, Wallowa County Fairgrounds, Enterprise. Horse and livestock shows, 4-H, and all the accoutrements of a county fair.

September: **Hells Canyon Mule Days** (1-888-323-3271; www.hellscanyonmuledays.com), second weekend, Wallowa County Fairgrounds, Enterprise. Mule show, quilt show, horse and mule sales, food, and cowboy poetry to celebrate the mule skinners of yore.

Juniper Jam Music Festival (541-426-3390; www.juniperjam.com), Sat. of Labor Day weekend, Wallowa County Fairgrounds, Enterprise. Music all day long—jazz, country, folk, and more.

POWDER RIVER–SUMPTER VALLEY–UKIAH AREA

The Queen City of the Inland Empire or the Queen City of the West—that's how Baker City styled itself back in the days of its two gold rushes, in the 1860s and 1880s. Miners scrabbled in the hills, and fine houses sprouted along the city streets like mushrooms. Today it's quieter, but the homes and some of the original businesses are still there. This area takes in the Queen City and a few smaller towns revolving in its orbit, quite a number of ghost towns and mining sites, and a lot of wild country, reaching from the sagebrush outskirts of Baker City to tiny Ukiah in the heart of the Blues. It's a land of contrasts.

GUIDANCE **Baker County Chamber of Commerce and Visitors Bureau** (1-800-523-1235; www.visitbaker.com), 490 Campbell Street, Baker City 97814.

City of Sumpter (541-894-2314; www.historicsumpter.com), 240 N. Mill Street, P.O. Box 68, Sumpter 97877.

Umatilla National Forest (541-278-3716; www.fs.fed.us/r6/uma), 2517 SW Hailey Avenue, Pendleton 97801; **North Fork John Day Ranger District** (541-427-3231), P.O. Box 158, Ukiah 97880.

Wallowa-Whitman National Forest (541-523-1405; www.fs.fed.us/r6/w-w), 1550 Dewey Avenue, Baker City 97814.

GETTING THERE *By car:* **I-84** is the north–south artery through Baker City and its surroundings, while **OR 86** runs eastward up the Powder River Valley, and **OR 7** approaches from the west. **US 395** and **OR 74** link Ukiah to the rest of the world.

GETTING AROUND *By trolley:* **Community Connection** (523-6591) operates a new trolley route providing transportation within Baker City Mon.–Sat. 7–7. Beyond the city, you'll need a car.

MEDICAL EMERGENCY **St. Elizabeth's Hospital** (541-523-6461), 3325 Pocahontas Road, Baker City.

✷ To See

FARMERS' MARKETS **Baker City Farmers' Market** (541-523-9761), Geiser-Pollman Park. Sat. 10–1 and Wed. 3:30–6:30, June–Oct.

FOR FAMILIES **Sumpter Valley Railroad** (541-894-2268; www.svry.com), Sumpter. Operational summer weekends Memorial Day–Labor Day. Round-trip adult fares $15, seniors $14, kids 6–16 $9, families $40, under six free; one way $10, $9, $7, and $30. For decades this narrow-gauge line brought logs from the mountains down to Baker City. It fell into disuse in 1956, but dedicated volunteers have restored the 5 miles of line between Sumpter and McEwen and collected vintage cars to run with one of the original steam locomotives. The result is a high-country ride through the forests and mining operations that made the county rich; only now you'll hear birdsong rather than the din of the gold dredge. Pets allowed on leash.

♿ **T&T Wildlife Tours** (541-856-3356; www.tnthorsemanship.com), 15477 Sky Ranch Lane, Haines. Tours offered weekends mid-Dec.–early Mar. Adults $7, children $5. If you happen to be here in winter, you can take a horse-drawn wagon ride to the Anthony Lakes elk feeding station (you can get there by car, too, snow permitting, from exit 185 off I-84 and N. Powder River Road, but that's obviously less fun). A 250-strong herd winters here, and Susan Triplett and Alice Trindle have been taking people to see them for nearly 20 years. The wagon is handicapped accessible, no less.

GHOST TOWNS Some lasted a few years, some several decades; all were rowdy Wild West towns in their day, some quite populous. Today they sit surrounded by forest, with perhaps a few ruined buildings marking the site. **Auburn,** off French Gulch Road 7 miles from Baker City via OR 30, grew from zero to six thousand in 1861, when Henry Griffen struck gold. Seven years later it was nearly empty. A

SUMPTER WAS A GOLD-MINING TOWN WITH A TRAIN STATION FOR SHIPPING SUPPLIES IN AND GOLD OUT.

high-clearance vehicle is advisable. **Bourne,** 7 miles north of Sumpter on Cracker Creek Road, was a busy placer mining camp that even had its own post office from 1895 to 1927 (though it was first called Cracker). A wild and lawless place, it was abandoned after the flood of 1927. A few structures remain. Accessible by passenger car. Aptly named **Cornucopia** produced $20 million in gold in its day and was a strangely law-abiding town, considering. Several buildings still stand at various gravity-defying angles. Twelve miles north of Halfway on Cornucopia Highway, it can be reached by passenger cars, but only in summer. **Granite,** 15 miles northwest of Sumpter off OR 7, is, strictly speaking, not a ghost town, as a few people still live there. It did last from 1862 to the early 1900s. **Greenhorn** got its start when two young easterners walked into a bar (really) and asked where to start digging for gold. Another patron pointed randomly to a hillside spot where they duly dug and came up with some extraordinary ore. Before the two got back, the locals had already named it the Greenhorn Mine, so that's what it remained till the inevitable happened. Several structures, including an outhouse, are still visible. **Sparta,** 12 miles north of Richland by OR 86 and 5 miles of gravel at the Sparta turnoff. All that remains here is an old stone house, built as a store in 1872 by the Cohn-Heilner brothers. Though the townspeople built a 32-mile ditch to bring water to the operations, gold ran out in 1915.

HISTORIC HOMES **Baer House,** 2333 Main Street, Baker City. This is the mirror image of the **Adler House** (see *Museums*), at the other end of the block. Both are Italianate homes with two-story bow windows and ornamental cornices. Samuel Baer was a merchant in the district's infancy, and his house was the first of the two, built in 1882. Private home.

Bowen Home, 1701 Washington Avenue, Baker City. Ira Bowen made the crossing with his parents and arrived in the area with his parents in 1862. He grew up with the country and became the editor of the Baker City newspaper, *The Bedrock Democrat,* and built this ornamented Victorian house (privately owned).

Luther Ison Home, 1790 Washington Avenue, Baker City. Ison was a district judge who built this formidable home using bricks from Portland and fireplaces from Holland. He only lived in it for two years, as he died in 1889, though his widow stayed on for several decades. Private home.

HISTORIC SITES **Battle Mountain Forest State Scenic Corridor,** 9 miles north of Ukiah on US 395. This roadside tract was set aside to protect a stand of larch, pine, and spruce. It was also the site of a battle in the Bannock War, in which Bannocks and Paiutes marched from Idaho in hopes of regaining territory. The Indian forces were defeated at this spot by Gen. O. O. Howard on July 8, 1878—one of the last such battles in the Northwest.

Historic Baker City (541-523-5442), 2101 Main Street, Baker City. Who will mine the miners? Baker City was a sprout nourished by two sources of gold: the mines in the nearby Wallowas and the Oregon Trail emigrants, who kept coming through the 1860s and 1870s and were glad for some provisions. To the list should be added the miners themselves—whether they found gold or not, they needed food and supplies. Baker City soon became a beacon of the intermountain west, boasting the best hotel between Salt Lake City and Spokane, fine dining, an opera house, and (let's face it) plenty of less fine pursuits as well. Pick up a self-guiding

walking tour of Baker's downtown and admire more than one hundred businesses and fine homes that sprang up from the 1860s to the early 1900s.

Saint Francis Cathedral, 2000 Church Street, Baker City. Completed in 1908 of volcanic tuff quarried a few miles away, this is the seat of the largest (in area) Catholic diocese in the contiguous United States, covering all Oregon east of the Cascades.

Sumpter Valley Dredge State Heritage Area, 30 miles west of Baker city by OR 7 and Sumpter Valley Highway. There is gold in these hills, and there used to be more. This site is one of the most recently active in the area, having operated from 1935 to 1954, during which time it picked up more than $4 million worth of gold by scouring the riverbanks. You can see the results in the gouges and gravel ponds now linked by trails, and the massive dredge itself.

MUSEUMS **Adler House Museum** (541-523-9308), 2305 Main Street, Baker City. Fri.–Mon. 10–2. General admission $5, seniors $4.50, under 16 free. It's said that when Leo Adler's teacher reproved him for poor penmanship on an essay, he responded, "I'll have a secretary type it for me." Even if apocryphal, it shows a certain directorial spirit. The son of German Jewish immigrants, Adler spent all his life in Baker City, most of it in this house. As a teenager he delivered magazines door to door. One thing led to another, and he became head of a magazine distribution empire reaching halfway across the United States and gave liberally to civic organizations and to international causes. Never married, he died at age 98 in 1993 and left a $22 million endowment to the county, which is used for tuition scholarships and community improvement projects. Twin to the **Baer House** (see *Historic Homes*) down the block, Adler's house still has the original furniture and lighting, and the tour recounts his life story.

Baker Heritage Museum (541-523-9308; www.bakerheritagemuseum.com), 2480 Grove Street, Baker City. Daily 9–5, late Mar.–Oct. General admission $5, seniors $4.50, under 16 free. Considering what many emigrants had to jettison as they struggled across the country, it's amazing what did survive: cutlery and china, clothing, and embroidery, items that would be used on the trail and were needed upon arrival. Much of what you see in this 1920 natatorium is that, donated by pioneer families—even a delicate violin handcarved by a pioneering Mr. Pouch. Beyond that is a hall devoted to the mining booms that built Baker and the phantom towns that didn't make it, and, appropriately, rock collections, including the sparkling 18-ton trove of two Baker City sisters.

Eastern Oregon Museum (541-856-3233), 610 Third Street, Haines. Wed.–Sun. 9:30–4:30, second Sun. in May–second Sun. in Sept. Admission $2; families $5. A little bit of everything from daily life in pioneer days—toys, farm equipment, clothes, household items, what have you.

♿ **National Historic Oregon Trail Interpretive Center** (541-523-1843; http://oregontrail.blm.gov), 2267 OR 86, Baker City, 5 miles east of town. Daily 9–6, Apr.–Oct. and daily 9–4, Nov.–Mar. Handicapped-accessible facility. Adults 16 and older $8 Apr.–Oct. and $5 Nov.–Mar., seniors $4.50 Apr.–Oct. and $3.50 Nov.–Mar., children under 16 free. You can still see the ruts curving around the base of the bluff—also a panoramic view of the territory lying behind and before the emigrants who had made it this far. The center itself is an illuminating guide to the life and ramifications of the trail, using sound, video, living-history programs, and good old-fashioned exhibits to bring it all to life. Four and a half miles of trails wander about the property; imagine walking hundreds of miles of such terrain.

Pine Valley Community Museum (541-742-5346), 115 Record Street, Halfway. Weekends 10–4, Memorial Day–Labor Day. Admission by donation. This small but proud local museum displays mining, farming, and homesteading tools, and a collection of mounted animals.

Sumpter Municipal Museum (541-894-2414; www.sumptermuseum.org), 245 S. Mill Street, Sumpter. Thurs.–Sun. 11–3, Wed. evening 5–7. Admission by donation. Formerly known as Sumpter Supply, this 1899 building now holds a collection of photos, and the logging, mining, and ranching equipment that made Sumpter what it is.

NATURAL WONDERS **Hole in the Wall.** View from OR 86 about 9 miles north of Richland. In 1984, heavy rains undermined the mountainside, which then slid down to the valley, blocking the river and road. An interpretive sign shows the path of the slide, clearly visible from the road.

OREGON TRAIL Besides the **Flagstaff Hill** site, where the **National Historic Oregon Trail Interpretive Center** is located (see *Museums*), the entire **Powder River Valley** formed the path of thousands of covered wagons, from the sagebrush hills east of Baker City to the green river valley now approximated by US 30 to North Powder. After that brief interlude, though, they faced the Blue Mountains.

SCENIC DRIVES The **Blue Mountain Scenic Byway** runs from 10 miles north of Granite scenically down to Ukiah along FR 53, then gradually down OR 74 through the plateau towns to the Columbia River, about 103 miles. In season you may see, through the trees, meadows of blue camas in bloom.

Elkhorn Drive Scenic Byway, a 106-mile loop from Baker City through the high country, circles through the ghosts of hard-rock mining towns, old gold dredges, the granite pillars towering over Anthony Lake, and back down to the Powder River Valley. The scenery is wild, and there is plenty of opportunity to stop, hike, or watch wildlife.

Baker City is one terminus of the **Hells Canyon Scenic Byway** (see "Wallowa Valley–Snake River Area").

✷ To Do

BICYCLING **Phillips Reservoir Shoreline Trail,** about 16 miles west of Baker City off OR 7 at Mason Dam, runs along the south shore of the reservoir; about 7 miles each way, or make it a loop by picking up OR 7 for 0.5 mile, then turning on to Hudspeth Lane. Also from Mason Dam, the **Dooley Summit Trail** runs about 18 miles on forest roads with views. In town, the **Leo Adler Memorial Parkway** is a paved path of about 3 miles along the Powder River, open to bikes and pedestrians. For further rides in the national forest, contact the **Wallowa-Whitman National Forest** (see *Guidance*).

BIRD-WATCHING Ponds east and west of I-84 in Baker City attract waterfowl; best access is on **Best Frontage Road,** exit 302 from I-84. OR 86 east of town, near Virtue Flat and the **National Historic Oregon Trail Interpretive Center**

(see *Museums*), is a good spot for desert birds, and if you continue up the Powder River you may have some surprises, such as Forster's terns and eastern kingbirds; plenty of raptors, too. OR 7 toward Sumpter, The ponds and rivers on OR 7 toward Sumpter are habitat for osprey and songbirds.

CAMPING There's lovely high-country camping in the **Wallowa-Whitman National Forest** (see *Guidance*): **Anthony Lakes Campground,** 30 miles northwest of Baker City via US 30, County Road 1146, and FR 73, is a scenic high-mountain site with 16 tent/trailer sites and 21 tent sites, water, toilet, swimming, and hiking trails. **Grande Ronde Lake,** 2 miles past Anthony Lakes; eight tent/trailer sites, water, hiking, swimming. **McCully Forks,** 33 miles southwest of Baker City by OR 7 and County Roads 410 and 520; six tent sites; no fee, no water. **Miller's Lane,** 27 miles southwest of Baker City by OR 7, County Road 667, and FR 2220; four tent/trailer sites, three tent sites; no fee, no water. **Mud Lake,** 31 miles northwest of Baker City by US 30, CR 1146, and FR 73; five tent/trailer sites, three tent sites, water. **Southwest Shore,** 21 miles southwest of Baker City by OR 7, CR 667, and FR 2220; 18 tent/trailer sites; no water. **Union Creek,** 20 miles southwest of Baker City on OR 7; 58 tent/trailer sites, 12 tent sites, restrooms, water, hiking, boating, swimming.

In the **North Fork John Day District** of **Umatilla National Forest** (see *Guidance*): **Bear Wallow,** on OR 244, 10 miles east of Ukiah; seven tent/trailer sites, ADA toilets, interpretive trail; no water. **Lane Creek,** 9 miles east of Ukiah on OR 244; six tent/trailer sites, ADA toilets; no water. **Frazier,** 16 miles east of Ukiah on OR 244; 16 tent/trailer sites, ADA toilets; no water; a mile from **Lehman Hot Springs** (see *Hot Springs*). **Olive Lake,** off FR 10 about 12 miles west of Granite; 21 tent/trailer sites, two tent sites, hiking trail, nearby wilderness; no water. **Tollbridge,** 17 miles south of Ukiah on FR 10; seven tent/trailer sites, water. **Drift Fence,** on the Blue Mountain Scenic Byway 7 miles southeast of Ukiah on FR 52; five trailer/tent sites, outhouses; no fee, no water. **North Fork John Day,** 10 miles west of Granite on FR 52; 14 tent/trailer sites, three tent sites; no water. **Oriental Creek,** 12 miles east of Dale on FR 5506; seven sites along the John Day River; no fee, no water; not recommended for trailers or low-clearance vehicles.

Hewitt-Holcomb County Park (541-893-6147), 41132 Robinette Road, Richland; 47 tent and RV sites, boat ramps, play areas, water, restrooms, showers; reservations available; electric hookups $17, tent sites $11.

Farewell Bend State Park, 25 miles northwest of Ontario off I-84. This historic site has 101 hookup sites, 30 tent-only sites, 2 cabins; water; ADA restrooms; and trails; reservations available May–mid-Oct. (a few sites open year-round).

Ukiah-Dale Forest State Scenic Corridor, 3 miles west of Ukiah on US 395, has 27 primitive sites along Camas Creek ($8) and restrooms; no reservations.

Unity Lake State Recreation Site (1-800-551-6949), on OR 245, 50 miles east of John Day, is a shaded spot by a reservoir in an otherwise dry area with 35 hookup sites ($13–15) and a hiker/biker camp, water, showers, ADA restrooms, and two handicapped-accessible rustic cabins ($38); open Apr.–Oct.; no reservations.

CANOEING AND KAYAKING Forty miles of the **North Fork John Day River,** where it falls from the foothills to the plain, are designated Wild and Scenic and a favorite of rafters, with some class II or class III rapids. There are several put-ins near Dale, and the take-out is at Monument. For information contact the ranger district at 541-427-3231.

For flat-water paddling, **Anthony Lake** (see *Camping*) nestles under the crags with pristine waters, and there's a handy campground nearby. Several of the campgrounds mentioned in *Camping* are also lakes or reservoirs, though at these powerboats may also be permitted.

GOLF **Quail Ridge Golf Course** (541-523-2358), 2801 Indiana Avenue, Baker City. Eighteen holes.

HIKING An easy 1-mile trail encircles lovely **Anthony Lake** (see *Camping*), with views of the lake and Elkhorn crags. Anthony Lakes is the hub of a larger trail network encompassing the 23-mile **Elkhorn Crest Trail** and the 1-mile **Black Lake Trail** (for maps and details call the Baker Ranger District at 541-523-1305). A nice workout culminating in a splendid view is the **Mount Ireland Trail,** 3.2 miles up to the peak of Mount Ireland, with its fire lookout; from Sumpter take FR 23, then turn north on FR 7370, which becomes FR 100 after about 4 miles; the trailhead is 0.25 mile farther on the left.

Closer to town, the **Leo Adler Memorial Parkway** is 3 miles of paved path open to walkers and bikers along the Powder River. And the **Phillips Reservoir** trails (see *Bicycling*) are open to hikers as well.

HOT SPRINGS **Lehman Hot Springs** (541-427-3015; www.lehmanhotsprings.com), OR 244, about 16 miles east of Ukiah. Closed Mon. and Tues. Soaking is $9 for everyone over the age of three. More than 50 sulfur springs come bubbling out of the earth here. Hunters Lehman and Teel stumbled over them in 1871, filed a claim, and immediately built guest facilities. They eventually burned down, but the resort rebuilt with a lodge, cabins, bunkhouse, and campsites, all focused on a series of pools ranging from 95 to 120 degrees.

WINTER SPORTS **Anthony Lakes Ski Resort** (541-856-3277), 19 miles west of I-84 exit 285, via Powder River Road, Ellis Road, and Anthony Lakes Highway. If it were less remote, the lift lines would be longer, but as it is, you get some of the driest powder and shortest lines in Oregon. Three lifts offer 900 vertical feet and a dozen runs for all skill levels, and there are 19 miles of groomed Nordic track. And really, it's not inaccessible at all once you're in the area.

✷ Wilder Places

PARKS **Fizz Springs County Park,** 13 miles northeast of Richland in the Eagle Cap Wilderness, is currently undeveloped but is the home of some naturally carbonated springs. Come and pick up your own soda water. Take OR 86, New Bridge Road, Eagle Creek Road, and FR 7735 (summer only).

Farewell Bend State Park (541-869-2365 or 1-800-551-6949), 25 miles northwest of Ontario off I-84. Today people visit the park on Brownlee Reservoir to water-ski or boat, or just picnic. But it's called Farewell Bend for a reason. Before the reservoir, this was a bend on the Snake River. Tired Oregon Trail emigrants who had followed the Snake for weeks paused there to rest and say farewell to the river, knowing they had to tackle many dry, hard miles up to the Blue Mountains and beyond. Displays and historical markers tell the story. Look up at the dry bluffs surrounding you and imagine facing this country without cars, air-conditioning, or comfortable clothes, and your shoes have holes. Camping and picnicking are available.

Ukiah-Dale Forest State Scenic Corridor, 3 miles west of Ukiah on US 395, is a restful road among old-growth pine and larch along Camas Creek and the North Fork John Day—a nice stop to admire wildflowers and pick berries. A campground is open mid-Apr.–mid-Sept.

Unity Forest State Scenic Corridor, along US 26, 50 miles east of John Day, is an undeveloped stretch of forest and meadow preserving habitat for cougar, bobcat, bear, and other large mammals. No fee.

Unity Lake State Recreation Site (1-800-551-6949), 50 miles east of John Day on OR 245, is an out-of-the-way reservoir on the Burnt River with High Desert all around. Picnicking, camping, and waterskiing are all options here. Open year-round (campground Apr.–Oct. only).

WILDERNESS AREAS **North Fork John Day Wilderness** (541-523-6391), 15 miles east of Ukiah and 25 miles northwest of Baker City, comprises four units shared between two national forests. Despite the fragmentation, it is a wilderness whose nearest towns (Granite and Ukiah) are themselves remote, and whose vistas consist of blue-green fir forests, meadows of camas and mariposa lilies, grassy tablelands, and very, very few people. Its primary purpose is the protection of the North Fork's headwaters and fish—the John Day is the only major watercourse in Oregon that remains undammed—but it draws those visitors who crave elbow room, whether on the river or on the hundred miles of trail.

WILDLIFE AREAS **Bridge Creek Wildlife Area** (541-276-2344), 5 miles south of Ukiah on Road 52. A land of grassy basalt breaks and the occasional pine, Bridge Creek is a haven for a thousand or so wintering elk. Songbirds and deer abound the rest of the year. Access is unlimited except Dec.–Apr., when a permit is needed.

♿ **Elkhorn Wildlife Area** (541-898-2826), 61846 Powder River Lane, North Powder. A large tract with handicapped-accessible viewing sites, camping, and trails, its terrain ranges from sagebrush steppe to forest, with a variety of animal life large and small. It's particularly known for elk but also houses birds of prey, grouse, songbirds, and mammals large and small. Closed Dec.–mid-Apr. Hunting and trapping are allowed in season.

✱ Lodging

BED & BREAKFASTS

Sumpter

Sumpter Bed and Breakfast (1-800-287-5234; www.sumpterbb.com), 344 NE Columbia Street. As an active mining town, Sumpter had its share of mishaps, so in 1900 this became Sumpter's hospital, with everything including an operating room. Today a happily restored bed & breakfast, it boasts tastefully chosen furniture of the period and six guest rooms sharing three baths. $49–100, double occupancy.

FOREST SERVICE RENTALS

Reserve the following through www.recreation.gov or by calling 1-877-444-6777.

Anthony Lakes Guard Station, adjacent to the **Anthony Lakes Campground** (see *Camping*). Open spring–fall. This two-story log cabin was a guard station in the 1930s and is luxuriously provided with a flush toilet, hot shower, electric lights, and an equipped kitchen. It can sleep eight in three bedrooms. $80.

Antlers Guard Station, 37 miles from Baker city via OR 7 and County Road 529. Open year-round. This one is rustic, with an outhouse and outdoor water pump. It sleeps four and has an equipped albeit simple kitchen and a propane fireplace. $45.

GUEST HOUSES

Halfway

The Birch Leaf Farm and Guest House (1-800-727-9977; www.thebirchleaf.com), 47830 Steel Hill Road. Out of the way of a town that was once halfway to somewhere, the Birch Leaf is a 1906 farmhouse that can sleep 10, with four bathrooms. Decks, a library, and a TV room let you relax with a book, a movie, or a herd of deer, and guests have use of a common kitchen. This is a base for outdoor pursuits—rafting, hiking, or trekking, or just strolling the orchards and gardens. The house rents for $195 for four, and $25 for each additional person; a variety of bed configurations is available.

HOTELS AND MOTELS

Baker City

Geiser Grand Hotel (1-888-434-7374; www.geisergrand.com), 1996 Main Street. When Baker City was the Queen City of the Mines, it obviously required a hotel in keeping with its importance. Not a bedbug-infested flophouse, nor a rowdy roadhouse, as in some other fledgling mining towns—no, a hotel of some dignity, appropriate for the major players who would doubtless be coming through, as well as for the concert musicians and divas who would (and did) perform at the opera house. And so the Geiser was finished in 1889, complete with cupola, stained-glass ceiling, chandeliers, a fine restaurant, and all modern conveniences of the time. Like so many ambitious hotels of the intermountain west, it eventually fell on hard times and was extensively renovated before coming into use again. Much of the stained glass over the dining room is new, and the rooms have been redone in a more contemporary style, though they retain their 10-foot windows and fine views. And the fine wood of the lobby is still in place, as is the detailed exterior. Wander through the exhibits in the basement and peruse a holiday menu from the early 1900s—the Waldorf probably didn't do much better. Doubles $79–139, suites $129–249.

Sumpter

🐾 **The Depot Inn Motel** (1-800-390-2522), 179 S. Mill Street. The 14-unit motel is popular in summer with road-trippers and history buffs, and in winter with snowmobilers. With prior approval, pets are accepted into these clean, unpretentious rooms. $75, double occupancy.

LODGES

Granite

The Lodge at Granite (541-755-5200), 1027 Milton Street. Nearly off the map, as befits a near ghost town, the 10-year-old lodge is a base for exploring the surrounding wilderness and mining history. Doubles $65.

Halfway

Cornucopia Lodge (1-800-742-6115; www.cornucopialodge.com), P.O. Box 608, Halfway 97834. Twelve miles north of Halfway, near the old Cornucopia mine, is a new lodge on the edge of the Eagle Cap Wilderness. Snug rustic cabins have one or two bedrooms and lots of privacy; lodge rooms sit above a large lobby strewn with sofas and a fireplace. Meals are available in the lodge (not included in room rates). Lodge rooms $70, cabins $75–95.

Pine Valley Lodge (541-742-2027; www.pvlodge.com), 163 Main Street. Halfway used to be halfway, more or less, from the supply center of Baker City to the Cornucopia mine—the logical stop on a freight run. The lodge occupies some weathered downtown buildings and has turned them into accommodation reminiscent of an old stage stop, except considerably more comfortable. It certainly looks Old West, with its simple gable roof and wraparound porch, and one freestanding rental has a tree growing out of the wall. The owners run Pine Valley Ranch, a 27,000-acre cattle operation. $80–150, with continental breakfast.

✷ Where to Eat

DINING OUT

Baker City

Geiser Grand Hotel (541-523-1889; www.geisergrand.com), 1996 Main Street. Daily for lunch and dinner, weekends for breakfast. The Geiser was and remains the city's premier dining venue. Eat in the saloon, with its original mahogany bar and brass fixtures, or in the dining room, where polished wood columns soar up to the stained-glass ceiling. The menu is weighted toward steaks and roasts but includes the best of Northwestern seafood and even some tasty vegetarian selections.

EATING OUT

Baker City

Mad Matilda's Coffee House (541-523-4588), 1917 Main Street. Mon.–Thurs. and Sat. 8:30–4, Fri. 8:30–6. A busy place to start the day, Matilda's is where folks go for waffles, breakfast wraps, and other breakfasty things, or a light lunch. Take-out, too.

✐ **Sumpter Junction Restaurant** (541-523-9437), 2 Sunridge Lane. Open for breakfast, lunch, and dinner. Sumpter is where the train is, and though this restaurant is in Baker City, it won't let you forget. A G-scale model train runs around the dining room, completing its circuit every four minutes or so. Appropriately, there's also a kids' menu—so with the inland American menu (nothing fancy, but satisfying) and friendly, small-town service, this is a great stop for families or train lovers.

Haines

Haines Steak House (541-856-3639; www.hainessteakhouse.com), US 30. Wed.–Sun. for dinner. Steak lovers flock here for the thick steaks and endless chuckwagon salad bar—though you can, if you wish, get a lobster tail. Or both. Caters to cowboy appetites.

✷ Events

May: **Sumpter Flea Market,** Memorial Day weekend, Fourth of July weekend, and Labor Day weekend, Sumpter Fairgrounds, Sumpter. Treasures old and new, fiddle music, and food.

July: **Haines Stampede** (541-423-7881), July Fourth weekend, Haines. Rodeo, royalty, and demolition derby.

JOHN DAY RIVER AREA

You might call this the country in between—between bustling Bend and the dowager Baker City, or between the famous John Day Fossil Beds and the wildly photogenic Wallowas. Or you could call it the undiscovered country. Grant County, within which most of this province lies, is extensive but counts only seven thousand souls, mostly engaged in ranching or farming. It has wild, scenic rivers (the John Day and Malheur), rough grasslands, three wilderness areas, and an impressive mountain range (the Strawberries), yet travelers seem to regard it as a stretch to cross between one end of the state and the other. True, there are as yet fewer tourist amenities than in other parts of the state, but that means open space, quiet campgrounds, and undisturbed trails—and there are plenty of those.

GUIDANCE **Grant County Chamber of Commerce** (1-800-769-5664), 301 W. Main Street, John Day 97845.

Malheur National Forest (541-575-3013; www.fs.fed.us/r6/malheur), 431 Patterson Bridge Road, John Day 97845; **Prairie City Ranger District** (541-820-3800), 327 SW Front Street, P.O. Box 337, Prairie City 97869 .

Umatilla National Forest (541-278-3716; www.fs.fed.us/r6/uma), 2517 SW Hailey Avenue, Pendleton 97801; **North Fork John Day Ranger District** (541-427-3231), P.O. Box 158, Ukiah 97880.

Wallowa-Whitman National Forest (541-523-1405; www.fs.fed.us/r6/w-w), 1550 Dewey Avenue, Baker City 97814; **Unity District** (541-446-3351), 214 Main Street, P.O. Box 39, Unity 97884.

GETTING THERE *By car:* The John Day area is traversed east–west by **OR 19** and north–south by **US 395.**

GETTING AROUND You will need a car.

MEDICAL EMERGENCY **Blue Mountain Hospital** (541-575-1311), 170 Ford Road, John Day.

✷ To See

HISTORIC HOMES **Joaquin Miller Cabin,** US 395, Canyon City. Miller was a peripatetic individual who was born in Indiana, came to Oregon as a child, lit out for California, the Klondike, and even London, returning occasionally to Oregon but never settling. Apparently he went through wives and lovers as often as through the countryside. With a penchant for versifying, he somehow became known as the Poet of the Sierras; though today his verse is largely forgotten and he is remembered, if at all, for his self-aggrandizing tall tales. On one of his Oregon forays he made his way to Canyon City, where he lived in this cabin and managed to become a judge before returning to California. This would have been less remarkable if he had ever obtained a law degree, but you can't call him inexperienced: he had been a schoolteacher, Pony Express rider, editor, Indian fighter, and more.

HISTORIC SITES **Kam Wah Chung & Co.** (1-800-551-6949), 125 N. Canton Street, John Day. Daily 9–5, May–Sept. Admission by donation. The mining centers of Oregon had a large though segregated Chinese population. Conceiving of America as Gold Mountain, they labored hard, sent money home, and often sent their bones home after death, if not before. Lung On and his partner, Ing "Doc" Hay, lived and ran their business in this modest house, selling such goods as Chinese medicines, opium (it was legal at the time), and ritual necessities to their compatriots. Ing Hay in particular was sought out for his medical skill, and not just by Chinese—folks didn't understand it, but it seemed to work as often as the alternative. The little house is as chockfull of supplies as it was in operation and is visited by guided tour only. After Hay died, hundreds of dollars of uncashed checks were found under the bed. An interpretive center across the street offers cultural background.

MUSEUMS **DeWitt Museum** (541-820-3603), Main and Bridge streets, Prairie City. Wed.–Sat. 10–5, mid-May–mid-Oct. Donations accepted. The building looks like an oversized train depot, and it is. The Sumpter Valley Railway, which now does tourist runs between Sumpter and McEwan, used to carry lumber, machinery, and passengers between Prairie City and Baker City, crossing the Elkhorn Range. Inside is a nicely restored waiting room, station agent's office, baggage claim, and all the other aspects of a busy frontier train station.

Grant County Historical Museum (541-575-0362), US 395, Canyon City. Mon.–Sat. 9–4:30, May–Sept. General admission $4, seniors $3.50, kids 7–17 $2. Canyon City was launched by its very own gold boom, which in turn lured ranchers and lumbermen, and was for a time the biggest city in Oregon. The exhibits take the viewer through its whole settlement periods to show how this portion of the West was won.

✐ **Grant County Ranch and Rodeo Museum** (541-575-5545), 241 E. Main Street, John Day. Thurs.–Sat. 10–4. General admission $3, children under 12 free. Here are all the artifacts of cowboy culture, from saddles to spurs, with photos and text to match—cowboy mythos and cowboy fact.

Oxbow Trade Company (541-575-2911), US 395, Canyon City. It's not exactly a museum, but it's fun to look at. Owners Jim and Mary became fascinated with horse-drawn vehicles—so fascinated that they bought a few, restored them, and a

THE STRAWBERRY MOUNTAINS

business was born. They and their craftsmen now comb the country for wagons, buggies, etc. and restore them. Or they build them from scratch! Whether you want a buckboard or a surrey with a fringe on top, this is the place, and you're welcome to come in and admire. Call ahead, as they may be on the road.

NATURAL WONDERS The **Strawberry Mountains** line the horizon south of John Day like a primitive saw. Thought to have started life as a buckling of the undersea floor, when all this region was under the Pacific, it later became volcanic; one of its eruptions buried a layer of the John Day Fossil Beds in ash. The range rises to 9,000 feet and is very unfrequented—the place to find solitary alpine lakes and fields of wildflowers (see *Wilderness Areas*).

SCENIC DRIVES The eastern half of the **Journey through Time Scenic Byway** runs from John Day to Baker City via US 26 and OR 7 through small towns that were, variously, way stages on The Dalles military road, gold-digging towns, and a former hot springs spa. Four miles east of Prairie City is a covered wagon and viewpoint overlooking the Strawberry Mountains, in memory of the Oregon Trail emigrants.

The 50-mile **South Fork John Day River Backcountry Byway** traces the river from Dayville to the Ochoco Mountains along County Roads 42 and 68. The country is pretty unpopulated (that's why it's called backcountry), so look out for bighorn sheep, bear, and even wild horses as you transit from dry rimrock to the higher forest. On the way you'll pass the Rockpile Ranch, established in the late 1800s and still ranching today, and a one-room schoolhouse.

✷ To Do

BICYCLING You can choose the level roads of the John Day Valley, or you can take your cycling to the next level in the Strawberry Mountains. From **Prairie City,** a couple of leisurely out-and-back rides: the **Strawberry Road** route is 4 miles each way, from the intersection of Front Street and Johnson to County Road 62, to the Oxbow Ranch (another 7 miles of steep gravel road takes you to the top of the mountain); and the **Indian Creek Road** route: from the same intersection take US 26 west for 4.6 miles to Indian Creek Road, turn left, and go as far as you like. Either way you'll have pleasant views. For a longer ride, the **Valley Loop** is about 14 miles, with a rise of 300 feet: start at Front and Bridge streets in Prairie City and ride on Bridge Street (CR 62) for 6 or so miles, turn left onto County Road 61, and keep going. This route is about half pavement and half gravel.

Up in the mountains, you'll have to avoid the wilderness areas where bikes are prohibited, but that still leaves you plenty of room: the **Horseshoe Trail** is quite a challenge for 6 miles, with a rise of 2,800 feet, but will reward you with magnificent views of the dissected mountainside; from Prairie City take CR 62, then FRs 14 and 13, and continue 12 miles to the trailhead. The 9-mile **Davis Creek Trail** is lower in elevation and nicely unpopulated: from US 26 take FR 2614, about a 0.25 mile west of Austin Junction. After 2 miles turn south on FR 2614229 and continue another 0.25 mile to the trailhead.

For further suggestions, contact the **Malheur National Forest** (541-575-3000).

CAMPING **Malheur National Forest** operates numerous campsites, most of which will be uncrowded. For reservations, when allowed, call 1-877-444-6777 or log onto www.reservusa.com. Some are:

In the **Blue Mountain Ranger District: Magone Lake,** 26 miles north of John Day on FR 3620; 20 tent/trailer sites, three tent sites, water, ADA restrooms, swimming, boat launch; reservations possible. **Dixie,** 8 miles northeast of Prairie City on US 26; 11 tent/trailer sites; no water, no reservations. **Middle Fork,** 9 miles northwest of Austin Junction on County Road 20; 10 tent/trailer sites; no water, no reservations. **Deerhorn,** 4 miles northwest of Austin Junction on CR 20; five tent/trailer sites; no water, no reservations. **Canyon Meadows,** 20 miles southeast of John Day on FR 1520; 18 tent/trailer sites; no water, no fee, no reservations. **Parish Cabin,** 11 miles east of Seneca on FR 16; 19 tent/trailer sites, water; no reservations. **Wickiup,** 18 miles southeast of John Day on FR 15; seven tent/trailer sites, four tent sites; no water, no fee, no reservations. **Starr,** 16 miles south of John Day on US 395; eight tent/trailer sites; no water, no reservations.

In the **Prairie City Ranger District: Trout Farm,** 15 miles southeast of Prairie City on CR 62; six tent/trailer sites, water; no reservations. **Slide Creek,** 9 miles south of Prairie City on FR 6001; three tent/trailer sites, hiking access; no water, no fee, no reservations. **Strawberry,** 11 miles south of Prairie City on FR 6001; 11 tent sites, water; no reservations. **Murray,** 21 miles east of Seneca on FR 924; five tent/trailer sites; no water, no reservations. **Big Creek,** 21 miles east of Seneca on FR 815; 15 tent/trailer sites, water, mountain biking; no reservations. **Elk Creek,** 25 miles southeast of Prairie City on FR 16; five tent/trailer sites; no water, no fee, no reservations. **North Fork Malheur,** 29 miles southeast of Prairie City on FR 1675; five tent/trailer sites, hiking by Wild and Scenic River; no water, no fee, no reservations. **Little Crane,** 30 miles southeast of Prairie City on FR 16; four tent/trailer sites; no water, no fee, no reservations. **Crescent,** 17 miles southeast of Prairie City on CR 62; five tent/trailer sites; no water, no fee, no reservations.

In the **Emigrant Creek Ranger District: Yellowjacket,** 30 miles northwest of Burns on FR 3745; 20 tent/trailer sites, water, boating; no reservations. **Idlewild,** 17 miles north of Burns on US 395; 24 tent/trailer sites, water, ADA restroom, cross-country skiing; no reservations. **Falls,** 30 miles northwest of Burns on FR 4300-050; six tent/trailer sites, water, hiking; no reservations. **Emigrant,** 32 miles northwest of Burns on FR 4340-050; six tent/trailer sites; no water, no reservations. **Delintment Lake,** 45 miles northwest of Burns on FR 41; 26 tent/trailer sites, six tent sites, water; no reservations. **Joaquin Miller,** 20 miles north of Burns on US 395; 18 tent/trailer sites; no water, no reservations.

Clyde Holliday State Recreation Site (1-800-551-6949), 8 miles west of John Day on US 26, is a handy jump-off site for the Strawberry Mountain Wilderness, or for hanging out along the John Day River; 31 hookup sites ($13–17), two tepees ($29), and a hiker/biker site ($4), with shower, water, restrooms; no reservations; open Mar.–Nov.

GOLF **Bear Valley Meadows Golf Course** (541-542-9309), 12 Valley Way, Seneca. Nine holes.

HIKING With so much public land in three national forests, there are plenty of choices of walks. This is just a sprinkling, all in the **Malheur National Forest:**

A series of short, easy trails in **Strawberry Basin,** high in the Strawberry Mountains, can take you around Strawberry Lake (0.6 mile), on to Slide and Little Slide lakes (0.5 mile), or around the basin itself (2.8 miles), with tie-ins to the larger wilderness trail system. From Prairie City take County Road 60 to the Strawberry Campground, about 12 miles. The **Joaquin Miller Trail,** on the edge of the Strawberry Mountain Wilderness, is altogether more challenging—6 miles rising 2,100 feet, one-way. Take US 395 south from John Day to County Road 65, take 65 for 4 miles, and turn left on FR 6510; park at the end of the road. The **Table Mountain Trail** climbs 1,600 feet in 6 miles. From US 395 take CR 65 for 6 miles, turn left onto FR 651, and drive for 3 miles to the trailhead. The 1-mile **Cedar Grove Trail** is both easy and botanically interesting: it leads through a stand of Alaskan yellow cedars, the only ones for several hundred miles around. From John Day take US 26 west about 18 miles to FR 21; turn south and go 9 miles, then turn west on FR 2150 and continue 5 miles to the trailhead.

HOT SPRINGS **Ritter Hot Springs** (541-421-3846; www.ritterhotsprings.com), Ritter Road, Ritter. Pool open daily 24/7 except Fri. night–Sat. night. Pool and/or mineral baths $3–5. The springs were a stagecoach stop on the old Ritter Stage Road from John Day to Pendleton. Riders on the rough track must have been relieved to find a general store, built in 1894; hot water for washing; and even, after 1903, a hotel. The hotel still exists, cleaned up and refurbished, with eight rooms running $30–36, a three-bedroom cabin with kitchen and bathroom for $81, and campsites for $11. From Mount Vernon take US 395 north 45 miles and turn west on Ritter Road. Go on for 10 miles, cross a bridge, and after 0.2 mile turn right into the gravel driveway.

✷ Wilder Places

PARKS **Clyde Holliday State Recreation Site** (541-932-4453 or 1-800-551-6949), on US 26, 8 miles west of John Day. At the base of the Strawberry Mountains, this quiet park is shaded by cottonwoods and pines. Picnicking, camping, and summer interpretive events are on offer. If you're lucky, you might see steelhead swimming upriver to spawn.

WILDERNESS AREAS **Black Canyon Wilderness** (**541-477-6900** or **541-416-6500**), 11 miles south of Dayville on FR 74. It's not a big wilderness, as these things go, but it's rugged—four-fifths of the acreage has at least a 30 percent gradient; it's a canyon, after all. There are 17 miles of trails, including the 12-mile Black Canyon Trail.

Monument Rock Wilderness (541-575-3000) lies in the Malheur National Forest, about 40 miles southeast of Prairie City by CR 62 and FRs 13 and 1370, in the eastern part of the Strawberry range. Its ridges get about twice as much precipitation as the surrounding countryside, due to the storm-tunnel effect of the John Day River Valley; the vegetation is based on native bunchgrasses and subalpine trees. A fire lookout on Table Mountain, near the entry to the wilderness, is a place for sweeping views.

The **Strawberry Mountain Wilderness** (541-575-3000), in the Malheur National Forest, is nearly 70,000 acres of rugged outback comprising five life zones, a hundred miles of trail, headwaters of half a dozen streams, and, usually, very few visitors. Named for the wild strawberries growing on the slopes, it's also remote enough to be home to bighorn sheep, cougar, and other large mammals, and a great variety of birds. Many acres of forest were burnt in a 2002 wildfire—a trauma for lovers of the mountain, but which gave rise to plentiful wildflowers. Access is from a sometimes rugged road from Prairie City.

WILDLIFE AREAS **Logan Valley** (541-573-1375), off FR 16, 17 miles east of Seneca. Along the southern edge of the Strawberries, the Logan Valley wetlands and riparian forests were acquired by the Burns Paiute tribe from the Nature Conservancy. Upland sandpiper and long-billed curlew don't nest in many places in Oregon, but they do here, along with other wetland-loving species.

✷ Lodging

BED & BREAKFASTS

Mount Vernon

Inn at Juniper Ridge (503-537-7570; www.innatjuniperridge.com), 23121 US 395 N. Owners Norbert and Mary Smith retired to this 1,000-acre spread, where they receive guest in their spacious Western-style home. You have two options: the Fish Room, with its cozy window seat and trout theme, or the Cowboy Suite, with with its own deck, kitchenette, and woodstove. $120–150, double occupancy, including full breakfast.

Prairie City

Riverside School House Bed and Breakfast (541-820-4731; www.riversideschoolhouse.com), 28076 N. River Road. It actually is a schoolhouse, with its original bell, that served local children from about 1900 to the 1960s. The one-room school is now a cheerful one-room B&B with a simply but comfortably furnished bedroom and living room, and breakfast delivered to your door. Lots of light, too—when did they stop building schools with those tall windows? It's six miles south of Prairie City on the way to the Strawberry Wilderness, on a working ranch right next to the John Day River—you're halfway to hiking heaven. $125, double occupancy.

✐ **Strawberry Mountain Inn** (1-800-545-6913; www.strawberrymountaininn.com), 710 NE Front Street. Situated on Prairie City's very subdued main artery 0.25 mile east of town, this former farmhouse is nicely situated for a stroll down Front Street (grocery store, antiques, Laundromat, Western wear) and for the recreational possibilities surrounding it on all sides. Three of the four guest rooms have private baths; there's a hundred-year-old orchard on one side and the Strawberry Mountains on the other. $95–125, with full or continental breakfast. Children welcome, and there's room in the barn for your horse.

COTTAGES AND CABINS

John Day

Up the Lazy River (541-575-5612), 907 E. Main Street. Enjoy the enclosed sleeping porch in this two-bedroom cabin (if you'd rather sleep indoors, no problem—there's a king-sized bed in one room and a queen in the other). A homemade breakfast—which you can enjoy on the deck over the burbling John Day River—arrives when you want it and should hold you over for several hours of river running or loafing. Doubles $85–95; ask about family rates.

Prairie City

Prairiewinkle Inn (1-888-820-4369), 134 Front Street. Prairiewinkle is really a one-bedroom town house on Prairie City's Front Street owned by the town dentist. A queen bed, twin bed, kitchen, and back deck make it a viable option for families, and the decor is homey. $70–125 (ask about extended-stay rates).

FOREST SERVICE RENTALS To reserve these former guardians of the forest, go to www.recreation.gov:

🐾 **Deer Creek Guard Station,** about 30 miles south of John Day by US 395, County Road 63, and FR 24. Built for firefighters in the 1950s, this is a rustic cabin that can sleep four. There's a woodstove for heat, a propane cookstove, and a propane refrigerator, but no water. There is an outhouse, though, and corrals for your horses. $40; pets welcome. Open spring, summer, and fall.

🐾 **Fall Mountain Lookout.** Take US 395 about 11 miles south from John Day, then take FRs 3920 and 4920; after 0.25 mile take FR 492067 and go 1 mile. This is an actual tower, with the fire watcher's cabin in almost original 1930s condition. The wilderness views are astonishing, and there is even electricity, cookstove, and refrigerator. No water though, nor indoor plumbing (there's an outhouse). Pets okay. $40. Open spring, summer, and fall, but check road conditions.

Two Color Guard Station, about 25 miles south of Medical Springs via OR 203, FR 77, and FR 7755. A CCC bunkhouse, this "cabin" sleeps 12 and has a furnished though simple kitchen, comfortable furniture, running water for drinking, and a flush toilet (in summer; in winter you use the outhouse, and there's no drinking water). $80 June–Sept., $60 Oct.–Dec. (*Caution:* In winter the road may be accessible only on snowmobiles.)

HOTELS

Prairie City

Hotel Prairie (541-820-4800), 112 Front Street. An old-fashioned hotel that was around when gold diggers of all kinds were flocking to Prairie City, it reopened in 2008 with a quiet atmosphere (a sight quieter, I'm sure, than in 1905), comfortable rooms, and the unself-conscious style of a frontier hotel. Two rooms have a shared bath—good for families—while the rest have private baths, and historic photos bring back the local past. $75–135, double occupancy.

✷ Where to Eat

EATING OUT

Bates

Austin House Café and Country Store (541-448-2526; www.austinhousecafecountrystore.com), 75805 US 26. Thurs.–Mon 8–8. It started as a passenger train lunch stop on the Sumpter Valley Railroad. Since there was already a sawmill on the site, Austin was already a town, albeit a small one. The tradition continues with hearty breakfasts, sandwiches, and the "best steaks and burgers around"—also the only ones around, since you are now miles from everywhere, but this is cattle country, so the odds are good. Sit by the stone fireplace in winter, and check out the huge, carved mahogany 1864 bar.

Prairie City

Oxbow Coffee House and Restaurant (541-820-4544), 128 W. Front Street. Thurs.–Sun. 10–8 in winter, Tues.–Sun. or Thurs.–Tues. 10–9 in summer. The building has been through many permutations—it's been a butcher shop, an auto repair shop, and a succession of bars and restaurants—and now offers coffee, breakfast burritos, ice cream, and pastries. More remarkable perhaps than the menu is the magnificent carved mahogany bar, which made its way from Milan to St. Louis to a Prairie City saloon, where it stayed till the saloon had nearly crumbled. It was fortunate to be rescued. It also houses a collection of trophy game heads that will stare at you broodingly as you drink your espresso.

✷ Events

May: **Seneca Oyster Feed** (541-542-2161), second weekend, Seneca. These are actual oysters, not the Rocky Mountain kind, and end up barbecued in the park alongside burgers, salads, and other summery foods (never mind that May is not summer at this altitude of 4,100 feet; Seneca has recorded the coldest ever winter temperature in Oregon). Proceeds go to maintain the community-built golf course.

Southeast Oregon

9

BURNS–MALHEUR REFUGE–
STEENS MOUNTAIN AREA

ONTARIO–NYSSA–VALE–
JORDAN VALLEY AREA

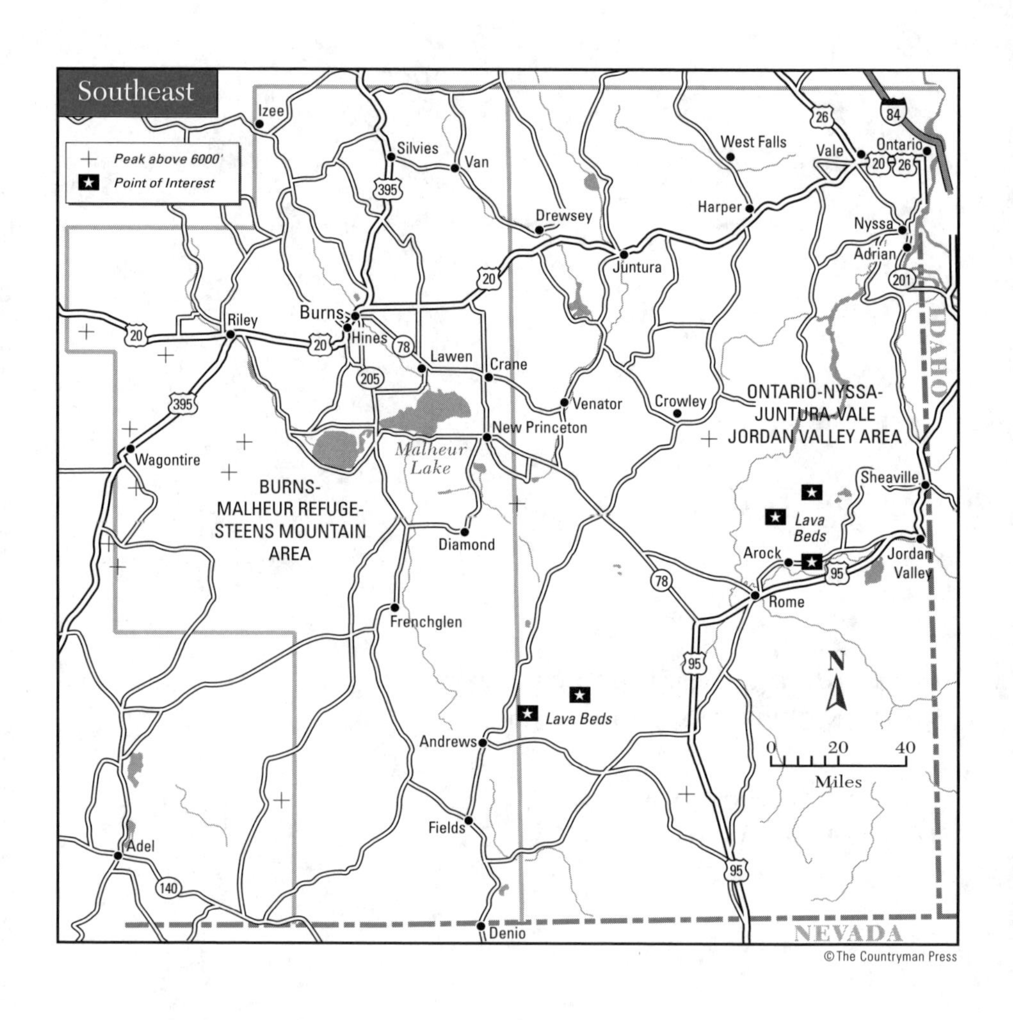
Southeast
Peak above 6000'
Point of Interest
Izee
Silvies
Van
395
West Falls
Vale
Ontario
84
26
20
Harper
Drewsey
Nyssa
Adrian
Juntura
201
Burns
Hines
Riley
78
Lawen
Crane
205
Venator
Crowley
ONTARIO-NYSSA-
JUNTURA-VALE
JORDAN VALLEY AREA
IDAHO
New Princeton
Malheur
Lake
Wagontire
BURNS-
MALHEUR REFUGE-
STEENS MOUNTAIN
AREA
Sheaville
Lava
Beds
Diamond
Arock
Jordan
Valley
95
Rome
Frenchglen
N
Lava Beds
Andrews
0
20
40
Miles
Fields
Adel
140
Denio
NEVADA
© The Countryman Press

SOUTHEAST OREGON

[We] passed down the creek a short distance & found boiling water running out of the ground . . . One of our company cooked a fish which he caught in about two minutes perfectly through.

—*Medorem Crawford, 1842*

The emigrants had the benefit of hot springs every so often to cook, do laundry, and wash themselves, dusty and road weary as they were. It was wilderness then, and much of it still is. Not so long ago there were sections of highway out here where you couldn't pick up a radio station. About 38,000 people occupy the 20,000 square miles of ranch and public lands that make up Harney and Malheur counties—just under three people per square mile. No wonder the Oregon Trail pioneers did their best to avoid it, usually cutting northeast over the Blue Mountains—rugged, but friendlier than the desert—to reach the Columbia. Ranchers, though, were a different story. Improbable rumors of grass as high as a horse's belly beckoned California cattlemen, and it turned out to be at least partially true: the Donner and Blitzen Valley and vast seasonal marshes grew quantities of giant wild rye, Indian ricegrass, and other forbs. Cattle barons like Peter French (see "Burns–Malheur Refuge–Steens Mountain Area"), each more or less a law unto himself, amassed spreads of hundreds of thousands of acres. Most of French's territory is now the Malheur National Wildlife Refuge, where you can still see some of his original buildings.

Much of this corner of the state presents typical basin and range topography: sagebrush flats broken by long, parallel mountains, complicated here by the occasional volcanic cone. Rainfall averages 10 inches a year, or less. East of the Steens the landscape breaks up into jagged canyons and steep brown hills, so you wonder how anyone could make a living out here at all. Barren it is, but where plains open up around Nyssa and Ontario, the land is given over to potatoes and onions, hay, grain, and cattle—the gift of dams on the Owyhee starting in 1939.

This piece of Oregon is huge but remote. Fill your tires and your tank, be prudent, and enjoy the treasure hidden in the desert.

BURNS–MALHEUR REFUGE–STEENS MOUNTAIN AREA

East of Bend the junipers thin out. Then they practically disappear, and you clock mile after mile of scrubby sage and bunchgrasses, with occasional greasewood where the soil turns salty, or alkali flats with nothing at all. You look longingly at the pines peppering the occasional mountain. At intervals traces of the old Bend-Burns road snake through the sage. The land looks so flat it could be a lake bed, which, in fact, it was for thousands of years.

This piece of the High Desert lies in the Great Basin, where water never reaches the sea; it flows into ephemeral lakes or just disappears. Ten thousand years ago the plains were filled with lakes whose rushy margins drew uncounted waterfowl and eager human hunters; today the few remnant lakes are still on the ancient flyway, visited seasonally by still-impressive flocks and eager birdwatchers (and hunters). It's lonely country with the particular beauty of sagebrush plains and broken rimrock. Weather and road conditions can be extreme in any season; always carry water. Beware of unpaved roads, which often require high clearance. And from time to time, get out of the car, smell the sage, and listen to the quiet.

GUIDANCE **Bureau of Land Management, Burns District** (541-573-4400), 28910 US 20 W., Hines 97738.

Harney County Chamber of Commerce (541-573-2636; www.harneycounty.com), 76 E. Washington Street, Burns 97720.

Malheur National Forest (541-575-3000), 431 Patterson Bridge Road, John Day 97845.

GETTING THERE *By car:* **US 20** traverses the area east to west, passing through Burns. **US 395** and **OR 205** are the north–south arteries, with **OR 78** taking off southeast from Burns toward the Sheepshead Mountains.

GETTING AROUND Horses used to be thought sufficient, but today you need a car.

MEDICAL EMERGENCY **Harney District Hospital** (541-573-7281), 557 W. Washington Street, Burns.

TOWNS Burns. George McGowan evidently loved poetry. Having settled in the High Desert, he named the town for Scottish poet Robert Burns, perhaps nostalgic for the lochs and braes of his homeland. In 1884, when it was incorporated, Burns was already a little boomtown catering to area ranchers and farmers, and it became county seat by the proven method of filching county records from competitor Harney City. Cattle and lumber are still the main industries, but in the past few decades Burns has grown from a sagebrush crossroads town to one boasting several motels and stores, thanks in large part to the recreation boom—especially birders flocking to nearby Malheur Wildlife Refuge.

Fields. Before the railroad, Charles Fields set up a roadhouse on the stagecoach line between Winnemucca, Nevada, and Burns (in 1881 there was apparently enough traffic to justify it). Travelers could get lodging, a meal, and even pick up some supplies at the mercantile before moving on. A railroad passing to the east eventually took away the traffic, but his place—now a motel, café, and store—still stands. There's not much more to Fields than that, and being 112 miles between Burns and nowhere, there likely won't be. But it too has become a favorite of birders and other lovers of the outdoors, who come to imbibe milk shakes, hamburgers, and the flavor of the Old West.

Wagontire, population two, sits amid thousands of square miles of desert 55 miles southeast of Burns and much farther from anywhere else. There's a motel and—hey—an airstrip.

* To See

FARMERS' MARKETS Harney County Farmers' Market (541-573-1809), Hines City Park. Sat. 9–noon, July–mid-Sept.

HISTORIC SITES Diamond, at the end of the road 56 miles south of Burns, had a post office back in 1887. It was named for the diamond-shaped brand of early rancher Mace McCoy. The Diamond Hotel, established in 1898, is still in business.

The Narrows, on the channel between Malheur Lake from Harney Lake, was a little farming community with a post office in the early 1900s. But farming was never easy here—for one thing, the lake water is brackish—and it disappeared during the Depression.

Peter French Round Barn, about 50 miles southeast of Burns by OR 78, Sod House Lane, and Lava Bed Road. Pete French was a legend in his own time, a cattleman who came up from California in the 1870s and ended up a cattle baron controlling hundreds of square miles. This round barn was Pete's idea for training horses in winter and is the only one of several in the area to have survived. Built of rock and juniper logs brought from 60 miles away, its intricate system of beams and supports make it a thing of beauty. French himself came to a bad end, shot in 1897 by one of the plentiful enemies he had made with his land-grabbing ways. A private visitors center nearby (541-493-2070) offers guided tours, but you can visit this State Historic Site on your own.

P Ranch, Frenchglen. The entire settlement of Frenchglen was once a headquarters of Peter French's ranch empire, complete with the hotel to house buyers and other travelers. Short trails from the Frenchglen Hotel lead to abandoned barns and equipment, and big skies over French's immense empire.

Riddle Brothers Ranch National Historic District (541-573-4400), about 30 miles southeast of Frenchglen. Open mid-June–Oct. The Bureau of Land Management has restored several buildings on this remote spread, so visitors can envision ranch life as it was. Walter, Ben, and Fred Riddle moved over here from the Willamette Valley in the early 1900s to ranch the vast, sparsely populated lower reaches of the Steens. Now you can explore their holdings by foot or on horseback, enjoying the silence, scenery, and wildlife. Call the district office, as the gate may be locked periodically. From Frenchglen take OR 205 south 10 miles, then turn left onto S. Steens Mountain Loop Road and continue 20 miles. There are no amenities except a vault toilet.

Sod House Ranch, on Sod House Lane between the refuge entrance and refuge headquarters. The Sod House was the northern center of operations for Pete French's spread, with eight remaining buildings including the sod-roofed stone cellar and the 116-foot-long Long Barn. Open seasonally with on-site interpreters; call 541-493-2612 for hours.

MUSEUMS **Harney County Historical Museum** (541-573-5618; www.burnsmuseum.com), 18 W. D Street, Burns. Tues.–Fri. 10–4 and Sat. 10–3, Apr.–Sept. General admission $4, couples $5, seniors $3, children 6–12 $1, family of four $6. A collection of all things defining Harney County: exhibits on Peter French and his operations, birds of this birding hot spot, lumbering history, and pioneer and Indian artifacts.

George Benson Memorial Museum (541-493-2612), 36931 Sod House Lane, Princeton. Next to the visitors center on the **Malheur National Wildlife Refuge,** the small museum houses taxidermy displays of many bird species found on the refuge. Call for hours.

NATURAL WONDERS **Alvord Desert,** just east of Steens Mountain, is an 11-mile-long, 6-mile-wide alkali flat, or playa. Most of such precipitation as arrives in this piece of the Great Basin is caught by the mountain itself; the rain shadow is a sparkling desert, popular in summer and fall for landsailing (except in spring, when snowmelt turns it into Alvord Lake). For thousands of years during the Ice Age, a huge, 200-foot-deep lake extended from here to Nevada. As it dried up, it left the accumulated mineral deposits of millennia. Below the lake bed lies the same basalt that caps Steens Mountain. Several hot springs bubble up along the fault line between mountain and desert (see *Hot Springs*). Native Lahontan cutthroat, a trout uniquely adapted to alkaline conditions, inhabit nearby Mann Lake.

Diamond Craters, east of OR 205 on Diamond Lane about 40 miles south of Burns, is a geologist's playground with examples of almost every kind of basaltic eruption—cinder cones, spatter cones, lava flows, domes—formed from activity about twenty-five thousand years ago. You almost have to be a geologist to see it, though, since not all the features are obvious. A detailed guide can be found online at www.gorp.away.com.

Glass Buttes, milepost 77 off US 20. They may look scrubby and dusty today, but much of that low vegetation covers obsidian that flowed from this 5-million-year-old volcano in the more recent past. Just get out of your car and find obsidian bits right beside the highway—black, red, flame, and other colors. The larger butte is mostly rhyolite, but Little Glass Butte and the plain alongside are favorites of rock hounds and flintknappers. Yes, you can collect! But you must use only hand tools. A dirt road leads from US 20 into the buttes. For collecting restrictions, call 541-493-4400.

Malheur and Harney lakes lie about 20 miles south of Burns. Huge but shallow, they are fed by the Silvies and Donner and Blitzen rivers running down from the Strawberry Range to the north and Steens Mountain to the south. Water levels can fluctuate widely depending on the winter's snow. The waters are somewhat brackish due to the alkaline soils and evaporation, but being wide mirrors of blue far from any other open water, they attract thousands of waterfowl and shorebirds in spring and fall (see *Bird-Watching*).

Steens Mountain, about 70 miles southeast of Burns. From Burns or anywhere in the steppe country round about, you look east and see the Steens lying like a long knife where the sky meets the earth. Evidently it's been cutting a cake, for it usually has a line of frosting on top. At 9,733 feet, it's a respectable peak, but you hardly notice that due to the fact that the mountain stretches north–south for 30 miles—the peak is just a bump on the blade. The Steens is a fault block—a chunk of earth's crust uplifted along a fault—rising gently from the west and dropping a mile to the Alvord Desert on its eastern side, much more typical of basin and range geology than of Oregon's volcanic and accreted ranges (other fault blocks in Oregon are Hart Mountain and Abert Rim, all part of the state's corner of the Great Basin). Several herds of wild horses roam its remote, glacier-carved canyons; bighorn sheep, pronghorn antelope, elk, and their predators are at home here. For its sweeping gorges, wildflowers, isolation, and sheer impressive hulk, the Steens was judged worthy of wilderness designation in 2000. Trails and a primitive road are open in summer. If you go, remember it's rugged and remote: don't count on cell phone service or amenities other than a very primitive road (see *Scenic*

MALHEUR LAKE IN THE GREAT BASIN

Drives). From Burns take OR 78 and OR 205 south to Frenchglen, about 60 miles, and turn left on N. Steens Mountain Loop.

SCENIC DRIVES **Diamond Loop National Backcountry Byway** is a remote, partially paved 69-mile route around **Diamond Craters** (see *Natural Wonders*) and surrounding sagebrush hills, marshes, and rimrock. Sights to be seen are as various as antelope and ibis, spatter cones and spires. Enter the byway at the junction of OR 205 and Diamond Lane, or from Princeton on OR 78, and make sure to get food, water, and gas in Burns or Frenchglen.

Lakeview to Steens Backcountry Byway, 90 miles, mostly gravel. Leaving OR 205 10 miles south of Frenchglen, you can strike off into the desert toward Lakeview in south central Oregon. The landscape is stark, with broad sagebrush flats broken by long, high mountains—this is really basin and range country. Hart Mountain, Warner Lakes, and Abert Rim are not much changed since the Fremont expedition came by in the 1840s. The country is remote with few services; make sure your car is in good shape and that you have adequate supplies. The descent down the scarp of Hart Mountain is not suitable for large trailers or RVs. In fact, it takes nerves in any vehicle.

Steens Mountain Loop, 52 miles up the Steens and down. Steens Mountain is as wild and remote as it gets in the Lower 48 (see *Natural Wonders*): the closest population center is Burns, which isn't exactly a metropolis. You can view the rugged terrain close up by taking the N. Loop Road from Frenchglen, rising through bands of sagebrush, juniper, grasses, and a few scattered aspen groves; walking or driving a 0.25-mile spur to the peak; and descending along ridges and switchbacks down the S. Loop Road to OR 205. But be warned: much of the road is dirt, rocky, rutted, and barely improved—a high-clearance vehicle is a must. And it's only open in the (short) summer. For conditions and information, call the Bureau of Land Management (541-493-4400).

✷ To Do

BICYCLING The gravel 35-mile Center Patrol Road of **Malheur National Wildlife Refuge** is open to bikes as well as cars. It is fairly level and has open marsh and mountain vistas all the way. Start at refuge headquarters and ride down to P Ranch at Frenchglen, or vice versa. Also at the refuge, the **East Canal Trail** is a dirt road of about 4 miles beginning at a gate across the Blitzen River and before Page Springs Campground.

In the **Malheur National Forest** (541-575-3000), the **Myrtle Creek Trail** runs through the canyon of a small stream for about 8 miles; from Burns take US 395 north 16 miles to FR 31, turn west, and drive 15 miles on FR 3100-226 to the trailhead. Also open to horses and hikers. The **Malheur Rail Trail,** deep in the mountains, was the right-of-way of the train line to Hines. At 12.5 miles, it offers varied terrain, some steep, some level. Take County Road 62 from Prairie City for 19 miles, then turn west on FR 16 to FR 1600-133; the trailhead is at the junction with FR 1600-097.

BIRD-WATCHING The star bird-watching location in eastern Oregon, if not in the entire state, is **Malheur National Wildlife Refuge** and its surroundings. The 187,000-acre refuge comprises wide **Malheur and Harney lakes,** wetlands, upland desert, nearby rimrock, and seasonally flooded fields. What with the rare expanse of water and varied habitat, Malheur attracts three hundred species of birds. Early spring brings ducks, geese, swans, sage grouse dancing on their leks, and early songbirds; later come the shorebirds and warblers; in July shorebirds already start reappearing, increasing through late summer; and then the waterfowl reappear in great clouds on their way south. A couple of hundred pairs of sandhill cranes nest on the refuge, and raptors are present year-round, including eagles and peregrine falcons.

More modestly, the highway **rest area** 10 miles east of **Riley** on US 20 is often honored with unusual sightings and is often good for raptors like ferruginous hawks.

Fields, 60 miles south of refuge headquarters, is an out-of-the-way but increasingly frequented bird-watching spot. Great horned owls often nest right outside the café, and the proximity of Malheur and remote mountains produces some interesting strays.

CAMPING **Chickahominy Reservoir,** a Bureau of Land Management site (541-573-4400) 5 miles west of Riley off US 20, has 28 sites, water, toilets, sun shelters, and boat ramp, but no showers; very exposed to the sun. The BLM also runs campgrounds on the Steens; see **Steens Mountain Wilderness** under *Wilderness Areas.*

In the **Malheur National Forest** (541-575-3000) six campgrounds fall within our area: **Yellowjacket,** 30 miles northwest of Burns via US 395 and FRs 31, 37, and 3745; 20 tent/trailer sites, water, boating, and an unexplained name. **Idlewild,** 17 miles north of Burns on US 395; 24 tent/trailer sites, ADA restroom, water; open winter and summer. **Falls,** 30 miles northwest of Burns via County Road 127, FR 43, and FR 4300-050; six tent/trailer sites, water, fishing. **Emigrant,** 32 miles northwest of Burns by CR 127, FR 43, FR 4340, and FR 4340-050; six tent/trailer sites; no water. **Delintment Lake,** 45 miles northwest of Burns by CR 127 and FR 41; 26 tent/trailer sites, six tent-only sites, water, swimming, and boating. **Joaquin Miller,** 20 miles north of Burns on US 395; 18 tent/trailer sites; no water.

GOLF **Valley Golf Club** (541-573-6251), 245 US 20 N., Hines. Nine holes.

HIKING Trails in the **Malheur National Forest** (541-575-3000) are lightly traveled and fairly remote: the **Craft Cabin Trail** follows Pine Creek for an 8-mile hike through some steep canyon. From Burns take US 20 east for 12 miles, turn left onto County Road 102/FR 28, turn right on FR 2850, turn right again on FR 2855, and follow signs. The 3-mile **Delintment Creek Trail** passes some springs and old-growth ponderosas; 12 miles north of Burns on CR 127, take FR 41, continue 45 miles, and turn left at junction. The **Devine Summit Trail** is an easy 2-mile walk on a self-guiding nature trail; brochures explain the different plant communities. It begins in the **Idlewild Campground,** 17 miles north of Burns on US 395. These are generally open spring to fall. See also *Bicycling.*

Steens Mountain offers some demanding but spectacular hikes, accessible summer only (except by ski): **Big Indian Gorge Trail** rises 8 miles from **South Steens Campground** through a deep glacial gorge, crossing wildflower meadows and ending at waterfalls springing from the canyon wall. The trail crosses three streams, which can be impassable at times. **Blitzen River Trail** starts at **Page Springs Campground** and follows the Donner and Blitzen River up to Fish Creek. East of the mountain, **Pike Creek Trail** starts a 1.5 miles north of **Alvord Hot Springs** on E. Steens Road and runs 3 miles to a hidden but official campsite. This trail is often snow-free when those above aren't; however, the trail is sporadically maintained and may be hard to follow, and stream crossings may be impossible in spring or early summer. **Wildhorse Lake Trail** is only 1.25 miles each way, but it's steep and unstable; park at the end of Wildhorse Lake Overlook Road.

HOT SPRINGS **Alvord Hot Springs,** 12 miles south of Mann Lake on E. Steens Road. One pool is enclosed by tin and another is open to the sky on the edge of a great playa (see **Alvord Desert** under *Natural Wonders*). They are on private property but are open, free, to the respectful public. Soaking in natural hot springs with open desert on one side and the sheer, 5,000-foot face of the Steens on the other is unforgettable. Stay in designated areas and keep children close, as nearby springs are scalding and dangerous.

Crystal Crane Hot Springs (541-493-2312; www.cranehotsprings.com), 59315 OR 74, Crane. Daily 9–9. Hot springs bubbling up to a large pond are open to day visitors at $3.50; or you can use an indoor bath for $7.50 per person per hour (children $4). Or make a night of it and stay in the campground or rustic cabins (see *Resorts*).

UNIQUE ADVENTURES You may or may not catch a glimpse of wild mustangs at the **Kiger Wild Horse Viewing Area,** but several herds roam the valley, so there is a chance. The rough access road begins 3 miles east of Diamond; do not attempt in or after rain or snow.

✷ Wilder Places

WILDERNESS AREAS The **Steens Mountain Wilderness** (541-573-4400) covers some 175,000 acres of Oregon's highest fault-block mountain, buffered by more than 400,000 acres managed for sustainable use. Wild rivers, rugged trails, and gorges half a mile deep invite explorers on foot or on horseback, and unlike most wildernesses, this one is accessible by a preexisting road (albeit a rough, difficult one; see *Scenic Drives*). Several campgrounds are on the mountain just outside the wilderness boundary: wooded **Page Springs,** 3 miles east of Frenchglen on N. Loop Road, has 36 sites, water, toilets, and a trailhead; 17 miles farther up the road is **Fish Lake,** at 7,300 feet, which offers 23 sites, water, restrooms, a boat ramp, and swimming (brr); 2 miles beyond is **Jackman Park,** with six sites, a trailhead, and toilets but no water; and **South Steens,** on the southern end of the loop road, has 36 family sites and 15 equestrian sites. From Frenchglen proceed south on OR 205 about 9 miles, then turn left on S. Steens Mountain Loop Road and drive 18 miles. Fees at the above sites are $6–8. *Caution:* Much of the road is impassable by RVs or campers; a high-clearance vehicle is highly recommended. **Mann Lake,** below the mountain's eastern face, is open to camping and has restrooms, but there are no designated sites (or fees).

WILDLIFE REFUGES **Malheur National Wildlife Refuge** (541-493-2612; www.fws.gov/malheur), 36391 Sod House Lane, Princeton. Open dawn–dusk; visitors center open daily 8–4, summer–Nov., then Mon.–Thurs. 8–4. Established by Theodore Roosevelt, the Rough Rider himself, in 1908, Malheur sprawls across 187,000 acres of High Desert that take in two broad lakes, the Donner and Blitzen River, meadows and marshes, rimrock, alkali flats, and very big skies. Much of it was once the empire of cattle baron Peter French, and at the south end of the refuge you can visit what remains of his P Ranch and the Frenchglen Hotel that he built. Besides the hundreds of bird species that pass through or nest, look for coyotes, pronghorn, deer, weasels, kangaroo rats, and 54 other mammal species. And at night, consider the stars, far from city lights (or any lights at all). No camping is allowed on the refuge, but **Malheur Field Station** (541-493-2629; www.malheurfieldstation.org), 34848 Sod House Lane, takes guests in mobile homes or kitchenette units Apr.–Oct., with the possibility of meal service as well. Kitchenettes $50 (double occupancy), mobile homes $70–120. RV full hookup sites are $19. Call for reservations.

IN THE COMMON KITCHEN AT MALHEUR FIELD STATION

✷ Lodging

BED & BREAKFASTS

Burns

Lone Pine Guest Ranch (541-573-2103), 51 Lone Pine Road. The two rooms in this little contemporary house on the sagebrush prairie look out onto the infinity of the steppe. Each has a deck, kitchenette, woodstove, and private bath, and there are horse corrals out back in case you arrive on horseback. Kids welcome, too. $95, double occupancy, with breakfast.

Sage Country Inn (541-573-7243; www.sagecountryinn.com), 351½ W. Monroe Street. The hundred-year-old farmhouse used to sit on 160 acres. It still occupies nearly a city block dotted with fruit trees and rose bushes—not to be taken for granted in this land of little rain. Three guest rooms each come with private bath and full breakfast. $95–125. Children over six welcome.

CABINS AND COTTAGES

Fields

Steens Country Cabin (541-495-2344; www.steenscountrycabin.com), 14 miles north of Fields on E. Steens Road. If you really want to experience wide-open spaces, this Western-lodge-style cabin may be for you. It's under the mile-high facade of the Steens facing the Alvord Desert, so you have plenty of elbow room. The cabin has two bedrooms, a complete kitchen, bathroom, living room, and air-conditioning—a luxurious homestead indeed. Continental breakfast is provided. Just remember to bring all the other food and supplies you'll need. $80–125, depending on number of guests.

Burns

Silver Spur Motel (541-573-2077; www.silverspurmotel.com), 789 N. Broadway Avenue. The rooms, with their wood paneling and oak furniture, look much as they have for the past 50 years. There's a fireplace in the lobby and nature at your doorstep for a price to please the frugal. Doubles $49–56.

Diamond

Hotel Diamond (541-493-1898), 10 Main Street. Open Apr.–Oct. Diamond had 50 inhabitants in its heyday and was a supply center for the ranchers and sheepmen scattered across the land. As at Fields, the 1898 hotel was intended as a stage stop, but a train line passed to the east, and the place catered to off-duty sheepherders and cowboys more than to sporadic travelers. Now fully renovated, the hotel still offers a backcountry atmosphere with period furniture and a screened porch. Upstairs are the five original rooms, sharing two bathrooms, and downstairs are three newer queen-bedded rooms with private baths. Children are welcome. $75–97, with expanded continental breakfast; dinner is available for $19, if you reserve 24 hours ahead.

Frenchglen

Frenchglen Hotel (541-493-2825), 39184 OR 205. Open mid-Mar.–Oct. Now owned by the State of Oregon, the clapboard hotel was a project of Peter French and his employer, partner, and father-in-law. This was the frontier, and it wasn't fancy, but it was, and is, solid and cozy. Eight upstairs rooms share two bathrooms on a single corridor, and downstairs is the lobby/restaurant. An addition called Drover's Inn has been built out back, where the five rooms have private baths. $67–105. Dinner at the Frenchglen is renowned, and getting a space at one of the family-style tables requires reservations. The food is hearty and Western—you'll find steaks, trout, roasts, and more depending on the evening. Breakfast and lunch don't require reservations and can bring you in touch with local people on lunch break.

RANCHES

Fields

Whitehorse Ranch (541-495-2222; www.whitehorseranch.info), 57735 Whitehorse Lane. To experience life on a remote working ranch minus the "dude" aspect, consider the historic Whitehorse. Claimed in 1869, it's the oldest ranch in the county, running livestock on 63,000 acres, with many times that amount in grazing rights. Stay in the three-bedroom stone guest house at $60 per person or in the bunkhouse, where private rooms share a bath and living room ($7 per person or $90 double occupancy). Meals are taken with the buckaroos at 6 AM, midday, and 6 PM—they're hearty, but they go fast and are served Apr.–mid-Oct.

RESORTS

Crane

Crystal Crane Hot Springs (541-493-2312; www.cranehotsprings.com), 59315 OR 74. Soak in the hot spring-fed lake under the big sky, then retire to your rustic but cozy cabin and listen to the coyotes. There's not much out here but sagebrush, stars, and wildlife. Four cabins sleep two or three and share a bathroom; the fifth has a half bath. Rates $45-60. Campsites are available at $12–20 for RV sites and $15 for tent sites. Well-behaved pets okay.

✷ Where to Eat

DINING OUT

Diamond

Hotel Diamond (541-493-1898), 49130 Main Street. Open daily for dinner. The dining room at the Hotel Diamond is another place (there aren't many out here) for dinners beyond meat and potatoes. Usually there is a set menu at $19 for a three-course meal of meat or fowl, several vegetables, homemade bread, salad, and dessert. The cooking is appreciated by inhabitants and visitors from miles around, and reservations are recommended.

Frenchglen

Frenchglen Hotel (541-493-2825), 39184 OR 205. See *Hotels and Motels*.

EATING OUT

Burns

Broadway Deli (541-573-7020), 530 N. Broadway. Open for breakfast and lunch. Sustaining soups and sandwiches, and, often, birding information.

Diamond

Frazier's (541-493-1898), 10 Main Street. Tues.–Sat. 11–2. The new log café at the **Hotel Diamond** (see *Hotels and Motels*) gives you your only chance for lunch between Frenchglen and Burns, neither of which is next door. Here you'll find salads, hot and cold sandwiches, even a bean stew to warm you up.

Fields

Fields Station Café (541-495-2275), 22276 Field Drive. Open for breakfast and lunch. No pretension here, just decent American road food—breakfast, burgers, sandwiches, thick milk shakes, and local gossip, such as the cougar that turned up dead in someone's woodpile.

✷ Events

April: **John Scharff Migratory Bird Festival** (541-573-2636; www.migratorybirdfestival.com), first full weekend. Thousands of migratory birdwatchers descend on the desert oases of Burns and nearby Malheur National Wildlife Refuge for three days of talks, food, festivities, and guided tours. Highlights can include thousands of snow geese, sandhill cranes, eagles, and much more.

ONTARIO–NYSSA–VALE–JORDAN VALLEY AREA

Known as Treasure Valley, at least since 1959 when the local chambers of commerce adopted the name, the region where the Malheur, Payette, and Owyhee join the Snake River doesn't refer to gold that was sporadically struck in nearby mountain ranges. It reflects the unlikely agricultural importance of this stretch of arid country. Beginning in the 1870s, cattle descended on the verdant ribbons bordering the rivers, and sheepherders drove their hardier flocks over the hills when the grasses came up in the spring. The railroad was a boon to both these groups when it came through in 1884. But the large dams built on the Snake and Owyhee in the 1940s brought crops to the alluvial soils (still shipped out by rail), and today the valley is a thriving agribusiness center.

Outside Treasure Valley, though, most of the county is dry and broken by gulches and impassable canyons. Hamlets like Juntura, Drewsey, or Jordan Valley are few and far between. Roads are often unpaved and ungraded; warnings against RVs and trailers on certain stretches are not idle. But the desert is rich in eagles, antelope, and other wild things. Keep your eyes and senses open.

GUIDANCE **Bureau of Land Management, Vale District** (541-473-3144), 100 Oregon Street, Vale 97918.

Nyssa Chamber of Commerce (541-372-2377; www.nyssachamber.com), 105 Main Street, Nyssa 97913.

Ontario Visitors and Convention Bureau (541-889-8012 or 1-866-989-8012; www.ontariochamber.com), 676 SW Sixth Avenue, Ontario 97914.

Vale Chamber of Commerce (541-473-3800; www.valechamber.com), P.O. Box 661, Vale 97918.

GETTING THERE *By bus:* There are **Greyhound** stations in Ontario at 191 SE Third Street and Vale at 151 Smith Street N.

By car: **US 20** and **US 26** converge on Vale from the west, while **I-84** crosses Ontario northwest to southeast. Getting to southern Malheur County entails a detour through Idaho on **US 95.**

GETTING AROUND Despite the two bus stations, you will need a car to get anywhere.

MEDICAL EMERGENCY **Holy Rosary Medical Center** (541-881-7000 or 1-877-225-4762), 351 SW Ninth Street, Ontario.

TOWNS **Ontario.** The hub of the Treasure Valley's agricultural triangle, Ontario houses Treasure Valley Community College as well as Holy Rosary, the county's only hospital. Dusty and dry, it was judged a fit location for hundreds of Japanese Americans during World War II; a series of dams along the Owyhee boosted farming, and a number of those internees stayed on, helping create the multiethnic farming community of today.

Nyssa. Was it named for the New York Sheep Shearing Association? Or by an engineer's daughter, who was studying her history book and had it open to a page on St. Gregory of Nyssa? These are the two competing legends; nobody knows for sure. Near the spot where the Oregon Trail crossed the Snake River, the water and associated greenery attracted ranchers, and when the train came, Nyssa took off. Dam building on the Owyhee made crops more feasible, and today a checkerboard of irrigated fields surrounds the town.

Vale. Vale grew up with the country, having started as a scattering of cabins along the Oregon Trail near the hot springs of the Malheur River. Emigrants quickly availed themselves of the springs and of local hospitality, and in 1872 the Rinehart Stone House began to lend the town solidity. The pleasant downtown is centered on buildings from the early 1900s, many of whose walls now sport murals depicting Oregon Trail scenes.

Jordan Valley. Lost in the far southeastern corner of the state, the Valley of Jordan Creek was settled remarkably early. Gold is where you find it, and a wandering band of prospectors found it here in 1863, idly panning the creek at an evening's campsite. In less than two weeks they had filed claims, and settlement began. The mineral rush didn't last long, but the green creek valley in remote, arid country brought ranchers who, with grain farmers and sheepherders, constitute the economic base of this town of 650. Descendants of the Basques who arrived from 1890 to 1918 cherish Basque food and traditions; the only pelota frontón (Basque handball court) in the state is here.

✷ To See

FARMERS' MARKETS **Nyssa Farmers' Market,** Main Street between Third and Fourth streets, Nyssa. Third Fri. 4:30–7:30, Aug.–Oct.

Ontario Farmers' Market (541-889-3616), the House that Art Built, 441 SW First Street, Ontario. Sat. 10–2, Sept.

FOR FAMILIES ✐ **Vale murals.** Thirty murals depicting life on the Oregon Trail adorn downtown Vale, a town that grew up on the trail.

HISTORIC HOMES **Rinehart Stone House** (541-473-2070), 255 Main Street S., Vale. Tues.–Sat. 12:30–4, Mar.–Oct. Free. This square sandstone house was built by Lewis Rinehart in 1872 and, as the finest house then in town—with a ballroom yet—immediately became the focus of weddings and other festivities. The Rineharts were hospitable people. This was just as well, because their home on the Oregon Trail often enough took in tired emigrants; during the Bannock Wars of 1878, settlers from all around crammed into the stone house for protection. The last owner bequeathed it to the county, which saw to its restoration, so that it is now a museum displaying Oregon Trail exhibits, period photos, and artifacts.

HISTORIC SITES **Grand Opera House,** 123 S. Main Street, Vale. Dating from 1895, the place was originally a saloon but was made over as an entertainment hall during Prohibition.

Union Pacific Train Depot (1-866-989-8012), 300 Depot Lane, Ontario. In 1882 the railroad came to Ontario, to the great joy of pioneer farmers, and a depot was put in a full year before the first train came through. Ontarians say the rail line built the town, and it certainly connected it to the rest of the world through a junction with the Portland–Wyoming line. The sizable depot you see today dates from 1907 and gives you some idea of the traffic level: quantities of wool, grain, and soldiers were shipped through it from 1907 through midcentury. It continues to carry eastern Oregon's agricultural products abroad.

Jean-Baptiste Charbonneau Gravesite, in Danner, about 15 miles west of Jordan Valley. Jean-Baptiste was the youngest member of Lewis and Clark's Corps of Discovery, having been born along the way and carried on his mother's back most of the time. Yes, this was the son of Sacagawea and Toussaint Charbonneau, the team's official interpreter. His life continued as eventfully as it had begun. Clark adopted him after his mother died; he obtained a good education and spent time in European capitals before returning to America to take up the trapping life. Mountain man, guide, and explorer, he died of pneumonia in the Oregon desert at the age of 61. Nearby are ruins of the old Inskip Stage Stop.

Oregon Trail sites. Emigrants entered what is now Oregon by crossing the **Snake River** from Old Fort Boise, on the Idaho side; there's an interpretive kiosk about a mile south of Nyssa on OR 201. People and livestock often drowned in the crossing, but "there are Indians who swim the river from morning till night it is fun for them, there is many a drove of cattle that could not be got over without their help, by paying them a small sum, they will take a horse by the bridle or halter, and swim over with him, the rest of the horses all follow," noted Amelia Knight in 1853.

After the crossing, they would follow what is now a secondary road running northwest across dry country, crossing **Keeney Pass,** where a trail leads to an overlook. Shortly before arriving in **Vale,** a signpost points toward the **grave of John Henderson,** who died on the trail; at the time a blacksmith in the wagon train chiseled the name onto a stone that still stands there, beside a later monument.

The trail crossed the **Malheur River** just before entering Vale. Hot springs in the river enabled the tired, dusty travelers to bathe and wash clothes. The city of Vale grew up from this site, and wagon ruts may be seen along **Lytle Boulevard.**

Then the rested pioneers turned north toward **Alkali Springs.** They called it Sulfur Spring, which says something about the water quality, and went on to camp at **Birch Creek.** Dirt roads and fencing make the route impractical for cars, but just a few miles away, on I-84, is **Farewell Bend,** where the trail met the Snake for the last time. "In about 4 miles more over hills came to Snake River for the last time. Here it runs through lofty and inaccessible mountains. so farewell Snake," wrote the Adams sisters, 1852. **Farewell Bend State Park** commemorates the thousands of emigrants who passed here.

MUSEUMS **Four Rivers Cultural Center and Museum** (541-889-8191; www.4rcc.com), 676 SW Fifth Avenue, Ontario. Mon.–Sat. 10–5. General admission $4; seniors, kids 6–14, and college students $3; children under six free. The four rivers are the Snake, great tributary of the Columbia, and the Payette, Malheur, and Owyhee, all flowing into the Snake near Ontario and largely responsible for the zone's agricultural success. For a remote area of the intermountain west, the Four Rivers attracted and retained quite a diverse population, which the museum traces along with the region's development: the Northern Paiutes and their removal to make way for cattle; the Basque sheepherders; settlers from the East Coast and Europe; Japanese Americans who in the 1940s were allowed work on the farms as an alternative to internment and stayed on; and Mexicans who to this day work the fields and ranches. Exhibits include elements of the various cultures, the evolution of irrigation, an internment camp barracks, and a large collection of Indian artwork and artifacts from around the West.

Oregon Trail Agricultural Museum (541-372-3574), 117 Good Avenue, Nyssa. Fri.–Sat. 10–4 and Sun. 1–4 in summer. Free. The Nyssa-Vale-Ontario area is far eastern Oregon's biggest agricultural zone, and this heritage is exposed in this 1930s feed store through early farm equipment and photos. Guided tours of the museum, the historic Green Lantern Saloon, and Hotel Western can be reserved for $5.

NATURAL WONDERS The **Owyhee River** flows through a **canyon** of towering cliffs—layers of rhyolite, basalt, and fossil-bearing sedimentary formations rising to a thousand feet above the river. Most of it is wild and remote, accessible only water. But a road runs from **Lake Owyhee State Park** along the river, with an interpretive site 10 miles north of the dam: from Adrian take OR 201 north for 3 miles, turn left and go 4 miles, then left again till you reach the overlook about 5 miles on.

Jordan Craters is a very remote clump of volcanic cones, lava fields, and craters. Turn off I-95 8 miles north of Jordan Valley, turn onto Cow Creek Road, and follow signs for Jordan Craters for 25 miles. Dangerous when wet.

SCENIC DRIVES **Leslie Gulch–Succor Creek Backcountry Byway.** This 52-mile dirt-and-gravel adventure starts at the junction of OR 201 and OR 19 and travels south along the Succor Creek canyon for a good example of the area's stark topography: bleak cliffs, strange rock formations, and bare hills. A side road leads to Leslie Gulch on the banks of Lake Owyhee. The road is steep, narrow, and rough, requiring high-clearance vehicles and definitely out of bounds for trailers and RVs. Generally it's open spring to fall, but it may be impassable after a summer rainfall.

* To Do

BIRD-WATCHING The **Owyhee River Canyon** abounds in bald and golden eagles and many other raptors, not to mention otters and bighorn sheep, but most of it is accessible only by raft. However, a road overlooks the tortuous canyon from the Owyhee Dam to its confluence with the Snake, and a **Watchable Wildlife Interpretive Site** stands at a viewpoint about 10 miles north of the dam.

CAMPING The Bureau of Land Management runs several semiremote sites in spectacular places: **Leslie Gulch,** beside the Owyhee amid bizarre tuff turrets and spires, offers campsites, toilets, and boat ramp; from Nyssa take I-95 south for 40 miles, then take McBride Road to Leslie Gulch Road and continue about 14 miles for a total of 70 miles. The roads are steep and narrow, inadvisable for trailers, and may be impassable when wet. **Birch Creek Historic Ranch** is the site of an early ranch in the Owyhee Canyon and is a take-out point for people rafting the wild, scenic river. Campers find five sites, toilet, trails, and boat ramps 28 miles west of Jordan Craters. **Spring Recreation Site,** about 3 miles north of Huntington (exit 345 from I-84), is on Brownlee Reservoir and is open year-round, with campsites, water, restrooms, fishing, and water in the summer.

Cow Lakes Recreation Area, about 19 miles from Jordan Valley via US 95 and Danner Loop Road, is a somewhat dilapidated campground beside Upper Cow Lake with 10 campsites and a restroom, surrounded by desert.

Farewell Bend State Recreation Area, 25 miles northwest of Ontario off I-84, has 101 electrical hookup sites, 30 tent sites, a hiker-biker camp, and 2 cabins (10 sites stay open in winter); reservable at 1-800-452-5687.

Lake Owyhee State Park, 25 miles northwest of Ontario off I-84, has two campgrounds with a total of 57 electrical hookup sites, 8 tent sites, 9 primitive sites, 2 tepees, and all amenities. Open mid-Apr.–Oct. To reserve call 1-800-452-5687.

Succor Creek State Natural Area, off OR 201 about 30 miles south of Nyssa, has a primitive camping area with six walk-in and 12 hike-in campsites; no potable water. Open Mar.–Nov.

CANOEING, KAYAKING, AND RAFTING **Owyhee Wild and Scenic River** is a wilderness rafting experience requiring expert rafters or guides. Deep canyon walls, bighorn sheep, antelope, and hidden archaeological sites are all there for the admiring; help and emergency services are not. The surrounding area is nearly unpopulated desert. "You must be prepared to handle all problems and emergencies on your own," says the Bureau of Land Management. That said, the experience is unique, and you can get a waterproof guidebook with map from the bureau's Vale office (541-473-3144), and outfitters such as **Northwest Voyageurs** (1-800-727-9977; www.voyageurs.com; 121 Old Pollock Road, Pollock, ID) or **Momentum River Expeditions** (1-866-663-5628; www.momentumriverexpeditions.com; 1257 Siskiyou Boulevard, Ashland) are glad to guide you.

GOLF **Country View Golf Course** (541-881-1171), 3780 Arabian Drive, Ontario. Nine holes.

Ontario Golf Course (541-889-9022), 1345 Golf Course Road, Ontario. Eighteen holes.

HIKING Hiking trails roam the wilderness at **Jordan Craters, Leslie Gulch,** and **Birch Creek Historic Site,** all BLM sites (see *Camping*).

✷ Wilder Places

PARKS **Farewell Bend State Recreation Area** (541-869-2365 or 1-800-551-6949), 25 miles northwest of Ontario off I-84, is where Oregon Trail travelers said farewell to the Snake River. Today Brownlee Reservoir offers the traveler some relief, but the brown hills all around give you some idea of what faced the pioneers. Historic displays explain the history, while the reservoir allows boating and waterskiing. A large campground has water, showers, and all amenities.

Lake Owyhee State Park (1-800-551-6949), 25 miles northwest of Ontario off I-84, sits beside 52-mile Lake Owyhee, which was formed by the Owyhee Dam. There's plenty of wildlife in the rimrock and sagebrush hills, and boating on the lake.

Ontario State Recreation Site (1-800-551-6949), a mile north of Ontario off I-84, is a green retreat along the Snake River with picnic sites, tall trees, and wildlife. Swim in the river or bring your boat for a lazy day. No fee.

Succor Creek State Park, off OR 201 about 30 miles south of Nyssa, sits on a rough unpaved road straddling a creek amid red cliffs. There are primitive campsites but no water and no staffing—this is a place to commune with rude nature. Free, even for camping. Use caution as the access road is rough, and dangerous when wet.

✷ Lodging

BED & BREAKFASTS

Drewsey

Blue Bucket Inn (541-493-2375; www.bluebucketinn.com), 82457 Ahmann Road. Stay at a 2,600-acre working ranch and help with chores, or watch wildlife, or gaze over the meadows and mountains. The ranch house dates from the 1940s and is entirely given over to guests; two upstairs rooms have private baths and go for $85, while two downstairs rooms share a bath and cost $65. A full breakfast is included, and a family-style supper can be ordered ahead of time for $12.50 (restaurants are scarce out here). Children over 12 welcome.

Jordan Valley

Old Basque Inn (541-586-2800), 306 Wroten Road. See *Eating Out*.

Vale

✐ 🐾 **Oregon Trail Inn** (541-473-3030; www.searshomebb.com), 484 N. 10th Street. This house has the distinction of being a 1908 Sears Roebuck model, ordered and shipped to Vale, turret and all, for its owner. Pretty behind its picket fence, it sits on the edge of town with six period-style rooms. $60–65; no credit cards. Pets welcomed with prior approval.

HOTELS AND MOTELS

Ontario

🐾 **Stockman's Motel** (541-889-4446; www.stockmansmotel.com), 81 SW First Street. Budget friendly and pet friendly, the Stockman's is downtown, close to shops and the Snake River. From $36. Free Wi-Fi, too.

Vale

Goodrich Hotel (541-881-9636; www.goodrichhotel.com), 229 A Street. One of the century-old buildings in downtown Vale, the hotel was built to keep up with the comings and goings of ranchers, cowboys, and traders. Now it's been remodeled; all rooms are quietly but pleasantly furnished suites with kitchen, living room, and private baths, with either one or two queen beds. $59.

✷ Where to Eat

EATING OUT

Jordan Valley
Old Basque Inn (541-586-2800), 306 Wroten Road. Summer hours: Mon.–Sat. 7–3 and 5–10, Sun. 8–3. What could be more appropriate in the New World's Basque country than a Basque restaurant? New owners Steve and Robin Henry serve both Basque and American dishes in their house under the cottonwoods, and they have rooms upstairs, too (see *Bed & Breakfasts*).

✷ Events

June: ✐ **America's Global Village Festival** (1-866-989-8012), first Sat., Ontario. "Villages" represent each of several ethnic groups important in area history: Scottish, German, Hawaiian, African, Basque, and more, with music, food, and performances.

July: **Japan Obon Festival** (541-889-8562), midmonth, Idaho-Oregon Buddhist Temple, Ontario. This traditional festival honoring the dead with dance, music, and food has been held here since the 1940s; all are welcome.

Nyssa Thunderegg Festival (541-372-3091), second weekend, 804 Adrian Boulevard, Nyssa. A rock hound's dream, the festival includes rock tours around the area, gem vendors, food, and crafts.

Vale Rodeo (541-473-3800), Fourth of July weekend, Vale Rodeo Grounds. Riders arrive at the grounds by racing their horses down Rinehart Butte and across the Malheur River.

INDEX

B

D

E

F

G

H

I

M

N

O

P

Q

R

S

T

U

V

W

DA JAN 3 1 2011

Y

Z